The Supreme Court and Its Work

CONGRESSIONAL QUARTERLY INC.
1414 22ND STREET, N.W.
WASHINGTON, D.C. 20037

Congressional Quarterly Inc.

Congressional Quarterly Inc., an editorial research service and publishing company, serves clients in the fields of news, education, business and government. It combines specific coverage of Congress, government and politics by Congressional Quarterly with the more general subject range of an affiliated service, Editorial Research Reports.

Congressional Quarterly was founded in 1945 by Henrietta and Nelson Poynter. Its basic periodical publication was and still is the CQ *Weekly Report,* mailed to clients every Saturday. A cumulative index is published quarterly.

CQ also publishes a variety of books. The CQ *Almanac,* a compendium of legislation for one session of Congress, is published every spring. *Congress and the Nation* is published every four years as a record of government for one presidential term. Other books include paperbacks on public affairs and textbooks for college political science classes.

The public affairs books are designed as timely reports to keep journalists, scholars and the public abreast of developing issues, events and trends.

They include such recent tiles as *President Reagan* and the second editions of *Energy Policy* and *Defense Policy.* College textbooks, prepared by outside scholars and published under the CQ Press imprint, include such recent titles as *The Supreme Court; Congress Reconsidered, Second Edition;* and *The Politics of Shared Power: Congress and the Executive.*

In addition, CQ publishes *The Congressional Monitor,* a daily report on present and future activities of congressional committees. This service is supplemented by *The Congressional Record Scanner,* an abstract of each day's *Congressional Record,* and *Congress in Print,* a weekly listing of committee publications.

CQ Direct Research is a consulting service that performs contract research and maintains a reference library and query desk for clients.

Editorial Research Reports covers subjects beyond the specialized scope of Congressional Quarterly. It publishes reference material on foreign affairs, business, education, cultural affairs, national security, science and other topics of news interest. Service to clients includes a 6,000-word report four times a month, bound and indexed semi-annually. Editorial Research Reports publishes paperback books in its fields of coverage. Founded in 1923, the service merged with Congressional Quarerly in 1956.

Library of Congress Cataloging in Publication Data

Main entry under title:

The Supreme Court and its work.

Bibliography: p.
Includes index.
1. United States. Supreme Court — History. 2. Judges — United States — Biography. I. Witt, Elder.
KF8742.S9   347.73'26'09   81-12622
ISBN 0-87187-210-2   347.3073509   AACR2

Editor: Elder Witt
Editorial Coordinator: Nancy Lammers
Major Contributors: Martha V. Gottron,
W. Allan Wilbur
Cover: Richard Pottern
Production Manager: I. D. Fuller
Assistant Production Manager: Maceo Mayo

Contents

Editor's Note. *The Supreme Court and Its Work* offers the reader a complete and up-to-date introduction to the history and workings of the U.S. Supreme Court. The opening chapter examines the origins of the court and its development over the last two centuries into one of the most powerful courts in the world. The second chapter explains the way in which the court has operated in earlier times and the manner in which it operates today. Biographical sketches of all 101 men who have served as justices as well as information on the first woman nominated to that bench, Sandra Day O'Connor, who was chosen by President Reagan in mid-1981, are included in the third chapter. The last chapter includes thumbnail summaries of each of the court's major decisions from its first term in 1790 through the summer of 1981. The latter part of the book contains a list of the Acts of Congress declared unconstitutional by the Supreme Court, the Rules of the Supreme Court (1980), a glossary of legal terms and a selected bibliography. *The Supreme Court and Its Work,* like other CQ public affairs books, is designed to provide journalists, scholars and citizens with the background information necessary for an understanding of current issues, events and trends.

Origins and Development

"We must never forget that it is a constitution we are expounding," Chief Justice John Marshall admonished his fellow justices in 1819. [1]

To modern ears, Marshall's words may seem a truism, yet they state with clarity the reason that the Supreme Court plays such an important role in shaping life and government in the United States.

The role of the court has been unique, a direct outgrowth of the new meaning that the word "constitution" assumed in the American experiment.

In 1789 every government and every society could be said to have some constitution. The word simply was used to refer to whatever principles and assumptions underlay the existing system.

But in the United States the word was invested with new significance. "A Constitution, in the American sense of the word," Justice Samuel Miller would write a century after its adoption, "is a written instrument by which the fundamental powers of the government are established, limited, and defined, and by which these powers are distributed among several departments, for their more safe and useful exercise for the benefit of the body politic."

Miller continued: In the Constitution of the United States "the people themselves have undertaken to frame an organic law governing the relations of the whole people, as well as of the individual states, to the federal government, and to prescribe in many cases the limits and rules of private and personal rights. It is the fundamental law pursuant to which the government is permanently organized and conducted." [2]

In the United States, then, the Constitution was far more than a passive description of the existing system. It was an active instrument, the charter of a new national system, the source of power and of the limits of power.

But the Constitution of the United States of America was hardly self-enforcing. As Chief Justice Marshall wrote:

A constitution, to contain an accurate detail of all the subdivisions of which its great powers will admit, and of all the means by which they may be carried into execution, would partake of a prolixity of a legal code. . . . It would probably never be understood by the public. Its nature, therefore, requires, that only its great outlines should be marked, its important objects designated, and the minor ingredients which compose those objects be deduced from the nature of the objects themselves. [3]

The question was obvious. Who would undertake these all-important deductions? Who would enforce the limits the Constitution set upon the powers of Congress, the president, the states? Who would fill in the broad outlines of the powers it granted? Who would ensure its continuing validity as circumstances changed?

The answer was not long — if ever — in doubt. The Supreme Court would serve this function, declared Marshall in the 1803 ruling in *Marbury v. Madison* — and that point has been underscored in almost every ensuing constitutional decision by the court. The "weakest branch" of the new system — six men — would undertake this critical responsibility; the court would become "the particular guardian of the terms of the written constitution." [4]

In the 190 years of its history, the Supreme Court — by virtue of this responsibility — has become the most powerful court the world has ever known.

It can override the will of the majority expressed in an act of Congress. It can forcefully remind a president that in this nation all persons are subject to the rule of law. It can require the redistribution of political power in every state of the Union. And it can persuade the nation's citizens that the fabric of their society must be rewoven into new patterns.

There have been mistakes and contradictions along the way; several constitutional amendments bear witness to the most notable of these. Constitutional development in the United States follows no tidy pattern. The court does not initiate cases, solicit issues, nor arrange the order in which it deals with them. It must take them as they come. And when it decides the cases before it, it often seems tentative and hesitant, zigging and zagging from case to case within a particular issue.

The pattern is not neat, but it is quintessentially human. For all the remoteness of the black-robed justices working in isolation within marble chambers, the court is the most human of government institutions.

Issues come to the court only when individuals disagree upon them. Black and white, merchant and consumer, prisoner and warden, president and pauper — they come before the court to seek resolution of their disputes.

The men before whom their case is made are neither monks nor oracles. They respond to the same concerns and influences as their fellow citizens. They hear the arguments, then they meet, talk, and vote. The court has decided. The justices write, comment, edit. The opinions are signed. The decision is announced. The dispute is resolved — and the role of the court in the continuing development of the American system is once again affirmed.

The court is the nation's balance wheel. As Justice Robert H. Jackson explained in 1954:

> In a society in which rapid changes tend to upset all equilibrium, the court, without exceeding its own limited powers, must strive to maintain the great system of balances upon which our free government is based. Whether these balances and checks are essential to liberty elsewhere in the world is beside the point; they are indispensable to the society we know. Chief of these balances are: first, between the Executive and Congress; second, between the central government and the States; third, between state and state; fourth, between authority, be it state or national, and the liberty of the citizen, or between the rule of the majority and the rights of the individual. [5]

This is the story of the court and those balances.

The Origins of Power

In contrast to Articles I and II of the Constitution, which set out in considerable length and detail the powers and prerogatives of Congress and the executive, Article III is brief, simply sketching the outline of a federal judiciary.

One scholar, Julius Goebel Jr., suggests that "to some delegates, provision for a national judiciary was a matter of theoretical compulsion rather than of practical necessity ... more in deference to the maxim of separation [of powers] than in response to clearly formulated ideas about the role of a national judicial system and its indispensability." [6]

At any rate, with little discussion and less debate, the Constitutional Convention approved language that simply declared in Article III:

> The judicial Power of the United States, shall be vested in one supreme Court, and in such inferior Courts as the Congress may from time to time ordain and establish.

Section 1 of the article goes on to state that the judges of these courts will hold their posts during good behavior, and that their salaries may not be diminished during their terms in office.

Article II already had provided that the members of the Supreme Court would be appointed by the president by and with the advice and consent of the Senate — and that judges, along with all other civil officers of the new national government, "shall be removed from office on Impeachment for, and Conviction of, Treason, Bribery, or other high Crimes and Misdemeanors."

Section 2 of Article III describes the reach of the judicial power. It includes some cases because of their subject — "all Cases, in Law and Equity, arising under this Constitution, the Laws of the United States, and Treaties made, or which shall be made, under their Authority . . . all Cases of admiralty and maritime Jurisdiction. . . ." And federal judicial power reaches other cases because of the parties involved — "all Cases affecting Ambassadors, other public Ministers and Consuls; . . . Controversies to which the United States shall be a Party; . . . Controversies between two or more States. . . ."

The Supreme Court would have original jurisdiction — the power to hear the initial arguments — in cases involving foreign dignitaries and those involving states. In all other types of cases, the Supreme Court's jurisdiction was to be appellate — it would only hear appeals from the rulings of lower courts.

There ended the Constitution's description of the nation's judicial branch. The remaining sections of Article III deal with jury trials, the place of trials, and the crime of treason.

The brevity of the constitutional description left to Congress and the court itself the task of filling in much of the substance and all of the details of the new judicial system. One early observer commented, "the convention has only crayoned in the outlines. It is left to Congress to fill up and colour the canvas." [7]

An Independent Branch

Although the Articles of Confederation had not provided for a system of national courts, the concept of a separate and relatively independent judiciary was generally accepted by the delegates to the Constitutional Convention. At the time of the adoption of Article III by the convention, six of the original 13 states had such judicial branches. [8]

There was some debate in the convention over the need for any inferior federal courts. Some delegates argued that state courts were adequate to handle all judicial business other than that which the Supreme Court would consider. That debate was resolved by leaving the final decision on the creation of lower federal courts to Congress.

There also was disagreement over whether Congress or the president should appoint the members of the Supreme Court — and whether the court should try impeachments. A compromise resulted in giving the President the power to name the court's members with the advice and consent of the Senate — and in granting the Senate the power to try impeachments.

To safeguard the independence of the judges, the "good behavior" and salary provisions were added. Alexander Hamilton wrote in *The Federalist Papers*:

> The standard of good behavior for the continuance in office of the judicial magistracy is certainly one of the most valuable of the modern improvements in the practice of government. In a monarchy it is an excellent barrier to the despotism of the prince; in a republic it is a no less excellent barrier to the encroach-

ments and oppressions of the representative body. And it is the best expedient which can be devised in any government to secure a steady, upright, and impartial administration of the laws. [9]

The provision for impeachment of judges would, on the other hand, wrote Hamilton, ensure the responsible conduct of their duties. [10]

Federal Supremacy

Neither the separateness nor the independence of the Supreme Court is truly unique. The most notable and peculiar of its characteristics is its power to review and nullify state and federal laws that collide with the Constitution.

This role was made necessary by the convention's adoption, in Article VI, of the declaration that:

This Constitution, and the Laws of the United States which shall be made in Pursuance thereof; and all Treaties made, or which shall be made, under the Authority of the United States, shall be the supreme Law of the Land; and the Judges in every State shall be bound thereby, any Thing in the Constitution or Laws of any State to the Contrary notwithstanding.

Article VI went on to state that all officials of the national and state governments were to take an oath to support the Constitution. Left unsaid — again — was who would enforce the provisions and prescriptions of the Constitution if some officials chose to ignore that oath.

Insofar as the supremacy of federal authority over state actions was concerned, that omission was remedied by the Judiciary Act of 1789, enacted by the First Congress. That statute gave the Supreme Court the power to review, and affirm or reverse, rulings where state courts rejected claims that state laws or actions conflicted with the U.S. Constitution, federal laws or treaties. It also specified that the Supreme Court would consist of a Chief Justice and five associate justices, meeting twice each year, in February and in August.

This provision for judicial review of state rulings was the famous Section 25 of the Judiciary Act, the subject of much criticism and many repeal efforts over the next three decades.

Judicial Review and Acts of Congress

Congress never granted the Supreme Court parallel authority to review acts of Congress for their constitutionality. And the Constitution itself is silent on whether the court can nullify an act of Congress.

In 1803 the court simply claimed this role for itself. Asserting the power for the first time, the court in the case of *Marbury v. Madison* struck down a portion of the same Judiciary Act that had granted it the power to review state court rulings. The offending section, wrote Chief Justice John Marshall, purported to enlarge the original jurisdiction of the court — and that Congress had no power to do.

Marbury v. Madison sparked a long scholarly debate over whether the Supreme Court was undertaking a role the Framers intended it to fill or was usurping more power than it had been intended to possess. Despite its sporadic intensity, the debate is irrelevant. The court's power to review the acts of Congress is firmly established in practice and has never been seriously challenged.

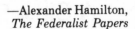

"Where the will of the legislature . . . stands in opposition to that of the people, declared in the Constitution, the judges ought to be governed by the latter. . . ."

—Alexander Hamilton,
The Federalist Papers

Most scholars view this role as envisioned by the members of the Constitutional Convention. They point to various comments during the convention debates — and during the ratification conventions in the states — as indicating that many members of the convention simply assumed that the Supreme Court would exercise this power.

Most enduring of the arguments of this early period are those set out by Alexander Hamilton in *The Federalist Papers.* Hamilton reasoned that this function of the court was essential to the existence of a limited constitutional government. The federal courts, he said, would serve as "bulwarks of a limited Constitution." [11]

After his often-quoted description of the judicial branch as "incontestably . . . beyond comparison the weakest of the three departments of power," Hamilton continued:

The complete independence of the courts of justice is peculiarly essential in a limited Constitution. By a limited Constitution, I understand one which contains certain specified exceptions to the legislative authority; such, for instance, as that it shall pass no bills of attainder, no *ex post facto* laws, and the like. Limitations of this kind can be preserved in practice no other way than through the medium of courts of justice, whose duty it must be to declare all acts contrary to the manifest tenor of the Constitution void. Without this, all the reservations of particular rights or privileges would amount to nothing. [12]

Hamilton rejected the counter-argument that to allow the court to declare acts of Congress invalid would elevate the "weakest branch" to a position superior to that of Congress:

. . . every act of a delegated authority, contrary to the tenor of the commission under which it is exercised, is void. No legislative act, therefore, contrary to the Constitution, can be valid. To deny this would be to affirm . . . that the representatives of the people are superior to the people themselves; that men acting by virtue of powers may do not only what their powers do not authorize, but what they forbid. . . .

. . . the courts were designed to be an intermediate body between the people and the legislature in order, among other things, to keep the latter within the limits assigned to their authority. The interpretation of the laws is the proper and peculiar province of the courts. A constitution is, in fact, and must be regarded by the judges as, a fundamental law. It therefore belongs to them to ascertain its meaning as well as the meaning of any particular act proceeding from the legislative body. If there should happen to be an irreconcilable variance between the two, that which has the superior obligation and validity ought, of course, to be preferred; or, in other words, the Constitution ought to be preferred to the statute, the intention of the people to the intention of their agents.

Nor does this conclusion by any means suppose a superiority of the judicial to the legislative power. It only supposes that the power of the people is superior to both, and that where the will of the legislature, declared in its statutes, stands in opposition to that of the people, declared in the Constitution, the judges ought to be governed by the latter. . . . [13]

A Slow Start: 1790-1800

On Sept. 24, 1789, President George Washington signed the Judiciary Act into law — and sent to the Senate his nominations for the first members of the Supreme Court.

One of the men so honored declined so that he could accept a state position; another accepted but never attended a formal session of the court; and John Jay, the first Chief Justice, would spend much of his tenure abroad, engaged in diplomatic duties, and would resign after six years to become governor of New York.

The First Justices

Washington's original selections — all of whom were active in the founding of the new government — were:

● Chief Justice John Jay, 44, of New York, co-author with Hamilton and James Madison of *The Federalist Papers.*

● John Rutledge of South Carolina, 50, a member of the Constitutional Convention.

● Robert Hanson Harrison of Maryland, 44, who declined the post to accept that of chancellor of Maryland.

● John Blair of Virginia, 57, a member of the Constitutional Convention and a leader in the effort to obtain Virginia's ratification of the new national charter.

● James Wilson of Pennsylvania, 47, signer of the Declaration of Independence, member of the Constitutional Convention, and a leader in obtaining ratification of the new charter by his state.

● William Cushing, of Massachusetts, 57, a state judge and leader of the state ratification effort.

After Hanson's refusal, Washington selected James Iredell of North Carolina, 38, for the fifth associate justice's seat. Iredell had led the initially unsuccessful effort to win North Carolina's vote in favor of the new Constitution.

Confirmation of the first set of nominees came within two days, on Sept. 26. Iredell was nominated early the next year, on Feb. 9, 1790, and confirmed Feb. 10.

The tenure of these original members, with the exception of Cushing, was brief. Jay resigned in 1795. Two other men would follow him as Chief Justice within the court's first decade.

Rutledge resigned in 1791, never having attended a formal session of the full court. Blair, after several years of irregular attendance, resigned because of his poor health in 1796. Wilson died in 1798. Iredell, the only member of the first court to move his family to the new nation's capital, New York, resigned in 1799. [14]

Cushing alone would serve into the 19th century, remaining on the court for 21 years until his death in 1810.

The First Terms

"The status of the federal judiciary in the 1790s," wrote Robert G. McCloskey, "was ambiguous and . . . comparatively minor. . . . The paramount governmental tasks were legislative and executive." [15]

The record of the Supreme Court's first decade bears out that statement.

Only three of the six justices were present for the court's opening session on Feb. 1, 1790. Jay, Wilson and Cushing, wearing robes and, at least in Cushing's case, a wig, met briefly in the Royal Exchange Building in New York.

By Feb. 2 Blair had arrived, making the quorum needed for transaction of business. But there was no business, aside from organizational matters, chief among which was the appointment of a clerk. After several days of admitting attorneys to practice before it, the court adjourned its first term on Feb. 10, 1790.

The second term lasted two days — Aug. 2-3, 1790. Iredell, confirmed in February, was present.

In 1791 the capital and the court moved to Philadelphia where the court shared, with the mayor's court, a room in the new City Hall. No cases were decided by the court in 1791 or 1792.

The court met in Philadelphia until 1800. Three times — in 1793, 1794 and 1797 — the court was forced by epidemics of yellow fever to cancel its August term. [16]

In 1791 Justice Rutledge resigned to take a state judgeship. Two of the men offered his seat declined, preferring to retain their seats in state legislatures. [17] President Washington then selected Thomas Johnson of Maryland, at 59, one of the court's oldest members. Johnson would hold the seat only 14 months.

In 1792 Chief Justice Jay conducted an unsuccessful passive campaign from the bench for the post of governor of New York. At that point he described the post of a Supreme Court justice as "intolerable." [18]

The First Major Decision

On Feb. 18, 1793, the court announced its decision in the case of *Chisholm v. Georgia,* its first major ruling. Within five years, the ruling was overturned by adoption of a constitutional amendment.

Reading the language of Article III literally, the court upheld the right of citizens of one state, South Carolina, to bring original suits in the Supreme Court against another state, Georgia. The vote of the court was 5-1. Iredell dissented. Each of the justices announced his opinion orally.

The states were shocked by the ruling, seeing in it the potential for their economic ruin. Early in 1798 the 11th Amendment was added to the Constitution. It declared that states could not be sued, without their consent, in federal courts by citizens of another state.

Circuit Duty

Despite the lack of many notable decisions by the full Supreme Court during these first years, the justices found themselves kept quite busy — and rather unhappy — due to the demands of their duty as circuit judges. For a full century, the justices worked to convince Congress to abolish this role for them.

The Judiciary Act of 1789 provided no separate set of judges for the federal circuit courts. The act instead provided that that Supreme Court justices would travel throughout the states to hold circuit court where and when necessary.

This aspect of judicial duty, though onerous, served an important function in the new nation. Historian Charles Warren notes that "it was . . . almost entirely through their contact with the judges sitting in the circuit courts that the people of the country became acquainted with this new institution, the federal judiciary." [19]

But the distances the justices were required to travel were long, traveling conditions difficult, and questions were raised about the propriety of the justices participating in cases at the circuit level that were then reviewed by the Supreme Court. As early as 1790 Chief Justice Jay asked Congress and the executive to remove this burden. Congress responded with minor changes in the system in 1793; the quickly repealed Judiciary Act of 1801 abolished this duty temporarily; and until late in the 19th century the requirement that justices fill this function remained on the statute books. [20]

The Court, Congress and the President

During this decade, the court, on two occasions, made clear its character as a purely judicial branch, declining to perform non-judicial functions assigned by Congress or to issue advisory opinions in response to executive queries.

In 1792 Congress imposed upon the circuit courts the duty of ruling upon claims of invalid pensioners. Justices Iredell, Blair and Wilson, sitting as circuit judges, refused to carry out that duty, declaring that Congress had overstepped itself by requiring them to undertake such non-judicial responsibilities. As a result of their protest, Congress amended the pension law. [21]

The following year, President Washington asked the court for advice on certain questions of foreign policy, neutrality and treaty law. The justices politely declined to give such advice, citing "the lines of separation, drawn by the Constitution between the three departments of the government" and "our being Judges of a Court in the last resort." The court thereby established its policy of issuing no advisory opinions. [22]

Early in 1793 Johnson resigned. He was quickly replaced by William Paterson of New Jersey, 44, one of the two key senators responsible for the drafting and enactment of the Judiciary Act of 1789. Paterson would serve until 1806.

During the February 1794 term the court heard the case of *Georgia v. Brailsford*, one of a handful of cases tried before it by a jury. [23] And in the last major case in which John Jay would participate, the court rejected the assertion that a foreign country had the right — independent of any treaty or other legal guarantee — to set up a prize court in the United States to decide the disposition of captured vessels. [24]

Two More Chiefs

In April 1794 Jay accepted an appointment as special ambassador to England; he never returned to his seat on the court. After concluding the treaty with Britain, he resigned in June 1795 to become governor of New York.

John Rutledge of South Carolina, the absentee justice of the court's first terms, was nominated by Washington — at Rutledge's own suggestion — to succeed Jay. Appointed while the Senate was in recess in 1795, Rutledge presided over the court's August 1795 term, but was then refused confirmation by the Senate in December. The Senate acted upon reports of Rutledge's criticism of the Jay Treaty — and on rumors of his mental instability, rumors to which Rutledge gave new credibility by attempting suicide after his rejection by the Senate.

Washington then, early in 1796, named Cushing, the senior justice, to lead the court. Although he was quickly confirmed, Cushing declined the post on the basis that at 64 he was too old. He would serve for 14 more years.

President Washington then offered the post of Chief Justice to Sen. Oliver Ellsworth of Connecticut, who, with Paterson, had drafted the Judiciary Act. Ellsworth, 51, was nominated March 3, 1796, confirmed the following day, and took his seat March 8.

Treaties and Taxes

Without Ellsworth, who was sworn in too late to take part in the decisions, the court during the February 1796 term decided the two most significant cases of the decade. They were the treaty case of *Ware v. Hylton* and the tax case of *Hylton v. United States.*

John Marshall argued *Ware v. Hylton* before the court, apparently his only appearance as an advocate before the tribunal he would lead for more than three decades. He lost the case.

In *Ware v. Hylton,* the court established the supremacy of federal treaty provisions over conflicting state laws. A Virginia law that allowed the confiscation, or payment in depreciated currency, of debts owed by Virginians to British subjects was invalid, held the justices, because it conflicted with provisions of the peace treaty with Britain, which ensured the collection of such debts.

Hylton v. United States brought to the court the first clear challenge to an act of Congress as unconstitutional.

John Jay   Oliver Ellsworth

There was no debate over the court's power to rule on that point. Each of the sitting justices — while on circuit duty — had indicated his belief that federal courts were empowered to resolve such challenges. [25]

Congress had imposed a tax on carriages. The tax was challenged as a direct tax, which the Constitution required be apportioned among the states by population. The definition of "direct tax" was unclear, but the court declared that the carriage tax was not a direct tax and thus was not subject to the apportionment requirement.

In its ruling the court declared that direct taxes were only those on land and on individuals, a definition that would stand for a century, until its repudiation by the court in 1895.

Justice Chase

A new member of the court took part in these two decisions — Samuel Chase of Maryland. Chase, a political maverick, would be the only justice in history to be impeached and tried by the Senate.

Chase was Washington's surprise choice to fill the seat left vacant by the resignation of Justice Blair. A signer of the Declaration of Independence, Chase had opposed ratifi-

---

"It was . . . almost entirely through their contact with the judges sitting in the circuit courts that the people of the country became acquainted with this new institution, the federal judiciary."

—Charles Warren
The Supreme Court in United States History

---

cation of the Constitution, arguing that it was an undemocratic document.

Nominated and confirmed in January 1796, he took his seat as the February 1796 term began — and voted with the majority in both the tax and the treaty cases. Chase and Ellsworth were the last of Washington's appointments to the court. With Cushing and Paterson, Chase would serve well into the next century.

The Adams Administration

The major decision of the court during the administration of John Adams came when the court in *Calder v. Bull* declared that the constitutional ban on *ex post facto* laws applied only to criminal, not civil, laws. Few other decisions of lasting significance were announced during the 1797-1801 terms.

With the deaths of Justices Wilson and Iredell, Adams had the opportunity to fill two seats on the court. To succeed Wilson, Adams named Bushrod Washington of Virginia, 36, President Washington's nephew. To succeed Iredell, he chose Alfred Moore, 44, of North Carolina. Washington would serve for more than three decades; Moore resigned in 1804 after barely five years on the bench.

The 1799 and 1800 terms of the court were uneventful. The August 1800 term was the last to be held in Philadelphia. Only three justices attended — Paterson, Moore and Washington. Ellsworth, named ambassador to France in February 1799, was abroad — as he would be for the remainder of his time as Chief Justice. Cushing was ill. Chase was campaigning, unsuccessfully, for the re-election of President Adams.

In the election of 1800 the staunch nationalist position of the court became a campaign issue, coupled with complaints about the ambassadorial service of Chief Justices Jay and Ellsworth, acting as agents of the Federalist administrations.

Notwithstanding such criticism, the court's first decade had been a cautious one. As Julius Goebel Jr. concluded:

> Its [the court's] posture toward acts of Congress, except for a few instances of individual critique, was one of respect. There were, indeed, occasions . . . that invited inquiry into the constitutional basis for congressional action where less deference would have been appropriate. These opportunities were not seized, nor was there succumbing to the temptation to a loose construction of statutory language sometimes advanced by counsel in argument.

> When the Court was constrained to explore the intendment of statutory language, it did so as a court of law in terms familiar to the profession and not by flights of fancy about the "spirit" of the Constitution. . . .

> The Supreme Court during its first decade . . . left the formulation of policy to the branches of government where it conceived such belonged. [26]

Establishment of Power: 1801-1835

The year 1801 was a watershed for both the nation and the court. A new president — Thomas Jefferson — and a new Chief Justice — John Marshall — took office. Although Jefferson and Marshall shared the home state of Virginia they were life-long antagonists — a fact that added to the natural tension between executive and judiciary at this point in the life of the young nation.

There was also a new capital in 1801. The seat of the government moved to Washington, D.C. The Capitol was under construction as the home of Congress; a residence was provided for the president, but no place was set aside for the Supreme Court to meet. At the last minute, it was allotted a small committee room in the unfinished Capitol. There it convened for its February 1801 term.

Ellsworth Steps Down

In 1800 Oliver Ellsworth, still in France on diplomatic assignment, resigned as Chief Justice.

President Adams first named former Chief Justice Jay to the seat. Confirmation was immediate; so was Jay's letter declining the honor. Jay noted his failing health and the continuing responsibilities of the justices for holding circuit court. He wrote:

> ...the efforts repeatedly made to place the Judicial Department on a proper footing have proved fruitless. I left the bench perfectly convinced that under a system so defective, it would not obtain the energy, weight and dignity which are essential to its affording due support to the National Government, nor acquire the public confidence and respect which, as the last resort of the justice of the nation, it should possess. [27]

Adams was a lame duck, defeated for re-election in 1800. (The tie in electoral votes between Jefferson and Aaron Burr remained unresolved until February 1801.) But Adams was not about to relinquish this opportunity. On Jan. 20, 1801, he named John Marshall Chief Justice. Marshall was then his secretary of State, after serving for a time on diplomatic assignment and in the House of Representatives.

After a brief delay by Federalist advocates of Justice Paterson's elevation to the chief justiceship, the Senate confirmed Marshall Jan. 27.

The Marshall Era Begins

Chief Justice Marshall was sworn in on Feb. 4, 1801, the second day of the court's first term in Washington. He was 45 years old. He would serve for 34 years, until his death.

On the day set for the opening of the term, Feb. 2, only Justice Cushing was present. By Feb. 4 there were four members present — Cushing, Chase, Washington and Marshall. No cases were reported as decided during the term.

But events outside the court's makeshift chamber were moving quickly with broad implications for the court and its new Chief Justice.

In February the House broke the electoral deadlock between Burr and Jefferson, and chose Jefferson as the new president. He took office March 4, 1801.

Only a few days before Jefferson's selection, Congress enacted the Judiciary Act of 1801. The act eliminated circuit duty for the justices, providing for a separate staff of circuit judges. It shifted the court's schedule, providing for June and December terms, instead of February and August sessions; and it reduced to five the number of seats on the court.

The law was widely viewed as a Federalist plan to allow Adams to name a last group of Federalist judges and to protect the Supreme Court from any immediate change through Jeffersonian appointments. Adams quickly filled the new judgeships with Federalist loyalists, confirming Jefferson's view that the federal judiciary would indeed remain a "strong fortress in the possession of the enemy." [28]

Another late-session law produced the situation that brought the case of *Marbury v. Madison* to the court. This second law created a number of justice-of-the-peace positions for the District of Columbia. On March 2 outgoing

"Let the end be legitimate, let it be within the scope of the Constitution, and all means which are appropriate ... which are not prohibited ... are constitutional."

—Chief Justice Marshall
McCulloch v. Maryland,
1819

President Adams appointed men to fill those posts; they were confirmed the following day. Their commissions were made out and signed. But still-acting Secretary of State John Marshall (also by now the sitting Chief Justice) failed to deliver all the commissions to all the nominees before the end of the Adams administration at midnight March 3.

President Jefferson appointed a number of these people to their sought-after posts, but not William Marbury, who came to the Supreme Court late in 1801, asking the justices to order Secretary of State James Madison to deliver him his commission.

Marbury filed an original suit with the court, asking that the justices use the authority granted them by the Judiciary Act of 1789 and issue a writ of *mandamus* to Madison.

Already the court was pursuing a path quite independent of the Jefferson administration. In August the justices declined Jefferson's offer to provide them with his views on the application of a certain law at issue in a case before them. The president's position, the court indicated, was not relevant to their consideration of the matter.

Then, in December, the court backed Jefferson's position in a prize vessel case. But also that month the court agreed to hear Marbury's case, setting arguments for the next term — the June 1802 term.

Jefferson was convinced that the court intended to use the Marbury case as a vehicle for interfering in the operations of the executive branch. That view — and the Jeffersonians' view of the Judiciary Act of 1801 — sparked repeal of that law early in 1802. Circuit court duty was reinstated for the justices, and a single annual term was set for the court, beginning each year in February.

Because the change in schedule was enacted after February 1802, this last provision delayed for 14 months the next term at which the arguments would be heard in *Marbury v. Madison.* The court did not meet from December 1801 until February 1803.

Marshall the Man

Two major decisions were announced in the 1803 term. In both their coupling and their resolution the skilled leadership of John Marshall already was evident.

Marshall's legal training was meager; he had little experience in the practice of law and none as a judge. Before his appointment as Chief Justice, he had been a politician and a diplomat, and it was those skills that characterized his tenure as Chief Justice. For three decades his personality dominated the court and the men who served with him.

More than at any other time in the court's history, the personal characteristics of the Chief Justice were of considerably more importance than his legal talents.

The court operated as a family firm, not a federal institution. The justices, most of whom came to Washington only for a few months each year, leaving their wives and families at home, lived together in a boardinghouse. After their dinners together, they often, over wine, discussed and resolved the cases brought before them. [29]

Marshall's contribution as Chief Justice has been often described. Alexander M. Bickel's words are among the most evocative:

Congress was created very nearly full blown by the Constitution itself. The vast possibilities of the presidency were relatively easy to perceive and soon, inevitably, materialized. But the institution of the judiciary needed to be summoned up out of the constitutional

---

". . . The institution of the judiciary needed to be summoned up out of the constitutional vapors, shaped and maintained; and the Great Chief Justice, John Marshall — not singlehanded, but first and foremost — was there to do it and did."

—Alexander M. Bickel
The Least Dangerous Branch

---

vapors, shaped and maintained; and the Great Chief Justice, John Marshall — not singlehanded, but first and foremost — was there to do it and did. [30]

The *Marbury* Ruling

Two years after Marshall assumed his post, the court announced its decision in *Marbury v. Madison*. On Feb. 24, 1803, the court at once claimed, exercised and justified its power to review and nullify acts of Congress it found to conflict with the Constitution.

But in so doing it neatly avoided the expected collision with the Jefferson administration, although it did manage to rebuke Jefferson for not delivering Marbury his delayed commission.

The court held that Marbury was due his commission, that it should be delivered to him, but that the court was powerless to order the delivery. The court lacked that power because it found the section of the Judiciary Act authorizing it to issue such orders to be unconstitutional and void, an impermissible expansion of its original jurisdiction.

This decision, one scholar has explained, "became authority . . . for the proposition — which had already been adopted in a majority of the states and which was destined to form a distinct feature of the whole political system of the United States — that a constitution is a fundamental law, that legislative and executive powers are limited by the terms of this fundamental law, and that the courts as interpreters of the law are expected to preserve and defend constitutions as inviolable acts, to be changed only by the people through the amending process." [31]

Judicial Restraint

During congressional debate over repeal of the 1801 Judiciary Act, the possibility was raised that the court might declare the repeal unconstitutional, an improper effort by Congress to encroach on the independence of the court.

One week after the *Marbury* decision, the court made clear that it would exercise its newly affirmed power with care. The court upheld the Repeal Act of 1802. This ruling, announced March 2, 1803, came in the case of *Stuart v. Laird*. [32]

It would be more than 50 years before the court again declared void an act of Congress.

The Chase Impeachment

The business before the court steadily increased during the first decade of the 19th century, but few of its decisions during that period were of as much significance for the future of the court and the country as some of the extrajudicial matters affecting the court.

Most notable of these was the impeachment, trial and acquittal of Justice Samuel Chase.

Chase, a maverick at the time of his selection to the court, continued, from his seat, to make enemies. He actively campaigned for President Adams in 1800. He strongly supported the hated Sedition Act of 1798 — and presided as the judge in the trials of a number of persons charged with violating it.

After a particularly partisan speech to a grand jury in Baltimore in May 1803, Chase became the object of an impeachment drive. The charges against him involved both his conduct during the Sedition Act trials and this particular charge to the Baltimore grand jury. On March 12, 1804, the House impeached Justice Chase by a vote of 73-32.

His trial in the Senate began early in 1805. Chase, who continued to participate in the court's functions, appeared in the Senate with his attorneys. Presentation of the evidence and arguments consumed a month. On March 1, 1805, he was acquitted. More than a majority of the senators voted to find him guilty on three of the charges against him, but the vote fell short of the two-thirds required for conviction.

The Chase acquittal ended the rumored plans of Republicans to impeach all four remaining Federalist justices — Marshall, Cushing, Paterson and Washington.

Furthermore, wrote historian Charles Warren, the acquittal represented a rejection of the Republican argument that impeachment could be used as "a means of keeping the courts in reasonable harmony with the will of the nation, as expressed through Congress and the executive, and that a judicial decision declaring an Act of Congress unconstitutional would support an impeachment and the removal of a judge. . . ."[33]

Reporting the Decisions

At the end of the 1804 term, William Cranch, then chief justice of the circuit court in the District of Columbia, began publication of Cranch's *Reports* of the decisions of the Supreme Court.

Alexander J. Dallas, a noted attorney in Pennsylvania, had reported some of the court's decisions during its terms in Philadelphia. But after the court moved to Washington, Dallas discontinued this service.

Cranch, who would perform this public service for a dozen years, first published a volume including the decisions from 1801 through 1804. "Up to that time, the opinions in the cases heard ... [during that period] had been practically unknown to the Bar and to the general public," writes Warren, "with the exception of the *Marbury Case*, a summary of which had been widely published and commented upon in the newspapers." [34]

In his preface to the first volume, Cranch expressed the hope that publication of the court's decisions would eliminate "much of that uncertainty of the law, which is so frequently, and perhaps so justly, the subject of complaint in this country."

Furthermore, wrote Cranch, reporting of the actual decisions of the court should limit judicial discretion:

> ... Every case decided is a check upon the judge. He cannot decide a similar case differently, without strong reasons, which, for his own justification, he will wish to make public. The avenues to corruption are thus obstructed, and the sources of litigation closed. [35]

New Justices

Early in Marshall's tenure — undoubtedly with the encouragement of Reporter Cranch — the court began to write down its decisions and opinions.

In addition, Chief Justice Marshall exerted all his considerable personal influence to convince his fellow justices to speak with one voice in these decisions. He persuaded them to drop the practice of *seriatim* opinions, under which each justice wrote and read his own views, and to adopt the "opinion of the court" approach, usually allowing him to write that opinion.

Appropriately enough, however, William Johnson, the first Republican justice, who served for most of Marshall's tenure, provided a counterbalance to the Chief Justice's push for judicial unanimity.

Johnson, known as the "father of dissent," was but 32 at the time of his appointment to the Supreme Court, but he nevertheless did not hesitate to voice his disagreement with the Chief Justice and the court.

President Jefferson filled two other seats on the court during his two terms in office. In 1806 Justice Paterson died and Jefferson named H. Brockholst Livingston of New York, 49, John Jay's brother-in-law, as Patterson's successor. Livingston served on the court for 16 years.

In 1807 increases in territorial and judicial business spurred Congress to create a new circuit that took in Kentucky, Tennessee and Ohio, and a seventh seat on the Supreme Court. Jefferson, after polling the members of Congress from those three states, named Thomas Todd, Kentucky's chief justice, to the new seat. Todd, 41, was nominated and confirmed in 1807, seated at the 1808 term, missed the 1809 term, and issued his first opinion — a dissent — in 1810. He served until 1826 but, like Livingston, his judicial career was notable mainly for his steady support of Chief Justice Marshall.

The Burr Trial

In 1807 the Jefferson administration brought former Vice President Aaron Burr to trial for treason. The charge was related to Burr's alleged efforts to encourage an uprising in and a movement for the independence of the western states from the United States. The actions of the Supreme Court and its Chief Justice in this affair further heightened the animosity felt by the president for the court.

Early in 1807 the Supreme Court, affirming its power to issue a writ of *habeas corpus* to challenge the detention of an individual by federal officials, held that there was insufficient evidence for the government to prosecute two of Burr's accomplices for treason. [36]

Jefferson, writes Charles Warren, regarded this ruling as "another deliberate attack by the court upon his executive authority" while the Federalists viewed it as "a noble example of the judicial safeguards to individual liberty." [37]

After the Supreme Court's term ended, Chief Justice Marshall traveled to Richmond to preside personally as circuit judge over the trial of Burr. His rulings that the government's evidence was insufficient to support a charge of treason were seen as directly contributing to Burr's acquittal later in the year. Jefferson, irate at the rulings and the outcome, suggested that the Constitution be amended to provide other means than impeachment for removing justices from the bench. The amendment was not approved.

Jefferson's feelings toward the court were further exacerbated during the national resistance to his administration's Embargo Act imposed during the conflict with Britain. Justice Johnson — one of Jefferson's own choices as a member of the court — declared illegal and void the president's effort to instruct customs officials to detain all vessels thought to be intending to evade the embargo. [38]

Fletcher v. Peck

In 1810 the Supreme Court for the first time exercised its power to strike down a state law as unconstitutional.

In the case of *Fletcher v. Peck*, the court invalidated a law passed by Georgia's legislature in 1796 to repeal a 1795 land grant law obtained through bribery of the members of the 1795 legislature.

The repeal was challenged by the innocent third parties who had acquired land under the 1795 grant and who now found their titles null and void. They argued that the legislative nullification was unconstitutional, a clear violation of the Constitution's language, which forbids states to impair the obligation of contracts.

The case was argued twice — in 1809 and 1810. One of the attorneys for the property owners bringing the challenge was 32-year-old Joseph Story of Massachusetts.

On April 16, 1810, the court — for whom Chief Justice Marshall spoke — held unconstitutional the legislative repeal of the land grant law and the nullification of the titles granted under it.

Story won his case — and the following year he was appointed, at 34, to the Supreme Court.

The Last of the First

In September 1810 Justice Cushing died — the last of the original six justices named to the court in 1790; he had outlived all his original colleagues by a decade or more.

The interest that attended the search for Cushing's successor on the bench provided some indication of the status the court had attained in its first decades. The court was then evenly divided between Federalists (Marshall, Washington, Chase) and Republicans (Johnson, Todd, and Livingston).

President Madison received much advice on the selection of a nominee, including some from his predecessor,

Thomas Jefferson. Notwithstanding all the advice — or perhaps because of it — Madison required four tries to fill Cushing's seat.

His first selection was Levi Lincoln, who had served as attorney general to Jefferson. Lincoln declined; Madison nominated him anyway; the Senate confirmed the nomination and Lincoln again firmly declined, early in 1811.

In February, Madison named Alexander Wolcott, a Republican leader in Connecticut, to the seat. Criticized as unqualified, Wolcott was rejected by the Senate: Only nine votes were cast in favor of his confirmation. Madison subsequently nominated John Quincy Adams, then ambassador to Russia; Adams was confirmed but declined the appointment.

Madison then waited for the better part of 1811 before making another choice. The 1811 term — for which there was neither a quorum of justices present nor any business — passed virtually unnoticed.

At mid-year Justice Chase died, creating a second vacancy. In November President Madison nominated Gabriel Duvall of Maryland, comptroller of the treasury for almost a decade, to fill the Chase seat; he named Story to the Cushing seat. Both were quickly confirmed and would serve long terms — Duvall, 23 years; Story, 34.

In Time of War

For the next several years, the conflict with England — the War of 1812 — was a dominant factor in the work of the court. After the Capitol was burned by the British in August 1814, the court met in temporary quarters for the next four terms, even holding some sessions in a tavern.

The cases before the court largely involved wartime issues — neutral rights, ship seizures, foreign affairs. The court made clear in these rulings that violations of neutral rights were to be resolved diplomatically, not judicially. And it affirmed broad power for the federal government over the person and property of enemies during wartime.

Challenge to Power

One result of *Fletcher v. Peck* was considerable state resistance to the court's exercise of its power to invalidate state actions. States began to question whether in fact Congress could authorize the court to curtail state power in such a final manner.

In 1816 the court itself considered that question. The case presenting it was *Martin v. Hunter's Lessee*, a long-running dispute over the ownership of a large parcel of land

William Johnson

Thomas Jefferson

in Virginia. Chief Justice Marshall did not participate in the court's consideration of the matter due to his own ties to the matter.

In 1813 the court had ruled on the substance of the case, deciding in favor of the British claim to the land, rejecting the Virginian's claim. But the Virginia courts refused to obey the decision, ruling that the Supreme Court could not constitutionally tell a state court what to do.

This direct challenge to its authority returned to the court in 1816. On March 20, 1816, it was firmly rebuffed. Justice Story wrote the court's opinion, upholding the power of Congress to grant the Supreme Court appellate jurisdiction over all matters involving federal laws, treaties and the U.S. Constitution — regardless of the court in which such cases had first been heard. This opinion, declared Charles Warren, "has ever since been the keystone of the whole arch of federal judicial power."[39]

In another 1816 ruling, however, the court left the large and controversial area of criminal law almost entirely to state courts. In the case of *United States v. Hudson and Goodwin*, the justices declared that federal courts had no jurisdiction over criminal activity — except for matters which Congress had specifically declared to be federal crimes.

New Questions, New Reporter

Warren describes the end of the 1816 term as the end of an era. With the end of the War of 1812, he writes, the attention of the people turned toward industrial and manufacturing endeavors, transportation, communication and economic change. Questions of war, prize vessels, and embargo acts — which had taken so much of the court's attention during the first years of the century — faded from the docket, to be replaced by questions of contract obligations, commerce regulation, and state powers.

Also at the end of this term, Cranch ended his work as unofficial reporter of the court's work. An official reporter, Henry Wheaton, was appointed; Congress authorized him a salary of $1,000 a year. He would hold that post for 11 years.

The 1819 Term

The term that convened in a new courtroom on Feb. 2, 1819, was one of the most notable in the court's history. The court announced three major constitutional decisions — in the cases of *Dartmouth College v. Woodward, McCulloch v. Maryland* and *Sturges v. Crowninshield.*

The court moved back into permanent quarters for this term; the courtroom under the Senate chamber had been rebuilt. Here the court would meet until the Civil War.

The court announced its decision in the *Dartmouth College* case on the opening day of the term. Argued for three days in the preceding term, the case had drawn little attention in the nation's press. The dispute between a small college in New Hampshire and the state legislature hardly seemed notable. But the issue it presented was of major significance for the nation's economic development: Did the Constitution's contract clause protect private corporate charters — as well as public grants — against impairment by the state?

With only Justice Duvall dissenting, the Supreme Court answered that question with a resounding "yes." Not only did the court protect Dartmouth College from legislative efforts to reshape its structure and purpose, the justices with this decision promised the corporations beginning to form that they too would be secure against this type of interference.

Two weeks later the court seemed to tie the hands of the states even further in economic matters. On Feb. 17 the court held invalid New York's insolvency law — enacted to ease the difficulties of debtors in default. The court held that the New York law violated the ban on state action impairing the obligation of contracts, because it allowed the discharge of debts contracted before its passage.

The day before this ruling the *National Intelligencer* became the first newspaper in the country to begin printing daily announcements of the actions of the Supreme Court. Notwithstanding this new channel of communication of its decisions, the decision in the New York insolvency case, *Sturges v. Crowninshield*, was misreported and misunderstood.

Until a second ruling came in 1827, it generally was thought that the states lacked any power to afford debtors this sort of relief. [40]

McCulloch v. Maryland

After these two rulings were announced, the court moved on to hear arguments — for nine days in late February and early March 1819 — in the case of *McCulloch v. Maryland.*

Daniel Webster, a young member of Congress from Massachusetts who had argued successfully for Dartmouth College, argued for the Bank of the United States in this case. Again, he won.

McCulloch v. Maryland posed two questions to the justices: Did Congress have the power to charter a national bank? Did states have the power to tax the operations of such a bank?

The court announced its decision on Saturday, March 6, affirming the power of Congress and curtailing the power of the states.

Writing for a unanimous court, Chief Justice Marshall declared that Congress had broad power under the "necessary and proper" clause to select the means to implement its powers specifically granted by the Constitution. "Let the end be legitimate, let it be within the scope of the Constitution," wrote Marshall, "and all means which are appropriate . . . which are not prohibited . . . are constitutional."[41]

The bank was a useful fiscal instrument for national economic stability, so Congress might properly decide to incorporate it.

Furthermore, this power could not be hampered by the states — and thus states could not tax the bank, for by taxing it, they could destroy it and frustrate the congressional purpose in chartering the bank. This decision aroused intense opposition, particularly in the South and the West where the bank was hated.

McCulloch v. Maryland, wrote Robert G. McCloskey, "is by almost any reckoning the greatest decision John Marshall ever handed down." In upholding the constitutionality of the bank's incorporation, he continues, Marshall "set down the classic statement of the doctrine of national authority. The argument he advanced was not new; its main outlines had been endlessly debated since the first Congress. . . . But Marshall deserves the credit for stamping it with the die of his memorable rhetoric and converting it from a political theory into the master doctrine of American constitutional law." [42]

Review and Reaction

In 1821 the court for the second time reaffirmed its own power to review the decisions of state courts.

The case of *Cohens v. Virginia* arose from different circumstances than had *Martin v. Hunter's Lessee,* but like the earlier case *Cohens* presented to the court a basic challenge to its power under Section 25 of the Judiciary Act.

With equal firmness, Chief Justice Marshall reiterated the points Justice Story had made in the 1816 ruling. It was the constitutional obligation of the court to review cases in which state courts rejected challenges that state actions were in conflict with the Constitution, U.S. laws or treaties, Marshall declared.

Those who approved the decision considered it "one of the chief bulwarks of American unity." Critics — still led by former President Jefferson — saw it as one more blow to state sovereignty. Jefferson complained that the court was "working like gravity . . . to press us at last into one consolidated mass." [43]

By 1825 the court had nullified as unconstitutional statutes of 10 states. These rulings set off an effort to remove or at least restrict the power of the court to review state court decisions.

Among the measures discussed were repeal of Section 25; a constitutional amendment providing that all cases involving a state would be appealed to the Senate, not the court; statutes requiring that five — or all seven — justices concur in holding a state law invalid.

Jefferson proposed that each justice should be required to issue a separate opinion — as in the pre-Marshall days. He suggested that Congress then denounce the views of those with whom it disagreed — and impeach the justices who did not respond with a change of view. None of these proposals were approved by both chambers of Congress.

Period of Stability

There were no changes in the court's membership from late 1811 until early 1823. Then in March 1823 Justice Livingston died. President Monroe chose Secretary of War Smith Thompson, also of New York and related by marriage to the Livingston clan, to fill the seat. Confirmed late in the year, Thompson took his seat in the February 1824 term. Due to his relationship to the Livingston family — to whom the contested steamboat monopoly involved in the case of *Gibbons v. Ogden* had been granted — Thompson did not participate in that case, the most important one decided by the court in his 20 years of service.

Congress and Commerce

The Constitution granted Congress the power to regulate interstate and foreign commerce. With the exception of an early law providing for the licensing of vessels in the coastal trade, Congress did not exercise this power to any degree in the first years of the nation's existence.

The states, however, passed a variety of laws regulating commerce and transportation within their borders. In the case of *Gibbons v. Ogden,* the court began the long process of defining the reach of federal commerce power and the limits it set to state power.

Gibbons v. Ogden brought before the justices a challenge to New York's grant of a steamboat monopoly to the Fulton-Livingston partnership, giving that company exclusive rights to run steamships on New York waterways. The monopoly provoked considerable interstate animosity threatening to destroy both the national peace and any sort of incipient national commercial network.

The challengers of the monopoly claimed that it interfered with the federal power to regulate interstate commerce because it excluded from New York waterways vessels licensed under the federal coasting law.

The case divided Republican against Federalist in Congress and in the states. It was argued for five days in February 1824. Daniel Webster argued for the challengers.

On March 3, 1824, Chief Justice Marshall, as usual in major cases, delivered the court's opinion. Commerce, the court held, was not merely buying and selling of goods, but included "intercourse" of all sorts. Commerce also included navigation.

Congress had licensed vessels in the coasting trade. The state monopoly conflicted with the free operation of those federally licensed vessels and so must be held invalid.

Gibbons v. Ogden ranks with *McCulloch v. Maryland* as one of the two major rulings of the Marshall era establishing national power and national supremacy. *Gibbons v. Ogden,* furthermore, served as the "emancipation proclamation of American commerce," [44] giving impetus to the development of the port of New York, the railroads and a national system of commerce.

Federal Authority Extended

A few weeks after *Gibbons,* the court approved further extension of federal authority at the expense of state prerogatives — holding in the case of *Osborn v. Bank of the United States* that the bank could sue state officials in federal court even if the state did not consent to the suit. The court went on to declare that a state official who acted in reliance upon an unconstitutional state law — or exceeded his proper authority — was not immune from being sued in federal court for his actions.

In 1825 the court held that if creditors could sue debtors in federal rather than state courts, the federal courts were free to disregard state laws enacted to ease the debtors' plight by, for example, allowing debts paid in depreciated currency. [45]

Also in that term the court for the first time considered a case involving slaves. The court held that slavery was not illegal under international law. [46]

Changes at Court

Congress responded to the court's steadily increasing workload by lengthening its term. Beginning in 1827, the court convened its term on the second Monday in January.

When the 1827 term began, the court had a new member. Justice Todd had died in 1826. President John Quincy Adams named federal Judge Robert Trimble of Kentucky as his successor. Trimble would serve only two terms before his death in 1828.

The 1827 term was a busy one. One historian reports that the court resolved 77 cases during the two-month session, leaving 109 for resolution in the next term. [47]

With the January 1828 term a new reporter took over the function of publishing the court's opinions. Richard Peters Jr. would fill that post for 15 years.

State Powers

Having firmly established federal supremacy and national power in *Marbury, McCulloch* and *Gibbons v. Og-*

den, the court in the 1827 term now upheld the right and power of states to act concurrently with the federal government in some areas.

In the case of *Ogden v. Saunders,* the court clarified the power of states to enact laws to help debtors. By an unusually close vote of 4-3, the justices upheld New York's revised insolvency law, which — as amended after the 1819 ruling in *Sturges v. Crowninshield* — applied only to debts contracted after its passage. For the first and only time in his career, Chief Justice Marshall was on the losing side in a constitutional case. Emphasizing the deference the court owed to the decision of state legislators, Justice Bushrod Washington wrote the majority opinion. Justices Duvall and Story joined Marshall in dissent.

Later in the term, the court upheld a state's power to abolish the penalty of imprisonment for debtors. This did not impair the obligation of a contracted debt, held the court in the case of *Mason v. Haile* but simply modified the remedy for defaulting on that obligation.

Advocates of state powers did lose a major case in the 1827 term, however. *Brown v. Maryland* posed to the justices the question of a state's power to tax persons who sold imported goods in the state. Arguing for the state was Roger B. Taney, who would follow Marshall as Chief Justice. As Marshall had lost the case of *Ware v. Hylton,* so Taney came out on the losing end in this contest.

The court held that a state could not tax persons who sold imported goods, that such a tax interfered with the federal power to regulate imports and impose import duties. So long as imported goods remained in their original package, held the court, they could not be taxed by the state.

Jackson's Justices

In 1828 Justice Trimble, the court's junior member, died. Despite his defeat for re-election that year, President Adams named John J. Crittenden of Kentucky to fill the Trimble seat. The Senate refused to consider the nomination.

Within a week after taking office, President Andrew Jackson named John McLean of Ohio, who had served Adams as postmaster general, to the empty seat.

McLean, a perennial presidential candidate during his 31 years as a justice, had served in the House, run unsuccessfully for the Senate, and had expanded the Post Office into the largest department in the executive branch. As one of the most political men who ever sat on the bench, McLean did not hesitate to use his judicial opinions for political ends. His insistence upon defending the power of Congress to exclude slavery from the territories would precipitate the unfortunate breadth of the Supreme Court's *Dred Scott* decision in 1857 denying that power.

In 1829 Justice Washington died after 32 years on the court. Jackson selected Henry Baldwin of Pennsylvania to the seat. Baldwin, one of the more eccentric men to serve on the court, would hold the seat for 14 years.

Business and Taxes

The 1829 term produced four major rulings on questions of state power. In the case of *Providence Bank v. Billings,* the court held that a state would not be assumed to have granted a corporation a tax exemption unless such a special privilege was explicitly included in the corporation's charter. In the case of *Weston v. City of Charleston,* the court denied cities and states the power to tax U.S. stock, holding such a tax an impermissible interference with the federal borrowing power.

In *Willson v. Blackbird Creek Marsh Co.*, the court upheld some state power to regulate its waterways and navigation thereupon, at least so long as Congress had not exercised its power over those waters.

But in the case of *Craig v. Missouri*, the court held that a state violated the constitutional ban on state bills of credit when it authorized the issuance of state loan certificates.

Another slavery question was before the court in the 1829 term. In *Boyce v. Anderson* the justices held that a slave who drowned in a steamboat accident was a passenger, not freight. The slave owners in the case were disappointed; their recovery would have been greater had the slave been considered cargo.

The Cherokee Crisis

Georgia's effort to bring the Cherokee Indians within its jurisdiction brought the Supreme Court and the state into collision in the last years of the Marshall era.

The Cherokees sought to file an original case in the Supreme Court asking for an order directing Georgia to stop enforcing the stringent new state laws affecting the Indians and their land. While this case was pending before the court late in 1830, the state ignored another court order staying the execution of an Indian convicted of murder under the challenged laws. The state executed the Indian before the court could hear his case.

In January 1831 the House rejected another move for repeal of the statute authorizing the court to review state court rulings. In March the court held that the Cherokees could not bring an original suit because they were not a separate nation in the eyes of the federal law.

But a second case arose quickly. Georgia had convicted and sentenced to hard labor two missionaries who had not complied with state law regarding white persons living in Indian territory. The missionaries took their case to the Supreme Court, arguing that the state lacked the power to impose or enforce such a requirement.

On March 3, 1832, Chief Justice Marshall announced the court's decision, holding the state law was unconstitutional. Federal jurisdiction over Indian matters was exclusive; the state had no power to pass such laws; the missionaries' conviction was reversed and they should be released.

Georgia refused to comply or release the missionaries. President Jackson openly sympathized with the state, allegedly remarking, "Well, John Marshall has made his decision, now let him enforce it."

For months the confrontation persisted. Chief Justice Marshall was most depressed, writing to Justice Story that he doubted that the Union would survive in the face of such rebellion by state authority.

But late in 1832 South Carolina's adoption of a declaration "nullifying" a new tariff law and barring appeals to the Supreme Court from decisions upholding state laws provoked Jackson to label such state resistance treason. He asked Congress to increase the power of federal courts to enforce federal laws in the face of such challenges.

It was abruptly made clear to Georgia officials that their resistance to the Supreme Court's order concerning the missionaries no longer could expect tacit presidential backing. The governor pardoned the missionaries. The case

Daniel Webster   Joseph Story

ended. In 1833 Congress approved Jackson's request for expanded federal judicial power.

The Bill of Rights

Marshall's last major constitutional opinion came in 1833. In the case of *Barron v. Baltimore*, the court held that the Bill of Rights was intended to limit only federal, not state, action. "It is a striking fact," wrote Charles Warren, "that this last of Marshall's opinions on this branch of law should have been delivered in limitation of the operations of the Constitution whose undue extension he had been so long charged with seeking." [48]

As a result of the decision in *Barron v. Baltimore*, it was a full century before the court addressed itself at length to questions of the rights of individuals rather than of institutions. And this decision made necessary the enactment of the 14th Amendment, which would eventually, in the 20th century, be read to extend the guarantees of the Bill of Rights against state action and thus would serve as the basis for an expansion of federal judicial power comparable to that of the Marshall era.

Three major cases were argued in the early 1830s but carried over to later terms because of the court's inability to resolve the questions they posed. These were the cases of *Charles River Bridge v. Warren Bridge*, *Briscoe v. Commonwealth Bank of Kentucky* and *New York v. Miln*. The court's pace was slowed: Marshall was nearing 80, Johnson and Duvall were ill and absent much of the time.

End of an Era

An era was coming to a close. In August 1834 Justice Johnson, the independent soul who fathered the court's tradition of dissent, died. To succeed him, Jackson named James M. Wayne of Georgia. Wayne would serve for 33 years, until 1867.

In January 1835 the aged Duvall resigned. Jackson named Roger B. Taney, former attorney general and Treasury secretary, to succeed him.

But Taney had played a key role in Jackson's war on the Bank of the United States, implementing the president's order to remove U.S. funds from the bank. In that post he had won many enemies. Whig opposition to the nomination convinced the Senate, on the last day of its 1835 session, to postpone consideration of the Taney nomination. The vote was 24-21. The Duvall seat remained empty.

Then, on July 6, 1835, Chief Justice John Marshall died. The court's great center chair was vacant.

Eulogies of Marshall were numerous and elaborate. But perhaps the most objective assessment of his accomplishment as Chief Justice came from abroad. After traveling through the United States in the last years of the Marshall era, Alexis de Tocqueville wrote of the Supreme Court:

The peace, the prosperity, and the very existence of the Union are vested in the hands of the seven Federal judges. Without them the Constitution would be a dead letter: the executive appeals to them for assistance against the encroachments of the legislative power; the legislature demands their protection against the assaults of the executive; they defend the Union from the disobedience of the states, the states from the exaggerated claims of the Union, the public interest against private interests, and the conservative spirit of stability against the fickleness of the democracy. Their power is enormous, but it is the power of public opinion. [49]

No single man had done more than John Marshall to establish that enormous power or to win the essential public respect for and support of the still-young Supreme Court of the United States.

State Power and Slavery: 1836-1860

It is perhaps a mark of how infrequently presidential nominees to the Supreme Court adhere to the views of their patron that the court never has been known by the name of a president, even if he named all or most of its members.

President Washington of course selected the entire original court; it was never referred to as the "Washington Court." The next president to name more than half the tribunal's members was Andrew Jackson. Jackson named six justices in eight years. Of the six, four served for more than a quarter of a century, well into the Civil War.

Jackson's first three nominees were McLean, Baldwin and Wayne. The fourth was Roger B. Taney.

After Jackson's nomination of Taney as an associate justice was postponed by the Senate early in 1835, Chief Justice Marshall's death opened a second vacancy on the court. When Congress convened late in 1835, Jackson sent it a second Taney nomination, this one for the post of Chief Justice.

To fill the vacant seat of an associate justice Jackson chose Philip B. Barbour of Virginia, who had argued the state's case in *Cohens v. Virginia.* Barbour had served several terms in the House, during which he had advocated proposals that required five of seven justices to concur in holding a statute unconstitutional; he also had served as a state and a federal judge. Barbour would have the briefest tenure of all the Jackson appointees. He died in 1841 after five years on the court.

The same political opposition that delayed action on Taney's first nomination to the court delayed confirmation of him as Chief Justice until March 15, 1836. Leaders of the opposition to his selection were two of the foremost Supreme Court advocates of the era, Daniel Webster and Henry Clay. Nevertheless, the Senate at length confirmed Taney's nomination by a vote of 29-15.

While the Senate considered the nomination, the court met without a Chief Justice for its 1836 term. Story, the senior sitting justice, presided.

Taney's First Term

In 1837, Chief Justice Taney's first term, the court finally decided the three major constitutional cases that had been pending throughout the last years of the Marshall era — *Charles River Bridge v. Warren Bridge, New York v. Miln* and *Briscoe v. Commonwealth Bank of Kentucky.*

Many saw the court's rulings in these cases as clear evidence that the Taney court would favor the rights of the states, which the court under Chief Justice Marshall consistently had curtailed.

A more measured assessment of the relationship between the court under Taney and that under Marshall is provided by Carl B. Swisher:

The work of the 1837 term . . . marked the beginning of a new order. The transition was not a sharp one, and those who saw it as such were mistaken. In spite of the radical doctrines sponsored by some Jacksonians of the time, the Court was careful to adhere to traditional patterns. . . . The change was limited . . . and yet it was there. There was a greater tendency to look to items of local welfare and to emphasize the rights of the states, a greater concern with living democracy in a rapidly changing society. [50]

Contracts

First and most famous of the decisions of this term is that in the *Charles River Bridge* case, first argued before the court in 1831. The issue was the constitutional ban on state action impairing the obligation of contracts.

The Charles River Bridge Co., originally chartered by the state to build a bridge to bear passenger traffic across the Charles River near Boston, challenged a subsequent state act allowing a second bridge to be built across that river. Daniel Webster argued for the original company that implicit in its charter was the exclusive privilege to carry such traffic. After five days of argument in January 1837, the court announced its opinion in February. Chief Justice Taney wrote the court's decision.

The court did not undercut its earlier rulings recognizing and protecting contract obligations, but it ruled against the Charles River Bridge Co. A charter, Taney explained, would not be construed to be more favorable to its corporate recipient — at public expense — than its express terms required. In the absence of an explicit grant of monopoly privilege, the state had not infringed the first charter by granting a second to another company.

Commerce and Credit

A few days after that ruling, the court held that a state might properly require shipowners to report all passengers on ships arriving in its ports. This reporting requirement had been challenged, in the case of *New York v. Miln,* as an infringement of the federal power to regulate foreign commerce. But the court held the requirement a legitimate exercise of the state police power.

The term's third major ruling also worked to give states more room in which to exercise their power. In the case of *Briscoe v. Commonwealth Bank of Kentucky,* like *Miln* first argued in the 1834 term, the court upheld a state law that authorized a state-chartered bank to issue bank notes. Henry Clay had argued for the victorious bank.

This law, like that struck down seven years earlier in *Craig v. Missouri,* had been challenged as infringing the constitutional ban on state bills of credit. But where the Marshall court had struck down the law in *Craig,* the Taney court upheld that in *Briscoe.* Justice Story dissented, as he had in the earlier two decisions, saying that Chief Justice Marshall would have disagreed too.

The Nine-Man Court

On the last day of President Jackson's term in office, Congress expanded the court to nine seats. Jackson immediately nominated John Catron of Tennessee and William Smith of Alabama to fill the two new seats.

Catron, the Tennessee campaign manager for the newly elected president, Martin Van Buren, was confirmed and served until 1865. Smith declined the second seat.

Van Buren then named Alabama senator-elect John McKinley to the seat. He was confirmed and served 15 years, although illness curtailed his participation in the court for half that period.

The Exercise of Power

During Taney's tenure as Chief Justice, the court continued sturdily to assert its own power and that of lower federal courts to resolve the increasingly frequent questions of the allocation of governmental authority. The *Dred Scott* decision provides dramatic example of the extreme to which this point could be carried.

But unlike that ruling, most of the court's pronouncements in this area simply consolidated and reinforced the position the court already had assumed in earlier years.

In 1838 Rhode Island came to the court asking the justices to resolve a boundary dispute with Massachusetts, the first such case to come to the court. Massachusetts moved to dismiss the case, arguing that the court lacked the power to hear it. Over the dissent of the Chief Justice, the court rejected the motion and proceeded with the case, which finally was resolved in favor of Massachusetts in 1846.

The 1838 term also brought the court's decision in the case of *Kendall v. United States,* upholding the power of a federal court to issue an order directing an executive branch official to perform non-discretionary "ministerial" duties — even if the court order was in direct conflict with presidential instructions to the official. Such orders, held the court, did not breach the separation of powers.

Cases and Corporations

The increase in the number of corporate enterprises operating within the United States brought questions of corporate rights and state powers before the court.

In 1839 the court held, on one hand, that states could forbid out-of-state companies to do business in their territory. But in the same case the court effectively moderated that holding by declaring that without clear evidence that a state intended to exercise this power, it would be assumed to consent to the operations of such "foreign" corporations.[51]

Five years later, the court opened the doors of the federal courts to corporate litigation by modifying the strict view of a corporation's "residence" adopted early in the Marshall era. The new rule allowed more cases involving corporations to be heard in federal courts, rather than state courts, on the basis that the corporation and the opposing party were residents of different states.[52]

Slavery and States' Rights

Advocates of state sovereignty tasted defeat in a number of rulings from the Taney court early in the 1840s. In *Holmes v. Jennison,* decided in 1840, the court made clear that the Constitution left states no power to engage in foreign affairs. Two years later the court held that federal courts were not bound by state judges' interpretations of state laws. In another case decided that term, the court held that states could not tax the income of federal officials.[53]

By the 1840s virtually all questions of states' rights seemed to tie back into the increasingly sensitive issue of slavery. The court had carefully avoided addressing this issue in any but peripheral ways, but by 1841, writes Swisher, "the court found itself in the thick of the slavery discussion, from which it did not actually escape until the close of the Civil War period, even though there were intervening years in which no such cases were actually decided."[54]

Thus, even when the issue was commerce in general, with no evident tie to the slavery issue, the court's opinions were closely perused and construed as expanding or curtailing state powers to deal with slavery.

The double-edged nature of the issue — and all judicial efforts to deal with it — was evident in the 1841 and 1842 rulings of the court and their public reception.

In 1841 the court decided the case of *Groves v. Slaughter* on a point other than the slavery questions presented. But Justice McLean's opinion, declaring the right of a state to exclude slavery, was interpreted by some southerners as upholding the right of a state to exclude free blacks as well.

The following year the court decided the case of *Prigg v. Pennsylvania.* It struck down a Pennsylvania law setting

John McLean   Roger B. Taney

up certain procedures for determining whether a black person was in fact the sought-after fugitive before he or she was removed from the state by a pursuer. Federal power over fugitive slaves was exclusive, leaving states no opportunity to pass such laws, held the court. But, wrote Swisher, "while upholding the power of the federal government to provide for the return of fugitive slaves, it nullified the obligations and seemed to nullify the power of the states to aid in the process, [and] it at once gave incentive to abolitionist activities and led the South to demand enactment of a Fugitive Slave Act which could be effectively administered without the aid of the states. Thereby it added to the furor of sectional conflict and the hysteria of competing parties." [55]

Court Vacancies

The court's efforts to deal with the increasingly difficult questions before it were hampered by the illness and disability of some of its members and then by long-vacant seats, the product of political turmoil outside the courtroom.

In this period occurred the longest vacancy in Supreme Court history to date. After the death of Justice Baldwin in April 1844, his seat remained empty for more than two years.

This extended vacancy was in large part the result of the political disaffection that marred the relationship between President John C. Tyler and Congress. Tyler had more nominations to the court rejected than any other president. Of his six nominations, only one was confirmed.

Before Tyler took office, there was another new justice. Justice Barbour died during the 1841 term. The lame-duck president, Van Buren, nominated — and the Senate quickly confirmed — Peter V. Daniel of Virginia, a federal judge, to Barbour's seat. Daniel served until 1860.

Tyler had his first opportunity to name a justice when Justice Smith Thompson died in 1843. He chose Treasury Secretary John Spencer; Spencer was rejected by the Senate in January 1844. Tyler next nominated Reuben Walworth of New York, state chancellor. Before its midyear adjournment, the Senate tabled that nomination.

In April, Justice Baldwin died. Tyler nominated Philadelphia lawyer James Edward King for that seat. The King nomination was also tabled by the Senate. Both the King and the Walworth nominations finally were withdrawn.

Early in 1845, Tyler, now a lame duck in addition to his other political disabilities, sent two more names to the Senate. To fill the Thompson seat he chose Samuel Nelson, a New York judge. Nelson, a well-respected figure, was quickly confirmed; he would serve on the court for 27 years, until 1872. But Tyler's selection of John M. Read as Baldwin's successor was ignored by the Senate. That seat remained empty for another full year.

Early in the Polk administration, Justice Story died. He had served longer than any other justice to that time — 34 years. Late in 1845 Polk nominated George W. Woodward of Pennsylvania to fill the Baldwin seat — and Sen. Levi Woodbury of New Hampshire to fill Story's chair. Woodbury — Taney's successor as secretary of the Treasury — was quickly confirmed early in 1846; he would serve only six years before his death in 1851. Woodward, his nomination opposed by one of his state's senators, was rejected.

Finally, in August, Polk named Pennsylvania judge Robert C. Grier to the Baldwin seat. He was quickly confirmed, ending the 28-month vacancy on the court. He served for 24 years, until his resignation in 1870.

For the next five years, the court's membership was complete and stable.

Commerce Confusion

Despite its stability of membership, the court's performance on the interlocking issues of commerce and slavery was confusing, to say the least. In the December 1846 term, the court again upheld the federal fugitive slave law.[56] But in the same term, it backed state power to regulate commerce in intoxicating liquor.

The diversity of reasoning among the justices in these latter cases — known as the *License Cases* — from Massachusetts, Rhode Island and New Hampshire reflected the court's increasing division over the location of the lines dividing state and federal power over commerce. Six justices wrote nine opinions in the *License Cases*.

In early 1849 this uncertainty of opinion flowered into complete confusion with the decision of the court in the *Passenger Cases*. These two cases, from New York and Boston, involved state laws that required masters of vessels to post bonds and to pay a tax for each immigrant landed in the state. The laws were challenged as infringing upon federal power to regulate foreign commerce. They were defended as a proper exercise of the state's police power to protect its public health and welfare.

After hearing each case argued three times, the court found these laws unconstitutional because they conflicted with federal power over foreign commerce. But beyond that point the court splintered, with eight justices writing separate opinions that took seven hours to read from the bench. The justices could not agree on whether the federal power over foreign commerce was exclusive, leaving no room for state regulation, or whether there might be such room if Congress had not exercised its power in a particular area.

There was no opinion of the court in these cases, and Reporter Benjamin C. Howard, exercising considerable wisdom, declined to summarize the ruling beyond the fact that it struck down the challenged laws. For details and reasoning, he simply referred the reader to the "opinions of the judges."

Political Questions

In the 1829 case of *Foster v. Neilson,* the court had refused to resolve an international boundary dispute because it said such a disagreement presented a "political question" that should be resolved by the representative branches of the government.

Twenty years later the court applied this doctrine in the case of *Luther v. Borden* and refused to decide which of two competing factions was the legitimate government of Rhode Island. This too was a political question, held the court, suitable for resolution by Congress, not the court.

Internal Changes

In 1844 Congress responded to the increasing workload of the court by lengthening its term. Opening day was moved back from January to the first Monday in December.

Other procedural changes during this time reflected the end of the days when the court considered only a few cases and did so at a leisurely pace that allowed time for lengthy arguments and required less record keeping. In 1839 the court required that all motions to it be filed in writing with the clerk. In 1849 the court limited the time for arguments, giving counsel for each side two hours to present his case, but no more, without special leave.

In 1843 Richard Peters, for 15 years the court's reporter, was fired by four of the justices acting in the absence of the Chief Justice and their other colleagues. Peters had fallen out of favor with several of the justices as a result of differences over the inclusion of their opinions in the reports.

Peters was replaced by Benjamin Howard of Maryland, a former member of Congress and a college friend of Justice Wayne. Howard would serve until 1861.

Public Confidence

Despite the personnel changes and philosophical difficulties endured by the court during the 1840s, public confidence in it continued to rise. Charles Warren reports that public esteem for the Supreme Court was at a peak in the last years of that decade. He wrote that "while there were extremists and radicals in both parties who inveighed against it and its decisions, yet the general mass of the public and the Bar had faith in its impartiality and its ability."[57]

The first decisions of the next decade — which would bring a precipitate drop in public respect for the court — appeared to bear out this confidence. The court exercised restraint in dealing with the slavery issue — and appeared to be clarifying its position on commerce matters.

In the December 1850 term the court heard arguments in the case of *Strader v. Graham.* The basic question presented was the same one that would arise in the *Dred Scott* case a few years later: Were slaves owned in Kentucky still slaves after they worked for a time in a free state and returned to Kentucky?

The court held that this matter should be resolved in the courts and under the laws of the state where the slaves were residing. This was not a matter for federal courts to resolve, held the justices.

Cooley, Curtis and Commerce

Late in 1851 Justice Woodbury died. As his successor, President Millard Fillmore chose Benjamin R. Curtis, 41, a noted Boston attorney. Confirmed in December 1851, Curtis would serve only six terms, but in that brief tenure he would leave his mark on history in several notable constitutional opinions.

The first of these rulings came during his first term in the case of *Cooley v. Board of Wardens of the Port of Philadelphia,* which required the justices to decide whether a city could enact ordinances concerning the use of pilots in its harbor. Philadelphia's ordinance regulating this matter was challenged as infringing on the federal power over commerce.

The court upheld the Philadelphia ordinance. Curtis wrote the majority opinion. The court declared that there were two categories of interstate and foreign commerce: one essentially local, which could be regulated locally, at least so long as it was not regulated by Congress; the other essentially national, which needed a uniform rule if it was to be regulated at all, and thus could never be regulated by the states.

In a sense, the Curtis opinion was no more than "an eloquent statement of indefiniteness," wrote Carl B. Swisher a century later, but "with the statement the indefiniteness came to seem in some way manageable, by contrast with the confusion of multiple opinions in the License Cases and the Passenger Cases. The opinion promised to give a more pragmatic, less conceptual and categorical direction to the Court's thinking concerning state regulation of commerce."[58]

The December 1851 term included two other decisions of importance in the area of navigation and commerce. In the case of *Pennsylvania v. Wheeling & Belmont Bridge Co.,* the court held that a bridge built by the state of Virginia across the Ohio River was too low and thus obstructed interstate commerce. The court ordered the bridge torn down. But Congress in 1852 passed a law that declared the bridge did not obstruct interstate commerce, allowing the bridge to stand. This was the first example of Congress overturning the court's decision by legislation.

Also that term, the court responded to the growing network of national commerce and transportation, substantially enlarging the federal government's admiralty jurisdiction to include all the nation's navigable waterways, not just those subject to the ebb and flow of tides.[59]

The Southern Seat

In July 1852 Justice McKinley died. To fill his place, President Fillmore chose Edward Bradford of Louisiana, who failed to win Senate confirmation during that session. Fillmore next named Sen. George E. Badger of North Carolina, whose nomination was effectively killed when the Senate, in an unusual breach of tradition, postponed consideration of it — by a one-vote margin — early in 1853. In the last week of his term, Fillmore sent still a third name to the Senate — that of Louisianan William C. Micou — but the Senate refused to confirm him.

The new president, Franklin Pierce, chose John A. Campbell of Alabama, 41, well known both for his scholarship and for his advocacy before the Supreme Court. Campbell was quickly confirmed and served until the outbreak of the Civil War.

Due Process

In 1856 the court began the long process of finding a definition of due process. In the case of *Murray v. Hoboken Land & Improvement Co.* the court held that the Fifth Amendment guarantee of due process applied to actions of Congress, as well as to executive and court actions.

John A. Campbell   **Benjamin R. Curtis**

And Justice Curtis, writing for the court, defined due process — by indirection — as procedures that did not conflict with specific written provisions of the Constitution or with the established practice in England at the time of the settlement of the New World colonies.

The *Dred Scott* Case

Also in 1856 the court heard arguments in the case of Dred Scott, a Missouri slave who claimed that he was free as a result of a sojourn in Illinois and other territories that were "free states" under the Missouri Compromise of 1820. Scott's case was argued Feb. 11, 1856. In May of that year the court ordered the case argued again. Reargument took place early in the December 1856 term. Justice Curtis' brother was one of the attorneys appearing in the case before the court.

Chief Justice Taney was aging. This factor, along with health and family problems of other members of the court, slowed its operations. Not until February 1857 — a year after the first arguments — was the *Dred Scott* case discussed at conference.

At the conference the court agreed the decision would follow that in *Strader v. Graham* a few years earlier — holding that Scott's status was a matter to be resolved under state law. The majority agreed not to consider the

---

As long as the Constitution endures, "this tribunal must exist with it, deciding in the peaceful forms of judicial proceedings the angry and irritating controversies between sovereignties, which in other countries have been determined by the arbitrament of force."

—Chief Justice Roger B. Taney
Albeman v. Booth, 1859

---

larger issue — whether Congress had the power to exclude slavery from some territories, as it had done in the now-repealed Missouri Compromise. Justice Nelson was assigned the task of writing this majority opinion.

But Justices McLean and Curtis, both convinced anti-slavery men, dissented, and announced their intention to declare in their opinions that the Missouri Compromise was proper, that Congress indeed did have the power to ban slavery from the territories.

The majority thus was compelled to revise its plan. Nelson's assignment was withdrawn. Chief Justice Taney took upon himself the task of writing the majority's main opinion.

Taney's illness delayed announcement of the decision until March 6, 1857, just after President Buchanan was inaugurated. Each justice wrote a separate opinion in this case; the reading of the opinions in court took two days.

The court declared blacks forever disabled from attaining citizenship, the Missouri Compromise unconstitutional, and Congress powerless to halt the spread of slavery.

The court had overreached its power in setting such limits to the hopes of black men and the powers of Congress. It forced the issue of slavery out of the courtroom and the legislative chambers and onto the battlefield. This was also the first of the "self-inflicted wounds" of the court.

One scholar summarized the weakening impact of this decision upon the court:

During neither the Civil War nor the period of Reconstruction did the Supreme Court play anything like its role of supervision, with the result that during the one period the military powers of the President underwent undue expansion, and during the other, the legislative powers of Congress. The court itself was conscious of its weakness. . . . [A]t no time since Jefferson's first administration has its independence been in greater jeopardy than between 1860 and 1870.[60]

The *Dred Scott* decision was endorsed by southern Democrats and denounced by northern Democrats, dividing the party into warring factions and enabling the Republican Party to win the White House in 1860. Thus, Charles Warren would write, "it may fairly be said that Chief Justice Taney elected Abraham Lincoln to the presidency."[61]

Curtis' Resignation

Another result of the *Dred Scott* decision was Justice Curtis' decision to resign after only six years on the court. His philosophical disagreement with his colleagues and his general lack of confidence in the court, compounded by an acrimonious exchange with Chief Justice Taney over access to the *Dred Scott* opinions, spurred him to leave the bench and return to his more lucrative practice of law. He resigned in September 1857. He would argue more than 50 cases before the court in subsequent years, including the first *Legal Tender Case,* which he lost.

To replace Curtis in the "New England seat," President Buchanan nominated former Attorney General Nathan Clifford. Clifford, considered a party hack by some in the Senate, was confirmed by a three-vote margin early in 1858. He served until his death in 1881.

Federal Judicial Power

Although Chief Justice Taney's name became almost synonymous with his *Dred Scott* opinion — and the damage it did to the nation and the court — his last major pre-war opinion was both far more eloquent and more enduring in its impact.

Two years after the *Dred Scott* ruling, the court decided the case of *Ableman v. Booth.* In speaking for the court, Chief Justice Taney delivered a ringing reaffirmation of federal judicial power.

The case of *Ableman v. Booth* involved an abolitionist in Wisconsin who was tried and convicted of violating the federal Fugitive Slave Act. Both before his trial and after his conviction, state judges ordered federal officials to release him, using the writ of *habeas corpus* and declaring his detention improper.

Finally the case came before the Supreme Court in January 1859. The state did not send anyone to argue its case. On March 7, 1859, the unanimous Supreme Court declared that state judges lacked the power to so interfere in federal judicial proceedings.

To allow such interference, wrote Chief Justice Taney, "would subvert the very foundations of this Government." As long as the Constitution endured, he continued, "this tribunal must exist with it, deciding in the peaceful forms of judicial proceedings the angry and irritating controversies between sovereignties, which in other countries have been determined by the arbitrament of force." [62]

The Taney Court: A Modern View

The *Dred Scott* decision and the conflict that followed it so colored historians' view of the Taney court that only after a century had passed was an objective assessment of its accomplishments possible.

In the concluding chapter of his history of the Taney era, published in 1974, Carl B. Swisher described the court's decisions and operations during this period:

By contrast with the work of the same tribunal in various other periods, the essence of its contribution was seldom focused in eloquent philosophical statement from the bench. The Taney Court was peculiarly unphilosophical.... [I]t tended to be assumed that the federal constitutional system was now generally understood so that the earlier forms of judicial explanation were unnecessary. The government was no longer experimental but was a going concern....

The Taney court fell upon evil times not because of Jacksonianism or even because of lack of ability on the part of its members, but because it was caught in the grinding pressures of sectional conflict. A Court committed to application of the law was bound to crash into difficulties when the nation itself divided over whether there was indeed a surviving body of constitutional law binding on all the states and all the people.

... [I]n this time of civil war the strident ... voice of Mars ... drowned out the voice of the law, with its stress upon reason and rightness rather than ruthless power.... [63]

War and Recovery: 1861-1872

The decade of the Civil War saw the Supreme Court sink to its lowest point in public esteem. This, Carl Swisher explains, was "not merely because it had handed down the Dred Scott decision but because the rule of law as interpreted by the judiciary had given way to a rage for unrestricted exercise of power — which seemed to flare with even greater violence once the battlefields were stilled. There could be a restoration of the prestige of the judiciary only with restoration of respect for the rule of law." [64]

During this period, which includes the last years of Chief Justice Roger B. Taney and almost the entire tenure of his successor, Chief Justice Salmon P. Chase, the court as an institution underwent considerable change.

It moved into a new courtroom, was expanded to 10 seats and contracted to eight, gained five new members — including the new Chief Justice — and found itself faced with the most sensitive questions to date concerning the powers of the president.

New Justices

In mid-1860 Justice Daniel died. His seat remained empty well into 1862.

Late in his term, President Buchanan named his former attorney general and secretary of State, Jeremiah S. Black, to fill Daniel's seat. But political opposition within both parties brought the rejection of Black's nomination by a vote of 25-26 in February 1861.

The Civil War broke out in April. That same month two more vacancies occurred. Justice McLean died and Justice Campbell resigned when his home state, Alabama, seceded. The court's other southern members — Wayne and Catron — continued to hold their seats through the war.

President Lincoln thus had three seats to fill. In January 1862 he selected Noah H. Swayne, an Ohio attorney, 57, to fill the McLean seat. Swayne would serve 19 years.

In July 1862 Lincoln filled the empty Daniel seat with Samuel Freeman Miller of Iowa, 46, the only justice trained in medicine as well as law. He would serve for 28 years, until 1890, writing 616 opinions.[65]

To the third seat Lincoln named his close friend and political adviser David Davis of Illinois, 47. Davis would serve 14 years, until he resigned to take a Senate seat.

In March 1863 Congress added a 10th seat to the court, giving Lincoln a fourth appointment. To that new seat he named Stephen J. Field, chief justice of the California Supreme Court, who would serve almost 35 years and be the only justice ever the target of an assassination attempt as a result of his rulings. When Field was appointed he had to travel to Washington by steamship and railroad across Panama. The transcontinental railroad was not completed until 1869.

New Chambers

When the court met for its December 1860 term, it met in a new courtroom. After four decades in the basement room under the Senate chamber, the court moved upstairs. The new wings of the Capitol housing the Senate and House had been completed; the old Senate chamber had been refurbished for the court at a cost of $25,000. The court would meet in this room for the next 75 years, until moving into its own building.

There was a new reporter for the court in 1861. Benjamin C. Howard resigned to run unsuccessfully for governor of Maryland. He was succeeded by Jeremiah Black, Buchanan's unsuccessful nominee for the Daniel seat. Black served for only two years, resigning in 1863 to resume his successful private practice of law full time. He was succeeded in 1864 by John William Wallace of Pennsylvania, who held the post until 1875.

Presidential War Powers

The Civil War began in April 1861. Congress did not meet until mid-summer. In the interim President Lincoln moved to deal with the emergency, calling for troops, imposing a blockade on southern ports, and in some circumstances authorizing military commanders to suspend the privilege of the writ of *habeas corpus*.

These actions marked the most dramatic expansion of executive power in the nation's history to that point and, not surprisingly, some of them were challenged as exceeding the president's constitutional authority.

Chief Justice Taney was among the first to declare Lincoln's actions unconstitutional. In May, the month after war had broken out, a military commander in Baltimore refused to comply with Taney's order — issued as a circuit judge, not a Supreme Court justice — to produce in court one John Merryman, a civilian imprisoned by the Union army for his anti-Union activities.

The commander cited, as grounds for his refusal, Lincoln's instructions allowing him to suspend the privilege of the writ of *habeas corpus*, the instrument used to inquire into the reasons justifying an individual's detention.

Taney responded with an opinion, which he sent to Lincoln himself, declaring that only Congress could suspend this privilege and that Lincoln's actions were thus unconstitutional. If such authority can be "usurped by the military power . . . the people of the United States are no longer living under a government of laws, but every citizen holds his life, liberty, and property at the will and pleasure of the army officer in whose military district he may happen to be found." [66]

Lincoln, undeterred, continued to insist that emergency conditions required the exercise of extraordinary power. Five years later, after both Taney and Lincoln were dead, the Supreme Court in the case of *Ex parte Milligan* would confirm Taney's position.

The *Prize Cases*

The legality of Lincoln's actions blockading southern ports was the major war issue resolved by the court during the war years. And it was decided in the *Prize Cases* in 1863 in favor of presidential power, if only by a vote of 5-4.

Had the vote tipped the other way, all of Lincoln's wartime actions would have been called into question, seriously undermining his ability to lead the nation in the conflict.

The majority upheld the president's power to institute the blockade even before Congress officially had authorized such an action. The vote made clear the importance of Lincoln's appointments to the court. The majority consisted of his first three nominees — Swayne, Miller and Davis — and Wayne and Grier, who wrote the majority opinion. Dissenting were Taney, Nelson, Catron and Clifford.

Having resolved that critical question, the court retreated to a position of restraint in dealing with issues of war. In the December 1863 term, Taney's last, the court held that it lacked jurisdiction to hear a challenge to the use of paper money as legal tender (necessary to finance the war),[67] or over a petition of *habeas corpus* ordering military officials to justify their detention of a civilian.[68] Within six years, the court would reverse both holdings.

The Court in 1865

From left: Court Clerk Daniel W. Middleton, Justices David Davis, Noah H. Swayne, Robert C. Grier, James M. Wayne, Chief Justice Salmon P. Chase, Justices Samuel Nelson, Nathan Clifford, Samuel F. Miller, Stephen J. Field.

A New Chief

In October 1864, as the war neared its end, Chief Justice Taney died. He was 87 years old and had served the nation as its Chief Justice for 28 years.

President Lincoln wished to name a man who would back the administration on the critical issues of emancipation — another exercise of extraordinary presidential powers that lacked any clear base in the Constitution — and legal tender. Congress had passed laws making paper money legal tender in place of gold to enable the Union to finance its war effort.

Lincoln chose Salmon P. Chase, a potential political rival who had, nevertheless, served until mid-1864 as secretary of the Treasury. After his re-election in 1864, Lincoln nominated Chase as Chief Justice. He was quickly confirmed and seated as the court began its December 1864 term. Chase was 56, three years younger than Taney when he had assumed the post, yet he would serve only nine years before his death in 1873.

Military Justice

"Never again would there be a term wherein so few questions of importance were answered as in that of 1864-65," wrote historian Charles Fairman.[69]

But the following term brought before the justices another facet of the problem that had confronted Chief Justice Taney in the *Merryman* case five years earlier: Can a president in wartime replace the nation's civilian courts with courts-martial, to which civilians as well as military men are subject?

In April 1866 the Supreme Court answered this question with an emphatic "no" — just as Taney had. The justices were unanimous in holding that Lincoln had acted illegally when he instituted trial by military commission for civilians in non-war areas where the civil courts continued to function.

The court divided 5-4 on the related issue of whether Congress and the president acting together could replace civilian justice with courts-martial in such areas.

The court's full opinions in this case of *Ex parte Milligan* were not released until December 1866 — eight months later. The majority opinion was written by Lincoln's personal friend, Justice Davis, who warned as Taney had that suspension of constitutional guarantees during wartime would lead to despotism.

These opinions and this ruling provoked violent criticism in Congress. There they were viewed as evidence that the court would — at its first opportunity — hold unconstitutional the military regimes imposed as Congress' effort to reconstruct the defeated South.

Congressional criticism took the forms of proposals for impeachment of the majority justices, "reorganization" of the court through the addition of new seats, curtailment of the court's appellate jurisdiction, and the requirement that the court be unanimous on constitutional rulings.

In fact, the court did undergo some reorganization at this point, due, however, more to the unpopularity of President Johnson than to the court's own rulings.

In May 1865 Justice Catron died after 28 years on the court, the last of which he had spent in virtual exile from his southern home. Johnson's April 1866 nomination of his close friend, Attorney General Henry Stanbery, died after the Senate abolished the vacant seat, and reduced the size of the court to seven by providing that both Catron's seat and the next two becoming vacant would not be filled.

In mid-1867 Justice Wayne — the court's other southern member — died after 32 years on the bench. He was the last of the Jackson justices; his service had spanned the Taney era. His seat was not filled; the court was now eight members.

The *Test Oath* Cases

The apprehensiveness of Reconstruction architects about the court's view of their measures was heightened early in 1867. The court struck down an act of Congress requiring persons wishing to practice law before the federal courts to take a "test oath" affirming their loyalty — past and present — to the Union.

Augustus H. Garland, a noted Supreme Court advocate, later attorney general, who had served in the Confederate government during the war, challenged this test oath requirement. A similar state law also was challenged.

In the cases of *Ex parte Garland* and *Cummings v. Missouri*, the court in 1867 held both state and federal oath requirements unconstitutional. The majority found them a violation of the Constitution's ban on *ex post facto* laws and bills of attainder. The only Lincoln justice voting with the majority was Field; the arguments of his brother, David Dudley Field, who had argued one of the cases before the court, apparently persuaded Justice Field to vote against the test oaths.

A Matter of Jurisdiction

After *Milligan* and the *Test Oath Cases*, however, the Supreme Court showed no stomach for battle with Congress on the overall issue of Reconstruction.

In the 1867 term — only months after deciding the Garland case — the court unanimously refused Mississippi's request that it order President Johnson to stop enforcing the Reconstruction Acts. Such an order, the court held in *Mississippi v. Johnson*, was outside its power and its jurisdiction. Similar reasoning brought rejection of a like request from Georgia the following month.

The following term, however, the application of a southern editor named McCardle to the court for a writ of *habeas corpus* to force military authorities in Mississippi to justify their holding him for trial brought to a peak the concern of Reconstruction advocates in Congress.

McCardle was being held for trial by a military commission on charges that his anti-Reconstruction articles were impeding the process of "reconstructing" the South.

The court heard arguments in the case the first week of March 1868, just as the Senate opened its impeachment trial of President Johnson. Three days after the court had taken the *McCardle* case under advisement, Congress revoked its jurisdiction over such cases. Johnson vetoed the bill. It was immediately repassed over his veto.

The court then considered the new issue — the impact of the repeal of its jurisdiction on the pending case. Later in the spring the court postponed final consideration of the case until the next term.

In May the Senate acquitted President Johnson.

The following April — 1869 — the court dismissed the *McCardle* case. The court held unanimously that when Congress revoked its jurisdiction over a category of cases, it was left powerless to do anything but dismiss all pending cases of that type.

The same day, in the case of *Texas v. White,* the court's majority endorsed the view that as a matter of law the seceding states never had left the union — that states had no power to secede — a moot point in 1869. Justices Swayne, Grier and Miller objected that the majority was endorsing a legal fiction and ignoring political reality.

Gold or Greenbacks?

To finance the war, Congress had passed the Legal Tender Acts, allowing the use of paper money in the payment of debts. These laws — which resulted in drastic change in the nation's economic system — repeatedly were challenged in federal courts.

In the December 1867 term, the Supreme Court heard such a challenge argued in the case of *Hepburn v. Griswold.* The justices ordered a second round of arguments that took place in December 1868; one of the attorneys arguing for the acts was the former justice, Benjamin R. Curtis, who had resumed an active legal practice upon resigning his seat.

Contemporary coverage of the case indicated little expectation that the court would hold the acts unconstitutional. After all, Chief Justice Chase had been Treasury secretary when the challenged laws were approved at the behest of the Lincoln administration.

But even after the second arguments, no decision was announced during the December 1868 term. The justices apparently did not reach a decision until November 1869 — and then their efforts were hampered by the vacillations of the aged Justice Grier, who voted in conference first to uphold the acts, then to strike them down.[70] The final vote in November was 5-3 against the validity of the Legal Tender Acts. The majority consisted of Chase, Nelson, Clifford, Field and Grier.

Congress in 1869 provided that a justice might retire and continue to receive half his salary. In December — before the court announced its decision in *Hepburn v. Griswold* — Justice Grier, 76, was persuaded to retire, effective Feb. 1, 1870.

Six days after his resignation, on Feb. 7, 1870, the court announced that by a 4-3 vote it found the statutes unconstitutional. They were inappropriate means for the exercise of the war powers, held the majority, and, as applied to debts contracted before the passage of the laws, they were a clear impairment of contract obligations. The dissenters were Justices Miller, Swayne and Davis.

Court Packing?

Even as Chase was reading the opinion in *Hepburn v. Griswold,* either the most effective court packing in the nation's history — or at least the best timing of appointments — was under way.

After Grant's election as president in 1868, Congress increased the size of the court to nine, giving Grant a new seat to fill. Grier's decision to retire opened a second vacancy.

Grant first chose Attorney General Ebenezer Hoar of Massachusetts for the new seat. But personal and political opposition developed to block that nomination in the Senate. To smooth the way for Hoar's confirmation, Grant nominated former Secretary of War Edwin M. Stanton — the choice of most members of Congress — for the Grier seat. Stanton was confirmed immediately, but died four days later. Hoar's nomination was rejected in February 1870; the vote was 24-33.

And so on Feb. 7, 1870, Grant sent two more nominations to the Senate — Joseph P. Bradley of New Jersey, 57, a railroad attorney, and Grier's personal choice as his successor; and William Strong of Pennsylvania, a state judge. Bradley and Strong were confirmed and seated in the spring of 1870.

Within weeks of their seating the court announced it would rehear the constitutional challenge to the Legal Tender Acts. The second *Legal Tender Case* — *Knox v. Lee* — was argued in the December 1870 term.

On May 1, 1871, 15 months after *Hepburn v. Griswold,* the court overruled itself. By a 5-4 vote, the court reversed the 4-3 vote in the earlier case. The five-man majority upheld the Legal Tender Acts as a proper exercise of the power of Congress. Justice Strong, who with Bradley converted the dissenters in *Hepburn* into the majority in *Knox,* wrote the majority opinion. The full opinions were not released until January of the following year.

This abrupt about-face — so clearly the result of a change in the court's membership — damaged the public confidence the court had been slowly regaining after the *Dred Scott* ruling and the war decade. It was, in the words of Charles Evans Hughes, 'the second of the court's self-inflicted wounds. Hughes declared that "there was no ground for attacking the honesty of the judges or for the suggestion that President Grant had attempted to pack the court." But he added: "Stability in judicial opinions is of no little importance in maintaining respect for the court's work." [71]

The Balance of Power: 1873-1888

The Union had been preserved. Indeed, in *Texas v. White,* a majority of the Supreme Court endorsed the legal fiction that it never had been disrupted. Now — as the critical war issues of the 1860s faded from its docket — the court set about restoring the state-federal balance of power.

Concern for the maintenance of the states as effective functioning units of the federal system was paramount in the minds of the justices. And so, to enhance state power, the court curtailed federal authority.

The court's power of judicial review of acts of Congress was wielded with new vigor. Between *Marbury* in 1803 and the *Slaughterhouse Cases* in 1873, the court held unconstitutional 10 acts of Congress. Six of the 10 were struck down between 1870 and 1873.

Another sign of the court's new sensitivity to the claims of states was its decision in 1871 that, even as the salaries of federal officials were not subject to state taxes, so state officials' salaries were immune from federal taxes.[72]

The 14th Amendment

No better example of the court's view of the proper balance between state and federal power can be found than its rulings interpreting the Civil War Amendments — in particular the 14th Amendment.

In 1865 the addition of the 13th Amendment had formally declared the abolition of slavery. In 1868 the 14th Amendment gave added protection to the rights and liberties of persons threatened by state action. And in 1870 the 15th Amendment guaranteed blacks the right to vote.

Intended as instruments of radical change in the nation's social fabric, these amendments were so narrowly construed by the court in the decades immediately after their adoption that they lay virtually useless for most of the ensuing century.

The effect of these rulings was to preserve state power over the rights of individuals by denying any expansion of federal authority in that area.

The *Slaughterhouse Cases*

The court's first ruling on the scope of the 14th Amendment came in 1873 with the *Slaughterhouse Cases.* It was indicative of the direction in which 14th Amendment protections would first be extended that these cases were brought by butchers seeking to protect their businesses rather than by blacks seeking to assert their newly granted civil rights.

Louisiana had granted one company a monopoly on the slaughtering business in New Orleans. That grant was challenged by other butchers as denying them the right to practice their trade. They argued that this right was protected by the 14th Amendment's guarantee of the privileges and immunities of U.S. citizenship, of equal protection of the laws, and of due process.

The *Slaughterhouse Cases* were first argued in January 1872, just before the court's opinions in the second *Legal Tender Case* were read. But those arguments were before an eight-man court. Justice Nelson, now 80, was absent. The court apparently was evenly divided, and ordered the cases reargued in the following term.

Before the December 1872 term began, Nelson resigned after 27 years of service. President Grant named Ward Hunt, a New York judge — as Nelson had been — to the seat. Hunt was seated in December 1872.

The *Slaughterhouse Cases* were reargued over a three-day period in February 1873. Attorney for the butchers was former Justice John Campbell.

The court announced its decision April 14, 1873. By a vote of 5-4, the court held that Louisiana had not violated the 14th Amendment by its grant of a slaughtering monopoly.

Writing for the court Justice Samuel Miller stated that the amendment did not increase the number of rights an individual possessed, but only extended new protection to those few rights, privileges and immunities that had their source in one's federal, rather than state, citizenship. The right to do business did not derive from one's U.S. citizenship, held the majority.

Any other decision, wrote Miller, would convert the court into "a perpetual censor upon all legislation of the States on the civil rights of their own citizens." [73]

Chief Justice Chase dissented, as did Swayne, Field and Bradley.

The next day, over Chase's lone dissent, the court held that a state did not deny a woman the privileges or immunities of U.S. citizenship when it refused, because of her sex, to license her to practice law in its courts.[74]

The Court in 1876

From left: Justices Joseph P. Bradley, Stephen J. Field, Samuel F. Miller, Nathan Clifford, Chief Justice Morrison R. Waite, Justices Noah H. Swayne, David Davis, William Strong, Ward Hunt.

Chief Justice Waite

Within the month, Chief Justice Chase was dead of a sudden stroke. His seat remained vacant for most of the following year.

President Grant tried unsuccessfully to place two of his personal friends in the seat — naming first Attorney General George Williams of Oregon and then Caleb Cushing, a former attorney general, of Massachusetts. Finally, he chose a little-known Ohio attorney, Morrison R. Waite, 58. Waite, who never had argued a case before the Supreme Court and who had no judicial experience, was quickly confirmed. He was seated in March 1874.

The term in which Waite began his 14 years as Chief Justice was the first to begin in October. Early in 1873 Congress had provided that the court's term would begin the second Monday in October rather than in December as it had since 1844.

Privileges and Immunities

Unlike his predecessor, Chief Justice Waite agreed fully with the court's narrow view of the privileges and immunities of federal citizenship.

In 1875 he wrote the court's opinion as it reinforced its decision in the *Slaughterhouse Cases*, holding that the right to vote was not a privilege or immunity of U.S. citizenship.[75]

The court under Waite was just as reluctant to acknowledge that the Civil War Amendments had expanded federal power to enforce individual rights as it was to admit that the amendments had expanded the list of protected rights.

In 1876 the court struck down several key portions of the laws Congress had enacted to enforce the 15th Amendment's guarantee of the right to vote and the 13th Amendment's abolition of slavery. Again, the new Chief Justice spoke for the court as it declared that Congress overreached

---

"For protection against abuses by Legislatures the people must resort to the polls, not to the courts."

—Chief Justice Morrison R. Waite
Munn v. Illinois, 1877

---

itself in enacting such a broad statute penalizing persons who employed violence to deny blacks the right to vote. The court reiterated that the right to vote came from the states; only the right to be free of racial discrimination in voting came from the U.S. Constitution. These rulings left Congress virtually powerless to protect the newly enfranchised black.[76]

The Election of 1876

The disputed presidential election of 1876 drew the court into political controversy when five of its members — Bradley, Miller, Strong, Field and Clifford — served on the Electoral Commission that resolved the dispute over electoral votes, and paved the way for the election of Republican Rutherford B. Hayes. Hayes subsequently placed Stan-

ley Matthews — the man who had helped negotiate the compromise which elected him — on the Supreme Court.

State Powers

Not surprisingly, the court of the 1870s, which refused to grant Congress broad power to enforce the civil rights of individuals, was quite willing to allow states to exercise their police power in ever-widening fields.

The rapid growth of large manufacturing and transport companies after the Civil War had prompted their customers to organize and seek state regulation of those businesses to curtail their power over the individual consumer. Among the most successful were farmer groups, including the Grange, which in some states obtained the passage of "Granger laws" setting limits on the rates railroads and grain elevator companies could charge for hauling or storing farm products and other goods.

Despite the failure of the butchers to win 14th Amendment protection of their right to do business in the *Slaughterhouse Cases*, the railroad and grain storage operators mounted a similar challenge to these Granger laws. They argued that the state, in passing these laws, deprived them of their liberty and property without due process of law.

The *Granger Cases*

In a group of cases known as the *Granger Cases* and by the title of one of them — *Munn v. Illinois* — the court in 1877 rejected this challenge to state regulatory laws.

Upholding the laws, Chief Justice Waite explained that in the court's view some private property, by virtue of its use, was so invested with a public interest that states could properly exercise their police power to regulate it. Justices Field and Strong dissented.

The majority also rejected the idea that federal courts should review such laws to determine if the regulations were reasonable. Chief Justice Waite acknowledged that the state might abuse this power to regulate business, but found that insufficient argument "against its existence. For protection against abuses by Legislatures the people must resort to the polls," he concluded, "not to the courts."[77]

Three years later, the court — again with Waite as its spokesman — found in the state police power a substantial qualification of the Constitution's ban on state impairment of contract obligations. In the case of *Stone v. Mississippi*, the court held that a legislature could never contract to place a subject beyond the exercise of this power. It upheld a decision of the Mississippi legislature to ban lotteries, even though this decision nullified the charter of a lottery corporation granted by a previous legislature.

New Justices

A week after the court's decision in *Munn v. Illinois*, Justice Davis resigned to take a Senate seat. As his replacement the new president, Hayes, chose a 44-year-old lawyer, a namesake of the first Chief Justice, John Marshall Harlan.

Harlan would serve well into the 20th century, his 34-year tenure characterized by a long line of opinions dissenting from the court's narrow view of the 14th Amendment.

At the turn of the decade, the court's personnel underwent further change. By 1881 only three of the justices who participated in the 1873 *Slaughterhouse* decision remained on the bench — Miller from the majority and Field and Bradley from the dissent.

By 1880 the court was operating under the handicap of having three members unable to fill their proper roles. Swayne, now 75, had been in failing mental health for three years.[78] Hunt suffered a stroke in 1879 and never returned to the bench. Clifford had been disabled for some time but refused to resign until a Democratic president could choose his successor.

But the first departure from the court of the 1880s was none of these but Justice Strong, who, although in his 70s, still was at the peak of his abilities. President Hayes chose William B. Woods of Georgia as Strong's successor. Woods, a federal circuit judge, was the first southerner named to the court since Justice Campbell was selected in 1852. Although only 56 at the time of his appointment, he served but six years before his death.

In January 1881, shortly after Woods was confirmed, Swayne resigned. To succeed him, Hayes selected Sen. Stanley Matthews, 56, also of Ohio. Matthews had been instrumental in the compromise that placed Hayes in the White House in 1877. Nominated first by Hayes and then by incoming President James J. Garfield, Matthews was confirmed by the narrow margin of one vote, 24-23. He served on the court for seven years, until his death in 1889.

Later in 1881 Justice Clifford died. To replace him President Arthur selected Horace Gray, chief justice of the Massachusetts supreme court. Gray, 53 at the time, served for 20 years.

Finally in 1882, after three years of absence from the bench, Justice Hunt resigned. After Arthur's first choice, Roscoe Conkling, declined, Arthur chose federal Judge Samuel Blatchford of New York to fill the seat. He served for 11 years.

Personal Rights

The 14th Amendment, ratified in 1868, proved a rich source of Supreme Court litigation. In the 15 years between the *Slaughterhouse Cases* — the court's first 14th Amendment ruling — and the end of Chief Justice Waite's term in 1888 — the court decided some 70 cases on the basis of that amendment. In the ensuing 30 years there would be 10 times as many — some 725 14th Amendment cases — decided by the court.[79]

In general, individuals who sought to invoke the protection of the amendment's privileges and immunities, due process or equal protection clauses had little success. The court on the whole was unresponsive to "social" legislation or to claims of individual rights, although there were exceptions.

Racial Equality

In 1878 the Supreme Court struck down a state law that required equal access for black and white passengers to railroads operating in the state. The law was impermissible state interference with interstate commerce, held the court in the case of *Hall v. DeCuir.*

In 1880 the court applied the 14th Amendment to deny states the freedom to restrict jury service to white persons. But three years later, in the *Civil Rights Cases,* the court made clear that it would condone use of the amendment only to reach clearly discriminatory *state* action.

Private Discrimination

In the *Civil Rights Cases,* the court declared Congress powerless to reach acts of *private* discrimination against blacks. With Justice Bradley writing the majority opinion, the court struck down the far-reaching Civil Rights Act of 1875, enacted to implement the guarantees of the Civil War Amendments.

The court declared that the 14th Amendment did not give Congress the power to regulate matters that traditionally had been left to state control. Congress could act only to correct — not to prevent — discrimination by the state.

In 1884, however, the court upheld the power of Congress to provide for the punishment of persons who beat up a black man to keep him from voting in a federal election.[80]

The Bill of Rights

The same day, however, the court demonstrated its reluctance to use the 14th Amendment to curtail state authority. Joseph Hurtado was convicted of murder under California law that did not provide for a grand jury indictment in serious crimes. Citing the Fifth Amendment guarantee of charge by indictment for serious federal crimes, Hurtado challenged his conviction as a violation of the 14th Amendment's due process guarantee. That guarantee, he argued, applied the indictment provision to the states.

The court rejected Hurtado's argument reaffirming the view — first set out in *Barron v. Baltimore* by Chief Justice Marshall — that the Fifth Amendment applies only against federal, not state, action. The 14th Amendment, held the court, did not extend the right to an indictment to persons charged with state crimes. Justice Harlan dissented from this ruling in *Hurtado v. California.*

In its first major ruling concerning the guarantees of the Fourth and Fifth Amendments against *federal* authority, however, the court just two years after *Hurtado* read those provisions to give broad protection to the individual.

The court's decision in *Boyd v. United States,* decided in 1886, was a ringing defense of individual privacy against the threat of governmental invasion. Justice Bradley, for the court, declared that "constitutional provisions for the security of person and property should be liberally construed. A close and literal construction deprives them of half their efficacy and leads to gradual depreciation of the right. . . ."[81]

And later that year, in one of the first successful equal protection cases brought by an individual, the court held that the equal protection guarantee extended to all persons, not just citizens, and meant that city officials could not deny all Chinese applicants the right to operate laundries.[82]

Property Rights

In the 1870s — most notably in the *Slaughterhouse* and *Granger* cases — the court steadfastly had rejected the efforts of businessmen to use the 14th Amendment as a shield against government regulation.

But in the 1880s that stance began to weaken.

In 1869 the court had held that corporations were not *citizens* and so could not invoke the protection of the 14th Amendment's privileges and immunities clause.[83]

But 17 years later, in 1886, Chief Justice Waite simply announced — before the court heard arguments in the case of *Santa Clara County v. Southern Pacific Railway* — that there was no need for the arguing attorneys to discuss whether corporations were *persons* under the protection of the 14th Amendment's equal protection clause: The court had decided that they were.

That same year the court sharply limited the power of the states to regulate railroad rates. In the case of *Wabash,*

St. Louis and Pacific Railway Co. v. Illinois, the court held that states could not set rates for railroads that formed part of an interstate network. Such regulation infringed the federal power over interstate commerce. This ruling cut back sharply the power that the court had seemed to grant to the states in *Munn v. Illinois,* just nine years earlier.

Yet in other areas the court of the late 1880s continued to back the exercise of the state police power. It upheld state laws regulating intoxicating liquors and colored oleo, refusing to find such laws either violations of the due process guarantee or burdens on interstate commerce.[84]

Changes in the Court

In 1887 Justice Woods died. President Cleveland filled this "southern seat" with Lucius Quintus Cincinnatus Lamar of Mississippi. Lamar, 62, had served both in the House and the Senate and was secretary of Interior at the time of his selection to the court. He was the first Democrat placed on the court in 25 years. Although the Republican-dominated Senate Judiciary Committee opposed confirmation, he was confirmed by a vote of 32-28. He served only five years, until his death in 1893.

In March 1888 Chief Justice Waite, 72, died of pneumonia.

As the new Chief Justice President Cleveland selected Melville W. Fuller, a successful Chicago attorney whose clients included several major railroads. Fuller had argued

> *"...Constitutional provisions for the security of person and property should be liberally construed. A close and literal construction deprives them of half their efficacy and leads to gradual depreciation of the right...."*
>
> —Justice Joseph Bradley
> *Boyd v. United States,* 1886

a number of cases before the court. He was 55 years old at the time of his selection. Nominated in May 1888, he was confirmed in July by a vote of 41-20. He would lead the court for 22 years, until his death in 1910.

By the end of its first century, the court had become more institutional and less personal in its operations. No longer did the justices live, as well as work, together. That practice had ended soon after the Civil War. And after Reporter Wallace left that post in 1875, the volumes of the court's decisions were no longer cited by the name of the Reporter, but by the impersonal "U.S." designation.

The Court in 1888

From left: Justices Joseph P. Bradley, Stanley Matthews, Samuel F. Miller, Horace Gray, Chief Justice Melville W. Fuller, Justices John Marshall Harlan, Stephen J. Field, Samuel Blatchford, Lucius Q. C. Lamar.

The Conservative Court: 1889-1919

Melville Fuller became Chief Justice of the United States at the end of the court's first century. His tenure would span the transition — chronologically, politically and socially — from the world of the 18th and 19th centuries to that of the 20th century. Vast change would come to the nation during this period, change that would bring new challenges to the Supreme Court. William Swindler describes it:

> The passing of the frontier, the rise of an interstate industrialism, the shift from a rural to an urban distribution of population, the breakdown of 19th century capitalism and the efforts to construct in its stead a twentieth-century capitalism, the breakthrough in science and technology, the change in the society of nations brought about by global wars and the militant dialectic of totalitarianism — the constitutional posture of the American people had to be readjusted in response to each of these.
> Fuller's court stood upon the watershed, with a powerful pull of ideological gravity toward the past. At least three of his colleagues when he came onto the bench dated from the constitutional golden age: Justices Bradley, Field and Miller all had begun their careers under men who in turn had known John Marshall and Joseph Story. From these venerated predecessors, who interpreted the Constitution with reference to a pioneer economy and an *ante-bellum* concept of the Federal function, Fuller and his intimate associates undertook to derive a jurisprudence to apply to issues never imagined by the early Federalist jurists.[85]

Justice Brewer

Within five years of Fuller's assuming the seat of Chief Justice, there were four other new members of the court — all chosen by President Benjamin Harrison and all men of conservative bent.

The first and most notable of Harrison's selections came in 1889. Justice Matthews died in March. As his successor, Harrison chose Federal Circuit Judge David J. Brewer of Kansas, Justice Field's nephew. Brewer, 52, was confirmed late in the year. During his 20 years on the court he would be one of its most articulate members.

Segregation and Substantive Due Process

On March 3, 1890, Justice Brewer delivered his first major opinion for the court.

In the case of *Louisville, New Orleans and Texas Railway Co. v. Mississippi*, the majority upheld a state law requiring railroads to provide separate accommodations for black and white passengers on trips within the state. Justices Harlan and Bradley dissented.

Accepting the state court's finding that the requirement applied only to intrastate trips, the Supreme Court majority held it no burden on interstate commerce.

Although the case rested on a different constitutional basis, it clearly marked the way to the position the court would take six years later in *Plessy v. Ferguson*, accepting the "separate but equal" doctrine as constitutional, and confirming the segregation of U.S. society into black and white compartments for the next 60 years.

Three weeks later, on March 24, 1890, the court majority for the first time accepted and declared the doctrine of substantive due process, the belief that the due process clause (included in the Fifth and the 14th Amendments) gives federal courts the power to review the substance of legislation, in this case legislation intended to regulate business.

In the case of *Chicago, Milwaukee & St. Paul Railway Co. v. Minnesota*, the court held that Minnesota denied businessmen their right to due process when it set the rates they could charge and did not provide for judicial review of the reasonableness of those rates.

No longer would the court defer to legislative judgment in rate-setting, as it had indicated it would in *Munn v. Illinois*. Now it assumed for itself the power to review the wisdom of these economic decisions.

Justice Brown

This ruling, which extended the protection of the 14th Amendment to business — a view the court had so firmly rejected in the *Slaughterhouse Cases* — came in the last term of Justice Samuel F. Miller, author of the *Slaughterhouse* opinion. In October 1890 Miller died after 28 years on the bench.

Harrison chose federal Judge Henry B. Brown, a Yale classmate of Brewer's, to succeed Miller. Brown, from Michigan, would serve on the court for 15 years.

The Circuit Court of Appeals Act

For the nation's first century, the Supreme Court was essentially the only body to hear appeals from the decisions of other federal courts. As a result of increasing litigation in the federal courts, the Supreme Court's workload mushroomed. From the end of the Civil War until 1891 it was not at all uncommon for a case to wait two or three years after being docketed before it was argued before the court.

The court adopted various changes in its operations to promote more expeditious handling of cases, but all such efforts were negated by the increasing volume of business.

Finally, in 1891, Congress eliminated the justices' obligation to ride circuit. It set up a system of federal appeals courts — between the old district and circuit courts, on the one hand, and the Supreme Court on the other. The decisions of these new circuit courts of appeals were final in many cases; the Supreme Court had complete discretion in deciding whether or not to hear appeals from them. The result, at least for a time, was a reduction in the press of business at the court.

Incrimination and Immunity

Early in 1892 the Supreme Court decided the case of *Counselman v. Hitchcock*, one of its rare 19th century rulings concerning the Bill of Rights. And, as in the case of *Boyd v. United States* six years earlier, the court construed those amendments to provide broad protection for individuals against federal authority. The court held the immunity provisions of the Interstate Commerce Act to be constitutionally insufficient. If a witness was to be compelled to testify and provide authorities with evidence against himself, held the unanimous court, the government must promise that it would not use that evidence in any way against him. This was the requirement of the Fifth Amendment guarantee that an individual would not be forced to incriminate himself.

New Justices

Within 10 days of the *Counselman* ruling, Justice Bradley died. As his successor, President Harrison chose George Shiras Jr., a Pennsylvania lawyer whose clients included the great iron and steel companies of Pittsburgh and the Baltimore & Ohio Railroad. Despite opposition to his nomination from the senators from his home state, Shiras was unanimously confirmed. He served on the court for a decade.

In January of the following year, 1893, Justice Lamar died. To succeed him, Harrison chose a friend from his Senate days — Howell E. Jackson of Tennessee, a federal circuit judge. Jackson, however, became ill within a year of his appointment and died after two years on the court, only a few months after the court's landmark income tax ruling of May 1895.

The Hazards of Riding Circuit

The attempted murder of Justice Stephen J. Field — by a litigant unhappy with one of his circuit decisions — may have hastened the passage of the Circuit Court of Appeals Act of 1891, which finally relieved Supreme Court justices of the duty of sitting as circuit judges.

In 1888 Field, sitting as a circuit judge in California, his home state, delivered an opinion that held invalid a purported marriage contract between Sarah Althea Hill and William Sharon. Sharon, a wealthy mine owner and senator from Nevada (R 1875-81), was by the time of the ruling deceased.

Hill, by now the wife of one of Field's former colleagues on the California Supreme Court, David Terry, was incensed at the ruling. As a result of a brawl in the courtroom upon announcement of the ruling, she and Terry were imprisoned for contempt of court.

In 1889 Field returned to California to hold circuit court. Concern for his safety led the attorney general to authorize protection for Field. Thus he was accompanied by David Neagle, an armed federal marshal. As Field and Neagle were traveling by train to Los Angeles where Field was to hold court, the Terrys boarded the train. While Field was eating breakfast, Terry accosted him and struck him. Neagle, thinking that Terry was reaching for a knife with the intent of attacking Field, shot and killed Terry.

Neagle was arrested and charged with murder by state officials. He contested his detention, arguing to the federal courts that the state could not hold him for actions taken in the performance of his duties under federal law.

The case came to the Supreme Court in 1890. Justice Field did not participate in the matter, but the court agreed with Neagle's argument and ordered his release. (*In re Neagle,* 135 U.S. 1, 1890).

In mid-1893 Justice Blatchford died. The seat he had filled had been held by a New Yorker since 1806, but this tradition came to an end in 1894. President Cleveland tried twice, without success, to place another New York attorney in the Blatchford seat. But the opposition of Sen. David Hill of New York blocked both the nominations of William Hornblower and Wheeler Peckham.

Finally in February 1894 Cleveland nominated Sen. Edward D. White of Louisiana, 48, to the seat. He was confirmed the same day. White would serve on the court 27 years. After 17 years as an associate justice, he would become the first sitting justice named Chief Justice, a post in which he would serve for a decade more.

The Protection of Property

The conservative character of the court of the 1890s was demonstrated with stunning force in the term that began in October 1894, one of the most notable single terms in court history. With three landmark decisions, the court placed itself firmly on the side of propertied interests, defending them against both federal power and organized labor.

Antitrust Act

On Jan. 21, 1895, the court by a vote of 8-1 held that the Sherman Anti-trust Act could not be used to outlaw manufacturing monopolies — because manufacturing was not commerce and so was not reachable under the federal commerce power, upon which the Sherman Act was based.

Chief Justice Fuller wrote the majority opinion in the case of *United States v. E. C. Knight & Co.,* agreeing with the argument of the attorneys representing the sugar refining monopoly that the United States could not challenge its concentration of power. The monopoly remained intact, and the antitrust law lay virtually useless as a means of controlling concentrated economic power.

Income Tax

On May 20, 1895, the court struck down the act of Congress imposing the nation's first general peacetime tax on personal income. The decision came in the twice-argued case of *Pollock v. Farmers' Loan and Trust Co.*

By a 5-4 vote, the court overturned a century-old precedent and declared the income tax a direct tax, subject to — and, in this case, in conflict with — the constitutional requirement that direct taxes be apportioned among the states according to population.

The ruling, which Justice Brown, one of the four dissenters, described as "nothing less than a surrender of the taxing power to the moneyed class," [86] resulted in the eventual addition of the 16th Amendment to the Constitution. In 1913 that amendment lifted the apportionment requirement for income taxes.

Again Chief Justice Fuller wrote the majority opinion. Dissenting were Justices Harlan, Brown, Jackson and White.

Strikes and Injunctions

Having fended off assaults upon property from the antitrust and the tax laws, the court was not yet finished. A week after the income tax decision, the court approved the use of federal judicial power to stop strikes.

In the case of *In re Debs,* the unanimous court upheld the contempt conviction of labor leader Eugene V. Debs for disobeying a court order to call off the Pullman strike that had halted rail traffic. Justice Brewer wrote the court's opinion.

As a result of this ruling, such court orders frequently were used by employers against labor unions. In the 37 years between *Debs* and enactment by Congress in 1932 of a statute forbidding this use of injunctions, such orders were sought in more than 120 major labor cases.[87]

In August 1895 Justice Jackson died. President Cleveland in December chose Rufus W. Peckham of New York — brother of his earlier unsuccessful nominee — for the seat. Peckham, 57, and a state judge, was quickly confirmed. During his 13 years on the court, he would serve as the court's spokesman in some of its most notable rulings in defense of property rights.

Separate and Equal

The economic conservatism of the Supreme Court of the 1890s was matched by similar views on social issues. The decision of May 18, 1896, in the case of *Plessy v. Ferguson* made that point clear.

By an 8-1 vote, the court upheld Louisiana law requiring separate cars for white and black passengers. This was no violation of the 14th Amendment's equal protection clause, declared Justice Brown for the majority. It was a reasonable exercise of the state police power to preserve the public peace and public order.

Reflecting the court's view of the inadequacy of laws as social instruments, Brown wrote that social equality of the races could not be accomplished by laws that conflicted with general community sentiment.

The government can secure its citizens equal legal rights and equal opportunities, but it can and should go no further. "Legislation is powerless to eradicate racial instincts or to abolish distinctions based upon physical differences, and the attempt to do so can only result in accentuating the difficulties of the present situation. If the civil and political rights of both races be equal one cannot be inferior to the other civilly or politically. If one race be inferior to the other socially, the Constitution of the United States cannot put them upon the same plane."[88]

In lonely if prophetic dissent, Justice Harlan warned that this decision would "in time, prove to be quite as pernicious as the decision made by this tribunal in the *Dred Scott* case."[89] He continued:

> If evils will result from the commingling of the two races upon public highways established for the benefit of all, they will be infinitely less than those that will surely come from state legislation regulating the enjoyment of civil rights upon the basis of race.[90]

This law, Harlan concluded, "is inconsistent with the personal liberty of citizens, white and black . . . and hostile to both the spirit and letter of the Constitution. . . ."[91]

Justice Field Resigns

Abraham Lincoln had nominated Justice Stephen J. Field of California to the court in 1863. Field was the only person ever to have held the new "western" seat.

In 1897 he was 81 years old; his health was failing and his irritability growing. Justice Harlan was selected by his colleagues to suggest that Field consider retirement. His reminder that Field had made such a suggestion to Justice

Grier 25 years earlier was met with an angry rejoinder. But after 34 years and nine months — the longest service of any man in the court's history — and a record unsurpassed for another 75 years — Field resigned in October 1897.

To succeed him President McKinley named Attorney General Joseph McKenna of California, 55, a political protégé of railroad magnate Leland Stanford, then a U.S. senator. McKenna, a former member of Congress, was

---

"If evils will result from the commingling of the two races upon public highways established for the benefit of all, they will be infinitely less than those that will surely come from state legislation regulating the enjoyment of civil rights upon the basis of race."

—Justice John Marshall Harlan, dissenting
Plessy v. Ferguson, 1896

---

confirmed, seated early in 1898, and served on the court well into the next century.

After McKenna filled Field's seat, there was no change in the court's membership for the next four years.

Freedom of Contract

The last major decisions of the 19th century provided the doctrinal foundation for the court's continuing insistence that the 14th Amendment should be used to protect businessmen against governmental interference in their economic decisions, but not to protect individuals against government infringement of their personal rights.

The court's increasing willingness to fend off state regulation of business matters produced a pair of decisions announced March 1, 1897. In *Allgeyer v. Louisiana,* Justice Peckham set out the court's view that the liberty protected by the 14th Amendment included "the right of the citizen . . . to earn his livelihood by any lawful calling; to pursue any livelihood or avocation, and for that purpose to enter into all contracts which may be proper, necessary and essential" to those ends.[92]

This doctrine of the freedom of contract would provide the court, for 40 years, with one of its most potent weapons against state laws intended to protect the individual worker by setting the maximum hours he might work and the minimum wage he should be paid.

In the second ruling announced that day, in the case of *Chicago, Burlington & Quincy Railway Co. v. Chicago,* the court — in a business context — acknowledged that some of the guarantees of the Bill of Rights might be of such a nature as to be included in the 14th Amendment's guarantee of due process against state action.

With Justice Harlan writing for the court, the justices upheld state police power to require railroads to maintain certain safety measures. In so doing, it stated that due process required the government to compensate the owner of private property for property "taken" for use in the public interest.

Hours, Rates and Wages

Despite its new freedom-of-contract doctrine, the court in 1898 upheld the first state maximum-hour law challenged as violating that freedom. In the case of *Holden v. Hardy,* the justices found that a law limiting the hours persons could spend working in underground mines was a proper exercise of the state's power to protect the health of its citizens.

The following week, the court in *Smyth v. Ames* reaffirmed the power of the judiciary to consider due process challenges to state regulation. When states set the rates that railroads may charge, wrote Justice Harlan for the majority, the rates must be set high enough to ensure the railways a fair return on their investment. And the courts will decide what return is fair.

In 1898 the court also demonstrated its continuing willingness to accept state laws governing the right to vote — even if those laws operated to deny Negroes that right. In the case of *Williams v. Mississippi* the court found no violation of the equal protection guarantee in a state law that required voters to pass a literacy test before being allowed to cast their ballot. Justice McKenna wrote the court's opinion, one of his first.

The Turn of the Century

In the *Slaughterhouse Cases* of 1873 the court had held that the right to do business was not a privilege or immunity of U.S. citizenship protected from state abridgment by the 14th Amendment. In later rulings it held that the right to vote was not such a privilege either.

But were the guarantees of the Bill of Rights — which clearly protected U.S. citizens against federal action — among those privileges and immunities? In one of its first 20th century rulings, the court answered that they were not.

The answer came in 1900 in *Maxwell v. Dow.* Justice Peckham, for the court, rejected the argument that the 14th Amendment required states to provide 12-person juries to try persons accused of crimes. Justice Harlan dissented.

The following year, the court showed equal reluctance to extend constitutional protections to any new groups of persons. In the *Insular Cases* decided in 1901, the court held that it was up to Congress to decide whether the Constitution and its guarantees applied to persons residing in territory newly acquired by the United States.

Justice Holmes

Late in 1902 Justice Gray resigned. As his successor President Theodore Roosevelt chose Oliver Wendell Holmes Jr., 61, chief justice of the Massachusetts Supreme Judicial Court.

Holmes served on the court for more than 29 years, through the terms of three Chief Justices and into a fourth. He was, by all measures, one of the nation's greatest justices. Like Harlan, he often found it necessary to dissent from the rulings of the conservative court of this era; also like Harlan, many of his dissents were later adopted as the views of the modern court.

The following year Justice Shiras resigned. Roosevelt chose Federal Circuit Court of Appeals Judge William R. Day as his successor. Day, 53, a successful railroad lawyer and McKinley's secretary of State before moving to the bench, would serve for 19 years.

The Expanding Federal Commerce Power

The first few years of Holmes' service saw the court give a broader reading to the federal commerce power than it had been willing to give in the last years of the 19th century.

The Court in 1897

From left: Justices Edward D. White, Henry B. Brown, Horace Gray, Stephen J. Field, Chief Justice Melville W. Fuller, Justices John Marshall Harlan, David J. Brewer, George Shiras Jr., Wheeler H. Peckham.

In 1903 the court recognized the existence of the federal police power, upholding in the case of *Champion v. Ames* an act of Congress forbidding the use of the mails for transmitting lottery tickets. But the vote was close — 5-4. Justice Harlan wrote the majority opinion; the dissenters were Chief Justice Fuller, Justices Brewer, Peckham and Shiras.

The following year the court enlarged on that ruling as it upheld a "police" use of the federal tax power to discourage the marketing of colored oleomargarine, holding that it would not inquire into the purposes of such a tax.[93]

In March 1904 the court began to revive the usefulness of the Sherman Anti-trust Act, ruling for the government in *Northern Securities Co. v. United States.*

Four of the justices, for whom Justice Harlan again spoke, read the Sherman Anti-trust Act literally — forbidding all restraints of trade. The four dissenting justices — White, Holmes, Peckham and Chief Justice Fuller — argued that the law forbade only unreasonable restraints of trade. The Harlan group became the majority through the concurrence of Justice Brewer, who found that the securities company was an unreasonable restraint of trade.

In a separate dissenting opinion, Justice Holmes set out one of his most often-quoted epigrams:

> Great cases, like hard cases, make bad law.... For great cases are called great, not by reason of their real importance in shaping the law of the future, but because of some accident of immediate overwhelming interest which appeals to the feelings and distorts the judgment.[94]

Holmes' comment appeared to be aimed directly at the man who had placed him on the bench — Theodore Roosevelt — whose intense interest in the success of the government's trust-busting effort, and this case, was well known. Roosevelt disregarded his nominee's comment and hailed the decision as a reversal of the 1895 holding in the sugar trust case.

In 1905 the court unanimously backed the government's prosecution of the beef trust. Justice Holmes wrote the opinion in the case of *Swift & Co. v. United States,* basing the ruling on a broad concept of commerce as a "current" among the states, a "stream" of which meatpacking was a part — and so was within the reach of the antitrust laws.

Due Process and State Power

Although the court was still willing to support the exercise of the state police power over a variety of subjects, its 1905 decision in the case of *Lochner v. New York* gave notice of its intention to curtail state efforts to interfere with wage and hour bargaining between employer and employee.

In February 1905 the court upheld state power to compel its citizens to be vaccinated against small pox. This, wrote Harlan, was a proper use of the police power.[95]

Six weeks later, in April, however, the court over the dissent of Harlan, Holmes, Day and White, decided in *Lochner* to strike down a New York law setting an eight-hour maximum work day for bakery employees.

Justice Peckham wrote the majority opinion, finding that the state law impermissibly interfered with the freedom of contract, protected by the 14th Amendment's due process clause. "It must . . . be conceded," wrote Peckham, "that there is a limit to the valid exercise of the police power by the state." And that limit was reached when the

state attempted to interfere with the liberty of bakers to contract as to their hours of work: "Clean and wholesome bread does not depend upon whether the baker works but ten hours per day or only sixty hours a week."[96]

Roosevelt's Last Justice

In 1906 Justice Brown resigned. President Roosevelt named his attorney general and close friend, William Moody, 52, as Brown's successor. Only four years later, Moody would retire from the court, an invalid due to acute rheumatism. Congress passed a bill allowing him to retire with special benefits.

Labor and the Court

The 1895 ruling in the case of Eugene V. Debs and the Pullman strike had made clear that the Supreme Court found the arguments and the tactics of the working man's labor movement uncongenial. The decisions of 1908 reaffirmed that point emphatically.

On Jan. 6, 1908, the court struck down an act of Congress enlarging the liability of railroads for injuries to their employees. By a 5-4 vote the court held that the law was invalid because it seemed to apply to intrastate aspects of interstate commerce.[97]

Three weeks later, the court invalidated an 1898 act that outlawed "yellow-dog" contracts, used by railroads to make their employees promise, as a condition of keeping their jobs, not to join labor unions.

Justice Harlan wrote the opinion of the court in the case of *Adair v. United States,* finding that such a federal restriction on the freedom of contract violated the due

---

> *"Great cases, like hard cases, make bad law.... For great cases are called great, not by reason of their real importance in shaping the law of the future, but because of some accident of immediate overwhelming interest which appeals to the feelings and distorts the judgment."*
>
> —Justice Oliver Wendell Holmes Jr.,
> dissenting, *Northern Securities Co. v. United States,* 1904

---

process guarantee of the Fifth Amendment, which operates against federal action. Holmes and McKenna dissented.

On Feb. 3, 1908, the court unanimously agreed that the Sherman Anti-trust Act applied to forbid secondary boycotts by labor unions; Chief Justice Fuller wrote the court's opinion in *Loewe v. Lawlor,* the *Danbury Hatters* case.

The 'Brandeis Brief'

This same term did bring one major victory for the workingman — and a key figure in that victory was a Boston lawyer named Louis D. Brandeis.

Oregon law set the maximum hours that women should work in laundries. The law was challenged, on the basis of *Lochner,* as a violation of the liberty of contract and thus of due process. The state engaged Brandeis as its counsel. He submitted a brief full of factual data supporting the argument that long hours of hard labor had a harmful effect upon women, and thus, through mothers, upon their children.

Brandeis won his case. A unanimous court upheld the law, modifying *Lochner* by allowing such interference with the liberty of contract when it could be justified as protecting the public health. Justice Brewer wrote the opinion in the case of *Muller v. Oregon.* And the name "Brandeis brief" came to be used to refer to briefs filled with factual, as well as legal, arguments.

Individual Rights

The court continued to hold its narrow views of the Constitution's protection for individual rights. In May 1908 the court — over the dissent of Justices Day and Harlan — upheld a state law that required Berea College in Kentucky to segregate black and white students in classes.[98]

And in November 1908 the court again declared, as it had in *Maxwell v. Dow,* that the 14th Amendment did not automatically extend the guarantees of the Bill of Rights to state defendants.

In the case of *Twining v. New Jersey,* the court refused to hold unconstitutional a state judge's comments on the failure of a defendant to testify in his own defense. That comment had been challenged as a violation of the Fifth Amendment guarantee against self-incrimination. But the court held that that guarantee did not apply in state trials. Justice Moody wrote the opinion; Justice Harlan dissented alone.

The Taft Justices

On March 4, 1909, William Howard Taft — solicitor general during the Harrison administration — was sworn in as president. During his term he appointed six members of the court; a dozen years later, he himself would become Chief Justice.

In 1909 Justice Peckham died. To succeed him Taft chose Horace H. Lurton, 65, with whom he had served on the court of appeals for the sixth circuit. Lurton had served on that court for 16 years at the time of his selection to the Supreme Court. He would serve there only four years before his death in 1914.

Edward D. White

Oliver Wendell Holmes Jr.

In 1910 Taft placed three more new members on the court — and elevated Justice White to the seat of Chief Justice.

Justice Brewer died in March after 20 years of service. Taft chose Charles Evans Hughes, 48, governor of New York, as his successor. Hughes would serve six years before resigning to run unsuccessfully for president in 1916. He would return to the court in 1930, Taft's successor as Chief Justice.

In July 1910 Chief Justice Fuller died. He had served as Chief Justice for 22 years. Taft broke precedent and named Justice Edward D. White as the court's new chief. White immediately was confirmed and served for more than 10 years in his new seat.

To fill White's now-vacant seat, Taft chose Joseph R. Lamar, 53, a Georgia attorney, whom he had met playing golf in Augusta. Lamar died after only five years on the court.

In November 1910 Justice Moody resigned. Taft named to the seat Willis Van Devanter of Wyoming, 51, a member of the circuit court of appeals for the eighth circuit. Van Devanter would serve for 26 years, Taft's longest serving appointee.

In October 1911 Justice Harlan died after a long and distinguished, if often lonely, career on the court. As his successor, Taft chose Mahlon Pitney of New Jersey, 54, a member of that state's supreme court. Pitney served until 1922.

With Harlan's death, only two members of the court remained from the court of the 1890s — White and McKenna.

The 'Rule of Reason'

For a few years after White replaced Fuller as Chief Justice, the court appeared to relax its conservative stance somewhat.

In Harlan's last term, the court adopted the "rule of reason" for applying the Sherman Anti-trust Act against restraints of trade, the rule that Harlan had so vigorously rejected in the *Northern Securities* case seven years earlier.

In mid-May 1911 the court by an 8-1 vote declared that the antitrust act outlawed only *unreasonable* restraints of trade, not *all* restraints of trade. The majority went on to order the break-up of the Standard Oil trust, which they found to be an unreasonable restraint. Chief Justice White wrote the majority opinion, declaring reasonableness the standard — which the courts would apply. Justice Harlan dissented.[99]

Two weeks later the court ordered the dissolution of the tobacco trust. Again Harlan dissented, arguing that the court was acting as a legislature, rewriting the law by adding the "rule of reason." [100]

Nevertheless, the court continued to use the "rule of reason" as the standard by which the federal antitrust laws would be applied against combinations charged with restraint of trade.

Federal Police Power

The court continued to back the exercise of a federal police power, upholding the Pure Food and Drug Act in 1911, a revised employers' liability act in 1912 and the White Slave Act in 1913.[101]

And other aspects of the federal commerce power were broadly construed. In the *Shreveport Rate* case of 1914, the court held that in some situations the federal commerce power authorized Congress, through the Interstate Commerce Commission, to set rates for railroads operating entirely within a state.

The Income Tax

With the antitrust rulings culminating in the oil and tobacco trust decisions, the court had resuscitated the Sherman Anti-trust Act, which its sugar trust ruling of 1895 had seemed to leave useless.

Congress and the states overrode the second of those landmark 1895 rulings — the income tax decision. In 1913 Congress and the states added to the Constitution the 16th Amendment, which declared that a federal income tax was not subject to the Constitution's apportionment requirement.

Congress quickly enacted a statute taxing incomes of more than $3,000 and $4,000 for single and married persons, respectively.

In the 1916 case of *Brushaber v. Union Pacific Railroad Co.,* the court upheld the act as constitutional. Chief Justice White wrote the opinion for the court, acknowledging that the clear intent of the new amendment was to overturn the court's reasoning in the 1895 *Pollock* case.

Rights and Remedies

In 1914 the court adopted the "exclusionary rule" to enforce the Fourth Amendment promise of personal security against unreasonable searches and seizures by federal agents.

In the case of *Weeks v. United States,* the unanimous court held that persons whose rights were violated by such searches could demand that any evidence so obtained against them be excluded from use in federal courts. Half a century later, when the court applied this rule against state action as well, it would become one of the most controversial of the court's rulings.

In 1915 the court applied the 15th Amendment to strike down Oklahoma's grandfather clause, which made it difficult for blacks to register to vote in the state. This decision in *Guinn v. United States,* however, did not settle the matter. Twenty-four years later, in the case of *Lane v. Wilson,* the court struck down a similarly discriminatory law Oklahoma adopted in place of the grandfather clause.

New Justices

President Woodrow Wilson named three men to the court, one of whom refused to speak to the other two for most of their tenure.

In 1914 Justice Lurton died. To succeed him, Wilson nominated his attorney general, James C. McReynolds, 52, of Tennessee. McReynolds, one of the most conservative men to serve on the court in the 20th century, also was one of the most difficult. He went out of his way to avoid dealing with Justices Louis D. Brandeis and Benjamin Cardozo — both Jewish — and refused to speak to Justice John Clarke, whom he considered unintelligent.[102]

Brandeis was Wilson's second nominee to the court, chosen to fill the seat left vacant by Justice Lamar's death in 1916. The nomination of Brandeis, 59, was opposed by a number of leaders of the American bar, including former President Taft, who considered him a dangerous radical. After five months of hearings, he was confirmed in June 1916 by a vote of 49-22. He served on the court for 23 years.

As soon as Brandeis was confirmed, Justice Hughes resigned to run unsuccessfully against Wilson for the White House. Federal Judge John H. Clarke of Ohio, 58, was Wilson's choice to fill this seat. Clarke resigned after six years on the bench, to work for the United States' entrance into the League of Nations. He lived for 23 more years, dying in 1945.

After Clarke joined the court, there were no other changes in its membership until 1921.

Maximum Hours

By 1917 the court appeared to have silently overruled *Lochner v. New York.* In two decisions early in the year, the court upheld maximum-hour statutes — in *Wilson v. New,* a federal law setting an eight-hour work day on interstate railroads, and in *Bunting v. Oregon,* a state law setting maximum hours for all industrial workers. The law upheld in *Bunting* also set minimum wages for women and children workers; by implication the court sustained those provisions as well.

But the votes were close on both cases. Day, Pitney, Van Devanter and McReynolds dissented from *Wilson. Bunting,* decided by only eight justices, found White, Van Devanter and McReynolds in disagreement with the majority.

Conservatism Confirmed

In the war years the court's liberal interlude came to an end.

In 1918 the court abruptly halted the steady expansion of federal police power since the turn of the century. By a 5-4 vote the court in *Hammer v. Dagenhart* struck down a 1916 act of Congress intended to outlaw child labor by barring from interstate commerce goods produced by child workers.

Justice Day wrote the court's opinion, returning to the distinction between manufacture and commerce set out in the 1895 sugar trust case, and holding that this act of Congress attempted to regulate manufacturing and so overreached its commerce power. Child labor was a subject left to state regulation, Day proclaimed. The court's most senior members, McKenna and Holmes, and its most junior ones, Brandeis and Clarke, dissented.

War and Freedom

World War I saw enactment of the Selective Service Act, providing for a military draft. In June 1917 nine and a half million men were registered for military service.[103] The law immediately was challenged as exceeding federal power and as violating the 13th Amendment, which abolished involuntary servitude.

In January 1918 the court unanimously upheld the law. Chief Justice White wrote the court's opinion in the *Selective Draft Cases.*

Wartime also brought enactment of an espionage act and a sedition act, the most repressive legislation since the Alien and Sedition Acts of 1798. But unlike their predecessors — which never were challenged before the court — the World War I legislation promptly was contested as violating the freedom of speech protected against federal action by the First Amendment.

In 1919 the court unanimously sustained the espionage act in the case of *Schenck v. United States.* Justice Holmes wrote the court's opinion, setting out his famous definition of the "clear and present danger" test for determining when government might permissibly curtail free speech.

The First Amendment, Holmes wrote, would "not protect a man . . . [who] falsely shout[ed] fire in a theater and caus[ed] a panic." The question to be asked, he continued, "is whether the words are used in such circumstances and are of such a nature as to create a clear and present danger that they will bring about the substantive evils that Congress has a right to prevent. It is a question of proximity and degree." [104]

Schenck was quickly followed by several other decisions upholding convictions under these challenged wartime statutes.

The court soon divided over the use of the "clear and present danger" test — but *Schenck* remains notable for its declaration that the First Amendment does not provide an absolute protection for free speech and as the first step in the court's effort to find and define the standards for deciding when government may permissibly curtail free speech.

New Times, Old Court: 1920-1937

In May 1921 Chief Justice White died suddenly. Former President William Howard Taft — who had made no secret of his long-held ambition to be Chief Justice — was chosen by President Harding as the 10th man to hold that post.

Taft was confirmed in June 1921. He would serve for nine years, during which he would play a key role in winning passage of the Judiciary Act of 1925, giving the court more control over its workload, and in initiating work on the court's own building.

Under Taft, the court's conservatism intensified. It revived the *Lochner* doctrine of freedom of contract and used it vigorously to restrain state efforts to regulate economic matters.

And it curtailed federal authority, persisting in the view that Congress could not regulate matters such as agricultural production and manufacturing, and converting the little-invoked 10th Amendment into a potent instrument for protecting state sovereignty and business matters from federal power.

During the Taft era the court accelerated its use of its power of judicial review. While the court had struck down only two acts of Congress in the years between the nation's founding and the Civil War, it struck down 22 federal laws in the period between 1920 and 1932. [105]

Despite such clearly conservative views, it was this same court that set the nation on its course toward the "due process revolution" of the 1960s.

Labor Law

In 1921 the court reaffirmed its willingness to allow management to convert the antitrust laws into a tool for halting labor union efforts to organize and improve the conditions of workers in the United States.

Congress in 1914 responded to some of the court's earlier rulings on this subject by including, in the Clayton Act of that year, a specific exemption for labor unions from the reach of the antitrust laws.

But in the 1921 decisions of *Duplex Printing Press v. Deering* and *American Steel Foundries v. Trade Council*, the court interpreted this exemption into uselessness. A decade later Congress finally forbade the use of federal injunctions in labor disputes.

Elections Regulation

The Taft court's narrowing view of federal power moved it to strike down acts of Congress regulating spending in primary elections — and attempting again to outlaw child labor.

In 1921 the court in the case of *Newberry v. United States* held that Congress could regulate spending only in general election campaigns — not primary campaigns — for federal office.

The effect of the decision striking down part of the 1911 Federal Corrupt Practices Act was to leave the subject of primary elections entirely under state control. The successful attorney in this case was former Justice Charles Evans Hughes.

Child Labor

In the 1904 ruling in *McCray v. United States* the court had declared that so long as the subject taxed by Congress was properly within federal power, the justices would not look behind the tax to ascertain its purpose.

Thus, after the court in 1918 struck down Congress' commerce-based effort to outlaw child labor, Congress passed the Child Labor Tax Act — placing a high tax on products made by industries which employed children.

The likelihood that such a tax would be sustained seemed high. In 1919 the court upheld a similar tax measure intended to outlaw narcotics. [106]

But even as the court under Chief Justice Fuller had found the due process clause useful for striking down state efforts to regulate business practices, so the Taft court found the little-used 10th Amendment a handy instrument for curtailing federal regulation.

The 10th Amendment, included in the first set of amendments (Bill of Rights) to the Constitution in 1791, states that "[t]he powers not delegated to the United States by the Constitution, nor prohibited by it to the States, are reserved to the States respectively, or to the people."

In May 1922 the court struck down the 1918 child labor tax law.

Chief Justice Taft wrote the majority opinion in the case of *Bailey v. Drexel Furniture Co.* The court declared that Congress — in using the tax power to ban child labor — was infringing upon the reserved rights of the states to regulate such matters.

The same day the court used the 10th Amendment to invalidate a 1921 law in which Congress had attempted to use the tax power to regulate the commodities futures trade. This too was a matter reserved to state control, wrote Chief Justice Taft.

If this sort of law were upheld, Taft wrote,

all that Congress would need to do hereafter, in seeking to take over to its control any one of the great number of subjects of public interest, jurisdiction of which the states have never parted with and which are reserved to them by the Tenth Amendment, would be to enact a detailed measure of complete regulation of the subject and enforce it by a so-called tax.... To give such magic to the word "tax" would be to break down all constitutional limitation of the powers of Congress and completely wipe out the sovereignty of the states.[107]

(Congress passed a new grain futures regulatory law based on the commerce power; the court upheld it in 1923.)

New Justices

After the close of Taft's first term, three of the justices resigned — Clarke in September 1922, Day in November and Pitney in December.

To fill the empty seats President Harding chose former Utah Sen. George Sutherland, 60; Minnesota corporate attorney Pierce Butler, 56; and federal Judge Edward T. Sanford of Tennessee, 57. Sutherland would serve for 16 years, Butler, 17, and Sanford, eight.

Early in 1925 Justice McKenna — the last of the 19th century justices — resigned after 26 years on the court; he was 82 years old. President Coolidge named Harlan Fiske Stone of New York, his attorney general, to the McKenna seat. Stone, 53 at the time of his appointment and for 15 years a professor of law, would serve for 16 years as an associate justice, becoming Chief Justice in 1941, and holding that post for five years until his death.

After Stone's confirmation, there were no further changes in the court's membership until Taft's death in 1930.

Lochner Revived

The court's rulings upholding state maximum-hour laws for workers were assumed by many to have silently overruled the *Lochner* principle that a state violated the 14th Amendment guarantee of due process when it interfered with this aspect of the liberty of contract.

But in April 1923 *Lochner* was revived with new force by the court's decision in *Adkins v. Children's Hospital.* The court by a vote of 5-3 struck down as invalid the act of Congress providing a minimum-wage law for women workers in the District of Columbia.

With Justice Sutherland writing one of his first and most important opinions, the court held that such a law unconstitutionally infringed on the freedom of the employer and the employee to make whatever contract they wished concerning wages.

Chief Justice Taft, Sanford and Holmes dissented. Brandeis did not participate in the case.

Taxpayers and Defendants

The year 1923 brought several other notable decisions. In *Frothingham v. Mellon* the court held that a federal taxpayer lacked sufficient personal interest in the use of tax monies to justify his bringing suit to challenge federal spending programs. For 45 years this decision insulated federal spending from such taxpayer challenges.

And the court began to edge toward the role it would adopt, later in the century, of ensuring that state criminal procedures adhered to fundamental standards of fairness.

In *Moore v. Dempsey* the court upheld federal intervention in a case where persons were convicted of a crime after a trial in a state court dominated by a mob. Through Justice Holmes the majority declared that in such a situation, where "the whole proceeding is a mask — that counsel, judge and jury were swept to the fatal end by an irresistible wave of public passion, and ... the state courts failed to correct the wrong," the federal courts must act to secure the defendants their constitutional rights to due process and a fair trial.[108]

Due Process and Free Speech

The court's role as balance wheel gives its work a paradoxical character at times. So it was in 1925 when the conservative court of the 1920s provided the spark that would flare into the "due process revolution" of the 1960s.

In the case of *Gitlow v. New York* the court upheld the conviction of Benjamin Gitlow, a left-wing socialist, for violating New York's criminal anarchy law by distributing a pamphlet calling for the overthrow of the government. Gitlow challenged his conviction as a violation of the First Amendment, which, he contended, was extended by the 14th Amendment to protect the individual against state, as well as federal, action.

Although the court upheld Gitlow's conviction, it also accepted this argument. Almost in passing, Justice Sanford stated that the court now assumed "that freedom of speech and of the press ... are among the fundamental personal rights and 'liberties' protected by the due process clause of the Fourteenth Amendment from impairment by the states." [109] In the 1930s, this announcement would provide the basis for the court's first decisions striking down state laws as encroaching upon the protected freedoms of the First Amendment.

Federal Law Enforcement

In the 1920s the court upheld as constitutional the practices of federal agents in searching vehicles without search warrants — when they suspected the car had been used in violating a law — and in employing wiretaps to obtain evidence. Neither practice, held the court in the 1925 case of *Carroll v. United States* and the 1928 case of *Olmstead v. United States,* violated the individual's right to be secure from unreasonable search and seizure. *Carroll* remains in effect; *Olmstead* protected electronic surveillance from constitutional challenge until 1967 when it was overturned.

Individual Rights

In 1927 the court for the first time overturned a state conviction because it did not comport with the due process guarantee of the 14th Amendment.

In the case of *Tumey v. Ohio* the court held that due process required that a person charged with a violation of the law be tried before an impartial judge. Thus it overturned the conviction of a person tried before a city court, whose judge was the mayor, and from which fines were deposited in the city treasury.

The court's definition of the liberty protected by the 14th Amendment was slowly beginning to expand in the area of personal rights, even as it had expanded earlier into the area of property rights.

In 1923 the court struck down a state law that forbade a teacher in the state schools to use any language but English.[110] The right of teachers to teach a foreign language — and of parents to engage teachers to teach their children such a subject — was protected by the 14th Amendment, held the court.

Two years later in the case of *Pierce v. Society of Sisters,* the court invalidated a state law that sought to ban private schools by requiring all children to attend public schools. Again, the court found the freedom of parents to choose private or public education to be within the protected area of personal liberty.

Negro citizens, however, continued to meet with little success in asserting their rights under the 14th Amendment. In 1926 the court in *Corrigan v. Buckley* clung to its 19th-century view that the 14th Amendment did not reach any form of private discrimination, and so could not be used to ban restrictive covenants limiting the sale of real estate to Negroes.

However, when state action was involved, the court was willing to exercise the power of the Civil War Amendments. In 1927 the court in *Nixon v. Herndon,* the first in a long line of "white primary" cases, struck down Texas' efforts to exclude Negroes from participating in the all-important Democratic primary elections.

The States' Police Power

In 1926 the court in *Euclid v. Ambler Realty Co.* firmly established the power of local government to control the use of its land through zoning ordinances. This, proclaimed the court, was a legitimate use of the police power. The following year, in *Buck v. Bell,* the court went even further, approving the use of the police power to sterilize mentally defective state residents.

But when the state asserted its power over economic transactions, it again collided with the court's insistence upon the freedom of contract protected by the due process guarantee.

Adkins in 1923 was followed by a 1924 decision striking down a state law regulating the weight of loaves of bread sold to the public. In 1927 the court held that the resale of theater tickets was a matter outside permissible state regulation, and in 1928 it placed employment agency practices beyond state reach.[111]

The Court in 1925

From left: Justices James C. McReynolds, Edward T. Sanford, Oliver Wendell Holmes Jr., George Sutherland, Chief Justice William Howard Taft, Justices Pierce Butler, Willis Van Devanter, Harlan Fiske Stone, Louis D. Brandeis.

Presidents and Tariffs

Executive power was upheld in two rulings during the 1920s.

In the 1926 case of *Myers v. United States* the court held that Congress could not deny the president the power to remove postmasters without its consent. The power to remove was a necessary corollary of the power to appoint, and was virtually unlimited, held Taft in the majority opinion. Congress could not properly force the president to retain subordinates whom he wished to remove.

Two years later, in the case of *J. W. Hampton Jr. & Co. v. United States*, the court upheld as proper Congress' decision to delegate power to the president to adjust tariff rates in response to competitive conditions.

Hoover and the Court

In February 1930 Chief Justice Taft resigned, a dying man. President Hoover selected Charles Evans Hughes to return to the court as Chief Justice. Hughes, then 67, would serve through the turbulent decade of the New Deal, resigning in 1941.

Taft died March 8, 1930. So — by coincidence — did his colleague Justice Sanford. To replace Sanford Hoover chose federal Judge John J. Parker of North Carolina. But opposition to the nomination from labor and Negro groups resulted in rejection of the nomination by the Senate in May. The vote was 39-41 against confirmation. It was the first rejection of a Supreme Court nominee in the 20th century, the first since Cleveland's New York nominees were blocked in 1894 by Sen. Hill.

Hoover then chose Owen J. Roberts of Pennsylvania to fill the Sanford seat. Roberts, 55, was a Philadelphia lawyer who had served as one of the two government prosecutors in the Teapot Dome scandal. He would serve on the court for 15 years.

In 1931 Justice Holmes was 90, the oldest man to serve on the court in its history. Hughes was the fourth Chief Justice with whom he had served.

Age had slowed his activities, and Chief Justice Hughes — for the court — gently suggested to Holmes that the time for retirement had come. On Jan. 12, 1932, he resigned after 28 years on the court. He died, at 93, in 1935, leaving his estate to the nation; it eventually would be used to fund a history of the court.

To replace Justice Holmes, Hoover selected New York Judge Benjamin Cardozo, 62, who had been almost unanimously proposed as Holmes' successor by leaders all over the nation. Cardozo's selection clearly represented the victory of merit over more mundane geographic or ethnic criteria. At the time, there were two New Yorkers already on the court — Hughes and Stone — and there was already a Jewish justice. Cardozo served only six years before his death in 1938.

After Cardozo took his seat on the court in early 1932, there were no further changes in the court personnel for more than five years.

The State and Free Expression

The first years of the 1930s were quiet ones at the Supreme Court. A nation devastated by the economic crash and resulting depression was preoccupied with survival and had little time for litigation.

In 1931 the court for the first time struck down a state law because it infringed upon the freedoms protected by the First Amendment.

In the case of *Stromberg v. California* the court divided 7-2 to invalidate California's law forbidding citizens to display a red flag as a symbol of opposition to organized government.

Chief Justice Hughes wrote the opinion, declaring that the opportunity for free political discussion was a fundamental principle of the U.S. constitutional system, both in itself and as a means of achieving lawful change and responsive government. Justices Butler and McReynolds dissented.

Two weeks after *Stromberg,* the court struck down yet a second state law on similar grounds. In *Near v. Minnesota* the court by a 5-4 vote found that a state law penalizing newspapers for criticizing public officials violated the guarantee of a free press. Joining Butler and McReynolds in dissent were Sutherland and Van Devanter. Hughes again wrote the majority opinion.

The *Scottsboro* Cases

Twice in the first half of the decade the court considered constitutional questions arising from the case of "the Scottsboro boys" — several young black men arrested in Alabama, away from their homes, and charged with raping two white women.

In 1932 the case of *Powell v. Alabama* came to the court. The issue was the right of these defendants — tried in state court — to have the effective aid of a lawyer in preparing a defense. This right to counsel is guaranteed defendants in federal trials by the Sixth Amendment, but the court had not before read the 14th Amendment guarantee of due process as extending this right to state defendants.

In November 1932 the court by a 7-2 vote held that these black men — represented only at the last minute by a local lawyer — had been denied their constitutional right to due process. In these particular circumstances, wrote Justice Sutherland for the court, the Constitution guaranteed these defendants the effective aid of an attorney. Justices Butler and McReynolds dissented.

Three years later — in the busy term of 1935 — the second *Scottsboro Case* came to the court. In *Norris v. Alabama* the issue was not the right to counsel but the right to trial by a fairly chosen jury.

On April 1, 1935, a unanimous court held that the Scottsboro defendants were denied their 14th Amendment rights when they were indicted and tried by all-white juries, the result of the state's consistent practice of excluding blacks from jury duty. Chief Justice Hughes wrote the court's opinion.

Voting Rights

On the same day that it announced its decision in *Norris v. Alabama,* the court decided *Grovey v. Townsend,* the third of its rulings concerning the persistent effort of the state of Texas to keep Negroes from voting in primary elections, the only significant elections in the Democratic-dominated South.

After the court in *Nixon v. Herndon* (1927) struck down the state law barring Negroes from voting in primary elections, the state delegated to state political parties the task of determining who could vote in its primary. In *Nixon v. Condon,* decided in 1932, the Supreme Court held that this delegation resulted in a denial of equal protection to Negro voters.

The state took no further action, but the Texas Democratic Party barred all Negroes from membership. In

Grovey v. Townsend the court held that the party's exclusion of Negroes was beyond the reach of the 14th Amendment because the party's action was not state action. The court was unanimous; Justice Roberts wrote the opinion.

State Powers

In 1934 the court lifted one long-standing restriction on state power to regulate business — and loosened another. In March of that year the court abandoned the view — first set out in *Munn v. Illinois* 57 years earlier — that states could regulate only businesses "affected with a public interest."

In the case of *Nebbia v. New York,* the court by a vote of 5-4 upheld a New York law setting milk prices, and declared that any business was subject to reasonable regulation. Roberts wrote the court's opinion; McReynolds, Butler, Sutherland and Van Devanter dissented. This decision was followed by rulings overturning the Taft court's decisions nullifying state regulation of bread weights, ticket sales and employment agencies.[112]

Earlier in the term, the court had upheld a state mortgage moratorium law against a challenge that it violated the Constitution's language protecting the obligation of contracts against state action. Again the vote was 5-4; the dissenters were the same as in *Nebbia.* Chief Justice Hughes wrote the opinion, finding the law a reasonable means of responding to the economic emergency of the Depression.[113]

The Court and the New Deal

"The court," wrote Robert H. Jackson in 1941, "is almost never a really contemporary institution. The operation of life tenure in the judicial department, as against elections at short intervals of the Congress, usually keeps the average viewpoint of the two institutions a generation apart. The judiciary is thus the check of a preceding generation on the present one; a check of conservative legal philosophy upon a dynamic people, and nearly always the check of a rejected regime on the one in being." [114]

Never was that point more dramatically made than in the events of 1935, 1936 and 1937. A court made up of men born in the mid-19th century, and appointed to their seats by Presidents Wilson, Harding, Coolidge and Hoover, looked with distaste upon radical legislative measures espoused by President Franklin D. Roosevelt and the Congress elected in the midst of national economic depression.

The 1935 Court

The court that began to consider the major legislation of the New Deal in 1935 was composed of six men in their 70s and three in their 60s. Roberts, at 60, was the court's youngest member. President Roosevelt was only 53.

The court's first ruling on New Deal measures came in the first week of January 1935. In *Panama Refining Co. v.*

The Court in 1932

From left: Justices Louis D. Brandeis, Owen J. Roberts, Willis Van Devanter, Pierce Butler, Chief Justice
Charles Evans Hughes, Justices Harlan Fiske Stone, James C. McReynolds, Benjamin N. Cardozo, George
Sutherland.

Ryan the court struck down part of the National Industrial Recovery Act (NIRA), finding it invalid because in it Congress delegated power to the executive without setting sufficiently specific limits or standards for its use. The vote was 8-1. Chief Justice Hughes wrote the opinion; only Cardozo dissented.

Six weeks later, in mid-February 1935, the court in the three *Gold Clause Cases* upheld the power of Congress to shift the nation away from the use of gold as its standard currency. The vote was 5-4; Hughes wrote the opinion; Sutherland, McReynolds, Butler and Van Devanter dissented. McReynolds, distressed by the rulings, added to his dissenting opinion the extemporaneous lament: "As for the Constitution, it does not seem too much to say that it is gone. Shame and humiliation are upon us now!" [115]

But the *Gold Clause Cases* would be the administration's solitary victory before the court in the October 1934 term.

On May 6, 1935, the dissenters in the gold decision were joined by Justice Roberts to form a majority invalidating an act of Congress setting up a comprehensive retirement system for the railroad industry. The court in *Railroad Retirement Board v. Alton Railway Co.* found the commerce power an insufficient basis for such a system.

The railroad decision was a harbinger of "Black Monday," which came three weeks later, on May 27, when a unanimous court handed President Roosevelt three major defeats. In the case of *Schechter Poultry Corp. v. United States,* the court held invalid key provisions of the NIRA as an excessive delegation of power from Congress to the president.

The court also found the Federal Farm Bankruptcy Act a violation of the due process guarantee and, in a third decision, the justices sharply limited the president's removal power, which it had envisioned as virtually unlimited only nine years earlier. [116]

The 1936 Term

When the court opened its next term, in early October 1935, it met for the first time in its own building. Chief Justice Taft had persuaded Congress to approve the idea in 1929; the cornerstone had been laid by Chief Justice Hughes in October 1932; and the court moved into the handsome marble building across from the Capitol for its 1936 term.

As the court convened, it was clear this would be a crucial term for the New Deal. A number of cases testing the validity of New Deal legislation were pending. And the justices — even before they addressed these cases — were clearly divided. As Arthur M. Schlesinger Jr. described it:

> They were already forming into distinct personal as well as constitutional blocs. The four conservatives used to ride to and from the Court together every day of argument and conference. To offset these riding caucuses, Stone and Cardozo began to go to Brandeis' apartment in the late afternoon on Fridays before conferences. Each group went over cases together and tried to agree on their positions. [117]

Hughes and Roberts were the two "swing men" between these two blocs.

On Jan. 6, 1936, the court struck down the Agricultural Adjustment Act, which adopted crop controls and price subsidies as measures to stabilize the agricultural produce market. By a vote of 6-3 the court held that Congress in this legislation intruded upon areas reserved by the 10th Amendment for state regulation. Justice Roberts wrote the opinion in *United States v. Butler.*

On May 18 the court by the same division struck down the Bituminous Coal Conservation Act with its decision in the case of *Carter v. Carter Coal Co.* The coal act was designed to control working conditions of coal miners and to fix prices for the sale of coal. This act was unconstitutional, held the court; coal mining was not commerce and so was outside the reach of federal authority. The same day, the court by a vote of 5-4 struck down the Municipal Bankruptcy Act. [118]

The administration could claim just one victory in the spring of 1936: the court upheld — as a proper exercise of the commerce power — the creation of the Tennessee Valley Authority. [119]

As the term ended, Justice Stone commented:

> I suppose no intelligent person likes very well the way the New Deal does things, but that ought not to make us forget that ours is a nation which should have the powers ordinarily possessed by governments, and that the framers of the Constitution intended that it should have.... We finished the term of Court yesterday, I think in many ways one of the most disastrous in its history. [120]

Due Process and Minimum Wages

In this same term, so devastating in its impact on the effort of federal authority to deal with the nation's economic difficulties, the court once again wielded the due process guarantee to strike down a state minimum-wage law.

In the case of *Morehead v. New York ex rel. Tipaldo* the same conservative majority that struck down the bank-

---

> *"As for the Constitution, it does not seem too much to say that it is gone. Shame and humiliation are upon us now!"*
>
> —Justice James C. McReynolds, dissenting
> *The Gold Clause Cases,* 1935

---

ruptcy act struck down New York's law setting the minimum wage to be paid women workers. Such a law, wrote Butler for the court, impaired the liberty of contract. Dissenting were Hughes, Stone, Brandeis and Cardozo.

Almost overlooked amid the New Deal controversy, the court in February 1936 took one more step toward imposing constitutional requirements on state criminal procedures. In the case of *Brown v. Mississippi* the unanimous court held that the 14th Amendment guarantee of due process denied states the power to use as evidence against a man a confession wrung from him by torture.

The Power of the President

In December 1936 the court — which held such a dim view of the president's efforts to deal with domestic crises — endorsed virtually unlimited power for the president in the field of foreign affairs.

In the case of *United States v. Curtiss-Wright Export Corp.*, the justices declared the president to be the sole negotiator of U.S. foreign policy. Justice Sutherland, author also of the opinions curtailing the removal power and striking down the coal act, described this aspect of presidential power as "plenary and exclusive."

Packing the Court

Highly frustrated by the court's adamant opposition to his efforts to lead the nation toward economic recovery, President Roosevelt began to look for a way to change the court's views.

His entire first term had passed without a court vacancy, despite the age and length of service of many of the justices. In part this may have been due to the fierce opposition of the conservative justices to Roosevelt's New Deal, but in part it was also due to much more practical considerations.

In 1936 there was no "retirement" system for justices; they could withdraw from full-time active service only by resigning. Upon resignation the largest pension a justice could draw was $10,000. Chief Justice Hughes later would say that he felt that both Van Devanter and Sutherland would have retired early in his term as Chief Justice, had the provisions for retirement income been more accommodating.[121]

'Judicial Reform' Plan

Roosevelt decided to create vacancies by convincing Congress that the court was handicapped by the advanced age of its members. Early in February, just after his inauguration for his second term, Roosevelt sent to Congress a "judicial reform" proposal — quickly labeled his "court-packing plan." The core of the proposal was that Congress should authorize him to appoint an additional member of the Supreme Court for each justice over 70 who did not resign. If approved, this would have enabled Roosevelt immediately to appoint six new justices, and in all likelihood, assured him a majority in favor of the New Deal.

The reaction to the proposal was adverse on all sides. Yet Congress began formal consideration of it. In a move that would prove crucial, Congress immediately separated out and passed a new Supreme Court Retirement Act on March 1. It provided that Supreme Court justices could retire and continue to receive their salary, just as other federal judges already were able to do.

The Senate Judiciary Committee then turned to consideration of the proposal's more controversial items.

The Court's Turnabout

Unknown to any but the justices themselves, however, the court already had begun to abandon its conservative effort to protect business from state and federal regulation. Signalling this change was its decision, reached before the court-packing proposal was made known, to abandon the *Lochner-Adkins* line of reasoning and uphold state minimum-wage laws. Implicit in this reversal was the willingness of a majority of the court to accept government authority to act to protect the general welfare of society — and to withdraw from its own role as the censor of economic legislation.

On March 29, 1937, while the Senate committee was still considering the Roosevelt plan, the court announced its decision in the case of *West Coast Hotel Co. v. Parrish.*

By a 5-4 vote the court upheld Washington State's minimum-wage law, overruling *Adkins* and effectively reversing the previous year's ruling in *Morehead v. New York.* Justice Roberts, who had voted to strike down the New York law, now voted to uphold the Washington law. Chief Justice Hughes wrote the majority opinion; Sutherland, Butler, McReynolds and Van Devanter dissented.

In his opinion, Chief Justice Hughes interred the doctrine of freedom of contract. No such freedom was mentioned in the Constitution, he pointed out. The "liberty" protected by the due process clauses of the Fifth and 14th Amendments, he continued, was not liberty of contract, but instead "liberty in a social organization which requires the protection of the law against the evils which menace the health, safety, morals and welfare of the people." [122] That liberty was protected by the minimum-wage law, which thus was fully constitutional.

The same day the court unanimously upheld two New Deal statutes — a second Federal Farm Bankruptcy Act, virtually identical to the one struck down on Black Monday, and a provision of the Railway Labor Act encouraging collective bargaining.[123]

Two weeks later, on April 12, the court — by the same 5-4 vote as in *Parrish,* upheld the National Labor Relations Act. Writing the majority opinion in the case of *National Labor Relations Board v. Jones & Laughlin Steel Corp.,* Chief Justice Hughes declared that the right to organize for collective bargaining, a fundamental right, was well within the scope of Congress' power over commerce.

On May 18 the Senate Judiciary Committee reported Roosevelt's court-packing bill, recommending against its enactment. Almost simultaneously, Justice Van Devanter, now 78, informed President Roosevelt that he intended to retire at the end of the current term.

Less than a week later, on May 24, the court confirmed the completeness of its turnabout. In the cases of *Steward Machine Co. v. Davis* and *Helvering v. Davis,* the court by votes of 5-4 and 6-3 upheld the unemployment compensation and old-age benefits programs set up by the Social Security Act. The court upheld the first as a proper use of the taxing power and the second as an appropriate means of acting to protect the general welfare. Justice Cardozo wrote the majority opinions in both cases.

Justice Black and the Due Process Revolution

To replace Van Devanter, Roosevelt chose Alabama Sen. Hugo L. Black as his first nominee to the court. Black, 51, was confirmed in August 1937. He would serve on the court until a week before his death in 1971.

In December 1937, soon after Black took his seat, the court announced its decision in the case of *Palko v. Connecticut.* With Cardozo writing for the majority, the court firmly declined to rule that the due process clause of the 14th Amendment automatically extended all the guarantees of the Bill of Rights against state, as well as federal action. Only those rights essential to a scheme of ordered liberty were binding upon the states through the due process guarantee, stated Cardozo. In Black's 34 years on the court, the justices would, one by one, place almost all of the guarantees of the Bill of Rights in this "essential" category.

The Court and the Rights of Persons: 1938-1969

On Oct. 4, 1937, Justice Hugo L. Black took his seat as the Supreme Court's most junior justice. It was the beginning of a new era.

The court-packing bill had been deflated into a judicial procedure reform bill, signed into law in August 1937. The first of the conservative quartet of justices had left the bench, the others would follow shortly. And the court had resigned its role as arbiter of the wisdom of economic legislation, and would now turn its attention to questions of individual rights and liberties.

In the next six years Roosevelt, who had waited five years to place a man of his choice on the court, would name eight justices and elevate a ninth to the position of Chief Justice. The men he would place on the court would, with a few exceptions, be young enough to be the sons of the men they succeeded, and the views of the court would change accordingly. Black, for example, was 51 when he replaced the 78-year-old Van Devanter.

The Roosevelt Justices

A few months after Black was seated, Justice Sutherland retired at 75. To that seat Roosevelt named Solicitor General Stanley F. Reed, 54. Reed served 19 years until retiring in 1957.

In mid-1938 Justice Cardozo died. In his place Roosevelt chose his close friend and adviser, Felix Frankfurter, a professor of law at Harvard. Frankfurter, 56, was seated early in 1939 and served for 23 years on the court.

Soon after Frankfurter took his seat, Justice Brandeis resigned. He was 82 years old and had served on the court 23 years. He was succeeded by a man literally half his age. William O. Douglas, the 40-year-old chairman of the Securities and Exchange Commission would serve on the court for 36-1/2 years — longer than any man in the court's history.

Late in 1939 Justice Butler died at 73. He was replaced by Attorney General Frank Murphy, 50, who served until his death in 1949. When Murphy took his seat in January 1940, Roosevelt nominees composed a majority of the court. Of the four staunch conservatives who had blocked Roosevelt's New Deal plans, only Justice McReynolds remained on the bench.

From Commerce to Civil Rights

The philosophical shift evident in the decisions of 1937 was reinforced by the rulings of the succeeding terms. Not only did the court redirect its efforts away from matters of property rights and toward issues of personal rights, but it also began to evolve different standards for the two types of cases.

The change was illustrated in *United States v. Carolene Products Co.* decided April 25, 1938. Over McReynolds' lone dissent, the court upheld a federal law barring the interstate transportation of certain milk products.

In the majority opinion, Justice Stone tentatively set out a double standard for constitutional cases. When a law was challenged as impinging upon economic rights, he said, the court would presume the law to be valid, unless the challenger could prove otherwise. But if a law was challenged as impinging upon personal liberties protected by the Bill of Rights, the court might be less inclined to assume the law's validity. As Stone worded it, "there may be narrower scope for operation of the presumption of constitutionality when legislation appears on its face to be within a specific prohibition of the Constitution, such as those of the first ten amendments." [124]

The reasoning behind such a double standard, Stone explained, was based upon the relationship of economic rights and personal rights to the political processes. Laws infringing upon the individual rights guaranteed by the Bill of Rights restricted the operation of the very processes that could be expected to produce the repeal of repressive legislation. Laws operating to curtail economic freedom, on the other hand, did not hinder the political processes that therefore could be used to repeal or modify the offending laws.

This new set of standards — plus the extension of the guarantees of the Bill of Rights to the states, begun with *Gitlow* 13 years earlier — provided the doctrinal underpinnings for the civil rights revolution to come. One observer calls the *Carolene Products* standard — set out in a footnote — "the manifesto in a footnote." [125]

The New View of Federal Power

In a steady line of decisions beginning with those announced on March 29, 1937, the court upheld revised versions of virtually all the major New Deal legislation it had struck down in 1935 and 1936. [126]

Abandoning its restrictive view of the relationship between states' rights and federal power, the court overturned its earlier decisions granting the incomes of federal officials immunity from state taxes and granting those of state officials similar immunity from federal taxation. [127]

This line of rulings — in which the court also renounced many of the various doctrines it had invoked to curtail state and federal power over economic matters — culminated on Feb. 3, 1941.

By a unanimous vote the court upheld the Fair Labor Standards Act of 1938, which prohibited child labor, set a maximum 40-hour workweek and a minimum wage of 40 cents an hour for workers in interstate commerce.

This decision, in the case of *United States v. Darby Lumber Co.*, specifically overruled *Hammer v. Dagenhart*, the 1918 ruling placing child labor beyond the reach of the federal commerce power. The court implicitly reaffirmed Hughes' earlier statement discarding the "freedom of contract" doctrine and declared the 10th Amendment of no relevance to questions of federal power. Writing for the court Justice Stone explained that the justices viewed that amendment as "but a truism [stating] that all is retained which has not been surrendered." [128]

With this decision, writes William F. Swindler, the court returned to Chief Justice John Marshall's view of the broad commerce power:

> ... after half a century of backing and filling, the court had come unequivocally to acknowledge that a plenary power over interstate commerce was vested in Congress, and that Congress was the sole judge of the appropriate use of this power. The new constitutionalism, in this, was returning to the concept enunciated by John Marshall a century before, that the commerce power "is complete in itself, may be exercised to its utmost extent, and acknowledges no limitations other than are prescribed in the Constitution." [129]

Later in this same term, in May 1941, the court extended federal power in another direction. In the case of *United States v. Classic,* the court asserted that Congress had the power to regulate primary elections when they were an integral part of the process of selecting members of Congress. This ruling overturned the statement to the contrary in *Newberry v. United States,* decided 20 years earlier.

Rights and Freedom

Already in Black's first term questions of individual freedom and civil rights were beginning to occupy more of the court's attention.

In March 1938 the court unanimously held that the First Amendment guarantee of freedom of religion was abridged when a city required Jehovah's Witnesses to be licensed before they could distribute religious literature on city streets. This decision came in the case of *Lovell v. Griffin.*

In May the court confirmed the broad scope of the Sixth Amendment guarantee — for federal defendants — of the right to counsel. In the case of *Johnson v. Zerbst* the court held that federal courts were constitutionally bound to provide defendants with legal counsel unless they waived that right.

And in December 1938 the court began seriously to test the constitutional validity of the "separate but equal" doctrine, which had made possible the pervasive racial segregation of much of American life.

In the case of *Missouri ex rel. Gaines v. Canada* the court held that the Constitution required a state providing white residents the opportunity for higher education to offer it to blacks as well. This promise of equal protection, wrote Chief Justice Hughes, was not fulfilled by a state's offering to pay the tuition for a black student to attend law school in another state.

The following term, the court decided the case of *Hague v. CIO,* striking down a city ordinance used to prevent union organizers from meeting and discussing labor union membership and related subjects. The First Amend-

The Court in 1940

From left: Justices Owen J. Roberts, William O. Douglas, James C. McReynolds, Stanley F. Reed, Chief Justice Charles Evans Hughes, Justices Felix Frankfurter, Harlan Fiske Stone, Frank Murphy, Hugo L. Black.

ment guarantee of the freedom of speech and assembly forbids such official restriction of these rights, held the court. And in 1940 the court in *Thornhill v. Alabama* extended this rationale to strike down a state law forbidding labor picketing. [130]

Also in 1940 the court in *Cantwell v. Connecticut* held that a state violated the First Amendment when it used a permit system to restrain and a breach-of-the-peace law to punish persons for making provocative statements about religion.

War and Patriotism

The war in Europe encouraged a resurgence of patriotic display in the United States. In 1940 the court's emerging views on state power and religious freedom were tested by the case of *Minersville School District v. Gobitis.* State efforts to inculcate patriotism prevailed, at least temporarily, over religious freedom.

By a vote of 8-1 the court upheld a state's right to require public school students to recite daily the national pledge of allegiance to the flag, even if the recitation conflicted with their religious beliefs. Justice Frankfurter wrote the majority opinion; only Justice Stone dissented.

The Changing of the Guard

Early in 1941 Justice McReynolds, after 26 years on the court, resigned. He was 78 years old, the last of the conservative foursome of the New Deal to leave the bench.

At the end of the 1941 term, Chief Justice Hughes retired. Roosevelt chose Justice Harlan Fiske Stone, a Republican with 16 years service on the court, to move to the center chair. Stone, then 69, served in that post until his death in 1946.

To fill McReynolds' seat, Roosevelt chose South Carolina Sen. James F. Byrnes, 62. Byrnes did not find the post a congenial one and resigned after one term, in October 1942, to take a more active role in the Roosevelt administration's war effort.

As Byrnes' successor Roosevelt chose federal Judge Wiley B. Rutledge, 48. Rutledge took his seat in February 1943 and served until his death six years later.

To fill the seat Stone left vacant upon becoming Chief Justice, Roosevelt in 1941 chose Attorney General Robert H. Jackson, 49, who served for 13 years.

Issues of War

The United States was forcibly brought into World War II early in Stone's first term as Chief Justice. The issues of personal liberty and governmental power raised by the war dominated the work of the court during his tenure in that post.

After his first term, a special session was called in July 1942 so that the court might consider the constitutional challenge brought by Nazi saboteurs, arrested in the United States, to Roosevelt's decision to have them tried by a military commission, not civilian courts. The court in *Ex parte Quirin* upheld the president's actions, as within the scope of the authority delegated to him by Congress.

In three later decisions in 1943 and 1944, the court also upheld against constitutional challenge the actions of the president and Congress restricting the liberty of persons of Japanese descent living on the West Coast through a program of curfews and removal from the coast to inland camps. The court conceded the odious nature of ethnic

distinctions, but found them justified in this particular wartime situation. [131]

In one of these cases, however, *Korematsu v. United States,* the court for the first time declared that "all legal restrictions which curtail the civil rights of a single racial group are immediately suspect . . . the courts must subject them to the most rigid scrutiny." [132] Thus, even in condoning severe infringements of personal liberty and individual rights in the war years, the court laid the foundation for later decisions expanding those rights.

The Flag and the First Amendment

A primary characteristic of the court of the early 1940s — unlike its immediate predecessor — was its experimental approach to constitutional law, its "readiness to change new landmarks as well as old" ones. [133]

This readiness was amply demonstrated in the mid-war term that began in October 1942. In that term the court reversed two of its own recent rulings concerning the First Amendment rights of Jehovah's Witnesses, a sect whose particular beliefs and evangelistic fervor brought its members into frequent collision with state and local authority.

In the 1940 *Gobitis* case the court had upheld Pennsylvania's rule that schoolchildren participate in the pledge of allegiance to the U.S. flag each day. In 1942 the court

---

"If there is any fixed star in our constitutional constellation, it is that no official, high or petty, can prescribe what shall be orthodox in politics, nationalism, religion or other matters of opinion or force citizens to confess by word or act their faith therein."

—Justice Robert H. Jackson
*West Virginia Board of Education
v. Barnette,* 1943

---

had upheld, in the case of *Jones v. Opelika,* a city ordinance requiring street vendors — including Jehovah's Witnesses passing out religious material — to obtain city licenses for their activity. [134] The vote was 5-4. Justice Reed wrote the majority opinion.

But three of the dissenters in *Opelika* — members of the majority in *Gobitis* — announced that they were ready to reverse the flag salute case. This unusual public confession of error came from Justices Black, Murphy and Douglas.

Eleven months later, on May 3, 1943, the court reversed *Jones v. Opelika,* returning to the view set out in 1938 in *Lovell v. Griffin.* By a 5-4 vote the court in the case of *Murdock v. Pennsylvania* struck down licensing requirements similar to those upheld in the *Opelika* case, finding that they burdened the free exercise of religion when they were applied to the Jehovah's Witnesses. Justices Frankfurter, Reed, Roberts and Jackson dissented.

Six weeks after *Murdock* the court reversed its *Gobitis* ruling. The vote in that case of *West Virginia Board of Education v. Barnette* was 6-3. The majority was composed of Stone, the lone dissenter in *Gobitis,* now joined by Black,

Douglas and Murphy, and the two new members of the court — Jackson and Rutledge. Dissenting were Frankfurter, Reed and Roberts.

Justice Jackson eloquently stated the view of the new majority:

> If there is any fixed star in our constitutional constellation, it is that no official, high or petty, can prescribe what shall be orthodox in politics, nationalism, religion, or other matters of opinion or force citizens to confess by word or act their faith therein. [135]

The Right to Counsel, The Right to Vote

In 1941 the court rejected the argument that the 14th Amendment required states to provide all criminal defendants with the aid of an attorney. This ruling in *Betts v. Brady* came over the dissenting votes of Justices Murphy, Black and Douglas; 22 years later, Black would write the opinion overruling it.

In 1944 the court in the case of *Smith v. Allwright* expanded its definition of state action to strike down, once again, Texas' effort to maintain its "white primary." Relying on *United States v. Classic*, the court held that when a primary election is an integral part of the process of electing officials, the action of a political party to exclude Negroes from voting is state action within the reach of the 14th Amendment.

Chief Justice Vinson

In mid-1945 Justice Roberts resigned after 15 years on the court. President Truman selected his friend, Republican Sen. Harold Burton of Ohio, 57, to fill the seat. Burton,

a Republican, served on the court for 13 years.

Despite the addition of Justice Burton to the bench, the court operated for its October 1945 term with only eight members present. Justice Robert H. Jackson was absent for the term, acting as prosecutor at the Nuremberg trials of German war criminals.

On April 22, 1946, the court — over the dissent of Stone, Reed and Frankfurter — overruled several earlier decisions to hold that conscientious objectors were eligible for naturalization as citizens, even if they were unwilling to bear arms in the defense of their adopted country.

As Stone spoke from the bench to register his dissent from this ruling in *Girouard v. United States,* his voice faltered. He then had to be helped from the bench. He died that evening.

"The bench Stone headed was the most frequently divided, the most openly quarrelsome in history," wrote one observer. [136] That point was quickly borne out by events following his death. A long-distance feud erupted between Jackson, still absent in Europe, and Justice Black, now the court's senior member. Many assumed that Truman would elevate Jackson to the post of Chief Justice; rumors flew that two other justices had said they would resign if he were appointed.

Hoping to smooth over the differences, Truman chose Secretary of the Treasury Fred M. Vinson to head the court. Vinson, 56, served for seven years, until his death in 1953.

Civil Rights, 'Political Questions'

After Stone's death, the court — now with only seven participating members — announced its decision to strike down state laws requiring separate seating for black and

The Court in 1941

From left: Justices Stanley F. Reed, James F. Byrnes, Owen J. Roberts, William O. Douglas, Chief Justice Harlan Fiske Stone, Justices Frank Murphy, Hugo L. Black, Robert H. Jackson, Felix Frankfurter.

white passengers on interstate buses. In the case of *Morgan v. Virginia,* the court held that such a rule was a burden on interstate commerce — that the subject of seating on such vehicles was a matter for uniform national regulation. This ruling effectively reversed the court's 1890 decision upholding such requirements.

Also, late in the October 1945 term, the court by a vote of 4-3 in the case of *Colegrove v. Green* declined to enter the "political thicket" of electoral malapportionment.

Freedom and Fairness

Questions of individual freedom came before the court in increasing numbers during the postwar terms. In its first rulings on the application of the First Amendment's establishment clause to state action, the court in 1947 began its long effort to determine when — and in what manner — a state may provide aid to parochial schools or students at such schools without infringing upon the amendment's guarantee.

In 1947 the court reaffirmed its view that the due process clause of the 14th Amendment did not require states to abide by all the provisions of the Bill of Rights. In that same term, however, the court simply assumed that the Eighth Amendment ban on cruel and unusual punishment did apply to state action. [137]

In 1949 the court in the case of *Wolf v. Colorado* declared that the states — like the federal government — were bound by the Fourth Amendment guarantee of security against unreasonable searches and seizures. But the court rendered this declaration of little practical effect by refusing to require state judges to exclude evidence obtained in violation of the guarantee.

Also, in 1948, the court effectively curtailed the use of restrictive covenants to perpetuate housing segregation. In the case of *Shelley v. Kraemer* the court held that although the 14th Amendment did not reach the covenant itself, an agreement between private individuals, it did reach — and forbid — state court action enforcing those agreements.

Justices Clark and Minton

In mid-1949 Justice Murphy died. President Truman selected Attorney General Tom C. Clark to fill the seat. Clark, 49, served on the court for 18 years.

Almost as soon as Clark was confirmed, Justice Rutledge died. Truman named Sherman Minton, 59, a colleague from his days as a senator, to that seat. Minton, who had become a federal judge, served on the court for seven years.

Subversion and Segregation

Cold War issues and the emerging civil rights movement dominated the work of the Supreme Court during most of the 1950s.

The intense national concern over the threat of world communism produced a variety of laws and programs intended to prevent domestic subversion. Many of these anti-subversive efforts were challenged as infringing on freedoms of belief and expression protected by the First Amendment.

In May 1950 the court ruled on the first of these challenges. In *American Communications Association v. Douds* the court upheld the Taft-Hartley Act's requirement that all labor union officers swear they were not members of the Communist Party.

Chief Justice Vinson explained the majority view that Congress, under its commerce power, had the authority to impose such a requirement to avoid politically based strikes impeding the flow of interstate commerce. Justice Black in dissent argued that the commerce clause did not restrict "the right to think."

In 1951 the court in *Dennis v. United States* upheld the Smith Act, which made it unlawful to advocate or teach the violent overthrow of government in the United States or to belong to an organization dedicated to the accomplishment of these ends. The court upheld the convictions of 11 leaders of the U.S. Communist Party under the act. Chief Justice Vinson wrote the opinion; Justices Black and Douglas dissented.

During this term the court also upheld the power of the attorney general to prepare a list of organizations considered subversive — and backed state power to require public employees to take an oath denying membership in the Communist Party. [138]

In a special term called in the summer of 1953, the court considered a stay of execution granted by Justice Douglas for Julius and Ethel Rosenberg, convicted under the Espionage Act of 1917 of passing atomic secrets to the Soviet Union. The court — over the dissents of Black and Douglas — lifted the stay, allowing the Rosenbergs to be executed. [139] Douglas' action in granting the stay sparked the first of two impeachment attempts against him.

The Steel Seizure Case

By 1950 President Truman had named four members of the court, including the Chief Justice. Thus, when he found himself before the court in May 1952, defending his decision to seize the nation's major steel companies to avoid a strike and disruption of steel production during the Korean conflict, he might have expected a favorable decision.

Instead, on June 2, 1952, the court by a vote of 6-3 rebuked Truman, ruling that he had acted illegally and without constitutional authority. In an opinion by Justice Black, the majority upheld a lower court's order blocking the seizure. Justices Burton and Clark voted against Truman; Chief Justice Vinson and Minton voted for him.

The decision in *Youngstown Sheet & Tube Co. v. Sawyer* marked one of the rare instances where the Supreme Court flatly told the president he had overreached the limits of his constitutional power. And it was a mark of the court's power that President Truman, fuming, complied.

Separate But Equal?

In June 1951 the court announced two unanimous decisions that called further into question the continuing validity of the "separate but equal" doctrine it had espoused in *Plessy v. Ferguson,* 55 years earlier.

In *Sweatt v. Painter,* the court ordered the University of Texas law school to admit a Negro student. The court found the educational opportunity provided by a newly created "black" law school in the state was in no way equal to that at the university law school. Thus the state did not fulfill the promise of equal protection under the 14th Amendment by providing a separate black law school, held the court in an opinion written by Chief Justice Vinson.

In *McLaurin v. Oklahoma State Regents,* the court rebuffed the effort of the University of Oklahoma, forced by court order to accept a Negro student, to segregate that student in all phases of campus life.

A year and a half later, in December 1952, the court heard arguments in a group of five cases challenging the segregation of public elementary and secondary schools. The cases are known by the title of one — *Brown v. Board of Education of Topeka.*

In June 1953 the court ordered reargument in the cases in the October 1953 term. Before the reargument took place, however, the court had a new Chief Justice.

Chief Justice Warren

Chief Justice Vinson's last years were difficult ones. The sensitive questions of anti-subversive legislation in the McCarthy era, the face-off with Truman over the steel seizure, the tense special session considering the Rosenberg case, all confirmed Justice Holmes' description of the court as the quiet center of national storms.

Less than three months after the Rosenberg decision, Vinson died, in September 1953.

President Dwight D. Eisenhower then had the task of selecting a new Chief Justice within his first year of taking office. He looked to California, and chose that state's governor — 62-year-old Earl Warren.

Warren, a Republican, had run unsuccessfully for vice president on the Dewey ticket in 1948. As governor during World War II he had supported the relocation of residents of Japanese ancestry. He had just announced that he would not run for a fourth gubernatorial term when Vinson died. Explaining his choice, President Eisenhower said that he had selected Warren for his "integrity, honesty, middle-of-the-road philosophy." [140]

Warren received a recess appointment and began serving as the October 1953 term opened. He was confirmed in March 1954. He served for 16 years, retiring in June 1969.

Brown v. Board of Education

When the *Brown* cases were reargued in December 1953, Warren presided over the court.

When they were decided on May 17, 1954, Warren spoke for the court. With his brief opinion, the unanimous Supreme Court reversed *Plessy v. Ferguson,* decided 58 years earlier when Earl Warren was but five years old.

Concluding this, his first major opinion, Chief Justice Warren said:

> We conclude that in the field of public education the doctrine of "separate but equal" has no place. Separate educational facilities are inherently unequal. [141]

Richard Kluger, 20 years later, assessed the impact of *Brown:*

> Having proclaimed the equality of all men in the preamble to the Declaration of Independence, the nation's founders had then elected, out of deference to the slaveholding South, to omit that definition of equalitarian democracy from the Constitution. It took a terrible civil war to correct that omission. But the Civil War amendments were soon drained of their original intention to lift the black man to meaningful membership in American society. The Court itself would do much to assist in that process, and *Plessy* was its most brutal blow. Congress passed no civil rights laws after the Court eviscerated one of 1875, and those that remained on the books were largely ignored by the states and unenforced by federal administrations. . . .

It was into this moral void that the Supreme Court under Earl Warren now stepped. Its opinion in *Brown v. Board of Education,* for all its economy, represented nothing short of a reconsecration of American ideals. . . . [142]

In April 1955 rearguments were held on the question of implementing the *Brown* ruling. In May 1955 the second *Brown* ruling set out the standard — the states should proceed to end segregation in public schools with "all deliberate speed." Again the court was unanimous; again, Warren was its spokesman.

Although the court had carefully limited its opinion to the subject of schools, "it became almost immediately clear that *Brown* had in effect wiped out all forms of state-sanctioned segregation." [143]

The impact of *Brown* was so fundamental — and the public reaction to it so broad and deep — that it tends to dominate all descriptions of the court's work during the 1950s. Yet — with the exception of its 1958 ruling in *Cooper*

"We conclude that in the field of public education the doctrine of 'separate but equal' has no place. Separate educational facilities are inherently unequal."

—Chief Justice Earl Warren
Brown v. Board of Education, 1954

The Warren court's "opinion in Brown v. Board of Education, for all its economy, represented nothing short of a reconsecration of American ideals. . . ."

—Richard Kluger, *Simple Justice*

---

v. Aaron rebuking Arkansas Gov. Orval Faubus for his resistance to desegregation — the court did not hand down another major civil rights decision until the 1960s.

In case after case challenging various forms of segregation, the court did not hear arguments but simply told lower courts to reconsider the facts in light of *Brown.*

Resistance to these rulings was fierce, and was soon felt in Congress. The period from 1954 to 1960, writes William F. Swindler, was one of "tension between the high tribunal and Congress unparalleled even by the early years of the 1930s." [144] But now the roles were reversed: The court was the vanguard of change — and Congress the bulwark of reaction.

Security and Due Process

The tension between Congress and the court created by the school desegregation decision was further heightened by subsequent decisions invalidating federal and state anti-subversive programs — and beginning to impose new due process requirements upon police practices.

In 1956 the court struck down a state sedition law, holding, in *Pennsylvania v. Nelson,* that Congress in passing the Smith Act had pre-empted state power to punish efforts to overthrow the federal government. The same term, the court in *Slochower v. Board of Education* held that a state could not automatically dismiss employees simply because they invoked their Fifth Amendment right to remain silent when questioned by congressional committees.

And in the same term the court applied the equal protection guarantee to require that a state provide an indigent defendant with a free transcript of his trial, so that he might appeal his conviction. In this case of *Griffin v. Illinois,* as in *Slochower,* Burton, Minton, Reed and Justice John Marshall Harlan dissented.

The Eisenhower Justices

Just as the October 1954 term opened, Justice Jackson died. As his second nominee to the court, President Eisenhower chose John Marshall Harlan, grandson and namesake of the famous dissenting justice whose career spanned the turn of the century. Harlan, a distinguished New York attorney, was 55 when he was appointed to the Supreme Court. He was confirmed in March 1955 and served for 16 years.

Two years later, in October 1956, Justice Minton retired. As his successor, Eisenhower named William Joseph Brennan Jr., 50, a judge on the New Jersey Supreme Court. Brennan was the first member of the court born in the 20th century.

Early in 1957 Justice Reed retired after almost two decades on the bench. Eisenhower nominated federal Judge Charles Whittaker, 56, of Kansas. Whittaker would serve only five years before resigning in 1962.

In October 1958 Justice Burton retired, giving Eisenhower his fifth and last vacancy to fill. Eisenhower chose Potter Stewart of Ohio, a 43-year-old federal judge. Seated in the fall of 1958 as a recess appointment (as were Harlan and Brennan), Stewart was confirmed in May 1959.

Cases and Controversy

The criticism already aroused by the court's decisions of the early years under Chief Justice Warren was intensified by several lines of decisions in the late 1950s.

In 1951 the court in *Dennis v. United States* upheld the Smith Act, under which the leaders of the U.S. Communist Party were prosecuted for advocating the violent overthrow of the federal government. On June 17, 1957, the court in the case of *Yates v. United States* set such a strict standard for convictions under the Smith Act that it made successful prosecutions under the law almost impossible. Justice Harlan wrote the court's opinion, making clear that only advocacy of subversive *activity* — not just advocacy of certain *doctrine* — could be penalized without infringing on the First Amendment.

The same day the court in *Watkins v. United States* reversed the contempt citation of a witness who had refused to answer questions from the House Un-American Activities Committee about the Communist Party membership of persons other than himself.

These opinions and two others announced that day led conservative critics to label June 17, 1957, "Red Monday" — as May 27, 1935, had been "Black Monday" to supporters of the New Deal — and March 29, 1937, "White Monday" for the same group. [145]

The Court in 1954

From left: Justices Felix Frankfurter, Tom C. Clark, Hugo L. Black, Robert H. Jackson, Chief Justice Earl Warren, Justices Harold H. Burton, Stanley F. Reed, Sherman Minton, William O. Douglas.

Public and political criticism of the court was intense as a result of these rulings. Legislation was proposed to reverse or circumvent them and to withdraw the court's jurisdiction over all matters of loyalty and subversion. Southerners critical of the desegregation rulings joined others unhappy over the anti-subversive rulings to raise congressional hostility toward the court to a point unprecedented in the 20th century. [146]

A week after "Red Monday" the court in the case of *Mallory v. United States* overturned a young man's conviction for rape because he had been interrogated by federal officers too long without being informed of his rights and held too long between his arrest and arraignment. The court was unanimous in this ruling; the criticism was almost as unified.

The same day, the court in *Roth v. United States* made clear that obscene material did not have First Amendment protection, beginning a long and difficult process of describing what is or is not obscene material.

In July 1957 after hearing arguments late in the term, the court cleared the way for Japanese courts to try an American soldier for killing a Japanese woman on an Army rifle range, another ruling that won the court few friends.[147]

In 1958 the court began to give full constitutional recognition to the freedom of association — striking down Alabama's efforts to force the National Association for the Advancement of Colored People (NAACP) to disclose its membership lists. [148]

An unusual special session was called late the summer of 1958 to consider the Little Rock, Ark., desegregation case. The court in *Cooper v. Aaron* unanimously rejected city officials' request for delay in implementing the desegregation plan for the city's schools.

The Reapportionment Revolution

In *Brown v. Board of Education* the Supreme Court set off a long overdue revolution in civil rights.

But after *Brown* the court played only a secondary role in the accelerating civil rights movement. The court left it to Congress to implement, at last, the guarantees of the Civil War Amendments through effective legislation. The court's role was crucial, but secondary. When that legislation was challenged, as it had been in Reconstruction, the court upheld it as constitutional.

But in the area of voting rights, the court did — unexpectedly — take the lead.

In 1946 the court had rebuffed a constitutional challenge to maldistribution of voters among electoral districts, declaring such a matter a political question beyond its purview.

In 1962 the court abandoned that cautious stance, and held that constitutional challenges to such malapportionment of political power were indeed questions the courts might decide.

This ruling was foreshadowed in the 1960 decision in *Gomillion v. Lightfoot.* In that case the court unanimously agreed that a state, in gerrymandering a district to exclude all black voters, had clearly violated the 15th Amendment.

Because such state action violated a specific constitutional guarantee, held the court, it was properly a matter for federal judicial consideration. It was from that ruling only a short step to *Baker v. Carr,* announced March 26, 1962.

Tennessee's failure to redistrict for most of the 20th century had produced electoral districts for the state legislature of grossly unequal population. This maldistribution of electoral power was challenged as violating the 14th Amendment guarantee of equal protection.

Abandoning the "political thicket" view of *Colegrove v. Green,* the majority held that this was clearly a case under the Constitution and thus within the jurisdiction of the federal courts.

New Justices

Later in 1962, Justices Whittaker and Frankfurter retired. President John F. Kennedy named Deputy Attorney General Byron R. White, 44, and Secretary of Labor Arthur Goldberg, 54, to fill the empty seats. White took his seat in April 1962; Goldberg was seated at the beginning of the October 1962 term.

'One Person, One Vote'

In March 1963 the court set out the standard for constitutionally valid reapportionment plans. In the case of *Gray v. Sanders,* Justice Douglas wrote for the court that the promise of political equality, contained in the nation's most basic documents, meant "one person, one vote."

A year later, in February 1964, the court applied that rule to congressional redistricting in the case of *Wesberry v. Sanders.* Four months later in the June 1964 ruling in *Reynolds v. Sims,* the justices held that the same standard applied to the electoral districts for the members of both houses of the states' legislatures.

The result of these rulings, which Warren considered the most important of his tenure, was the redistribution of political power in Congress and every state legislature.

In 1969 the court in *Kirkpatrick v. Preisler* reaffirmed its commitment to this standard, requiring congressional districts within a state to be mathematically equal in population.

State Trials and Due Process

Involving itself in still another area traditionally left to state control, the court in the 1960s accelerated the step-by-step application of due process requirements to state law enforcement and criminal procedures. By 1969 the court had required states to abide by virtually every major provision of the Bill of Rights — until then applicable only to federal action.

The first major ruling in this "due process revolution" came on June 19, 1961. By a 5-4 vote, the court held in *Mapp v. Ohio* that evidence obtained in violation of the Fourth Amendment guarantee of security against unreasonable search and seizure must be excluded from use in state, as well as federal, courts. Justice Clark wrote the opinion; Justices Stewart, Harlan, Frankfurter and Whittaker dissented.

A year later, the court for the first time applied the Eighth Amendment ban on cruel and unusual punishment to strike down a state law. In *Robinson v. California* the court held that a state could not make narcotics addiction a crime.

In 1963 the court declared in *Gideon v. Wainwright* that states must provide legal assistance for all defendants charged with serious crimes. If the defendant is unable to pay for an attorney, the state must provide one, wrote Justice Black for the unanimous court, overruling the court's earlier refusal, in the 1941 case of *Betts v. Brady,* to extend this right to state defendants.

On June 15, 1964, the same day that it decided *Reynolds v. Sims,* the court held that states must observe the Fifth Amendment privilege against compelled self-incrimination. The vote in *Malloy v. Hogan* was 5-4; Brennan wrote the opinion; Harlan, Clark, Stewart and White dissented.

A week later, by the same vote, the court held, in the case of *Escobedo v. Illinois,* that a suspect has a right to legal assistance as soon as he is the target of a police investigation.

In April 1965 the court overruled its 1908 decision in *Twining v. New Jersey,* and held that state judges and prosecutors may not comment adversely upon the failure of a defendant to testify in his own defense. Such comment infringes upon the Fifth Amendment right to remain silent rather than incriminate oneself, declared the court in *Griffin v. California.*

The most controversial single Warren court criminal law ruling came the following term, on June 13, 1966.

In the case of *Miranda v. Arizona,* the court held by a vote of 5-4 that police may not interrogate a suspect in custody unless they have informed him of his right to remain silent, of the fact that his words may be used against him, and of his right to have the aid of a lawyer. If the suspect wishes to remain silent — or to contact his attorney — interrogation must cease until he wishes to speak or until his attorney is present. Statements obtained in violation of this rule could not be used in court. Chief Justice Warren wrote the majority opinion; dissenting were Harlan, Clark, Stewart and White.

The next term, as criticism of the court mounted in Congress and in statehouses across the nation, the court extended to state defendants the right to a speedy trial, enlarged the due process guarantees for juvenile defendants, and brought wiretapping and electronic surveillance under the strictures of the Fourth Amendment warrant requirement. [149]

This step-by-step process of applying the Bill of Rights against state, as well as federal, action was completed with the 1968 ruling in *Duncan v. Louisiana,* extending the right to a jury trial to state defendants and the extension of the guarantee against double jeopardy in *Benton v. Maryland,* announced on Warren's last day as Chief Justice.

Loyalty and Freedom

Questions of freedom of belief and association, arising from the anti-subversive measures of the 1950s, were still before the court during the 1960s.

Generally, the court scrutinized these restrictive measures closely, and often it found some constitutional flaw.

In 1961 the court upheld the constitutionality of the Subversive Activities Control Act of 1950, under which the Communist Party was required to register with the Justice Department. But this ruling in the case of *Communist Party v. Subversive Activities Control Board* (SACB) came by a 5-4 vote. Four years later a unanimous court held in *Albertson v. SACB,* that individuals could not be compelled to register under the law without violating the Fifth Amendment protection against self-incrimination.

In 1966 the court closely circumscribed the use of state loyalty oaths and in 1967 it struck down the portion of the Subversive Control Act that made it a criminal offense for a member of a "subversive" group to hold a job in the defense industry.[150]

The Court and Civil Rights

Congress in 1964 reasserted its long-dormant power to implement the promises of the Civil War Amendments through legislation. Passage of the comprehensive 1964 Civil Rights Act was followed in 1965 by the Voting Rights Act, and in 1968 by the Fair Housing Act.

The modern Supreme Court — unlike the court of the 1870s and 1880s — reinforced congressional action, holding that these revolutionary statutes were clearly constitutional.

In late 1964 the court upheld the contested public accommodations provisions of the 1964 Act with its ruling in *Heart of Atlanta Motel v. United States.* Justice Clark wrote the opinion for a unanimous court.

In 1966 the court rebuffed a broad challenge to the Voting Rights Act of 1965 as violating state's rights. In *South Carolina v. Katzenbach* the court, with only Justice Black dissenting in part, upheld the sweeping statute as well within the power of Congress to enforce the 15th Amendment guarantee against racial discrimination in voting.

And a few months after passage of the modern Fair Housing Act, the court in *Jones v. Mayer* reinterpreted the Civil Rights Act of 1866 to prohibit racial discrimination in the sale of real estate.

School Segregation

Throughout the 1960s the court continued to exercise a supervisory role over the desegregation efforts of school systems across the country. In its first major school ruling since 1954, the court in the 1964 case of *Griffin v. County School Board of Prince Edward County* said that a state could not avoid the obligation of desegregating its public schools by closing them down.

Four years later, in *Green v. County School Board of New Kent County,* the court declared that "freedom-of-choice" desegregation plans were acceptable only when they were effective in desegregating a school system. The court made clear that, in its view, there had been entirely too much deliberation and not enough speed in the nation's effort to implement the *Brown* decrees.

Personal Liberty

The court during this decade substantially expanded constitutional protection for matters within the private concerns of individuals.

In 1965 the court in *Griswold v. Connecticut* struck down as unconstitutional a state law that forbade all use of contraceptives, even by married couples. The justices could not agree on the exact constitutional basis for this ruling, but they did agree there were some areas so private that the Constitution protected them from state interference.

Two years later the court, using similar reasoning in the case of *Loving v. Virginia,* held it unconstitutional for a state to forbid a person of one race to marry a member of another race.

School Prayer

The criticism the Warren court engendered by its rulings on security programs, segregation and criminal procedures was further intensified by its interpretation of the First Amendment's "establishment" clause in the so-called "school prayer" decisions.

On the basis of this ban on state action "establishing" religion, the court in 1962 held that a state may not prescribe a prayer or other religious statement for use in public schools. This ruling in *Engel v. Vitale* was followed in 1963 by the holding that a state could not require Bible reading as a daily religious exercise in public schools. [151]

Libel and Symbols

The court also expanded the meaning of other provisions of the First Amendment. In the landmark libel case of *New York Times v. Sullivan,* decided in March 1964, the court enlarged the protection the First Amendment provided the press by stating that public officials and public figures could recover damages for libelous statements made by the news media only if they could prove the statements were published with "actual malice."

And early in 1969 the court held that the First Amendment's protection for symbolic speech guaranteed students the right to engage in peaceful non-disruptive protest of the war in Vietnam through the wearing of black armbands to school. [152]

Federal Courts

Also during the 1960s, in decisions that drew far less public attention, the court made it easier for state prisoners, federal taxpayers and persons threatened by state action to come into federal court for assistance.

On March 18, 1963, the same day that it announced its decisions in *Gray v. Sanders* and *Gideon v. Wainwright,* the court in *Fay v. Noia* relaxed the requirements placed upon state prisoners who wished to challenge their detention in federal courts. Two years later, in *Dombrowski v. Pfister,* the court indicated that federal judges should not hesitate to intervene and halt ongoing state proceedings under a law challenged as violating the First Amendment.

And in 1968 the court in *Flast v. Cohen* substantially modified its 1923 holding that federal taxpayers generally lacked the qualifications to bring lawsuits challenging the use of their tax monies.

Justices Fortas and Marshall

Impatient to place a man of his own choosing on the Supreme Court, President Lyndon B. Johnson in 1965 persuaded Justice Goldberg to leave the court for the post of ambassador to the United Nations.

In the vacated seat Johnson placed Washington attorney Abe Fortas, his close friend and adviser and the successful advocate in the case of *Gideon v. Wainwright.* Fortas, 55, took his place on the bench just before the October 1965 term began.

Two years later, when his son, Ramsey Clark, became attorney general, Justice Tom Clark retired. To fill Clark's seat, Johnson nominated the nation's first black justice, Thurgood Marshall, who had argued the *Brown* cases for the NAACP Legal Defense Fund. Marshall, 59, began his service just before the opening of the October 1967 term.

Warren's Retirement

In 1968 Chief Justice Warren informed President Johnson that he intended to retire as soon as his successor was confirmed. Johnson promptly moved to elevate Justice Fortas to the post of Chief Justice.

Johnson was a lame duck; he had announced in March that he would not run for re-election. The Republicans had hopes of winning the White House — and wished to have their candidate, Richard Nixon, select the new Chief Justice. These hopes were given added significance by the fact that the court itself was among the major campaign issues sounded by candidate Nixon. He criticized the court for "coddling criminals" and promised to appoint justices who would turn a more receptive ear to the arguments of policemen and prosecutors.

Charges of cronyism — related to Fortas' continued unofficial role as adviser to Johnson — and conflict of interest further compounded the difficulties of his nomination as Chief Justice. After a filibuster stymied the nomination in October 1968, Johnson withdrew it at Fortas' request. Simultaneously, Johnson withdrew his nomination of federal Judge Homer Thornberry of Texas to succeed Fortas as associate justice.

The following May, Fortas resigned his seat under threat of impeachment, the result of a magazine article charging him with unethical behavior. Fortas asserted his innocence in his letter of resignation, and said he left the court to avoid placing it under unnecessary stress.

The Contemporary Court

On June 23, 1969, Chief Justice Warren retired. With President Richard M. Nixon looking on, Warren E. Burger took his oath of office as the nation's 15th Chief Justice.

Despite the controversy surrounding Fortas — who had resigned only a week before the announcement of Burger's selection — Nixon's nomination of Burger, 61, a conservative court of appeals judge, moved easily through the Senate. Burger, of Minnesota, had caught the new president's attention earlier by voicing concern that the Warren court was ruling too often in favor of criminal defendants without sufficient concern for the societal costs of such rulings.

Haynsworth and Carswell

But Nixon's effort to appoint a second conservative to fill Fortas' seat ran into more difficulty than any nomination in decades. The seat Fortas resigned on May 14, 1969, remained vacant for a year.

In August 1969 Nixon selected Appeals Court Judge Clement F. Haynsworth Jr. of South Carolina. In November the Senate denied Haynsworth confirmation by a vote of 45-55. It was the first time since 1930 that a presidential nominee to the court had been rejected. The rejection came in part because of charges of conflict of interest against

Haynsworth, in part as a liberal backlash to the Fortas resignation.

Early in 1970 Nixon named G. Harrold Carswell of Florida, another appeals court judge, to fill the empty seat. But Carswell too was denied confirmation. In April 1970 the Senate rejected his nomination, 45-51. It had been opposed by a wide variety of groups because of his racial views and his undistinguished career record.

Soon after the Carswell defeat, Nixon selected Harry A. Blackmun, an appeals court judge from Minnesota and a longtime friend of Chief Justice Burger. Blackmun, 61, was quickly confirmed. He took his seat in June 1970.

The Conservative Court

President Nixon had promised to give the court a more conservative character, and some of the rulings of the court in the 1970s did narrow the effect of the landmarks of the Warren era. But none of those landmarks were overturned in the 1970s — and the so-called conservative court itself set out a few surprising decisions, particularly in areas of the law not dealt with by earlier courts.

Burger's first term was relatively uneventful, except for the controversy over efforts to fill the empty Fortas seat.

But Blackmun's first full term — beginning in October 1970 — produced several major rulings. In the case of *Swann v. Charlotte-Mecklenburg County Board of Education* the court unanimously upheld the use of such controversial methods as busing, racial balance ratios and gerrymandered school districts to remedy school segregation. Burger wrote the opinion, which made clear that the court had no intention of retreating from *Brown*.

In *Harris v. New York* the justices modified the *Miranda* decision by allowing some limited in-court use of statements obtained from suspects who were not given their *Miranda* warnings. And in a set of cases known as *Younger v. Harris* the court curtailed the impact of its 1965 ruling allowing federal judges to halt enforcement of state laws challenged as infringing upon First Amendment rights.

But the court in 1970-71 for the first time held invalid a state law discriminating against women, finding it a denial of equal protection. And during this term it declared alienage, like race, always a suspect classification for lawmakers to use. [153]

The most dramatic ruling of the term came on June 30, 1971, when the court resoundingly rejected the Nixon administration's effort to halt publication of newspaper articles based upon the classified "Pentagon Papers." [154]

The Court in 1979

From left: Justices Byron R. White, William H. Rehnquist, William J. Brennan Jr., Harry A. Blackmun, Chief Justice Warren E. Burger, Justices Lewis F. Powell Jr., Potter Stewart, John Paul Stevens, Thurgood Marshall.

New Justices

Just two weeks before the opening of the October 1971 term, Justices Black and Harlan, both in failing health, resigned. Black, 85, had served 34 years; Harlan, 72, had served almost 17 years.

Nixon chose Lewis F. Powell Jr., a former president of the American Bar Association and a successful Virginia attorney, to fill the Black seat. He named William H. Rehnquist of Arizona, an assistant attorney general, to the Harlan seat. Powell, 64, and Rehnquist, 47, were confirmed in December 1971. Not since Warren Harding had one president in his first term placed four men on the court.

The 'Nixon Court'?

But despite the fact that four of its members had now been handpicked by President Nixon for their conservative views, the court's decisions hardly justified the label "the Nixon court."

In the first term in which all four Nixon nominees participated, the court struck down all existing death penalty laws, expanded the right to counsel still further than *Gideon v. Wainwright,* and refused to allow the administration to use electronic surveillance without a warrant in national security cases. [155]

In the growing controversy over a woman's right to have an abortion, President Nixon had expressed his opposition to this right. Yet in January 1973, in the same week as his second inaugural, the Supreme Court by a 7-2 vote upheld this right. Justice Blackmun wrote the court's opinion. Only Justices Rehnquist and White dissented from the court's ruling in *Roe v. Wade* and *Doe v. Bolton.*

In that same term, the court rejected a constitutional challenge to the use of property taxes as the basis for financing public schools, but it extended desegregation requirements to non-southern school systems. [156] The justices formulated a new definition of obscenity, and held that state legislative districts need not always meet the standard of strict equality they had applied in 1969 to congressional districts. [157]

The most stunning blow dealt by the court to President Nixon was a peculiarly personal one. The Watergate scandal had set off full-scale investigations in the Senate and under the direction of a special prosecutor.

In the course of these investigations, the special prosecutor subpoenaed the president for certain taped recordings of White House conversations that could be used as evidence in the trial of former White House aides charged with obstructing justice.

Nixon refused to comply with the subpoenas, asserting executive privilege — the privilege to refuse with impunity to comply with such a court order to protect the confidentiality of his conferences with his aides.

In June 1974 the case came to the Supreme Court, which heard *United States v. Nixon* argued in a special late-term session in July. On July 24 the court — by a unanimous vote of eight members — informed Nixon he must comply with the subpoena. Only Rehnquist did not participate.

The conservative court reasserted the power claimed by Chief Justice John Marshall — to say what the law is — and flatly denied Nixon's claim.

Nixon said he would comply and, as a result of the information disclosed in his compliance, he resigned his office early in August 1974 to avoid impeachment.

Justice Douglas Retires

In 1973 Justice William O. Douglas had surpassed Justice Stephen Field's record to become history's longest serving justice. Disabled by a stroke early in 1975, Douglas retired from the bench in November 1975. He had served on the court 36-1/2 years since his appointment by President Roosevelt in 1939. He retired at the age of 77.

To replace Douglas, President Gerald R. Ford selected John Paul Stevens, 55, a federal appeals court judge from Chicago. Stevens quickly was confirmed and was sworn in as the court's 101st member on Dec. 19, 1975.

With the addition of Stevens to the court, it was a bench almost completely selected by conservative Republican presidents — Eisenhower, Nixon and Ford. Only White and Marshall had been chosen by Democratic Chief Executives. But despite this fact, the court in the late 1970s and early 1980s did not produce a steady flow of consistently conservative opinions. To the contrary, its rulings on most major issues were just as likely to disturb conservatives as to unsettle liberals.

Speech and Spending

Political speech won a new measure of protection from the court early in 1976 when the justices invalidated the spending limits that Congress had approved in 1974 for federal political campaigns. With its decision in the case of *Buckley v. Valeo,* the court held that by curtailing spending in a campaign Congress impermissibly curtailed political speech in violation of the First Amendment.

Two years later, the court ruled that states could not restrict spending by a corporation in behalf of one side of an issue in a referendum; and in 1980, the court held that states could not forbid public utilities to mail out statements of their positions on public issues along with their bills. [158]

Press Freedom

As the 1971 Pentagon Papers ruling illustrated, the court during this period remained a vigilant guard against undue encroachment by government on press freedom. The court ruled that "gag orders" forbidding press coverage should be used only when all other measures failed to protect a defendant's right to a fair trial. [159] And although it ruled in 1979 that a judge could exclude press and public from a pre-trial hearing in a murder case, in 1980 the court declared that the First Amendment guaranteed newsman and citizen alike a right to attend criminal trials. [160]

However, the court rebuffed news media claims of various forms of special privilege. The court refused to allow the press, with impunity, to withhold information sought by prosecutors, or to demand that police use subpoenas, rather than search warrants, to obtain information from newsmen, or to demand special access to public institutions, such as prisons. [161]

The Court and Congress

In 1976, the court — for the first time since the days of the New Deal — struck down an Act of Congress because it found that Congress had overstepped its power to regulate commerce and had infringed upon the rights of states.

The court, ruling in the case of *National League of Cities v. Usery,* declared that Congress had gone too far in interfering in state and local matters when it amended the Fair Labor Standards Act to extend minimum wage and overtime standards to state and local governments. It was up to those governments, wrote Justice Rehnquist for the five-man majority, to decide how much to pay their employees and how to compensate them for overtime work.

The court held several other federal statutes unconstitutional in part, including two provisions of the Social Security Act that, the court held, discriminated unfairly between men and women.[162] In 1978 the court held that Congress ran afoul of the Fourth Amendment when it authorized federal occupational safety and health inspectors to conduct warrantless searches of business premises.[163]

And in December 1980, the justices gave themselves a raise, ruling in the case of *United States v. Will* that Congress had acted improperly in rescinding two cost-of-living increases in federal judicial salaries.

But, on the other hand, the court in 1980 and 1981 upheld three major Acts of Congress against constitutional challenge. In 1980 the court backed the power of the legislature to restrict the use of federal funds for abortions.[164] In 1981 the court held that Congress had the power to exclude women from the military draft and to require the careful restoration of strip-mined lands.[165]

The Court and the President

Just before the end of his term in January 1981, President Jimmy Carter resolved one of the most difficult situations of his four years in the White House. In order to gain release of 52 Americans held hostage by Iran for more than 14 months, Carter agreed to return to Iran more than $1 billion in Iranian assets held in the United States and to place that much again in an escrow fund pending settlement of claims against Iran by American businesses. In addition, Carter agreed that all such claims would be transferred to an international tribunal from U.S. courts.

This agreement, which did win return of the hostages, was immediately challenged by various American companies who had won court orders attaching some of those Iranian assets as potential payment to the U.S. companies of claims against Iran. Late in the October 1980 term, after oral arguments for the year had been concluded, the Supreme Court agreed to hear one more case argued. On June 24, 1981, the case of *Dames & Moore v. Regan* was argued, airing the statutory and constitutional challenges of business to the executive agreement reached by Carter with Iran. Within eight days the court announced its ruling. On July 2, it unanimously upheld the agreement as within the power of the president. Writing for the court, Justice Rehnquist found the agreement a proper exercise by the president of power that Congress had granted to him.

Death and Confession

In 1972 the court struck down all existing death penalty statutes as unconstitutionally capricious. Four years later, in 1976, the court, however, declined to outlaw capital punishment altogether. Death was not, in all circumstances, a cruel and unusual — thus unconstitutional — punishment, declared the court in a trio of cases decided at the end of the October 1975 term.

Ruling in five different cases that day, the court held that states could not declare death the mandatory punishment for all those convicted of first-degree murder — but that states could impose a death penalty if they used a two-part procedure in which a jury first considered and determined a defendant's guilt or innocence, and then, in a separate hearing, considered the question of penalty.[166]

By the time the Warren Court's controversial *Miranda*

ruling reached its 15th anniversary in 1981, it was clear that that decision was a permanent part of the nation's legal landscape.

In May 1981, the court announced a pair of decisions, extending and affirming the Warren Court's basic ruling. In the case of *Estelle v. Smith*, Chief Justice Burge wrote for the court that a person in custody must be advised of his constitutional rights to silence and to counsel before he underwent a court-ordered psychiatric examination.

The same day, the court held in *Edwards v. Arizona*, that once a suspect invokes his right to legal counsel, police must halt all questioning of the suspect until the attorney is present or until the suspect himself initiates a new round of conversation.

Civil Rights

As the modern civil rights movement marked the 25th anniversary of the landmark school desegregation ruling in *Brown v. Board of Education* (1954), the Supreme Court found itself faced with a variety of complex civil rights cases.

On affirmative action, the court seemed to zig and zag. In the celebrated *Bakke* case of 1978, it held that state medical schools could not use racial quotas in their admissions process, but in 1979, the court ruled that private employers could voluntarily adopt affirmative action plans to eliminate clear racial imbalance in certain job areas.[167]

And in 1980, the court upheld the power of Congress to require that 10 percent of the funds provided in a public works jobs bill be set aside for awards to minority businesses.[168]

In several civil rights cases challenging job qualification tests and zoning decisions as racially discriminatory, the court seemed to move toward a stiffer test for those who claimed discrimination. Without proof that such tests and decisions were deliberately discriminatory, held the court, a plaintiff could not bring a successful constitutional challenge to them.[169]

Sex Discrimination

Early in the 1970s, the court struck down several state laws and federal rules as discriminatory because they were based on an outdated stereotype of women's abilities and activities. Then in 1976, the court seemed to set a new standard against which laws should be measured to determine whether or not they discriminated unfairly against women. In the case of *Craig v. Boren*, in which different legal drinking ages for men and women were challenged, the court declared that a sex-based distinction was invalid unless it was shown to be substantially related to the achievement of an important governmental goal.

But five years later, when it considered the constitutional validity of the all-male draft, the court appeared to discard that standard, upholding the power of Congress to draft only men because only men could go into combat.

The First Woman Justice

In mid-June 1981, Justice Potter Stewart, one of the younger members of the aging court, announced that he would retire at the end of the term after 23 years on the court. On July 7, Reagan announced that he would nominate Arizona Court of Appeals Judge Sandra Day O'Connor, 51, to the vacant seat. O'Connor, a law school classmate of Justice William H. Rehnquist, had served for two terms in the Arizona legislature before moving to the state bench. *(See p. 186)*

Footnotes

[1] *McCulloch v. Maryland*, 4 Wheat. 316 at 407 (1819).

[2] Samuel F. Miller, *Lectures on the Constitution of the United States* (New York and Albany: Banks & Brothers, 1891), pp. 71, 73-74.

[3] *McCulloch v. Maryland*, 4 Wheat. 316 at 407 (1819).

[4] Charles Grove Haines, *The American Doctrine of Judicial Supremacy* (Berkeley, Calif.: University of California Press, 1932; reprint ed., New York: Da Capo Press, 1973), p. 23.

[5] Robert H. Jackson, *The Supreme Court in the American System of Government* (Cambridge: Harvard University Press, 1955), p. 61.

[6] Julius Goebel Jr., *History of the Supreme Court of the United States:* Vol. I, *Antecedents and Beginnings to 1801* (New York: Macmillan Publishing Co., 1971), p. 206.

[7] Ibid. p. 280.

[8] Charles Warren, *Congress, the Constitution and the Supreme Court* (Boston: Little, Brown & Co., 1925), p. 23.

[9] James Madison, Alexander Hamilton and John Jay, *The Federalist Papers,* with an Introduction by Clinton Rossiter (New York: New American Library, Mentor Books, 1961), No. 78, p. 465.

[10] Ibid., No. 79, p. 474.

[11] Ibid., No. 78, p. 469.

[12] Ibid., p. 466.

[13] Ibid., pp. 467-468.

[14] Goebel, *Antecedents and Beginnings*, p. 554.

[15] Robert G. McCloskey, "James Wilson" in Leon Friedman and Fred L. Israel, eds. *The Justices of the United States Supreme Court, 1789-1969: Their Lives and Major Opinions*, 4 vols. (New York: Chelsea House Publishers in association with R. R. Bowker Co., 1969) I:93.

[16] Charles Warren, *The Supreme Court in United States History*, rev. ed., 2 vols. (Boston: Little, Brown & Co., 1922, 1926), I:102.

[17] Ibid., p. 57.

[18] Ibid., p. 89.

[19] Ibid., p. 58.

[20] Goebel, *Antecedents and Beginnings*, pp. 556-559, 566-569.

[21] Ibid., pp. 560-565; Warren, *Supreme Court in U.S. History*, I: 70-82.

[22] Warren, *Supreme Court in U.S. History*, I:108-111.

[23] Ibid., p. 104, note 2.

[24] *Glass v. The Sloop Betsey*, 3 Dall. 6 (1794).

[25] Goebel, *Antecedents and Beginnings*, pp. 589-592.

[26] Ibid., p. 792.

[27] Warren, *Supreme Court in U.S. History*, I:173.

[28] Ibid., p. 194.

[29] Ibid., p. 791-792.

[30] Alexander M. Bickel, *The Least Dangerous Branch* (Indianapolis: Bobbs-Merrill Co., 1962), p. 1.

[31] Haines, *Judicial Supremacy*, pp. 202-203.

[32] *Stuart v. Laird*, 1 Cr. 299 (1803).

[33] Warren, *Supreme Court in U.S. History*, I:293.

[34] Ibid., p. 288.

[35] William Cranch, Preface to Volume I of *Reports of Cases Argued and Adjudged in the Supreme Court of the United States in August and December Terms, 1801, and February Term, 1803.*

[36] *Ex parte Bollman*, 4 Cr. 75 (1807).

[37] Warren, *Supreme Court in U.S. History*, I:307.

[38] Ibid., p. 326.

[39] Ibid., p. 339.

[40] Ibid., p. 494.

[41] *McCulloch v. Maryland*, 4 Wheat. 316 at 421 (1819).

[42] Robert G. McCloskey, *The American Supreme Court* (Chicago: University of Chicago Press, 1960), pp. 66-67.

[43] Warren, *Supreme Court in U.S. History*, I:550.

[44] Ibid., p. 616.

[45] *Wayman v. Southard*, 10 Wheat. 1 (1825).

[46] *The Antelope*, 10 Wheat. 66 (1825).

[47] Warren, *Supreme Court in U.S. History*, I:699.

[48] Ibid., p. 780-781.

[49] Alexis de Tocqueville, *Democracy in America* (New York:

Alfred A. Knopf Inc. and Random House, Vintage Books, 1945) pp. 156-157.

[50] Carl B. Swisher, *History of the Supreme Court of the United States:* Vol. V, *The Taney Period, 1836-1864* (New York: Macmillan Publishing Co., 1974), p. 97.

[51] *Bank of Augusta v. Earle*, 13 Pet. 519 (1839).

[52] *Louisville Railroad v. Letson*, 2 How. 497 (1844).

[53] *Swift v. Tyson*, 16 Pet. 1 (1842); *Dobbins v. Erie County*, 16 Pet. 534 (1842).

[54] Swisher, *The Taney Period*, p. 535.

[55] Ibid., p. 546.

[56] *Jones v. Van Zandt*, 5 How. 215 (1847).

[57] Warren, *Supreme Court in U.S. History*, II: 207.

[58] Swisher, *The Taney Period*, p. 407.

[59] *Propeller Genesee Chief v. Fitzhugh*, 12 How. 443 (1852).

[60] Edward S. Corwin, "The Dred Scott Decision in the Light of Contemporary Legal Doctrine" in the *American Historical Review* quoted in Warren, *Supreme Court in U.S. History*, II: 316-317.

[61] Warren, *Supreme Court in U.S. History*, II: 356.

[62] *Ableman v. Booth*, 21 How. 506 at 525, 521 (1859).

[63] Swisher, *The Taney Period*, pp. 973-974.

[64] Ibid., pp. 974-975.

[65] William Gillette, "Samuel Miller" in Friedman and Israel, *The Justices of the Supreme Court*, II:1023.

[66] *Ex parte Merryman*, Federal Cases 9487, p. 152.

[67] *Roosevelt v. Meyer*, 1 Wall. 512 (1863).

[68] *Ex parte Vallandigham*, 1 Wall. 243 (1864).

[69] Charles Fairman, *History of the Supreme Court of the United States:* Vol. IV, *Reconstruction and Reunion, 1864-1888, Part One* (New York: Macmillan Publishing Co., 1971), p. 32.

[70] Frank Otto Gatell, "Robert C. Grier" in Friedman and Israel, *The Justices of the Supreme Court*, II:883.

[71] Charles Evans Hughes, *The Supreme Court of the United States* (New York: Columbia University Press, 1928), p. 53.

[72] *Collector v. Day*, 11 Wall. 113 (1871).

[73] *The Slaughterhouse Cases*, 16 Wall. 36 at 78 (1873).

[74] *Bradwell v. Illinois*, 16 Wall. 130 (1873).

[75] *Minor v. Happersett*, 21 Wall. 162 (1875).

[76] *United States v. Reese, United States v. Cruikshank*, 92 U.S. 214, 542 (1876).

[77] *Munn v. Illinois*, 94 U.S. 113 at 134 (1877).

[78] William Gillette, "Noah H. Swayne" in Friedman and Israel, II:998.

[79] Warren, *Supreme Court in U.S. History*, II: 599.

[80] *Ex parte Yarbrough*, 110 U.S. 651 (1884).

[81] *Boyd v. United States*, 116 U.S. 616 at 635 (1886).

[82] *Yick Wo v. Hopkins*, 118 U.S. 356 (1886).

[83] *Paul v. Virginia*, 8 Wall. 168 (1869).

[84] *Mugler v. Kansas*, 123 U.S. 623 (1887); *Powell v. Pennsylvania*, 127 U.S. 678 (1888).

[85] William F. Swindler, *Court and Constitution in the 20th Century: The Old Legality, 1889-1932* (Indianapolis: Bobbs-Merrill Co., 1969), pp. 1-2.

[86] *Pollock v. Farmers' Loan and Trust Co.*, 158 U.S. 601 at 695 (1895).

[87] Swindler, *Court and Constitution: 1889-1932*, p. 60.

[88] *Plessy v. Ferguson*, 163 U.S. 537 at 551-552 (1896).

[89] Id. at 559.

[90] Id. at 562.

[91] Id. at 563.

[92] *Allgeyer v. Louisiana*, 165 U.S. 578 at 589 (1897).

[93] *McCray v. United States*, 195 U.S. 27 (1904).

[94] *Northern Securities Co. v. United States*, 193 U.S. 197 at 400 (1904).

[95] *Jacobson v. Massachusetts*, 197 U.S. 11 (1905).

[96] *Lochner v. New York*, 198 U.S. 45 at 57 (1905).

[97] *First Employers' Liability Case*, 207 U.S. 463 (1908).

[98] *Berea College v. Kentucky*, 211 U.S. 45 (1908).

[99] *Standard Oil Co. v. United States*, 221 U.S. 1 (1911).

[100] *United States v. American Tobacco Co.*, 221 U.S. 106 (1911).

[101] *Hipolite Egg Co. v. United States*, 220 U.S. 45 (1911); *Second Employers Liability Case*, 334 U.S. I (1912); *Hoke v. United States*, 227 U.S. 308 (1913).

[102] David Burner, "James C. McReynolds" in Friedman and Israel, III:2023.

[103] Swindler, *Court and Constitution: 1889-1932*, p. 197.

[104] *Schenck v. United States*, 249 U.S. 47 at 52 (1919).

[105] Arthur M. Schlesinger Jr., *The Politics of Upheaval* (Cambridge: Houghton Mifflin Co., 1960) p. 455.

[106] *United States v. Doremus*, 249 U.S. 86 (1919).

[107] *Hill v. Wallace*, 259 U.S. 44 at 67-68 (1922); *Chicago Board of Trade v. Olsen*, 262 U.S. 1 (1923).

[108] *Moore v. Dempsey*, 261 U.S. 86 at 91 (1923).

[109] *Gitlow v. New York*, 268 U.S. 652 at 666 (1925).

[110] *Meyer v. Nebraska*, 262 U.S. 390 (1923).

[111] *Burns Baking Co. v. Bryan*, 264 U.S. 504 (1924); *Tyson & Bro. v. Banton*, 273 U.S. 418 (1927); *Ribnik v. McBride*, 277 U.S. 350 (1928).

[112] See, for example, *Olsen v. Nebraska*, 313 U.S. 236 (1941).

[113] *Home Building & Loan Association v. Blaisdell*, 290 U.S. 398 (1934).

[114] Robert H. Jackson, *The Struggle for Judicial Supremacy* (New York: Alfred A. Knopf, 1941), p. 315.

[115] William F. Swindler, *Court and Constitution in the 20th Century: The New Legality, 1932-1968* (Indianapolis: Bobbs-Merrill Co., 1970), p. 37.

[116] *Louisville Joint Stock Land Bank v. Radford*, 295 U.S. 555 (1935); *Humphrey's Executor v. United States*, 295 U.S. 602 (1935).

[117] Schlesinger, *Politics of Upheaval*, p. 468.

[118] *Ashton v. Cameron County District*, 298 U.S. 513 (1936).

[119] *Ashwander v. TVA*, 297 U.S. 288 (1936).

[120] Schlesinger, *Politics of Upheaval*, p. 483.

[121] Swindler, *Court and Constitution: 1932-1968*, p. 5.

[122] *West Coast Hotel Co. v. Parrish*, 300 U.S. 379 at 391 (1937).

[123] *Wright v. Vinton Branch*, 300 U.S. 440 (1937); *Virginia Railway Co. v. System Federation*, 300 U.S. 515 (1937).

[124] *United States v. Carolene Products*, 304 U.S. 144 at 152 (1938).

[125] Leo Pfeffer, *This Honorable Court: A History of the United States Supreme Court* (Boston: Beacon Press, 1965), p. 342.

[126] *NLRB v. Jones & Laughlin Steel Corp.* 301 U.S. 1 (1937); *Steward Machine Co. v. Davis*, 301 U.S. 548 (1937); *Helvering v. Davis*, 301 U.S. 619 (1937); *Alabama Power Co. v. Ickes*, 302 U.S. 464 (1938); *United States v. Bekins*, 304 U.S. 27 (1938); *Mulford v. Smith*, 307 U.S. 38 (1939); *United States v. Rock Royal Cooperative*, 307 U.S. 533 (1939); *Chicot County Drainage District v. Baxter State Bank*, 308 U.S. 371 (1940); *Sunshine Coal Co. v. Adkins*, 310 U.S. 381 (1940).

[127] *Helvering v. Gerhardt*, 304 U.S. 405 (1938); *Graves v. New York ex rel. O'Keefe*, 306 U.S. 466 (1939).

[128] *United States v. Darby Lumber Co.*, 312 U.S. 100 at 124 (1941).

[129] Swindler, *Court and Constitution: 1932-1968*, p. 104.

[130] *Thornhill v. Alabama*, 310 U.S. 88 (1940).

[131] *Hirabayashi v. United States*, 320 U.S. 81 (1943); *Korematsu v. United States*, 323 U.S. 214 (1944); *Ex parte Endo*, 323 U.S. 283 (1944).

[132] *Korematsu v. United States*, 323 U.S. 214 at 216 (1944).

[133] Swindler, *Court and Constitution: 1932-1968*, p. 139.

[134] *Jones v. Opelika*, 316 U.S. 584 (1942).

[135] *West Virginia Board of Education v. Barnette*, 319 U.S. 624 at 642 (1943).

[136] Alpheus T. Mason, *The Supreme Court from Taft to Warren* (Baton Rouge: Louisiana State University, 1958) p. 154.

[137] *Adamson v. California*, 332 U.S. 46 (1947); *Louisiana ex rel. Francis v. Resweber*, 329 U.S. 459 (1947).

[138] *Joint Anti-Fascist Refugee Committee v. McGrath*, 341 U.S. 123 (1951); *Garner v. Board of Public Works*, 341 U.S. 716 (1951).

[139] *Rosenberg v. United States*, 346 U.S. 273 (1953).

[140] Anthony Lewis, "Earl Warren" in Friedman and Israel, IV:2728.

[141] *Brown v. Board of Education*, 347 U.S. 483 at 495 (1954); Richard Kluger, *Simple Justice* (New York: Knopf, 1967), p. 707.

[142] Kluger, *Simple Justice*, pp. 709-710.

[143] Ibid., p. 750.

[144] Swindler, *Court and Constitution: 1932-1968*, p. 235.

[145] Ibid., p. 243.

[146] Ibid., p. 246.

[147] *Wilson v. Girard*, 354 U.S. 524 (1957).

[148] *NAACP v. Alabama ex rel. Patterson*, 357 U.S. 449 (1958).

[149] *Klopfer v. North Carolina*, 386 U.S. 213 (1967); *In re Gault*, 387 U.S. 1 (1967); *Katz v. United States*, 389 U.S. 347 (1967).

[150] *Elfbrandt v. Russell*, 384 U.S. 11 (1966); *United States v. Robel*, 389 U.S. 258 (1967).

[151] *Abington School District v. Schempp*, 374 U.S. 203 (1963).

[152] *Tinker v. Des Moines Independent Community School District*, 393 U.S. 503 (1969).

[153] *Reed v. Reed*, 404 U.S. 71 (1971); *Graham v. Richardson*, 403 U.S. 365 (1971).

[154] *New York Times Co. v. United States, United States v. The Washington Post*, 403 U.S. 713 (1971).

[155] *Furman v. Georgia*, 408 U.S. 238 (1972); *Argersinger v. Hamlin*, 407 U.S. 25 (1972); *United States v. U.S. District Court, Eastern Michigan*, 407 U.S. 297 (1972).

[156] *San Antonio Independent School District v. Rodriguez*, 411 U.S. 1 (1973); *Keyes v. Denver School District No. 1*, 413 U.S. 921 (1973).

[157] *Miller v. California*, 413 U.S. 15 (1973); *Mahan v. Howell*, 410 U.S. 135 (1973).

[158] *First National Bank of Boston v. Bellotti*, 435 U.S. 765 (1978); *Consolidated Edison Co. v. New York Public Service Commission*, 447 U.S. 530 (1980).

[159] *Nebraska Press Assn. v. Stuart*, 427 U.S. 539 (1976).

[160] *Gannett Co. Inc. v. DePasquale*, 443 U.S. 368 (1979); *Richmond Newspapers Inc. v. Virginia*, 448 U.S. 555 (1980).

[161] *Branzburg v. Hayes*, 408 U.S. 665 (1972); *Zurcher v. Stanford Daily*, 436 U.S. 547 (1978); *Houchins v. KQED Inc.*, 438 U.S. 1 (1978).

[162] *Jimenez v. Weinberger*, 417 U.S. 628 (1974); *Califano v. Westcott*, 443 U.S. 76 (1979).

[163] *Marshall v. Barlow's Inc.*, 436 U.S. 307 (1978).

[164] *Harris v. McRae*, 448 U.S. 297 (1980).

[165] *Rostker v. Goldberg* (1981); *Hodel v. Indiana* (1981).

[166] *Gregg v. Georgia, Proffitt v. Florida, Jurek v. Texas*, 428 U.S. 153, 242, 262 (1976); *Woodson v. North Carolina, Roberts v. Louisiana*, 428 U.S. 380, 325 (1976).

[167] *Regents of University of California v. Bakke*, 438 U.S. 265 (1978); *United Steelworkers v. Weber*, 443 U.S. 193 (1979).

[168] *Fullilove v. Klutznick*, 448 U.S. 448 (1980).

[169] *Washington v. Davis*, 426 U.S. 229 (1976); *Village of Arlington Heights v. Metropolitan Housing Development Corporation*, 429 U.S. 252 (1977).

2

The Court at Work

Constitutionally and politically, the Supreme Court is a branch of the federal government coequal with Congress and the presidency. In some ways it is the most powerful, since it can declare the actions of the president illegal and the legislation of Congress unconstitutional.

Still, the Supreme Court seems dwarfed by the sprawling bureaucracies of the legislative and executive components of government. The court is, after all, only nine men, housed within a single building at One First Street Northeast in the nation's capital. Its budget is but a fraction of those appropriated each year for Congress and the executive branch.

Nevertheless, the court is hardly aloof from the long-range and everyday problems of management, procedure, maintenance and personnel faced by any other institution. Like Congress — or the local department store, for that matter — it must be administered, budgeted, staffed and locked up after work each day. And it is the apex of a substantial federal judicial system that includes 95 district courts, 12 courts of appeal and three special courts, along with their judges and attendant staff.

The administrative aspects of the court's operations are, then, considerable, even if they do not rival those that have spawned the huge bureaucracies that serve the executive branch and Congress. Chief Justices from John Jay to Warren Burger have wrestled with the problems of ensuring smooth functioning of the court's managerial machinery in order to allow the judges to concentrate on dispassionate consideration of matters of law.

The ideal tableau of the court — and certainly the image that it has sought to perpetuate over the years — is one of nine wise, just and serene jurists sitting to render, with irreproachable integrity, decisions crucial to the conduct of national life.

That this image has been maintained so well for nearly two centuries testifies, to a remarkable degree, to its accuracy. The high standards necessary both to effective judicial performance and public trust have indeed been consistently maintained by a succession of mostly able jurists who were also men of exemplary personal demeanor. There have been few scandals involving the justices, and the embarrassments the court has suffered have been resolved openly and expeditiously. With some notable exceptions, the political affinities of the justices have been more implicit than overt.

The Court's Image

But to some extent the court's sacrosanct image is also more apparent than real. The court, of course, has no public relations mechanism as such, but the longstanding internal traditions of the institution effectively serve that function. Its insistence on the secrecy of its deliberations, in particular, protects the justices from disclosure of any of the fractiousness or ineptitude that certainly must occur from time to time. The elaborate courtesy and obeisance to seniority on the court also serve its image as an august deliberative body aloof from contentious bickering and disharmony. Its imposing headquarters, the "marble palace," softens the memory of the many years during which the justices were shunted from one "mean and dingy" makeshift office to another. The image notwithstanding, the court as a bureaucracy and administrative body continues to face many workaday challenges.

These involve matters much more important than the mere operation and upkeep of the court itself, although these are substantial. Most centrally, the court must select which cases to review, and when to review them, from the burgeoning volume of litigation that seeks its attention every year, and to render decisions after adequate consideration and in definitive language.

These problems have mushroomed during the past two, increasingly litigious, decades. Between 1960 and 1976, the number of new cases filed in federal district courts rose from 89,112 to 171,617. It is from this labyrinth of casework that the Supreme Court is expected judiciously to cull the legal issues most worthy of its judgment. In the same period — 1960 to 1976 — the court's own docket more than doubled, from 2,296 to 4,730.

So the august tribunal of justices is also, perforce, a beleaguered bureaucracy. In March 1971, the present Chief Justice, Warren E. Burger, told the National Conference on the Judiciary that he had begun work

. . .by giving priority to methods and machinery, to procedure and techniques, to management and administration of judicial resources, even over the much-needed re-examination of substantive legal institutions that are out of date. That re-examination is important, but it is inevitably a long-range undertaking and it can wait. . . .[1]

Operations of the Court

The Constitution makes the Supreme Court the final arbiter in "cases" and "controversies" arising under the Constitution or the laws of the United States. As the interpreter of the law, the court is often viewed as the least mutable and most tradition-bound of the three branches of the federal government.

Yet as the Supreme Court nears the end of its second century of existence, it has undergone innumerable changes. A few of these changes have been mandated by law. Almost all of them, however, were made because members of the court felt they would provide a more efficient or a more equitable way of dealing with the court's responsibilities. Some of the charges are embodied in court rules; others are informal adaptations to needs and circumstances.

The Schedule of the Term

The court's annual schedule reflects both continuity and change. During its formal annual sessions, certain times are set aside for oral argument, for conferences, for the writing of opinions and for the announcement of decisions. With the ever-increasing number of cases they face each year, the justices are confronted with a tremendous — some say excessive — amount of work during the regular term, which now lasts between eight and nine months.

Their work does not end when the session is finished, however. During the summer recess, the justices receive new cases to consider. About a fourth of the applications for review filed during the term are read by the justices and their law clerks during the summer interim.

Annual Terms

By law, the Supreme Court begins its regular annual term on the first Monday in October "and may hold a special term whenever necessary." [2]

The regular session, known as the October term, now lasts about nine months. Adjournment, which is not determined by statute or court rules, generally occurs in late June or early July of the following year when the court has taken action on the last case argued before it during the term. The increasing caseload that has faced the court has resulted in longer terms. Adjournment of the 1954 term, for example, occurred on June 6, 1955, while the October 1975 term did not end until July 6, 1976.

Adjournment takes place when a court order, announced by the Chief Justice in open court and entered in the court's journal, is issued. It states that "All cases submitted and all business before the Court at this term in readiness for disposition having been disposed of, it is ordered by this Court that all cases on the docket be, and they are hereby, continued to the next term." [3]

Over the years, the annual sessions of the court have been changed a number of times. During the first decade of its existence, 1790-1801, the court met twice a year, in February and August. The justices had few cases during these years and the early sessions were devoted largely to organization and discussions of lawyers' qualifications. The first case did not reach the court until 1791; the first formal opinion was not handed down until 1792, in the court's third year.

Despite the dearth of casework during the early semi-annual sessions, the Chief Justice and five associate justices had enough to do. The Judiciary Act of 1789, in addition to mandating the February and August sessions, required the justices to travel through the country to preside over the circuit courts — a time-consuming task that continued, except for a brief period, until circuit riding was finally abolished in 1891 and circuit courts of appeal were established.

The Judiciary Act of 1801 called for court terms beginning in June and December. The Judiciary Act of 1802 restored the February term of the court but not the August term. This resulted in a 14-month adjournment — from December 1801 until February 1803.

At the beginning of the 1827 term, Congress changed the opening day of the new term to the second Monday in January. This was done to give the justices more time to ride their circuits.

The opening day of the term was changed to the second Monday in December by an act of June 17, 1844. By this statute, Charles Warren wrote, the justices "were relieved of holding more than one Term of the Circuit Court within any District of such Circuit, in any one year. The result of this provision was to enable the Court to sit later each spring in Washington; and in alternate years thereafter it made a practice of sitting through March, adjourning through April and sitting again in May." [4]

An act of Jan. 24, 1873, moved the beginning of the term from the first Monday in December to the second Monday in October. Since 1917 terms have begun on the first Monday in October.

Special Sessions

The statute and rule covering the annual session of the court also permit the justices to hold special terms after the regular session is over. Special sessions are called to deal with urgent matters that cannot be postponed until the next session.

There have been few special sessions in the court's history: only four cases have been decided in special session. It has been far more common for the court to consider important cases that arise toward the end of the term simply by delaying the end of the regular term until action is completed.

The four cases for which special sessions were called are:

● *Ex parte Quirin.* The court convened a special term, July 29, 1942, heard arguments on July 29 and July 30 and, on July 31, upheld a military court's jurisdiction over the trial of Nazi saboteurs smuggled ashore from a German submarine. A formal opinion in the case was released on Oct. 29, 1942.

● *Rosenberg v. United States.* Three days after the end of the October 1952 term, the Supreme Court on June 18, 1953, convened a special term to consider a stay of execution ordered by Justice William O. Douglas for Ethel and Julius Rosenberg, convicted of divulging information about the atomic bomb to the Soviet Union. Arguments were heard on June 18, and the court vacated the stay on June 19. The Rosenbergs were executed that day. The court's opinion in the case was released July 16, 1953.

● *Cooper v. Aaron.* In a special session convened Aug. 28, 1958, the court unanimously upheld a lower court order enforcing a desegregation plan for Little Rock High School. The order was opposed by state officials in Arkansas. The court heard arguments on Aug. 28 and Sept. 11, and issued its decision on Sept. 12. City schools were to open in Little Rock on Sept. 15, but Gov. Orval Faubus closed them after the court's decision. A formal opinion in the case was released Sept. 29, 1958.

● *O'Brien v. Brown.* The court convened a special session July 6, 1972, to consider the seating of delegates from California and Illinois at the Democratic National Convention which was to open July 10. The court decided, by a vote of 6-3 on July 7, 1972, to return the California and Illinois cases to the convention and to let the convention itself, rather than the court, decide the matter.

Among the decisions made by the court after postponing adjournment of the regular term, the most famous is *United States v. Nixon.* In that case the court on July 24, 1974, unanimously denied President Richard M. Nixon's claim of absolute executive privilege to withhold documents requested by the Watergate Special Prosecutor.

On June 24, 1981, more than a month after the end of arguments in the 1980-1981 term, the court heard argued the case of *Dames & Moore v. Regan* concerning the executive agreement with Iran concluded early in 1981 to win return of the U.S. citizens held hostage by Iran. On July 2, the court upheld the agreement.

Other important decisions handed down after delaying adjournment include *Wilson v. Girard* in 1957, and *New York Times v. U.S., U.S. v. Washington Post* in 1971. The former involved the right of Japanese courts to try American soldiers; the latter rebuffed the effort by the Nixon administration to bar publication of the Pentagon Papers.[5]

Opening Day

Opening day ceremonies of the new term have changed considerably since the court first met on Feb. 1, 1790. Chief Justice John Jay was forced to postpone the first formal session for a day because some of the justices were unable to reach New York City — at that time the nation's capital and home of the court. It began proceedings the next day in a crowded courtroom and with an empty docket.

From 1917 until 1975, the opening day — the first Monday in October — and the rest of that week were spent in conference. The justices discussed cases that had not been disposed of during the previous term and some of the petitions that had reached the court during the summer recess. On the second Monday in October the court announced decisions reached during this initial conference.

At the beginning of the October 1975 term, this practice was changed. That year the justices reassembled for this initial conference during the last week in September. When the justices convened formally on Monday, Oct. 6, 1975, oral arguments began.

At least four justices must request that a case be argued before it can be approved for a hearing. Until 1955, the court often heard oral arguments five days a week. Friday arguments were dropped when the court's conference was moved to that day. Arguments are now heard on Monday, Tuesday, Wednesday and, rarely, Thursday, for about seven two-week sessions, beginning in the first week in October and ending in the last week of April or the first week of May.

There usually are two consecutive weeks of oral arguments during this period, with two-week or longer recesses during which the justices consider the cases and deal with other court business.

Since the early 1800s — when justices heard oral arguments from 11 a.m. until 4 or 5 p.m. — the schedule for hearing arguments has been changed several times in continuing efforts toward a more manageable daily calendar.

The present schedule for oral arguments — 10 a.m. to noon and 1-3 p.m. — began during the 1969 term. Since most cases receive one hour apiece for argument, that means the court can hear twelve cases a week.

The time provided for oral argument had been limited to two hours — one hour for each side — under a rule of the court adopted March 12, 1849. Cases which the court felt could be covered in a shorter period were placed on a "summary calendar," under which arguments were limited to a half hour for each side. That practice was revived during the 1940s and one hour's argument became the current limit in 1970. Exceptions to the hour-per-case time limit must be sought and granted before arguments begin.

Schedule of Conferences

In the court's early years, conferences often were held in the evenings or on weekends, sometimes in the common boardinghouse that the justices shared. The number of cases for which review was sought and the cases awaiting a final decision determined when and how often conferences were held. Later, Saturday was set aside as the regular conference day. In 1955, the court stopped hearing arguments on Friday and Friday became conference day.

Until recently, a court held its first conferences during opening week, following its formal call to order on the first Monday in October. But in 1975, to streamline the procedure, the justices began holding their initial conference the last week in September, before the official convening of the annual session.

At its initial conference, the court attempts to resolve leftover matters — appeals, petitions for certiorari, etc. — from the previous session. The September conference allows the court to announce its orders on these matters by opening day rather than a week after the formal convening.

During its term, the court holds conferences each Friday during the weeks when oral arguments are heard, and on the Friday just before the two-week oral argument periods. To reduce the workload of its Friday sessions, the court in recent years also has begun holding Wednesday conferences during the weeks when oral arguments are scheduled.

It is in conference that the justices discuss the cases which have been argued during the preceding weeks, and the appeals and petitions asking the court to grant review and hear arguments in other cases. Prior to each of the Friday conferences, the Chief Justice circulates a "discuss list" — a list of cases in which review is sought which are deemed important enough for discussion in conference.

Appeals are placed on the "discuss list" almost automatically, but as many as three-quarters of the petitions for certiorari are never placed on the list and are denied review without discussion by the court. No case is denied review, however, without at least an initial examination by the justices or their clerks. Any justice can have any case placed on the court's conference agenda for discussion.

Most of the cases scheduled for the "discuss list" are also denied review in the end, but only after discussion by the justices during the conference.

Although the last oral arguments have been heard by late April or early May of each year, the justices continue to meet in conference until the end of the term to consider cases remaining on the court's agenda.

All conferences are held in strict secrecy, with no legal assistants or staff present. The attendance of six justices constitutes a quorum. Conferences begin with handshakes all around. The Chief Justice is the first to speak in discussing a case; he is followed by each justice in order of seniority.

Decision Days

In the court's early years, conferences were held whenever the justices decided one was necessary — sometimes in the evening or on weekends. Similarly, decisions were announced whenever they were ready. There was no formal or informal schedule for conferences or for the announcement of decisions.

The tradition of announcing decisions on Monday — "Decision Monday" — began in 1857, apparently without any formal announcement or rule to that effect. This practice continued until the court announced on April 5, 1965, that "commencing the week of April 26, 1965, it will no longer adhere to the practice of reporting its decisions only at Monday sessions and that in the future they will be reported as they become ready for decision at any session of the Court." [6]

Like the announcement of opinions, the day for release of the court's "orders list" — the summary of the court's action granting or denying review — has changed over the years.

During the 19th century, the court's summary orders were often announced on Friday, which was called "Motion Day." The practice of posting orders on Monday evolved gradually.

During the first three months of the 1971 term, orders were announced on Tuesday; on Jan. 10, 1972, Monday was established as the day for posting orders. When urgent or important matters arise, the court's summary orders may be announced on a day other than Monday. And when the last oral arguments of the term have been heard, the court may release decisions and written opinions, as well as the orders list, on Mondays.

At present, the orders list is posted at the beginning of the Monday session. It is not orally announced and can be obtained from the clerk and the public information officer.

Unlike its orders, decisions of the court are usually announced orally in open court. The justice who wrote the opinion announces the court's decision, and justices writing concurring or dissenting opinions may state their views as well. When more than one decision is to be rendered, the justices who wrote the opinion make their announcements in reverse order of seniority.

Sometimes all or a large portion of the opinion is read aloud. More often, the author will summarize the opinion or simply announce the result and state that a written opinion has been filed.

Reviewing Cases

In determining whether to accept a case for review, the court has considerable discretion, subject only to the restraints imposed by the Constitution and Congress.

Article III, Section 2 of the Constitution provides that "In all Cases affecting Ambassadors, other public Ministers and Consuls, and those in which a State shall be Party, the supreme Court shall have original Jurisdiction. In all the other Cases ... the supreme Court shall have appellate Jurisdiction, both as to Law and Fact, with such Exceptions, and under such Regulations as the Congress shall make."

Original jurisdiction refers to the right of the Supreme Court to hear a case before any other court does. Appellate jurisdiction is the right to review the decision of a lower court. The vast majority of cases reaching the Supreme Court are appeals from rulings of the lower courts; generally only a handful of original jurisdiction cases are filed each term.

Since enactment of the Judiciary Act of 1925, the Supreme Court has had almost complete discretion to decide for itself what cases it would hear. [7]

Methods of Appeal

Cases come to the Supreme Court in several ways. They may come through writs of certiorari, appeals, petitions and requests for certification.

In seeking a writ of certiorari, a litigant who has lost a case in a lower court petitions the Supreme Court to review the case, setting out the reasons why review should be granted. If the petitition is granted, the court requests from the lower court a certified record of the case.

Supreme Court rules provide that:

Whenever a petition for writ of certiorari to review a decision of any court is granted, an order to that effect shall be entered, and the Clerk forthwith shall notify the court below and counsel of record. The case will then stand for briefing and oral argument. If the record has not previously been filed, the Clerk of this Court shall request the clerk of the court possessed of the record to certify it and transmit it to this Court. A formal writ shall not issue unless specially directed. [8]

The main difference between the certiorari and appeal routes is that the court has complete discretion to grant a request for a writ of certiorari but is under more obligation to accept and decide a case which comes on appeal.

Most cases reach the Supreme Court by means of the writ of certiorari. In the relatively few cases to reach the court by means of appeal, the appellant must file a jurisdictional statement explaining why his case qualifies for review and why the court should grant it a hearing. With increasing frequency in recent years, the justices have been disposing of these cases by deciding them summarily, without oral argument or formal opinion.

Those whose petitions for certiorari have been granted by the court must pay the court's standard $300 fee for docketing the case and the cost of printing briefs. Persons unable to afford the fee or the often considerable cost of printing briefs may file *in forma pauperis* (in the character or manner of a pauper) petitions. The rules governing *in forma pauperis* proceedings state:

...[A]ny court of the United States may authorize the commencement, prosecution or defense of any suit, action or proceeding, civil or criminal, or appeal therein, without prepayment of fees and costs or security therefor, by a person who makes affidavit that he is unable to pay such costs or give security therefor. Such affidavit shall state the nature of the action, defense or appeal and affiant's belief that he is entitled to redress. . . . An appeal may not be taken in forma pauperis if the trial court certifies in writing that it is not taken in good faith. [9]

Another seldom used method of appeal is certification, the request by a lower court — usually a court of appeals — for a final answer to questions of law in a particular case. The Supreme Court, after examining the certificate, may order the case argued before it.[10]

Process of Review

Each year the court is asked to review some 4,000 to 5,000 cases. All petitions are examined by the clerk of the court and his staff; those found to be in reasonably proper form are placed on the docket and given a number. Prior to 1970, there were two dockets, an appellate docket for petitions for certiorari and appeals in cases where the docketing fee was paid, and a miscellaneous docket for *in forma pauperis* petitions and appeals and other requests not qualifying for the appellate docket. When a case on the miscellaneous docket was accepted for review, it was transferred to the appellate docket and renumbered.

In 1970 the numbering system was revised and all cases except those falling within the court's original jurisdiction are now placed on a single docket. Only in the numbering of the cases is distinction made between prepaid and *in forma pauperis* cases on the docket. Beginning with the 1971 term, prepaid cases were labeled with the year and the number. The first case filed in 1978, for example, would be designated 78-1. *In forma pauperis* cases contain the year and begin with the number 5001. The second *in forma pauperis* case filed in 1978 would thus be number 78-5002.

Cases on the original docket were unaffected by the 1970 revision. The original docket remains a separate and distinct docket, but cases on it that are carried over to the next term are not renumbered; they retain the docket numbers assigned to them when they were filed.

Each justice, aided by his law clerks, is responsible for reviewing all cases on the dockets. In recent years a number of justices have used a "cert pool" system in this review. Their clerks work together to examine cases, writing a pool memo on several petitions. The memo is then given to the justices, who determine if more research is needed. (Other justices prefer to use a system in which they or their clerks review each petition themselves.)

Former Justice William O. Douglas called the review of cases on the dockets "in many respects the most important and interesting of all our functions." Others, apparently, have found it time-consuming and tedious and support the "cert pool" as a mechanism to reduce the burden on the justices and their staffs.

Justice John Paul Stevens, however, withdrew from the pool, saying that it did not save him or his clerks any time.

Petitions on the docket vary from elegantly printed and bound documents, of which multiple copies are submitted to the court, to single sheets of prison stationery scribbled in pencil and filled with grammatical and spelling errors. All are considered by the justices, however, in the process of deciding which ones merit review.

To Grant or Deny Review

The decision whether to grant or deny review of a case is made in conference. Conferences are held in the conference room adjacent to the Chief Justice's chambers. Justices are summoned to the conference room by a buzzer, usually between 9:30 and 10:00 a.m. They shake hands with each other, take their appointed seats, and the Chief Justice begins the discussion.

The 'Discuss List'

A few days before the conference convenes, the Chief Justice compiles a "discuss list" — a list of cases deemed important enough for discussion and a vote.

Appeals are placed on the "discuss list" almost automatically, but as many as three-quarters of the petitions for certiorari are denied a place on the list and thus rejected without further consideration. Any justice can have a case placed on "discuss list" simply by requesting that it be done.

Conferences are held in strict secrecy; only the justices attend, and no legal assistants or staff are present. The junior associate justice acts as doorman and messenger, sending for reference material and receiving messages and data at the door. The secrecy has worked well; unlike other parts of the federal government, there have been very few leaks about what transpires during the conferences.

At the start of the conference, the Chief Justice makes a brief statement outlining the facts of each case. Then each justice, beginning with the senior associate justice, comments on the case.

The last to speak, the junior associate justice, discusses the case and votes on whether the court should accept the case for review. The other justices, in reverse order of seniority, then vote on whether to grant review. (This is the same procedure followed in deciding cases already argued.) A longstanding but unwritten rule specifies that it takes four affirmative votes to have a case scheduled for oral argument.

The 'Orders List'

Petitions for certiorari, appeal, and *in forma pauperis* that are approved for review or denied review during conference are placed on a certified orders list to be released the following Monday in open court, announcing what cases will be set for later argument and which have been denied a hearing.

Arguments

The clerk of the court, once the court announces it will hear a case, arranges the schedule for oral argument. In general, cases are arranged in the order in which they are ordered set down for argument, "subject to modification in the light of the availability of appendices, extensions of time to file briefs, orders advancing, postponing or specially setting arguments, and other relevant factors." [11]

Cases generally are heard not sooner than three months after the court has agreed to review them. Under special circumstances, the date scheduled for oral argument can be advanced or postponed.

About two to three weeks before oral argument takes place, the justices receive the briefs and records from counsel in the case. The measure of attention the brief receives — from a thorough and exhaustive study to a cursory glance — depends both on the nature of the case and the work habits of the particular justice who is reading the brief.

Changes in the Workload of the Supreme Court

The Supreme Court's caseload more than doubled from 1960 to 1980. The increased workload is responsible for advancing the court's first conference from early October to the last week in September; for the inclusion of Wednesdays in the conference schedule and other changes in procedures; and for increasing the number of staff members available to cope with the growing number of cases facing the court each term.

Chief Justice Warren E. Burger has warned repeatedly that unless something is done to curb that workload it may be soon be "impossible" for a Chief Justice "to perform his duties well and survive very long." [1]

A glance at the number of cases on the court's docket over the years illustrates its growing burden. In 1803, 13 years after the court first convened, there were only 51 cases on the docket; seven years later, the number was 98. As the number of cases filed each year increased, Congress in 1837 created two additional circuits and added two justices to the seven then on the Supreme Court.

By 1845 there were 173 cases on the docket, and the number kept increasing. It grew to 253 cases in 1850, 310 in 1860, and 636 in 1870. A temporary increase in the number of justices to 10 in 1863 and the creation of several more circuit judges in 1869 did little to stem the tide. In 1880 there were 1,212 cases on the docket and a decade later there were 1,816.

More and More Cases

The Court of Appeals Act of 1891 had a dramatic impact on the caseload of the Supreme Court. The number of new cases dropped to 379 in 1891 and to 275 in 1892.

In the years that followed, however, Congress passed a spate of new laws creating opportunities for litigation, which consequently increased the court's workload. There were 723 cases on the court's docket in the 1900 term and 1,116 in the 1910 term.

Although the Judiciary Act of 1925 gave the court considerable discretion in granting review and greatly reduced the number of cases requiring oral arguments, the number of cases on the docket continued to increase. There were 1,039 cases on the docket in 1930; 1,109 in 1940; 1,321 in 1950; 2,296 in 1960; 4,212 in 1970; and 4,781 in 1980.

The dramatic rise in the court's caseload, particularly after 1960, was due primarily to the increase in *in forma pauperis* filings and to congressional enactment of environmental, civil rights, consumer, safety, and social welfare legislation. Petitions *in forma pauperis* grew from 517 in 1951 to about 2,000 a year in the early 1970s.

But while the number of cases filed each year and the number on each term's docket have increased enor-

mously, the number scheduled for oral argument has grown hardly at all. As one observer of the court pointed out in 1975, the court "was hearing about 150 cases on the merits in 1925; it was hearing about 150 cases on the merits twenty-five years ago. It hears about 150 cases on the merits today." [2]

Studying the Problem

The growing gap between the number of cases on the docket and the number in which oral arguments are heard has aroused concern that the court is neglecting many important cases.

To investigate the matter, several study groups were formed in the 1970s. One, the Study Group on the Caseload of the Supreme Court, was set up by Chief Justice Warren E. Burger in the fall of 1971 and headed by Professor Paul A. Freund of Harvard Law School. Another, the Commission on Revision of the Appellate Court System, was set up by Congress in 1972 and headed by Sen. Roman L. Hruska (R Neb.).

The court's study group issued its report in December 1972, warning that:

> . . .The statistics of the Court's current workload, both in absolute terms and in the mounting trend, are impressive evidence that the conditions essential for the performance of the Court's mission do not exist. For an ordinary appellate court, the burgeoning volume of cases would be a staggering burden; for the Supreme Court, the pressures of the docket are incompatible with the appropriate fulfillment of its historic and essential functions. [3]

To ease the burden on the court, the study group recommended the creation of a National Court of Appeals. The new court would be headquartered in Washington and — except for cases involving original jurisdiction — be given jurisdiction to consider all cases now within the Supreme Court's jurisdiction. The National Court of Appeals would screen all cases coming to the Supreme Court, denying review in some, deciding some itself and certifying the more important cases to the Supreme Court for disposition.

The Hruska commission likewise endorsed the creation of a new National Court of Appeals in its 1975 report. But the function of the proposed new court had changed. Instead of sending cases on to the justices, this new body would decide cases of lesser importance referred to it by the Supreme Court. [4]

The high court, the judicial branch and the legal profession have divided on these and other recommendations to lessen its workload. Until there is some consensus there is little likelihood that any dramatic measures will be forthcoming.

---

[1] "The Role of the Judiciary in America," speech sponsored by the American Enterprise Institute for Public Policy Research, Dec. 14, 1978.

[2] Erwin N. Griswold, "Rationing Justice — The Supreme Court's Caseload and What the Court Does Not Do," 60 *Cornell Law Review* 339 (1975).

[3] *Report of the Study Group on the Caseload of the Supreme Court* (Washington, D.C.: U.S. Government Printing Office, 1972).

[4] *Report of the Commission on Revision of the Appellate Court System* (Washington, D.C.: U.S. Government Printing Office, 1975).

Essential, or a Formality?

As one of the two public functions of the court, oral arguments are viewed by some as very important. Others dispute their significance, contending that by the time a case is heard most of the justices have already made up their minds.

A number of justices have indicated that oral arguments serve a useful purpose. Chief Justice Charles Evans Hughes wrote that "the desirability . . . of a full exposition by oral argument in the highest court is not to be gainsaid" because it provides "a great saving of time of the court in the examination of extended records and briefs, to obtain the grasp of the case that is made possible by oral discussion and to be able more quickly to separate the wheat from the chaff." [12]

More recently, Justice William J. Brennan, Jr. was quoted as saying: "Oral argument is the absolute indispensable ingredient of appellate advocacy. . . . Often my whole notion of what a case is about crystallizes at oral argument. This happens even though I read the briefs before oral argument." [13]

Time Limits

Like many other aspects of the court's operations, the time allotted for oral argument, as well as the atmosphere in which arguments are heard, has undergone considerable change over the years. In the early years of the court, arguments in a single case would often continue for days on end.

For the spectators who crowded the courtroom, oral arguments provided high entertainment. Women in Washington once flocked to hear the popular and dashing Henry Clay argue before the court in the 19th century. In one case, a case was reargued so that a late-arriving woman could hear the part she had missed.[14]

The increasing number of cases heard by the court made the continuation of such practices impossible. Under a rule of the court adopted March 12, 1849, counsel was allowed no more than two hours to present his argument. The two-hour allowance for oral argument continued until the early 20th century.

In between his terms on the court, Charles Evans Hughes wrote in 1928: "In the early period when cases were few, the Court could permit extended argument. At a more recent time, and until a few years ago, two hours was the regular allowance to each side and in very important cases, that time was extended. This allowance has been reduced to an hour, unless special permission is granted, and even in cases of great importance the Court has refused to hear arguments for more than an hour and a half on each side. This restriction is due to the crowded calendar of the court." [15]

In 1970 the time allowed each side for oral argument was reduced from one hour to 30 minutes. Again, the period for oral argument was reduced to save the court's time.

Since the time allotted must include time for any questions the justices may wish to ask, the actual time for any lawyer to make a formal presentation of his argument may be considerably shorter than 30 minutes.

Under the present rules of the court, only one lawyer will be heard for each side, except by special permission when there are several parties on the same side. Divided arguments are not favored by the court. Before 1970, when cases were allowed one hour per side, the court allowed two counsel to be heard for each side.

Although more than one attorney participating in an argument per side is "not favored" by the court, counsel for an *amicus curiae* may participate in oral argument if the party supported by the *amicus* allows him to use part of its argument time or the court itself grants a motion allowing argument by counsel for the "friend of the court." (*Amicus curiae* — literally "a friend of the court" — is a person who volunteers or is invited to take part in matters before the court but is not a party in the case.) That motion must show, the rules state, that the *amicus'* argument "is thought to provide assistance to the court not otherwise available." [16]

Because the court is reluctant to extend the time that each side is given for oral argument and because *amicus curiae* participation in oral argument would often necessitate such an extension, the court rarely grants such motions. And counsel in a case is usually equally unreceptive to a request that he give an *amicus* counsel any of the precious minutes which he has to argue the case.

Court rules provide advice to counsel presenting oral arguments before the court: "Oral argument should undertake to emphasize and clarify the written argument appearing in the briefs theretofore filed." That same rule warns that the court *"looks with disfavor on any oral argument that is read from a prepared text."* [17] During the 1974 term, two justices interrupted an attorney who was reading from a prepared text and called his attention to the rule. Most attorneys appearing before the court use an outline or notes to make sure they cover the important points.

Circulating the Argument

The Supreme Court has tape-recorded oral arguments since 1955. In 1968 the court, in addition to its own recording, began contracting with private firms to tape and transcribe all oral arguments. The contract stipulates that the transcript "shall include everything spoken in argument, by Court, counsel, or others, and nothing shall be omitted from the transcript unless the Chief Justice or Presiding Justice so directs." But "the names of Justices asking questions shall not be recorded or transcribed; questions shall indicated by the letter 'Q'." [18]

The marshal of the court keeps the court's tape during the term when oral arguments are presented. During that time use of these tapes usually is limited to the justices and their law clerks. At the end of the term, the tapes are sent to the National Archives. Three years after an argument has been heard, persons wishing to listen to the tape or buy a copy of the transcript can apply to the marshal for permission to do so.

Transcripts made by the private firm can be acquired more quickly. These transcripts usually are available less than a week after oral arguments are heard. Four copies are delivered to the marshal of the court, who transmits them to the Library of Congress. Interested persons can copy them in longhand or by typewriter but cannot photograph or photocopy them.

Those who purchase the transcripts from the firm must agree that they will not themselves, and will not permit any other party, "to make a photographic, electrostatic or other facsimile copy" of any of the transcripts. [19] Transcripts usually run from 40 to 50 pages for one hour of oral argument. During the 1980 term, transcripts were sold at a rate of $3.75 per page.

In recent years there have been many proposals that arguments should be taped for television and radio use. To date, the court has shown little enthusiasm for these proposals.

Use of Briefs

A major problem facing counsel in preparing an oral argument is his uncertainty about the extent to which the justices and their law clerks have examined his briefs. Nearly twenty years ago Justice Brennan wrote that "most of the members of the present Court follow the practice of reading the briefs before argument. Some of us, and I am one, often have a bench memorandum prepared before argument. This memorandum digests the facts and the arguments of both sides, highlighting the matters about which I may want to question counsel at the argument. Often I have an independent research made in advance of argument and incorporate the results in the bench memorandum." [20]

Nevertheless, an attorney cannot be sure that other justices will devote such attention to their briefs. If the brief has been thoroughly digested by the justices, he can use his arguments to highlight certain elements. But if it has merely been scanned — and perhaps largely forgotten — in the interval between the reading and the oral argument, he will want to go into considerable detail about the nature of the case and the facts involved. Most lawyers therefore prepare their argument on the assumption that the justices know relatively little about their particular case but are well-acquainted with the general principles of relevant law.

The brief of the petitioner or appellant must be filed within 45 days of the court's announced decision to hear the case.

Except in *in forma pauperis* cases, 40 copies of the brief must be filed with the court. For *in forma pauperis* proceedings, the party must file one typed copy with the clerk and send one typed copy to each of the other parties in the case.

The opposing brief from the respondent or appellee is to be filed within 30 days of his receipt of the brief of the petitioner or appellant. Either party may appeal to the clerk for an extension of time in filing the brief.

The form and organization of the brief is covered by rules 33 and 34 of the court.

Court rules adopted in 1980 for the first time set a limit on the number of pages in a brief. Most briefs asking the court to review a case, or opposing such a request, are limited to 30 printed pages. Briefs arguing the merits of a case may be as long as 50 pages.[21] Briefs that do not comply with these requirements will not be accepted by the clerk.

The court's rules 33 and 34 set out the elements of a brief to the court. They include: 1) the questions presented for review, 2) a list of all parties to the proceeding in the court below, 3) a table of contents and table of authorities, 4) citations to the opinions and judgments delivered in the courts below, 5) a statement of the grounds on which the jurisdiction of the Supreme Court is invoked, 6) the constitutional provisions, treaties, statutes, ordinances and regulations which the case involves, 7) a concise statement of the case containing all information material to the consideration of the questions presented, 8) a summary of the argument, 9) the argument "exhibiting clearly the points of fact and of law being presented, citing the authorities and statutes relied upon," and 10) a conclusion "specifying with particularity the relief to which the party believes himself entitled."

Questioning

During oral argument the justices may interrupt with questions or remarks as often as they wish. On the average, questions are likely to consume about a third of counsel's allotted half-hour of argument. Unless counsel has been granted special permission extending his 30-minute limit, he can continue talking after his time has expired only to answer questions.

The frequency of questioning, as well as the manner in which questions are asked, depends on the style of the justices and their interest in a particular case. Former Justice William O. Douglas, for example, had a reputation for asking relatively few but very incisive questions. Justice Lewis F. Powell Jr. tends to be extremely courteous. Justice Thurgood Marshall often shows considerable impatience with overblown rhetoric.

Questions from the justices have been known to upset and unnerve counsel by interrupting his rehearsed argument and introducing an unexpected element. Nevertheless, questioning has several advantages. It serves to alert counsel about what aspects of the case need further elaboration or more information. For the court, questions can bring out weak points in an argument — and sometimes strengthen it.

The late Chief Justice Charles Evans Hughes wrote:

The judges of the Supreme Court are quite free in addressing questions to counsel during argument. The Bar is divided as to the wisdom of this practice in courts of last resort. Some think that as a rule the court will get at the case more quickly if counsel are permitted to present it in their own way. Well-prepared and experienced counsel, however, do not object to inquiries from the bench, if the time allowed for argument is not unduly curtailed, as they would much prefer to have the opportunity of knowing the difficulties in the minds of the court and of attempting to meet them rather than to have them concealed and presented in conference when counsel are not present. They prefer an open attack to a masked battery. From the standpoint of the bench, the desirability of questions is quite obvious as the judges are not there to listen to speeches but to decide the case. They have an irrepressible desire for immediate knowledge as to the points to be determined. [24]

It is advisable that attorneys answer the justices' questions immediately and directly. Several justices have made known their annoyance when informed by counsel that their inquiry will be answered later in the oral argument.

As Justice Robert H. Jackson advised in 1951, "never . . . postpone answer to a question, for that always gives an impression of evasion. It is better immediately to answer the question, even though you do so in short form and suggest that you expect to amplify and support your answer later." [25]

Court anecdotes probably tell as much about the proceedings of the court during oral argument as does any careful study of the rules and procedures.

Perhaps the most famous anecdote concerns the late Chief Justice Charles Evans Hughes. Hughes, a stickler for observance of the time limit for oral argument, is reported to have informed a leader of the New York Bar that his argument was over when the lawyer was in the middle of the word "If."[26]

In the late 19th century the justices occasionally left to have lunch behind a curtain in back of the bench when argument was particularly lengthy and inconsequential. Argument proceeded without the justices and amidst a clatter of china. [27]

The late Justice Felix Frankfurter was renowned for treating counsel, as well as his fellow justices, much as he had his students when he was a professor. This annoyed many lawyers presenting arguments and was resented by other justices who complained about Frankfurter's professorial questioning and his pedantic, if erudite, lectures.[28] Former Justice Douglas was known to write opinions or articles during the presentation of oral argument. [29]

Conferences

Cases on which oral argument has been heard are decided in conference. During the Wednesday afternoon conference, the four cases that were argued the previous Monday are discussed and decided. At the all-day Friday conference, the eight cases argued on the preceding Tuesday and Wednesday are discussed and decided. These conferences also consider new motions, appeals and petitions.

Conferences are conducted in complete secrecy. No secretaries, clerks, stenographers or pages are allowed into the room.

This practice began many years ago when the justices became convinced that there was a leak, a premature report of a decision. Suspicion focused on two page boys who waited upon the justices in the conference room. Despite the fact that the pages were later cleared when a member of the bar confessed that he had merely made an educated guess about the court's decision in a particular case, conferences have henceforth been attended only by the justices themselves.

In 1979 the substance of an opinion — and even the identity of its author — were correctly reported in the press several days before its announcement. A typesetter assigned to the court was then dismissed. *(Box, p. 71)*

In the court's early years conferences were held in the Washington boardinghouses in which the justices resided. The justices now meet in the elegant, oak-paneled, book-lined conference chamber near the Chief Justice's suite. There are nine chairs around the large rectangular table, each bearing the nameplate of the justice who sits there. The Chief Justice sits at the east end of the table and the senior associate justice at the west end. The other justices take their place in order of seniority. The junior justice is charged with sending for and receiving documents or other information the court needs. Justice Tom C. Clark, the junior justice from 1949 until 1954, once remarked: "For five years, I was the highest-paid doorkeeper in the world." [30]

Discussion Procedure

On entering the conference room the justices shake hands with each other, a symbol of harmony that began in the 1880s. The Chief Justice begins the conference by calling the first case to be decided and discussing it. When he is finished, the senior associate justice speaks, followed by the other justices in order of seniority.

The justices theoretically can speak for as long as they wish without any time limitation imposed. Nevertheless, Chief Justice Charles Evans Hughes — impatient with long

and occasionally irrelevant discourses during conference — convinced the other justices to limit the time they spent discussing a case. The record of the number of cases decided during Hughes' tenure as chief justice reflects this speedier pace in discussion and debate of the cases. As the number of cases considered during conference has grown, subsequent courts have tended to follow Hughes' example.

Similarly, the justice whose turn it is to speak during conference is supposed never to be interrupted. But according to an often-repeated story, Justice Oliver Wendell Holmes Jr. did just that to Justice John Marshall Harlan early in this century. As Harlan was presenting his argument in a particular case, Holmes interrupted with "That won't wash! That won't wash!" Chief Justice Melville W. Fuller allegedly relieved the tension with the remark: "But I just keep scrubbing away, scrubbing away." [31]

Other than these procedural arrangements, little is known about what actually transpires in conference. Athough discussions generally are said to be polite and orderly, they occasionally can be acrimonious. Likewise, consideration of the issues in a particular case is usually full and probing, but decisions sometimes are reached before all the justices are satisfied that the issues have been fully explored.

Voting

Once a case has been discussed, voting begins with the junior justice — the last in order of discussion and the first to vote. Voting proceeds up the order of seniority, a custom thought to have been instituted to protect the young justices from being influenced by their elders. The Chief Justice is the last to vote. It takes a majority vote to decide a case — five votes if all nine justices are participating.

Opinions

After the justices have voted on a case, the writing of the opinion or opinions begins. An opinion is a reasoned argument explaining the legal issues in the case and the precedents on which the decision is based.

Any justice may decide to write a separate opinion. If he is in agreement with the court's decision but disagrees with some of the reasoning in the majority opinion, he may write a concurring opinion giving his reasoning. If he disagrees with the majority, he may write a dissenting opinion or simply go on record as a dissenter without an opinion. More than one justice can sign a concurring or a dissenting opinion.

Writing opinions is often a long and tedious process but a highly important one. The way in which a majority opinion is written can have a tremendous impact on the lives of Americans.

The impact of a particular opinion depends to some extent on who writes it, how he writes it and the extent of support of or dissent from the opinion by the other justices.

The amount of time consumed between the vote on a case and the announcement of the decision varies from case to case. In simple cases where few points of law are at issue, the opinion sometimes can be written and cleared by the other justices in a week or less. In more complex cases, especially those with several dissenting or concurring opinions, it can take six months or more. Some cases may have to be reargued or the initial decision reversed after the drafts of opinions have been circulated.

Assignment Procedure

Soon after a case is decided in conference, the task of writing the majority opinion is assigned. The Chief Justice assigns the task in cases in which he voted in the majority. In cases in which he was in the minority, the senior associate justice voting with the majority assigns the job of writing those majority opinions.

The assigning justice may consider the points made by majority justices during the conference discussion, the workload of the other justices, the need to avoid the more extreme opinions within the majority and expertise in the particular area of law involved in a case. (For an example of this last factor, the court's landmark 1973 rulings on the issue of abortion were explained through a majority opinion written by Justice Harry A. Blackmun, who developed his expertise in medical law during his legal career, which included work with the famous Mayo Clinic in Minnesota, his home state.)

Chief Justice Charles Evans Hughes sometimes assigned "conservative" opinions to "liberal" justices and "liberal" opinions to "conservative" justices to avoid giving any impression that the court was divided along ideological lines.

The assignment of opinions can create morale problems among members of the court. Justices have become annoyed and angered when not assigned to write opinions in cases of particular interest to them or directed to write them in routine, uninteresting cases. In 1898 Justice John Marshall Harlan wrote to Chief Justice Melville W. Fuller and complained: "Two Saturdays in succession you have not assigned to me any case but have assigned cases and important ones to Justice [Horace] Gray. I was in the majority in each case assigned to him." [32]

More recently, rumors circulated about ill-will between Chief Justice Warren E. Burger and former Justice William O. Douglas. In a 1972 abortion case, Douglas was said to believe that Burger had abused his power by voting with the majority in order to assign the writing of the majority opinion although, Douglas alleged, Burger's sympathies lay with the minority. Douglas threatened to file a scathing dissent on Burger's alleged misuse of the assignment powers but was dissuaded from doing so by his colleagues, who argued that the court's reputation would suffer if the dissent were publicized. [33]

Methods of Writing

The style of writing a court opinion, a majority opinion or concurring or dissenting opinions depends primarily on the individual justice. In some cases, the justice may prefer to write a restricted and limited opinion; in others, he may prefer a broader approach to the subject. His decision is likely to be influenced by the need to satisfy the other justices who voted with him in the majority.

The time spent in preparing an opinion varies widely from justice to justice and from case to case. Justice Oliver Wendell Holmes Jr. was reportedly able to write an opinion over a weekend. Justices Hugo L. Black and Louis D. Brandeis were noted for reading widely on all aspects of a case before writing their opinions. Justice Frankfurter was a perfectionist who often prepared as many as 30 or more drafts for each opinion.

Justices use their law clerks to obtain and sift through the material needed to write an opinion. There has been speculation that some clerks actually ghostwrite a justice's opinion — or at least that justices sometimes tell a clerk what they want in an opinion and allow the clerk to write the first draft.

On the other hand, Justice Douglas was said to give his clerks little or nothing to do in writing or organizing his written opinions. The traditional secrecy which surrounds each justice's office and work habits makes verification of such reports about the clerks' role in opinion-writing very difficult.

When a justice is satisfied that the opinion he has written is conclusive or "unanswerable," it is sent to the print shop in the court's basement. There the draft of the opinion is printed under rigid security. Each copy of the draft opinion is numbered to prevent the removal of extra copies from the premises.

Circulation of Drafts

Once the drafts are printed and circulated, the justices — particularly those in the majority and those filing joint concurring or dissenting opinions — discuss the drafts by memo, at lunch or over a private telephone line that does not go through the switchboard.

Often the suggestions and criticisms require the author carefully to juggle opposing views. To retain a majority, the author of the draft opinion frequently feels he must make major emendations to oblige justices who are unhappy with the initial draft. Some opinions have to be rewritten repeatedly before the majority is satisfied.

The Nixon Opinion. One illustration of the difficulty of writing a majority opinion is provided by Chief Justice Burger's problems in the case of the Nixon White House tapes. In mid-1974 the court voted unanimously that the president must turn over the tapes sought as evidence in the Watergate "coverup" case, rejecting the argument that he could invoke executive privilege to withhold them.

After the decision had been reached, Burger assigned the opinion to himself. To save time, Burger circulated the draft opinion piece-by-piece. The other justices were dissatisfied with what they were seeing. Many began writing their own version of the opinion. Burger, while annoyed, was forced to compromise. The final result, handed down on July 24, 1974, in *United States v. Nixon,* [34] was a rather unusual joint product, with a number of justices writing various parts of the final opinion. But, although a joint effort, the final opinion was issued in Burger's name. [35]

Vote Changes

One reason for the secrecy surrounding the circulation of drafts is that some of the justices who voted with the majority may find the majority draft opinion so unpersuasive — or one or more of the dissenting drafts so convincing — that he may change his vote.

If enough justices alter their votes, the majority may shift, so that a former dissent becomes instead the majority opinion. When a new majority emerges from this process, the task of writing, printing and circulating a new majority draft begins all over again.

Tradition of Unanimous Opinions

Over the past few decades there has been considerable concern about the lack of unanimity in court decisions and the frequent use of dissenting and concurring opinions. The chief argument in favor of greater unanimity is that it increases the authority of — and hence the respect for — the court's decisions. More than 20 years ago Judge Learned Hand wrote that "disunity cancels the impact of monolithic solidarity on which the authority of a bench of judges so largely depends." [36]

Such disunity actually has a long tradition, at odds with the relative harmony the court likes to project. It was not until Chief Justice John Marshall took his seat on the court in 1801 that the aspiration toward unanimity became the norm. Before Marshall, each justice would announce his own opinion and the reason for it. These separate (or *seriatim)* opinions were the custom during the first decade of the court's existence.

During Marshall's 35 years on the high court, the practice of *seriatim* opinions was largely abandoned. In his first four years as Chief Justice, 26 opinions were handed down. Of these, Marshall delivered 24 and the senior associate justice only two. The court's ostensible unanimity was disturbed only once during these four years, by a one-sentence concurring opinion by Justice Samuel Chase in 1804. [37]

While Marshall's insistence on unanimity did much to dispel the early court's image as a bickering and dissension-filled forum and to increase its respect and esteem by the public, it did not meet with universal approval.

Jefferson and Marshall. One of Marshall's strongest critics was President Thomas Jefferson, a Republican who often — and vociferously — expressed displeasure over the court's decisions under Marshall, a Federalist.

In a letter to Thomas Richie, dated Dec. 25, 1820, Jefferson wrote that he had long favored a return to "the sound practice of the primitive court" of delivering *seriatim* opinions. Of Marshall's changes, he wrote: "An opinion is huddled up in conclave, perhaps by a majority of one, delivered as if unanimous, and with the silent acquiescence of lazy or timid associates, by a crafty chief judge, who sophisticates the law to his own mind, by the turn of his own reasoning." [38]

The Tradition of Dissent

During the first decade of its existence, the court followed the custom of the King's Bench of Great Britain in issuing *seriatim* opinions. Unlike the King's Bench, however, the Supreme Court delivered *seriatim* opinions in reverse order of seniority. The first case in which a full opinion was published was *State of Georgia v. Brailsford* (1792). The first opinion in the published record of that case was given by a justice who disagreed with the majority in the case. [39]

The first real dissent, and most of the few other dissents to surface during Marshall's tenure, came from William Johnson of South Carolina, a Jefferson appointee. Soon after coming to the court, Johnson delivered what amounted to a dissenting opinion in *Huidekoper's Lessee v. Douglass* (1805). [40]

In a letter to Jefferson, dated Dec. 10, 1822, Johnson complained about the adverse reaction to his concurring or dissenting opinions. "Some Case soon occurred in which I differed from my Brethren, and I felt it a thing of Course to deliver my Opinion. But, during the rest of the Session, I heard nothing but lectures on the Indecency of Judges cutting at each other." [41]

Under Marshall's successor, Chief Justice Roger B. Taney, dissent became more frequent. Unlike Marshall, Taney did not insist upon delivering the sole opinion for the court.

Nevertheless, Marshall's tradition of court unity continued for many years after his death. Until the early years of this century, the court generally gave single opinions with only an occasional concurrence or dissent. Concurring or dissenting opinions were issued in only about a tenth of the cases decided in the middle and late 19th century.

While the increasing use of concurring and dissenting opinions after Marshall's death has been criticized, particularly during this century, it was, according to some observers, almost inevitable. Charles P. Curtis Jr., for example, has written that "if you require unanimity, you make compromise inevitable, in the Court as everywhere else. Compromise is as alien to the feelings of the judicial process as what Solomon offered to do with the baby was to the feelings of the mother." [42] Even the high apostle of unanimity, John Marshall, filed nine dissents and one special concurrence during his 35 years as Chief Justice.

The tradition of dissent is often defended by a recitation of cases in which a carefully reasoned dissent became, in time, the basis of a new majority opinion. But such turnabouts are infrequent. Justice Oliver Wendell Holmes Jr., the "Great Dissenter," issued 173 formal dissents — but fewer than 10 percent of these had any impact on subsequent reversals of court decisions.

A dissenting justice may hope that his dissent will convince a majority of the other justices that his opinion is the correct one or that a later court will vindicate his views. A dissenting justice is able to avoid the process of revising and compromising his opinion which often faces the author of the majority opinion. The dissenter generally has only himself to please, a fact which makes many well-written and well-reasoned dissents more memorable than the majority opinion in the case.

The most frequently quoted defense of dissent on the court was given by Chief Justice Charles Evans Hughes, who wrote that "[a] dissent in a court of last resort is an appeal to the brooding spirit of the law, to the intelligence of a future day, when a later decision may possibly correct the error into which the dissenting judge believes the court to have been betrayed." [43]

Hughes was by no means an unqualified advocate of dissent and is believed on a number of occasions to have yielded his dissent to join the majority without further argument. The words preceding his statement about "an appeal to the brooding spirit of the law" are probably more indicative of Hughes' feelings about dissent:

There are some who think it desirable that dissents should not be disclosed as they detract from the forces of the judgment. Undoubtedly, they do. When unanimity can be obtained without sacrifice of conviction, it strongly commends the decision to public confidence. But unanimity which is merely formal, which is recorded at the expense of strong conflicting views, is not desirable in a court of last resort, whatever may be the effect upon public opinion at the time. This is so because what must ultimately sustain the court in public confidence is the character and independence of the judges. They are not there simply to decide cases, but to decide them as they think they should be decided, and while it may be regrettable that they cannot always agree, it is better that their independence should be maintained and recognized than that unanimity should be secured through its sacrifice. [44]

A list of the "great dissenters" compiled by Karl M. ZoBell includes those few who exercised dissent "in a manner which was — either because of a particular notable dissenting opinion, or because of the sheer weight of dissents filed — of historical or jurisprudential significance." According to ZoBell, the great dissenters were:

● Justice William Johnson (1804-1834), who "did not choose to conceal his ideas when they differed from those of the majority." During his time on the court he wrote almost half of the 70 dissenting opinions filed in those years. Johnson differed with the majority most frequently in three areas — judicial versus legislative power, the sanctity of property and the role of the states.

● Justice Benjamin R. Curtis (1851-1857), who "seldom dissented" during his six years on the court. But his last opinion — a dissent in the case of *Dred Scott v. Sandford,* (1857) — "was subsequently vindicated by the will of the people, and constitutional amendment; it is thus recalled as a landmark opinion in the history of American judicature."

● Justice John Marshall Harlan (1877-1911), a prodigious dissenter who delivered 380 dissents. He is most famous for his lone dissent against the "separate but equal" doctrine upheld in *Plessy v. Ferguson.*

"It was Harlan's lot to read the law differently than did the majority of his brethren in numerous cases, only to have his views adopted by the legislature or by the court years after his death," ZoBell said.

● Justice Oliver Wendell Holmes Jr. (1902-1932), who "actually dissented less frequently during his tenure than did the average of his brethren — once in every 33 cases." But "Holmes' dissents had a way of later becoming correct expositions of the law, as defined by the court or as effected by the Legislature, not only more frequently, but sooner than did those of Harlan." The effect of Holmes on the use of dissent cannot be overestimated. During the so-called Holmes era, "dissent became an instrument by which justices asserted a personal, or individual, responsibility which they viewed as of a higher order than the institutional responsibility owed by each to the court, or by the court to the public." [45]

Other justices who almost certainly should be added to any list of "great dissenters" are Louis D. Brandeis (1916-1939), Benjamin N. Cardozo (1932-1938), Chief Justice Harlan Fiske Stone (1925-1946) and Felix Frankfurter (1939-1962). All served during a time of increasing court division and dissension, when New Deal legislation was being tested in the courts.

Concurring Opinions

For those convinced that dissents damage the prestige of the court and the impact of its decisions, concurring opinions are similarly distasteful. Concurrence is, in many ways, a variation on the *seriatim* opinions of the 1790s. A concurring opinion indicates that the justice who wrote it agrees in general with the majority opinion but has reservations about the way it was written, the reasoning behind it, or specific points in it.

During John Marshall's tenure as Chief Justice, dissents were often masked as concurring opinions. Justice Johnson was a master at this, too. He also wrote a number of concurring opinions supporting decisions of the Federalist majority but not the reasoning behind those decisions. In the case of *Martin v. Hunter's Lessee,* for example, Johnson wrote in a concurring opinion: "I flatter myself that the full extent of the constitutional revisory power may be secured to the United States, and the

benefits of it to the individual, without ever resorting to compulsory or restrictive process upon the state tribunals; a right which, I repeat again, Congress has not asserted; nor has this court asserted, nor does there appear any necessity for asserting." [46]

The case of *United States v. United Mine Workers,* decided in 1947, provides one example of the problems and vexations accounting for and arising from the use of concurring opinions. [47] Chief Justice Fred M. Vinson and Justices Stanley F. Reed and Harold H. Burton voted against the United Mine Workers for two reasons. Justices Wiley B. Rutledge and Frank Murphy both dissented on the same grounds. Justices Frankfurter and Robert H. Jackson agreed with Vinson, Reed and Burton on one of the grounds but rejected the other. Justice Hugo L. Black and William O. Douglas concurred with Vinson for the reason that Frankfurter and Jackson had rejected, but rejected the argument that Frankfurter had approved. The result was that five justices supported the result for one reason, five justices supported it for another reason, and four justices were opposed for both reasons.

Issuing the Opinion

When the drafts of an opinion — including dissents and concurring views — have been written, circulated, discussed and revised, if necessary, the final versions are sent to be printed.

After the opinion is put into final form in the justices' chambers, it is given to the printer in the Supreme Court building. Between the time that the print shop receives the opinions and they are announced in court, they are kept under the same rigid security as the original drafts. After they are printed, they are proofread in the office of the reporter of decisions. Shortly before the case is announced in court, the reporter adds a "headnote" or syllabus summarizing the decision, accompanied by a "lineup" showing how each justice voted.

Beginning late in 1981, the court's decisions will be printed by computer. The opinions will be typed into word processors in the justices' chambers and then transmitted, by a push of a button, to a typesetting computer in the Supreme Court building. From that computer, the opinion will then go to two offset presses for printing.

Only about 200 copies of this "bench opinion" — or "slip opinion" — are made. As the "bench opinions" are announced in court, copies are distributed to lawyers and reporters in the courtroom and to journalists and others in the public information office. Another copy, with any necessary corrections on it, is also sent to the U.S. Government Printing Office where it is reprinted in *United States Reports,* the official record of Supreme Court opinions.

Announcement of Opinions

The public announcement of opinions in court is probably the court's most dramatic function. It also may be the most expendable. Depending on who delivers the opinion and how, announcements can take a considerable amount of the court's time. Opinions are simultaneously given to the public information officer and reporter of decisions for distribution.

Nevertheless, those who are in the courtroom to hear the announcement of a ruling are participating in a very old tradition. The actual delivery may be tedious or exciting, depending on the nature of the case and the eloquence of the opinion and the style of its oral delivery.

Differences between the opinion as actually spoken and its written counterpart, while of little legal or practical importance, can add a certain interest. Once, Justice James C. McReynolds allegedly became so agitated in delivering one dissent that he added: "The Constitution is gone." [48] This remark was not included in the opinion.

In this century, the court has reduced the amount of time spent in delivering opinions. Before Charles Evans Hughes became Chief Justice in 1930, the court generally read long opinions word for word. Some opinions took days to announce early in the court's history. As the workload increased, this practice came to be regarded as a waste of the court's time. Hughes encouraged the delivery of summaries of the opinion. The justice who has written the majority opinion now generally delivers only a summary, and dissenting justices often do the same with their opinions.

Reporting of Decisions

The importance — and difficulty — of adequately reporting Supreme Court decisions cannot be underestimated. Few people read the full Supreme Court opinions, and accounts in the news media often are superficial. Consequently, the American public frequently has little idea of the reasons for and meaning of decisions that affect their lives.

Justice Felix Frankfurter was acutely aware of this problem. "The evolution of our constitutional law is the work of the initiate," he wrote in 1932. "But its ultimate sway depends upon its acceptance by the thought of the nation. The meaning of the Supreme Court decisions ought not therefore to be shrouded in esoteric mystery. It ought to be possible to make clear to lay understanding the exact scope of constitutional doctrines that underlie decisions." [49]

In a 1967 magazine article, Gilbert Cranberg of the Des Moines, Iowa, *Register and Tribune* quoted one columnist who described the Supreme Court as:

...the worst reported and the worst judged institution in the American system of government....

The wholesale shunning of what the Court says leaves most of the country dependent on second-hand reports. It would be difficult to devise handicaps more devastating to an understanding of the Court than those that hobble news reporting of its rulings.... Where Congressmen, subordinate administrators and Presidents are frequently eager to explain and defend their policies, Justices of the Supreme Court emerge from isolation only to read their opinions.... No Justice is available to discuss or clarify the opinion he has written.

Formal Reporting

Cranberg estimated that in 1967 "the total circulation of Supreme Court opinions is probably no more than 20,000. Most of the texts are located in forbidding legal libraries and inaccessible private law offices. Because there are no more than 300,000 lawyers in the United States, it's apparent that even many of the nation's attorneys do not actually read the court opinions."

While total circulation of formal court opinions is now considerably higher than it was in 1967, the psychological impediments to reading them are still there. As Cranberg noted, "poring over Supreme Court texts seemed about as inviting as an evening of wading through a technical manual. Indeed, the deadly, all-but-indigestible legalese I expected to find was there in abundance, but to my delighted surprise there was also a gold mine of information and often exciting, absorbing reading." [50]

As noted earlier, the reporter of decisions edits the opinions and supervises their publication in the official *United States Reports.* The court's decisions first appear in the preliminary prints of the *United States Reports,* usually a few months after the opinions have been issued. On the cover of each preliminary report, there is a message to users requesting them "to notify the Reporter of Decisions ... of any typographical or other formal errors, in order that corrections may be made before the bound volume goes to press." The bound volume usually appears a few months after the preliminary prints.

Copies of preliminary prints are sold by the U.S. Government Printing Office for $50 a term, payable in advance. Each bound volume, which generally contains two to four of the preliminary prints, seldom exceeds 900 pages. The price of a bound volume depends on its length; in recent years the price has ranged from $10 to $20. Individual slip-sheet opinions are sold by the same source at $120 a term. Single copies of a specific court decision vary in size with the length of the opinion and can range in price from 35 cents to more than $2.

The Office of the Clerk of the Court sends copies of the opinions to counsel in each case. A limited number of opinions are available in the clerk's office within a few days after the opinion is announced. There is no charge for these. The opinions are also included in *The United States Law Week,* published by The Bureau of National Affairs, Inc., and *Supreme Court Bulletin,* published by Commerce Clearing House.

News Media

Relatively few people make the effort and take the time to read the opinions of the court, so most Americans must rely on the news media to learn what the court has decided.

Since the late 18th century, however, many — perhaps most — of the opinions handed down by the court have not even been reported by most newspapers.

Nevertheless, efforts have been made in the mid-20th century to improve media coverage of the Supreme Court. Justice Felix Frankfurter played a considerable role in that improvement. His biographer, Liva Baker, wrote:

Frankfurter's concern for public understanding of the Supreme Court took him into a long running fight with *The New York Times.* The press, Frankfurter believed, had a semipublic function and a semipublic responsibility. The *Times,* as the one documentary paper in the nation, should, he thought, furnish its readers the kind of competence in its reporting of the Supreme Court that it furnished in other fields. It should, Frankfurter was fond of saying, cover the Supreme Court at least as well as the World Series.

Beginning in 1933, Frankfurter barraged Arthur Hays Sulzberger, publisher of the *Times,* with letters in which he was outspokenly critical of its failings — and equally outspokenly congratulatory of its triumphs. Finally, in the mid-1950s, a young reporter and Pulitzer Prize winner named Anthony Lewis was sent to Harvard Law School for a year, then assigned to cover the Supreme Court. The *Times* expanded and deepened its Court coverage; a significant by-product of this development was the effect on other prominent newspapers which, encouraged by the *Times,* sought to improve their reporting of Court news and bring it up to World Series levels. [51]

Supreme Court justices have long felt that their opinions must speak for themselves and that efforts by the justices or by the public information office to explain or interpret the court's opinions are unnecessary. Nevertheless, the court has taken a number of actions in recent years to make it easier for the news media to digest the written opinions in the limited time available and report them fully and accurately.

In 1965 the court announced that decisions would be released on other days of the week as well as Monday. By spreading out the announcement of decisions, the court gives reporters fewer cases each day. It is now the practice for decisions to be announced more often on Tuesday or Wednesday than on Monday, particularly late in the term.

In 1970, the court began the practice of having the reporter of decisions add a headnote to each slip opinion. This note summarizes the case, the court's holding, and the lineup of justices on the issues. This gives reporters some guide to the hundreds of pages of written opinions issued each term.

The court's public information officer releases opinions to the news media shortly after they are announced. Some of the country's major newspapers and national news media have their own offices near the public information office, so court opinions can be transmitted quickly to their headquarters.

Other Channels

In addition to the formal and press reporting of court opinions, there are a number of other, often impromptu, methods of publicizing its rulings. Various lobbying groups are rarely shy about speaking out on court opinions which meet with their approval or provoke their disapproval. In the 1960s and early 1970s, court decisions on issues like school desegregation, prayer in the schools, capital punishment and abortion resulted in an avalanche of publicity both from groups supportive of and hostile to the opinions.

When Supreme Court justices were still riding circuit, they usually maintained strong contacts with people, particularly lawyers and local judges, in the communities they served. Through these contacts, they were able to inform community leaders about recent court rulings and the legal principles on which those opinions were based.

In those days and at the present time, the legal fraternity also has provided a forum for discussing and clarifying court opinions through meetings of bar associations and publication of scholarly articles.

Traditions of the Court

Tradition plays a major role in the operations of the Supreme Court. The court's insistence on the historic continuity of its procedures, and its strict adherence to conventions of secrecy and formal decorum, have yielded little to the changing moods and social patterns of the contemporary world outside its chambers.

At best, this overlapping network of traditions gives the court an aura of substance, dignity and caution that befits the nation's highest institution of law — and the public's confidence in the integrity, sobriety of purpose and independence from outside pressure of its justices. But to some critics, much of the court's tenacious adherence to its formal traditions of procedure and behavior reflect an anachronistic set of values that undergird and constrict the effective functioning of the modern court.

Despite continuing efforts to streamline its procedures and find more efficient ways to cope with change, the court remains the most traditional of the three major branches of government.

Some traditional aspects of the court seem merely quaint. Modern justices are still reluctant to take part in Washington's cocktail party circuit, a regular stop for congressmen, diplomats and administration officials. Justices still employ a full-time seamstress to mend their robes and use quill pens made from the feathers of purebred white geese. While most lawyers no longer don frock coats and striped trousers to appear before the court, attorneys from the solicitor general's office still dress in the cutaways.

Other traditions are much more substantive and more controversial. Proposed changes in convention such as the mandatory retirement of justices, televising court sessions and security measures to prevent press leaks are issues which continue to generate debate.

Even the more informal or irreverent of the justices have found the traditions of the court of sufficient importance to observe and preserve them. Justice Felix Frankfurter, for example, was a man who "brought a sense of informality and impish humor to the august tribunal. He would wave from the bench at friends among the spectators. He once escorted the child of a visiting Australian law school dean into the empty courtroom and let her sit on each of the justices' chairs. When Mrs. Charles Fahy came to court to hear her husband, the solicitor general from 1941 to 1945, argue a case, Frankfurter once teased her with this note scribbled from the bench: 'Anyhow — I'm for your hat!' He teased his own law clerks incessantly. He whistled in the marble halls, anything from 'The Stars and Stripes Forever' to the sextet from 'Lucia.' "

But "underneath the gaiety and banter there was a seriousness of purpose equal to anything Frankfurter had undertaken in his life. He approached the court with a kind of religious awe; he was indefatigable in guarding its traditions, and he felt, said Chief Justice Earl Warren, 'the burden of carrying on the traditions of the court more than any man.' " [52]

Secrecy

Among the court's most important traditions is secrecy. Secrecy applies not only to formal deliberations but to disclosure of personal disagreements and animosities among the justices as well. The unwritten code of secrecy has made the court the most leakproof of Washington institutions. Nevertheless, there have been and continue to be occasional glimpses into its inner workings and conflicts.

The practice of allowing no one except the justices themselves in the conference room began years ago with the mistaken impression that a page, secretary, clerk or stenographer had leaked a decision. Subsequent leaks, including several instances from 1973 through 1981, have moved the justices to take measures to prevent further premature disclosures or unwarranted gossip. *(Box this page)*

In addition to the rather infrequent revelations by an inquisitive press, justices and their law clerks have occasionally revealed something about the court's inner workings and conflicts in their writings and speeches. Probably the two best known examples were the use of the papers of Chief Justice Harlan Fiske Stone and Justice Louis D. Brandeis.

When Stone died in 1946, his widow turned over all the Chief Justice's files and papers to Alpheus T. Mason. In his biography of Stone,[53] Mason revealed much of the court's day-to-day operations, including feuds between liberal and conservative justices. Alexander Bickel used Brandeis' papers to show the justice's contribution to court solidarity, quoting Chief Justice William Howard Taft as saying of Brandeis, "He thinks much of the court and is anxious to have it consistent and strong, and he pulls his weight in the boat." [54]

Justices have good reason to maintain the veil of secrecy that surrounds their conference deliberations and their personal relations with other members of the court. Widespread disclosure of what goes on in conference could reduce public esteem for the court and its rulings. When leaks do occur, the court refuses to confirm or deny their accuracy, and the justices are loath to reveal instances of infighting and conflict among themselves lest they demean the dignity of the court and encourage further quarreling among the justices.

Courtesy

Both in and out of court, the justices seek to present an image of formality and courtesy. Before they go into the courtroom and at the beginning of their private conferences, the justices shake hands with each other. This practice began in the late 19th century when Chief Justice Melville W. Fuller decided that it was a good idea to remind the justices that differences of opinion did not preclude overall harmony of purpose.[55] In court and in their written opinions, the justices address each other as "my brother" or "my dissenting brothers." But the image of fraternal harmony is occasionally undermined by personal, ideological and legal differences among justices with strong views and even stronger egos.

In his book on Justice Samuel F. Miller (1862-90), Charles Fairman quoted Miller as having told a friend that Chief Justice Morrison R. Waite (1874-88) was "mediocre" and that "I can't make a great Chief Justice out of a small man." Miller was equally critical of fellow Justices Nathan Clifford, Noah Haynes Swayne and David Davis. "I can't make Clifford and Swayne, who are too old, resign, or keep the Chief Justice from giving them cases to write opinions in which their garrulity is often mixed with mischief. I can't hinder Davis from governing every act of his life by his hope of the Presidency." [56]

More than a decade before his appointment as Chief Justice, President William Howard Taft indicated his dis-

Inside the Conference Room

An unusual and well-publicized leak from the Supreme Court occurred in 1979 when ABC-TV news reporter Tim O'Brien broadcast the results of two cases which had not yet been formally announced in open court. On April 16 O'Brien revealed that Justice Byron R. White would deliver the majority opinion in an important libel case which would allow public figures offended by a report to inquire into the journalist's "state of mind."

Two days later the court, with Justice White speaking for the majority, ruled that public figures could indeed look into the "state of mind" of a journalist and the editorial process when suing for allegedly libelous reporting. O'Brien also reported that during the conference discussion of the case, the justices became involved in an angry and vociferous shouting match about the decision.

On April 17 O'Brien reported that Chief Justice Warren E. Burger had written the opinion in a still unannounced case in which the court ruled against the effort of prison inmates to expand their "due process" rights in parole hearings. After the two ABC-TV broadcasts, Burger was said by court sources to have ordered an immediate investigation.

The court itself made no public comment about the O'Brien reports, and O'Brien refused to reveal how or from whom he obtained the information. Within a week, however, it was reported that Chief Justice Burger had fired a typesetter from the court's print shop. The typesetter, John Tucci, worked for the U.S. Government Printing Office in the court's basement printing shop. Tucci, who would have had access to the opinion before it was released in court, denied that he had leaked the information to O'Brien.

taste for some of the justices. "The condition of the Supreme Court is pitiable, and yet those old fools hold on with a tenacity that is most discouraging," Taft said in 1910. "Really, the Chief Justice Fuller is almost senile; Harlan does no work; Brewer is so deaf that he cannot hear and has got beyond the point of the commonest accuracy in writing his opinions; Brewer and Harlan sleep almost through all the arguments. I don't know what can be done. It is most discouraging to the active men on the bench." [57]

Once he became Chief Justice in 1921, Taft was publicly far less critical of the other justices. Still, Taft's efforts to control the disputes and acrimony among the justices "at times exhausted his supply of good nature, and he sometimes betrayed his own irritations by very sharp remarks in letters." One of these letters, written in 1929, when Justice Harlan Fiske Stone was being considered as Taft's successor, alleged that "Stone is not a leader and would have a good deal of difficulty in massing the Court." John P. Frank recounts how, when Stone was appointed in 1925, "he was welcomed into the little extra-court meetings of the Taft bloc of conservative justices, and then, after a time, was dropped from those conventions when it appeared that he might be dangerously 'progressive.' " [58]

Perhaps the most publicized public airing of judicial antagonisms was the attack by Justice Robert H. Jackson against Justice Hugo L. Black in 1946. Jackson had wanted and expected to become Chief Justice when Harlan Fiske Stone died. Instead, President Truman nominated Fred M.

Vinson, and Jackson blamed Black for blocking his appointment as Chief Justice.

When Vinson was nominated, Jackson was serving as chief of a tribunal trying German war criminals in Nuremberg. Jackson responded to news of the appointment with a vitriolic letter to the Senate and House Judiciary committees. In that letter, Jackson denounced Black for participating in a case in which, Jackson charged, Black should have disqualified himself. That case involved the United Mine Workers, who were being represented by a former law partner of Black's, Crampton Harris. Unmentioned in the letter was the fact that Black and Harris had ceased being partners 19 years earlier and had seen each other hardly at all since that time. Black did not reply to the charge, nor did he mention that he had disqualified himself in all cases involving the Federal Communications Commission because his brother-in-law was a member of the FCC.

An earlier example of lack of judicial courtesy involved Chief Justice Roger B. Taney and Justice Benjamin R. Curtis in the famous *Dred Scott* decision of 1857. [59] In that case nine separate opinions were filed, with Taney speaking for the majority of the court. Taney represented the southern point of view and Curtis the northern, or abolitionist, side on the question of slavery in the territories. The Chief Justice made it difficult for Curtis to write his dissent in the case by refusing to allow Curtis to see the other opinions before completing his dissent. Shortly after the opinions were finally released, Curtis resigned from the court.

Justice James C. McReynolds is often cited as a man whose lack of courtesy made life on the court difficult for his fellow justices. McReynolds, who was appointed by President Woodrow Wilson in 1914 and served until 1941, was described by John P. Frank as "the total antithesis of everything Wilson stood for and . . . the most fanatic and hard-bitten conservative extremist ever to grace the Court." [60] McReynolds showed considerable antagonism to the more liberal members of the court and to the Jewish justices, Louis D. Brandeis and Benjamin N. Cardozo.

Discourtesies Rare

Frank has noted that "far more striking than the Court's disputes over the years is the absence of personal friction among the judges, and the extent to which normal tendencies of irritability are controlled rather than exposed. When one considers how easily a bench of nine could march off in nine different directions, one's principal impression may well be not how often but how seldom this occurs. An instance of a [Justice James C.] McReynolds snarling in bare-toothed anti-Semitic hostility at his Jewish brothers on the Court is overbalanced by the real personal sympathy" among the justices. "This degree of respectful personal interrelations is by no means restricted to Justices who . . . were essentially like-minded." [61]

The desire of most justices to maintain these "respectful personal interrelations" has made outbursts like Justice Jackson's rare. Disagreements among justices are far more likely to be exhibited in subtler ways.

A common method of criticizing another justice is to cite his words or previous opinions to prove the inconsistency of his views on a particular issue or opinion. Jackson, for example, was fond of quoting the statements that Justice Black had made when he was a senator from Alabama. Many of these criticisms are so subtle that they go unnoticed by everyone except those privy to the relationships between the justices.

Seniority

The system of seniority governs such court procedures as conference discussion and voting on decisions, and seating in the courtroom. It is also a determining factor in assignment of office space.

Only the Chief Justice is exempt from such traditional obeisance to seniority.

During conferences, discussion of cases begins with the Chief Justice and proceeds down the line of seniority to the junior associate justice. The junior justice has the task of sending for and receiving documents or other information the court may need. Voting on the cases begins with the junior justice and proceeds up the line of seniority to the Chief Justice.

The justices' seating in the courtroom also reflects their respective seniority. The Chief Justice is seated in the center of the winged mahogany bench. The senior associate justice sits at the immediate right of the Chief Justice and the second senior associate justice at the immediate left. In alternating order of seniority, the other justices take their places, with the junior associate justice at the far left of the bench and the second newest appointee at the far right.

Like the seating on the bench, the three-room offices of the justices are assigned according to seniority. Since there are only seven suites inside the so-called "golden gates" — the large bronze doors that seal the justices off from the public — the two junior justices usually occupy the offices on the public corridor just outside. One exception to this rule was Justice William O. Douglas, who until 1962 chose to keep the office he had been assigned as the most junior justice when he came to the court in 1939. Over the next 23 years, 12 justices with less seniority than Douglas moved to suites inside the door. In 1962, when Justice Frankfurter retired, Douglas at last decided to move inside the "golden gates."

In 1981, Justices William H. Rehnquist and John Paul Stevens occupy space outside the gates.

Continuity

Continuity is not merely an image that the court seeks to perpetuate but is inherent in the nature of the institution.

The main factor in the continuity of the court, of course, is that its justices are appointed for life — and for most members, that has been literally true. The majority of justices either have died while still on the bench or retired near the end of their careers.

Only 102 justices have been confirmed for court service in the nearly two centuries since its establishment. (One — Edwin M. Stanton — died after confirmation before taking his seat on the bench.) None has been removed from the bench involuntarily — although several have resigned under pressure — and few have given up the prestige and accoutrements of the court for another career. Just as change is central to Congress and the presidency through periodic elections, continuity is built into the court through longevity of service. The average length of service of all justices of the court, including current members, has been about 15 years. More than half of them served for at least that long.

William O. Douglas served longer than any other justice in the court's history. When he retired on Nov. 12, 1975, he had been on the high bench for more than 36 years.

Augustus H. Garland once reportedly told President Grover Cleveland, who wished to appoint him to the court, that he thought himself unqualified because a justice should serve for at least 20 years and he doubted that he would live that much longer.

Turnover

The justices' long service on the court is the most integral aspect of its continuity. With a new member added only every two years or so, successive courts assume their own collective identity, as the same justices work together over the space of decades. Each new member, however different in ideology and temperament from his associates, can make only an incremental difference. He is influential as an instrument of change by a factor of only one-ninth — less so, really, given the deferential role imposed upon him by the tradition of seniority.

While it is customary to refer to influential courts by the names of their Chief Justices — "The Marshall Court" or "The Warren Court" — such designations are somewhat misleading. Although the leadership and judicial ideology of each Chief Justice is without doubt a strong element in the direction "his" court takes and the innovations it generates, the makeup of each court is to a large degree fortuitous.

The Chief Justice, after all, usually inherits his associates when he takes office and does not himself choose new ones as vacancies occur — although his counsel may be covertly sought by a president. For the most part, a Chief Justice works with the associates he has been given, often nominated by a president and confirmed by a Congress of a different political persuasion from his own.

"The Warren Court," for example, is considered the most liberal and activist of modern times. Yet its chief, Earl Warren, was a Republican appointee who took command of a bench manned by eight veteran justices appointed by the liberal Democratic Roosevelt-Truman administrations. In subsequent years — although the court absorbed four nominees of Warren's sponsor, Dwight Eisenhower — the "Warren Court" also came to include four appointees of Democratic Presidents Kennedy and Johnson.

The direction of the clearly more conservative "Burger Court" can easily be attributed to the judicial attitudes of its Chief Justice, Warren E. Burger, and his three fellow-Nixon appointees. But it also encompasses three Eisenhower-Kennedy-Johnson holdovers and a moderate, John Paul Stevens, appointed by Nixon's successor, Gerald Ford.

Whether tending to be monolithic in its judgments or closely divided along liberal/conservative lines — or simply unpredictable — the membership of the court is, in other words, determined in large part by slowly evolving circum-

stances: by the political party in power as vacancies occur, by the length of time a court has sat together, and finally by the mere durability of each justice, surviving changes in the court and in the times.

Precedent

Another substantive factor in the court's essential continuity is its reliance on precedent in arriving at decisions. Except in rare cases where there is no judicial opinion to be cited, any decision is based primarily on earlier relevant opinions of the Supreme Court or lower courts as interpreted in light of the case under consideration.

The most dramatic and far-reaching of the court's decisions have been instances where a court has arrived at a clear-cut reversal of an earlier court's landmark opinion, especially one where basic constitutional questions are involved. The 1954 decision in *Brown v. Board of Education* represented a watershed reversal of more than a century of earlier court decisions in civil rights cases — decisions which the "Warren Court," in effect, declared to have been unconstitutional.

But whatever the court's decision — and it is far more common to uphold or modify an earlier court's judgment than to reverse it outright — it is so rooted in precedent that it marks a further stage in a judicial continuum rather than an original judgment that stands on its own.

For some justices, precedent has been a primary consideration. Justice Owen J. Roberts, for example, issued this scathing dissent in January 1944 when the court overturned an admiralty case it had decided 16 years earlier. "The evil resulting from overruling earlier considered decisions must be evident," Roberts contended. "[T]he law becomes not a chart to govern conduct but a game of chance.... [T]he administration of justice will fall into disrepute. Respect for tribunals must fall when the bar and the public come to understand that nothing that has been said in prior adjudication has force in a current controversy." [62]

Justice Frankfurter joined in Roberts' dissent in the case. Yet four years earlier, Frankfurter had this to say about reversing previous court decisions: "We recognize that *stare decisis* [adherence to precedent] embodies an important social policy. It represents an element of continuity in law, and is rooted in the psychologic need to satisfy reasonable expectations. But *stare decisis* is a principle of policy and not a mechanical formula of adherence to the latest decision, however recent and questionable, when such adherence involves collision with a prior doctrine more embracing in its scope, intrinsically sounder, and verified by experience.... This Court, unlike the House of Lords, has from the beginning rejected a doctrine of disability at self-correction." [63]

The Chief Justice

For the most part, the office of Chief Justice of the United States has developed through the leadership and initiative of the men who have held the job.

There is scant statutory authority for the office or its duties. The Constitution only mentions the title once: "When the President of the United States is tried, the Chief Justice shall preside,"[64]

The Judiciary Act of 1789 specifies only "That the supreme court of the United States shall consist of a chief justice and five associate justices."

Indeed, in the very early years of the court, there was little indication that the title of Chief Justice would become such an important and prestigious one. As John P. Frank noted:

> The great and yet intangible difference between the Chief and his Associates is the prestige that, rightly or wrongly, tradition attaches to the Chief Justiceship. Popular mythology makes the Chief Justiceship much of what it is, in part because there have been some very great Chief Justices whose personal glory has rubbed off on the office, and partly because of popular esteem for the very idea of 'Chief.'

Yet because of tradition, popular perception of the office, or other intangible factors, the Chief Justice is widely perceived as more than *primus inter pares,* or "first among equals." Although he casts only one vote in accepting and deciding cases, as Frank pointed out:

> ...his formal title is a trifle different: he is Chief Justice of the United States, and his fellows are Justices of the Supreme Court. He administers the oath of office to the President. He presides when the Court is in public session, and at its secret conferences. He also presides over the judicial conference of the judges of the lower courts, and he has the not inconsiderable duty of assigning the writing of most of the opinions of his brothers. He is the chief administrative officer of the Court.[65]

First Among Equals

The first three Chief Justices were not held in especially high esteem. The first, John Jay, came to the court in 1789 and resigned six years later, on June 29, 1795, after having concluded the Jay treaty with England and having been elected governor of New York.[66]

His successor, John Rutledge, had first been appointed to the court in 1790 but resigned as a justice the next year to accept the post of chief justice of South Carolina. After Jay's election, Rutledge wrote to President Washington that he would accept the Chief Justiceship "if you think me as fit as any other person and have not made choice of one to succeed him [Jay]."[67]

Washington immediately accepted Rutledge's suggestion, and Rutledge was sworn in as Chief Justice on Aug. 12, 1795. But before the Senate came back into session to confirm him, reports of Rutledge's earlier criticism of the Jay Treaty provoked a storm of controversy. When the Senate returned in December, there were, in addition to the outrage arising from Rutledge's criticism of the Jay Treaty, persistent rumors that the new Chief Justice was mentally unbalanced. Later that month, the Senate rejected the nomination by a vote of 14 to 10.

Washington next offered the Chief Justiceship to Henry Clay, but Clay declined the offer, as did Justice William Cushing. Washington then nominated Oliver Ellsworth, who served from 1796 until he reigned in 1800. President John Adams named former Chief Justice Jay to succeed Ellsworth, but Jay refused to return to his old post, largely because of the onerous circuit duties imposed upon the justices. Adams then chose John Marshall.

John Marshall

Marshall's great achievement was to increase public respect for the Supreme Court. When he became Chief Justice in 1801 the court was held in low esteem, and its rulings, embodied in often unclear and confusing *seriatim* opinions, did little to enhance the prestige of the third branch of the government.

By his insistence on unanimity and the avoidance of dissenting and concurring opinions, Marshall — and to a far lesser extent, his successor, Roger B. Taney (1836-64) — gave the court the prestige it needed to deal effectively with many of the conflicts and controversies that were confronting the country. President Thomas Jefferson, who sought to break Federalist control of the court, encouraged dissent but was successful only in his appointment of Jeffersonian loyalist William Johnson. Following the deaths of Justices William Cushing and Samuel Chase, Jefferson wrote to his successor, James Madison, in 1811 that "it will be difficult to find a character of firmness enough to preserve his independence on the same bench with Marshall."

According to Frank, a Chief Justice:

> ...must get his real eminence not from the office but from the qualities he brings to it. He must possess the mysterious quality of leadership. In this respect the outstanding Chief was Marshall, who for 35 years presided over a Court largely populated by Justices of an opposing political party. Moreover, his Court, because of the very newness of the Constitution it was expounding, dealt with some of the greatest questions of history. Nonetheless, Marshall dominated his Court as has no other Chief Justice. He wrote most of its important opinions, and his dissents are remarkable for their rarity. . . . More important, Marshall brought a first-class mind and a thoroughly engaging personality into second-class company. The Court when he came to it was lazy and quite willing to let him do the work.[68]

William Howard Taft

The only Chief Justice who had served as president (1909-1913), William Howard Taft, came to the court in 1921 and immediately embarked on efforts to modernize the U.S. judicial system. His greatest contributions to the court came in his role as administrator rather than as judge or legal scholar.

A year after his appointment, Taft succeeded in persuading Congress to establish the Judicial Conference of Senior Circuit Judges — now the Judicial Conference of the United States — the governing body for the administration of the federal judicial system.

More important to the Supreme Court itself was Chief Justice Taft's work in convincing Congress to enact the Judiciary Act of 1925. That law gave the court — then burdened by a severe backlog of cases — almost unlimited discretion in deciding which cases to accept for review. As a result, the caseload — at least for a time — became more manageable, and the court was able to devote more time and energy to constitutional issues and important questions of federal law.

James F. Simon described Taft's contributions as Chief Justice:

> Some experts rate Chief Justice William Howard Taft as one of the Court greats, not because of his opinions, but because of his devoted efforts to reform an antiquated court system. . . . In his first year as Chief Justice Taft crisscrossed the country in a whistle stop campaign for reform of the courts. He spoke to bar associations, argued his case in legal periodicals and testified at length before the House and Senate judiciary committees. His efforts were handsomely rewarded the next year when Congress passed a judicial reform act that streamlined the federal judicial system by coordinating the activities of the far-flung federal districts and bringing them under surer executive control of the Chief Justice. That accomplished, Taft turned his attention to the problem of court congestion in the Supreme Court docket. "We made our preparations with care," he later said, "and it proved to be easier than we supposed." (Taft's reward was the Judges Bill of 1925. . . .) Before he was through, Chief Justice Taft's arm-twisting (he thought nothing of calling the chairman of the judiciary committee or even talking to the president about his reforms) had succeeded in winning the Court its first permanent home — the present Supreme Court building.[69]

Charles Evans Hughes

Another great Chief Justice, Charles Evans Hughes, called attention to the "personality and character" of the office before he himself assumed it in 1930:

> The Chief Justice as the head of the Court has an outstanding position, but in a small body of able men with equal authority in the making of decisions, it is evident that his actual influence will depend upon the strength of his character and the demonstration of his ability in the intimate relations of the judges. It is safe to say that no member of the Supreme Court is under any illusion as to the mental equipment of his brethren. Constant and close association discloses the strength and exposes the weaknesses of each. Courage of conviction, sound learning, familiarity with precedents, exact knowledge due to painstaking study of the cases under consideration cannot fail to command that profound respect which is always yielded to intellectual power conscientiously applied. That influence can be exerted by any member of the Court, whatever his rank in order of precedence.[70]

Hughes served as an associate justice from 1910-16 under the often indecisive, occasionally rambling Chief Justice Edward D. White. During those years, Hughes became acutely aware of the need for leadership by a Chief Justice in conference discussions and in the assignment of opinions. He also came to appreciate the value of harmony among the nine justices.

Constitutional Duty

In the only presidential impeachment trial in the nation's history, Chief Justice Salmon P. Chase — as presiding officer of the trial — may well have prevented President Andrew Johnson's conviction by the Senate in 1868. Mary Ann Harrell has pointed out that "Johnson's political enemies wanted a quick conviction. The Constitution, however, required the Chief Justice to preside; and Chase insisted on presiding as a judge, while the Senate tried legal issues as a court should. The Radicals had to let him rule on points of law; Chase gave the President's lawyers a chance to be heard. Johnson escaped conviction by one vote."

Source: Mary Ann Harrell, *Equal Justice Under Law: The Supreme Court in American Life* (Washington, D.C.: The Foundation of the Federal Bar Association with the cooperation of the National Geographic Society, 1975), p. 53.

Years after Hughes' death, former Justice Owen J. Roberts described Hughes as "the greatest of a great line of Chief Justices." During conferences, Roberts said, "his presentation of the facts of a case was full and impartial. His summary of the legal questions arising out of the facts was equally complete, dealing with opposing contentions so as to make them stand out clearly. . . . After the Chief Justice had finished his statement of the case and others took up the discussion, I have never known him to interrupt or to get into an argument with the Justice who was speaking. He would wait until the discussion had closed and then briefly and succinctly call attention to the matters developed in the discussion as to which he agreed or disagreed, giving his reasons."[71]

During oral argument and in assigning opinions, Hughes was said to show similar control and consideration. Counsel who were nervous or long-winded were often saved by a simple question from Hughes which sought to clarify or rephrase arguments they had presented poorly. "I know of no instance," Justice Roberts said, "where a lawyer had reason to feel rebuked or hurt by anything the Chief Justice said or did."[72]

Hughes described the assigning of opinions as "my most delicate task. . . . I endeavored to do this with due regard to the feelings of the senior Justices and to give to each Justice the same proportion of important cases while at the same time equalizing so far as possible the burden of work. Of course, in making assignments I often had in mind the special fitness of a Justice for writing in the particular case."[73]

In assigning opinions, Hughes also tried to avoid extreme points of view and let the centrist view prevail. As Merlo Pusey pointed out in his study of Hughes, "When a Justice with a reputation as a liberal voted with the majority on the conservative side of a question, he usually got the opinion to write. The same was true in the case of a conservative voting on the liberal side. Hughes' constant effort was to enhance public confidence in the entire court as an independent and impartial tribunal."[74]

Hughes also could be extremely considerate of the other justices. When he had voted with the majority at the Saturday conference, he usually had the opinion-writing assignment delivered to the appropriate justice that same night. Knowing that Justice Cardozo, who had suffered a heart attack before coming to the court in 1932, would

Earl Warren and the *Brown* Decision

Chief Justice Warren's personal qualities and his amiable relationship with the other justices played a major role in the court's unanimous ruling in *Brown v. Board of Education*. That landmark decision, written by Warren and handed down on May 17, 1954, declared racial segregation in public schools inherently discriminatory and therefore in contravention of the equal protection clause of the Fourteenth Amendment.

The *Brown* decision was a catalyst for the civil rights revolution of the late 1950s and 1960s. The opinion doubtless would have been far less important and far-reaching had it not been unanimous. Had there been dissenting or concurring opinions, the impact of the decision would have been reduced, and opponents of desegregation would have been given the opening to challenge the decision. Warren's achievement in securing unanimity was remarkable in itself. Equally remarkable was the fact that he had been Chief Justice only a few months when the decision was handed down.

In *Simple Justice*, a book on the *Brown* decision, Richard Kluger wrote that:

...some time between late February and late March, the court voted at one of its Saturday conferences on the school-segregation cases. The date is in doubt because the justices had agreed that the case was of such magnitude that no word ought to leak out before the decision was announced. . . . The vote was apparently eight to strike down segregation and one, [Justice Stanley F.] Reed, to uphold it. But it was far from certain whether Jackson was going to file a separate concurrence or whether Frankfurter might or whether the two of them might agree on one. . . . Warren, of course, wished to avoid concurring opinions; the fewer voices with which the Court spoke, the better. And he did not give up his hope that Stanley Reed, in the end, would abandon his dissenting position. The Chief assigned himself the all-important task of writing the majority opinion.

On March 30, Justice Jackson suffered a serious heart attack. It was suspected that Jackson, along with Frankfurter, might issue a concurring opinion in the case.

Warren, who had been working on the majority opinion, did not circulate his draft until May 7. Justices Burton, Black, Douglas, Minton and Clark responded quickly and enthusiastically, making only a few minor suggestions for change.

"It was with the three remaining members of the Court [Frankfurter, Jackson, Reed] that Warren could have anticipated problems: any of them might still choose to write his own opinion," Kluger wrote. But Frankfurter "had from the beginning been working for a unified Court. Nothing could have been worse, for the Court or the nation itself, than a flurry of conflicting opinions that would confuse and anger the American people. So long as the Chief was willing to fashion his opinion in a frank, carefully modulated way, Frankfurter had intended to go along." Warren's draft apparently met with Frankfurter's approval.

"Warren personally delivered his draft opinions to Jackson's hospital room and left them for the ailing Justice to study." After having his clerk, Barrett Prettyman, read the draft, Jackson "was willing to settle for one whose principal virtue seemed to be its temperate tone." Prettyman was quoted by Kluger as saying that the "genius of the Warren opinion was that it was so simple and unobtrusive. [Warren] had come from political life and had a keen sense of what you could say in this opinion without getting everybody's back up. His opinion took the sting off the decision, it wasn't accusatory, and it didn't pretend that the Fourteenth Amendment was more helpful than the history suggested — he didn't equivocate on that point."

Justice Reed then remained the only holdout. According to Kluger, Reed's position on the *Brown* case "stemmed from a deeply held conviction that the nation had been taking big strides in race relations and that the Court's decision to outlaw separate schools threatened to impede that march, if not halt it altogether." Warren met many times with Reed and, according to Reed's clerk, George Mickum, had this to say in one of their last meetings: "Stan, you're all by yourself in this now. You've got to decide whether it's really the best thing for the country."

Warren, according to Mickum, "was not particularly eloquent and certainly not bombastic. Throughout, the Chief Justice was quite low-key and very sensitive to the problems that the decision would present to the South. He empathized with Justice Reed's concern. But he was quite firm on the Court's need for unanimity on a matter of this sensitivity." Mickum added that "I really think he [Reed] was really troubled by the possible consequences of his position. Because he was a Southerner, even a lone dissent by him would give a lot of people a lot of grist for making trouble. For the good of the country, he put aside his own basis for dissent." At a conference on May 15, the justices at last accepted — unanimously — Warren's opinion in the *Brown* case.

Source: Richard Kluger, *Simple Justice: Brown v. Board of Education and Black America's Struggle for Equality* (New York: Alfred A. Knopf, 1976), pp. 694-699.

begin work on an assignment immediately after getting it, Hughes delayed the delivery of Cardozo's assignments until Sunday. And — so that Cardozo would not be aware of this practice — he also delayed delivering the assignments to Justice Van Devanter, who lived in the same apartment house as Cardozo. Similar tact was used when the other justices gave Hughes "the highly unpleasant duty" of asking for the resignation of 90-year-old Justice Holmes.

Harlan Fiske Stone

In contrast to Hughes' efficient administration of court business, his successor as Chief Justice, Harlan Fiske Stone, was unable or unwilling to maintain such control of the court. Stone allowed conference discussions to go on as long as the other justices wished and made little effort to minimize disagreements and dissents. According to John P. Frank, "Stone is a notable example of a judge completely competent in his own individual duties of judging who was yet unable to function well as Chief."

During Stone's tenure as Chief Justice, Frank continued, "the high efficiency of the Court began to deteriorate, the Court was much more frequently divided than usual, and the opinions of at least some of its members indulged in a stridency of tone which diminished the prestige of the tribunal. Personal relations within the Court were most unhappy. Why? Stone's occasional testiness and vanity made him very difficult to work with. A partisan battler himself, he could not rise above the fray to bring calm leadership into the controversies of others. . . . He was given to tactless comment about his colleagues." [75]

Earl Warren

Chief Justice Earl Warren was temperamentally the opposite of Stone in many respects. Toward the other justices, he was usually temperate and good-natured. Warren had been named Chief Justice by President Eisenhower in October 1953 and had been confirmed unanimously by the Senate on March 1, 1954. Three days after his confirmation, columnist James Reston of *The New York Times* wrote that the new Chief Justice appeared to display at conferences and in court "an ability to concentrate on the concrete; a capacity to do his homework; a sensitive, friendly manner, wholly devoid of pretense, and a self-command and natural dignity so useful in presiding over the court." [76]

Warren's affability and low-key persuasiveness — as much as the liberal affinities of the associate justices he inherited from Democratic presidents — were responsible for leading the Supreme Court into a revolutionary era of ideological decision-making. *Brown v. Board of Education*[77] and other opinions of the Warren era were catalysts of social reform. They also unleashed a storm of protest from those who feared expanding the rights of blacks, the poor, criminals and the underprivileged. *(Box, p. 76)*

Despite his low-keyed, amiable relationships with his fellow justices, however, Warren could show a gritty leadership. On two occasions in early 1962, Warren publicly rebuked senior justice Felix Frankfurter for expanding his written opinion as he announced it in open court and for lecturing the other justices when he delivered a dissenting opinion.

Warren E. Burger

Since becoming Chief Justice in 1969, Warren E. Burger, like his conservative predecessor William Howard Taft, has functioned more as an administrator of the U.S. court system and as a representative of the courts before Congress than as a leader in judicial philosophy. Burger has been tireless in his efforts to streamline the courts and to make the ever-increasing caseload of both the Supreme Court and the lower federal courts more manageable. *(See box p. 62)*

Burger has been subjected to considerable criticism as a Chief Justice. He has been blamed for antagonizing some of the other justices and for failing to control the "increasingly unharmonious" relations on the court.

Nevertheless, a lawyer who clerked on the court during the 1977 term defends the Chief Justice and points out that "Burger has tried more than most to bring the justices together by compromising his own position. Some are strong-willed people who just won't bend — and he can't force them." [78]

Head of the Judicial System

In addition to his duties on the Supreme Court, the Chief Justice is also chairman of the Judicial Conference of the United States, chairman of the board of the Federal Judicial Center, and supervisor of the Administrative Office of the United States Courts. Chief Justice Burger has estimated that he spends about a third of his time on administrative tasks that do not directly involve the other justices.

Judicial Conference of the U.S. The Judicial Conference, the body which governs administration of the federal judicial system, was set up in 1922 by Chief Justice William Howard Taft. A former lower court judge as well as a former president, Taft felt the federal judiciary needed a forum for coordination.

The conference consists of the Chief Justice, its chairman, and 24 members — the 11 chief justices of the U.S. courts of appeal, a district court judge elected by his peers in each circuit, and the chief judges of the Court of Claims and the Court of Customs and Patent Appeals. *(See p. 93)*

Federal Judicial Center. The center was created by Congress in 1967 as a research, training and planning arm of the federal judiciary. Headquartered in Washington, D.C., its seven-member board meets four times a year. It was in his capacity as chairman of the Federal Judicial Center that Chief Justice Burger established the Study Group on the Caseload of the Supreme Court in 1972. *(See p. 93)*

Administrative Office of the U.S. Courts. The Administrative Office serves as the "housekeeper" and statistician for the federal court system. It was established by Congress in 1939 to take over the administrative duties that had been performed by the attorney general's office. Among other things, it fixes the salaries of all lower-court personnel except judges and supervises the administrative functions of these courts. *(See p. 93)*

Extra-Judicial Roles

In addition to his responsibilities as head of the Supreme Court and of the federal judicial system, Congress has also made the Chief Justice a member of the Board of Regents of the Smithsonian Institution and a member of the Board of Trustees of the National Gallery of Art and of the Joseph H. Hirshhorn Museum and Sculpture Garden.

The Constitution gives justices of the Supreme Court no other duty than to serve as justices, and the Chief Justice no other additional duty than to preside over Senate impeachment proceedings. Nevertheless, a number of Chief Justices have taken on additional tasks, and several of them have been severely criticized for involving the court in controversial non-judicial issues.

Political Involvement

A number of the Chief Justices have been active politically before their appointment and have retained an activist political temperament upon assuming command of the high court. John Marshall, Roger Taney, Salmon P. Chase, Charles Evans Hughes, Harlan Fiske Stone and Fred M. Vinson had been Cabinet members. William Howard Taft had been president. Edward D. White had been a U.S. Senator. Earl Warren had been Governor of California. In fact, only two Chief Justices have come from strictly legal backgrounds: Morrison R. Waite (1874-1888) and Melville W. Fuller (1888-1910).

Advising the President

During his first term, President Washington, seeking judicial advice, sent the court 29 questions on international law and treaties at a time when he was trying to keep the new country out of the war between Britain and France. The court refused to give advice, maintaining that the Constitution gave them no authority to share executive power or to issue advisory opinions to a president.

Nevertheless, Chief Justice Warren E. Burger has pointed out that "although the members of the first Supreme Court wisely resisted President Washington's request for advisory opinions and declined to perform other functions which they deemed to be executive in nature, there is little doubt that Chief Justice Jay gave advice to Washington over the dinner table and even in writing." [79]

Diplomatic Missions

Jay did more for President Washington than just that. Before becoming Chief Justice, he had served as interim secretary of state. At the president's request, Jay undertook a successful diplomatic mission to Great Britain in 1794 to try to patch up quarrels over British troops in the American Northwest and private debts to British creditors.

The Jay Treaty, which the Chief Justice negotiated during the visit, may have prevented another war between Britain and the United States, but it involved Jay and the court in partisan controversy. (So did Jay's decision to run twice for governor of New York while still Chief Justice.)

While the Senate confirmed Jay's nomination as envoy to Britain by a vote of 18 to 8 on April 19, 1794, objections to such double duty were raised that would resurface when Jay was renominated to the Chief Justiceship in 1800.

During three days of Senate debate on the nomination, a resolution was offered which maintained that "to permit Judges of the Supreme Court to hold at the same time any other office of employment emanating from and holden at the pleasure of the Executive is contrary to the spirit of the Constitution and as tending to expose them to the influence of the Executive, is mischievous and impolitic."

Similar, although more subdued, criticism befell Jay's successor Oliver Ellsworth for accepting President Adams' appointment as envoy to France in early 1799.

Chief Justice Harlan Fiske Stone referred to the impact on the court of the Jay and Ellsworth missions in a letter to President Franklin D. Roosevelt on July 20, 1942.

"We must not forget that it is the judgment of history that two of my predecessors, Jay and Ellsworth, failed in the obligation of their office and impaired their legitimate influence by participation in executive action in the negotiation of treaties," Stone wrote. "True, they repaired their mistake in part by resigning their commissions before resuming their judicial duties, but it is not by mere chance that every Chief Justice since has confined his activities strictly to the performance of his judicial duties." [80]

Investigatory Commissions

Chief Justice Stone's letter to Roosevelt was written in response to the president's suggestion that Stone conduct an investigation into the uses of rubber during World War II. Stone declined the offer, saying, "I cannot rightly yield to my desire to render for you a service which as a private citizen I should not only feel bound to do but one which I should undertake with zeal and enthusiasm."

Stone's main reason for rejecting the assignment was that "a judge and especially the Chief Justice cannot engage in political debate or make public defense of his acts. When his action is judicial he may always rely upon the support of the defined record upon which his action is based and of the opinion in which he and his associates unite as stating the grounds for decision. But when he participates in the action of the executive or legislative departments of government he is without those supports. He exposes himself to attack and indeed invites it, which because of his peculiar situation, inevitably impairs his value as a judge and the appropriate influence of his office." [81]

Chief Justice Earl Warren proved more willing to accept a non-judicial public duty. After the assassination of President Kennedy in 1963, Warren chaired the Commission To Report Upon the Assassination of President John F. Kennedy, the so-called Warren Commission.

Perquisites

The Chief Justice has a number of special perquisites. In addition to an annual salary of $92,400 a year and to the attention and respect that surrounds the office, he also has four law clerks (including a special assistant), three secretaries and a messenger. The Chief Justice is also provided with a car and chauffeur, paid for by the government.

In 1972 Congress authorized the Chief Justice to "appoint an Administrative Assistant who shall serve at the pleasure of the Chief Justice and shall perform such duties as may be assigned to him by the Chief Justice." The statute authorizing the appointment of an administrative assistant says nothing about the functions and duties of such a position; it is left to the Chief Justice to determine how and in what areas he will work.

Chief Justice Burger has had his administrative assistant operate "exclusively in areas outside the Chief Justice's judicial functions as a member of the Supreme Court."

This assistant has provided "(1) research and analysis supportive of the Chief Justice's public addresses and statements; (2) monitoring of literature and developments in the fields of judicial administration and court improvement; (3) liaison with the many legal and judicial groups and individuals dealing with problems in those fields, including assistance in organizing legal conferences; (4) assistance in the task of explaining to the public the role of the Supreme Court and the federal judicial system; and (5) assistance to the Chief Justice in his overall supervisory responsibilities with respect to the institutional operations of the Supreme Court, such as the supervision and coordination of the various offices of the Court." [82]

The Justices

From 1790 through 1980, only 101 men have served as Supreme Court justices. On average, a new justice joins the court every 22 months. With the exception of Jimmy Carter, every president who has served a full term or more has made at least one appointment. That so few justices have served is due in part to the fact that justices are appointed for life.

How Large a Bench?

Another factor in the low turnover has been the fact that the court has remained the same size since 1869. In the Judiciary Act of 1789, Congress established the number of justices, including the Chief Justice, at six. The Judiciary Act of 1801, enacted one month before President John Adams' term expired, reduced the number to five, to prevent the newly-elected president, Thomas Jefferson, from filling any vacancies. Congress in 1802 repealed the 1801 law, bringing the number of Supreme Court justices back to six.

The Judiciary Act of 1807 increased the number to seven, primarily because of the increasing judicial work. In 1827 Congress added two new seats, bringing the number to nine, the size it has remained ever since, except during the Civil War period. The Judiciary Act of 1863 increased the number of justices to ten, but in 1866 Congress cut the court's size down to seven to prevent President Andrew Johnson from filling vacancies with appointees who would reflect his views about the unconstitutionality of Reconstruction legislation.

The last adjustment in court size came with the Judiciary Act of 1869, which increased it to nine seats. The act mandated "That the Supreme Court of the United States shall hereafter consist of the Chief Justice of the United States and eight associate justices, any six of whom shall constitute a quorum; and for the purposes of this act there shall be appointed an additional associate justice of said court."

The last major effort to change the number of members on the court was President Franklin D. Roosevelt's aborted "court-packing" attempt in 1937 to add justices who ostensibly would be more sympathetic to his New Deal legislative proposals than were the sitting justices. In opposition to the plan, several justices argued "that a Court of nine is as large a court as is manageable. The Court could do its work, except for writing of the opinions, a good deal better if it were five rather than nine. Every man who is added to the Court adds another voice in counsel, and the most difficult work of the Court . . . is that that is done around the counsel table; and if you make the Court a convention instead of a small body of experts, you will simply confuse counsel. It will confuse counsel within the Court, and will cloud the work of the Court and deteriorate and degenerate it." [83]

Since the failure of Roosevelt's plan, there have been no further efforts to increase the number of justices, nor are there likely to be any in the foreseeable future. During the 19th century, the main reason for increasing the number of justices was the burden of circuit duty: as new circuits were added, more justices were needed to attend sessions of the courts in these circuits. Circuit-riding duties of the justices ended in 1891. *(See box, next page)*

In the past — but to a lesser extent today — a justice usually was appointed from the circuit which he was to oversee. Factors other than regional ones that a president generally considers in nominating a person to be a justice of the Supreme Court are the likelihood of his winning Senate confirmation, his ability and reputation, his ideological position, his political affiliation and beliefs and his religion.

Confirmation

Since the late 18th century, the Senate has formally rejected only 11 court nominees. (The last two were President Richard Nixon's appointees Clement F. Haynsworth Jr. and G. Harrold Carswell.) In addition to the nominations that the Senate has formally rejected, 13 others have been denied confirmation without a vote.

A Judicial 'Family'

Depending on shifting traditions and circumstances, members of the court have sometimes behaved more like a close-knit, chummy family, at others more like a group of dignitaries on their most scrupulously formal behavior.

In the early years of the court, particularly after John Marshall became Chief Justice in 1801, the justices usually lived together during the term in the same boardinghouse and shared their meals together. During the Marshall years, when the court was in session, the justices were together during oral arguments, usually from 11 a.m. until 4 p.m. each day and during conference after 7 p.m. After the conferences, the justices often dined and socialized with each other.

During the early years of the 19th century, Charles Warren has written, "the Judges of the Court appear to have been assiduous diners-out." [84] John Quincy Adams, then secretary of state, wrote in his diary on March 8, 1821: "We had the Judiciary company to dine with us, this day. Chief Justice Marshall, the Judges Johnson, Story and Todd, the Attorney-General Wirt, and late District Attorney Walter Jones; also Messrs. Harper, Hopkinson, D. B. Ogden, J. Sergeant, Webster, Wheaton and Winder, all counsellors of the Court. . . . We had a very pleasant and convivial party." [85]

At this time, the justices "lived for the most part in the same lodgings," Warren continued, and "their intercourse was necessarily of the closest kind, off as well as on the bench." Charles Sumner, later the radical Republican senator from Massachusetts and outspoken abolitionist, wrote in a letter of March 3, 1834: "All the judges board together, having rooms in the same house and taking their meals from the same table, except Judge McLean whose wife is with him, and who consequently has a separate table, though in the same house. I dined with them yesterday. . . . No conversation is forbidden, and nothing which goes to cause cheerfulness, if not hilarity. The world and all its things are talked of as much as on any other day." [86]

In a letter of March 8, 1812, Justice Joseph Story described the life of the justices in their common boardinghouse. "It is certainly true, that Judges here live with perfect harmony, and as agreeably as absence from friends and families could make our residence. Our intercourse is perfectly familiar and unrestrained, and our social hours, when undisturbed with the labors of the law, are passed in gay and frank conversation, which at once enlivens and instructs." [87]

Many of the justices continued to share a common boardinghouse until after the Civil War. In the late 19th century, however, as the terms of the court grew longer, the justices abandoned the boardinghouses, moved their families to Washington and set up their own homes.

Some of the familial aspects of the earlier days remain. It is rare for one justice to allow his animosity toward another to come to public attention. Justices rarely criticize the views of their colleagues, except in their written opinions. And there have been repeated instances when the other justices have taken on extra work or exhibited extra kindness toward a justice who was physically or mentally unwell. Still, the secrecy and isolation of the court tend to make the camaraderie of the boardinghouse days all but impossible today.

Individualism

History, tradition and the nature of the court's work limit severely the opportunities of its members to demonstrate their individual views and traits.

In the early years of the court, several factors encouraged the growth of individualism. One was the practice of delivering *seriatim* opinions, instead of the issuance of one, single opinion of the court. Chief Justice Marshall ended *seriatim* opinions, but the increasing use of dissenting and concurring opinions after his tenure had a similar effect.

Of judicial independence and individualism, Wesley McCune wrote:

Were it not for one institution, the dissenting opinion, anyone who accepted appointment to the Court would almost immediately lose his individual identity, except for what he could retain in Washington society or during summer vacations. If justices wrote only majority opinions, blended to fit the views of five or more justices, the name on the opinion would mean little and the Court would become as impersonal as a big bank. But through dissents justices have asserted their personal views. Thus, each justice can build a reputation even after arriving on the Court, in addition, of course, to shaping future law by protesting that of the present. [88]

The justices' early circuit-riding responsibilities also encouraged individualism. While on the circuit, the justices operated not as a group but as individual judges with as much discretionary power as they wished to exert.

Another factor favoring independence was the lack of office space before the new court building was completed in 1935. Until then, most of the justices worked in their own homes, seeing the other justices only when oral arguments were heard or conferences held.

Even after occupying their offices in the new court building, however, the justices seldom approached the "old-boy" closeness of the boardinghouse days. After taking his seat on the court in 1972, Justice Lewis F. Powell Jr. confessed:

I had thought of the Court as a collegial body in which the most characteristic activities would be consultation and cooperative deliberation aided by a strong supportive staff. I was in for more than a little surprise. . . . The Court is perhaps one of the last

Circuit-Riding

Circuit-riding was a tremendous burden for most justices, and there were numerous complaints from the justices about the intolerable conditions that circuit duties imposed on them.

In a letter to the president on Aug. 19, 1792, for example, all the justices wrote:

We really, sir, find the burdens laid upon us so excessive that we cannot forbear representing them in strong and explicit terms. . . . That the task of holding twenty-seven Circuit Courts a year, in the different States, from New Hampshire to Georgia, besides two sessions of the Supreme Court at Philadelphia, in the two most severe seasons of the year, is a task which, considering the extent of the United States and the small number of Judges, is too burdensome. That to require of the Judges to pass the greater part of their days on the road, and at inns, and at a distance from their families, is a requisition which, in their opinion, should not be made unless in cases of necessity.[1]

The president transmitted that letter to Congress, but Congress, then and for almost 100 years thereafter, refused to abolish the circuit-riding duties. Thus the justices, many of them old and in ill health, faced days of difficult and often impossible travel, inadequate lodgings, bad food and epidemics and disease.

In a speech on the Senate floor on Jan. 12, 1819, Sen. Truman Lacock, D-Pa., summed up the major reasons for retaining circuit duties. If the justices were relieved of circuit duties, Lacock argued, they would become "completely cloistered within the City of Washington, and their decisions, instead of emanating from enlarged and liberalized minds, would assume a severe and local character." They might also become "another appendage of the Executive authority" to be subjected to the "dazzling splendors of the palace and the drawing room" and the "flattery and soothing attention of a designing Executive."[2]

Congress finally acted to end the justices' circuit-riding duties when it approved the Circuit Court of Appeals Act of 1891. That act established a new set of appeals courts between the district courts and the Supreme Court.

Each justice stil has jurisdiction over one or more of the 12 federal circuits and may issue injunctions, grant bail or stay an execution in these circuits. Requests for an injunction, bail or a stay of execution go first to the presiding justice in that circuit. If denied, the application may then be made to one of the other justices.

[1] Charles Warren, *The Supreme Court in United States History*, I:88-89.
[2] Ibid. p. 674.

citadels of jealously preserved individualism. . . . Indeed a justice may go through an entire term without being once in the chambers of all the other members of the Court.

Powell describes the justices and their staffs as "nine small independent law firms."[89]

Retirement

Neither the Constitution nor the law has anything to say about when or under what circumstances a justice should retire from service on the Supreme Court. Justices are appointed for life and "shall hold their Offices during good Behavior," according to Article III, Section 1 of the Constitution.

Forty-four justices have resigned from the court; one was impeached, tried and acquitted; a few others have been threatened with impeachment.

Of the 44 who resigned, most did so because of old age or mental or physical ill health.

Forty-seven justices died while on the court. Three who had announced their retirements died before their resignations took effect. Other reasons for resigning have included matters of conscience, the desire to do other work and the threat of scandal or impeachment.

Until 1869, to keep drawing a salary, many older justices stayed on the job. Until that year, a retired justice received no compensation for his service after retirement. The Judiciary Statute of 1869 provided that any judge who had served on any federal court for at least 10 years, and was 70 or older, could resign from the bench and continue to receive his regular salary until he died.

The law now provides that a justice, if he wishes, may retire at age 70 after having served 10 years or at age 65 after 15 years of service, with compensation commensurate with his salary.

But despite old age or poor health, a number of justices have resisted leaving their seats until subjected to considerable pressure from their colleagues on the court.

After the election of President Andrew Jackson in 1832, Chief Justice John Marshall and Justice Gabriel Duvall (1811-1835), both in failing health, were reluctant to resign because they feared that the "radical" new president would choose equally "radical" new justices to take their places. Marshall remained on the court until his death in 1835, and Duvall submitted his resignation the same year after learning that Jackson intended to nominate as his successor Roger B. Taney, of whom Duvall approved.

By 1869 it was apparent that Justice Robert C. Grier (1846-1870) was both physically and mentally unable to carry out his duties. Early the next year, all the other justices formed a committee to tell Grier that "it was their unanimous opinion that he ought to resign." Soon after being told that by the committee, Grier submitted his resignation.

In his book on the Supreme Court, Charles Evans Hughes recounts the difficulties that the justices had in convincing Justice Stephen J. Field (1863-1897) to resign.

Some justices have stayed too long on the bench. An unfortunate illustration was that of Justice Grier who had failed perceptibly at the time of the first argument of the legal tender case. As the decision was delayed, he did not participate in it. A committee of the Court waited upon Justice Grier to advise him of the desirability of his retirement and the unfortunate consequences of his being in a position to cast a deciding vote in an important case when he was not able properly to address himself to it.

Justice Field tarried too long on the bench. . . . It occurred to the other members of the Court that Justice Field had served on a committee which waited upon Justice Grier to suggest his retirement, and it was thought that recalling that to his memory might aid him to decide to retire. Justice Harlan was deputed to make the suggestion. He went over to Justice Field, who was sitting alone on a settee in the robing room apparently oblivious of his surroundings, and after arousing him gradually approached the question, asking if he did not recall how anxious the Court had become with respect to Justice Grier's condition and the feeling of the other Justices that in his own interest and in that of the Court he should give up his work. Justice Harlan asked if Justice Field did not remember what had been said to Justice Grier on that occasion. The old man listened, gradually became alert and finally, with his eyes blazing with the old fire of youth, he burst out:

"Yes! And a dirtier day's work I never did in my life!"

That was the end of that effort of the brethren of the Court to induce Justice Field's retirement; he did resign not long after. [90]

In recounting the Grier and Field resignations, Hughes also described the "agreeable spectacle of Justice Holmes at eighty-five doing his share of work, or even more, with the same energy and brilliance that he showed twenty years ago." [91] But in 1932 after he had become Chief Justice, Hughes was obliged to suggest to Holmes, then 90 years old, that he resign. Holmes, doubtless recalling the Grier and Field cases, resigned immediately.

Motives for Resignation

At least three justices have resigned because of the dictates of conscience. Justice John A. Campbell (1853-1861) resigned soon after the outbreak of the Civil War to return to his native Alabama despite the fact that he had opposed secession and had freed all of his own slaves. Justice Benjamin R. Curtis (1851-1857) resigned after disagreeing with Chief Justice Taney over the Dred Scott decision; Curtis, a strong advocate of freedom for slaves once they were on free territory, felt he could no longer serve on a court which had issued the Dred Scott decision, and retired, for that and other reasons. Justice Tom C. Clark (1949-1967) resigned to avoid any possible charges of conflict-of-interest after his son, Ramsey, was appointed attorney general.

A number of justices left the court to run for elective office or to take other work. The first Chief Justice, John Jay, resigned in 1795 to become governor of New York. Five years later, he declined reappointment as Chief Justice because he felt that the court lacked "the energy, weight and dignity which are essential to its affording due support to the national government." [92]

Justice Charles Evans Hughes resigned in 1916 to run unsuccessfully for the presidency. Fourteen years later he returned as Chief Justice. Arthur J. Goldberg resigned in 1965 to become U.S. ambassador to the United Nations.

Abe Fortas, the only justice ever to resign amidst charges of judicial misconduct, submitted his resignation on May 14, 1969, a few days after *Life* magazine had published reports that Fortas, during his first year on the court, had received the first of what were to be annual fees of $20,000 from the family foundation of Louis Wolfson. Wolfson was later convicted of violating federal securities laws. In submitting his resignation, Fortas denied any wrongdoing, saying that the fee in question had been returned and the relationship terminated. He was resigning

Compulsory Retirement?

There have been repeated — if so far unsuccessful — suggestions that a constitutional amendment be enacted to require justices of the Supreme Court to retire at age 70 or 75. Justice Owen J. Roberts expressed his support for such a proposal more than 30 years ago:

"I believe it is a wise provision. First of all, it will forestall the basis of the last attack on the court, the extreme age of the justices, and the fact that superannuated old gentlemen hung on there long after their usefulness had ceased. More than that, it tends to provide for each administration an opportunity to add new personnel to the Court, which, I think, is a good thing."[1]

Charles Fairman has written that "there are two distinct reasons for urging some scheme for compulsory retirement" of Supreme Court justices. "There is, first, the actual impairment of mental and physical powers. . . . A second reason for insuring renewal of the Court involves considerations of a different order. Rigidity of thought and obsolescence of social outlook, though more objective, may be no less real than the waning of bodily powers. When a majority of the Court cling to views of public policy no longer entertained by the community or shared by the political branches of government, a conflict arises which must be resolved."[2]

[1] Speech to the Association of the Bar of the City of New York, Dec. 11, 1948.

[2] Charles Fairman, "The Retirement of Federal Judges," *Harvard Law Review,* January 1938, p. 397.

nevertheless, he said, to quiet the controversy and enable the court to "proceed with its work without the harassment of debate concerning one of its members."[93]

Impeachment Attempts

Only a few justices have faced impeachment. The first was Samuel Chase (1796-1811). Of the eight articles of impeachment that the House voted against him in late 1804, six concerned his alleged arbitrary and improper actions at the treason and sedition trials of John Fries and James G. Callender in 1800. In its articles of impeachment, the House charged that his partisan behavior in and out of court amounted to "high Crimes and Misdemeanors" under the Constitution.

The Senate trial began on Feb. 4, 1805. Although 25 of the 34 members of the Senate were Republicans, Chase was acquitted on all counts on March 1. Soon after the acquittal, Chase's and Marshall's adversary, President Jefferson, acknowledged that the impeachment of justices was "a farce which will not be tried again."

Jefferson proved prophetic, except for several inchoate efforts in recent years to impeach Justice William O. Douglas (1939-1975) and Chief Justice Earl Warren (1953-1969).

The first impeachment attempt against Douglas came after he had stayed the execution of convicted spies Julius and Ethel Rosenberg in 1953. That resolution was tabled by the Senate Judiciary Committee after a one-day hearing.

The second effort came on April 15, 1970, a week after the Senate's rejection of President Nixon's nomination of G. Harrold Carswell to the Supreme Court. In a speech on the House floor on that date, Minority Leader Gerald R. Ford, R-Mich., charged that Douglas (1) had not disqualified himself from a 1970 Supreme Court case involving Ralph Ginzburg, publisher of *Eros* magazine, although Douglas had received $350 for a 1969 article in another magazine published by Ginzburg; (2) had allegedly sanctioned revolution in his book, *Points of Rebellion* (Random House, 1970); (3) was the author of an article entitled "Redress in Revolution" in the April 1970 issue of *Evergreen Review,* which contained a number of nude photographs; (4) practiced law in violation of federal statutes by assisting in the establishment of the Albert Parvin Foundation in 1960 and in giving the foundation legal advice; and (5) served as a consultant of the "leftish" Center for the Study of Democratic Institutions at a time when the center was the recipient of Parvin Foundation funds.

On Dec. 3, 1970, a special House subcommittee created to investigate the charges against Douglas concluded that there were no grounds for impeachment.

The efforts to impeach Chief Justice Warren never got as far as those against Douglas. Most of the opposition to Warren came from right-wing groups angered over the Warren Court's expansion of individual, civil and criminal rights. The demand for Warren's impeachment was confined, for the most part, to the fulminations of the John Birch Society and to a grass-roots bumper-sticker campaign throughout the South.

Extra-Judicial Activities

A Supreme Court justice cannot be compelled to take any extra-judicial assignments but is free to engage in such activities if he wishes to. The use of this freedom has sparked considerable controversy both inside the court and among its critics. It was Justice Douglas' extra-judicial activities that prompted the 1970 impeachment effort against him.

A Yen for Politics

The extra-judicial activities that cause most concern are those which seem to have a political motive. Before 1900, the political activities of the justices involved a generally less-than-subtle quest for elective office or outright endorsement of or opposition to political candidates.

As Justice Owen J. Roberts pointed out in a 1948 speech, "every justice who has ever sat on that Court who was bitten by political ambition and has actively promoted his own candidacy for office has hurt his own career as a judge and has hurt the Court."[94]

The early justices did not hesitate to campaign openly for their party's candidates. Justices Samuel Chase (1796-1811) and Bushrod Washington (1799-1829) campaigned actively for presidential candidates John Adams and Charles Pinckney, respectively, in 1800. Chase's campaigning was denounced by the anti-Federalist press, which complained, somewhat disingenuously, that he was neglecting his court duties.

Other political-minded 19th century justices included Smith Thompson (1823-1843), John McLean (1830-1861), Salmon P. Chase (the Chief Justice — 1864-1873 — who presided over the Senate impeachment trial of President Andrew Johnson), David Davis (1862-1877) and Stephen J.

Field (1863-1897). Like Chief Justice Jay before him, Justice Thompson, a Democrat, ran for governor of New York in 1828 but, unlike Jay, conducted an all-out campaign — which he lost.

Justice McLean, who before coming to the court in 1830 had served in the Cabinets of Presidents James Monroe and John Quincy Adams, sought and failed to receive his party's presidential nomination in 1836, 1848, 1852 and 1856. Referring to McLean specifically and to the tendency of justices during that period to become involved in politics, Alexander Bickel wrote "that the recurrence of justices with manifest political aspirations would in time destroy an institution whose strength derives from consent based on confidence." The conduct of justices acting upon their "manifest political aspirations," Bickel continued, "is awkward, unseemly and may give occasion for dire suspicions." [95]

Before his appointment as Chief Justice in 1864, Salmon P. Chase had been a U.S. senator, a governor, a Cabinet member and a presidential candidate. His political activities did not cease on the court. From the bench in 1868 he unsuccessfully sought the presidential nomination of both parties.

Justice David Davis accepted nomination as a minor party candidate for president in 1872 before resigning from the court in 1877 to serve in the Senate. Stephen J. Field periodically indicated his availability for the Democratic presidential nomination.

Far fewer justices have sought elective office in the 20th century. Charles Evans Hughes resigned his seat on the court to run for president in 1916. Justice Robert H. Jackson was approached to run for governor of New York. Presidents Roosevelt in 1944 and Truman in 1948 both considered Justice William O. Douglas as a running mate. After President Eisenhower suffered a heart attack, Chief Justice Earl Warren was widely considered a possible Republican presidential nominee in 1956.

1876 Electoral Commission

One ostensibly public-spirited activity on the part of five justices ended up involving the court in one of its most serious political controversies when Justices Nathan Clifford (1858-1881), Samuel F. Miller (1862-1890), Stephen J. Field (1863-1897), William Strong (1870-1880) and Joseph P. Bradley (1870-1892) were appointed to serve on the electoral commission which resolved the disputed presidential election between Democratic candidate Samuel J. Tilden and Republican candidate Rutherford B. Hayes in 1876.

Congress set up the commission in January 1877 and specified that it be composed of 15 members: three Republicans and two Democrats from the Senate, two Republicans and three Democrats from the House and two Democrats and two Republicans from the Supreme Court. The court itself was to choose a fifth justice. The court finally selected Bradley, a Republican. Dexter Perkins and Glyndon G. Van Deusen wrote that "Justice Bradley, at first in favor of giving Florida's electoral vote to Tilden, changed his mind between midnight and the morning of the day the decision was announced; there is considerable evidence that he yielded to Republican pressure." [96] The commission's vote, announced Feb. 10, 1877, favored Hayes, and Congress acquiesced on March 2, 1877.

Charles Warren pointed out that the justices' service on this commission did not enhance the court's prestige.

"The partisan excitement caused by this election and by the inauguration of Hayes led some newspapers to assert that public confidence in the judges had been weakened, and that the country would be the less willing to accept the doctrines laid down by the Court." [97]

'Public Service'

Some 20th century justices have ignored the lesson of the Hayes-Tilden Electoral Commission that participation on supposedly non-partisan commissions or investigative bodies can involve the court in political controversy. Among these instances were the participation of Justice Joseph R. Lamar (1911-1916) in international arbitration cases; Justice Owen J. Roberts' role on the German-American Mixed Claims Commission and the Pearl Harbor Review Commission and, most controversially, Justice Robert H. Jackson's prosecution of Nazi war criminals at the Nuremberg Nazi trials, and Chief Justice Earl Warren's role as head of a seven-member commission to investigate the assassination of President John F. Kennedy.

Jackson at Nuremberg. Several justices were troubled by Jackson's one-year absence (1945-1946) because of his war-trial duties. Chief Justice Harlan F. Stone had opposed Jackson's acceptance of the assignment, and some of the other justices were angry about the extra work that Jackson's absence imposed on them. The situation became even worse after Stone's death in April 1946.

As John P. Frank wrote: "Taking a justice away from his primary duty can be done only at the expense of that duty. Stone's acute bitterness over the burdens placed upon the court by the absence of Jackson (who, Stone sputtered, was off running a lynching bee at Nuremberg) is understandable. Such extra-judicial work may also involve justices in controversies that lower the prestige so valuable to the court." [98]

But the fact that the court did suffer some loss of prestige because of Jackson's role at Nuremberg had less to do with the workload burdens placed on the other justices than with Jackson's assault on Justice Hugo L. Black, issued from Nuremberg. "The most recent direct outbreak of one justice against another was Jackson's attack on Black at the time of the appointment of Chief Justice Vinson in 1946. Jackson, who was abroad at Nuremberg trying German war criminals at the time and who had deeply desired the place for himself, apparently felt that Black was in some way responsible for the appointment of Vinson. He issued a vitriolic public statement denouncing Black for having participated in a certain case in which Jackson felt that Black should have disqualified himself." Amidst the publicity that the statement received, Justice Black "maintained a complete silence," wrote Frank.[99]

Somewhat surprisingly, Justice Felix Frankfurter did not share his colleagues' resentment of Jackson's role in the Nuremberg trials. Years before his appointment to the Supreme Court in 1939 and after his retirement in 1962, Justice Frankfurter opposed the participation of justices in any public activities that were not strictly relevant to their judicial responsibilities.

In 1929, for example, Professor Frankfurter had written that "In suggesting that judges engage in public activities off the bench, we are in danger of forgetting that it is the business of judges to be judges. . . . It is necessary for judges to be less worldly than others in order to be more judicial." [100] After his retirement as a Supreme Court justice in 1962, Frankfurter also criticized Chief Justice Earl Warren's decision to head the investigation of President Kennedy's assassination.

Although Frankfurter resigned immediately from the American Civil Liberties Union, the National Association for the Advancement of Colored People and even the Harvard Club when named to the court, he nevertheless served on several presidential and national commissions while serving as a member of the court.

The Warren Commission. To ascertain all the facts and circumstances relating to the assassination of President Kennedy, President Johnson created a seven-man investigating commission on Nov. 29, 1963. Chief Justice Warren agreed to head the commission, which also included Sens. Richard B. Russell, D-Ga., and John Sherman Cooper, R-Ky.; Reps. Hale Boggs, D-La., and Gerald R. Ford, R-Mich.; Allen W. Dulles, former director of the CIA; and John J. McCloy, former disarmament adviser to President Kennedy.

The Warren Commission released its findings on Sept. 27, 1964, concluding that Lee Harvey Oswald, "acting alone and without advice or assistance," had shot President Kennedy. Before the report was released, critics of Warren's performance on the court denounced the Chief Justice for neglecting his judicial duties and for participating in such a "political" undertaking. After the findings were released, those convinced that there had been a conspiracy to kill Kennedy joined in the criticism.

White House Advisers

Justice Frankfurter's continuing interest in political and other non-judicial matters was particularly evident in his role as adviser to President Franklin D. Roosevelt on a variety of matters, foreign and domestic. During the spring and summer of 1939, for example, Frankfurter sent almost 300 notes to Roosevelt warning of the threat posed by Hitler and advising the president of the actions that should be taken to counter the German threat. These and subsequent actions led observers to label Frankfurter the "outside insider in the Roosevelt administration." [101]

Supreme Court justices have been giving advice to presidents and other elected officials since the time of the first Chief Justice, John Jay. This informal relationship generally has resulted in criticism of the justices and the court. When President Roosevelt indicated at a press conference in September 1939 that he had discussed the situation in Europe with Justices Harlan Fiske Stone and Felix Frankfurter, there was a storm of protest over the involvement of justices in the foreign policy deliberations and decisions of the executive branch. Stone thereafter refused all invitations to confer with the president. Frankfurter, however, continued advising Roosevelt and his successors.

A more recent example is the advice that Justice Abe Fortas continued to give President Lyndon Johnson after Fortas' appointment to the court in 1965. Fortas' role as an adviser to Johnson was a major factor in his failure to win Senate confirmation as Chief Justice in 1968. It likely played some part in events leading to Fortas' resignation from the court in May 1969.

James F. Simon described the circumstances leading to Fortas' resignation. In the summer of 1968: "President Johnson named Associate Justice Abe Fortas to succeed Chief Justice Warren. At first, anti-Fortas forces, led by Republican Senator Robert P. Griffin of Michigan, opposed the nomination primarily because it had been made by a

'lame duck' president. At the Senate's confirmation hearings, Fortas ran into deeper trouble. The chief justice-designate, it was learned, had counseled the president on national policy and had even done some behind-the-scenes lobbying on the president's behalf while sitting on the Supreme Court. Later, when Fortas admitted that he had received $15,000 for conducting a series of seminars at American University, his ethics as well as his politics were brought into question. As a result, his nomination as Chief Justice languished and was finally withdrawn by President Johnson." [102]

Fortas retained his seat as an associate justice. But in May 1969, *Life* magazine revealed that since becoming a justice Fortas had accepted — and then returned several months later — $20,000 from a charitable foundation controlled by the family of indicted stock manipulator Louis E. Wolfson. Shortly thereafter, Fortas resigned. In a letter to Chief Justice Earl Warren on May 14, 1969, Fortas stated:

> There has been no wrongdoing on my part....
> There has been no default in the performance of my judicial duties in accordance with the high standards of the office I hold. So far as I am concerned, the welfare and maximum effectiveness of the Court to perform its critical role in our system of government are factors that are paramount to all others. It is this consideration that prompts my resignation which, I hope, by terminating the public controversy, will permit the Court to proceed with its work without the harassment of debate concerning one of its members. [103]

Perquisites

The scandal surrounding Justice Fortas' acceptance of a fee from the Wolfson Foundation prompted Chief Justice Warren, shortly before his resignation, to urge adoption of a judicial code of ethics requiring judges to file an annual report on investments, assets, income, gifts and liabilities and prohibiting them from accepting compensation other than their judicial salaries.

In 1973 the Judicial Conference, under Chief Justice Warren Burger, adopted resolutions asking judges to report gifts of more than $100 and any income from outside work. Indebtedness or stock earnings need not be reported. The ethics code for federal judges does not require Supreme Court justices to file income disclosure reports. But since passage of the 1978 Ethics in Government Act (PL 95-521), the justices have been required to file annual statements disclosing their income and assets.

Since each justice is paid an annual salary of $88,700 — the Chief Justice makes $92,400 — there is little need for a justice to seek outside sources of income. This was not always the case, however. Some of the early justices were so strapped for money and so penuriously reimbursed for their services on the court that they were obliged to seek additional sources of income. *(Salaries of the Justice, p. 100)*

The other perquisites of the justices' office include two secretaries, a messenger and three law clerks. Like the Chief Justice, they also have their own offices, the services of a court barber and the use of the court dining room, exercise room and library. Unlike the Chief Justice, however, the associate justices are not provided with a government-paid car and chauffeur and must get to and from work on their own.

Supporting Personnel

Compared to the executive and legislative branches of the federal government, the Supreme Court employs few people and spends relatively little money. Only about 300 people now work for the court, and its recent annual budgets have been in the comparatively modest $10-million range.

Some court employees, like the clerk of the court, the marshal, the reporter of decisions, the press officer, the librarian and their staffs, as well as pages and security officers, are appointed by the court. The law clerks are chosen by the justices themselves. In addition, several other groups work with the court but are not employees of it. These include the Office of Solicitor General, the Supreme Court bar, the Federal Judicial Center, the Administrative Office of the U.S. Courts, the U.S. Judicial Conference and the Supreme Court Historical Association.

Solicitor General

The solicitor general, the third highest-ranked official in the Department of Justice, is appointed by the president to represent the U.S. government before the Supreme Court. He decides which cases the government should ask the court to review and what the government's legal position toward them will be. He and his staff prepare the government's briefs and supporting data and argue the government's case before the court. When he chooses not to argue a case himself he assigns the task to one of his staff. A few cases of particular importance may be argued by the attorney general, the solicitor general's superior.

One observer who spent many years in the Office of the Solicitor General wrote that the solicitor general "may not unfairly be described as the highest government official who acts primarily as a lawyer. He has few administrative responsibilities; he can devote his time to studying the legal problems which come before him. Moreover, he must stand on his own feet when he is presenting the most important government cases to the Supreme Court. . . . The solicitor general regards himself — and the Supreme Court regards him — not only as an officer of the executive branch but also as an officer of the Court." [104]

The principal duties of the solicitor general's office are to decide which cases the government should appeal from the lower courts, to review the briefs in those cases written by branches of the Justice Department or the independent agencies of the government, and to participate in oral arguments before the court. The briefs that are reviewed can be approved without change or totally rewritten. Most are revised and modified to some extent in collaboration with the author of the draft.

The Office of the Solicitor General has a heavy workload. During the October 1975 term, for example, the solicitor general participated in 2,219 cases — about 47 percent of the court's total caseload. And of the 179 cases argued in that term, the solicitor general was a party or *amicus curiae* in 121 of them. Lawyers from the solicitor general's office are the only attorneys who still wear frock coats and striped trousers when presenting oral arguments.

The solicitor general is under considerable pressure to limit the number of cases that he brings before the court. As Robert L. Stern noted, this pressure is "partly self-serving and partly not." On the more objective level, the solicitor general

> . . .is aware of the necessity from the standpoint of the effective administration of the judicial system of restricting the number of cases taken to the Supreme Court to the number that the Court can hear. This alone permits the Court to give adequate consideration to the important matters which the highest tribunal in the land should decide. . . . A heavy additional burden would be imposed on the Court if the government, with its great volume of litigation, disregarded that policy and acted like the normal litigant who wants to take one more shot at reversing a decision which is obviously wrong because he lost.

> The selfish reason for the Solicitor General's self-restraint in petitioning for certiorari is to give the Court confidence in government petitions. It is hoped and believed — although no one who has not been on the Court can be sure — that the Court will realize that the Solicitor General will not assert that an issue is of general importance unless it is — and that confidence in the Solicitor General's attempt to adhere to the Court's own standards will cause the Court to grant more government petitions. [105]

The post of solicitor general was created by Congress in 1870 with the establishment of the Department of Justice. Before that time, the functions of the solicitor general were carried out by the attorney general. Congress explained that its purpose in establishing the new office was to provide "a staff of law officers sufficiently numerous and of sufficient ability to transact this law business of the Government in all parts of the United States." The law also said that the solicitor general should be "a man of sufficient learning, ability and experience that he can be sent . . . into any court wherever the government has any interest in litigation, and there present the case of the United States as it should be presented." [106]

At present, the solicitor general is paid the Executive Level III salary of $55,387.50 a year.

As far as the general public is concerned, solicitors general are fairly anonymous figures, although several — Taft, Reed, Jackson and Thurgood Marshall — later became justices of the Supreme Court. One recent exception was Robert H. Bork (1973-77). Bork's notoriety, however, had nothing to do with his court-related duties but, rather, with his role in the famous "Saturday Night Massacre" following President Nixon's decision to fire special Watergate prosecutor Archibald Cox — himself a former solicitor general (1961-65) — on Oct. 20, 1973. Attorney General Elliot Richardson and Deputy Attorney General William Ruckelshaus resigned rather than obey Nixon's order to fire Cox. After the resignations of Richardson and Ruckelshaus, Bork, as the highest-ranked official left in the Justice Department, took command and fired Cox.

Clerk of the Court

The clerk of the court is the chief administrative officer of the court, and his office is responsible for conducting almost all its business. The office was established by the

Solicitors General

Name	Term		State of Origin	President
Benjamin H. Bristow	Oct. 11, 1870	Nov. 15, 1872	Kentucky	Grant
Samuel F. Phillips	Nov. 15, 1872	May 3, 1885	North Carolina	Grant
John Goode	May 1, 1885	Aug. 5, 1886	Virginia	Cleveland
George A. Jenks	July 30, 1886	May 29, 1889	Pennsylvania	Cleveland
Orlow W. Chapman	May 29, 1889	Jan. 19, 1890	New York	Harrison
William Howard Taft	Feb. 4, 1890	Mar. 20, 1892	Ohio	Harrison
Charles H. Aldrich	Mar. 21, 1892	May 28, 1893	Illinois	Harrison
Lawrence Maxwell Jr.	Apr. 6, 1893	Jan. 30, 1895	Ohio	Cleveland
Holmes Conrad	Feb. 6, 1895	July 8, 1897	Virginia	Cleveland
John K. Richards	July 1, 1897	Mar. 16, 1903	Ohio	McKinley
Henry M. Hoyt	Feb. 25, 1903	Mar. 31, 1909	Pennsylvania	Roosevelt
Lloyd Wheaton Bowers	Apr. 1, 1909	Sept. 9, 1910	Illinois	Taft
Frederick W. Lehman	Dec. 12, 1910	July 15, 1912	Missouri	Taft
William Marshall Bullitt	July 16, 1912	Mar. 11, 1913	Kentucky	Taft
John William Davis	Aug. 30, 1913	Nov. 26, 1918	West Virginia	Wilson
Alexander C. King	Nov. 27, 1918	May 23, 1920	Georgia	Wilson
William L. Frierson	June 1, 1920	June 30, 1921	Tennessee	Wilson
James M. Beck	June 30, 1921	June 7, 1925	New Jersey	Harding
William D. Mitchell	June 4, 1925	Mar. 5, 1929	Minnesota	Coolidge
Charles Evans Hughes Jr.	May 27, 1929	Apr. 16, 1930	New York	Hoover
Thomas D. Thacher	Mar. 22, 1930	May 4, 1933	New York	Hoover
James Crawford Biggs	May 4, 1933	Mar. 24, 1935	North Carolina	Roosevelt
Stanley Reed	Mar. 23, 1935	Jan. 30, 1938	Kentucky	Roosevelt
Robert H. Jackson	Mar. 5, 1938	Jan. 17, 1940	New York	Roosevelt
Francis Biddle	Jan. 22, 1940	Sept. 4, 1941	Pennsylvania	Roosevelt
Charles Fahy	Nov. 15, 1941	Sept. 27, 1945	New Mexico	Roosevelt
J. Howard McGrath	Oct. 4, 1945	Oct. 7, 1946	Rhode Island	Truman
Philip B. Perlman	July 30, 1947	Aug. 15, 1952	Maryland	Truman
Walter J. Cummings Jr.	Dec. 2, 1952	Mar. 1, 1953	Illinois	Truman
Simon E. Sobeloff	Feb. 10, 1954	July 19, 1956	Maryland	Eisenhower
J. Lee Rankin	Aug. 4, 1956	Jan. 23, 1961	Nebraska	Eisenhower
Archibald Cox	Jan. 24, 1961	July 31, 1965	Massachusetts	Kennedy
Thurgood Marshall	Aug. 11, 1965	Aug. 30, 1967	New York	Johnson
Erwin N. Griswold	Oct. 12, 1967	June 25, 1973	Massachusetts	Johnson
Robert H. Bork	June 26, 1973	Jan. 20, 1977	Connecticut	Nixon
Wade Hampton McCree Jr.	March 4, 1977	June 30, 1981	Michigan	Carter
Rex E. Lee	Aug. 6, 1981		Utah	Reagan

first formal rule of the court, adopted in February 1790. Through the years, the clerk's duties have increased enormously. The clerk now has the largest staff at the court — more than thirty people.

The responsibilities of the clerk include:

(a) the administration of the court's dockets and argument calendars;

(b) the receipt and recording of all motions, petitions, jurisdictional statements, briefs and other documents filed with the court;

(c) the distribution of those various papers to the justices;

(d) the collection of filing fees and the assessment of costs;

(e) the preparation and maintenance of the court's order list and journal, upon which are entered all the court's formal judgments and mandates;

(f) the preparation of the court's formal judgments and mandates;

(g) the notification to counsel and lower courts of all formal actions taken by the court, including written opinions;

(h) the supervision of the printing of briefs and appendices after review has been granted in *in forma pauperis* cases;

(i) the requesting and securing of the certified record below upon the grant of review or other direction of the court;

(j) the supervision of the admission of attorneys to the Supreme Court bar, as well as occasional disbarments;

(k) the constant giving of procedural advice, by telephone, mail and in person, to those counsel and litigants who need assistance as to the court's rules and procedures.

To help the clerk and his staff carry out these many functions, a computerized information system was installed in 1976. [107]

To date, there have been only 16 clerks of the court. Four of them served for a quarter of a century or more: Elias B. Caldwell (1800-1825); William T. Carroll (1827-1863); J. H. McKenney (1880-1913) and C. Elmore Cropley (1927-1952). The first clerk, John Tucker, was selected on the third day of the court's first session, Feb. 3, 1790, to oversee the courtroom and library, manage subordinate

Clerks of the Supreme Court

Name	Term	State of Origin
John Tucker	1790-1791	Massachusetts
Samuel Bayard	1791-1800	Pennsylvania
Elias B. Caldwell	1800-1825	New Jersey
William Griffith	1826-1827	New Jersey
William T. Carroll	1827-1863	Maryland
D. W. Middleton	1863-1880	District of Columbia
J. H. McKenney	1880-1913	Maryland
James D. Maher	1913-1921	New York
William R. Stansbury	1921-1927	District of Columbia
C. Elmore Cropley	1927-1952	District of Columbia
Harold B. Willey	1952-1956	Oregon
John T. Fey	1956-1958	Virginia
James R. Browning	1958-1961	Montana
John F. Davis	1961-1970	Maine
E. Robert Seaver	1970-1972	Missouri
Michael Rodak Jr.	1972-1981	West Virginia
Alexander L. Stevas	1981-	Pennsylvania

employees, collect the salaries of the justices and find them lodgings when necessary.

The 1790 rule that established the position of clerk prohibited him from practicing law before the court while he was a clerk. In the early years the clerk performed many of the duties later taken over by the reporter and the marshal. So varied were the responsibilities of the early clerks that they were described as a combination business manager-errand boy for the justices and the lawyers who appeared before the court.

The importance of the clerk was summed up nearly a century ago by a man who had had considerable experience with the clerk's office, Augustus H. Garland, former governor of Arkansas, former Democratic senator from that state and former U.S. attorney general.

Garland wrote:

It is well to note that it is quite important for lawyers practicing in that Court to see much of the Clerk's office and to know its workings. If any motion is to be had or proceedings asked in Court not specifically provided for by law or rule, it is wise to seek advice there beforehand.... Many useless and sometimes unpleasant collisions between the Court and counsel are avoided by this precaution. Even the oldest and most experienced attorneys are not ashamed to consult the Clerk's office and they do not hesitate to do so.[108]

Although the Office of the Clerk of the Court was established in 1790, provision was not made for his salary until nine years later. In 1799 Congress provided "That the compensation to the Clerk of the Supreme Court of the United States shall be as follows, to wit: for his attendance in Court, ten dollars per day, and for his other services, double the fees of the clerk of the Supreme Court of the state in which the Supreme Court of the United States shall be holden." [109]

For almost 100 years the office of the clerk was self-supporting. It paid salaries and other expenses of its operations out of filing fees. The generous fees and other allowances gave some of the early clerks a handsome annual stipend. In 1881, for example, the clerk's net income was almost $30,000 a year — only slightly less than the president's and considerably more than the justices'.[110] Strict accountability for the court's funds was not imposed until 1883. The filing fees now go to the U.S. Treasury, and Congress appropriates the money for the salaries and expenses of the clerk's office. The clerk now has an annual salary of $56,500.

Marshal of the Court

The post of marshal of the court was not formally established until 1867. Many of the duties assigned to the marshal at that time were performed by the marshal of the district in which the court was located. Between 1794 and 1867, for example, the 12 men who served as marshal of the District of Columbia also served, informally, as marshal of the court. The first of these was David Lennox and the last was David Gooding.

In the Judiciary Act of 1867, Congress first gave the court authority to appoint a marshal and, if necessary, to remove him from his post, and to fix his compensation. Several of his tasks, which included ensuring the security of the court, overseeing its protocol functions and supervising payment of its expenses, formerly had been performed by the clerk of the court.

The marshal's current functions include maintaining order in the building and in the courtroom: he directs the court's police force of seventy men and women. They supervise the security of the building and check the briefcases and purses of all visitors who enter the building. The marshal and his aides also receive visiting dignitaries and escort the justices to formal functions outside the court. He supervises inaugural ceremonies for new justices and arranges memorial services for those who have died.

During public sessions of the court, the marshal (or his deputy) and the clerk — both dressed in cutaways — station themselves at either end of the bench. At exactly 10 a.m., the marshal pounds the gavel and announces: "The Honorable, the Chief Justice and the Associate Justices of the Supreme Court of the United States." As the justices take their seats, he calls for silence by crying "Oyez" ("Hear ye") three times and announces: "All persons having business before the honorable, the Supreme Court of the United States, are admonished to draw near and give their attention, for the court is now sitting. God save the United States and this honorable Court."

The marshal is responsible for seating arrangements during the public sessions and may refuse admission to

Marshals of the Court

Richard C. Parsons (1867-1872)
John C. Nicolay (1872-1887)
John Montgomery Wright (1888-1915)
Frank Key Green (1915-1938)
Thomas E. Waggaman (1938-1952)
T. Perry Lippitt (1952-1972)
Frank M. Hepler (1972-1976)
Alfred Wong (1976-   )

anyone whose attire or conduct does not meet court standards. During oral argument, the marshal or his assistant flashes the white and red lights to warn counsel that his time for presenting arguments is about to expire.

The marshal also serves as the court's business manager and paymaster. He pays the salaries of the justices and all other court employees and disburses other court funds. In addition, the marshal is directed to "serve and execute all process and orders issued by the Court or a member thereof." Today, the marshal of the court delegates the actual serving of papers — usually disbarment orders — to U.S. marshals. In earlier days, serving of papers was sometimes more dramatic.

Marshal Frank K. Green (1915-38), for example, served a subpoena on business tycoon J. Pierpont Morgan Jr. when government officials were trying to regain possession of Martha Washington's will, which Morgan's father had allegedly stolen. Upon receiving the subpoena, Morgan returned the will.

The marshal also appoints and has jurisdiction over the court's messengers, who replaced the court pages in the early 1970s.

The marshal currently receives an annual salary of $49,000.

Reporter of Decisions

The reporter of decisions is responsible for editing the opinions of the court and supervising their printing and publication in the official *United States Reports*. Publication is a slow process. The reporter and his staff of ten check all citations after the opinions of the justices have been delivered, correct typographical and other errors in the opinions and add the headnotes, the voting lineup of the justices and the names of counsel that now appear in the published version of the opinions.

The court's orders and decisions are first circulated as "Preliminary Prints." Users of these preliminary prints are "requested to notify the reporter of decisions ... of any typographical or other formal errors, in order that corrections may be made before the bound volume goes to press." The orders and decisions are printed by the U.S. Government Printing Office and sold by the Superintendent of Documents.

The post of reporter of decisions had a rather informal beginning. The first reporter, Alexander J. Dallas (1790-1800), was self-appointed. Before the court moved to Philadelphia, Dallas had published a volume on Pennsylvania court decisions. When the court began meeting in Philadelphia in 1791, Dallas' book contained the cases of both the Pennsylvania court and the Supreme Court. Most accounts of the early Supreme Court indicate that Dallas, a lawyer, undertook the first reports as a public service. Dallas — who was also a journalist, editor, patron of the arts and secretary of the Treasury (1814-1816) — published four volumes of decisions covering the Supreme Court's first decade.

Dallas was succeeded in his unofficial post by William Cranch in 1802.

While reporting on the court's decisions, Cranch continued to sit as a judge and later chief justice of the circuit court in Washington, D.C. During Cranch's service as reporter of decisions, the justices began supplementing their oral opinions with written texts in important cases. This was of immeasurable assistance to Cranch and subsequent reporters. Cranch, whose reports were highly praised

Reporters of Decisions

Name	Term of Office
Alexander J. Dallas	1790-1800
William Cranch	1801-1815
Henry Wheaton	1816-1827
Richard Peters Jr.	1828-1842
Benjamin C. Howard	1843-1860
Jeremiah S. Black	1861-1862
John W. Wallace	1867-1874
William T. Otto	1875-1882
J. C. Bancroft Davis	1883-1902
Charles Henry Butler	1902-1915
Ernest Knaebel	1916-1943
Walter Wyatt	1946-1963
Henry Putzel Jr.	1964-1979
Henry C. Lind	1979-

for their accuracy and clarity, believed that public scrutiny of opinions was needed to keep the justices from making arbitrary decisions.

Cranch's successor, Henry Wheaton, was the first reporter formally appointed by the court. In 1816 Congress provided for publication of court decisions and, a year later, set the reporter's salary at $1,000 a year. The Judiciary Act of 1817 mandated that, for this salary, the reporter had to publish each opinion within six months of a decision and provide 80 copies to the secretary of state for distribution. The reports continued to be sold to the public, at $5 a volume, and the reporter was still able to share in the profits, such as they were.

After he retired in 1827 to become minister to Denmark, Wheaton and his successor, Richard Peters Jr., became involved themselves in a Supreme Court case.[111]

Peters was determined to increase the then-meager sales of the reports and his own profits as well. He therefore decided to revise and streamline the earlier reports and publish them in "Peters' Condensed Reports" at a price of $36. Since the purchase of Peters' reports would make it unnecessary for the interested public to purchase Wheaton's reports, the former reporter of decisions sued Peters, charging a violation of copyright. The court ruled, however, that court opinions were in the public domain.

As Augustus H. Garland noted in his book on the Supreme Court, "The office of the Reporter is not a ... bed of roses. The work is constant, arduous and exacting. A failure to give full scope in the syllabus ... to the utterances of a judge brings wrath upon him."[112] Reporters Benjamin C. Howard (1843-1860) and John W. Wallace (1867-1874) felt the wrath of several justices.

In 1855 Justice Peter V. Daniel (1842-1860) wrote to reporter Howard complaining that his name had not been inserted at the beginning of his dissenting opinion and that he was henceforth uncertain that he would allow his dissents to be published in the reports. Unfortunately for Howard, he had omitted Daniel's name. Justices Noah H. Swayne (1862-1881) and Nathan Clifford (1858-1881) complained that reporter Wallace failed to publish their opinions or butchered them with his editing.

Wallace was the last reporter to have his name identified with the court's published reports. The first 90 volumes of the reports were titled 1-4 Dall.; 1-15 Cranch; 1-12

Wheat. 1-16 Pet.; 1-24 How.; 1-2 Black and 1-23 Wall. After 1874 the name of the reporter was no longer used as part of the formal citation.

The reporter of decisions is now paid an annual salary of $54,500. The first two reporters, Dallas and Cranch, were paid no salary at all and relied on the sale of their reports or on outside jobs for their income. Congress provided an annual stipend of $1,000 in 1816 but reporters were still obliged to rely on sales of the reports to supplement their incomes. Henry Wheaton, for example, argued a number of cases before the Supreme Court and then reported them.

Supreme Court Bar

When the Supreme Court first convened in February 1790, one of its first actions was to establish qualifications for lawyers who wished to practice before the court. Rule 2, adopted at that time, provided that "it shall be requisite to the admission of attorneys and counsellors to practice in this court, that they shall have been such for three years past in the Supreme Court of the State to which they respectively belong, and that their private and professional character shall appear to be fair."

Qualifications

The two requirements for admission to the Supreme Court bar — acceptable personal and professional character, and qualification to practice before a state's or territory's highest court — have remained the same since 1790. In nearly 200 years since the court was established, some 150,000 attorneys have been admitted to the Supreme Court bar. Some 6,000 are now admitted each year.

The bar of the Supreme Court has been called "a heterogeneous collection of individual lawyers located in all parts of the nation. There is no permanent or formal leadership." [113] Although some lawyers seek admission to the Supreme Court bar merely for their own personal prestige, membership does have a real function. No attorney can enter an appearance in a case or by himself process any case to completion unless he is a member of the Supreme Court bar.[114] A non-member may work on a case, but at least one member of the bar must sponsor any case filed with the court.

The Royal Exchange, New York City, first home of the U.S. Supreme Court.

New Offices

During the 1970s two new support offices were added at the Supreme Court — the legal office and the curatorial office.

Created in 1973, the legal office is composed of two attorneys, known as legal officers, who assist the court with procedural questions arising from petitions for writs of certiorari and applications for extraordinary relief. They also aid some justices with their circuit duties.

The curatorial office was created in 1974 to maintain records of gifts to the court, to care for its historical collection, to develop exhibits and to answer questions from the public concerning court history and the historical collection.

An attorney who has been admitted to practice before the highest court in his home state for three years and who believes himself to have the other qualifications may apply for admission to the bar of the Supreme Court. To apply, he must submit: 1) a certificate from the presiding judge or the clerk of his home court proving his admission to its bar and his good standing, and 2) an executed copy of a court-approved form containing a personal statement from him and the statement of two sponsors, members of the Supreme Court bar who know, but are not related to, the applicant, endorsing the correctness of his statement.[115]

Before 1970 lawyers had only one means of entry which still applies — an oral motion in open court. The attorney selects a day when the court is in public session and notifies the clerk. The applicant then finds a standing member of the Supreme Court bar who is willing and able to appear in court with him. Early on the morning of his swearing-in, he appears at the office of the admissions clerk and pays a $100 admission fee. When the court convenes at 10 a.m. on the appointed day, the Chief Justice announces that admissions will be entertained at that time. The clerk then calls the sponsor to the rostrum, he requests that the applicant be admitted to the bar, and the Chief Justice announces that the motion is granted.

After all the motions have been made and granted, the new members are welcomed by the Chief Justice, and the clerk of the court administers the oath to the group.

In 1970, largely as a result of the increasing amount of time being spent on the oral motions in open session, the court began allowing applicants to submit written motions without making a formal appearance. These so-called "mail-order admissions" now constitute 80 percent or more of all admissions to the Supreme Court bar.

Attorneys can be disbarred or can resign from the Supreme Court bar. Disbarment generally follows a showing that an attorney has been disbarred from practice in some jurisdiction or "engaged in conduct unbecoming a member of the bar of this Court." [116]

To some observers, including John P. Frank, modern members of the Supreme Court bar seem to lack the dramatic flair and oratorical genius that 19th century legal luminaries like Daniel Webster, Henry Clay, John C. Calhoun and Augustus H. Garland exhibited when presenting arguments before the court.

"The most striking difference between the argument of the 19th century and that of today is the difference in the lawyers themselves. In the 19th century, there was a Supreme Court bar, a group of lawyers in or about Washington for at least portions of the year to whom other lawyers sent their cases in the same fashion that a New York lawyer today might send a piece of San Francisco business to a San Francisco lawyer," writes Frank.[117]

But, he continued, "the ease of modern transportation coupled with the desire of individual lawyers to have the experience of appearing in the Supreme Court have almost totally destroyed the system of a Supreme Court bar, so that today a very small number of appearances makes a man an unusually experienced Supreme Court practitioner. The number of lawyers under the age of sixty engaged solely in private practice who have appeared before the court a substantial number of times could be quickly counted. Today the lawyer from Little Rock takes in his own case, whereas in 1880 he would have retained A. H. Garland, who as attorney general and private counsel argued 130 cases. Jeremiah Sullivan Black presented 16 cases between 1861 and 1865 and won 13, including eight reversals of lower courts. Today a very experienced private practitioner may have argued five cases in a lifetime." [118]

Press Officer

The court's press (or public information) office is responsible for answering questions from the public and the news media and distributing information about the court and the justices. The press officer is the public spokesman for the court in matters other than the interpretation of its opinions and orders. As has been noted, the justices believe that their opinions and orders must speak for themselves.

The public information office releases the opinions and orders of the court to the press soon after they are announced in open court. The court's informal orders, the schedule of court sessions and conferences, the activities of the justices, and changes in court procedures are usually placed on a bulletin board in the public information office. Special announcements about the court or the justices are released by the office.

Some of the major news media have offices next to the public information office. The press and the public also can read the file on current petitions, motions, briefs, responses and jurisdictional statements there.

The current public information officer is only the court's third since the post was established in 1935. His salary is $48,000 a year. The public information office has a staff of three.[119]

Librarian

The Supreme Court library, which contains about 250,000 volumes, is located on the third floor of the court building. Rule 2(1) of the court limits its use to court personnel, members of the bar of the court, members of Congress, their legal staffs, and attorneys for the United States, its departments and agencies. Usually, however, the library will grant access to its books to members of the public or press who specify a particular research interest.

Since 1887, when the post of librarian was created, there have been seven court librarians. The librarian's salary is now $54,500 a year.

In the early years of the court, the justices had no library of their own, and it was not until 1812 that Congress allowed the justices to use the Library of Congress. In 1832, after repeated refusals to give the court its own library, Congress gave the justices the 2,011 law books in the Library of Congress but insisted that congressmen retain

Old City Hall, Philadelphia, home of the Supreme Court, 1791-1800.

the right to use them as well. Since the court had no librarian at the time, the clerk of the court was put in charge of the books. By 1863 the number of law books had increased to almost 16,000. In 1884 the marshal of the court was given responsibility for the court's collection of books. The post of librarian, created in 1887, remained in the marshal's department until Congress made it a separate office in 1948.

The library has the most complete available set of the printed briefs, records and appendices of court cases. It also contains all federal, state and regional reports; federal and state statutory codes; legal periodicals; legal treatises; and digests and legislative and administrative source material. There are also special collections in international law, military law, British law, patent and trademark law and Supreme Court history.

When the clerk was in charge of the library in the 19th century, lawyers and others allowed to use the library could borrow no more than three books from the library at one time. The books had to be returned within a "reasonable" time. For books that were not returned within a "reasonable" time, the clerk imposed a fine of $1 a day on the borrower. If a book was lost, the borrower had to pay twice the value of the lost book. This rule was changed to protect the court's collection. Books and other material cannot now be removed from the building, although members of the Supreme Court bar may request that material be sent to them when they are arguing a case.

Law Clerks

As the number of cases has increased over the years, the justices have relied more and more on their law clerks. In 1981 there were 32 law clerks serving the nine justices — almost twice the number employed in 1969. The Chief Justice and five of the associate justices had four clerks each, while the other three justices managed with two or three clerks. The clerks were hired by the individual justices, usually for one year, and are paid $23,087 a year for their services. Some clerks, however, stay longer than a year.

The justices have complete discretion in hiring the law clerks they want. The clerks are generally selected from candidates at the top of their classes in the country's most prestigious law schools. Some have previously clerked for a lower court judge. The nature and amount of a clerk's work depends on the work habits of the particular justice. Years ago, Justice Brandeis once asked his clerk to check every page of every volume of *United States Reports* for information that Brandeis wanted. Justice Hugo L. Black insisted that some of his clerks play tennis with him. Chief Justice Stone liked his clerks to accompany him on his walks.

As John P. Frank, who clerked for Justice Black in the early 1950s, pointed out, "the tasks of the clerks are very much the product of the whims of their justices. In general, it is the job of the clerk to be eyes and legs for his judge, finding and bringing in useful materials." [120] The two major functions of the clerks are to read, analyze and often prepare memoranda for the justices on the thousands of cases that reach the court each year and to help otherwise in whatever way a justice expects in preparing an opinion that he will deliver.

Over the years, law clerks occasionally have been the subject of controversy. In the late 1950s, for example, conservative critics claimed that the court was a hotbed of radicalism and even communism. Because some of these critics were convinced that the clerks had a strong effect on the court's more liberal opinions, they convinced a few conservative congressmen to propose that appointments of law clerks be subject to Senate confirmation. While these efforts failed, there has been continuing debate and concern about just how much influence the clerks have on the opinions of the justices.

It has even been charged that law clerks have on occasion written the opinion issued in the name of the justices, but there has been no proof that any clerk has actually authored an opinion. How much of the preliminary writing a clerk may do is a well-guarded secret.

Three of the current justices served as law clerks: Justice Byron R. White clerked for Chief Justice Fred M. Vinson in 1946-47, Justice John Paul Stevens clerked for Justice Wiley B. Rutledge in 1947-48, and Justice William H. Rehnquist clerked for Justice Robert H. Jackson in 1952-53. All three tend to minimize the influence the clerks have on the justices and their opinions.

Justice Stevens has written that "an interesting loyalty develops between clerks and their Justices. It is much like a lawyer-client relationship, close and confidential. Like a lawyer, a clerk can't tell his client, the Justice, what to do. He can only suggest what can happen if he does or doesn't do something." [121]

Justice White has said that "we couldn't get our work done without the clerks. But I don't think they influence the results here all that much. I like 'em around to hear their various views. When I served as a clerk, I don't think anything I ever did or said influenced my Justice. I felt I was doing Chief Justice Vinson a service by making sure that relevant considerations were placed before him, such as opinions from other courts, law journals, ideas of my own — things he wouldn't have time to dig up on his own." [122]

More than 20 years ago, William H. Rehnquist described his activities as clerk to Justice Jackson. "On a couple of occasions each term, Justice Jackson would ask each clerk to draft an opinion for him along lines which he suggested. If the clerk were reasonably faithful to his instructions and reasonably diligent in his work, the Justice would be quite charitable with his black pencil and paste pot. The result reached in these opinions was no less the product of Justice Jackson than those he drafted himself; in literary style, these opinions generally suffered by compari-

son with those which he had drafted. . . . The specter of the law clerk as a legal Rasputin, exerting an important influence on the cases actually decided by the Court, may be discarded at once. No published biographical materials dealing with any of the Justices suggest any such influence. I certainly learned of none during the time I spent as Clerk." [123]

Rehnquist — considered perhaps the most conservative member of the current court — criticized the clerks of the early 1950s not for their influence but their political bias. "After conceding a wide diversity of opinion among the clerks themselves, and further conceding the difficulties and possible inaccuracies inherent in political cataloguing of people, it is nonetheless fair to say that the political cast of the clerks as a group was to the 'left' of either the nation or the Court. Some of the tenets of the 'liberal' point of view which commanded the sympathy of a majority of the clerks I knew were: extreme solicitude for the claims of Communists and other criminal defendants, expansion of federal power at the expense of State power, great sympathy toward any government regulation of business — in short, the political philosophy now espoused by the Court under Chief Justice Earl Warren." [124]

Whatever the impact of the clerks on the justices and their opinions has been, they almost always remain in the shadows, inaccessible to the public and the press. The clerks talk among themselves about the views and personalities of their justices, but rarely has a clerk discussed clashes among the justices or leaked news about an opinion until it is announced in court. Such unwritten rules, as well as a clerk's loyalty to the justice he serves, account for the anonymity that surrounds the clerks during their time as staff members of the court.

The first law clerk was hired by Justice Horace Gray in 1882. As early as 1850 the justices had sought congressional approval for the hiring of an "investigating clerk" to help each justice and to copy opinions. When that request was not granted, some of the justices used employees of the court clerk's office to help them.

Justice Gray's law clerk, who had been the top graduate of Harvard Law School, served primarily as a servant and a barber, paid by the justice himself. It was not until 1886 that Congress provided $1,600 a year for a "stenographic clerk" for each justice. In the years that followed, clerks often served considerably longer than the one year they generally serve now. Chief Justices Charles Evans Hughes and William Howard Taft and Justice Frank Murphy employed law clerks who served for five years or more.

Messengers

The former page system — similar to that still used in the Congress — has been phased out in recent years and replaced by a messenger system. Messengers now are selected by the marshal of the court and perform most of the duties that the pages had performed. Each justice has one personal messenger of his own, and the court employs about six additional full-time messengers. The messengers, some of whom are college students or even college graduates, earn from $9,391 to $16,920 a year.

Before they were replaced by messengers, pages were appointed by the marshal. The early pages were chosen when they were high school freshmen; in later years, some of the young men and women who were chosen were night law school students.

When the court was in session, the pages waited behind the bench to pass notes from one justice to another, to fill water glasses or to obtain reference material from the library. When the court was not in session, they performed whatever errands the justices or other court officials needed. Robert Higbie, a former page who now works in the court's library, recounts how, as a young teen-ager, he and another page raced to open a door for Justice William O. Douglas. Once Higbie slipped and Douglas admonished him: "Next time, young man, wear rubbers."

Supporting Organizations

Four other organizations have an impact directly or indirectly on how the court operates, on its workload or the amount of public interest in the court. These organizations are the U.S. Judicial Conference, the Administrative Office of the U.S. Courts, the Federal Judicial Center and the Supreme Court Historical Association.

U.S. Judicial Conference

The Judicial Conference of the United States is the governing body for the administration of the federal judicial system. It has been called the system's "board of trustees" or "board of directors." By law, the conference is charged with carrying on "a continuous study of . . . the general rules of practice and procedure" and recommending "such changes in and addition to those rules as the Conference may deem desirable to promote simplicity in procedure, fairness in administration, the just determination of litigation and the elimination of unjustifiable expense and delay." [125]

The conference has committees or panels on court administration, budget, judicial conduct, judicial activities, review, the federal magistrates system, the bankruptcy system, the probation system, criminal law, the jury system, intercircuit assignments, rules of practice and procedure, Pacific territories, admission to practice standards and, since 1977, a special "Committee on the Bicentennial of Independence and the Constitution."

Congress, at the urging of Chief Justice William Howard Taft, created the judicial conference, then called the Judicial Conference of Senior Circuit Judges, in 1922. The conference originally consisted of the Chief Justice of the Supreme Court, the chief judges of the nine circuit courts of appeal, and the attorney general, who was at that time responsible for the administrative affairs of the courts.

Until 1940 the reports of the conference were included in the annual reports of the attorney general. When the Administrative Office of the United States Courts was created in 1939, administrative responsibility over the courts was transferred from the attorney general to the new office. The administrative office has operated under the supervision and direction of the judicial conference since that time.

The number of members on the conference has more than doubled since 1922. In the 1950s the chief judge of the U.S. Court of Claims and the U.S. Court of Customs and Patent Appeals as well as a district court judge representing each judicial circuit joined the Chief Justice and the chief judges of the 11 circuits as members of the judicial conference. In late 1978 two bankruptcy judges were added, bringing the number of members to 27. The conference has no separate budget of its own, and whatever staff assistance is needed is provided by the Administrative Office of the U.S. Courts.

Administrative Office

As its name indicates, the administrative office is responsible for supervising the administration, pay and employee benefits of the support personnel of the federal court system, except for the Supreme Court. The administrative office also reports on the procedures and caseloads of the federal courts, again except for the Supreme Court. The director and deputy director are appointed by the Supreme Court and are responsible for preparing and submitting the budgets of all 12 U.S. circuit courts of appeal and the U.S. district courts.

The administrative office is responsible for supervising federal probation officers. It also publishes, in cooperation with the Bureau of Prisons, a quarterly magazine called *Federal Probation,* which describes itself as a journal "of correctional philosophy and practice." The office's bankruptcy division administers the offices of the United States bankruptcy judges and, since 1968, the administrative affairs of United States magistrates. When the federal public defender organizations and community defender organizations were created by the Criminal Justice Act of 1970, the administrative office was given the responsibility for their budgets and payrolls as well.

Created by Congress in 1939, the Administrative Office of the U.S. Courts operates under the direction of the Judicial Conference of the United States. The director submits a report about the activities of the office, the situation of the federal courts and any recommendations for improvement to the annual meeting of the judicial conference, to Congress and to the attorney general. In fiscal year 1978, about 450 people worked in the administrative office, which had a budget of $11,750,000.

Federal Judicial Center

The Federal Judicial Center was created by Congress in 1967 "to further the development and adoption of improved judicial administration in the courts of the United States." The center serves as the research, training and development arm of the federal judiciary. Its seven-member board, headed by the Chief Justice, includes two judges from the U.S. circuit courts, three from the U.S. district courts and the director of the Administrative Office of the U.S. Courts. The board meets four times a year and the center's policy decisions are made at these meetings.

The center, located in the Dolley Madison House in Washington, D.C., holds about 100 education and training seminars each year and undertakes research projects. One such project is the development of a computerized management information system for improved administration in the courts.

The results of the center's research projects are often passed on to the U.S. Judicial Conference to assist it in making recommendations for improvement in the federal court system. The center's staff — about 100 people — is employed to carry out the board's policy decisions and the center's educational and research projects. The center's annual budget is about $8 million.

The center's most publicized and controversial project was its 1972 report of the Federal Judicial Center Study Group on the Caseload of the Supreme Court. As chairman of the center, Chief Justice Warren E. Burger chose seven respected court-seasoned lawyers to serve on the study group. The group, chaired by Professor Paul A. Freund of Harvard Law School, studied the problem for a year.

In December 1972 its report was issued. One of its major conclusions was that "The statistics of the Court's current workload, both in absolute terms and in the mounting trend, are impressive evidence that the conditions essential for the performance of the Court's mission do not exist. For an ordinary appellate court the burgeoning volume of cases would be a staggering burden; for the Supreme Court the pressures of the docket are incompatible with the appropriate fulfillment of its historic and essential functions." [126]

The study group's first and most controversial recommendation for relieving the court's workload was the creation of a National Court of Appeals. *(See box, p. 62)*

Historical Society

The Supreme Court Historical Society was founded in November 1974 as a non-profit group to increase public interest in and knowledge about the Supreme Court and the federal court system. The society collects and preserves data and memorabilia about the court's early history. The brainchild of Chief Justice Warren E. Burger, it is modeled after the White House and Capitol historical societies. It publicizes the judiciary's — particularly the Supreme Court's — contribution to the country's history on both scholarly and popular levels.

The money to operate the society comes primarily from its 2,200 members. Membership fees range from $25 a year for a regular member to $50,000 for a "benefactor" or top-ranked life member. Members include students (who pay only $5 a year), individuals, firms and foundations. The society has committees for acquisitions, exhibits, oral history and publications and publishes a quarterly newsletter and an annual yearbook. The staff includes a director, three office employees and four researchers.

The brochure sent to prospective members contends that the society "receives no governmental financial support." In September 1976, however, it did receive a five-year, $25,000-a-year matching grant from a division of the National Archives — the National Historical Publications and Records Commission — to prepare a comprehensive documentary history of the Supreme Court from 1789-1800. The need to raise matching funds from private sources for the project has encouraged the society to solicit new members and to publicize the increasing number of items it offers for sale to members and to the public in a kiosk in the Supreme Court foyer.

Supreme Court Chamber, U.S. Capitol, 1860-1935.

Housing the Court

Between Feb. 1, 1790, when the Supreme Court first met in New York City, and Oct. 7, 1935, when the justices first convened in their present building at One First Street Northeast in Washington, D.C., the court held session in about a dozen different places. Thus, during the court's first 145 years of existence, the justices moved, on average, once every 12 years.

Early Days

Some of these early courtrooms were shared with other courts. After the court moved to Washington in 1801, it held formal sessions in various rooms of the Capitol and, according to some sources, in two taverns as well. [127] Some of the premises provided for the court in the Capitol have been described by commentators of that time as "mean and dingy" and "little better than a dungeon." [128] Their present headquarters, by contrast, has been called a "marble palace." [129]

New York City

The Supreme Court first met on Feb. 1, 1790, in New York City, then the nation's temporary capital. The court held session at the Royal Exchange Building at the intersection of Broad and Water Streets in what is now Manhattan's financial district. The courtroom occupied the second floor of the gambrel-roofed, cupola-topped building. There was an open-air market on the first floor of the building and the courtroom on the second floor was a room 60 feet long with a vaulted ceiling.

The justices stayed in New York for two terms. The first lasted from Feb. 1-Feb. 10, 1790, and the second for only two days, Aug. 2-3, 1790. There were no cases on the court's docket during these two terms and the justices spent their time at such duties as appointing a court crier — now called clerk of the court — and admitting lawyers to the bar.

Philadelphia

Before the end of the second term, Congress had voted on July 16, 1790, to move the capital from New York to Philadelphia. The Supreme Court joined the rest of the federal government there for its next session, which began on Feb. 7, 1791, at Independence Hall, then known as "The State House." With no cases to attend to, the court adjourned the next day.

When the court was moved to Philadelphia, it was understood that the justices would sit in City Hall, but that building was not completed until the summer of 1791, in time for the court's August 1791 term. The justices met in the east wing of the new City Hall, which also housed the state and municipal court.

Those courts usually met at different times from the Supreme Court. In March 1796, however, the "Mayor's Court" was scheduled to hold a session in the same first-floor courtroom that the Supreme Court was using. As a result, the Supreme Court vacated the courtroom and held session in the chambers of the Common Council on the second floor of the building.

The court remained in City Hall until the end of the August 1800 term. City Hall also housed the U.S. Congress, which occupied the west wing, and the Pennsylvania legislature, which met in the central part of the building. The records indicate that while in City Hall, the justices often kept late hours to hear oral arguments and that there they began wearing robes for the first time.

Washington, D.C.

The act of July 16, 1790, which transferred the seat of the federal government from New York to Philadelphia, also provided for a subsequent and permanent move to Washington, D.C. That law specified that the final move would take place on the "first Monday in December, in the year one thousand eight hundred." By that time, enough of the Capitol and the White House had been completed for the government to move. Congress and the president were subjected to considerable criticism because the buildings they were to occupy were labeled too palatial and extravagant for a young democracy.

For the Supreme Court, however, there were no accommodations at all. A House committee in 1796 had pointed out that a "building for the Judiciary" was needed, and in 1798 Alexander White, a commissioner for the Federal City, had suggested appropriating funds for one. But two weeks before the court moved to Washington, it was still seeking a place to conduct its business.

Courtrooms in the Capitol

Faced with the imminent convening of the homeless Supreme Court in Washington, Congress on Jan. 23, 1801, passed a resolution providing that "leave be given to the Commissioners of the City of Washington to use one of the rooms on the first floor of the Capitol for holding the present session of the Supreme Court of the United States."

Since only the north wing of the Capitol was ready for occupancy at that time, Congress assigned the court a small room — 24 feet by 30 feet, 31 feet high and rounded at the south end — in the east basement, or first floor, entrance hall. There, the court held its first session in Washington on Feb. 2, 1801. It was the first of a series of often makeshift, hand-me-down quarters assigned by Congress to the court before the completion of its present building in 1935.

By 1807 the entire north wing of the Capitol was in dire need of renovation. In a letter to Chief Justice John Marshall on Sept. 17, 1807, Benjamin Henry Latrobe, the Architect of the Capitol and Surveyor of Public Buildings, suggested that the court move "for the next session into the Library formerly occupied by the House of Representatives."

There the court remained for the February and summer 1808 terms. But as Latrobe indicated in a letter to President James Monroe on Sept. 6, 1809, "the Library became so inconvenient and cold that the Supreme Court preferred to sit at Long's Tavern" during the February 1809 term. Long's Tavern, where the first inaugural ball was held, was located on First Street Southeast, where the Library of Congress now stands.

On Feb. 5, 1810, the court returned to the Capitol and met in a courtroom especially designed for it. Located in the basement beneath the new Senate chamber, the court-

Statue "The Contemplation of Justice" at entrance of Supreme Court Building.

room was also used by the U.S. Circuit Court and probably by the Orphan's Court of the District of Columbia. The noted Philadelphia lawyer, Charles J. Ingersoll, provided this description of the new courtroom:

> Under the Senate Chamber, is the Hall of Justice, the ceiling of which is not unfancifully formed by the arches that support the former. The Judges in their robes of solemn black are raised on seats of grave mahogany; and below them is the bar; and behind that an arcade, still higher, so contrived as to afford auditors double rows of terrace seats thrown in segments round the transverse arch under which the Judges sit.... When I went into the Court of Justice yesterday, one side of the fine forensic colonnade was occupied by a party of ladies, who, after loitering some time in the gallery of the Representatives, had sauntered into the hall, and, were, with their attendants, sacrificing some impatient moments to the inscrutable mysteries of pleading. On the opposite side was a group of Indians, who are here on a visit to the President in their native costume, their straight black hair hanging in plaits down their tawny shoulders, with mockassins on their feet, rings in their ears and noses, and large plates of silver on their arms and breasts. [130]

The court remained in the new courtroom until the Capitol was burned by the British on Aug. 24, 1814, during the War of 1812. The British are said to have used Supreme Court documents to start the fire. When the Capitol was burned, Congress moved to the temporary "Brick Capitol" at the site of the present Supreme Court building, then — during the two years that the Capitol was being restored — to a house rented from Daniel Carroll. That house, which the court used from Feb. 6, 1815, until July 1, 1816, subsequently became Bell Tavern.

The court returned to the Capitol for its February 1817 term and occupied an undestroyed section in the north wing until 1819. It was this room that was described as "mean and dingy" and "little better than a dungeon." [131] The court remained there until the February 1819 term, when its regular courtroom beneath the Senate chamber was repaired.

The courtroom, which the justices were to occupy until 1860, was the object of both praise and criticism. It was on the court's first day in the restored courtroom — Feb. 2,

1819 — that the decision in the Dartmouth College Case was announced, a decision that made the court headline news throughout the country. [132] On the same day that the Dartmouth case was decided, the *National Intelligencer* reported: "We are highly pleased to find that the Courtroom in the Capitol is in a state fit for the reception of the Supreme Court. . . . It is . . . considerably more agreeable than that which was produced on entering the same apartment, previous to the re-modification of it made necessary by the conflagration of the interior of the Capitol." [133]

Many observers took a dimmer view of the courtroom. The *New York Statesman,* for example, described it as "not in a style which comports with the dignity of that body, or which wears a comparison with the other halls of the Capitol. In the first place, it is like going down cellar to reach it. The room is on the basement story in an obscure part of the north wing. In arriving at it, you pass a labyrinth, and almost need the clue of Ariadne to guide you to the sanctuary of the blind goddess. A stranger might traverse the dark avenues of the Capitol for a week, without finding the remote corner in which Justice is administered to the American Republic." [134] Other critics noted that the chamber was so small that the justices had to put on their robes in full view of the spectators.

Whatever its shortcomings, the courtroom at least lent a new aura of stability and permanence to the previously peripatetic court. The court remained in the basement courtroom for 41 years, surviving fires in 1851 and 1852. After the court moved to its new chambers in 1860, the courtroom became part of the law library of Congress.

In 1860, with the Civil War imminent, the court moved from the basement to the old Senate chamber on the first floor of the Capitol. The new courtroom was located on the east side of the main corridor between the rotunda and the current Senate chamber. The large room, with a dozen anterooms for office space and storage, was by far the most commodious and imposing quarters the court had occupied. The galleries had been removed when the Senate moved to its new chambers, giving the courtroom an aura of spaciousness.

The justices sat on a raised platform behind a balustrade. In back of the balustrade was an arched doorway topped by a gilded American eagle and flanked by ten marble columns. The justices faced a large semi-circular colonnaded chamber. The area just in front of the bench was used for the presentation of arguments and it was ringed by wooden benches for the spectators. There were red drapes and carpets, and busts of former Chief Justices lined the walls.

Despite the dignity and spaciousness of the courtroom, the adjoining office space was cramped and inadequate. There was no dining hall, for example, and the justices were forced to use the robing room for their meals. The conference room, where the justices met to discuss cases and render their decisions, also served as the court's library. Because of the reluctance of some of the justices to opening the conference room windows, the room was frequently closed and stuffy. The clerk's office was similarly close and cluttered.

None of the justices had individual office space in the Capitol, and each had to provide for his own and his staff's working quarters at a time when spacious housing in Washington was difficult to find. Nevertheless, the justices held sessions in these quarters for 75 years, with two exceptions. An explosion of illuminating gas on Nov. 6, 1898, forced the court to hold the Nov. 7 and Nov. 14

sessions in the Senate District of Columbia Committee room. During reconstruction of the courtroom from October to Dec. 9, 1901, sessions were held in the Senate Judiciary Committee room.

President — later Chief Justice — William Howard Taft began promoting the idea of a separate building for the Supreme Court around 1912. Taft continued to advocate the construction of a Supreme Court building when he became Chief Justice in 1921. At Taft's persistent urging, Congress finally relented in 1929 and authorized funds for the construction of a permanent dwelling for the court. During the construction of the new building, the court continued to sit in the old Senate chamber. Its last major decision announced there, at the end of the 1934 term, was that striking down President Roosevelt's National Industrial Recovery Act.

New Court Building

The Supreme Court held its first session in the new building at One First Street Northeast, across the plaza from the Capitol, on Oct. 7, 1935. A hundred and forty-five years after it first met in New York, 134 years after it moved to Washington and six years after Congress had appropriated $9,740,000 for a permanent residence, the nation's highest tribunal finally had a home of its own.

In laying the cornerstone for the new building on Oct. 13, 1932, Chief Justice Charles Evans Hughes paid tribute to his predecessor, William Howard Taft, who had died two years before. "This building," Hughes said, "is the result of his intelligent persistence." The site chosen for the new court had been the location of the "Brick Capitol" that was used by Congress after the British burned the Capitol in 1814.

Architect Cass Gilbert was commissioned to design the edifice and, in May 1929, submitted a plan for "a building of dignity and importance suitable for its use as a permanent home of the Supreme Court of the United States." Chief Justice Taft died in 1930 and Gilbert in 1934, but the project was continued under Chief Justice Hughes and architects Cass Gilbert Jr. and John R. Rockart, under the supervision of Architect of the Capitol David Lynn.

The architects chose the Corinthian style of Greek architecture which would blend most harmoniously with the congressional buildings on Capitol Hill. The dimensions of the building were 385 feet east and west, from front to back, and 304 feet north and south. At its height, the building rises four stories above the ground level.

Marble was selected as the primary material to be used, and more than $3 million — almost a third of the building's cost — was spent on domestic and foreign marble. Pure Vermont marble was used for the exterior of the building. A thousand freight cars were needed to haul the stone from Vermont. Georgia marble flecked with crystal was quarried for the four inner courts, while a creamy Alabama marble was used for most of the walls and floors of corridors and entrance halls.

For the court's Great Hall — its showcase — and the courtroom at the end of the Great Hall, architect Gilbert insisted on Ivory Vein Marble from Spain for the walls and Light Sienna Old Convent marble from the Montarrenti quarry in Italy for the huge columns. The Italian marble was shipped to finishers in Knoxville, Tenn., and they made the blocks into 30-foot columns and shipped them to Washington. Darker Italian and African marble was used for the floor.

Most of the floors are of oak, and the doors and walls of most offices are of American-quartered white oak. Bronze and mahogany were also used. The roof was made from cream-colored Roman tile set on bronze strips over lead-coated copper on a slab of watertight concrete. As Wesley McCune noted, the "Court might succumb to a political storm, but it will never be driven out by any kind of inclement weather." [135] The building includes two self-supporting marble spiral staircases from the garage to the top floor. The only other spiral staircases like those in the court are in the Vatican and the Paris Opéra.

Since its completion in 1935, the Supreme Court building has been a subject of both outspoken praise and equally outspoken criticism. It has been described as both a "marble palace" and a "marble mausoleum." Its admirers speak in terms of structural simplicity, austerity, beauty, and dignity. For them, it is a fitting monument epitomizing the words on the front entrance of the building, "Equal Justice Under Law."

Despite general public approval of the new building, it has had numerous critics. In the 1930s, the authors of the Federal Writers' Project *Guide to Washington* wrote that "the building has a cold, abstract, almost anonymous beauty but is lacking in that power which comes from a more direct expression of purpose." Chief Justice Harlan Fiske Stone called it "almost bombastically pretentious" and "wholly inappropriate for a quiet group of old boys such as the Supreme Court." Another justice said that the court would be "nine black beetles in the Temple of Karnak." Another asked: "What are we supposed to do, ride in on nine elephants?" [136]

The building was designed so that the justices need not enter public areas except when hearing oral arguments and announcing their opinions. A private elevator connects the underground garage with the corridor, closed to the public, where the justices' offices are located.

The basement of the Supreme Court building contains — in addition to the garage — a printing press and offices for the guards and maintenance help.

The second floor contains the justices' dining room and library and the Office of the Reporter of Decisions and other offices.

On the third floor is the library, paneled in hand-carved oak, and on the fourth floor there is a gymnasium and storage area.

The public is allowed to see only the ground floor, where the public information office is located, and the first floor, which houses the courtroom.

When Congress in 1929 authorized $9,740,000 for the construction of the court building, it was expected then that extra funds for necessary furnishings would have to be appropriated. Nevertheless, the final and complete cost of the building, in addition to all the furnishings, was below the authorization, and $94,000 was returned to the U.S. Treasury. It is estimated that replacing the building today would run to well over $100 million.

Architecture

On the steps to the main entrance of the building are a pair of huge marble candelabra with carved panels representing justice, holding sword and scales, and the "three fates," who are weaving the thread of life. On either side of the steps are two marble figures by sculptor James Earle Fraser. On the left side is a female — the "contemplation of justice" — and on the right is a male — the "guardian or authority of law."

At the entrance of the building is a pediment filled with sculptures representing "liberty enthroned," guarded by "order" and "authority." On either side are groups depicting "council and research." Panels on the main door were sculptured by John Donnelly Jr. and depict scenes in the development of the law. Along both sides of the great hall are busts of former Chief Justices, heraldic devices and medallion profiles of lawgivers.

From the great hall, oak doors open into the courtroom, or court chamber. Measuring 82 feet by 91 feet with a 44-foot ceiling, the room has 24 columns of Italian marble. Overhead, along all four sides of the room, are marble panels sculptured by Adolph A. Weinman. Directly above the bench are two figures, depicting "majesty of the law" and "power of government." Between these figures is a tableau of the Ten Commandments. At the far left is a group representing "safeguard of the rights of the people" and "genii of wisdom and statecraft." At the far right is "the defense of human rights."

On the wall to the right of incoming visitors are figures of historical lawmakers of the pre-Christian era — Menes, Hammurabi, Moses, Solomon, Lycurgus, Solon, Draco, Confucius and Augustus. These are flanked by figures symbolizing "fame" and "history." To the left of visitors are lawmakers of the Christian era — Napoleon, Marshall, Blackstone, Grotius, Saint Louis, King John, Charlemagne, Mohammed and Justinian. They are flanked by figures representing "liberty," "peace" and "philosophy."

New Quarters?

When the building was finished in 1935, it was widely regarded as the permanent home of the United States Supreme Court. But in recent years, court officials have complained that the building "is bursting at the seams" [137] and that the court needs more space. In 1978, Chief Justice Warren E. Burger gave his blessing to a group of federal planners who are attempting to find an alternate location for the court.

The present building, these planners contend, could not be expanded without destroying the architectural integrity of the building. Among the alternatives being considered are to move the court to a new location on Capitol Hill and convert the present building into a legal museum or turn it over to the Library of Congress for a visiting scholars center; to expand below ground level and take over adjacent property; and to select as a site a new "judicial campus" in "monumental Washington" — somewhere between the Lincoln Memorial and the Capitol.

Those favoring a move from Capitol Hill to a new "judicial campus" contend that the court has remained in the shadow of Congress since 1800 and needs a new and separate location to symbolize its role as the third and co-equal branch of the government. Planning is still in the early stages and a final decision, which will require years of study and the approval of several federal agencies, the court and Congress, is not expected for at least several years.

Cost of the Court

Compared to its two coequal branches of the government, the executive branch and Congress, the Supreme Court seems a relatively inexpensive operation. In fiscal year 1979, for example, the high court received $9,690,000 for the salaries of the nine justices and more than 300 employees and other expenses, and $1,450,000 for care of the building and grounds. That same fiscal year, the Executive Office of the President requested $83.2 million, and Congress, with more than 18,000 employees, asked for $1.2 billion. [138]

Supreme Court Budget

The Supreme Court budget for each fiscal year is drawn up in the Office of the Marshal of the Court. It is submitted by Oct. 15 — nearly a year in advance — to the Office of Management and Budget (OMB). (The fiscal year begins the following Oct. 1.)

The OMB is prohibited by statute from making any changes in the proposed budget for the federal judiciary before submitting it — along with proposed executive and legislative budgets — to Congress in January.

Supreme Court requests in the president's budget document have been divided into two categories — salaries and expenses of the Supreme Court, and care of buildings and grounds — since fiscal year 1977. Before that, there were five categories: salaries; printing; miscellaneous expenses; car for the Chief Justice; and books for the Supreme Court.

Federal Judiciary

For the 95 district courts, the 12 circuit courts, the Court of Claims, the Court of Customs and Patent Appeals and the Customs Court, the budget process before submission to Congress involves several steps that are not applicable to the Supreme Court. The budget of each lower court requires consideration by the Administrative Office of the U.S. Courts and the Judicial Conference of the United States, which have no jurisdiction over the Supreme Court.

The various offices of the district courts submit their budget requirements for the next fiscal year to the chief judge of their district, who sends them to the administrative office in Washington by May 1 of the preceding fiscal year. The chief judge of the three special courts follows the same procedure.

The chief judge of each of the 12 circuit courts has been assisted since 1972 by a "circuit executive" whose duties include preparing the budget requests. Like those of the district and special courts, the proposed budget for the circuits must be submitted to the administrative office by May 1.

Budget requests are evaluated by specialists on the basis of productivity, in May and June. The conclusions are reviewed by the director of the administrative office, then sent to a committee of judges for review before they are delivered to the judicial conference for approval.

Committees of the judicial conference review the requests, make recommendations and send them to the budget committee for evaluation and further recommendations.

The judicial conference meets, usually in September, to consider the committees' recommendations and prepare a final version of the requests, which are then returned to the financial management division of the administrative office and submitted to the Office of Management and Budget (OMB) by Oct. 15.

The fiscal 1979 budget request for the federal judiciary — minus Supreme Court funds — was $521.1 million.

Congressional Consideration

Before the president sends the budget to Congress, the Administrative Office of the U.S. Courts submits justifications for the funds requested to the subcommittees of the congressional appropriations committees that will first consider the requests — the Senate subcommittee on State, Justice, Commerce and the Judiciary and the House subcommittee on the Departments of State, Justice and Commerce, the Judiciary and Related Agencies. Subcommittee hearings on the proposed budget generally begin in late January or early February.

The subcommittees hold public hearings at which a justice of the Supreme Court, the chairman of the Judicial Conference Budget Committee, the chief judges of the special courts and experts on the budget from the Administrative Office of the U.S. Courts are called to justify the budget requests. When the hearings are over, the subcommittees vote on appropriations bills and send them to a vote by the full Senate and House Appropriations Committees, followed by a final vote on the floors of the House and Senate. The Judiciary's budget requests are often reduced by Congress.

The funds Congress appropriates for the Supreme Court now go directly to the court and are spent by the marshal for salaries of the justices and other employees and for court needs. Before 1935, Congress channeled money for the Supreme Court through the Justice Department. The allocation of funds for the other federal courts is handled by the financial management division of the Administrative Office of the U.S. Courts. The division submits recommendations on the allocation to the director of the administrative office, who makes the final decision on how the money is disbursed.

Salaries of the Justices

Supreme Court justices in recent years have expressed no complaint about their current salaries — $88,700 a year for justices, and $92,400 for the Chief Justice. In 1975, Congress passed a law providing cost-of-living salary increases for the federal judiciary.

Service on the Supreme Court was not always so remunerative. On Sept. 23, 1789, Congress set the salary of an associate justice at $3,500 a year and for the Chief Justice at $4,000 a year.

That salary was not increased until 1819. When Congress was urged to raise the salaries in 1816, Justice Joseph Story (1812-1845) prepared a memorandum complaining that "the necessaries and comforts of life, the manner of living and the habits of ordinary expenses, in the same rank of society, have, between 1789 and 1815, increased in price from one hundred to two hundred percent. The business of the Judges of the Supreme Court, both at the Law Term in February and on the Circuits, has during the same period increased in more than a quadruple ratio and is increasing annually." [139] Congress was unreceptive at that time to Story's and other pleas for a pay raise for the justices.

Late in 1980, the court gave itself a raise when it ruled in the case of *United States v. Will* that Congress had improperly tried to rescind the cost-of-living increases due the justices and all other federal judges for fiscal years 1977 and 1980. The result of that ruling was a sizable increase for all federal judges, the justices included, retroactive to Oct. 1, 1980. *(See box this page)*

Retirement System

For almost a century, many Supreme Court justices were caught in a dilemma: low salaries and no retirement plan. Many left the bench to accept more lucrative employment elsewhere. Justice Story, for one, did not. In 1816, when Congress refused to increase his and the other associate justices' salaries from $3,500, Story declined an offer to take over Charles Pinckney's law practice in Baltimore. Had he accepted the offer, he would have been assured of an income of at least $10,000 a year.

Until 1869 justices who were unable to carry out their duties because of age or disability often hesitated to submit resignations because there were no retirement benefits.

It was in large measure the incapacity of Justices Robert C. Grier (1846-1870) and Samuel Nelson (1845-1872) that prompted Congress to provide in the Judiciary Act of April 10, 1869, "that any judge of any court of the United States, who, having held his commission as such at least ten years, shall, after having attained the age of seventy years, resign his office, shall thereafter, during the residue of his natural life, receive the same salary which was by law payable to him at the time of his resignation."

The Judiciary Act of 1869 made no provisions for retirement benefits for a justice who became incapacitated before reaching age 70 or before 10 years of service on the court. That omission was subsequently remedied, and the U.S. Code now contains provisions for resignation or retirement for age and retirement for disability.

Before 1937, justices who left the court for any reason had to resign rather than retire, which meant that their pensions were subject to fluctuating civil service guidelines. That policy was changed with the Supreme Court Retirement Act of 1937. *(Details, p. 81)*

The law now provides that:

Any justice or judge of the United States appointed to hold office during good behavior who resigns after attaining the age of seventy years and after serving at least ten years continuously or otherwise shall, during the remainder of his lifetime, continue to receive the salary which he was receiving when he resigned. Any justice or judge of the United States . . . may retain his office but retire from regular active service after attaining the age of seventy years and after serving at least ten years continuously or other-

Salaries

Years	Chief Justice	Associate Justices
1789-1819	$ 4,000	$ 3,500
1819-1855	$ 5,000	$ 4,500
1855-1871	$ 6,500	$ 6,000
1871-1873	$ 8,500	$ 8,000
1873-1903	$10,500	$10,000
1903-1911	$13,000	$12,500
1911-1926	$15,000	$14,500
1926-1946	$20,500	$20,000
1946-1955	$25,500	$25,000
1955-1964	$35,500	$35,000
1964-1969	$40,000	$39,500
1969-1975	$62,500	$60,000
1975-1977*	$65,625	$63,000
1977-1980	$75,000	$72,000
1980-	$92,400	$88,700

* A cost of living adjustment equal to 5 percent of regular salary.

wise, or after attaining the age of sixty-five years and after serving at least fifteen years continuously or otherwise. He shall, during the remainder of his lifetime, continue to receive the salary of the office. [140]

Any justice or judge of the United States appointed to hold office during good behavior who becomes permanently disabled from performing his duties may retire from regular active service. . . . Any justice or judge of the United States desiring to retire under this section shall certify to the President his disability in writing. Whenever an associate justice of the Supreme Court, a chief judge of a circuit or the chief judge of the Court of Claims, Court of Customs and Patent Appeals or Customs Court, desires to retire under this section, he shall furnish to the President a certificate of disability signed by the Chief Justice of the United States. . . . [141]

Each justice or judge retiring under this section after serving ten years continuously or otherwise shall, during the remainder of his lifetime, receive the salary of the office. A justice or judge retiring under this section who has served less than ten years in all shall, during the remainder of his lifetime, receive one-half the salary of the office. [142]

A justice of the Supreme Court who is unable to perform his duties cannot be forced to resign. Congress, however, has provided that any other federal judge deemed to be "unable to discharge efficiently all the duties of his office by reason of permanent mental or physical disability" can be replaced by the president with Senate approval. [143]

Footnotes

¹ "Court Reform — Priority to Methods and Machinery," Speech by Chief Justice Warren E. Burger, March 12, 1971, to the National Conference on the Judiciary, Williamsburg, Va.

² Supreme Court Rule 3(1).

³ Robert L. Stern and Eugene Gressman, *Supreme Court Practice* (Washington, D.C.: Bureau of National Affairs, 1978), p. 4.

⁴ Charles Warren, *The Supreme Court in United States History*, rev. ed., 2 vols. (Little, Brown & Co., Boston, 1922, 1926) II:148.

⁵ *United States v. Nixon*, 419 U.S. 683 (1974); *Wilson v. Girard*, 354 U.S. 524 (1957); *New York Times Co. v. United States, Washington Post v. United States*, 403 U.S. 713 (1971).

⁶ *Supreme Court Journal*, April 5, 1965; quoted in Stern and Gressman, *Supreme Court Practice* p. 10.

⁷ John P. Frank, *Marble Palace: The Supreme Court in American Life* (New York: Alfred A. Knopf, 1958), p. 15.

⁸ Supreme Court Rule 23(2).

⁹ 28 U.S.C. 1915(a).

¹⁰ Supreme Court Rules 24, 25.

¹¹ Supreme Court Rule 37(2).

¹² Charles Evans Hughes, *The Supreme Court of the United States* (New York: Columbia University Press, 1928), pp. 62-63.

¹³ Quoted in Harvard Law School Occasional Pamphlet Number Nine (1967), p. 22.

¹⁴ Frank, *Marble Palace*, pp. 91-92.

¹⁵ Hughes, *The Supreme Court of the United States*, p. 61.

¹⁶ Supreme Court Rule 38(7).

¹⁷ Supreme Court Rule 38(1).

¹⁸ Stern and Gressman, *Supreme Court Practice*, p. 741.

¹⁹ Ibid.

²⁰ William J. Brennan Jr., "State Court Decisions and the Supreme Court," 31 *Pennsylvania Bar Association Quarterly* 403-404 (1960).

²¹ Supreme Court Rules 15(3); 16(3); 21(4); 22(2); 34(3).

²² Supreme Court Rules 33 and 34.

²³ *Huffman v. Pursue, Ltd.*, 419 U.S. 892 (1974).

²⁴ Hughes, *The Supreme Court of the United States*, p. 62.

²⁵ Robert H. Jackson, "Advocacy Before the Supreme Court: Suggestions for Effective Case Presentations," 101 *American Bar Association Journal* 862 (1951).

²⁶ Frank, *Marble Palace*, p. 92.

²⁷ Ibid., p. 93.

²⁸ Ibid., p. 105.

²⁹ Ibid.

³⁰ Quoted by Richard L. Williams, "Justices Run 'Nine Little Law Firms' at Supreme Court," *Smithsonian*, February 1977.

³¹ Willard L. King, *Melville Weston Fuller* (New York: Macmillan Publishing Co., 1950), p. 290.

³² Ibid., p. 245.

³³ Glen Elsasser and Jay Fuller, "The Hidden Face of the Supreme Court," *Chicago Tribune Magazine*, April 23, 1978, p. 50.

³⁴ *United States v. Nixon*, 419 U.S. 683 (1974).

³⁵ Elsasser and Fuller, "The Hidden Face," pp. 50-57.

³⁶ Learned Hand, *The Bill of Rights* (Cambridge: Harvard University Press, 1958), p. 72.

³⁷ *Head & Amory v. Providence Ins. Co.*, 2 Cr. 127 (1804).

³⁸ Quoted in Warren, *The Supreme Court in United States History*, I:654.

³⁹ *State of Georgia v. Brailsford*, 2 Dall. 402 (1792).

⁴⁰ *Huidekoper's Lessee v. Douglass*, 3 CR. 1 (1805).

⁴¹ Warren, *The Supreme Court in U.S. History*, I:655.

⁴² Charles P. Curtis Jr., *Lions Under the Throne* (Fairfield, N.J.: Kelley Press, 1947), p. 76.

⁴³ Hughes, *The Supreme Court of the United States*, p. 68.

⁴⁴ Ibid., p. 67-68.

⁴⁵ Karl M. ZoBell, "Division of Opinion in the Supreme Court: A History of Judicial Disintegration," 44 *Cornell Law Quarterly* 186-214 (1959).

⁴⁶ *Martin v. Hunter's Lessee*, 1 Wheat. 304 at 381 (1816).

⁴⁷ *United States v. United Mine Workers*, 330 U.S. 258 (1947).

⁴⁸ Frank, *Marble Palace*, p. 121.

⁴⁹ *The New York Times*, Nov. 13, 1932.

⁵⁰ Gilbert Cranberg, "What Did the Supreme Court Say?" *Saturday Review*, April 8, 1967.

⁵¹ Liva Baker, *Felix Frankfurter* (New York: Coward-McCann, 1969), p. 218.

⁵² Ibid., pp. 216-217.

⁵³ Alpheus T. Mason, *Harlan Fiske Stone* (New York: Viking Press, 1956).

⁵⁴ Alexander Bickel, *The Unpublished Opinions of Justice Brandeis* (Cambridge: Harvard University Press, 1957), p. 203.

⁵⁵ Mary Ann Harrell, *Equal Justice Under Law: The Supreme Court in American Life* (Washington, D.C.: The Foundation of the American Bar Association with the cooperation of the National Geographic Society, 1975), p. 127.

⁵⁶ Charles Fairman, *Mr. Justice Miller* (Cambridge: Harvard University Press, 1939), pp. 373-374.

⁵⁷ Henry F. Pringle, *Life and Times of William Howard Taft*, 2 vols. (New York: Farrar & Rinehart, 1939), I:529-530.

⁵⁸ Frank, *Marble Palace*, pp. 76, 81, 264-265.

⁵⁹ *Dred Scott v. Sandford*, 19 How. 393 (1857).

⁶⁰ Frank, *Marble Palace*, p. 45.

⁶¹ Ibid., p. 259.

⁶² *Mahnich v. Southern Steamship Co.*, 321 U.S. 96 at 112-113 (1944).

⁶³ *Helvering v. Hallock*, 309 U.S. 106 at 119, 121 (1940).

⁶⁴ Art. I, section 3, clause 6.

⁶⁵ Frank, *Marble Palace*, p. 71.

⁶⁶ Warren, *The Supreme Court in United States History*, I:124.

⁶⁷ Quoted in Warren, *The Supreme Court in United States History*, I:127.

⁶⁸ Frank, *Marble Palace*, pp. 78-79.

⁶⁹ James F. Simon, *In His Own Image: The Supreme Court in Richard Nixon's America* (New York: David McKay Company, 1973), pp. 92-93.

⁷⁰ Hughes, *The Supreme Court of the United States*, p. 57.

⁷¹ Address to the Association of the Bar of the City of New York, Dec. 12, 1948.

⁷² Ibid.

⁷³ Merlo Pusey, *Charles Evans Hughes*, 2 vols. (New York: Columbia University Press, 1963), II:678.

⁷⁴ Ibid., p. 679.

⁷⁵ Frank, *Marble Palace*, pp. 80-81.

⁷⁶ *The New York Times*, March 4, 1954.

⁷⁷ *Brown v. Board of Education*, 347 U.S. 483 (1954).

⁷⁸ Quoted by David F. Pike, "Supreme Court: Trials and Tribulations," *U.S. News & World Report*, March 26, 1979, p. 34.

⁷⁹ Address to the National Archives, Sept. 21, 1978.

⁸⁰ Letter to Franklin D. Roosevelt, July 20, 1942.

⁸¹ Ibid.

⁸² Stern and Gressman, *Supreme Court Practice*, pp. 26-27.

⁸³ Charles Evans Hughes, Letter to Congress, March 21, 1937.

⁸⁴ Charles Warren, *The Supreme Court in United States History*, I:471.

⁸⁵ Ibid., p. 87.

⁸⁶ Ibid., p. 792.

⁸⁷ Ibid., p. 473.

⁸⁸ Wesley McCune, *The Nine Young Men* (New York: Harper & Brothers, 1947), p. 238.

⁸⁹ Quoted by Richard L. William, "Justices Run 'Nine Little Law Firms' at Supreme Court," *Smithsonian*, February 1977, p. 89.

⁹⁰ Hughes, *The Supreme Court of the United States*, pp. 75-76.

⁹¹ Ibid., p. 76.

⁹² Warren, *The Supreme Court in United States History*, I:173.

⁹³ Letter to Chief Justice Earl Warren, May 14, 1969.

⁹⁴ Address to the Association of the Bar of the City of New York, Dec. 11, 1948.

⁹⁵ Alexander Bickel, *Politics and the Warren Court* (New York: Harper & Row, 1965), p. 137.

⁹⁶ Dexter Perkins and Glyndon G. Van Deusen, *The United States of America*, 2 vols. (New York: Macmillan Publishing Co., 1962), II:64.

[97] Warren, *The Supreme Court in United States History,* II:583.

[98] Frank, *Marble Palace,* p. 269.

[99] Ibid., pp. 258-259.

[100] *The Boston Herald,* Nov. 15, 1929.

[101] Baker, *Felix Frankfurter,* p. 237; see also, Joseph P. Lash, *From the Diaries of Felix Frankfurter* (New York: W. W. Norton and Company, 1975).

[102] Simon, *In His Own Image: The Supreme Court in Richard Nixon's America,* p. 102.

[103] Letter to Chief Justice Earl Warren, May 14, 1969.

[104] Robert L. Stern, "The Solicitor General and Administrative Agency Litigation," *American Bar Association Journal,* Feb. 1960, pp. 154-155.

[105] Ibid., p. 156.

[106] 28 U.S.C. 505.

[107] Stern and Gressman, *Supreme Court Practice,* pp. 17-18.

[108] Augustus H. Garland, *Experience in the Supreme Court of the United States, with Some Reflections and Suggestions as to That Tribunal* (Washington, D.C.: John Byrne and Company 1898), p. 12., quoted in Stern and Gressman, *Supreme Court Practice,* p. 18.

[109] 1 Stat. 624, 625.

[110] Charles Fairman, "The Retirement of Federal Judges," *Harvard Law Review,* January 1938, p. 417.

[111] *Wheaton v. Peters,* 8 Pet. 591 (1834).

[112] Garland, *Experience in the Supreme Court of the United States,* quoted in Supreme Court Information Office, "The Docket Sheet," Vol. 13, No. 3 (Summer, 1976), p. 4.

[113] Stern and Gressman, *Supreme Court Practice,* pp. 909-910.

[114] Supreme Court Rule 5, 6.

[115] Supreme Court Rule 5(2).

[116] Supreme Court Rule 8.

[117] Frank, *The Marble Palace,* p. 93.

[118] Ibid., pp. 93-94.

[119] Telephone interview with Barrett McGurn, April 16, 1979.

[120] Frank, *The Marble Palace,* p. 116.

[121] Quoted by Richard L. Williams in "Justices Run 'Nine Little Law Firms' at Supreme Court," *Smithsonian,* February 1977, p. 88.

[122] Id., pp. 90-91.

[123] William H. Rehnquist, "Who Writes Decisions of the Supreme Court," *U.S. News & World Report,* Dec. 13, 1957, p. 74.

[124] Ibid., p. 75.

[125] 28 U.S.C. 331, as amended in 1961.

[126] *Report of the Study Group on the Caseload of the Supreme Court* (Federal Judicial Center, 1972), p. 8.

[127] "The Supreme Court — Its Homes Past and Present," American Bar Association Journal, Vol 27 (1941):283-289.

[128] Warren, *The Supreme Court in United States History,* I:164.

[129] Frank, *Marble Palace.*

[130] Quoted by Warren, *The Supreme Court in United States History,* I:457-458.

[131] Id., p. 459.

[132] *Dartmouth College v. Woodward,* 4 Wheat. 518 (1819).

[133] *National Intelligencer,* Feb. 2, 1819, quoted in Warren, *The Supreme Court in United States History,* I:460.

[134] *New York Statesman,* Feb. 7, 1824, quoted in Warren.

[135] McCune, *The Nine Young Men,* p. 2.

[136] Quoted in Harrell, "Equal Justice Under Law: The Supreme Court in American Life," p. 116.

[137] Quoted by Lawrence L. Knutson, Associated Press, Jan. 16, 1978.

[138] *Appendix to the Budget for Fiscal Year 1980, The Budget of the U.S. Government* (Washington, D.C.: U.S. Government Printing Office, 1979), pp. 51-52.

[139] William Waldo Story, ed., *Life and Letters of Joseph Story,* 2 vols. (Boston: Little & Brown, 1851), I:302.

[140] 28 U.S.C. 371.

[141] 28 U.S.C. 372.

[142] Ibid.

[143] 28 U.S.C. 372(b).

3

Members of the Court

At the time of its 190th birthday in 1980, the Supreme Court had had only 101 members, making it one of the most exclusive government bodies in the world. All 101 justices had been men, and all but one white. All but 11 had been Protestants. But this changed in 1981 with the nomination of Sandra Day O'Connor as the first woman justice.

Yet the court has exhibited diversity in other ways — politically, geographically, and in the age, personality and previous service of its individual members. And there have been periodic breakthroughs when appointees with innovative ideas or controversial backgrounds first attained a seat on the court. The first Roman Catholic was appointed in 1835, the first Jew in 1916, the first black in 1967. No woman has yet been nominated to the court, although two women were on a list being considered by President Richard M. Nixon in 1971.

There are in fact no constitutional or statutory qualifications at all for serving on the Supreme Court. The Constitution simply states that "the judicial power of the United States shall be vested in one Supreme Court" as well as any lower federal courts the Congress may establish (Article III, Section 1) and that the president "...by and with the Advice and Consent of the Senate, shall appoint ... Judges of the Supreme Court...." There is no age limitation, no requirement that judges be native-born citizens, nor even a requirement that appointees have a legal background.

Naturally, informal criteria for membership quickly developed. Every nominee to the court has been a lawyer. And over the years a myriad of other factors have entered into the process of presidential selection. Some of them became long-lasting traditions with virtually the force of a formal requirement. Others were as fleeting as the personal friendship between an incumbent president and his nominee.

The First Justices

George Washington, as the first president, had the responsibility of choosing the original six justices of the Supreme Court. The type of men he chose and the reasons he chose them foreshadowed the process of selection carried out by his successors.

In naming the first justices, Washington paid close attention to their politics, which at that time meant primarily loyalty to the new Constitution. Of the six original appointees, three had attended the Philadelphia convention which formulated the Constitution, and the other three had supported its adoption. John Jay, the first Chief Justice, was co-author with Alexander Hamilton and James Madison of *The Federalist Papers*, a series of influential essays published in New York supporting ratification of the Constitution.

During his two terms of office (1789-97), Washington had occasion to make five additional Supreme Court appointments. All were staunch supporters of the Constitution and the new federal government.

Another of Washington's major considerations was geographical. The new states were a disparate group that had barely held together during the fight for independence and the confederation government of the 1780s. To help bind them more closely together, Washington consciously tried to represent each geographical area of the country in the nation's new supreme tribunal.

His first six appointees consisted of three northerners — Chief Justice John Jay from New York and Associate Justices William Cushing of Massachusetts and James Wilson of Pennsylvania — and three southerners — John Blair of Virginia, James Iredell of North Carolina and John Rutledge of South Carolina. The five later appointees were Oliver Ellsworth of Connecticut, Thomas Johnson and Samuel Chase of Maryland, William Paterson of New Jersey and Rutledge, appointed a second time. Thus by the time Washington left office, nine of the original 13 states had already achieved representation on the Supreme Court.

Appointment Opportunities

With a total of 11, Washington still holds the record for the number of Supreme Court appointments made by any president. The second highest total — nine — belongs to President Franklin D. Roosevelt, the only president to serve more than two terms. Roosevelt also came closest since Washington to naming the entire membership of the court — only two justices who served prior to the Roosevelt years were still on the court at the time of his death. And one of them — Harlan Fiske Stone — Roosevelt elevated from associate justice to Chief Justice.

Presidents Andrew Jackson (1829-37) and William Howard Taft (1909-13) had the next highest number of justices appointed with six each. Taft holds the record for a one-term president. Next in order are Abraham Lincoln

103

Longest Vacancies

The longest vacancy in the court's history lasted for two years, three months and 23 days. During that period the Senate rejected four nominations by two presidents to the seat, and future President James Buchanan declined three invitations to fill the vacancy.

When Justice Henry Baldwin died April 21, 1844, John Tyler was president. Elected vice president on the Whig ticket in 1840, Tyler broke with the party after he had become president upon William Henry Harrison's death in 1841. From then on, he was a president essentially without a party or personal popularity. At the time of Baldwin's death, one Tyler nomination to the court had already been rejected and a second was pending. Tyler first offered the Baldwin vacancy to Buchanan, who, like Baldwin, was a Pennsylvanian. When he declined, the president nominated Philadelphia attorney Edward King to the seat.

Followers of Henry Clay, however, who controlled the Senate, thought Clay would win the presidency in that year's election, and they voted in June 1844 to postpone consideration of both King's nomination and Tyler's pending appointment of Reuben H. Walworth to the second vacancy. Tyler resubmitted King's name in December. Again the Senate refused to act, and Tyler was forced to withdraw the appointment.

By this time, Tyler was a lame duck president and Clay had lost the election to Democrat James K. Polk. Nonetheless, Tyler in February 1845 named John M. Read, a Philadelphia attorney who had support among the Democrats and the Clay Whigs in the Senate. But the Senate failed to act on the nomination before adjournment, and the vacancy was left for Polk to fill.

Polk had only slightly better luck with his appointments. After six months in office he offered the position to Buchanan, who again refused it. Another few months passed before Polk formally nominated George W. Woodward to the Baldwin vacancy in December 1845.

Woodward turned out to be a hapless choice. He was opposed by one of the senators from his home state, Pennsylvania, and his extreme "American nativist" views made him unpopular with many other senators. His nomination was rejected on a 20-29 vote in January 1846. Polk then asked Buchanan once again to take the seat. Buchanan accepted but later changed his mind and declined a third time. The president then turned to Robert C. Grier, a district court judge from Pennsylvania who proved acceptable to almost everyone. The Senate confirmed him Aug. 4, 1846, the day following his nomination.

Daniel Vacancy

The second-longest vacancy lasted almost as long as the first — two years, one month and 16 days. It occurred when Justice Peter V. Daniel of Virginia died May 31, 1860. At this point four of the remaining justices were northerners; four were from the South. Naturally, the South wanted then-President James Buchanan to replace Daniel with another southerner; the North urged a nomination from one of its states.

Buchanan took a long time making up his mind. In February 1861, nearly eight months after the vacancy occurred, he nominated Secretary of State Jeremiah S. Black, a former chief justice of the Pennsylvania supreme court and U.S. attorney general. Black might have proved acceptable to southern senators, but many of them had already resigned from the Senate to join the Confederacy. Though he supported the Union, Black was not an abolitionist, and his nomination drew criticism from the northern anti-slavery press. Black also was opposed by Democrat Stephen A. Douglas, who had just lost the presidential election to Abraham Lincoln. Finally, Republicans in the Senate were not anxious to help fill a vacancy that they could leave open for the incoming Republican president. Had Buchanan acted earlier, it is likely that Black would have been confirmed. As it was, the Senate rejected his nomination by a one-vote margin, 25-26.

Buchanan made no further attempt to fill the Daniel vacancy. Lincoln, who soon had two more seats on the court to fill, did not name anyone to the Daniel seat until July 1862 — more than a year after his inauguration. His choice was Samuel F. Miller, a well-respected Iowa attorney. Miller's nomination had been urged by a majority of both the House and Senate and by other politicians and members of the legal profession. The Senate confirmed his nomination within half an hour of receiving it July 16, 1862.

Sources: Henry J. Abraham. *Justices and Presidents: A Political History of Appointments to the Supreme Court.* New York: Oxford University Press, 1974; Charles Warren. *The Supreme Court in United States History,* rev. ed. 2 vols. Boston: Little, Brown & Company, 1922, 1926.

(1861-65) and Dwight D. Eisenhower (1953-61) with five each.

Four presidents of the United States — of whom Jimmy Carter was the only one to serve a full term — made no appointments to the Supreme Court. William Henry Harrison (1841) and Zachary Taylor (1849-50) both died in office before any vacancies occurred. Andrew Johnson (1865-69), who served just six weeks short of a full term, had no chance to make a court appointment because of his rancorous political battle with Congress over Reconstruction. So bitter did the struggle become that Congress in effect took away Johnson's power of appointment by passing legislation in 1866 to reduce the court to seven members from 10 as vacancies should occur.

The legislation was occasioned by the death of Justice John Catron in 1865 and Johnson's nomination in 1866 of Henry Stanbery to replace him. The Senate took no action on Stanbery's nomination and instead passed the bill reducing the size of the court. When Justice James Wayne died in 1867, the membership of the court automatically dropped to eight. In 1869, when the Republicans had recaptured the White House, they enacted legislation increasing the court to nine seats, allowing President Ulysses S. Grant to make a nomination.

Non-partisan Appointments

As political parties became an established fact of American political life, each of the major parties sought to appoint members to the Supreme Court who would espouse their view of what the federal government should and should not do.

As Washington had appointed supporters of the new Constitution, so most presidents have selected nominees with whom they were philosophically and politically in accord. Whenever a president goes to the opposite political party to find a nominee, it is the exception rather than the rule.

The first clear-cut instance of a president of one party appointing a member of the other to the Supreme Court was Republican Abraham Lincoln's selection of Democrat Stephen J. Field of California in 1863. President John Tyler, elected vice president as a Whig in 1840, appointed Democrat Samuel Nelson to the court in 1845, but by that time Tyler was no longer identified with either major political party.

After Lincoln's example, Republican presidents occasionally appointed Democrats to the court. President Benjamin Harrison selected Democrat Howell E. Jackson of Tennessee in 1893; Warren G. Harding appointed Democrat Pierce Butler in 1922; Herbert Hoover appointed Democrat Benjamin N. Cardozo in 1932; Dwight D. Eisenhower appointed Democrat William J. Brennan Jr. in 1956; and Richard Nixon appointed Democrat Lewis F. Powell Jr. in 1971. Republican William Howard Taft was the only president to appoint more than one member of the opposite party to the court. Three of his six nominees to the court were Democrats — Edward D. White, whom he elevated from associate justice to Chief Justice, and Horace Lurton and Joseph R. Lamar, southern Democrats appointed respectively in 1909 and 1910.

Only three Democrats appointed Republicans to the court. Woodrow Wilson named Louis D. Brandeis, a nominal Republican, to the bench in 1916. Franklin D. Roosevelt elevated Republican Harlan Fiske Stone from associate justice to Chief Justice in 1941. Harry S Truman appointed Republican Sen. Harold H. Burton of Ohio, an old friend and Senate colleague, in 1945.

Lobbying for a Nomination

Presidential selection of justices is usually the result of a balancing of factors and a sifting of potential candidates before the president finally makes up his mind. But on a few occasions in American history, a president's choice has all but been made for him by overwhelming pressure for a particular nominee.

One of the more dramatic instances of this process occurred in 1853, when President Franklin Pierce nominated John A. Campbell of Alabama for a spot on the court. Campbell was a 41-year-old lawyer who had such a brilliant reputation that the Supreme Court justices decided they wanted him as a colleague. As a result, the entire membership of the court wrote to Pierce requesting Campbell's nomination. To emphasize their point, they sent two justices to the president to deliver the letters in person. Pierce complied, and Campbell was confirmed within four days.

In 1862 President Lincoln was looking for a new justice from the Midwest. The Iowa congressional delegation began pressing for the appointment of Samuel F. Miller, a doctor and lawyer who had helped form the Iowa Republican Party and had a strong reputation for moral and intellec-

tual integrity. The movement grew rapidly until 129 of 140 House members and all but four senators had signed a petition for Miller's nomination. With such massive and unprecedented congressional support, Miller received Lincoln's approval despite his lack of any judicial experience. He became the first justice from west of the Mississippi River.

In 1932 a strong national movement began for the appointment of Benjamin Cardozo, chief judge of the New York court of appeals, to the Supreme Court. Cardozo was a Democrat, while the president who was to make the appointment, Herbert Hoover, was a Republican. Furthermore, Cardozo was Jewish and there was already one Jew on the court, Louis D. Brandeis. Under these circumstances, it was considered unlikely Hoover would make the nomination.

But Cardozo's record was so impressive that a groundswell of support arose for him. Deans and faculty members of the nation's leading law schools, chief judges of other state courts, labor and business leaders, and powerful senators all urged Hoover to choose Cardozo. Despite his desire to appoint a western Republican, Hoover finally yielded and nominated Cardozo, who was confirmed without opposition.

Geographical Factors

George Washington's weighing of geographical factors in appointing the first justices continued as a tradition for over a century. It was reinforced by the justices' duty under the Judiciary Act of 1789 to attend circuit court sessions. Presidents strove not only for geographical balance in their appointments, but considered it important that each justice be a native of the circuit over which he presided.

But the burdensome attendance requirement was curtailed by legislation during the 19th century until it became optional in 1891 and was abolished altogether in 1911. In the 20th century, geography became less and less a consideration in Supreme Court nominations, although as recently as 1970 President Nixon made an issue of it in the failure of the Senate to confirm two southerners — Clement Haynsworth Jr. and G. Harrold Carswell — to the court. Nixon claimed the Senate would not confirm a conservative southerner and turned to Minnesotan Harry A. Blackmun instead.

In its heyday, the geographical factor was sometimes almost sacrosanct. The most enduring example was the so-called New England seat, which was occupied by a New Englander, usually from Massachusetts, from 1789 to 1932. There was also a seat for a New Yorker from 1806 to 1894 and a Maryland-Virginia seat from 1789 to 1860. (Details, box, next page)

Geography had strong political ramifications as well. This was especially so in the case of the South. With the growth of sectional differences, particularly over the slavery issue, before the Civil War, the South felt itself to be on the defensive. One of the ways it sought to defend its interests was to gain a majority on the Supreme Court. And, indeed, five of the nine justices in 1860 were from slaveholding states.

With the coming of the Civil War, the sectional balance of power shifted. Four of the five southern justices died between 1860 and 1867, and another — Justice John A. Campbell of Alabama — resigned to join the Confederate cause.

Regional Seats on the Supreme Court

Geography was a prime consideration in the appointment of Supreme Court justices throughout the 19th century. Presidents found it expedient to have each of the expanding nation's rival sections represented on the court. Whenever a justice died or resigned, his replacement usually came from the same state or a neighboring one. In addition, the justices' circuit duties, which required them to attend court sessions in their circuits periodically, made it desirable for each justice to be a native of the circuit over which he presided.

The 'New England Seat'

The most notable instance of geographical continuity was the seat traditionally held by a New Englander. William Cushing of Massachusetts was appointed an associate justice by President George Washington in 1789. From then until 1932, the seat was held by a New England appointee, usually from Massachusetts.

When Cushing died after 21 years on the court, President James Madison looked to New England for a successor. He offered the post to both former Attorney General Levi Lincoln and John Quincy Adams, both from Massachusetts, but they declined. After Madison's nomination of Alexander Wolcott of Connecticut was turned down by the Senate, the president turned back to Massachusetts and selected Joseph Story, at 32 the youngest justice ever chosen.

Story served 34 years, dying in 1845. James K. Polk, who was then president, chose to continue the New England tradition of holding the seat by appointing Levi Woodbury of New Hampshire, a prominent Jacksonian who had served as governor, U.S. senator, secretary of the Navy, and secretary of the Treasury.

Woodbury's tenure lasted less than six years, and it fell to President Millard Fillmore to find a successor. He chose Benjamin Curtis, another Massachusetts native.

Curtis resigned in 1857 after only five and a half years, largely because of his acrimonious relations with other members of the Taney court. President James Buchanan, mindful of the continued need for a New Englander on the court, chose Nathan Clifford of Maine, a former attorney general.

Clifford served until his death in July 1881, shortly after President James A. Garfield was shot. When Garfield died in September his successor, Chester Arthur, chose the chief justice of the Massachusetts supreme court, Horace Gray, to replace Clifford.

Gray served until 1902, when he was succeeded by another Massachusetts supreme court chief justice, Oliver Wendell Holmes Jr., appointed by President Theodore Roosevelt.

By the time of Holmes' appointment, however, the significance of geography had declined as a qualification for selection to the Supreme Court. President Theodore Roosevelt, in particular, was disdainful of such a prerequisite and it was mostly accidental that Holmes came from Massachusetts. Nevertheless, his selection extended for another 30 years the tradition of the "New England seat."

After Holmes' resignation in 1932, President Herbert Hoover chose as his successor Benjamin N. Cardozo, chief judge of New York State's highest court, thus ending the Supreme Court's longest-lasting geographical tradition. And while Cardozo's successor, Felix Frankfurter, was a resident of Massachusetts, that fact apparently played no role in his selection.

The 'New York Seat'

New York was another longtime holder of a specific seat on the Supreme Court. With the appointment of Justice Henry Brockholst Livingston by President Thomas Jefferson in 1806, a tradition began which continued until New Yorkers themselves ended it in 1894 by their internal quarreling.

Livingston served until his death in 1823. President James Monroe offered the post indirectly to Martin Van Buren, then a U.S. senator, but received a non-committal response. The president then chose Smith Thompson of New York, his secretary of the Navy. Thompson served for 20 years. His death in 1843 came at an inopportune moment politically: President John Tyler was disliked by both Democrats and Whigs and had little political leverage. His attempts to choose a successor to Thompson met with repeated failure, the Senate defeating one nominee and forcing another to withdraw. Finally, at the last moment before leaving office in 1845, Tyler found a New Yorker acceptable to the Senate for the post. He was Samuel Nelson, who continued to serve until his resignation in December 1872.

Two more New Yorkers held the seat after Nelson's retirement, Ward Hunt from 1873 to 1882 and Samuel Blatchford from 1882 to 1893. But then a bitter quarrel between New Yorkers over the seat ended the tradition.

The two main New York antagonists were President Grover Cleveland and Sen. David B. Hill, old political enemies. Cleveland twice nominated a New Yorker for the post, and twice Hill used senatorial courtesy to object to the nominees. In both cases, the Senate followed its own tradition of honoring a senator's objection to a nominee of his own party from his own state and rejected Cleveland's choices. On his third try to fill the vacancy, Cleveland abandoned New York and chose U.S. Senator Edward D. White of Louisiana, who was confirmed immediately by his colleagues.

The 'Virginia-Maryland Seat'

Virginia and Maryland shared a seat on the Supreme Court from the first appointments in 1789 until the Civil War. John Blair of Virginia, appointed by President Washington, served until 1796. Washington chose as his successor Samuel Chase of Maryland. After his death in 1811, another Marylander, Gabriel Duvall, was given the seat. Upon his resignation in 1835, the seat went back to Virginia, with Philip P. Barbour holding it from 1836 to 1841 and Peter V. Daniel from 1841 to 1860. With the coming of the Civil War, there was a realignment of circuits as well as the desire of the new Republican administration to appoint more northerners and westerners to the court. The Maryland-Virginia tradition was ended when Iowan Samuel F. Miller was appointed as Daniel's successor by President Abraham Lincoln.

Not one of these justices was replaced by a southerner. Thus by 1870 every Supreme Court seat was held by a northerner or westerner. But with the gradual decline of bitterness over the war, southern members again began to appear on the court. President Rutherford B. Hayes, who sought to reconcile relations between the North and South, made the first move by appointing William B. Woods of Georgia in 1880. Woods was not a native southerner, having migrated there after the Civil War. But despite this "carpetbagger" background, he was never identified with the corruption and profligacy associated with the Reconstruction era. As a federal judge for the fifth — deep-South — circuit, he gained the respect of his neighbors for his fairness and honesty.

The first native southerner appointed to the court after the Civil War was Woods' successor, Lucius Q. C. Lamar of Mississippi, appointed by President Grover Cleveland in 1888. Lamar had personally drafted Mississippi's ordinance of secession in 1861 and had served the Confederacy both as a military officer and as a diplomatic envoy to Europe. So his accession to the court was an even more significant symbol of reconciliation between the sections than Woods' appointment eight years earlier.

Thirty-one states have contributed justices to the Supreme Court. New York has by far the highest total, with 13, followed by Ohio with ten and Massachusetts with eight. Several major states have had only one justice, including Texas, Indiana and Missouri — as have such small states as Utah, Maine and Wyoming.

Of the 19 states which have never had a native on the court, most are smaller western states. Only six of the 19 are east of the Mississippi River. The largest state never to have had a justice is Florida, the ninth most populous state according to the 1970 census.

The lack of representation on the court from some of the smaller states resulted in a controversy during the 1950s when North Dakota's outspoken maverick Sen. William Langer began opposing all non-North Dakotan Supreme Court nominees as a protest against big-state nominees. Langer was chairman of the Senate Judiciary Committee during the 83rd Congress (1953-55). In 1954 he joined in delaying tactics against the nomination of Earl Warren as Chief Justice, managing to hold off confirmation for two months. He continued his struggle for the next six years, until his death in 1959.

Only Lawyers

All of President Washington's appointees were lawyers, and no president has deviated from this precedent. The legal education of the justices has changed radically over the years, however. Until the mid-19th century, it was traditional for aspiring lawyers to study privately in a law office until they had learned the law sufficiently to pass the bar. There were no law schools as such in the early years, although some universities had courses in law. John Marshall, for example, attended a course of law lectures at William and Mary College in the 1770s. Two of the earliest justices — John Rutledge and John Blair — received their legal education in England, at the Inns of Court. A modern justice, Frank Murphy (1940-49), also studied there.

Of the 54 justices (including Rutledge and Blair) who attended law school, by far the largest number (12) attended Harvard. Yale taught eight justices law and Columbia five. The first justice to receive a law degree from an American university was Benjamin R. Curtis, who got his from Harvard in 1832.

But it was not until 1957 that the Supreme Court was composed, for the first time, entirely of law school graduates. Before that, many had attended law school, but had not received degrees. The last justice never to have attended law school was James F. Byrnes, who served from 1941 to 1942. The son of poor Irish immigrants, Byrnes never even graduated from high school. He left school at the age of 14, worked as a law clerk and eventually became a court stenographer. Reading law in his spare time, Byrnes passed the bar at the age of 24.

The last justice not to have a law degree was Stanley F. Reed, who served from 1938 to 1957. He attended both the University of Virginia and Columbia law schools, but received a degree from neither.

Pre-court Experience

Judges. Most justices have been active either in politics or in judicial office before coming to the Supreme Court. In fact, only one justice — George Shiras Jr. — had never engaged in political or judicial activities before his appointment. A total of 60 justices had some judicial experience — federal or state — before coming to the Supreme Court. Surprisingly, there have been many more who had experience on the state level (42) than on the federal level (25). (There is an overlap in the figures because seven justices had both federal and state judicial offices.)

All except two of President Washington's appointees had state judicial experience, the president believing that such experience was important for justices of the new federal court. But it was not until 1826 that a justice with previous federal judicial experience was appointed. He was Robert Trimble, who had served nine years as a U.S. district judge before being elevated to the Supreme Court.

Even after Trimble's appointment, judges with federal judicial experience continued to be a rarity on the Supreme Court. By 1880 only two other federal judges — Philip P. Barbour in 1836 and Peter V. Daniel in 1841 — had made it to the highest court. After 1880, when federal circuit judge William B. Woods was appointed, the pace picked up, and federal judicial experience became an increasingly important criterion for appointment to the Supreme Court. In 1980 five of the nine sitting justices, a majority, had held previous federal judicial office.

Politicians. Many justices have come from a political background, serving in Congress, as governors or as members of a Cabinet. One president, William Howard Taft, was later appointed to the court, as Chief Justice, in 1921.

More than a fourth of all justices — 27 — held congressional office before their elevation to the court. An additional six justices sat in the Continental Congress in the 1770s or 1780s.

The first justice who had a congressional background was William Paterson, who had served in the Senate from 1789 to 1790. Chief Justice John Marshall was the first justice with Cabinet experience, having held the post of secretary of State from 1800 to 1801.

Only a few incumbent members of Congress have been directly nominated to the Supreme Court. Only one incumbent House member, James M. Wayne in 1835, has ever been named to the court, and six incumbent senators: Oliver Ellsworth in 1796, John McKinley in 1837, Levi Woodbury in 1846, Edward D. White in 1894, Hugo L. Black in 1937 and Harold H. Burton in 1945.

The Senate has traditionally confirmed its own members without much debate. But in January 1853 when lame-

Catholic and Jewish Justices

The overwhelming Protestant complexion of the Supreme Court has been broken only 11 times; 90 of the 101 justices have been of Protestant background.

The first Catholic nominee, Chief Justice Roger B. Taney, was controversial not because of his religion, but because of his close alliance with his sponsor, the highly political Andrew Jackson.

Not until 1894 — 30 years after Taney's death — was the second Catholic, Edward D. White, appointed; he became Chief Justice 16 years later. White's religion, like Taney's, was not an issue. Both men were from traditional Catholic regions, and their faith had not been a factor during their long political careers. In President McKinley's 1897 appointment of Catholic Joseph McKenna, geography was the overriding factor; he replaced another Californian, Stephen J. Field.

Pierce Butler was the next Catholic appointee. President Warren G. Harding named him to the bench in 1922, largely because of Butler's political base. He was a Democrat, and Harding wanted to make a show of bipartisanship.

On Butler's death in late 1939, President Franklin D. Roosevelt picked as his successor Frank Murphy, an Irish Catholic politician who had been mayor of Detroit, governor of Michigan, and was then serving as Roosevelt's attorney general. In 1949, when Murphy died, President Truman broke the continuity of a Catholic seat on the court by naming a Protestant, Tom C. Clark. For the first time since 1894, there was no Catholic on the court.

Of all the Catholic appointments, that of William J. Brennan Jr. by President Eisenhower in 1956 attracted the most notice, although it too was relatively non-controversial. But it was an election year and the Republicans were making a strong appeal to normally Democratic Catholic voters in the big cities. Some saw Brennan's appointment as part of that GOP strategy, although Eisenhower insisted it was an appointment made purely on merit.

Much more controversial than any of the Catholic nominees was Louis D. Brandeis, the first Jewish justice, named by President Wilson in 1916. Brandeis was already a figure of great controversy because of his views on social and economic matters. Conservatives bitterly fought his nomination, and there was an element of anti-Semitism in some of the opposition. When Brandeis took his seat on the court, Justice McReynolds refused to speak to him for three years and once refused to sit next to him for a court picture-taking session.

Herbert Hoover's nomination of Benjamin N. Cardozo in 1932 established a so-called Jewish seat on the Supreme Court. Justice Felix Frankfurter replaced Cardozo in 1939. He in turn was replaced by Justice Arthur J. Goldberg in 1962. And when Goldberg resigned his court position to become U.S. Ambassador to the United Nations, President Lyndon B. Johnson chose Abe Fortas to replace him.

But with Justice Fortas' resignation in 1969, President Richard M. Nixon broke the tradition of a "Jewish seat" by choosing Harry A. Blackmun of Minnesota, a Protestant.

duck President Millard Fillmore nominated Whig Sen. George Badger of North Carolina to the court, the Democratic Senate postponed the nomination until the close of the congressional session in March. Then the new Democratic president, Franklin Pierce, was able to nominate his own man. The postponement of Badger's nomination was a polite way of defeating a colleague's nomination, avoiding an outright rejection.

Sen. White's nomination came about after a bitter quarrel between President Grover Cleveland and Sen. David B. Hill of New York resulted in the Senate's rejection of two Cleveland nominees from New York. Cleveland then turned to the Senate for one of its own members, White, and that body quickly approved him.

Sen. Hugo L. Black's 1937 nomination was surrounded by controversy. Sen. Joseph T. Robinson of Arkansas, the Senate majority leader who had led the fight for President Franklin D. Roosevelt's so-called "court-packing" plan, was expected to get the nomination but died suddenly. So Roosevelt picked Black, one of the few southern senators other than Robinson who had championed the president in the court battle. Black's support of the controversial bill — plus what some felt was his general lack of qualifications for the Supreme Court — led to a brief but acrimonious fight over his nomination. After he was confirmed, publicity grew over his one-time membership in the Ku Klux Klan, and charges were made that he was still a member. But in a nationwide radio address, Black denied any racial or religious intolerance on his part and defused the criticism.

The last Supreme Court appointee with any previous congressional service was Sherman Minton in 1949. He had served as a U.S. senator from Indiana from 1935 to 1941, then was appointed to a circuit court of appeals judgeship. Since the retirement of Justice Black in 1971, no Supreme Court member has had any congressional experience.

Cabinet Members. Since John Adams' secretary of state, John Marshall, was appointed to the Supreme Court, 22 other Cabinet secretaries became justices, 13 of them appointed while still serving in the Cabinet. Heading the list of Cabinet positions that led to Supreme Court seats is that of attorney general. Nine attorneys general, including seven incumbents, have been appointed to the court. Next came secretaries of the Treasury (four), secretaries of state (three) and secretaries of the Navy (three). One postmaster general, one secretary of the interior, one secretary of war and one secretary of labor were appointed to the court.

The appointment of incumbent attorneys general has been largely a 20th-century phenomenon: Six of the seven appointments occurred after 1900. The other occurred just before that, when President William McKinley appointed his attorney general, Joseph McKenna. The 20th-century incumbents named to the court were William H. Moody, appointed by Theodore Roosevelt in 1906; James C. McReynolds (Wilson, 1914); Harlan Fiske Stone (Coolidge, 1925); Frank Murphy (Franklin D. Roosevelt, 1940); Robert H. Jackson (Roosevelt, 1941); and Tom C. Clark (Truman, 1949).

In the 19th century two men who had served as attorney general eventually were elevated to the Supreme Court, but appointment followed their Cabinet service by some years. They were Roger B. Taney, appointed Chief Justice by President Andrew Jackson in 1835, after serving as Jackson's attorney general from 1831 to 1833, and Nathan Clifford, appointed to the court by President James Buchanan in 1857 after service as James K. Polk's attorney general from 1846 to 1848.

Foreign-Born Justices

Since the Constitution makes no stipulation that Supreme Court justices must be native-born Americans, presidents are free to name foreign-born members to the court.

In all, six Supreme Court justices were born outside the United States, although one was the son of an American missionary who was temporarily living abroad. Of the remaining five, four were born in the British Isles. Only one — Felix Frankfurter — was born in a non-English-speaking country.

President George Washington appointed three of the foreign-born justices. The others were selected by Presidents Benjamin Harrison, Warren G. Harding and Franklin D. Roosevelt.

The six justices born outside the United States, in order of their appointment, are:

● James Wilson, born Sept. 14, 1742, in Caskardy, Scotland. Wilson grew up in Scotland and was educated at St. Andrews University in preparation for a career in the ministry. But in 1765 he sailed for America, where he studied law and went into land speculation. A signer of the Declaration of Independence, Wilson also was a member of the 1787 Constitutional Convention and its committee of detail, which was responsible for writing the first draft of the Constitution. In 1789 President Washington appointed Wilson one of the original members of the Supreme Court. In the late 1790s, Wilson's land speculations failed and he was jailed twice for debt while riding circuit and died in a dingy inn in North Carolina.

● James Iredell, born Oct. 5, 1751, in Lewes, England. Iredell was born into an old English family allegedly descended indirectly from Oliver Cromwell's son-in-law. Through family connections, Iredell received an appointment as colonial comptroller of customs at Edenton, N.C., at the age of 17. After six years he was promoted to collector of the port of Edenton. Iredell identified with the colonial cause and resigned his job as collector in 1776. While serving in his colonial offices, Iredell had studied law and began practice in 1770. In 1788 he was a strong supporter of the new federal Constitution and worked for its ratification by North Carolina. President Washington appointed him a Supreme Court justice in 1790. He served until his death in 1799 at the age of 48, the youngest justice ever to die on the court.

● William Paterson, born Dec. 24, 1745, in County Antrim, Ireland. Paterson emigrated to America with his parents when he was only two years old. He received his education at Princeton University and then read law,

opening his own law practice in 1769. Paterson was active in New Jersey affairs during the Revolutionary and Confederation periods, and served as a delegate to the Constitutional Convention in 1787. He was a member of the First Senate in 1789-90 and as a member of the Judiciary Committee helped write the Judiciary Act of 1789. Later, he codified the laws of the state of New Jersey, and in association with Alexander Hamilton laid out plans for the industrial city of Paterson. He was appointed to the Supreme Court by President Washington in 1793 and served until his death in 1806.

● David J. Brewer, born Jan. 30, 1837, in Smyrna, Turkey. Brewer was a member of an old New England family whose father was serving as a Congregational missionary in Turkey. The family returned to the United States soon after Brewer's birth. Brewer sought his fortune in Kansas and spent most of his career in the Kansas court system and lower federal courts. He was elevated to the Supreme Court by President Benjamin Harrison in 1890. Brewer's mother was the sister of Supreme Court Justice Stephen J. Field (1863-97) and Cyrus W. Field, promoter of the first Atlantic cable.

● George Sutherland, born March 25, 1862, in Buckinghamshire, England. Sutherland's father converted to Mormonism about the time of George's birth and moved his family to the Utah Territory. Although the senior Sutherland soon deserted the Mormons, the family remained in Utah, where George was educated at Brigham Young University. When Utah entered the Union as a state in 1896, Sutherland was elected to the state legislature. In 1900 he won a seat in the U.S. House and went on to serve two terms in the U.S. Senate (1905-17) before being defeated for re-election. While in the Senate, he formed a close friendship to a fellow senator, Warren G. Harding of Ohio. When Harding became president, he appointed Sutherland to the Supreme Court. Later, Sutherland was one of the justices known as implacable foes of President Franklin D. Roosevelt's New Deal.

● Felix Frankfurter, born Nov. 15, 1882, in Vienna, Austria. Frankfurter came to the United States with his parents in 1894 and grew up on the lower East Side of New York City. He achieved a brilliant academic record at City College and Harvard Law School, entering practice in New York City. In 1914 he joined the Harvard Law faculty and remained there, with time out for some governmental service during World War I, until his appointment to the Supreme Court by President Franklin D. Roosevelt in 1939.

The last Supreme Court justice with Cabinet experience was Tom C. Clark (1949-67), once Truman's attorney general.

Governors. Only five governors or former governors have ever been appointed to the Supreme Court. The most recent — and the most famous — was California Gov. Earl Warren, appointed Chief Justice by President Eisenhower in 1953. Warren had a long political career behind him, having served as attorney general of California before winning three terms as governor of his state. In 1948 he was

the Republican nominee for vice president and was briefly a candidate for the presidential nomination in 1952.

The only other incumbent governor ever appointed to the court was Charles Evans Hughes of New York, chosen by President Taft in 1910. Hughes was a reform governor who had conducted investigations into fraudulent insurance practices in New York before being elected governor in 1906. He left the court in 1916 to run for president on the Republican ticket, losing narrowly to Woodrow Wilson. Later he served as secretary of state under Presidents

Harding and Coolidge and returned to the court in 1930 as Chief Justice.

The three other former governors appointed to the Supreme Court were Levi Woodbury of New Hampshire in 1846 (governor, 1823-24), Salmon P. Chase of Ohio in 1864 (governor, 1856-60), and Frank Murphy of Michigan in 1940 (governor, 1937-39).

Generation Gaps

The age at which justices joined the court has varied widely. The oldest person ever initially appointed was Horace H. Lurton, who was 65 when he went on the court in 1910. Two Chief Justices were older than that when they achieved their office, but they had already served on the court previously: Harlan Fiske Stone was 68, in 1941; and Charles Evans Hughes 67, in 1930.

Representing the younger generation, Justices William Johnson and Joseph Story were both only 32 when they were appointed in 1804 and 1811 respectively. Story was younger than Johnson by about a month.

Only two other justices were under 40 when appointed: Bushrod Washington, nephew of the president, who was 36 when appointed in 1798, and James Iredell, who was 38 when appointed in 1790. Iredell also was the youngest justice to die on the court — 48 when he died in 1799.

The youngest justice in the 20th century was William O. Douglas, who was 40 when appointed in 1939.

The oldest justice ever on the court was Oliver Wendell Holmes, who retired at 90 in 1932, the court's only nonagenarian. The second-oldest member, Chief Justice Roger B. Taney, was 87 when he died in 1864. All other justices who reached 80 retired from the bench. They were Louis D. Brandeis and Gabriel Duvall, both 82, Joseph McKenna and Stephen J. Field, both 81, and Samuel Nelson, 80.

The youngest member ever to leave the court was Benjamin Curtis, who resigned in 1857 at 47. Others who left the court before the age of 50 were Justices Iredell, dead at 48, Alfred Moore, who retired at 48, and John Jay and John A. Campbell, who retired at 49. Jay also holds the record for number of years survived after leaving the court — 34 years. In modern times, Justice James F. Byrnes lived 29 years after resigning from the court in 1942.

Longevity

Length of service on the court has also varied greatly, from 15 months to 36 years. Justice James F. Byrnes served the shortest term, being confirmed by the Senate June 12, 1941, but resigning on Oct. 3, 1942, to become director of the World War II Office of Economic Stabilization.

Justice Thomas Johnson, who served from 1791 to 1793, was on the court only 16 months. Although he retired because of ill health, he lived another 26 years, dying at the age of 87.

Edwin Stanton, the controversial secretary of war during the Lincoln and Andrew Johnson administrations, was nominated for the Supreme Court by President Grant. The Senate confirmed him on Dec. 20, 1869, but Stanton died suddenly of a heart attack on Dec. 24. Since he did not have a chance to begin his service on the court, he is not considered to have been a justice.

In January 1974 Justice William O. Douglas broke the old longevity record for service on the court, held since December 1897 by Stephen J. Field, who had served 34 years and nine months when he resigned. Douglas went on to serve until November 1975, when he resigned after 36 years and seven months on the court.

Chief Justice John Marshall established the first longevity record by serving for 34 years and five months between 1801 and 1835. That record held until Field broke it in 1897.

Other justices who served 30 years or longer include Hugo L. Black (34 years, 1 month), the first John Marshall Harlan and Joseph Story (33 years each), James Wayne (32 years), John McLean (31 years), and Bushrod Washington and William Johnson (30 years each).

Black's 34 years occurred in an era of such changing membership on the court that he served at one time or another with 28 different justices, more than a quarter of the court's entire membership throughout its history.

Four or five years is usually the longest the court goes without a change in justices. But there was one lengthy period — 12 years — when the court maintained the same membership intact. That was from 1811, when Joseph Story was confirmed, to 1823, when Justice Henry Brockholst Livingston died.

Infirmity

Longevity of service sometimes leads to questions of disability, as justices age and are no longer capable of carrying a full load of casework. By early 1870, Justice Robert C. Grier was nearly 76. His mental and physical powers were obviously impaired and he often seemed confused and feeble. Grier complied when a committee of his fellow justices finally approached him to urge his resignation. He died eight months later.

Among the justices urging Grier's retirement was Stephen J. Field. Ironically, a quarter of a century later, Field found himself in the same position as Grier. His powers had visibly declined and he was taking less and less part in court proceedings. The other justices finally began hinting strongly that Field resign. But Field insisted on staying on the court long enough to break Chief Justice John Marshall's record for length of service on the court.

A Disabled Court. In 1880 the court was manned by an especially infirm set of justices; three of the nine were incapacitated. Justice Ward Hunt had suffered a paralytic stroke in 1879 and took no further part in court proceedings, but he refused to resign because he was not eligible for a full pension under the law then in effect. Finally, after three years, Congress passed a special law exempting Hunt from the terms of the pension law, granting him retirement at full pay if he would resign from the court within 30 days of enactment of the exemption. Hunt resigned the same day.

Justice Nathan Clifford also had suffered a stroke which prevented him from participating in court activities. But Clifford also refused to resign, hoping to live long enough for a Democratic president to name a successor. At the time, Clifford was the only Democrat left on the court who had been named by a Democratic president. But he died while Republicans were still in power.

While Hunt and Clifford were both incapacitated, Justice Noah Swayne's mental acuity was noticeably declining. He was finally persuaded to resign by President Rutherford B. Hayes, with the promise that Swayne's friend and fellow Ohioan Stanley Matthews would be chosen as his successor.

The most recent case of a court disability was that of Justice William O. Douglas, who suffered a stroke in January 1975. At first, Douglas attempted to continue his duties, but in November 1975 he resigned, citing the pain and physical disability resulting from the stroke.

Controversial Justices

The only time a justice clearly has been driven from the court by outside pressure occurred in 1969, when Justice Abe Fortas resigned. The resignation followed by less than eight months a successful Senate filibuster against President Lyndon B. Johnson's nomination of Fortas to be Chief Justice. Fortas' departure from the court climaxed a furor brought on by the disclosure early in May 1969 that he had received and held for 11 months a $20,000 fee from the family foundation of a man later imprisoned for illegal stock manipulation.

A year after Fortas' resignation, an attempt was made to bring impeachment charges against Justice Douglas. General dissatisfaction with Douglas' liberal views and controversial lifestyle — combined with frustration over the Senate's rejection of two of President Nixon's conservative southern nominees — seemed to spark the action. House Republican leader Gerald R. Ford of Michigan, who led the attempt to impeach Douglas, charged among other things that the justice had practiced law in violation of federal law, had failed to disqualify himself in cases in which he had an interest, and violated standards of good behavior by allegedly advocating revolution. A special House Judiciary subcommittee created to investigate the charges found no grounds for impeachment.

The only Supreme Court justice ever to be impeached was Samuel Chase. A staunch Federalist who had rankled Jeffersonians with his partisan political statements and his vigorous prosecution of the Alien and Sedition Acts, Chase was impeached by the House in 1804. But his critics failed to achieve the necessary two-thirds majority in the Senate for conviction.

Questionable Behavior

Other, less heralded cases, have occurred from time to time that resulted in increased criticism of the justices. One early controversy surfaced in 1857, when the nation was awaiting the court's decision in the *Dred Scott* case. Justices Robert C. Grier and John Catron wrote privately to the incoming president, James Buchanan, detailing the court's discussions and foretelling the final decision. Buchanan was glad of the news and was able to say in his inaugural address that the decision was expected to come soon and that he and all Americans should acquiesce in it. But divulging the court's decision before it is publicly announced is generally considered to be unethical.

Another controversy arose 14 years later in the so-called Legal Tender Cases. The court, with two vacancies, had found the Civil War legal tender acts unconstitutional. But then President Grant named two justices to fill the vacancies, and the court voted to rehear the case. With the two new justices — William Strong and Joseph P. Bradley — voting with the majority, the court now found the legal tender acts constitutional. It was charged that Grant had appointed the two knowing in advance that they would vote to reverse the court's previous decision. But historians have not turned up any evidence that there was any explicit arrangement involved.

Political activity by Supreme Court justices has usually been frowned upon — especially in the 19th century, when several justices manifested a hunger for their party's presidential nomination.

Justice John McLean entertained presidential ambitions throughout his long Supreme Court career (1829-61)

Relatives on the Court

Several sets of relatives have served as Supreme Court justices. In two instances, they were on the court at the same time. There have been no father-son combinations, but one grandfather-grandson, one uncle-nephew and one father-in-law-son-in-law tandem. At least one pair of cousins served on the court.

The two John Marshall Harlans were grandfather and grandson. The elder Harlan, a Kentucky politician, was put on the court by President Rutherford B. Hayes in 1877 and served until 1911 — one of the longest periods of service in court history. His grandson and namesake was born and grew up in Chicago, but made his career as a highly successful Wall Street lawyer. His service extended from his appointment by President Dwight D. Eisenhower in 1954 until his resignation in September 1971.

Stephen J. Field was appointed to the Supreme Court by President Abraham Lincoln in 1863. Twenty-six years later, in 1889, he was still on the court when President Benjamin Harrison named his nephew, David J. Brewer, as an associate justice. Brewer was Field's sister's son. The two served together on the court from 1889 to Field's death in 1897.

Although Justice Stanley Matthews was only four years older than Justice Horace Gray, Matthews posthumously became Gray's father-in-law. Both justices were appointed in 1881, Matthews by President James A. Garfield and Gray later in the year by President Chester Arthur. They served together on the court until Matthews' death in March 1889. In June of the same year, Gray, a 61-year-old bachelor, married Matthews' daughter Jane.

The two Lamars who served on the court — Lucius Quintus Cincinnatus Lamar of Mississippi and Joseph Rucker Lamar of Georgia — were cousins. They were descendants of a Huguenot family that settled in the colonies in the 1600s. Lucius served on the court from 1888 to 1893, the first native-born southerner to be appointed after the Civil War. Joseph, appointed by President William Howard Taft, served from 1910 to 1916. Other prominent members of the same family were Mirabeau Buonaparte Lamar, second president of the Republic of Texas (1838-41), and Gazzaway Bugg Lamar, merchant, banker, and Confederate agent.

and flirted with several political parties at various stages. In 1856 he received 190 votes on an informal first ballot at the first Republican national convention. He also sought the Republican presidential nomination in 1860.

Chief Justice Salmon P. Chase had aspired to the presidency before going on the bench, losing the Republican nomination to Lincoln in 1860. In 1864, while serving as Lincoln's secretary of the Treasury, he allowed himself to become the focus of an anti-Lincoln group within the Republican Party. During his service on the court, in both 1868 and 1872, he made no secret of his still-burning presidential ambitions and allowed friends to maneuver politically for him.

In 1877 the Supreme Court was thrust into the election process when a dispute arose as to the outcome of the 1876 presidential election. To resolve the problem, Congress created a special electoral commission that included five

Supreme Court justices. Each chamber of Congress also chose five members, the Democratic House choosing five Democrats and the Republican Senate choosing five Republicans.

The five justices were supposed to be divided evenly politically — two Democrats, Nathan Clifford and Stephen J. Field, two Republicans, Samuel F. Miller and William Strong, and one independent, David Davis. Davis, however, withdrew from consideration because he had been elected a U.S. senator from Illinois. Justice Joseph P. Bradley, a Republican, was substituted for Justice Davis, making the overall lineup on the commission 8 to 7 in favor of the Republicans.

The three Republican justices loyally supported the claims of Republican presidential aspirant Rutherford B. Hayes on all questions, and the two Democratic justices backed Democratic nominee Samuel J. Tilden.

The result was the election of Hayes. Justice Clifford, the chairman of the commission, was so contemptuous of the outcome that he called Hayes an illegitimate president and refused to enter the White House during his incumbency.

Biographies of the Justices

This directory includes vital statistics and brief accounts of the lives and public careers of each of the 101 justices of the Supreme Court through mid-1981. Also included is biographical data on Sandra Day O'Connor, selected for the court by President Ronald Reagan in July 1981. The justices are listed in the chronological order of their appointment to the court; the dates beneath each justice's name indicate his period of service.

Sources used in compiling these biographies included: individual biographies of the justices; *The Justices of the United States Supreme Court 1789-1969: Their Lives and*

Major Opinions, ed. Leon Friedman and Fred L. Israel, R. R. Bowker Company, New York, 1969; *Dictionary of American Biography,* Charles Scribner's Sons, New York, 1928-1936; *Encyclopedia of American Biography,* ed. John A. Garraty, Harper & Row, New York 1974; *Encyclopedia Americana,* Americana Corp., New York, 1968; *Encyclopedia Britannica,* Encyclopedia Britannica Corp., Chicago, 1973; *Who Was Who in America,* Marquis-Who's Who, Inc., Chicago, 1968; and several histories, chiefly Charles Warren, *The Supreme Court in United States History,* 2 vols, Little, Brown & Co., Boston, 1922, 1926.

John Jay
(1789-1795)

Born: Dec. 12, 1745, New York, N.Y.

Education: privately tutored; attended boarding school; graduated from King's College (later Columbia University), 1764; clerked in law office of Benjamin Kissam, admitted to the bar in 1768.

Official Positions: secretary, royal boundary commission, 1773; member, New York Committee of 51, 1774; delegate, Continental Congress, 1774, 1775, 1777, president, 1778-79; delegate, New York provincial congress, 1776-77; chief justice, New York State, 1777-78; minister to Spain, 1779; secretary of foreign affairs, 1784-89; envoy to Great Britain, 1794-95; governor, New York, 1795-1801.

Supreme Court Appointment: nominated Chief Justice by President George Washington Sept. 24, 1789; confirmed by the Senate Sept. 26, 1789, by a voice vote; replaced on the court by Oliver Ellsworth, nominated by President Washington.

Family: married Sarah Van Brugh Livingston, April 28, 1774, died 1802; five daughters and two sons.

Died: May 17, 1829, Bedford, N.Y.

Personal Background

John Jay, the first Chief Justice of the United States, was descended from two of New York's most prominent families. His mother was Dutch, his father a wealthy merchant descended from French Huguenots.

The youngest of eight children, Jay grew up on the family farm at Rye, N.Y. He was taught Latin by his mother and attended a boarding school in New Rochelle for three years. Following more private tutoring, he entered

King's College and graduated at the age of 19. He was admitted to the bar four years later.

In 1774 Jay married Sarah Van Brugh Livingston, daughter of William Livingston, later governor of New Jersey during the Revolution. The couple had seven children, one of whom became a lawyer and active abolitionist. John Jay, Jay's grandson, served as minister to Austria in the early 1870s.

In his retirement years, Jay pursued his interest in agriculture and devoted time to the Episcopal Church. He was one of the founders of the American Bible Society and was elected its president in 1821. He opposed the War of 1812.

Public Career

During his many years of public service, Jay developed a reputation for fairness and honesty. Prior to the presidential election of 1800, Alexander Hamilton urged Governor Jay to call a special session of the New York legislature and change the state's election laws to ensure New York would deliver Federalist votes. Although a strong Federalist, Jay refused, writing to Hamilton that he would be "proposing a measure for party purposes which I think it would not become me to adopt."

Jay represented his state at both the first and second Continental Congresses. Although he was not present for the signing of the Declaration of Independence, he worked for its ratification in New York. At this time he also helped to draft the new state constitution.

In December 1778 Jay was elected president of the Continental Congress. The following September, he was sent to Spain in an attempt to win diplomatic recognition and large amounts of economic aid. Although the mission was at best only a modest success, it did provide Jay with important diplomatic experience. In 1783 Jay helped negotiate the Treaty of Paris, which formally ended the Revolutionary War.

Although he was not a member of the Constitutional Convention in 1787, Jay recognized the need for a stronger union while serving as secretary of foreign affairs. He contributed five essays to *The Federalist Papers* arguing for support of the new Constitution. In the presidential election of 1789 Jay received nine electoral votes.

While organizing his first administration, George Washington first offered Jay the position of secretary of state. When Jay declined, the president named him Chief Justice of the new Supreme Court. In this position, Jay helped pave the way for a strong, independent national judiciary.

In 1794 Jay, while still Chief Justice, was sent to England in an effort to ease growing hostilities between that country and the United States. The result was the controversial Jay Treaty, which outraged many at home who felt it surrendered too many American rights.

When he returned from the treaty negotiations Jay discovered he had been elected governor of New York, a position he had run for and lost in 1792. He promptly resigned as Chief Justice and served as governor for two three-year terms.

During his tenure Jay supported the gradual freeing of slaves and instituted a revision of the state criminal code. He became interested in prisoner welfare and recommended the construction of a model penitentiary. He also reduced the number of crimes carrying the death penalty.

Following the resignation of Oliver Ellsworth, President Adams, in December 1800, nominated Jay for a second term as Chief Justice. Although he was immediately confirmed by the Senate, Jay refused the office for health reasons and also, as he wrote Adams, because the court lacked "the energy, weight, and dignity which are essential to its affording due support to the national government."

Jay lived in retirement on his 800-acre estate in Westchester County, N.Y., for 28 years until his death at 83 in 1829.

John Rutledge
(1789-1791)

Born: ca. September 1739, Charleston, S.C.

Education: privately tutored; studied law at the Middle Temple in England; called to the English bar in 1760.

Official Positions: member, South Carolina Commons House of Assembly, 1761-76; South Carolina attorney general pro tem, 1764-65; delegate, Stamp Act Congress, 1765; member, Continental Congress, 1774-76, 1782-83; president, South Carolina General Assembly, 1776-78; governor, South Carolina, 1779-82; judge of the Court of Chancery of South Carolina, 1784-91; chief, South Carolina delegation to the Constitutional Convention, 1787; member, South Carolina convention to ratify U.S. Constitution, 1788; chief justice, South Carolina Supreme Court, 1791-1795; member, South Carolina Assembly, 1798-99.

Supreme Court Appointment: nominated associate justice by President George Washington September 24, 1789; confirmed by the Senate Sept. 26, 1789, by a voice vote; replaced on the court by Thomas Johnson, nominated by President Washington.

Family: married Elizabeth Grimké, May 1, 1763, died 1792; ten children.

Died: June 21, 1800, in Charleston, S.C.

Personal Background

Sarah Hext Rutledge was only 15 years old when she gave birth to her first son, John, in 1739. When her husband, Dr. John Rutledge, died in 1750, she was left a wealthy widow with seven children at the age of 26.

As a youth, John Rutledge studied law in the office of Andrew Rutledge, who was Speaker of the South Carolina Commons House of Assembly. Later he read for two years under Charleston lawyer James Parsons and then sailed for England, where he studied at the Inns of Court in London.

The wealthy Rutledge family, together with the Pinckneys, exerted great influence over South Carolina politics toward the end of the 18th century. John Rutledge's brother Edward, a law partner of Thomas Pinckney, was a signer of the Declaration of Independence and a delegate to the Constitutional Convention in Philadelphia; he was elected governor of South Carolina in 1798. Hugh Rutledge, another brother, also was a member of the South Carolina bar.

In 1763 Rutledge married Elizabeth Grimké, member of an old Charleston family and aunt of Angelina and Sarah Moore Grimké, two of South Carolina's most famous abolitionists and reformers. One of Rutledge's children, John Jr., became a member of the U.S. House of Representatives.

Public Career

Almost immediately upon his return to South Carolina from England in 1761, Rutledge became a leading member of the local bar. He had been home only three months when he was elected to the provincial legislature. In 1764 he was appointed attorney general by the King's governor in an attempt to win his support in a power struggle between the crown and the assembly. Rutledge held the position for 10 months but did not take sides against the assembly.

At the age of 25 Rutledge was the youngest delegate to the Stamp Act Congress in New York in 1765. There he served as chairman of the committee that drafted a petition to the King demanding repeal of the Stamp Act. The demand was met the following year.

In 1774 Rutledge headed the South Carolina delegation to the Continental Congress, which included his brother Edward and Edward's father-in-law, Henry Middleton. At the Congress in Philadelphia, Rutledge allied with other conservatives in supporting colonial rights but opposing separation from the mother country. When the Congress proposed an economic boycott against Britain, he convinced them to allow one product to continue to be traded — South Carolina's principal export, rice.

Rutledge continued to serve in the Continental Congress in 1775 but returned to South Carolina in December of that year to help form a new state government. A new constitution was written, calling for the formation of a new state assembly. Rutledge was elected president of the assembly in March 1776. In 1778 he resigned rather than accept a new, more liberal and democratic state constitution. In the face of a British invasion the following year, however, he was made governor by the assembly and given broad emergency powers.

South Carolina fell to the British in the summer of 1780. After the British army moved to Virginia in 1781, Rutledge returned to South Carolina to help restore civil authority. In 1784 he was appointed chief judge of the new state court of chancery.

At the Constitutional Convention in 1787 Rutledge served on the select committee that produced the first draft of the Constitution. He is responsible for writing the "supremacy clause," which states that the Constitution and laws of the United States "shall be the supreme law of the land."

Most of his attention, however, was directed toward protecting wealthy, anti-democratic interests. He successfully opposed, for example, an immediate ban on the slave trade. In 1789 South Carolina's electors cast their vice-presidential votes for Rutledge, in recognition of his service to the state.

Rutledge accepted President Washington's offer to become an associate justice of the Supreme Court in 1789. But although he participated in circuit court duties, he never sat as a justice due to personal illness and the inaction of the court. In February 1791 Rutledge resigned to accept what he considered to be a more prestigious position — chief justice of the supreme court of South Carolina.

The importance of the U.S. Supreme Court was gradually increasing, however, and in 1795 Rutledge wrote Washington of his desire to succeed John Jay as Chief Justice. Although he presided as a recess appointee over the August term of the court, his nomination as Chief Justice was rejected by the Senate in December 1795 because of his public opposition to the Jay Treaty with England.

Rutledge attempted to drown himself after hearing news of his Senate rejection and suffered lapses of sanity until the end of his life. He died in June 1800 at the age of 60.

William Cushing
(1789-1810)

Born: March 1, 1732, Scituate, Mass.

Education: graduated Harvard, 1751, honorary LL.D., 1785; honorary A.M., Yale, 1753; studied law under Jeremiah Gridley, admitted to the bar in 1755.

Official Positions: judge, probate court for Lincoln County, Mass. (now Maine), 1760-61; judge, Superior Court of Massachusetts Bay province, 1772-77; chief justice, Superior Court of the Commonwealth of Massachusetts, 1777-80, Supreme Judicial Court, 1780-89; member, Massachusetts Constitutional Convention, 1779; vice president, Massachusetts Convention, which ratified federal constitution, 1788; delegate to electoral college, 1788.

Supreme Court Appointment: nominated associate justice by President George Washington Sept. 24, 1789; confirmed by the Senate Sept. 26, 1789, by a voice vote; replaced on court by Joseph Story, nominated by President Madison.

Family: married Hannah Phillips, 1774.

Died: Sept. 13, 1810, Scituate, Mass.

Personal Background

William Cushing was a member of one of colonial Massachusetts' oldest and most prominent families. He

---

Margins of Confirmation

More often than not, the Senate's actual confirmation of a Supreme Court nominee is a formality. Deference to the president usually prevails over whatever reservations members may have aired during committee and floor debate, so that 73 nominees have been approved by voice vote with no recorded opposition. (Five men confirmed in this fashion subsequently declined to serve.)

Three justices were confirmed by unanimous roll-call votes. In two other cases, the nominee was officially confirmed by voice vote, but an individual senator put his opposition into the record: Sen. Joseph McCarthy, R-Wis., to the confirmation of Justice William J. Brennan Jr. in 1957, and Sen. Strom Thurmond, R-S.C., to Arthur J. Goldberg in 1962.

Close Calls

A number of justices, however, were approved for court service by the skin of their teeth. One vote allowed the confirmation of Stanley Matthews, confirmed by a 24-23 vote in 1881; a three-vote margin, 26-23, confirmed Nathan Clifford in 1858; and Lucius Q. C. Lamar squeaked by, 32-28, in 1888.

Other nominees who attracted substantial opposition — more than 10 votes against confirmation — were Chief Justice Roger B. Taney, 29-15 in 1836; Philip P. Barbour, 30-11, 1836; William Smith, 23-18, 1837 (Smith declined the seat); John Catron, 28-15, 1837; Edwin M. Stanton, 46-11, 1869; Roscoe Conkling, 39-12, 1882 (he declined); Chief Justice Melville W. Fuller, 41-20, 1888; David J. Brewer, 53-11, 1889; Mahlon Pitney, 50-26, 1912; Louis D. Brandeis, 47-22, 1916; Chief Justice Charles E. Hughes, 52-26, 1930; Hugo L. Black, 63-16, 1937; Sherman Minton, 48-16, 1949; John M. Harlan, 71-11, 1955; Potter Stewart, 70-17, 1959; Thurgood Marshall, 69-11, 1967; and William H. Rehnquist, 68-26, 1971.

Also-Rans

A few votes also made the difference in Senate decisions to reject court appointees. Among the almost-justices were Jeremiah S. Black, defeated by a single vote, 25-26, in 1861; John J. Parker, 39-41, 1930; John Rutledge's appointment as Chief Justice, 10-14, 1795; John C. Spencer, 21-26, 1844; George W. Woodward, 20-29, 1845; Ebenezer R. Hoar, 24-33, 1870; William B. Hornblower, 24-30, 1894; Wheeler H. Peckham, 32-41, 1894; Clement Haynsworth Jr., 45-55, 1969; and G. Harold Carswell, 45-51, 1970. (Confirmation votes for each justice appear in these pages, and in the list of appointments, pp. 243-245.)

---

was descended on his mother's side from John Cotton, the 17th century New England Puritan minister. Both his father and grandfather served in the government of the Massachusetts Bay province.

Cushing graduated from Harvard in 1751. After teaching for a year in Roxbury, Mass., he began studying law under Jeremiah Gridley in Boston. In 1755 he opened private practice in his home town of Scituate.

In 1760 Cushing moved to what is now Dresden, Maine, to become justice of the peace and judge of pro-bates. He was not an accomplished lawyer and seemed unable to make decisions. Before long, he had lost most of his corporate business to other lawyers.

In 1774 Cushing married Hannah Phillips of Middletown, Conn.

Public Career

When Cushing's father, John Cushing, decided to retire from the provincial superior court in 1772, he insisted that his son succeed him as judge. Although William Cushing was not the colonial government's first choice, he nonetheless was appointed to the position that year.

In 1774 Cushing reluctantly allied himself with the colonials by refusing to accept his salary through the British government. Although his decision did not come until the state legislature began preparing impeachment proceedings against him, he now began to be perceived as a supporter of the revolutionary cause. This belief was strengthened when he was denied a seat on the governor's council because of his stand.

In 1775 the new revolutionary government of Massachusetts reorganized the judicial system but retained Cushing as senior associate justice of the superior court. In 1777 he was elevated to chief justice.

Although Cushing played only a small role in the state constitutional convention of 1779, he actively supported ratification of the Constitution. He also served as vice president of the state convention that ratified the document in 1788.

Cushing was one of Washington's original appointees to the Supreme Court in 1789. He was the only justice to wear a full wig but quickly abandoned that practice.

In 1794 Cushing was persuaded to run against Samuel Adams for governor of Massachusetts — while retaining his court seat — but lost by a two-to-one margin. In 1795 he declined an offer from Washington to succeed John Jay as Chief Justice. As senior associate justice, however, he presided over the court when Chief Justice Ellsworth was absent.

Cushing remained on the bench until his death in 1810, the longest-serving of the original justices.

James Wilson
(1789-1798)

Born: Sept. 14, 1742, Caskardy, Scotland.

Education: attended University of St. Andrews (Scotland); read law in office of John Dickinson, admitted to the bar in 1767; honorary M.A., College of Philadelphia, 1776, honorary LL.D., 1790.

Official Positions: delegate, first Provincial Convention at Philadelphia, 1774; delegate, Continental Congress, 1775-77, 1783, 1785-87; delegate, U.S. Constitutional Convention, 1787; delegate, Pennsylvania convention to ratify U.S. Constitution, 1787.

Supreme Court Appointment: nominated associate justice by President George Washington Sept. 24, 1789; confirmed by the Senate Sept. 26, 1789, by a voice vote; replaced on the court by Bushrod Washington, nominated by President John Adams.

Family: married, first, Rachel Bird, Nov. 5, 1771, died 1786, six children; second, Hannah Gray, Sept. 19, 1793, one son died in infancy.

Died: Aug. 21, 1798, Edenton, N.C.

Personal Background

James Wilson was born in the Scottish Lowlands, the son of a Caskardy farmer. Though the family had little money, his devout Calvinist parents were determined that James be educated for the ministry.

After study in local grammar schools, Wilson at 14 won a scholarship to St. Andrews University and matriculated in the fall of 1757. During his fifth year, he entered the university's divinity school but was forced to leave for financial reasons when his father died.

To help support his family, he took a job as a private tutor but left the position to study accounting and book-keeping in Edinburgh. In 1765 he decided against becoming a clerk and sailed for America.

After studying law in the new country, Wilson became one of its foremost legal scholars. Described as a man of extreme energy, he was driven by a desire for wealth and fame, constantly involved in various speculation schemes, primarily in land. He was part-owner of the Somerset Mills on the Delaware River and president of the Illinois and Wabash Co., which had vast western land holdings.

From 1777 to 1787, Wilson devoted most of his energy to developing new business interests. As his financial commitments built, he continued to seek new investments. But the credit cycle eventually caught up with Wilson. As an associate justice, he travelled the southern circuit in constant fear of being thrown in jail for bad debts.

Public Career

Wilson arrived in Philadelphia in the fall of 1765 and immediately obtained a tutorship at the College of Philadelphia. Teaching tired him, however, and he saw a better opportunity in law. He soon began reading in the office of John Dickinson, a prominent attorney who had studied at the Inns of Court.

In 1768 Wilson opened private practice in Reading, Pa. Two years later, he moved west to Carlisle, where his practice expanded rapidly. By 1774 he was practicing in seven counties, specializing in land law.

In 1775 Wilson was elected a delegate to the Continental Congress, where he served on several committees. He aligned himself with other members of the Pennsylvania delegation in opposing separation from England. In the end, however, he followed the state assembly's instructions and signed the Declaration of Independence.

Wilson's opposition to the Pennsylvania constitution of 1776 attracted criticism from state populists and earned him a reputation as a conservative aristocrat. That reputation grew when he developed an active practice in Philadelphia defending wealthy Tories and other rich businessmen. In 1779 he was forced to barricade his home against an armed attack by a riotous mob angered over high inflation and food shortages. He eventually had to go into hiding.

At the Constitutional Convention in 1787, Wilson was a member of the committee of detail, responsible for writing the first draft of the Constitution. Although his populist foes refused to believe it, Wilson was a fervent advocate of popular sovereignty and democracy who supported popular election of the president and members of both the Senate and House. One of the first to envision the principle of judicial review, Wilson fought for a strong national judiciary and a powerful presidency. He saw no conflict between the ideal of popular rule and a strong national government since, in his view, the national government existed only by virtue of the popular will. Wilson is credited with incorporating this idea of popular sovereignty into the Constitution.

As the new national government was being formed, Wilson hoped for federal office and offered his name to Washington as Chief Justice of the new Supreme Court. Washington appointed John Jay instead and named Wilson an associate justice.

Of the original Washington appointees to the Supreme Court, Wilson was its most accomplished legal scholar. A pamphlet he had published in 1774 presaged the concept of "dominion status" that serves today as the official guiding principle of the British Commonwealth.

His defense of the Bank of North America in 1785 anticipated constitutional opinions delivered by Chief Justice Marshall at least 25 years later. In 1964 Associate Justice Hugo Black cited Wilson in *Wesberry v. Sanders* as a supporting source for the "one-man-one-vote" principle.

Around 1796 Wilson's investment schemes began to collapse around him. While riding circuit, he was chased by angry creditors who caught up with him in Burlington, N.J., and had him jailed. He then sought refuge in Edenton, N.C. — the hometown of fellow Justice James Iredell — but was soon discovered and imprisoned again. Eventually released, he remained in Edenton in ill health. He died at 55 in a dingy inn next to the Edenton Court House.

John Blair Jr.
(1789-1796)

Born: 1732, Williamsburg, Va.

Education: graduated with honors from College of William and Mary, 1754; studied law at Middle Temple, London, 1755-56.

Official Positions: member, Virginia House of Burgesses, 1766-1770; clerk, Virginia Governor's Council, 1770-75; delegate, Virginia Constitutional Convention, 1776; member, Virginia Governor's Council, 1776; judge, Virginia General Court, 1777-78, chief justice, 1779; judge, first Virginia Court of Appeals, 1780-89; delegate, U.S. Constitutional Convention, 1787; judge, Virginia Supreme Court of Appeals, 1789.

Supreme Court Appointment: nominated associate justice by President George Washington Sept. 24, 1789; confirmed by the Senate Sept. 26, 1789, by a voice vote; replaced on court by Samuel Chase, nominated by President Washington.

Family: married Jean Balfour, died 1792.

Died: Aug. 31, 1800, Williamsburg, Va.

Personal Background

John Blair Jr. was the son of one of Virginia's most prominent colonial officials, a member of the House of Burgesses and a member of the Governor's Council. He was also acting governor of the state in 1758 and 1768.

The family owned rich land holdings, and young John — one of 10 children — was given an excellent education. In 1754 he graduated from the College of William and Mary, which had been founded by his great-uncle James Blair. After studying law at the Middle Temple in London, he returned home to Williamsburg and began practicing law.

A slightly built man, six feet tall with thinning red hair, Blair toward the end of his life suffered from chronic headaches, possibly brought on by the rigors of riding circuit. His wife, Jean Balfour, died in 1796 from a chronic illness which was described at the time as hysteria.

Public Career

Blair entered the Virginia House of Burgesses in 1766 at the age of 34. A conservative, he opposed the defiant resolutions of Patrick Henry condemning the Stamp Act, but joined with leading merchants in agreeing to boycott specific British imports.

In 1770 Blair resigned his seat to become clerk of the governor's council, the first of several state offices and judgeships. In 1782, while serving as a judge on the state's first court of appeals, he sided with the majority decision in *Commonwealth v. Caton* that the court could declare legislative acts unconstitutional.

Although not a leading participant in the Constitutional Convention of 1787, Blair firmly supported ratification and was one of three Virginia delegates who signed the new document.

When the Virginia judicial system was reorganized in 1789, Blair sat on the new supreme court of appeals for three months until his appointment as one of the original justices of the U.S. Supreme Court. Because of his wife's illness and the relative inactivity of the court, he did not attend all its sessions. He finally resigned in January 1796 after his wife's death.

In 1799 Blair wrote to his sister of being "struck with a strange disorder . . . depriving me of nearly all the powers of mind." He died on Aug. 31, 1800, at his home in Williamsburg.

James Iredell
(1790-1799)

Born: Lewes, England, Oct. 5, 1751.

Education: educated in England; read law under Samuel Johnston of North Carolina; licensed to practice, 1770-71.

Recess Appointments

If a vacancy occurs on the Supreme Court when the Senate is not in session, the president may make a recess appointment. The appointee may be sworn in as a justice and participate actively in the deliberations and decisions of the court. When the Senate reconvenes, the president must then formally nominate the appointee, who is then subject to Senate confirmation. If confirmed, the justice will be sworn in a second time.

Of the 15 recess appointments in the court's history, only five have taken their seats on the bench before being confirmed by the Senate. Four of these men were eventually confirmed when the Senate reconvened — Benjamin R. Curtis, appointed and confirmed in December 1851; Earl Warren, appointed as Chief Justice in September 1953 and confirmed in March 1954; William J. Brennan Jr., appointed in October 1956 and confirmed in 1957; and Potter Stewart, appointed in October 1958 and confirmed in May 1959.

The fifth recess appointee who took his seat before his confirmation was ultimately rejected by the Senate. When John Jay resigned as the nation's first Chief Justice in June 1795, John Rutledge asked President Washington to appoint him to the vacancy. A Federalist, Rutledge had served for a year and a half as one of the first associate justices, resigning in 1791.

Washington complied with the request and gave Rutledge a recess appointment. Rutledge presided over the August 1795 term of the court at which two cases were heard and decided. When the Senate convened at the end of the year, it refused to confirm Rutledge's formal nomination, rejecting him Dec. 15, 1795, by a 10-14 vote. Reports that Rutledge suffered a mental disability no doubt played some role in his rejection. But the deciding factor was his outspoken opposition to the Jay Treaty, which made him appear disloyal to his own political party.

The ten men who received recess appointments but who did not take their place on the court until after formal confirmation by the Senate were: Thomas Johnson, confirmed in 1791; Bushrod Washington, confirmed in 1798; Alfred Moore, confirmed in 1799; Brockholst Livingston, confirmed in 1806; Smith Thompson, confirmed in 1823; John McKinley, confirmed in 1837; Levi Woodbury, confirmed in 1846; David Davis, confirmed in 1862; John Marshall Harlan, confirmed in 1877; and Oliver Wendell Holmes Jr., confirmed in 1902.

Sources: Henry J. Abraham. *Justices and Presidents: A Political History of Appointments to the Supreme Court.* New York: Oxford University Press, 1974. U.S. Senate Judiciary Committee. *Nomination of Potter Stewart.* Executive Rept. No. 2, 86th Cong., 1st Sess., Minority Views.

Official Positions: comptroller of customs, Edenton, N.C., 1768-1774; collector of customs, Port of North Carolina, 1774-76; judge, Superior Court of North Carolina, 1778; attorney general, North Carolina, 1779-1781; member, North Carolina Council of State, 1787; delegate, North Carolina convention for ratification of federal Constitution, 1788.

Supreme Court Appointment: nominated associate justice by President George Washington Feb. 8, 1790; confirmed by the Senate Feb. 10, 1790, by a voice vote; replaced on court by Alfred Moore, nominated by President John Adams.

Family: married Hannah Johnston, July 18, 1773; three children.

Died: Oct. 20, 1799, Edenton, N.C.

Personal Background

James Iredell was born into an English family reputedly descended from Oliver Cromwell's son-in-law, Henry Ireton. The family was forced to change its name, so the story goes, following the return of Charles II to the throne.

When James' merchant father, Francis, became ill in the early 1760s, James was able through family connections to acquire a position in America in 1868 as comptroller of the customs in Edenton, N.C. During his six years in that job he read law in the office of Samuel Johnston and began practice in December 1770. In 1773 he married his mentor's sister, Hannah Johnston.

Because of a slight lisp, Iredell was not effective as a public speaker but was a prolific writer of letters and essays. Many of these writings survive today and reveal a clear, candid style.

Public Career

Although a new immigrant and an employee of the British, Iredell nevertheless soon found himself in support of the American revolutionary cause. In 1776 he resigned from his job as collector for the crown at the port of Edenton.

Iredell then served on a commission to redraft North Carolina law in conformance with the state's new independent status. When a new state judicial court system was created the following year, he was chosen one of three superior court judges — a position he reluctantly accepted. But the rigors of travelling circuit were burdensome for him, and he resigned after a few months to return to private law practice.

From 1779 to 1781, Iredell served as state attorney general. In 1787 the legislature appointed him to collect and revise all state laws; the new code appeared in 1791.

After the war Iredell had aligned himself with conservative leaders who favored a strong government and adherence to the peace treaty terms of 1783. In 1786 he stated that the state constitution had the power to limit the state legislature — a novel idea at the time.

Iredell's most influential work, written under the pen name of "Marcus," was his defense of the new federal Constitution. The tract, which appeared at the same time as the first issues of the Jefferson-Hamilton-Jay pro-Constitutional *Federalist Papers,* refuted George Mason's 11 objections to the document.

At the state ratification convention in 1788, Iredell served as floor leader of the Federalists, a position that brought him to the attention of George Washington. When Robert Harrison declined to serve on the Supreme Court in 1790, the president decided to appoint Iredell because, as Washington noted in his diary, "in addition to the reputation he sustains for abilities, legal knowledge and respectability of character, he is of a State of some importance in the Union that has given no character to a federal office."

Iredell served on the court for nine years, riding the southern circuit five times between 1790 and 1794. In dissent from *Chisholm v. Georgia,* he argued that a state could not be sued by a citizen from another state — a position later added to the Constitution by the 11th

Amendment. In 1798 he set a precedent for *Marbury v. Madison* in arguing for the right of courts to declare laws unconstitutional *(Calder v. Bull)*.

Iredell died in 1799 at 48 in his home in Edenton.

Thomas Johnson
(1791-1793)

Born: Nov. 4, 1732, Calvert County, Md.

Education: educated at home; studied law under Stephen Bordley; admitted to the bar, 1760.

Official Positions: delegate, Maryland Provincial Assembly, 1762; delegate, Annapolis Convention of 1774; member, Continental Congress, 1774-1777; delegate, first constitutional convention of Maryland, 1776; first governor of Maryland, 1777-1779; member, Maryland House of Delegates, 1780, 1786, 1787; member, Maryland convention for ratification of the federal Constitution, 1788; chief judge, general court of Maryland, 1790-91; member, board of commissioners of the Federal City, 1791-94.

Supreme Court Appointment: nominated associate justice by President George Washington Nov. 1, 1791, to replace John Rutledge, who resigned; confirmed by the Senate Nov. 7, 1791, by a voice vote; replaced on court by William Paterson, nominated by President Washington.

Family: married Ann Jennings, Feb. 16, 1766, died 1794; three boys and five girls, one of whom died in infancy.

Died: Oct. 26, 1819, Frederick, Md.

Personal Background

Born to Thomas and Dorcas Sedgwick Johnson in 1732, Thomas Johnson was one of 12 children. He received no formal education as a youth but trained in the office of Thomas Jennings, clerk of the Maryland provincial court in Annapolis. Following that apprenticeship, Johnson worked and studied in the office of Stephen Bordley, an Annapolis attorney. He was admitted to the bar in 1760.

During the Revolution Johnson served as first brigadier-general of the Maryland militia. In 1777 he was responsible for leading almost 2,000 men from Frederick, Md., to Gen. Washington's headquarters in New Jersey.

After the war Johnson revived a plan he had dreamed of as early as 1770 — to improve navigation along the Potomac River and open a passageway to the west coast. To this end, he helped organize the state-chartered Potomac Company in 1785, with his good friend George Washington as its president. The company eventually proved unprofitable.

In 1766 Johnson married Ann Jennings, the daughter of his old employer in the provincial court. They were married for 28 years, until her death in 1794.

Public Career

Johnson began his career as a Maryland statesman in 1762 when he was chosen a delegate to the Maryland

Provincial Assembly from Anne Arundel County. As a member of the first Continental Congress in Philadelphia, he served on the committee that drafted a petition of grievances to King George III. In 1775 it was Thomas Johnson who placed the name of George Washington in nomination before the Congress for the position of commander-in-chief of the Continental Army.

Johnson was absent from Philadelphia the day the Declaration of Independence was signed. However, he thoroughly supported the document and voted for Maryland's independence on July 6, 1776. He also helped to write the new state constitution that year.

During the Revolution Johnson served three consecutive terms as governor of Maryland and played a key role in keeping Washington's army manned and equipped.

Declining to serve a fourth term as governor, Johnson entered the Maryland house of delegates in 1780, where he helped prepare legislation determining the jurisdiction of the state admiralty court. As a member of the state ratification convention in 1788, he worked for approval of the new federal Constitution. Two years later he became chief judge of the Maryland general court.

Johnson was nominated associate justice of the Supreme Court in August 1791. Hesitant because of the rigors of riding circuit, he was assured by Chief Justice Jay that every attempt would be made to bring him relief. When assigned to the southern circuit, however, including all territory south of the Potomac, he was unable to persuade Jay to rotate assignments. Citing ill health, he resigned from the bench after serving little more than a year. He wrote only one opinion during his tenure.

Johnson, however, continued in public life as a member of the commission appointed by Washington to plan the new national capital on the Potomac. That commission selected the design submitted by Pierre L'Enfant and voted to name the new city "Washington." Johnson was present when the cornerstone of the new Capitol building was laid in September 1793.

In 1795 Johnson refused an offer from President Washington to serve as secretary of state. He retired to Frederick, Md., where he died at the age of 86.

William Paterson
(1793-1806)

Born: Dec. 24, 1745, County Antrim, Ireland.

Education: graduated from College of New Jersey (Princeton), 1763, Master of Arts, 1766; studied law under Richard Stockton; admitted to the bar, 1769.

Official Positions: member, New Jersey Provincial Congress, 1775-76; delegate, New Jersey State Constitutional Convention, 1776; New Jersey attorney general, 1776-83; delegate, U.S. Constitutional Convention, 1787; U.S. senator, 1789-1790; governor, New Jersey, 1790-93.

The Men Who Never Served

One Supreme Court nominee was confirmed by the Senate but died before he could take his seat on the court.

Edwin M. Stanton — President Lincoln's fiery secretary of war who became the chief cabinet opponent of Lincoln's successor, Andrew Johnson — resigned his post in 1868 after Congress' effort to impeach Johnson failed.

The next year, Stanton's congressional supporters persuaded President Grant to appoint Stanton, already in failing health, to a court seat. He was quickly confirmed, on Dec. 20, 1869, but died four days later.

Seven other nominees were confirmed but declined the appointment.

Supreme Court Appointment: nominated associate justice by President George Washington March 4, 1793, to replace Thomas Johnson, who resigned; confirmed by the Senate March 4, 1793, by a voice vote; replaced on court by H. Brockholst Livingston, nominated by President Jefferson.

Family: married, first, Cornelia Bell, Feb. 9, 1779, died 1783, three children; second, Euphemia White, 1785.

Died: September 9, 1806, Albany, N.Y.

Personal Background

Born in Ireland, William Paterson emigrated to America with his parents when he was two years old. The family lived in several places before settling in Princeton, N.J., where William's father, Richard, began manufacturing tin plate and selling general merchandise. He also made successful real estate investments which helped to pay for William's education.

At the college of New Jersey (Princeton), Paterson was a fellow student of Oliver Ellsworth, who would later become Chief Justice of the Supreme Court. With Ellsworth and others, Paterson founded the Well-Meaning Society (later the Cliosophic Club) as a forum for lively discussions on the political issues of the day.

In 1766 Paterson received a Master of Arts degree from Princeton and the same year began reading law in the office of Richard Stockton. In 1769 he opened his own practice in New Bromley, about 30 miles from Princeton. There was little demand for his services, however, and in 1772 he returned to the college town.

Paterson married twice. With his first wife, Cornelia Bell, he lived on a farm on the Raritan River west of New Brunswick. She died in 1783 after the birth of their third child. Two years later Paterson married her close friend, Euphemia White.

Public Career

Paterson was elected as a delegate from Somerset County to the provincial congress of New Jersey in 1775, where he served as assistant secretary and later secretary. In 1776 he helped write the state constitution and was chosen attorney general. During this period Paterson also was a member of the state legislative council, a county minuteman officer and a member of the council of safety.

In May 1787 Paterson was chosen a delegate to the Constitutional Convention in Philadelphia, where he was responsible for introducing the New Jersey Plan, proposing a unicameral legislature giving each state an equal vote. Despite failure of that plan, Paterson signed the Constitution and worked for its adoption in New Jersey.

As a member of the judiciary committee of the new U.S. Senate, Paterson was responsible, along with his old classmate Oliver Ellsworth, for writing the Judiciary Act of 1789. He left the Senate in 1790 when he was chosen governor and chancellor of the state of New Jersey.

In this capacity, Paterson codified the laws of the state and updated the procedural rules for the common-law and chancery courts. With the assistance of Alexander Hamilton, he laid plans for an industrial town on the Passaic River, to be named Paterson.

Appointed to the Supreme Court in 1793, Paterson — while riding circuit — tried several cases arising out of the Whiskey Rebellion in western Pennsylvania. He took a Federalist position in a number of sedition trials.

When Oliver Ellsworth resigned as Chief Justice in 1800, President Adams refused to elevate Paterson to the position because of his close alliance with Alexander Hamilton. In 1804 Paterson missed a session of the court because of failing health and in 1806 decided to travel to Ballston Springs, N.Y., for treatment. He made the trip only as far as his daughter's home in Albany, where he died on Sept. 9.

Samuel Chase
(1796-1811)

Born: April 17, 1741, Somerset County, Md.

Education: tutored by father; studied law in Annapolis law office; admitted to bar in 1761.

Official Positions: member, Maryland General Assembly, 1764-84; delegate, Continental Congress, 1774-78, 1784-85; member, Maryland Committee of Correspondence, 1774; member, Maryland Convention and Council of Safety, 1775; judge, Baltimore Criminal Court, 1788-96; chief judge, General Court of Maryland, 1791-96.

Supreme Court Appointment: nominated associate justice by President George Washington Jan. 26, 1796, to replace John Blair, who resigned; confirmed by the Senate Jan. 27, 1796, by a voice vote; replaced on court by Gabriel Duvall, nominated by President Madison.

Family: married, first, Anne Baldwin May 21, 1762, who died; second, Hannah Kilty Giles, March 3, 1784, four children.

Died: June 19, 1811, Baltimore, Md.

Personal Background

Samuel Chase's mother, Martha Walker, died when he was still a child. His father, Thomas Chase, an Episcopal clergyman, tutored him at home and gave him a foundation in the classics. At 18, Chase began studying law in the office of Hammond and Hall in Annapolis. Two years later, in 1761, he was admitted to the bar and began practicing in the mayor's court of Annapolis. Chase lived in the state capital until 1786, when he moved to Baltimore.

During his lifetime Chase invested in several business schemes that later caused him embarrassment. In 1778, when his efforts to corner the flour market through speculation were discovered, he was dismissed as a member of the Maryland delegation to the Continental Congress for two years.

Chase also was involved in two war-supply partnerships and owned many iron and coal properties. These businesses were largely failures, and in 1789 he was forced to declare personal bankruptcy.

About six feet in height, Chase had a large head and brownish-red complexion that earned him the nickname "bacon face" among his law colleagues. He was a signer of the Declaration of Independence and a fervent patriot whose career was marked by turbulence, sensation and controversy.

Public Career

When Chase entered the Maryland general assembly in 1764 he took immediate opposition to the policies of the British-appointed governor of the colony. As a member of the "Sons of Liberty," he participated in riotous demonstrations, incurring the wrath of the Annapolis mayor and aldermen who called him a "busy, restless incendiary, a ringleader of mobs, a foul-mouthed and inflaming son of discord."

In 1778 Chase served on no fewer than 30 committees of the Continental Congress. As a delegate from Maryland, he urged that the colonies unite in an economic boycott of England. He served with Benjamin Franklin and Charles Carroll on a commission sent to Montreal to persuade Canada to join with the colonies against Great Britain. The mission failed.

Instrumental in achieving support in Maryland for the Declaration of Independence, Chase did not favor adoption of the new Constitution, arguing it would institute an elitist government and not a government of the people. He wrote a series of articles against ratification under the pen name of "Caution."

As a judge, his abusive and overbearing manner won him few friends. Displeased over the fact that Chase held two judgeships simultaneously, the Maryland assembly at one point tried to strip from him all public offices, but the vote fell short.

It was his impeachment trial in 1805 that was to bring him the most publicity. By the time Chase reached the Supreme Court he had become a radical Federalist. As an associate justice, he took an active part in Federalist politics and campaigned hard for the Alien and Sedition Acts. Biased and dogmatic, he sought the indictment of Republican newspaper editors who sided against the Federalists.

Chase's greatest political impropriety came on May 2, 1803, when he gave an impassioned speech to a grand jury against democratic "mobocracy." He was impeached by the House on March 12, 1804. Although most senators agreed that Chase had acted poorly on the bench, there were not enough votes to convict him of "high crimes," and he kept his seat on the court. There have been no other impeachments of Supreme Court justices.

Following the trial, Chase sank into oblivion. By then, John Marshall dominated the court, and Chase was often ill from gout and unable to attend meetings. He died in 1811.

Oliver Ellsworth
(1796-1800)

Born: April 29, 1745, Windsor, Conn.

Education: B.A., Princeton, 1766; honorary LL.D., Yale (1790), Princeton (1790) and Dartmouth (1797).

Official Positions: member, Connecticut General Assembly, 1773-1776; state's attorney, Hartford Co., 1777-85; delegate to Continental Congress, 1777-84; member, Connecticut Council of Safety, 1779; member, Governor's Council, 1780-85, 1801-07; judge, Connecticut Superior Court, 1785-89; delegate, Constitutional Convention, 1787; member, U.S. Senate 1789-96; commissioner to France, 1799-1800.

Supreme Court Appointment: nominated Chief Justice by President George Washington March 3, 1796, to replace John Jay, who resigned; confirmed by the Senate March 4, 1796, by a 21-1 vote; succeeded on court by John Marshall, nominated by President John Adams.

Family: married Abigail Wolcott, 1771; four sons and three daughters survived infancy.

Died: Nov. 26, 1807, Windsor, Conn.

Personal Background

Oliver Ellsworth's great-grandfather immigrated in the middle of the 17th century from Yorkshire, England, to Windsor, Conn., where the future second Chief Justice was born to captain David Ellsworth and Jemima Leavitt in 1745.

After studying under a Bethlehem, Conn., minister, Ellsworth entered Yale at 17. For reasons that are now unclear, he left Yale at the end of his sophomore year and enrolled in Princeton, where he engaged in lively discussions about colonial politics and sharpened his debating skills.

After graduating from Princeton, Ellsworth began studying for the ministry at the urging of his father. Theology did not hold his interest long, however, and he soon turned to law. After four years of training he was admitted to the bar in 1777.

Ellworth had little money in the early years of his practice. After marrying 16-year-old Abigail Wolcott in 1772, he settled on a farm that had belonged to his father and worked the land himself. When the Hartford court was in session, he walked to the town and back, a total of 20 miles.

Ellsworth's financial situation changed dramatically, however, as his practice grew. By 1780 he had become a leading member of the Connecticut bar and was well on his way toward acquiring a large fortune.

According to contemporary accounts, Ellsworth was a good conversationalist and elegant dresser who enjoyed frequent pinches of snuff. A tall, robust man, he was in the habit of talking to himself and was prone to obstinacy. Aaron Burr is said to have remarked: "If Ellsworth had happened to spell the name of the Deity wih two d's, it would have taken the Senate three weeks to expunge the superfluous letter."

Deeply religious, Ellsworth was an active member of the Congregationalist Church and returned to the study of theology after his retirement from the court. He also advocated improved farming techniques for Connecticut and wrote a regular advice column on the subject.

Public Career

Although his name is not among the signers of the Constitution, Ellsworth deserves to be included in any list of the nation's "founding fathers." Principal author of the Judiciary Act of 1789 and co-author of the Connecticut Compromise, Ellsworth originated the name for the new American government when he suggested the appellation "United States" in a resolution being considered by the Constitutional Convention.

Ellsworth's political career began in 1773 when he was elected to the Connecticut general assembly. In 1775 he was appointed one of five members of the committee of the pay table, which controlled the state's Revolutionary War expenditures. He also was a Connecticut delegate to the Continental Congress during the Revolution and served on many of its committees, including one that heard appeals from admiralty courts.

In 1787 Ellsworth was elected a member of the Connecticut delegation to the Constitutional Convention and helped devise the famous "Connecticut Compromise" that ended the dispute between large and small states over representation in the federal legislature.

Ellsworth had to leave the convention before it ended to attend to judicial business in Connecticut, and was not present for the signing of the newly drafted Constitution. He worked hard for its ratification in Connecticut, however.

In 1789 Ellsworth became one of Connecticut's first two U.S. senators. His administrative skills were immediately put to use as he helped draft the first set of Senate rules and organize the army, a U.S. Post Office and a census. Ellsworth engineered the conference report on the Bill of Rights and helped draft the measure that admitted North Carolina to the union. It was Ellsworth's idea to force Rhode Island to join the federation by imposing an economic boycott.

A staunch supporter of Hamilton's monetary policies, Ellsworth had by this time become a strong Federalist. His most important work in the Senate came when he was chosen to head a committee to draft a bill organizing the federal judiciary. The bill, which provided for the initial structure of the Supreme Court, the district courts and the circuit courts, became the Judiciary Act of 1789.

When John Jay resigned as Chief Justice of the United States in 1795, President Washington appointed John Rutledge as his successor. The Senate refused to confirm Rutledge, however, and Washington chose to elevate Associate Justice William Cushing. When Cushing declined, the nomination fell to Ellsworth.

Ellsworth had been on the court only three years when President Adams sent him to France with two other envoys in an effort to soften hostilities between France and the United States. The mission, plagued by transportation difficulties and only partially successful, took its toll on Ellsworth's health.

Before returning home, Ellsworth notified Adams of his resignation as Chief Justice. He lived on his estate in Windsor until his death in 1807.

Bushrod Washington
(1798-1829)

Born: June 5, 1762, Westmoreland County, Va.

Education: privately tutored; graduated College of William and Mary, 1778; read law under James Wilson; member, Virginia bar; honorary LL.D. degrees from Harvard, Princeton and University of Pennsylvania.

Official Positions: member, Virginia House of Delegates, 1787; member, Virginia convention to ratify U.S. Constitution, 1788.

Supreme Court Appointment: nominated associate justice by President John Adams Dec. 19, 1798, to replace James Wilson, who died; confirmed by the Senate Dec. 20, 1798, by a voice vote; succeeded on court by Henry Baldwin, nominated by President Jackson.

Family: married Julia Ann Blackburn, 1785; no children.

Died: Nov. 26, 1829, in Philadelphia, Pa.

Personal Background

Bushrod Washington received his first name from his mother, Hannah Bushrod, a member of one of Virginia's oldest colonial families. His father, John Augustine Washington, was a brother of George Washington and served as a member of the Virginia legislature and magistrate of Westmoreland County, Va.

As a boy Bushrod was privately tutored. He graduated from the College of William and Mary at 16 and was a founding member of Phi Beta Kappa, then a secret social club. He was a student in George Wythe's law course at the same time as John Marshall.

Toward the end of the Revolution, Washington enlisted as a private in the Continental Army. He was present when Cornwallis surrendered at Yorktown in October 1781. After the war, Washington studied law for two years under the Philadelphia lawyer James Wilson, whom he would later succeed on the Supreme Court.

Biographical sources remember Bushrod Washington as a confirmed user of snuff and an untidy dresser, blind in one eye. According to most accounts, he also was considered to be a diligent and methodical student of the law. In the words of his colleague, Justice Joseph Story: "His mind was solid, rather than brilliant; sagacious and searching, rather than quick or eager; slow, but not torpid...."

In 1785 Washington married Julia Ann Blackburn, the daughter of an aide-de-camp to Gen. Washington during the Revolution. She is said to have been at his side constantly, even when he made his rounds as a circuit judge. She was with him when he died in Philadelphia and died herself during the trip home to attend the funeral.

When George Washington died in 1799 with no children of his own, he left his Mount Vernon estate, including all his public and private papers, to his nephew Bushrod. The former president had provided that his slaves be freed when his wife Martha died. But Bushrod refused to carry out this request and in 1821 sold more than 50 of the slaves to two men from Louisiana, separating families in the process.

For this action he was bitterly attacked in several journals of the day. He dismissed the criticism by arguing the slaves were his property to do with as he saw fit. In 1816 Washington had been elected the first president of the American Colonization Society, established to transport free blacks to Africa — a movement that was criticized by abolitionists.

Public Career

Washington began private law practice in Westmoreland County, Va., and later in Alexandria, Va., where he specialized in chancery cases. In 1787, with encouragement from his uncle, he ran for the Virginia House of Delegates and was elected. The following year he was sent as a delegate to the state ratification convention and successfully argued, along with Marshall and Madison, for state approval of the new federal Constitution.

Around 1790 Washington moved to Richmond, where he developed a successful law practice and trained many law students, including Henry Clay. During this period he also served as reporter for the court of appeals and spent much of his time writing two volumes of reports of cases argued before the court.

During his tenure on the court, Washington was often associated with Chief Justice Marshall and Justice Story. Indeed, Justice William Johnson, another member of the Marshall court, once complained that Marshall and Washington "are commonly estimated as a single judge." Washington and Marshall disagreed in only three cases during their joint tenure.

Alfred Moore
(1799-1804)

Born: May 21, 1755, New Hanover County, N.C.

Education: educated in Boston; studied law under his father; received law license, 1775.

Official Positions: member, North Carolina legislature, 1782, 1792; North Carolina attorney general, 1782-91; trustee, University of North Carolina, 1789-1807; North Carolina Superior Court judge, 1799.

Supreme Court Appointment: nominated associate justice by President John Adams, Dec. 6, 1799, to replace James Iredell, who died; confirmed by the Senate Dec. 10, 1799, by a voice vote; succeeded on court by William Johnson, nominated by President Jefferson.

Family: married Susanna Eagles.

Died: Oct. 15, 1810, Bladen County, N.C.

Personal Background

Alfred Moore was born in 1755, the son of a North Carolina colonial judge. He was descended from Roger

Moore, a leader of the 1641 Irish Rebellion, and James Moore, governor of South Carolina in the early 18th century.

Seeking the best education for their son, Moore's parents sent him to school in Boston. After completing his studies there, Moore returned home and read law under his father. At the age of 20 he was licensed to practice law.

During the Revolution Moore served as a captain in a Continental regiment commanded by his uncle, Colonel James Moore. He saw action in several successful battles, but, after his father died in 1777, left the army and returned to the family plantation to be with his mother. He continued his activities against the British by joining the local militia and participating in raids on troops stationed in Wilmington. The British plundered his property in retaliation.

Public Career

Following brief service in the North Carolina legislature, Moore became state attorney general in 1782, succeeding James Iredell, his predecessor on the Supreme Court, and during that time became a leader of the state bar.

A strong Federalist, Moore was instrumental in getting North Carolina finally to ratify the Constitution in 1789.

Moore resigned as attorney general in 1791 when the state legislature created a new office of solicitor general, giving it the same powers and salary as the attorney general. Moore claimed the new office was unconstitutional.

In 1792 Moore was elected to the state legislature again, but three years later lost a race for the U.S. Senate by one vote in the legislature. In 1798 he was appointed by President John Adams as one of three commissioners to negotiate a treaty with the Cherokee Indians, but he withdrew from the discussions before the treaty was signed. In 1799 he served as a judge on the North Carolina Superior Court.

When Justice James Iredell died in 1799, Adams looked to North Carolina for a replacement. William R. Davie was apparently the first choice, but he had just been made a diplomatic agent to France, so the nomination went to Moore.

Moore exerted little influence during his five years on the court and wrote only one opinion. He resigned in 1804, citing ill-health, and returned home to work on the development of the University of North Carolina. He died in North Carolina on Oct. 15, 1810, at the home of his son-in-law.

John Marshall
(1801-1835)

Born: Sept. 24, 1755, Germantown, Va.

Education: tutored at home; self-taught in law; attended one course of law lectures at College of William and Mary, 1780; member, Phi Beta Kappa.

Official Positions: member, Virginia House of Delegates, 1782-85, 1787-90, 1795-96; member, Executive Council of State, 1782-84; recorder, Richmond City Hustings Court, 1785-88; delegate, state convention for ratification of federal Constitution, 1788; minister to France, 1797-98; member, U.S. House of Representatives, 1799-1800; U.S. secretary of state, 1800-1801; member, Virginia Constitutional Convention, 1829.

Supreme Court Appointment: nominated Chief Justice by President John Adams Jan. 20, 1801, to replace Oliver Ellsworth, who resigned; confirmed by the Senate Jan. 27, 1801, by a voice vote; replaced on court by Roger B. Taney, nominated by President Jackson.

Family: Married Mary Willis Ambler, Jan. 3, 1783, died Dec. 25, 1831; ten children.

Died: July 6, 1835, Philadelphia, Pa.

Personal Background

The first of 15 children, John Marshall was born in a log cabin on the Virginia frontier near Germantown. His father, descended from Welsh immigrants, was an assistant surveyor to George Washington and member of the Virginia House of Burgesses. His mother was the daughter of an educated Scottish clergyman.

As a youth, Marshall was tutored by two clergymen but his primary teacher was his father, who introduced him to the study of English literature and Blackstone's Commentaries.

During the Revolutionary War, young Marshall participated in the siege of Norfolk as a member of the Culpeper Minute Men and was present at Brandywine, Monmouth, Stony Point and Valley Forge as a member of the third Virginia Regiment. In 1779 he returned home to await another assignment but was never recalled. He left the Continental Army with the rank of captain in 1781.

Marshall's only formal instruction in the law came in 1780 when he attended George Wythe's course of law lectures at the College of William and Mary. He was admitted to the bar that same year and gradually developed a lucrative practice, specializing in defending Virginians against their pre-Revolutionary War British creditors.

In January 1783 Marshall married Mary Willis Ambler, daughter of the Virginia state treasurer, and established a home in Richmond. The couple had ten children, only six of whom survived to maturity. Marshall spent many years attending to the needs of his wife, who suffered from a chronic illness and nervousness.

From 1796 until about 1806, Marshall's life was dominated by the pressures of meeting debts incurred by a land investment he had made in the northern neck of Virginia. It has been speculated that his need for money motivated him to write *The Life of George Washington,* which appeared in five volumes from 1804 to 1807. The book was written too quickly, and when Jefferson ordered postmasters, who doubled as salesmen for the book's publisher, not to take orders for it, the opportunity for large sales was lost.

The leisurely pace of the Supreme Court in its early days was well suited to the personality of Marshall, who had grown to enjoy relaxation and the outdoors as a boy. The Chief Justice enjoyed socializing in the clubs and saloons of Richmond and kept a fine supply of personal wines. He is said to have excelled at the game of quoits (similar to horseshoes), and was also known to take a turn at whist, backgammon and tenpins.

Marshall was Master of his Masonic lodge in Richmond and served as Masonic Grand Master of Virginia for several years. He was a member of the American Colonization Society, which worked toward the transfer of freed slaves to Africa, and belonged to the Washington Historical Monument Society and several literary societies.

Public Career

Marshall was elected to the Virginia House of Delegates from Fauquier County in 1782 and 1784. He reentered the House in 1787 and was instrumental in Virginia's ratification of the new U.S. Constitution. At the state ratifying convention his primary attention was directed to the need for judicial review. By 1789 Marshall was considered to be a leading Federalist in the state.

Marshall refused many appointments in the Federalist administrations of Washington and Adams, including U.S. attorney general in 1795, associate justice of the Supreme Court in 1798 and secretary of war in 1800. In 1796 he refused an appointment by President Adams as minister to France, but the following year agreed to serve as one of three special envoys sent to smooth relations with that country. This mission, known as the "XYZ affair," failed when French diplomats demanded a bribe as a condition for negotiation. Congress, however, was greatly impressed by the stubborn resistance of the American emissaries, and Marshall received a generous grant as a reward for his participation.

In 1799 Marshall was persuaded by Washington to run for the U.S. House of Representatives as a Federalist from Richmond. His career in the House was brief, however, for in 1800 he became secretary of state under Adams. When Adams retired to his home in Massachusetts for a few months that year, Marshall served as the effective head of government.

When Oliver Ellsworth resigned as Chief Justice of the United States on Sept. 30, 1800, Adams offered the position to John Jay, who had been the court's first Chief Justice. When Jay declined, the Federalists urged Adams to elevate associate Justice William Paterson. But Adams nominated Marshall instead.

As the primary founder of the American system of constitutional law, including the doctrine of judicial review, Marshall participated in more than 1,000 Supreme Court decisions, writing more than 500 of them himself. In 1807 he presided over the treason trial of Aaron Burr in the Richmond circuit court, locking horns with Jefferson, who sought conviction. Burr was acquitted.

In 1831, at age 76, Marshall underwent successful surgery in Philadelphia for the removal of kidney stones. Three years later, he developed an enlarged liver and his health declined rapidly. When Marshall died on July 6, 1835, three months short of 80, the Liberty Bell cracked as it tolled in mourning.

William Johnson
(1804-1834)

Born: Dec. 17, 1771, Charleston, S.C.

Education: graduated Princeton, 1790; studied law under Charles Cotesworth Pinckney; admitted to bar in 1793.

Official Positions: member, South Carolina House of Representatives, 1794-98, Speaker, 1798; judge, Court of Common Pleas, 1799-1804.

Supreme Court Appointment: nominated associate justice by President Thomas Jefferson on March 22, 1804, to replace Alfred Moore, who resigned; confirmed by the Senate March 24, 1804, by a voice vote; replaced on court by James M. Wayne, nominated by President Jackson.

Family: married Sarah Bennett, March 20, 1794; eight children, six of whom died in childhood; two adopted.

Died: Aug. 4, 1834, Brooklyn, N.Y.

Personal Background

William Johnson's father, also named William, was a blacksmith, legislator and Revolutionary patriot who moved from New York to South Carolina in the early 1760s. When the British captured Charleston during the war, the Johnson family was exiled from their home and William's father sent to detention in Florida. After several months, the family was eventually reunited in Philadelphia and returned to South Carolina together.

Young William graduated first in his class from Princeton in 1790. Returning to Charleston, he began reading law under Charles Cotesworth Pinckney, a prominent adviser to President Washington who had studied at the Inns of Court. Johnson joined the bar in 1793.

The following year, Johnson married Sarah Bennett, sister of Thomas Bennett, who later would become governor of South Carolina. The couple had eight children but only two survived to maturity. They eventually adopted two refugee children from Santo Domingo.

A member of the American Philosophical Society, Johnson retained an interest in education and literature all his life. He was one of the primary founders of the University of South Carolina and in 1822 published a two-volume biography of Revolutionary War General Nathanael Greene. Johnson also published a *Eulogy of Thomas Jefferson* in 1826.

Public Career

Johnson's political career began in 1794 when he entered the South Carolina house of representatives as a member of Jefferson's new Republican party. Following service as speaker in 1798, Johnson was chosen one of three judges to sit on the state's highest court, the Court of Common Pleas. Here, he gained experience riding circuit and dealing with the burgeoning judicial questions concerning federal and state relations. In 1804 Johnson became Jefferson's first Republican nominee to the Supreme Court, replacing Alfred Moore.

At least until 1830, Johnson was the most independent of the justices on the Marshall Court, and has been called "the first great Court dissenter." Fighting against the wishes of powerful — some would say dictatorial — Chief Justice Marshall, Johnson eventually succeeded in establishing dissenting opinions as accepted court practice.

Johnson once wrote Jefferson that the court was no "bed of roses," and in the first part of his career on the bench tried to obtain another appointment. He remained on the court, however, until his death following surgery in 1834 in Brooklyn.

Henry Brockholst Livingston
(1806-1823)

Born: Nov. 25, 1757, New York City.

Education: graduated from College of New Jersey (Princeton), 1774; honorary LL.D., Harvard (1810), Princeton; studied law under Peter Yates; admitted to bar in 1783.

Official Positions: member, New York Assembly, 12th session, 24th session, 25th session; judge, New York State Supreme Court, 1802-07.

Supreme Court Appointment: nominated associate justice by President Thomas Jefferson Dec. 13, 1806, to replace William Paterson, who died; confirmed by the Senate Dec. 17, 1806, by a voice vote; replaced on court by Smith Thompson, nominated by President Monroe.

Family: married, first, Catharine Keteltas, five children; second, Ann Ludlow, three children; third, Catharine Kortright, three children.

Died: March 18, 1823, Washington, D.C.

Personal Background

As a member of the powerful Livingston family of New York, Brockholst Livingston was born into the colonial aristocracy. His father, William Livingston, was governor of New Jersey and a leader in the New York opposition to British colonial policies.

Young Livingston was graduated from Princeton in 1774, where he was a classmate of James Madison, and joined the Continental Army at the outbreak of the Revolution. As a commissioned major, he served under Generals Schuyler and St. Clair and participated in the siege of Ticonderoga. He was also an aide to Benedict Arnold during the Saratoga campaign and was present at Gen. John Burgoyne's surrender in 1777. Livingston left the army with the rank of lieutenant colonel.

After the war, Livingston travelled to Spain to serve as private secretary to his brother-in-law, John Jay, then serving as the American minister there. During this time, Livingston began to form a personal dislike for Jay.

Although Livingston was considered an affable and genial man, there appears to have been a violent side to his personality. He killed one man in a duel in 1798 and is believed to have fought several others. An assassination attempt was made on his life in 1785.

Livingston married three times and had a total of 11 children. A devotee of history, he was co-founder of the New York Historical Society and one of its vice-presidents. He served as trustee and treasurer of Columbia University from 1784 until the end of his life and was instrumental in organizing the New York public school system.

Public Career

Livingston — who began emphasizing the middle name Brockholst, probably to avoid confusion with two cousins also named Henry — was elected to the New York Assembly in 1786. He also began practicing law at this time, working closely with Alexander Hamilton.

During these years, Livingston began a conversion, along with other members of his family, from Federalism to anti-Federalism. By 1792 he was bitterly attacking the campaign of John Jay for the New York governorship and succeeded in denying Jay a crucial bloc of votes. When Jay returned from negotiating a treaty with England in 1794, Livingston was at the forefront of voices critical of Jay and his agreement.

As the New York anti-Federalist alliance of the Burr, Clinton and Livingston factions reached its height around 1800, several Livingstons received high appointments. In 1802 Brockholst Livingston joined two of his relatives-by-marriage on the New York supreme court. He served for five years, specializing in commercial law.

In 1804 Livingston was considered seriously for an opening on the Supreme Court, but the position went instead to William Johnson. In 1806, however, Livingston was nominated by Jefferson to fill the vacancy created by the death of William Paterson.

Livingston died in 1823, after serving 16 years on the bench.

Thomas Todd
(1807-1826)

Born: Jan. 23, 1765, King and Queen County, Va.

Education: graduated from Liberty Hall (now Washington and Lee University), Lexington, Va., 1783; read law under Harry Innes; admitted to bar in 1788.

Official Positions: clerk, federal district for Kentucky, 1792-1801; clerk, Kentucky house of representatives, 1792-1801; clerk, Kentucky court of appeals (supreme court), 1799-1801; judge, Kentucky court of appeals, 1801-1806; chief justice, 1806-07.

Supreme Court Appointment: nominated associate justice by President Thomas Jefferson on Feb. 28, 1807, to fill a newly created seat; confirmed by the Senate March 3, 1807, by a voice vote; replaced on court by Robert Trimble, nominated by President John Q. Adams.

Family: married, first, Elizabeth Harris, 1788, five children; second, Lucy Payne, 1812, three children.

Died: Feb. 7, 1826, Frankfort, Ky.

Personal Background

Thomas Todd was only 18 months old when his father died. He was 11 when his mother died, and from then on was raised by a guardian. The family owned large tracts of land handed down since the 17th century. But Thomas was excluded from inheriting any of this by primogeniture.

Todd's mother, Elizabeth, managed to leave her son money she had accumulated through managing a successful boarding house, and Thomas used it to acquire a solid education in the classics. Most of the inheritance, however,

was eventually lost because of mismanagement on the part of the guardian.

At age 16, Todd served in the Revolutionary War for six months, returning home to attend Liberty Hall (now Washington and Lee University) in Lexington, Va. After graduation, he accepted an invitation from Harry Innes, a distant relative and respected member of the Virginia legislature, to tutor Innes' daughters in exchange for room, board and law instruction.

In 1784, when Innes was asked to move to Danville, Ky. (then part of Virginia), to set up a district court in the area, Todd made the move with the family. It was at this time that the Kentucky area of Virginia held the first of five conventions seeking admission to the Union as a separate state. Through his friendship with Innes, Todd was able to act as clerk for each convention.

With his first wife, Elizabeth, Todd had five children, one of whom, Charles Stewart, became Minister to Russia in 1841. When Elizabeth died in 1811, Todd married Dolley Madison's sister, Lucy Payne, in the East Room of the White House the following year.

During his lifetime, Todd accumulated over 7,200 acres in Kentucky. He also owned stock in two companies involved in waterway and public highway transportation.

Public Career

Todd joined the Virginia bar in 1788 and soon developed a specialty in land law. When Kentucky became a state in 1792, he served as secretary to the new Kentucky legislature. In 1799, when the state supreme court was created, Todd was chosen to be its chief clerk.

In 1801 Kentucky Governor James Garrard appointed Todd to fill a newly created fourth seat on the state court. At the age of 41, Todd was named its chief justice. Most of the cases handled by the court during his tenure involved land title disputes, and the chief justice developed a reputation for being fair and honest in settling complicated land controversies.

In 1807 the federal Judiciary Act of 1789 was amended to create a new federal court circuit made up of Tennessee, Kentucky and Ohio. On the recommendation of the congressmen from those states, President Jefferson chose Todd to preside over this new circuit as the sixth associate justice on the Supreme Court.

During his years on the bench, Todd missed five entire court terms because of personal and health reasons. He delivered only 14 opinions during his tenure, and of these, only one was a dissent.

Joseph Story
(1811-1845)

Born: Sept. 18, 1779, Marblehead, Mass.

Education: attended Marblehead Academy; graduated from Harvard, 1798, LL.D., 1821; read law under Samuel Sewall and Samuel Putnam; admitted to bar, 1801.

Official Positions: member, Massachusetts legislature, 1805-1808; speaker of the house, 1811; U.S. Representative, 1808-09; delegate, Massachusetts constitutional convention, 1820.

Supreme Court Appointment: nominated by President James Madison Nov. 15, 1811, to replace William Cushing, who died; confirmed by the Senate Nov. 18, 1811, by a voice vote; replaced on court by Levi Woodbury, nominated by President Polk.

Family: married, first, Mary Lynde Oliver, Dec. 9, 1804, died June 1805; second, Sarah Waldo Wetmore, Aug. 27, 1808, seven children.

Died: Sept. 10, 1845, Cambridge, Mass.

Personal Background

Joseph Story was descended from an old New England family. His father participated in the Boston Tea Party in 1773. Following a disagreement with a fellow classmate, Joseph was forced to leave Marblehead Academy before completing his college preparatory studies. By constantly studying on his own through the fall of 1794, however, he was able to enroll in Harvard in time for the 1795 term. Such drive and diligence were to characterize much of Story's life.

After graduating (second in his class) from Harvard in 1798, Story began reading law, sometimes for 14 hours a day, in the Marblehead office of Samuel Sewall, later chief justice of the Massachusetts supreme court. When Sewall was appointed to a judgeship, Story completed his studies under Samuel Putnam in Salem, Mass.

Admitted to the bar in 1801, Story began practice in Salem. The county bar was dominated by the Federalist establishment, however, and Story, a Republican-Democrat, was exposed to a good deal of prejudice. In the beginning he considered moving to Baltimore, but as his practice grew in prestige and influence, he chose to remain in Salem.

Story was an ardent poetry lover throughout his life. He was known by his hometown friends as "the poet of Marblehead." In 1805 he published "The Power of Solitude," a long, effusive poem written in heroic couplets. When his father and his wife of only seven months both died in 1805, Story, in a fit of sorrow, burned all copies of the poem he could find. Story experienced tragedy several times in his life; he lost five of his seven children by his second marriage.

An avid conversationalist, Story enjoyed music, drawing and painting. Besides being a writer, Story was an able public speaker and eulogist. He delivered the annual Fourth of July oration in Salem in 1804 and in 1826 delivered the Phi Beta Kappa oration at Harvard.

Public Career

Story served for three years in the Massachusetts legislature and then entered the U.S. Congress in 1808. During his one term of service in the House, he was blamed by Jefferson for the repeal of Jefferson's foreign trade embargo, and lost further points with his party by calling for a plan to strengthen the U.S. Navy. In January 1811 Story returned to the Massachusetts legislature and was elected speaker of the house. By November of that year he had become one of the two youngest men ever to sit on the Supreme Court. (The other was William Johnson.)

Only 32 years old and with no court experience, Story had not been Madison's first choice for the job, but Levi Lincoln and John Quincy Adams had both declined. Alexander Wolcott had been rejected by the Senate. Although he had a few financial reservations about taking the job, Story accepted the position as a great honor.

A supporter of higher learning for women, Story retained an active interest in education for most of his life. In 1819 he was elected to the Harvard Board of Overseers and became a fellow of the Harvard Corporation six years later. In 1829, Story moved from Salem to Cambridge, Mass., to become professor of law at his alma mater. He played a key role in the foundation of Harvard Law School. He is also credited, along with Chancellor James Kent of New York, with founding the equity system of jurisprudence as practiced in the United States today.

While teaching at Harvard, Story wrote his nine *Commentaries* on the law. Each of these works went through many editions, and one — *Commentaries on the Constitution* (1833) — was published in French, Spanish and German. By this time Story had achieved an international reputation.

In addition to the *Commentaries,* Story wrote legal essays for the North American Review and the American Law Review, and contributed unsigned articles to the *Encyclopedia Americana.* His court opinions, though often accused of being tedious, are seminal works in the history of American national law.

On the court, Story rarely disagreed with the strong nationalism of Chief Justice Marshall. In fact, it was Story's opinion in *Martin v. Hunter's Lessee* (1816) that established the appellate supremacy of the Supreme Court over state courts in civil cases involving federal statutes and treaties.

When Marshall died in 1835, Story undoubtedly coveted the chief justiceship, and his colleagues generally agreed he should be appointed. But Story was anathema to Andrew Jackson (he once called Story the "most dangerous man in America"), and Roger Taney received the nomination instead.

Story's nine years on the Taney Court were spent largely in dissent and by the beginning of the 1845 term he was prepared to resign. He refused to leave until he had attended to all his unfinished business, however, and in the fall of 1845 suddenly became ill and died on September 10, 1845.

Gabriel Duvall
(1812-1835)

Born: Dec. 6, 1752, Prince Georges County, Md.

Eduation: classical preparatory schooling; studied law.

Official Positions: clerk, Maryland Convention, 1775-77; clerk, Maryland House of Delegates, 1777-87; member,

Maryland State Council, 1782-85; member, Maryland House of Delegates, 1787-94; U.S. Representative, 1794-96; chief justice, General Court of Maryland, 1796-1802; presidential elector, 1796, 1800; first comptroller of the Treasury, 1802-1811.

Supreme Court Appointment: nominated associate justice by President James Madison, Nov. 15, 1811, to replace Samuel Chase, who died; confirmed by the Senate Nov. 18, 1811, by a voice vote; replaced on court by Philip Barbour, nominated by President Jackson.

Family: married, first, Mary Bryce, July 24, 1787, died March 24, 1790, one son; second, Jane Gibbon, May 5, 1795, died April 1834.

Died: March 6, 1844, Prince Georges County, Md.

Personal Background

Descended from a family of French Huguenots, Gabriel Duvall was the sixth of ten children born on the family plantation known as "Marietta." The farm land, located on the South River near Buena Vista, Md., had been assigned to Duvall's great-grandfather by Lord Baltimore.

Duvall was active in the Revolutionary War, serving as mustermaster and commissary of stores for the Maryland troops, and later as a private in the Maryland militia. Toward the end of the war, he helped protect confiscated British property.

In 1787, at the age of 35, Duvall married Mary Bryce, daughter of Captain Robert Bryce of Annapolis. She died three years later, shortly after the birth of their son. In 1795 Duvall married Jane Gibbon, who died in 1834 shortly before Duvall resigned from the Supreme Court.

Public Career

Duvall's first public appointment came in 1775 when he was made clerk of the Maryland Convention. When the Maryland state government was created in 1777, he was named clerk for the house of delegates.

In 1787 Duvall was elected to the Maryland house of delegates, where he served until 1794. He was also chosen to attend the Constitutional Convention in Philadelphia, but decided along with the four others elected from Maryland not to attend.

Duvall entered the third Congress of the United States in 1794 as a Republican-Democrat. Two years later he resigned to become chief justice of the general court of Maryland. As chief justice, Duvall also served as recorder of the mayor's court in Annapolis, and it was in this capacity that he heard Roger Taney deliver his first speech as a member of the bar.

Duvall was chosen by President Thomas Jefferson to be the first comptroller of the Treasury in 1802. Nine years later he was nominated by President James Madison to serve on the Supreme Court.

During his 23 years on the bench, Duvall generally voted with Chief Justice Marshall. His most notable dissent came in the Dartmouth College case, although he wrote no formal opinion.

By the end of his tenure on the court, Duvall was 82 years old. His deafness and frequent absence had become an embarrassment and his resignation in 1835 came as a great relief to court observers.

Duvall spent his last years working on his family history and devoting attention to his son and nieces and nephews. He died in 1844 at the age of 91.

Smith Thompson
(1823-1843)

Born: ca. Jan. 17, 1768, Dutchess County, N.Y.

Education: graduated Princeton, 1788; read law under James Kent; admitted to bar, 1792; honorary law doctorates from Yale, 1824, Princeton, 1824, and Harvard, 1835.

Official Positions: member, New York state legislature, 1800; member, New York Constitutional Convention, 1801; associate justice, New York Supreme Court, 1802-14; appointed to New York State Board of Regents, 1813; chief justice, New York Supreme Court, 1814-18; U.S. secretary of Navy, 1819-23.

Supreme Court Appointment: nominated associate justice by President James Monroe Dec. 8, 1823, to replace Brockholst Livingston, who died; confirmed by the Senate Dec. 19, 1823, by a voice vote; replaced on court by Samuel Nelson, nominated by President Tyler.

Family: married, first, Sarah Livingston, died Sept. 22, 1833, two sons and two daughters; second, Eliza Livingston, two daughters and one son.

Died: Dec. 18, 1843, Poughkeepsie, N.Y.

Personal Background

Smith Thompson's public career was inevitably shaped by his personal ties and social connections. His father, Ezra Thompson, was a successful New York farmer and a well known anti-Federalist in state politics. More important, however, were Thompson's links to the powerful Livingston family, an important force in New York politics at the end of the 18th century.

Thompson was born in 1768 — the exact date is unclear — in Dutchess County, N.Y., between the Hudson River and the Connecticut border. After graduating from Princeton in 1788, he taught school and read law under James Kent, a well-respected jurist, then working in Poughkeepsie. In 1793 Thompson joined the law practice of Kent and Gilbert Livingston, an old friend of his father.

Thompson married Livingston's daughter, Sarah, in 1794, and thus became a member of that fractious family. When Sarah died in 1833, he married her first cousin, Eliza Livingston. By this time, however, the family's influence was on the decline.

Public Career

Thompson's public career got off to a quick start in 1800 when he entered the state legislature as a member of the Livingston wing of the anti-Federalist Republican party. The next year he attended the state constitutional convention and received an appointment as district attorney for the middle district of New York. Before he had a chance to assume those duties, however, he was appointed to the state supreme court and immediately assumed that position.

During his tenure on the state bench, Thompson served with two of his cousins by marriage. One of these men, Brockholst Livingston, preceded Thompson to the U.S. Supreme Court in 1806.

In addition to his family relations, Thompson was joined on the state court by James Kent, his old friend and mentor. When Kent stepped down as its chief justice in 1814 to become chancellor of New York, Thompson succeeded him.

Thompson became secretary of the Navy under President Monroe in 1819, probably through the influence of Martin Van Buren, a rising young New York politician and ally of Thompson. As Navy secretary, Thompson had few administrative duties and spent a good deal of his time dabbling in New York politics, working, at times, with Van Buren. He also made no secret of his presidential ambitions during this period.

When Brockholst Livingston died in 1823, Thompson was immediately thought of as a contender for the vacancy on the Supreme Court, along with Chancellor Kent. Thompson delayed expressing formal interest in the seat, however, hoping with Van Buren's help to mount a campaign drive for the 1824 presidential election. Van Buren disappointed him in the end, however, and Thompson accepted the court appointment from Monroe. Thompson continued to harbor political ambitions while on the Supreme Court and in 1828 decided to run for governor of New York. He lost to his old friend, Martin Van Buren, in a bitter and dramatic campaign.

While on the court, Thompson became part of a group that began to pull away from the strong nationalism of Chief Justice John Marshall. In 1827 he voted with the majority against Marshall in *Ogden v. Saunders* supporting state bankruptcy laws. His most notable opinion came in *Kendall v. United States* (1838) when he argued against President Jackson that the executive branch was not exempt from judicial control. The passage was later omitted from the printed opinion at the request of the U.S. attorney general.

Robert Trimble

(1826-1828)

Born: Nov. 17, 1776, Augusta County, Va.

Education: Bourbon Academy; Kentucky Academy; read law under George Nicholas and James Brown; admitted to bar in 1803.

Official Positions: Kentucky state representative, 1802; Kentucky Court of Appeals Judge, 1807-09; U.S. District Attorney for Kentucky, 1813-17; U.S. District Judge, 1817-26.

Supreme Court Appointment: nominated associate justice by President John Quincy Adams on April 11, 1826, to replace Thomas Todd, who died; confirmed on May 9,

1826, by a 27-5 vote. Replaced on court by John McLean, nominated by President Jackson.

Family: married Nancy Timberlake, Aug. 18, 1803; at least 10 children.

Died: Aug. 25, 1828, Paris, Ky.

Personal Background

Robert Trimble was the son of an early Kentucky pioneer who hunted game and scouted for Indians. It appears young Trimble studied at the Bourbon Academy in Kentucky and after teaching for a short time attended the Kentucky Academy (later Transylvania University) in Woodford County. Following his study at the Kentucky Academy, Trimble read law under George Nicholas and James Brown, who later became Minister to France.

Public Career

Trimble began private practice in Paris, Ky., in about 1800. In 1802 he entered the Kentucky House of Representatives and in 1807 was appointed justice of the Kentucky Court of Appeals. He resigned the judgeship in 1808, claiming the yearly salary of $1,000 was too low to support his large and growing family.

Trimble also refused the chief justiceship of Kentucky in 1810 for financial reasons, and declined to run for the U.S. Senate in 1812. Although he twice refused to accept the law professorship at Transylvania University, he served as a trustee of the school for many years.

Trimble's decision to concentrate on his private law practice instead of public service proved profitable. By 1817 he had earned a sizable amount of money and owned a number of slaves. That year he decided to accept the nomination by President Madison to be the federal district judge for Kentucky. He served for eight years.

Trimble — Adams' only appointment to the U.S. Supreme Court — was chosen for his judicial belief in strong national power over state power, a position that had not won him many friends in Kentucky. During his two years on the Supreme Court bench, he was a strong supporter of Chief Justice Marshall, although they disagreed in *Ogden v. Saunders* over the power of the states to enact insolvency laws.

John McLean

(1829-1861)

Born: March 11, 1785, Morris County, N.J.

Education: attended local school; privately tutored; read law in office of Arthur St. Clair Jr.

Official Positions: examiner, U.S. Land Office, 1811-12; U.S. Representative, 1813-16, chairman, Committee on Accounts; judge, Ohio Supreme Court, 1816-22; commissioner, General Land Office, 1822-23; U.S. postmaster general, 1823-29.

Supreme Court Appointment: nominated associate justice by President Andrew Jackson March 6, 1829, to replace Robert Trimble, who died; confirmed by the Senate March 7, 1829, by a voice vote; replaced on court by Noah H. Swayne, nominated by President Lincoln.

Family: married, first, Rebecca Edwards, 1807, died 1840, four daughters and three sons; second, Sarah Bella Ludlow Garrard, 1843, one son, died in childbirth.

Died: April 4, 1861, Cincinnati, Ohio.

Personal Background

John McLean's father, Fergus, was a Scotch-Irish weaver who immigrated to New Jersey in 1775. After his marriage to a New Jersey woman and the birth of several children, Fergus moved his family first to western Virginia, then Kentucky and finally in 1797 settled on a farm near Lebanon, Ohio, about forty miles north of Cincinnati. Young John attended the county school and later earned enough money as a farmhand to hire two Presbyterian ministers to tutor him.

In 1804 he began two years of work as an apprentice to the clerk of the Hamilton County Court of Common Pleas in Cincinnati. At the same time, he was able to study law with Arthur St. Clair, a respected Cincinnati lawyer.

Following his admission to the bar in 1807, McLean married Rebecca Edwards of Newport, Ky., and returned to Lebanon, where he opened a printing office. In a short time, he began publishing the Lebanon *Western Star* newspaper, a weekly journal supportive of Jeffersonian politics. In 1810, however, McLean relinquished the printshop to his brother, Nathaniel, and devoted all of his time to law practice.

McLean experienced a profound religious conversion in 1811 and remained a devout Methodist for the rest of his life. He participated actively in church affairs and was chosen honorary president of the American Sunday School Union in 1849.

Public Career

McLean was elected to Congress in 1812. During his two terms of service, he supported the war measures of the Madison administration, and opposed creation of the second Bank of the United States. In 1816 McLean resigned from the House and was elected to one of four judgeships on the Ohio Supreme Court, serving for three years.

McLean worked hard for the nomination and election of James Monroe to the presidency in 1816, and in 1822 Monroe returned the favor by appointing McLean commissioner of the General Land Office. A year later he was made postmaster general.

McLean was well-liked by the postal employees and proved to be a skilled administrator. The postal service greatly expanded under his leadership, and by 1828 the department was the largest agency in the executive branch.

By this time, McLean had become an astute politician. He managed to keep his job as postmaster general under John Quincy Adams while establishing ties with many of Andrew Jackson's men at the same time. When Jackson became president in 1829, Robert Trimble's seat on the Supreme Court was still vacant because of Senate political maneuverings, and McLean was nominated to fill it. His most famous opinion during his 36 years on the bench was his dissent in the *Dred Scott* case, which was eventually reflected in the 14th Amendment to the Constitution.

McLean entertained presidential ambitions throughout his Supreme Court career and flirted with several political parties at various stages. In 1856 he received 190 votes on an informal presidential ballot taken at the first Republican national convention in Philadelphia. Thaddeus Stevens pushed his candidacy four years later, but the effort was blocked by Ohio Republicans.

McLean died of pneumonia in 1861.

Henry Baldwin
(1830-1844)

Born: Jan. 14, 1780, New Haven, Conn.

Education: Hopkins Grammar School, 1793; Yale College, 1797, LL.D., 1830; studied law under Alexander J. Dallas.

Official Positions: U.S. Representative, F-Pa., 1817-1822; chairman, Committee on Domestic Manufactures.

Supreme Court Appointment: nominated associate justice by President Andrew Jackson, Jan. 4, 1830, to replace Bushrod Washington, who died; confirmed by the Senate Jan. 6, 1830, by a 41-2 vote; replaced on court by Robert C. Grier, nominated by President Polk.

Family: married, first, Marianna Norton, 1802, died 1803, one son, Henry; second, Sally Ellicott, 1805.

Died: April 21, 1844, Philadelphia, Pa.

Personal Background

Born in New Haven, Conn., Baldwin was the product of a New England heritage going all the way back to the seventeenth century. His half-brother, Abraham, was a representative to both the Continental Congress and the Constitutional Convention and a U.S. Senator from Georgia.

As a boy, Henry lived on the family farm near New Haven but moved to the city when he entered Yale College. Upon graduation in 1797, he clerked in the law office of Alexander J. Dallas, a prominent Philadelphia attorney, and was soon admitted to the Philadelphia bar. Following this, Baldwin decided to settle in Pittsburgh, then a young city which afforded opportunities for a beginning lawyer.

Baldwin settled easily and quickly into the Pittsburgh community, joining the county bar and making many friends. With Tarleton Bates and Walter Forward, he formed a successful law firm known as the "Great Triumvirate of Early Pittsburgh." During this period, Baldwin developed a reputation for his well-written law briefs, which he prepared in his large personal law library, considered to be one of the finest in the "West."

In only a short time, Baldwin and his law partners became known for their political leadership as well as their legal skill. Together, they published a newspaper called *The Tree of Liberty,* which supported a faction of the Republican party in western Pennsylvania. Through his work in the party and in Pittsburgh civic affairs, Baldwin became a popular and prominent leader in the community by his mid-twenties. Before long, he was affectionately known as the "Idol of Pennsylvania" and the "Pride of Pittsburgh."

Despite all of his political and legal activity, Baldwin found time to involve himself in business affairs. He was part owner of at least three mills in Pennsylvania in addition to a profitable woolen mill in Steubenville, Ohio.

Public Career

Baldwin, the manufacturer, entered Congress in 1817 as a supporter of higher tariffs and as a spokesman for Pittsburgh's economic growth interests. He resigned from the House in 1822 for health reasons, but after two years of rest returned to his role as unofficial political leader of Allegheny County. In 1823 he urged Andrew Jackson to run for the presidency and throughout John Quincy Adams' administration was a close adviser to Jackson on western Pennsylvania politics.

When Justice Bushrod Washington died in 1829, President Jackson decided to nominate Baldwin to fill the seat, against the wishes of Vice President Calhoun, who supported another candidate.

Baldwin's career on the bench was erratic. In the beginning, he supported the liberal interpretations of Chief Justice Marshall, but later refused to embrace either strict or broad construction of the Constitution.

Baldwin is reported to have suffered temporary mental derangements toward the end of his life. Biographical sources do not elaborate on this except to say he did not get along well with other justices on the bench, and his closest friends were suspicious of his nonconforming and peculiar habits. As early as 1832, Roger B. Taney had advised President Jackson not to take legal action against the Bank of the United States because the case would be tried in Philadelphia and Baldwin would be unreliable as presiding judge. Baldwin, then 52, had already begun to suffer lapses of reason.

Baldwin was said to be occasionally violent and ungovernable on the bench toward the end of his life. In 1844, when he died of paralysis, he was deeply in debt and his friends had to take up a collection to pay his funeral expenses.

James Moore Wayne

(1835-1867)

Born: ca. 1790, Savannah, Ga.
Education: Princeton University, 1808, honorary LL.B., 1849; read law under three lawyers including Judge Charles Chauncey of New Haven.
Official Positions: member, Georgia House of Representatives, 1815-16; mayor, Savannah, 1817-19; judge, Savannah Court of Common Pleas, 1820-22; Georgia superior court, 1822-28; U.S. Representative, D-Ga., 1829-35, chairman, Committee on Foreign Relations.
Supreme Court Appointment: nominated associate justice by President Andrew Jackson, Jan. 7, 1835, to replace William Johnson, who died; confirmed by the Senate Jan. 9, 1835 by a voice vote.

Family: married Mary Johnston Campbell, 1813; three children.
Died: July 5, 1867, Washington, D.C.

Personal Background

James Wayne was born in Georgia, the son of a British army officer. He was the twelfth of thirteen children. As a boy, James lived on the family rice plantation outside of Savannah and was educated by an Irish tutor. He progressed so quickly in his studies that he was ready to enter the College of New Jersey (now Princeton) at the age of 14. Shortly after his graduation in 1808, James' father died and his brother-in-law, Richard Stites, became his guardian.

Wayne had begun to study law under a prominent Savannah lawyer, John Y. Noel, and after his father's death, he studied at Yale under Judge Charles Chauncey for almost two years. Upon returning to Savannah, he read in the office of his brother-in-law and in 1810 went into partnership with Samuel M. Bond.

During the War of 1812, Wayne served as an officer in a volunteer Georgia militia unit called the Chatham Light Dragoons. In 1813 he married Mary Johnston Campbell of Richmond, Va. The couple had three children.

Public Career

In 1815 Wayne was elected to the Georgia legislature, serving two years. At age 27 he became mayor of Savannah, but resigned after two years to resume his law practice. At the end of 1819, he was elected to sit on Savannah's Court of Common Pleas and in 1822 was appointed to a superior court judgeship. The court provided him with much hard work and the opportunity for public recognition.

Wayne entered Congress in 1829 and served for three terms. During this period he became a strong ally of the Jackson administration. By 1835 he was considered a leading Unionist Democrat and was nominated to the Supreme Court by President Jackson.

Unlike his colleague, Justice Campbell of Alabama, Wayne refused to leave the bench when secession came and remained a strong Union supporter throughout the Civil War. It was an agonizing period for the justice, who was disowned by his home state and accused of being an enemy alien by a Confederate court.

At war's end, Wayne opposed the punitive Reconstruction measures taken against the South and refused to hold circuit court in states under military Reconstruction rule. He did not live to see the end of Reconstruction, dying of typhoid in 1867.

Roger Brooke Taney

(1836-1864)

Born: March 17, 1777, Calvert County, Md.
Education: graduated from Dickinson College in Pennsylvania, 1795, honorary LL.D.; read law in office of Judge Jeremiah Chase in Annapolis.

Official Positions: member, Maryland House of Delegates 1799-1800; Maryland State Senator, 1816-21; Maryland Attorney General, 1827-31; chairman, Jackson Central Committee for Maryland, 1827-28; U.S. Attorney General, 1831-33; acting Secretary of War, 1831; U.S. Secretary of the Treasury, 1833-34 (appointment rejected by Senate).

Supreme Court Appointment: nominated Chief Justice by President Andrew Jackson, Dec. 28, 1835, to replace John Marshall, who died; confirmed by Senate on March 15, 1836, by a 29-15 vote; replaced on court by Salmon P. Chase, nominated by President Lincoln.

Family: married Anne P. C. Key, Jan. 7, 1806; six daughters, one son died in infancy.

Died: Oct. 12, 1864, Washington, D.C.

Personal Background

Roger Taney was descended on both sides from prominent Maryland families. His mother's family, named Brooke, first arrived in the state in 1650, complete with fox hounds and other trappings of aristocracy. The first Taney arrived about 1660 as an indentured servant but was able to acquire a large amount of property and became a member of the landed Maryland tidewater gentry.

Taney was born in Calvert County, Md., on his father's tobacco plantation. He was educated in local rural schools and privately tutored by a Princeton student. In 1795, at the age of 18, he graduated first in his class from Dickinson College in Pennsylvania.

As his father's second son, Taney was not in line to inherit the family property and so decided on a career in law and politics. For three years, he was an apprentice lawyer in the office of Judge Jeremiah Chase of the Maryland General Court in Annapolis. He was admitted to the bar in 1799.

In 1806 Taney married Anne Key, daughter of a prominent farmer and the sister of Francis Scott Key. Since Taney was a devout Roman Catholic and his wife an Episcopalian, they agreed to raise their sons as Catholics and their daughters as Episcopalians.

Public Career

Taney began his political career as a member of the Federalist party, serving one term in the Maryland legislature from 1799 to 1800. After being defeated for re-election, he moved from Calvert County to Frederick, where he began to develop a profitable law practice.

In 1803 Taney was beaten again in an attempt to return to the House of Delegates. Despite this setback, he began to achieve prominence in the Frederick community as a lawyer and politician. He was to live there for more than 20 years.

In supporting the War of 1812, Taney split with the majority of Maryland Federalists. But in 1816, as a result of shifting political loyalties, he was elected to the state senate and became a dominant figure in party politics.

Taney's senate term expired in 1821. In 1823 he settled in Baltimore, where he continued his successful law practice and political activities. By this time, the Federalist party had virtually disintegrated and Taney threw his support to the Jackson Democrats. He led Jackson's 1828 presidential campaign in Maryland and served as the state's attorney general from 1827 until 1831. At that time, he was named U.S. attorney general for the Jackson administration and left Baltimore for Washington.

It was at this stage in his career that Taney played a leading role in the controversy over the second Bank of the United States, helping to write Jackson's message in 1832 vetoing the bank's recharter. The next year, when Secretary of Treasury William Duane refused to withdraw federal deposits from the national bank, Duane was dismissed by Jackson and replaced by Taney, who promptly carried out the action.

Taney held the Treasury job for nine months, presiding over a new system of state bank depositories called "pet banks." Jackson, who had delayed as long as he could, was eventually forced to submit Taney's nomination as Treasury secretary to the Senate. In June 1836, Taney was rejected by the Senate and forced to resign.

In 1835 Jackson appointed Taney to replace aging Supreme Court Justice Gabriel Duvall, but the nomination was indefinitely postponed by a close Senate vote. Ten months later, Jackson proposed Taney's name again, this time to fill the seat left vacant by the death of Chief Justice Marshall. To the horror of the Whigs, who considered him much too radical, Taney was confirmed as Chief Justice on March 15, 1836.

Philip Pendleton Barbour
(1836-1841)

Born: May 25, 1783, Orange County, Va.

Education: read law on his own; attended one session at College of William and Mary, 1801.

Official Positions: member, Virginia House of Delegates from Orange Co., 1812-14; U.S. Representative, 1814-25, 1827-30; Speaker of the House, 1821-23; state judge, General Court for the Eastern District of Virginia, 1825-27; president, Virginia Constitutional Convention, 1829-30; U.S. district judge, court of eastern Virginia, 1830-36.

Supreme Court Appointment: nominated associate justice by President Andrew Jackson, Dec. 28, 1835, to replace Gabriel Duvall, who resigned; confirmed by the Senate, March 15, 1836, by a 30-11 vote; replaced on court by Peter Vivian Daniel, nominated by President Van Buren.

Family: married Frances Todd Johnson, 1804; seven children.

Died: Feb. 25, 1841, in Washington, D.C.

Personal Background

Philip Barbour was a country gentleman from one of Virginia's oldest families. Descended from a Scottish merchant who settled in the state in the seventeenth century, Philip's father, Thomas Barbour, was a member of the Virginia House of Burgesses and a prosperous Orange County planter. James Barbour, Philip's older brother, was a Virginia governor, a U.S. senator and secretary of war under President John Quincy Adams.

As a boy, Philip received his early education in the local schools, excelling in languages and classical literature. At the age of 17, he read law for a short time and then moved to Kentucky to begin practice. He soon returned to his home state, however, and borrowed money to enroll in the College of William and Mary. He attended only one session and left to resume his law practice. After two years, he had earned enough money to marry Frances Johnson, the daughter of an Orange County landowner. James Barbour had married Frances' sister 12 years earlier.

Public Career

Philip Barbour was elected to the Virginia House of Delegates in 1812. Two years later he won a seat in the U.S. Congress and, in a philosophical split with his brother, allied with a group of older Republicans who espoused strict construction and limited federal power.

Barbour served as Speaker of the House from 1821 until he was defeated by Henry Clay in 1823. In 1824 he chose not to run for re-election to his House seat.

After declining an offer from Thomas Jefferson to teach law at the University of Virginia, Barbour became a state judge on the general court for the eastern district of Virginia, serving for almost two years. In 1827 he returned to Congress and ran again for speaker, losing this time to fellow-Virginian Andrew Stevenson.

By this time Barbour was politically aligned with the Democratic forces of Andrew Jackson. After being passed over for a Jackson cabinet position in 1829, he was chosen president of the Virginia Constitutional Convention to replace the ailing James Monroe. In votes taken by the convention, he sided with the landed interests of the conservative eastern slaveholders against the claims of the westerners who later were to form a separate state, West Virginia.

In 1830 Barbour accepted an appointment as federal district court judge for eastern Virginia. During the national election of 1832, he was touted as a vice presidential candidate over Jackson's choice, Martin Van Buren. But party regulars, fearing the election might be thrown into the Senate, persuaded Barbour to withdraw his candidacy and support Van Buren as the nominee.

Barbour became an associate justice at the age of 53. In his short term on the bench — only five years — he generally followed the Taney court's drift toward a narrowing of corporate immunity and greater consideration of social and economic concerns.

Barbour became ill in early February 1841. By the end of the month, however, his health seemed to have improved and on Feb. 24 he attended a conference with other justices until ten o'clock at night. The next morning he was found dead of a heart attack.

Official Positions: judge, Tennessee Supreme Court of Errors and Appeals, 1824-31; first chief justice of Tennessee, 1831-34.

Supreme Court Appointment: nominated associate justice by President Andrew Jackson March 3, 1837, to fill a newly created seat; confirmed by the Senate March 8, 1837, by a 28-15 vote. Seat abolished by Congress; later recreated and filled by Joseph P. Bradley, nominated by President Grant.

Family: married, wife's name not available.
Died: May 30, 1865, Nashville, Tenn.

Personal Background

Little is known about John Catron's early years. Born about 1786, of German ancestry, he is believed to have lived first in Virginia and then Kentucky. His family was poor, and young Catron probably had little formal education, if any. In 1812 Catron moved to the Cumberland Mountain region of Tennessee and served under Andrew Jackson in the War of 1812. He joined the bar in 1815 and practiced in the Cumberland Mountain area until 1818, when he settled in Nashville and became an active member of the Davidson County bar. By this time he had developed a specialty in land law.

Catron was a successful businessman as well as a lawyer. With his brother George and a third partner, he owned and operated the profitable Buffalo Iron Works from 1827 until 1833 when he sold his interest in the business. He later reinvested in the company but kept himself out of its management.

Public Career

In 1824 the Tennessee legislature created a new seat on the Supreme Court of Errors and Appeals — the state's highest court — and Catron was elected to fill the post. In 1831 he became the court's first chief justice but resigned in 1834 when the court was abolished by judicial reorganization.

After leaving the bench, Catron turned his attention to private practice and politics. In 1836 he directed Martin Van Buren's presidential campaign in Tennessee. As a result of his party loyalty and diligence, Catron was picked by outgoing President Jackson in 1837 to fill one of two newly created seats on the Supreme Court. (The other was filled by John McKinley.) The appointment came on Jackson's final day in office.

On the court, Catron supported states' rights and in 1857 sided with the "pro-Southern" majority in the *Dred Scott* case. He refused to support the Confederacy, however, and was forced to leave Nashville after Tennessee seceded from the Union.

John Catron
(1837-1865)

John McKinley
(1837-1852)

Born: ca. 1786, Pennsylvania.
Education: self-educated.

Born: May 1, 1780, Culpeper County, Va.

Education: read law on his own and was admitted to the bar in 1800.

Official Positions: Alabama state representative, sessions of 1820, 1831 and 1836; U.S. Senator, 1826-31 and 1837; U.S. Representative, 1833-35.

Supreme Court Appointment: nominated associate justice by President Martin Van Buren Sept. 18, 1837, for a newly created Supreme Court seat; confirmed by the Senate Sept. 25, 1837, by a voice vote; replaced by John A. Campbell, nominated by President Pierce.

Family: married, first, Juliana Bryan; second, Elizabeth Armistead.

Died: July 19, 1852, Louisville, Ky.

Personal Background

Born in Virginia, McKinley at an early age moved to frontier Kentucky with his family. His father, a physician, gave McKinley an interest in studying for an acceptable profession. Young McKinley read law and was admitted to the bar in 1800.

After practicing in Frankfort, the state capital, and in Louisville, the state's main commercial center, McKinley set out for Alabama, a newly-thriving territory about to be admitted to the union. He settled in Huntsville, and soon became a part of the so-called Georgia machine, a group of locally prominent lawyers, planters and businessmen, mostly from Georgia, who dominated north Alabama socially and politically.

Public Career

Once settled in Huntsville, McKinley entered politics. He was elected to the Alabama legislature for the session of 1820. Then, in 1822, he missed election by the state legislature to the U.S. Senate by only one vote. Four years later, the seat opened up again with the death of the incumbent, and this time McKinley took it, by a margin of three votes.

During his term in the Senate, he stood for strict construction of the Constitution and a liberal reform of federal land policies, defending small landholders against speculators. McKinley was defeated for re-election to the Senate by Alabama Gov. Gabriel Moore in 1831.

During the 1820s McKinley had switched from support of Henry Clay to Andrew Jackson. Thereafter, he remained an ardent Jacksonian. In 1832 he was elected to the U.S. House and supported Jackson's campaign against the Bank of the United States. McKinley further proved his loyalty to Jackson by supporting Martin Van Buren, Jackson's choice for the vice presidency in 1832 and for the presidency in 1836.

Elected once again to the U.S. Senate in 1837, McKinley was picked for the Supreme Court by President Van Buren before the new Congress met, so he never got to serve his second Senate term. Congress had enacted a bill increasing the court from seven members to nine in the waning days of Jackson's term. After William Smith of Alabama had turned down Jackson's nomination to one of the new seats, it fell to the newly inaugurated President Van Buren to pick another man. His choice was McKinley.

McKinley's fifteen years on the bench were quiet. He stood by his states' rights and pro-slavery views to the last.

McKinley's circuit-riding duties — which he estimated at 10,000 miles a year — contributed to his failing health. When he died in 1852, Chief Justice Taney eulogized him as a "sound" lawyer, "faithful and assiduous. . . ."

Peter Vivian Daniel
(1841-1860)

Born: April 24, 1784, Stafford County, Va.

Education: attended Princeton University, 1802-03.

Official Position: member, Virginia House of Delegates, 1809-12; Virginia Privy Council, 1812-35; lieutenant governor of Virginia, 1818-35; U.S. district judge, eastern district of Virginia, 1836-41.

Supreme Court Appointment: nominated associate justice by President Van Buren Feb. 26, 1841, to replace Justice Philip Barbour, who died; confirmed by the Senate March 2, 1841, by a 22-5 vote; replaced on court by Samuel F. Miller, nominated by President Lincoln.

Family: married, first, Lucy Randolph, 1809, died 1847; second, Elizabeth Harris, 1853; two children.

Died: May 31, 1860, Richmond, Va.

Personal Background

Daniel was a member of an old Virginia family which went back to the early days of the colony. It was a landed family, with a sizeable estate, "Crow's Nest," where Daniel was born and brought up. His early education was by private tutors. He spent one year at Princeton, but returned to Virginia and moved to Richmond to study law in the office of Edmund Randolph.

Randolph had been both attorney general and secretary of state in George Washington's administration, and Daniel's association with him gained him access to the inner circle of Virginia political power. Daniel's marriage to Randolph's daughter Lucy further cemented the connection.

Public Career

In 1809 Daniel was elected to the Virginia house of delegates, where he served until elected to the Virginia privy council, an executive advisory and review body, in 1812. In 1818 he was chosen lieutenant governor of Virginia while continuing to serve on the privy council. He remained in both capacities for the next 17 years.

A loyal Jacksonian Democrat, Daniel supported President Andrew Jackson in his attack on the Bank of the United States. At one point, Jackson offered him the post of attorney general, but Daniel turned it down because of its inadequate salary. Because of his support of Jackson, Daniel was denied re-election in 1835 to his positions as privy councilor and lieutenant governor. The next year, Jackson appointed him federal district judge for eastern Virginia.

Daniel's elevation to the Supreme Court came suddenly. Justice Philip Barbour died Feb. 24, 1841, only a week before Democratic President Martin Van Buren was to turn over his office to the new Whig administration of William Henry Harrison. To ensure that the court seat remained in Democratic hands, Van Buren nominated

Daniel only two days after Barbour's death, and the Democratic-controlled Senate confirmed the appointment on March 2, two days before adjournment.

Daniel remained on the court for 19 years, a vestige of the Jeffersonian school's advocacy of states' rights and a weak central government. He died on the eve of the Civil War and was not replaced on the court for two years. The delay occurred because the Republicans took power and restructured the circuit court system to cut the number of southern circuits and increase those in the midwest and west.

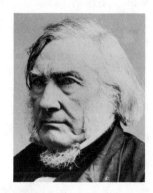

Samuel Nelson
(1845-1872)

Born: Nov. 10, 1792, Hebron, N.Y.

Education: graduated, Middlebury College, 1813.

Official Positions: postmaster, Cortland, N.Y., 1820-23; presidential elector, 1820; judge, sixth circuit of New York, 1823-31; associate justice, New York Supreme Court, 1831-37; chief justice, New York Supreme Court, 1837-45; member, Alabama Claims Commission, 1871.

Supreme Court Appointment: nominated associate justice by President John Tyler Feb. 4, 1845, to replace Justice Smith Thompson, who died; confirmed by the Senate Feb. 14, 1845, by a voice vote; replaced on court by Ward Hunt, nominated by President Grant.

Family: married, first, Pamela Woods, 1819, died 1822, one son; second, Catherine Ann Russell, ca. 1825, two daughters, one son.

Died: Dec. 13, 1873, Cooperstown, N.Y.

Personal Background

Descended from Scotch-Irish parents who immigrated to America in the 1760s, Nelson spent his boyhood on farms in upstate New York. He attended local district schools, where his interest in his studies at first led him to plan a career in the ministry.

After graduation from Middlebury College in 1813, however, Nelson decided to study law instead. He clerked in a law office in Salem, N.Y., was admitted to the bar in 1817, and settled in Cortland, a small but thriving county seat in central New York. After establishing a successful law practice there, Nelson became involved in politics, identifying with the Democratic-Republicans and later with the Jackson-Van Buren wing of the Democratic party.

Public Career

In 1820 Nelson served as a presidential elector, voting for President James Monroe, and was appointed postmaster of Cortland, a position he held for three years. Also during that period, in 1821, Nelson was a delegate to the state constitutional convention, where he advocated the abolition of property qualifications for voting.

Beginning in 1823, Nelson embarked on a career in the judiciary which was to last for nearly 50 years. His first judicial position was as a judge of the sixth circuit of New York (1823-31). In 1831 he was elevated to the state supreme court and in 1837 became chief justice. From there he went to the U.S. Supreme Court in 1845.

Nelson's nomination for the Supreme Court in the waning days of the Tyler adminstration came as a complete surprise. Two previous Tyler nominees had been turned down by the Senate, and several other prominent persons had declined offers of appointment. But Nelson's reputation as a careful and uncontroversial jurist, combined with his Democratic background, were received favorably, and the Democratic-controlled Senate confirmed him with little contention.

Most of Nelson's 27 years on the court were unspectacular. He achieved some brief notoriety in the secession crisis of 1860-61 when he joined with Justice John A. Campbell to try to conciliate the North and South and avoid the Civil War. Nelson was also considered for the Democratic presidential nomination in 1860, but nothing came of it.

In 1871 President Grant appointed Nelson a member of the commission to settle the Alabama claims dispute against Great Britain. It was his hard work on the commission which finally broke Nelson's health, and he retired from the court the next year.

Levi Woodbury
(1845-1851)

Born: Dec. 22, 1789, Francestown, N.H.

Education: Dartmouth College, graduated with honors, 1809; Tapping Reeve Law School, ca. 1810.

Official Positions: clerk, New Hampshire state senate, 1816; associate justice, New Hampshire superior court, 1817-23; governor, New Hampshire, 1823-24; speaker, New Hampshire state house, 1825; U.S. Senator, 1825-31 and 1841-45; secretary of the Navy, 1831-34; secretary of the Treasury, 1834-41.

Supreme Court Appointment: nominated associate justice by President James K. Polk Dec. 23, 1845, to replace Justice Joseph Story, who died; confirmed by the Senate Jan. 3, 1846, by voice vote; replaced on court by Benjamin R. Curtis, nominated by President Fillmore.

Family: married Elizabeth Williams Clapp, June 1819; four daughters, one son.

Died: Sept. 4, 1851, Portsmouth, N.H.

Personal Background

The second of ten children, Woodbury was born into an old New England family which traced its American roots back to 1630. Originally settled in Massachusetts, some of the family's descendants moved to New Hampshire in the late 1700s, where Woodbury was born in 1789.

Woodbury graduated from Dartmouth College with honors in 1809 and then began the study of law. While he studied privately with practicing lawyers — as was then the custom — he also briefly attended a law school in Litchfield, Conn., making him the first Supreme Court justice to have attended a law school.

After being admitted to the bar in 1812, Woodbury practiced in his native Francestown and in nearby Portsmouth, the main commercial center of the state, from 1812 to 1816. But his interests soon turned to politics, and he held some kind of political office almost constantly from 1816 to his appointment to the Supreme Court in 1845.

Public Career

Woodbury started his climb up the political ladder in 1816 when he was appointed clerk of the state senate. After serving a year, he was put on the New Hampshire superior court, where he remained until 1823, when he became a successful insurgent candidate for governor of New Hampshire, beating the entrenched Democratic-Republican machine of Isaac Hill.

Woodbury was defeated for re-election in 1824, but came back the next year to win a seat in the state house and was elected speaker. Shortly thereafter, the legislature elected him to the U.S. Senate, where he served from 1825 to 1831.

Upon his retirement from the Senate, Woodbury was made secretary of the Navy in President Andrew Jackson's cabinet reorganization of 1831. He made little mark in that office, but in 1834 he was suddenly elevated to the crucial post of secretary of the Treasury in the midst of Jackson's war on the Bank of the United States. Jackson had gone through three Treasury secretaries, including later Chief Justice Roger B. Taney, in a little over a year. Woodbury loyally cooperated with Jackson's policies, although with some reservations, and remained as head of the Treasury through the administration of Martin Van Buren (1837-41).

Upon leaving the cabinet, Woodbury was chosen to serve once again in the U.S. Senate, where he was sitting when Polk tapped him for the Supreme Court.

Woodbury served for less than six years on the court, dying in 1851. He was a contender for the Democratic presidential nomination in 1848, but lost to Lewis Cass.

Aug. 4, 1846, by a voice vote; replaced on court by William Strong, nominated by President Grant.

Family: married Isabella Rose, 1829.
Died: Sept. 26, 1870, Philadelphia, Pa.

Personal Background

The eldest of 11 children, Grier was born into a family of Presbyterian ministers. Both his father and his maternal grandfather followed that vocation.

Grier was taught by his father until the age of 17, then entered Dickinson College as a junior and finished in one year. He then became a teacher in the Northumberland Academy, succeeding his father as principal in 1815.

But Grier's interests turned to the law, which he studied privately, passing the bar in 1817. He set up practice first in Bloomsburg, but soon moved to the county seat of Danville, Pa., where he became a prominent local attorney.

Public Career

A solid Jacksonian Democrat, Grier came to the attention of the Democratic politicians in Harrisburg. As a result, he got a patronage appointment as president judge of the district court of Allegheny County in 1833, a job he held for the next 13 years, establishing a reputation as a thorough and knowledgeable judge.

In 1844 Supreme Court Justice Henry Baldwin of Pennsylvania died, and a long effort began to fill his seat. It took more than two years for the spot to be filled finally by Grier. President Tyler had made two nominations; the first was withdrawn and the second got no action from the Democratic Senate. Tyler left office in March 1845, and the task of filling the vacancy fell to President Polk.

Polk also had difficulty finding a justice, first offering the position to future president James Buchanan. When Buchanan turned it down, Polk nominated George Woodward, but the Senate refused to confirm him. Finally, Polk selected Grier, who was confirmed.

Grier served on the court for nearly a quarter-century. Toward the end of his service, his mental and physical powers waned to the point that he was barely functioning. Finally, a committee of his colleagues called on him to urge his retirement. He took their advice and resigned in February 1870. He died seven months later.

Robert Cooper Grier
(1846-1870)

Born: March 5, 1794, Cumberland County, Pa.
Education: Dickinson College, graduated 1812.
Official Positions: president judge, district court of Allegheny Co. Pa., 1833-46.
Supreme Court Appointment: nominated associate justice by President James K. Polk Aug. 3, 1846, to replace Justice Henry Baldwin, who died; confirmed by the Senate

Benjamin Robbins Curtis
(1851-1857)

Born: Nov. 4, 1809, Watertown, Mass.
Education: Harvard University, graduated 1829 with highest honors; Harvard Law School, graduated 1832.
Official Positions: Massachusetts state representative, 1849-51.

Supreme Court Appointment: nominated associate justice by President Millard Fillmore Dec. 11, 1851, to replace Justice Levi Woodbury, who died; confirmed by the Senate Dec. 29, 1851, by a voice vote; replaced on court by Nathan Clifford, nominated by President Buchanan.

Family: married, first, Eliza Maria Woodward, 1833, died 1844, five children; second, Anna Wroe Curtis, 1846, died 1860, three children; third, Maria Malleville Allen, 1861, four children.

Died: Sept. 15, 1874, Newport, R.I.

Personal Background

Curtis was the son of a Massachusetts ship captain whose ancestors settled New England in the 1630s. His father died while on a voyage abroad when Curtis was a child. He was raised by his mother with help from his half-uncle, George Ticknor, a Harvard professor and author.

When Curtis was ready to enter Harvard University in 1825, his mother moved to Cambridge and ran a boarding school for students there to support herself and her family. Curtis graduated from Harvard in 1829 and immediately entered Harvard Law School, from which he graduated in 1832 after taking a year off in 1831 to set up a law practice in Northfield, Mass., a small town in the Connecticut River Valley.

In 1834 Curtis moved to Boston to join the law practice of his distant cousin, Charles Pelham Curtis. After the death of his first wife, Curtis married his law partner's daughter in 1846.

Public Career

Elected to the Massachusetts house in 1849, Curtis chaired a commission which designed a sweeping reform of judicial proceedings in the state. A conservative Whig, Curtis was a strong supporter of Daniel Webster. He rallied behind the senator during the crisis of 1850 when Webster was working for compromise of the territorial and slave issues and was being denounced for his efforts by Massachusetts abolitionists.

In 1851, when President Fillmore was looking for a replacement for the late Justice Levi Woodbury, Webster, then serving as Fillmore's secretary of state, recommended Curtis. Curtis' relations with his colleagues on the court, especially with Chief Justice Taney, became so acrimonious during court arguments over the *Dred Scott* case and other pre-Civil War controversies that he decided to leave the court and resigned on Sept. 30, 1857.

Curtis believed strongly in preserving the Union through compromise. In his court activities, he upheld and enforced the unpopular fugitive slave law. But he drew the line at the *Dred Scott* decision; he was one of two justices who dissented from that highly criticized decision.

Curtis devoted the remainder of his life to a lucrative law practice in Boston. He appeared before the Supreme Court on numerous occasions to argue for his clients. Politically, he remained a conservative, objecting to some of the emergency measures taken by President Lincoln, including the Emancipation Proclamation and the suspension of *habeas corpus*.

He also opposed the radical Reconstruction policies of congressional Republicans during Andrew Johnson's administration. In 1868 he served as the leading counsel for President Johnson during the impeachment proceedings. Johnson offered Curtis the position of attorney general, but he declined.

John Archibald Campbell
(1853-1861)

Born: June 24, 1811, Washington, Ga.

Education: Franklin College (now the University of Georgia), graduated with first honors, 1825; attended U.S. Military Academy at West Point, 1825-28.

Official Positions: Alabama state representative, sessions of 1837 and 1843; assistant secretary of war, Confederate States of America, 1862-65.

Supreme Court Appointment: nominated associate justice by President Franklin Pierce March 22, 1853, to replace Justice John McKinley, who died; confirmed by the Senate March 25, 1853, by a voice vote; replaced on court by David Davis, nominated by President Lincoln.

Family: married Anna Esther Goldthwaite in the early 1830s; five children.

Died: March 2, 1889, Baltimore, Md.

Personal Background

Born into a family of Scotch and Scotch-Irish descent, Campbell was a child prodigy. He entered college at the age of 11, graduating at 14. He then attended West Point for three years before withdrawing to return home to support the family after the death of his father. A year later, at the age of 18, he was admitted to the bar by special act of the Georgia legislature.

In 1830 Campbell moved to Alabama to begin his legal career, settling first in Montgomery, where he met and married Anna Esther Goldthwaite, member of a prominent Alabama family. They moved to Mobile in 1837 and Campbell was elected to the first of two terms in the state legislature.

Public Career

Campbell quickly became one of the leading lawyers in Alabama, and before long his reputation spread nationally. Twice he declined appointment to the Alabama supreme court. He was a delegate to the Nashville convention of 1850, convened to protect southern rights in the face of what they saw as northern encroachment, especially on the slavery question. Campbell was a moderating influence at the convention, writing many of the resolutions which finally were adopted.

Campbell was selected for the Supreme Court after a Democratic Senate had refused to act on three choices nominated by Whig President Millard Fillmore. When Fillmore was replaced by Democrat Franklin Pierce in March 1853, Democrats were able to appoint one of their own to the court. Campbell's selection was made in an unprecedented fashion. The Supreme Court justices wanted the new president to nominate Campbell and sent a delegation to Pierce to make their wish known. Pierce complied.

Campbell's service on the bench was cut short by the Civil War. He opposed secession and was hopeful that slavery would slowly disappear if the South was left alone. He himself freed all his slaves upon his Supreme Court appointment, and thereafter hired only free blacks as servants. During the secession crisis, he attempted to serve as a mediator between the seceding states and the new Lincoln administration.

But when the die was cast and hostilities broke out, he resigned his court position and returned to the South, settling in New Orleans. In 1862, he was invited to join the Confederate government and accepted the position of assistant secretary of war in charge of administering the conscription law. He remained in that position until the fall of the Confederacy in 1865.

After a few months of detention by the Union, Campbell was freed and returned to New Orleans, where he built up a prosperous and prestigious law practice. He argued before the Supreme Court on numerous occasions in the quarter-century before his death.

Nathan Clifford
(1858-1881)

Born: Aug. 18, 1803, Rumney, N.H.

Education: studied law in office of Josiah Quincy in Rumney, admitted to New Hampshire bar, 1827.

Official Positions: Maine state representative, 1830-34; attorney general of Maine, 1834-38; U.S. Representative, 1839-43; U.S. Attorney General, 1846-48; Minister to Mexico, 1849-49.

Supreme Court Appointment: nominated associate justice by President James Buchanan Dec. 9, 1857, to replace Benjamin R. Curtis, who resigned; confirmed by the Senate Jan. 12, 1858, by a 26-23 vote; replaced on court by Horace Gray, nominated by President Arthur.

Family: married Hannah Ayer, ca. 1828; six children.

Died: July 25, 1881, Cornish, Maine.

Personal Background

Clifford was the son of a New Hampshire farmer whose American roots went back three generations. His grandfather was an officer in the Revolutionary War.

Clifford attended the local academies for his early education, then studied law in the office of Josiah Quincy, a prominent attorney in Rumney, N.H. Clifford was admitted to the bar in 1827 and moved to Newfield, Maine, to begin practice. There he met and married a local woman, Hannah Ayer.

Clifford was a staunch Jacksonian Democrat, maintaining his early political beliefs throughout his long life and political career.

Public Career

Clifford entered public life soon after beginning his law practice in Maine. In 1830, at the age of 27, he was elected to the lower house of the Maine legislature. He was re-elected for three more one-year terms, and served the last two years as speaker. He was then elected attorney general of the state by the legislature, serving four years. After that, he won two terms in the U.S. House, but was defeated for election to a third term.

Clifford's defeat in 1843 marked the end of the first phase of his political career. He then returned to law practice in Maine for three years. He had earned a reputation as a hard worker and received attention for the thoroughness of his preparation.

In 1846 President Polk chose Clifford as attorney general. Polk needed New England representation in his Cabinet, and Clifford supported the administration's ideas.

During his service in the Polk Cabinet, Clifford played a key role in mediating the many disputes between Polk and his secretary of state, James Buchanan. Polk was vigorously pursuing his war with Mexico, while Buchanan advocated a more cautious policy. Buchanan liked and trusted Clifford, and when he became president would appoint Clifford to the Supreme Court.

In 1848 Polk entrusted Clifford with a diplomatic mission. He was sent to Mexico with the purpose of getting Mexico to ratify the peace treaty ending the war. Clifford did so and stayed on to become U.S. minister to the Mexican government from 1848-49. With a new Whig adminstration in Washington in 1849, Clifford returned to Maine to resume law practice, this time in the more populous and prosperous city of Portland.

When a Supreme Court vacancy occurred in late 1857, Buchanan chose Clifford to fill it. There was strong criticism against the nomination; Clifford was looked upon in the North as a "doughface" — a northern man with southern principles. Clifford had supported Buchanan administration policies which many northerners thought favored the South. But Clifford was confirmed in a close vote.

In 1877, Clifford — still on the court — served as chairman of the electoral commission set up to decide the disputed presidential election of 1876. He voted with the Democrats for Tilden, but the Republican, Rutherford B. Hayes, won by one vote. Clifford always considered Hayes an illegitimate president, and refused to enter the White House during his presidency.

In 1880 Clifford suffered a stroke which prevented him from taking any futher active role in court proceedings. He refused to resign, however, hoping to live until a Democratic president could name his successor. But he died while the Republicans were still in power.

Noah Haynes Swayne
(1862-1881)

Born: Dec. 7, 1804, Frederick County, Va.

Education: studied law privately and was admitted to the bar in Warrenton, Va., in 1823.

Official Positions: Coshocton County prosecuting attorney, 1826-29; Ohio state representative, 1830 and 1836; U.S. attorney for Ohio, 1830-41; Columbus City councilman, 1834.

Supreme Court Appointment: nominated associate justice by President Abraham Lincoln Jan. 21, 1862, to replace John McLean, who died; confirmed by the Senate Jan. 24, 1862, by a 38-1 vote; replaced on court by Stanley Matthews, nominated by President Hayes and renominated by President Garfield.

Family: married Sarah Ann Wager, 1832; four sons, one daughter.

Died: June 8, 1884, New York City.

Personal Background

Although born in the slave-holding state of Virginia, Swayne was the son of antislavery Quaker parents of Pennsylvania origin. He studied medicine as a youth, but after the death of his teacher he switched to law.

Following his admission to the bar, Swayne migrated to the free state of Ohio because of his opposition to slavery. During his long legal career in that state, he was involved in cases defending runaway slaves. When he married Sarah Ann Wager, a Virginian who owned slaves, she freed them at his insistence.

Public Career

Shortly after settling in Ohio, Swayne became involved in politics as a Jacksonian Democrat. He was elected prosecuting attorney of Coshocton County in 1826 and to the Ohio legislature in 1829. In 1830 President Andrew Jackson appointed him U.S. attorney for Ohio, and he served throughout the rest of Jackson's administration as well as that of Martin Van Buren. During his service as U.S. attorney, he also developed a successful private law practice and served on the Columbus city council and once again in the state legislature.

Swayne's political activity ebbed in the 1840s, but resurged in the 1850s when the slavery issue began tearing the nation apart. Swayne's antislavery convictions drove him from the Democratic Party, and he supported the presidential candidate of the new Republican Party, John Charles Fremont, in 1856. Swayne also served in the 1850s as a member of a state committee overseeing Ohio's finances, which had fallen into disorder.

Although Swayne had no judicial experience and was not well known outside Ohio, Lincoln nevertheless made him his first appointment to the Supreme Court. The vacancy was caused by the death of Justice John McLean, a close friend of Swayne's, and McLean had let it be known that he wanted Swayne to succeed him on the court. In addition, Swayne was close to the governor of Ohio, William Dennison, who personally came to Washington to lobby for Swayne. The Ohio congressional delegation also recommended him.

Swayne fulfilled Republican hopes that he would uphold the extraordinary Civil War measures of the national government, and he continued to take a generally nationalist stance in his decisions throughout his years on the court. During his court service, he also lobbied for passage of the 15th Amendment, guaranteeing voting rights for blacks. His own state of Ohio was crucial to the ratification of the amendment and Swayne used all his influence in his adopted state on behalf of approval.

Twice Swayne maneuvered for the Chief Justiceship — in 1864, when Roger B. Taney died, and again in 1873 when Salmon P. Chase died. But he was disappointed both times. With his mental acuity noticeably declining by 1881, Swayne was persuaded by President Hayes to resign with the promise that his friend and fellow-Ohioan Stanley Matthews would be chosen as his successor.

Samuel Freeman Miller
(1862-1890)

Born: April 5, 1816, Richmond, Ky.

Education: Transylvania University, M.D., 1838; studied law privately, admitted to the bar in 1847.

Official Positions: justice of the peace and member of the Knox County, Ky., court, an administrative body, in the 1840s.

Supreme Court Appointment: nominated associate justice by President Abraham Lincoln July 16, 1862, to replace Justice Peter V. Daniel, who died; confirmed July 16, 1862, by a voice vote; replaced on court by Henry B. Brown, nominated by President Benjamin Harrison.

Family: married, first, Lucy Ballinger, ca. 1839, died ca. 1854, three children; second, Elizabeth Winter Reeves, widow of his law partner, 1857, two children.

Died: Oct. 13, 1890, Washington, D.C.

Personal Background

The son of a Pennsylvania-German father and a mother from North Carolina, both of whom migrated to Kentucky at the turn of the nineteenth century, Miller began his career as a medical doctor. After graduating from the medical department of Transylvania University in 1838, he set up practice in Barboursville in Kentucky's small, mountainous Knox County.

Miller soon developed an interest in legal and political matters. He joined a debating society and studied law on the side, passing his bar exam in 1847. He favored gradual emancipation of slaves, and when the Kentucky constitutional convention of 1849 strengthened the position of slavery in the state, Miller freed his own slaves and moved west to Iowa, a free state.

Public Career

In Iowa, Miller abandoned medicine and set up a prosperous law practice in Keokuk. With political tensions rising in the 1850s, Miller joined the public arena and helped organize the Republican Party in Iowa, serving as chairman of the Keokuk County GOP organization. By 1860 Miller was one of the leading Republican figures in the state and a strong backer of Abraham Lincoln for the party's presidential nomination. In 1861 Miller made a try for the Republican gubernatorial nomination but was defeated by incumbent Gov. Samuel J. Kirkwood.

Miller's appointment to the Supreme Court came despite his lack of judicial experience. With the creation of a new circuit west of the Mississippi, western congressmen and politicians, including a unanimous Iowa delegation, pressed for Miller's appointment. Lincoln's agreement to choose him made Miller the first Supreme Court justice from west of the Mississippi.

Miller was one of the five justices to serve on the electoral commission in 1877 to resolve the disputed presidential election of 1876 between Democrat Samuel J. Tilden and Republican Rutherford B. Hayes. Miller voted down the line with the Republican majority to give the presidency to Hayes.

Twice Miller was considered for Chief Justice — in 1873 and 1888 — but was passed over both times. His name was also mentioned for the presidency in 1880 and 1884, but no significant movement developed. Miller worked on the court almost up to the point of his death on Oct. 13, 1890.

David Davis
(1862-1877)

Born: March 9, 1815, Cecil County, Md.

Education: graduated Kenyon College, 1832; Yale Law School, 1835.

Official Positions: Illinois state representative, 1845-47; member, Illinois constitutional convention, 1847; Illinois state circuit judge, 1848-62.

Supreme Court Appointment: nominated associate justice by President Lincoln Dec. 1, 1862, to replace John A. Campbell, who resigned; confirmed by the Senate Dec. 8, 1862, by a voice vote; replaced on court by John Marshall Harlan, nominated by President Hayes.

Family: married, first, Sarah Woodruff, Oct. 30, 1838, died 1879; second, Adeline Burr, March 14, 1883, two daughters.

Died: June 26, 1886, Bloomington, Ill.

Personal Background

Davis was born in Maryland of Welsh ancestry. After studying law, he sought his fortune in the West.

Settling first in Pekin, Ill., he moved within a year to Bloomington, which became his lifelong home. He was active in Whig politics, running a losing race for the state senate in 1840 but winning a state house seat in 1844. It was during this period that he first became acquainted with Abraham Lincoln, a relationship that deepened over the years and was to have a major effect on Davis' life.

Public Career

After one term in the state house, Davis was chosen a member of the Illinois constitutional convention of 1847. At the convention, he fought for a popularly-elected judiciary, replacing the system of election by the legislature. Davis' position prevailed, and in 1848 he was elected a judge of the eighth state judicial circuit, a position he was re-elected to twice and which he held until his appointment to the Supreme Court.

Among the prominent lawyers who practiced before Judge Davis in Illinois were Abraham Lincoln and Stephen Douglas. Davis became close to Lincoln in the 1850s and joined the new Republican party with him when their Whig party fell apart. Davis became Lincoln's campaign manager in 1860 and was perhaps the most important person in securing Lincoln the Republican presidential nomination that year.

Lincoln appointed Davis to the Supreme Court vacancy created by the resignation of Justice John A. Campbell, an Alabaman who withdrew to join the Confederate effort.

Davis' interest in politics never faded. After Lincoln's death, he became disenchanted with the Republican Party. In 1872 he was nominated for president by the Labor Reform Party, a splinter group. Davis hoped to use this nomination to further his candidacy for the Liberal Republicans, a group of anti-Grant Republicans. But when the Liberals chose Horace Greeley instead, Davis declined the Labor Reform nomination.

Tired of his career on the Supreme Court, Davis accepted his election in 1877 by the Illinois legislature to the U.S. Senate and resigned from the court. The timing was unfortunate, for Davis had been expected to be a key member of the electoral commission set up to decide the disputed presidential election of 1876. Davis' political independence would have made him the swing vote on an otherwise evenly-divided commission. His replacement was a Republican, Justice Joseph P. Bradley, who voted with the Republicans and gave the election to Republican Rutherford B. Hayes. At the time, it was thought that Davis might have voted with the Democrats on at least some of the disputed electoral votes, but he indicated later that he did not disagree with the commission's decisions.

Davis served one term in the Senate (1877-83), voting independently, and then retired. From 1881 to 1883, he was president pro tem of the Senate, which under the succession law then in effect made him next in line for the presidency if anything had happened to President Arthur.

Stephen Johnson Field
(1863-1897)

Born: Nov. 4, 1816, Haddam, Conn.

Education: graduated Williams College, 1837, class valedictorian; studied law in private firms, admitted to the bar in 1841.

Official Positions: Alcalde of Marysville, 1850; California state representative, 1850-51; California Supreme Court justice, 1857-63.

Supreme Court Appointment: nominated associate justice by President Abraham Lincoln March 6, 1863, for a newly created seat; confirmed by the Senate March 10, 1863, by a voice vote; replaced on court by Joseph McKenna, nominated by President McKinley.

Family: married Virginia Swearingen, June 2, 1859; no children.

Died: April 9, 1899, in Washington, D.C.

Personal Background

The son of a New England Congregational clergyman, Field was born into a family which produced several prominent members. His brothers included David Dudley Field, a noted New York lawyer and politician; Cyrus West Field, a promoter of the first Atlantic cable; and Henry Martyn Field, a leading clergyman and author. Field's nephew, David J. Brewer, was himself a Supreme Court justice (1889-1910) and served with Field on the court for the last eight years of Field's service.

Field studied law with his brother Dudley and with John Van Buren, son of President Martin Van Buren. He was admitted to the New York bar in 1841 and for the next seven years practiced in partnership with his brother.

But in 1849, after a trip to Europe, he decided to strike out on his own and moved to California. Settling in Marysville, in the heart of the gold fields, Field lived the rough-and-tumble life of a frontier entrepreneur.

Public Career

Field served in 1850 as Maryville's alcalde (the chief local administrative office under the old Spanish system). He quarreled with a local judge and was twice disbarred and once sent to jail for contempt of court.

Field was elected to the California house in 1850 and during his year of service was the chief drafter of the civil and criminal codes for the new state. After being defeated in a bid for the state senate in 1851, he resumed his legal career for a time and then was elected to the California Supreme Court as a Democrat in 1857.

In 1863 Congress authorized an additional seat on the U.S. Supreme Court, partly to gain a new justice who would support the Civil War measures of the federal government, and partly because there was a need for a new circuit for the west coast. Many cases concerning land and mineral issues were coming to the court from California, and westerners wanted someone on the court familiar with those issues.

The California and Oregon congressional delegations unanimously recommended Field for the new seat, even though he was a Democrat. He had staunchly supported the Union cause and was an acknowledged expert in land and mining issues. So Lincoln appointed him.

During his service on the court, Field served, in 1877, on the electoral commission which decided the contested presidential election in favor of Republican Rutherford B. Hayes. Field voted on the losing Democratic side on all questions.

Field's name was mentioned for the Democratic presidential nomination in 1880 and 1884, but his candidacy did not advance very far. He aspired to be Chief Justice in 1888, when Waite died, but President Cleveland picked Melville W. Fuller instead.

In the 1890s, Field's mental powers were visibly declining, and he was taking less and less part in court proceedings. Finally, the other justices strongly hinted that he resign. Ironically, Field himself had been part of an effort to persuade aging Justice Robert C. Grier to resign in 1877. Field did finally quit the court in late 1897, but only after surpassing Marshall's record of 34 years and five months of service.

Salmon Portland Chase
(1864-1873)

Born: Jan. 13, 1808, Cornish, N.H.
Education: Dartmouth College, 1826.
Official Positions: U.S. Senator from Ohio, 1849-55, 1861; Governor of Ohio, 1856-60; U.S. secretary of the Treasury, 1861-64.

Supreme Court Appointment: nominated Chief Justice by President Abraham Lincoln, Dec. 6, 1864, to replace Chief Justice Roger B. Taney, who died; confirmed by the Senate Dec. 6, 1864, by a voice vote; replaced on court by Morrison R. Waite, appointed by President Grant.

Family: married, first, Katherine Jane Garniss, March 4, 1834, died Dec. 1, 1835; second, Eliza Ann Smith, Sept. 26, 1839, died Sept. 29, 1845; third, Sara Belle Dunlop Ludlow, Nov. 6, 1846, died Jan. 13, 1852, six daughters, only two of whom lived beyond infancy.

Died: May 7, 1873, New York City.

Personal Background

Chase grew up and made his career in Ohio but was born in New Hampshire of a prominent family that traced its roots in this country back to 1640. An uncle, Dudley Chase, served as a U.S. senator for Vermont (1813-17 and 1825-31), and another uncle, Philander Chase, was the Protestant Episcopal Bishop of Ohio (1818-31). Chase's father was a tavern-keeper who held various local political offices.

Upon his father's death in 1817, Chase went to live with his uncle Philander in Ohio and was brought up under his stern discipline. Throughout his life, Chase retained a strong and righteous religious streak, inculcated in his early years by his uncle.

After graduation from Dartmouth, Chase went to Washington, D.C., opened a private school, and studied law under Attorney General William Wirt. He was admitted to the bar in 1829, then moved west to Cincinnati to begin his distinguished legal career.

Chase became involved early in the anti-slavery movement and took a prominent role in defending runaway slaves, arguing one case up to the Supreme Court. For his activities, he became known as the "attorney general for runaway negroes."

Public Career

Chase's opposition to slavery soon moved him into politics, and he became a leader of the anti-slavery Liberty Party in the 1840s. In 1848 he joined the Free Soilers and helped write part of the party's platform. The following year, when the Free Soilers held the balance of power in the Ohio legislature, they helped the Democrats organize the legislature in return for the Democrats' support in electing Chase to the U.S. Senate.

In the Senate, Chase joined such anti-slavery stalwarts as William Seward and Benjamin Wade. When the old party system broke up, he helped to form the new Republican party.

In 1855 Chase was elected governor of Ohio and re-elected in 1857. He was mentioned for the Republican presidential nomination in both 1856 and 1860, but did not receive many votes. In 1861 he was elected once again to the U.S. Senate, but resigned after only two days to take a seat in President Lincoln's cabinet. As Lincoln's Treasury secretary, Chase was responsible for financing the war, first with large borrowings and then with the issue of paper money. He also devised a new federal banking system which became the cornerstone of American finance for the next half-century.

But Chase was not happy with Lincoln's leadership and allowed himself to become the focus of an anti-Lincoln group within the Republican party, which wanted to dump the president in 1864. Twice that year, efforts were made to substitute Chase for Lincoln, but the efforts of the radicals were not successful. Chase also had a series of running quarrels with Lincoln over other matters and submitted his resignation several times. Lincoln finally accepted it in the summer of 1864.

When Chief Justice Taney died in October, Chase was Lincoln's first choice for the post. Despite their differences, Lincoln had high regard for Chase's abilities. And the Republicans wanted someone on the court who they felt would sustain the extraordinary measures taken by the federal government during the war and others contemplated for the postwar period.

Chase was probably the most politically-involved Chief Justice in American history, both because of his own ambitions and because of the tumultuous state of the country. In the spring of 1865, Chief Justice Chase made a tour of the South to study conditions there and report to President Andrew Johnson. Later, in 1868, Chase presided at the impeachment trial of Johnson and fought with the radical Republicans for his rights as presiding officer of the trial. In both 1868 and 1872, Chase made no secret of his still-burning presidential ambitions and allowed friends to maneuver politically for him. But as in the past, he was disappointed in his hopes for the nation's highest office.

Born: May 6, 1808, Somers, Conn.
Education: Yale College, B.A., 1828; M.A., 1831.
Official Positions: U.S. Representative, 1847-51; Pennsylvania Supreme Court justice, 1857-68.
Supreme Court Appointment: nominated associate justice by President Ulysses Grant Feb. 7, 1870, to replace Robert C. Grier, who retired; confirmed by the Senate Feb. 18, 1870, by a voice vote; replaced by William B. Woods, nominated by President Hayes.
Family: married, first, Priscilla Lee Mallery, Nov. 28, 1836, died 1844, two daughters, one son; second, Rachel Davis Bull, a widow, Nov. 22, 1849, two daughters, two sons.
Died: Aug. 19, 1895, Lake Minnewassa, N.Y.

Personal Background

Strong was born into an old New England family which traced its ancestry in America back to 1630. He was the eldest of eleven children of a Presbyterian clergyman. After getting an M.A. from Yale in 1831, Strong taught school in Connecticut and New Jersey and studied law briefly at Yale Law School. But he moved to Pennsylvania to begin his legal career and was admitted to the Philadelphia bar in 1832. He then began practice in Reading, a thriving industrial town in the heart of the rich Pennsylvania-Dutch country. Since many of his clients did not speak English, Strong mastered the local German dialect and soon developed a thriving practice.

Public Career

After establishing himself as a member of Reading's elite through his successful law career, Strong was elected to two terms in the U.S. House as an anti-slavery Democrat (1847-51). Then, in 1857, he was elected to a fifteen-year term on the Pennsylvania Supreme Court. He was elected to the court as a Democrat, but with the coming of the Civil War, Strong joined the Republican party.

In 1864, when Chief Justice Roger B. Taney died, Lincoln considered Strong as a potential replacement, but finally chose Salmon P. Chase instead. Strong resigned from the Pennsylvania court in 1868 to devote himself to making money, but in 1869 his name came up again for a court vacancy, this time as an associate justice. Justice Grier had announced his retirement because of age and infirmity, and President Grant's advisers recommended Strong for the spot. But there was great sentiment in the country and the Congress for Edwin M. Stanton, the former secretary of war. Members of Congress circulated a petition for Stanton which was signed by a large majority of both houses; as a result Grant sent up Stanton's name instead of Strong's. Stanton was confirmed Dec. 20, 1869, but died suddenly four days later, never having had a chance to participate in court proceedings.

With Stanton's death, the way was finally clear for Strong to go onto the court. His selection was clouded by charges that Grant was trying to "pack" the court to reverse a decision unfavorable to the Civil War legal tender acts.

During his court service, he was known for his strong intellect and the forceful and articulate manner in which he presented his arguments. He was appointed a member of the Electoral Commission of 1877 which decided the disputed presidential election of 1876 in favor of Republican Rutherford B. Hayes. Strong supported Hayes on all the votes of the commission.

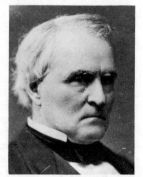

William Strong
(1870-1880)

Strong's court career lasted only 10 years. He retired at the peak of his intellectual abilities.

After his retirement from the court, Strong — then 72 — devoted himself to religious work, something which he had begun while still on the bench. From 1883 to 1895, he was president of the American Sunday School Union; he also served as vice president of the American Bible Society from 1871 to 1895, and was president of the American Tract Society from 1873 to 1895.

Joseph P. Bradley
(1870-1892)

Born: March 14, 1813, Berne, N.Y.
Education: Rutgers University, graduated 1836.
Official Positions: None.
Supreme Court Appointment: nominated associate justice by President Ulysses Grant Feb. 7, 1870, succeeding James Wayne, who died in 1867 and whose seat remained vacant by act of Congress until 1870; confirmed by the Senate March 21, 1870, by a 46-9 vote; replaced on court by George Shiras Jr., nominated by President Benjamin Harrison.
Family: married Mary Hornblower in 1844; seven children.
Died: Jan. 22, 1892, Washington, D.C.

Personal Background

Bradley's life and career exemplify the traditional American "Horatio Alger" success story. The oldest of eleven chidren, Bradley was raised on a small farm in penurious circumstances. But he showed an early aptitude for learning and after going to a country school, began teaching at the age of 16. A local minister took an interest in him and sponsored his entrance to Rutgers University, where he was graduated in 1836.

Bradley then studied law in the office of Archer Gifford, collector of the port of Newark, N.J., and passed the bar in 1839. His assiduous legal work soon paid off in a successful law practice. Specializing in patent, commercial, and corporate law, he became counsel for various railroads, the most important being the powerful Camden and Amboy Railroad. Another fillip to his career came when he married Mary Hornblower in 1844, daughter of the chief justice of the New Jersey Supreme Court.

Bradley had a lifelong interest in mathematics and geology. He devised a perpetual calendar designed to determine the day of the week any date fell on throughout history. And he researched and wrote a treatise on the origins of the steam engine. Always an avid reader, he had a library numbering 16,000 volumes.

The middle initial "P" did not stand for a middle name, but Bradley adopted its use some time during his early life, perhaps after his father's name, Philo.

Public Career

Bradley was a Whig before the Civil War, and went to Washington, D.C., in the winter of 1860-61 to lobby for a compromise settlement of issues between the North and South. But once the war broke out, he supported the Union cause and the Lincoln administration unreservedly. He ran a losing race for the U.S. House as a unionist in 1862. After the war, he identified with the radical wing of the Republican party and ran unsuccessfully as a Grant presidential elector in 1868.

Grant nominated Bradley for a seat on the court in February 1870, the same day he chose William Strong for another court vacancy. (The choices raised a storm later because they made possible the reversal of a crucial court decision, *Hepburn v. Griswold*, involving the validity of the Civil War legal tender acts).

The other major controversy of Bradley's court career came in 1877 when he served on the electoral commission established to determine the outcome of the disputed presidential election of 1876. With the commission divided seven-to-seven along partisan lines, Supreme Court Justice David Davis, an independent, was to have been the fifteenth and deciding member. But Davis withdrew from the commission because the Illinois legislature had chosen him to be a U.S. senator, and Bradley was substituted as the next least partisan justice. But he voted with the Republicans on all the issues, awarding all 20 disputed electoral votes to Republican Rutherford B. Hayes, thus making him president by one vote. Though he was excoriated in the Democratic press, Bradley always contended that he voted on the basis of the legal and constitutional questions and not on a partisan basis.

The rest of Bradley's career on the court was quieter. He was known for careful research and thoughtful analysis. He worked until practically the day of his death, Jan. 22, 1892.

Ward Hunt
(1873-1882)

Born: June 14, 1810, Utica, N.Y.
Education: graduated with honors from Union College, 1828.
Official Positions: New York state assemblyman, 1839; Mayor of Utica, 1844; member, New York state court of appeals, 1866-69; New York state commissioner of appeals, 1869-73.
Supreme Court Appointment: nominated associate justice by President Ulysses Grant Dec. 3, 1872, to replace Samuel Nelson, who retired; confirmed by the Senate Dec. 11, 1872, by a voice vote; took his seat on the court Jan. 9, 1873; replaced by Samuel Blatchford, nominated by President Arthur.

Family: married, first, Mary Ann Savage, 1837, died 1845; second, Marie Taylor, 1853, two children.

Died: March 24, 1886, Washington, D.C.

Personal Background

Hunt was born and made his career in the upstate New York city of Utica. His father was a banker there, and Hunt was descended from early New England settlers. After graduation from Union College, Hunt studied law, first at a private academy in Litchfield, Conn., and then with a local Utica judge, Hiram Denio. After admission to the bar in 1831, he formed a partnership with the judge and built a lucrative practice.

Public Career

While practicing law, Hunt became actively engaged in politics. He was elected to the New York state assembly (lower house) as a Jacksonian Democrat in 1838, and served a one-year term. Later he served a year as mayor of Utica in 1844.

Hunt's ties with the Democratic party began to loosen in the 1840s, when he opposed the annexation of Texas and the expansion of slavery. In 1848 he broke with the party to back Martin Van Buren's presidential bid on the anti-slavery Free Soil ticket.

In 1853 Hunt lost a bid for the state supreme court (the state court of original jurisdiction in New York) as a Democrat, partly because many Democrats refused to back him due to his apostasy in 1848. With the increasing sharpness of the slavery issue thereafter, Hunt finally broke permanently with the Democratic party and helped found the Republican party in New York in 1855-56. During the process, he formed an alliance with fellow Utica native Roscoe Conkling, who was to become the boss of New York Republican politics and to whom Hunt was to owe his appointment to the Supreme Court.

In 1865 Hunt was elected to the New York state court of appeals, the state's highest court, and became its chief judge in 1868. Following a court reorganization in 1869, he became commissioner of appeals, a position he held until his Supreme Court appointment.

Several other more famous names were presented to President Grant for the court vacancy, but Conkling, Grant's close ally, prevailed on the president to choose Hunt.

Hunt's service is considered one of the more inconspicuous in the court's history, and he was responsible for few major opinions.

After only six years service he suffered a paralytic stroke which incapacitated him from further service, but he did not retire from the court for another three years. The law then in effect granted a full pension only to justices who had reached the age of 70 and had served on the court for ten years.

Finally, with the court in danger of becoming bogged down because of Hunt's illness and the increasing age of several other justices, Congress passed a special law exempting Hunt from the terms of the pension law, granting him retirement at full pay if he would resign from the court within thirty days of enactment of the exemption. He resigned the day the law went into effect and died four years later.

Hunt's sponsor, Roscoe Conkling, was nominated by President Arthur to succeed Hunt. But Conkling declined, and the seat went to Samuel Blatchford.

Morrison Remick Waite

(1874-1888)

Born: Nov. 29, 1816, Lyme, Conn.

Education: Graduated from Yale College, 1837.

Official Positions: Ohio state representative, 1850-52; President of the Ohio constitutional convention, 1873-74.

Supreme Court Appointment: nominated Chief Justice by President Ulysses Grant Jan. 19, 1874, to replace Salmon P. Chase, who died; confirmed by the Senate Jan. 21, 1874, by a 63-0 vote; replaced on court by Melville W. Fuller, nominated by President Cleveland.

Family: married his second cousin, Amelia C. Warner, Sept. 21, 1840; five children.

Died: March 23, 1888, Washington, D.C.

Personal Background

Born into an old New England family, Waite counted among his forebears a chief justice of the Connecticut state supreme court, a prominent Connecticut justice of the peace, and a Revolutionary War hero. He attended one of New England's most prestigious institutions of higher learning, Yale College, graduating in the famous class of 1837. (Other members of the class included Samuel J. Tilden, later governor of New York and Democratic presidential nominee in 1876; William Evarts, later secretary of state under President Hayes (1877-81), and Edwards Pierrepont, later attorney general under President Grant (1875-76).)

Seeing greater opportunity in the frontier than in Connecticut, Waite moved to northwest Ohio in 1838 and studied law with Samuel D. Young, a prominent attorney in Maumee City. Waite was admitted to the bar in 1839 and practiced in Maumee City until 1850, when he moved to the booming city of Toledo on Lake Erie. There he made a name for himself as a specialist in railroad law and developed a large business clientele.

Public Career

While Waite came to the Supreme Court as one of the least experienced and least known Chief Justices — he had never held a judicial position nor practiced before the Supreme Court before his appointment — he nevertheless had been involved in public affairs on and off for almost thirty years. Twice he ran for Congress from the northwest Ohio district encompassing Toledo, as a Whig in 1846 and as an independent Republican in 1862, but lost both times. He was elected to the state house in 1849, serving one term. Throughout the Civil War, Waite was strongly pro-Union, and by speeches and writing attempted to rally the population to the Union cause.

Waite was offered a seat on the Ohio Supreme Court in 1863 but decline in favor of an informal advisory role to the governor. The major break which brought Waite to the attention of the national administration headed by President Grant occurred in 1871 when he was appointed a member of the U.S. delegation to the Geneva Arbitration, which was to settle the Alabama claims case. The U.S. was demanding compensation from Great Britain for allowing Confederate vessels to be fitted out in British ports and operate from them during the Civil War. Waite's hard work during the arbitration proceedings and the final award to the United States of $15.5 million dollars brought Waite a measure of national attention and praise.

Upon returning to the United States, Waite was elected to the Ohio constitutional convention in 1873 and was unanimously chosen its president. It was while he was presiding over the convention that he received word that President Grant had nominated him as Chief Justice. The selection came as a complete surprise to both the nation and to Waite. Waite was in effect Grant's fourth choice for the post, with his first choice refusing to accept the job and his next two withdrawing under threat of being rejected by the Senate.

At first, Waite was treated with some condescension by his fellow court members because of his inexperience, but he soon asserted his authority. By the end of his service he received praise for his industriousness if not his boldness or imaginativeness.

Waite also made efforts to protect his post from being involved in national politics, as it had been under his predecessor, Salmon P. Chase, who had angled for the presidential nomination. Waite refused to allow his name to be considered for the 1876 Republican presidential nomination. And he also declined to make himself available for service on the electoral commission formed in 1877 to determine the outcome of the disputed 1876 presidential contest.

Even while fulfilling his duties on the court, Waite assumed an additional load of civic responsibilities. He served as trustee of the Peabody Education Fund from 1874 to 1888 and was a member of the Yale Corporation from 1882 to 1888.

John Marshall Harlan
(1877-1911)

Born: June 1, 1833, Boyle County, Ky.

Education: Centre College, A.B., 1850; studied law at Transylvania University, 1851-53.

Official Positions: adjutant general of Kentucky, 1851; judge, Franklin County, 1858; state attorney general, 1863-67; member, Louisiana Reconstruction Commission, 1877; member, Bering Sea Tribunal of Arbitration, 1893.

Supreme Court Appointment: nominated associate justice by President Rutherford B. Hayes Oct. 17, 1877, to replace David Davis, who resigned; confirmed by U.S. Senate Nov. 29, 1877, by a voice vote; replaced on court by Mahlon Pitney, nominated by President Taft.

Family: married Malvina F. Shanklin Dec. 23, 1856; six children.

Died: Oct. 14, 1911, Washington, D.C.

Personal Background

Harlan was born into a prominent Kentucky political family, with both ancestors and descendants taking important roles in public life. His father, James Harlan, an admirer of Henry Clay's patriotism and John Marshall's leadership on the court, was a U.S. Representative from Kentucky (1835-39) and also served as attorney general and secretary of state of Kentucky. Justice Harlan's son, John Maynard Harlan (1864-1934), became a prominent Chicago lawyer and was the unsuccessful Republican nominee for mayor of Chicago in 1897 and 1905. And his grandson and namesake John Marshall Harlan (1899-1971) was himself a Supreme Court justice (1955-71).

Young Harlan studied law at Transylvania University, known as the "Harvard of the West," and then completed his legal education in his father's law office. He was admitted to the bar in 1853.

Public Career

Harlan's only judicial experience before his appointment to the Supreme Court was his first office, Franklin County judge, from 1858 to 1859. After that one-year experience on the bench, Harlan turned to politics. He ran for the U.S. House in 1859 as the candidate of a coalition of anti-Democratic groups, including the Whigs and Know-Nothings, but lost by 67 votes.

As a slaveholder and a member of the southern aristocracy, Harlan had difficulty following many of the nation's Whigs into the new Republican party. In the presidential election of 1860, he backed the Constitutional Union party, which stood for a compromise settlement of the increasingly bitter sectional conflict. But when the Civil War came, Harlan chose to stay loyal to the Union and served as an officer in the northern forces.

Upon the death of his father in 1863, Harlan resigned his commission and ran successfully for attorney general of Kentucky on the pro-Union ticket. Although opposed to many policies of the Lincoln administration — he supported Democrat George B. McClellan against Lincoln in 1864 — and believing the postwar constitutional amendments ending slavery and attempting to guarantee the rights of blacks were a mistake, Harlan eventually gravitated into the Republican party and was its nominee for governor of Kentucky in 1875. He was also prominently mentioned as a Republican vice-presidential candidate in 1872. But the major impact Harlan had on the national political scene came in 1876, when he headed the Kentucky delegation to the Republican national convention. At a critical moment during the deadlocked proceedings, Harlan swung the state's votes to Ohio Gov. Rutherford B. Hayes, thus helping start a bandwagon moving in Hayes' direction. Hayes was nominated and elected and acknowledged his debt to Harlan by considering him for appointment as attorney general. Although other political considerations intervened so that no Cabinet post was open for Harlan, Hayes kept him in mind. The new president appointed him to head a commission to settle the rival claims of two factions for control of Louisiana in the spring of 1877. Then, when Supreme Court Justice Davis resigned to enter the U.S. Senate, Hayes nominated Harlan to fill the vacancy.

Harlan's tenure on the court — almost 34 years — was one of the longest in the court's history, being exceeded by only four other justices. During his service on the court, he was called on by President Benjamin Harrison in 1892 to serve as the U.S. representative in the arbitration of the Bering Sea controversy with Great Britain.

He had a lively temperament, often delivering his opinions extemporaneously, in the style of an old-fashioned Kentucky stump speech. His vigorous attacks on several famous majority decisions earned him the title of "great dissenter." He was also one of the "last of the tobacco-spitting judges," a habit that was rapidly disappearing by the time of Harlan's death.

William Burnham Woods
(1880-1887)

Born: Aug. 3, 1824, Newark, Ohio.

Education: attended Western Reserve College for three years; graduated from Yale University, 1845.

Official Positions: mayor of Newark, Ohio, 1856; Ohio state representative, 1858-62, speaker in 1858-60 and minority leader in 1860-62; chancellor, middle chancery district of Alabama, 1868-69; U.S. circuit judge for fifth judicial circuit, 1869-80.

Supreme Court Appointment: nominated associate justice by President Rutherford B. Hayes Dec. 15, 1880, to replace William Strong, who resigned; confirmed by the Senate Dec. 21, 1880, by a 39-8 vote; replaced by Lucius Q. C. Lamar, nominated by President Cleveland.

Family: married Anne E. Warner, June 21, 1855; one son and one daughter.

Died: May 14, 1887, Washington, D.C.

Personal Background

Woods was a native Ohioan, born in Newark in the central part of the state. His father, a farmer and merchant, was from Kentucky, while his mother came from New England. Following his education at Western Reserve University and Yale, Woods studied law with S. D. King, a prominent lawyer in his home town of Newark. After passing the bar in 1847, he joined in partnership with his mentor, King, until the Civil War changed the course of his life.

Public Career

Following a rise to local prominence through the practice of law in Newark, the county seat of Licking County, Ohio, Woods was chosen mayor of his native city in 1856. The following year, he was elected to the state legislature, and was chosen speaker. An ardent Democrat, he opposed the rise of the newly established Republican party. When the Democrats lost control of the statehouse in the 1859 elections, Woods became the minority leader.

At first, he opposed the war policy of President Lincoln, but as the conflict continued he became convinced of the necessity of victory over the South. He joined the Union army in 1862, seeing action in the battles of Shiloh and Vicksburg and marching with Sherman through Georgia. He rose to the rank of brigadier general in 1865 and was brevetted a major general just before being mustered out of service in February 1866. His brother, Charles Robert Woods (1827-1885), was a well-known officer in the Union army.

After the war, Woods settled in Alabama, engaging in cotton planting, investing in an iron works, and resuming the practice of law. His decision to reside in the South invited the charge of being a "carpetbagger," but his name was never linked to the corruption and profligacy associated with that term.

By this time, Woods had become a Republican and was elected chancellor of the middle chancery division of Alabama on his new party's ticket in 1868. When President Grant and the national Republican party came to power the next year, Woods received an appointment as a circuit court judge for the fifth circuit (Florida, Georgia, Alabama, Mississippi, Louisiana, and Texas). Despite his northern origins and Union military background, he gained the respect of his southern neighbors and colleagues. Among his efforts to master his job was the necessity of learning the Louisiana law, which was based on the Napoleonic code. In 1877 Woods moved to Atlanta.

In 1880, when President Hayes was looking for a southerner to appoint to the court, he decided on Woods. Hayes made a constant effort throughout his administration to bring southerners back into the federal government. Woods became the first Supreme Court justice appointed from a southern Confederate state since 1853.

Woods served only six and a half years on the court, and was partially incapacitated by illness during the last months. The tradition of a new southern seat on the court was continued when President Cleveland picked as Woods' successor Lucius Q. C. Lamar of Mississippi.

Stanley Matthews
(1881-1889)

Born: July 21, 1824, Cincinnati, Ohio.

Education: Kenyon College, A.B., 1840.

Official Positions: assistant prosecuting attorney, Hamilton County, 1845; clerk, Ohio House of Representatives, 1848-49; judge, court of common pleas, Hamilton Co., 1851-53; member, Ohio Senate, 1855-58; U.S. attorney for southern Ohio, 1858-61; judge, superior court of Cincinnati, 1863-65; counsel, Hayes-Tilden electoral commission, 1877; member, U.S. Senate, R-Ohio, 1877-79.

Supreme Court Appointment: nominated associate justice by President Rutherford B. Hayes Jan. 26, 1881, to replace Noah Swayne, who resigned; no action by Senate; renominated by President Garfield March 14, 1881; confirmed by U.S. Senate May 12, 1881, by a 24-23 vote; replaced by David J. Brewer, nominated by President Benjamin Harrison.

Family: married, first, Mary Ann Black, Feb. 1843, died 1885, eight children; second, Mary Theaker, 1887.

Died: March 22, 1889, Washington, D.C.

Personal Background

Thomas Johnson and Isabella Brown Matthews' first child, born in Cincinnati in 1824, was named Thomas Stanley. He preferred to be called Stanley and dropped his first name when he became an adult. His maternal grandfather, Col. William Brown, was an Ohio pioneer who settled in Hamilton County in 1788. His father, a Virginian, served as Morrison professor of mathematics and natural history at Sylvania University in Lexington, Ky., for a number of years before becoming president of Cincinnati's Woodward High School, which his son attended.

Matthews entered Kenyon College as a junior and graduated in 1840. After reading law for two years in Cincinnati, he moved to Maury County, Tenn., where he passed the bar at the age of 18 and began his legal practice and the editorship of the *Tennessee Democrat,* a weekly paper supporting James K. Polk for president.

In 1844 Matthews married Mary Ann Black, the daughter of a prosperous Tennessee farmer. They had eight children. After her death in 1885 he wed Mary Theaker of Washington, D.C.

Public Career

Matthews left Tennessee when he was 20 and returned to Cincinnati. Within a year he was appointed assistant prosecuting attorney for Hamilton County and made editor of the *Cincinnati Morning Herald.* His strong stance against slavery won him election as clerk of the Ohio house of representatives in 1848. Three years later he was elected one of three judges in the court of common pleas in Hamilton County. Matthews served in the Ohio state senate from 1855-58 and as U.S. attorney for southern Ohio from 1858-61, a post to which he was appointed by President Buchanan. Although personally opposed to slavery, as U.S. attorney Matthews upheld the Fugitive Slave Act and prosecuted W. B. Connelly, a reporter who helped two slaves escape.

An officer in Ohio's 23rd and 51st regiment of volunteers, Matthews resigned his command in 1863 to accept election to Cincinnati's superior court. Two years later he returned to his private practice of railroad and corporate law. During Reconstruction Matthews was active in Republican politics as a presidential elector in 1864 and 1868, temporary chairman of the Liberal Republican convention in 1872 and GOP congressional candidate in 1876. He failed to win a seat in the 45th U.S. Congress in part because of the unpopularity of his prosecution of Connelly before the war.

Matthews campaigned for presidential candidate Rutherford B. Hayes and was one of the principal spokesmen on his behalf at the 1877 electoral commission. When Senator John Sherman of Ohio was appointed secretary of the Treasury in Hayes' cabinet, Matthews was elected by the legislature to fill his Senate seat. In January 1878 he introduced the "Matthews resolution" for the remonetization of silver.

Matthews' nomination to the Supreme Court by President Hayes upon the resignation of Justice Swayne of Ohio was not confirmed by the Senate. The appointment was criticized as merely a reward for Matthews' aid in Hayes' disputed victory over Samuel J. Tilden. The president was accused of cronyism; he and Matthews were fellow students at Kenyon College, lawyers in Cincinnati and officers in the 23rd Ohio infantry.

Matthews was renominated by President Garfield, Hayes' successor, but received continued opposition. Some feared Matthews' defense of large corporations and railroads during his legal practice would hinder his ability to dispense justice impartially on the court. A vote on the nominee was finally taken on May 12, 1881; he was confirmed 24-23.

Matthews died in Washington, D.C., during his eighth year on the court.

Horace Gray
(1881-1902)

Born: March 24, 1828, Boston, Mass.

Education: Harvard College, A.B., 1845; Harvard Law School, 1849.

Official Positions: reporter, Massachusetts supreme judicial court, 1854-64; associate justice, 1864-73, chief justice, 1873-81.

Supreme Court Appointment: nominated associate justice by President Chester Arthur Dec. 19, 1881, to replace Nathan Clifford, who died; confirmed by Senate Dec. 20, 1881, by a 51-5 vote; replaced on court by Oliver Wendell Holmes Jr., nominated by President Theodore Roosevelt.

Family: married Jane Matthews, June 4, 1889.

Died: Sept. 15, 1902, Nahant, Mass.

Personal Background

Harriet Upham Gray gave birth to her first child March 24, 1828, and named him Horace after her father, a businessman in the iron industry. His grandfather, Lieutenant-Governor William Gray, was the son of a poor New England shoemaker. He made his fortune as one of the first American merchants and shipowners to trade with Russia, India and China. Horace Gray's uncle, Francies Calley Gray, was a Massachusetts legal historian and his younger half-brother, John Chipman Gray, a renowned professor at Harvard Law School.

Gray graduated from Harvard in 1845 and traveled abroad. Reversals in the family business forced him to return to Boston to choose a business career. Although Gray's chief interest had always been natural history, he chose the legal profession and at Harvard Law School studied industriously. Reading law with Judge John Lowell and clerking in the attorneys' offices of Sohier & Welch completed Gray's preparation for the bar, which he passed in 1851. He practiced in Boston for 13 years.

As a young Boston lawyer Gray was a member of the Free Soil Party, which advocated free homesteads and opposed the expansion of slavery into the territories. Late in his life Gray married Jane Matthews, the daughter of Supreme Court Justice Stanley Matthews.

Public Career

Gray's career in the Massachusetts judiciary began in 1854 as a reporter for the state supreme court. After six years as a reporter he ran for state attorney general but failed to obtain the nomination of the Republican party, which he joined soon after its founding. Gov. John A. Andrews promoted Gray to the position of associate justice on August 23, 1864. Gray was 36 years old, the youngest appointee in the history of the supreme court of Massachusetts. The death or resignation of senior justices elevated Gray to the chief justiceship in 1873.

During his 17 years of service on the state court, Gray dissented only once and during his lifetime none of his decisions were overruled. Gray was respected for his careful historical research and knowledge of legal precedent. As chief justice he employed as his law clerk a bright young Harvard student, Louis D. Brandeis.

President James A. Garfield considered nominating Horace Gray to the Supreme Court after the death of Justice Nathan Clifford on July 25, 1881. But Garfield died prior to making the appointment. His successor, Chester Alan Arthur, appointed Gray associate justice on December 19, 1881. The Senate, anxious to fill Clifford's seat, which had been vacant for five months, confirmed Arthur's nominee the following day by a 51-5 vote.

On July 9, 1902, after 20 years of service, the 74-year-old Supreme Court justice informed President Theodore Roosevelt of his resignation. He died in September in Nahant, Mass.

Samuel Blatchford
(1882-1893)

Born: March 9, 1820, New York City.

Education: Columbia College, A.B., 1837.

Official Positions: judge, southern district of New York, 1867-72; judge, second circuit of New York, 1872-82.

Supreme Court Appointment: nominated associate justice by President Chester Arthur March 13, 1882, to replace Ward Hunt, who resigned; confirmed by Senate March 27, 1882, by a voice vote; replaced on court by Edward D. White, nominated by President Cleveland.

Family: married Caroline Appleton, Dec. 17, 1844.

Died: July 7, 1893, Newport, R.I.

Personal Background

Samuel Blatchford, born in New York City in 1820, was the son of the former Julia Ann Mumford, daughter of a well-known publicist, and Richard M. Blatchford, counsel for the Bank of England and the Bank of the United States and a Whig in the New York legislature. His paternal grandfather, a British clergyman and sire of 17 children, immigrated to Lansingburg, N.Y., in 1795.

At the age of 13, Blatchford entered Columbia College and four years later graduated at the top of his class. From 1837-41 he prepared for the bar as the private secretary of his father's friend, New York Governor William H. Seward. Blatchford passed the bar in 1842, practiced law with his father for three years and joined Seward's law firm in Auburn, N.Y. In 1844 he married Caroline Appleton of Lowell, Mass.

Public Career

After nine years as a partner with Seward & Morgan, Blatchford and Seward's nephew established the New York City firm, Blatchford, Seward & Griswold. He declined a seat on the New York supreme judicial court in 1855 to devote himself to his admiralty and international law practice.

During his legal career Blatchford reported extensively on federal court decisions. *Blatchford's Circuit Court Reports* (1852) included cases from New York's second circuit since 1845 and *Blatchford's and Howland's Reports* (1855) contributed to the extant knowledge of admiralty cases in the southern district. His extensive research into the state's judicial history as well as his expertise in admiralty law qualified Blatchford for the post of district judge for southern New York to which he was appointed in 1867 and for his subsequent appointment to the second circuit court in 1872.

After 15 years in the federal judiciary, Judge Blatchford was nominated to the Supreme Court by President Arthur. Roscoe Conkling, a New York lawyer and politician, was the president's first choice to fill the vacancy on the court created by the retirement of Justice Ward Hunt of New York. Although confirmed by the Senate, Conkling declined the appointment. Arthur's second choice, Sen. George F. Edmunds of Vermont, also declined. Blatchford accepted and the Senate readily confirmed the president's third nominee — Blatchford, a moderate Republican from an influential New York family, a successful lawyer and an experienced district and circuit court judge.

Blatchford served as trustee of Columbia University from 1867 until his death in 1893 in Newport, R.I.

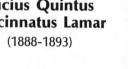

Lucius Quintus Cincinnatus Lamar
(1888-1893)

Born: Sept. 17, 1825, Eatonton, Ga.

Education: Emory College, A.B., 1845.

Official Positions: member, Georgia House of Representatives, 1853; member, U.S. House of Representatives, 1857-60, 1873-77; member, U.S. Senate, 1877-85; secretary of interior, 1885-88.

Supreme Court Appointment: nominated associate justice by President Grover Cleveland Dec. 6, 1887, to replace William Woods, who died; confirmed by U.S. Senate Jan. 16, 1888, by a 32-28 vote; replaced on court by Howell Edmunds Jackson, nominated by President Benjamin Harrison.

Family: married, first, Virginia Longstreet, July 15, 1847, died 1884, one sone, three daughters; second, Henrietta Dean Holt, Jan. 5, 1887, no children.

Died: Jan. 23, 1893, Vineville, Ga.

Personal Background

Of French Huguenot ancestry, Lamar was born into the landed aristocracy of the prewar South in 1825. The fourth of Lucius Quintus Cincinnatus' and Sarah Bird Lamar's eight children, he attended the Georgia Conference Manual Labor School, an institution that combined farm work with academics. Lamar graduated from Emory College in 1845 and two years later wed its president's daughter, Virginia Longstreet.

Lamar read law in Macon, Ga., passed the bar in 1847 and shortly thereafter followed his father-in-law to Oxford, Miss. The Reverend Augustus B. Longstreet became president of the University of Mississippi and Lamar taught mathematics and practiced law. The two men were devoted to one another. Longstreet had lost his only son; Lamar's own father had committed suicide when Lamar was nine years old.

Public Career

In 1852 Lamar returned to Georgia and established a successful legal practice with a close friend, E. C. Walthall, in Covington. The following year he was elected to the state legislature. The dissolution of his partnership and his failure to obtain the Democratic nomination to Congress prompted Lamar's return to Mississippi in 1855. He settled on a plantation and began practicing law and participating in state politics. A Jefferson Davis supporter and states' rights extremist, Lamar was elected to Congress in 1857 but resigned before his term expired. He personally drafted the state's ordinance of secession at the Mississippi Secession Convention of 1861.

Lamar served the Confederacy as colonel of the 18th Mississippi Regiment until an attack of apoplexy, an ailment since childhood, forced him to retire from active duty in May 1862. As special envoy to Russia he attended diplomatic briefings in Europe in 1863, but because of lack of support for the Confederate cause never went to Russia. He spent the remainder of the war as a judge advocate for the Army of Northern Virginia.

When General Lee surrendered, Lamar was 40 years old. Two of his brothers had died in battle; his friend Jefferson Davis was in prison; he was in debt. Disqualified from public office, he returned to Mississippi to practice law and teach metaphysics at the university.

Although a partisan sectionalist before the war, Lamar publicly advocated reconciliation and cooperation during the difficult days of Reconstruction. Pardoned for his role in the Confederacy, he was re-elected to Congress in 1872. His

eulogy of Massachusetts unionist Charles Sumner, heralded by the Boston *Advertiser* as the most significant and hopeful word from the South since the war, won Lamar national acclaim as the "great pacificator." A representative of the new South, Lamar reached the Senate in 1877. His reputation as a politician guided by more than sectional interests was strengthened by his refusal to follow the directive of the Mississippi legislature to support legislation authorizing the free coinage of silver. Anxious to demonstrate the South's desire to serve the entire nation, Lamar resigned from his second Senate term to accept a cabinet appointment. As Grover Cleveland's secretary of the interior, he directed the reclamation of thousands of acres of public lands and the establishment of a new Indian policy. While in office Lamar married Henrietta Dean Holt.

The death in 1887 of Justice William Woods, a Georgia Republican, created the first vacancy on the Supreme Court in six years. Although Lamar's appointment by President Cleveland was strongly opposed by many Republican senators, senators Stanford of California and Stewart of Nevada argued persuasively that Lamar's rejection would be interpreted as a ban against all Confederate veterans. The 63-year-old nominee was narrowly confirmed by the Senate, 32-28.

Lamar served on the court for five years. He died from apoplexy in his native Georgia on January 23, 1893. Seventeen years later the Lamar family could boast of another member on the bench — Joseph Rucker Lamar.

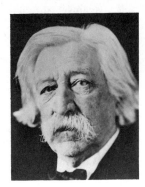

Melville Weston Fuller
(1888-1910)

Born: Feb. 11, 1833, Augusta, Maine.

Education: Bowdoin College, A.B., 1853; studied at Harvard Law School and read law, 1853-55.

Official Positions: member, Illinois house of representatives, 1863-1864; member, Venezuela-British Guiana Border Commission, 1899; member, Permanent Court of Arbitration at the Hague, 1900-1910.

Supreme Court Appointment: nominated Chief Justice by President Grover Cleveland April 30, 1888, to replace Morrison R. Waite, who died; confirmed by U.S. Senate July 20, 1888, by a 41-20 vote; replaced as Chief Justice by Edward D. White, nominated by President Taft.

Family: married, first, Calista Ophelia Reynolds, June 28, 1858, died 1864, two daughters; second, Mary E. Coolbaugh, May 30, 1866, five daughters, one son.

Died: July 4, 1910, Sorrento, Maine.

Personal Background

The second son of Frederick Augustus Fuller and the former Catherine Martin Weston was born in Augusta, Maine, in 1833. When Melville Weston Fuller was two months old, his mother divorced his father on the grounds of adultery and took her son to live with his grandfather, a judge on the Maine Supreme Court. Although she remarried when Fuller was 11, he continued to live with Judge Weston in Augusta.

Fuller attended Bowdoin College, where he was active in politics and a prolific writer of verse. He graduated Phi Beta Kappa in 1853 and, like both his grandfathers and his own father, chose the legal profession. Fuller read law in Bangor and after six months at Harvard Law School passed the bar. He began to practice in Augusta at the age of 22 and the same year took an editorial position on *The Age*, a local Democratic paper owned by his father's brother. At the age of 24 he was elected president of the common council and appointed city solicitor.

Like many young men in the 1850s, Fuller was lured west by the promise of a better life in the frontier. He settled in the booming railroad town of Chicago and started practicing real estate and commercial law.

Fuller was married twice. His first wife, Calista Ophelia Reynolds, died of tuberculosis six years after they were married. Mary Ellen Coolbaugh, the daughter of the president of Chicago's Union National Bank, and Fuller were wed in 1866. She bore him a son and five daughters. He had two daughters by his previous marriage.

Public Career

In Chicago, Fuller pursued a political as well as a legal career. He managed Stephen Douglas' presidential campaign against Abraham Lincoln in 1858, attended the Illinois Constitutional Convention three years later and served in the Illinois House of Representatives from 1863-64.

Meanwhile Fuller's legal practice and real estate investments on the North Shore prospered; his earnings by the 1880s reached an estimated $30,000 a year. Fuller acted as Chicago's counsel in litigation over the city's rights to Lake Michigan shore property. He also defended — in a nationally publicized case — the Reverend Charles E. Cheney, rector of Christ Church in Chicago, who was accused of canonical disobedience by an ecclesiastical tribunal because of his "low church" practices. A high Episcopalian himself, Fuller opened the way for the founding of the Reformed Protestant Episcopal Church in America.

Grover Cleveland met Melville Fuller during a western presidential tour and was impressed by his "sound money," low-tariff economic philosophy.

Although Fuller had previously declined the positions of civil service chairman and solicitor general in Cleveland's administration, he accepted the appointment of Chief Justice on April 30, 1888. The Republican Senate soon voiced its objections to the Democratic nominee. Midwesterners were wary of his ties with big corporations. Northerners accused him of anti-Union sentiment and circulated the pamphlet "The War Record of Melville Fuller," which was discredited only after Robert T. Lincoln, son of the former president, attested to his loyalty. The Philadelphia *Press* claimed that Cleveland's nominee was the most obscure man ever appointed Chief Justice.

Although Fuller had never held federal office, his professional credentials were sound and his appointment geographically expedient. Since Justice Davis' resignation in 1877, the seventh judicial circuit, comprising Illinois, Indiana and Wisconsin, had been unrepresented on the bench. Fuller was confirmed by the Senate, 41-20, nearly three months after his appointment.

During his court tenure, Fuller served on the Venezuela-British Guiana Border Commission and the Permanent Court of Arbitration in the Hague. An efficient and courteous leader of the court for 22 years, he was well-respected by his colleagues, particularly by Justice Holmes.

When Cleveland returned to the presidency he offered Fuller the position of secretary of state, but Fuller declined, believing his acceptance would lower the dignity of the court in the mind of the public. He died of heart failure at the age of 77 at his summer home in Sorrento, Maine.

David Josiah Brewer
(1889-1910)

Born: Jan. 20, 1837, Smyrna, Asia Minor.

Education: Wesleyan University, 1852-53; Yale University, A.B., 1856; Albany Law School, LL.B., 1858.

Official Positions: commissioner, U.S. circuit court in Leavenworth, Kansas, 1861-62; judge of probate and criminal courts, Leavenworth County, 1863-64; judge, first judicial district of Kansas, 1865-69; Leavenworth city attorney, 1869-70; justice, Kansas Supreme Court, 1870-84; judge, eighth federal circuit, 1884-89; president, Venezuela-British Guiana Border Commission, 1895.

Supreme Court Appointment: nominated associate justice by President Benjamin Harrison Dec. 4, 1889, to replace Stanley Matthews, who died; confirmed by U.S. Senate Dec. 18, 1889, by a 53-11 vote; replaced on court by Charles Evans Hughes, nominated by President Taft.

Family: married, first, Louise R. Landon, Oct. 3, 1861, died 1898; second, Emma Miner Mott, June 5, 1901.

Died: March 28, 1910, Washington, D.C.

Personal Background

Brewer was born in 1837 in Smyrna, Asia Minor, now Izmir, Turkey, where his father was a Congregational missionary. With his infant son and wife Emilia (Field), the daughter of a New England clergyman, Reverend Josiah Brewer returned to America to become chaplain of St. Francis Prison, in Wethersfield, Conn. Young Brewer had three notable uncles: David Dudley Field, a jurist; Cyrus W. Field, a financier and promoter of the trans-Atlantic telegraph cable; and Stephen Johnson Field, a Supreme Court justice from California from 1863-97.

Brewer attended Wesleyan University for two years before enrolling in his father's alma mater, Yale University, from which he was graduated with honors in 1856. After reading law for a year in David Field's office, Brewer attended Albany Law School. He passed the New York bar in 1858 and the Kansas bar the following year, having decided to go west as his uncle Stephen had done.

When he was 24 Brewer married Louise R. Landon of Burlington, Vt., who died 37 years later. At the age of 64 he wed Emma Miner Mott of Washington, D.C.

Public Career

Brewer's first official position was administrative. He was appointed U.S. commissioner of the circuit court in Leavenworth, Kansas, in 1861. After two years he was nominated judge of probate and criminal courts. From 1865-69 Brewer served as state district attorney and the following year as city attorney for Leavenworth until his election at the age of 33 to the Kansas Supreme Court. When Kansas passed a prohibition amendment in 1881, Judge Brewer sought to defend the rights of manufacturers against the confiscation of their property without compensation. Brewer's 14 years of service on the state court ended in 1884 when he was appointed to the eighth federal circuit by President Arthur.

When Justice Stanley Matthews died, Republican senators Plumb and Ingalls of Kansas urged President Benjamin Harrison to appoint Brewer to the court. During his consideration of the nomination, the president received a letter from Brewer himself recommending the appointment of Henry Billings Brown, a Michigan district court judge who had been in his class at Yale. Impressed by Brewer's generous comments about his friend, Harrison nominated the circuit court judge from Kansas instead. Although Brewer's appointment was opposed by some prohibitionists, he was confirmed by the Senate by a 53-11 vote.

During his 20 years on the Supreme Court, Brewer spoke out freely on the issues of the day. He advocated independence for the Philippines, suffrage for women and residency rights for Chinese aliens in America. Brewer was one of the original officers in the American Society of International Law and in 1895 presided over the congressional commission to oversee the disputed Venezuela-British Guiana boundary. A lecturer on American citizenship at Yale and corporate law at Columbian University, now George Washington University, Brewer also edited collections of the world's best orations and essays and wrote numerous books and articles. He was a lifelong member of the Congregational Church and active in missionary work.

Brewer died suddenly on March 28, 1910, in Washington, D.C.

Henry Billings Brown

(1891-1906)

Born: March 2, 1836, South Lee, Mass.

Education: Yale University, A.B., 1856; studied briefly at Yale Law School and Harvard Law School.

Official Positions: U.S. deputy marshal, 1861; assistant U.S. attorney, 1863-68; circuit judge, Wayne County, 1868; federal judge, eastern district of Michigan, 1875-90.

Supreme Court Appointment: nominated associate justice by President Benjamin Harrison Dec. 23, 1890, to replace Samuel Miller, who died; confirmed by U.S. Senate Dec. 29, 1890, by a voice vote; replaced on court by William H. Moody, nominated by President Theodore Roosevelt.

Family: married, first, Caroline Pitts, July 1864, died 1901; second, Josephine E. Tyler, June 25, 1904.

Died: Sept. 4, 1913, New York City.

Personal Background

The son of a prosperous merchant, Brown was born in the small town of South Lee, Mass., and raised in a middle-class Protestant home. His parents, Billings and Mary (Tyler) Brown prepared their son for the legal career they had chosen for him with a private secondary school and Yale University education. A moderately good student, he graduated from Yale in 1856 and went abroad for a year of further study.

Brown began his legal education as a law clerk in Ellington, Conn. After a few months he returned to Yale to attend lectures at the law school. Brown also studied briefly at Harvard Law School.

In 1859 the 23-year-old law student moved to Detroit. Within a year he finished his legal apprenticeship and passed the bar. Wealthy enough to hire a substitute, Brown escaped military service in the Civil War and immediately began his private practice.

Caroline Pitts, a member of a prosperous Detroit family, was Brown's wife for 37 years until her death in 1901. Three years later, at the age of 67, he married Josephine E. Tyler from Crosswicks, N.J., the widow of a lieutenant in the U.S. Navy.

Public Career

In the early days of the Lincoln administration, Brown was appointed deputy U.S. marshal for Detroit, his first official position. After two years he was promoted to assistant U.S. attorney for the eastern district of Michigan. Detroit was a busy Great Lakes port, and Brown became an expert in admiralty law.

Republican Governor Henry H. Crapo appointed Brown interim circuit judge for Wayne County in 1868. Defeated in his bid for election to a full term, Brown returned to private practice and formed a partnership with J. S. Newberry and Ashley Pond that specialized in shipping cases. After an unsuccessful congressional campaign in 1872, he resumed his practice until a welcome appointment three years later by President Grant to the post of district judge of eastern Michigan.

During his 14 years as district judge, Brown won a national reputation as an authority on admiralty law. Howell Edmunds Jackson, a sixth federal circuit court judge, urged President Harrison to appoint Brown to the Supreme Court after the death of Justice Miller. Harrison had served with Jackson in the Senate and followed the advice of his former colleague. Nominated associate justice on December 23, 1890, Brown was confirmed by the Senate within the week. Three years later Justice Brown returned Jackson's favor by recommending his appointment to the court.

Brown is considered to have been a centrist on the court, seldom dissenting and always seeking the middle ground.

Despite an attack of neuritis in 1890 which blinded him in one eye, Brown served on the court for 15 years. At the age of 70, severely handicapped by his impaired vision, he resigned. He lived in semi-retirement in Bronxville, N.Y., until his death on September 4, 1913, at the age of 77.

George Shiras Jr.
(1892-1903)

Born: January 26, 1832, Pittsburgh, Pa.

Education: Ohio University, 1849-51; Yale, B.A., 1853, honorary LL.D., 1883; studied law at Yale and privately, admitted to the bar in 1855.

Supreme Court Appointment: nominated associate justice by President Benjamin Harrison July 19, 1892, to replace Joseph P. Bradley, who died; confirmed by U.S. Senate July 26, 1892, by a voice vote; replaced on court by William R. Day, nominated by President Theodore Roosevelt.

Family: married Lillie E. Kennedy, December 31, 1857; two sons.

Died: August 2, 1924, Pittsburgh, Pa.

Personal Background

Shiras was born January 26, 1832, in Pittsburgh, Pa., into a family which had been in America since the 1760s. His father, of Scotch ancestry, married a Presbyterian minister's daughter, Eliza Herron, and was successful enough in the family brewery business to retire in his early thirties to a farm near the Ohio River. Here young Shiras, with his two brothers, spent his early years helping in his father's orchards.

In 1849 he left to attend Ohio University at Athens, Ohio, but after two years transferred to Yale, where he graduated in 1853. He then read law at Yale (without graduating) and in the Pittsburgh law office of Judge Hopewell Hepburn before being admitted to the Allegheny County bar in November 1855. Before settling down in Pittsburgh in 1858 to become Judge Hepburn's law partner, he spent several years practicing law in Dubuque, Iowa, with his brother, Oliver Perry, who later became a federal district judge in northern Iowa.

On December 31, 1857, he married a Pittsburgh manufacturer's daughter, Lillie E. Kennedy, with whom he had two sons. Both offspring followed him into the law profession, and one, George S. III, served as U.S. Representative from Pennsylvania to the 58th Congress from 1903-1905.

Upon the death of Judge Hepburn in 1862, Shiras maintained a successful independent practice until his accession to the Supreme Court in 1892. In more than 30 years of law practice in his native city, Shiras maintained a reputation of absolute integrity, of moderation in politics and manner, of restraint and good judgment, and of dignity and wit. The years Shiras prospered and plied his trade in Pittsburgh were those when the iron and steel, coal, and railroad magnates were amassing their fortunes. Despite his financial success and lucrative practice, Shiras remained modest, unostentatious and respected by his peers. In 1883 he received from Yale an honorary LL.D. degree, the first alumnus to do so.

To the end he preferred quiet living among family and friends and his pursuits as a naturalist rather than seeking the limelight. His moderation seemed to be reflected in both his professional and personal lives.

Public Career

Shiras' life was centered mainly in the private sector and he held no public offices until his Supreme Court appointment. In 1881 he refused the Pennsylvania state legislature's offer of the U.S. Senate nomination. A moderate Republican, he remained aloof from party politics and the state political machine, facts which favored his appointment to the high court. In 1888 he served as a presidential elector.

In July 1892, at the age of 60, he was nominated by President Harrison to be an associate justice of the Supreme Court to replace Joseph P. Bradley of New Jersey, who had died in January. Although Shiras had the support of the Pennsylvania bar, of the iron and steel interests (including Andrew Carnegie's personal support) and of U.S. Representative John Dalzell, the U.S. senators who headed the state Republican machine vigorously opposed his appointment. President Harrison had sent Shiras' name to the Senate without first consulting Senators James Donald Cameron and Matthew S. Quay as senatorial courtesy dictated. However, when the press and prominent persons including former Yale classmates came to his defense and the opposition was shown to be purely political, the matter was resolved and he was confirmed by unanimous consent.

Respected for his analytical powers and as a legal technician, Shiras exhibited a quiet competence and bore his share of the workload during his ten years on the court.

He resigned, as he had earlier resolved to do, at the age of 71, and lived out the years of his retirement in quiet comfort, shuttling between homes in Florida and the Lake Superior region of northern Michigan until his death in 1924 at age 92.

Howell Edmunds Jackson
(1893-1895)

Born: April 8, 1832, Paris, Tenn.

Education: West Tennessee College, A.B., 1849; University of Virginia, 1851-52; Cumberland University, 1856.

Official Positions: custodian of sequestered property for Confederate states, 1861-65; judge, court of arbitration for western Tennessee, 1875-79; state legislature, 1880; U.S. Senate, 1881-86; judge, 6th federal circuit court, 1886-91; circuit court of appeals, 1891-1893.

Supreme Court Appointment: nominated associate justice by President Benjamin Harrison Feb. 2, 1893, to replace Lucius Q. C. Lamar, who died; confirmed by U.S. Senate Feb. 18, 1893, by a voice vote; replaced on the court by Rufus W. Peckham, nominated by President Cleveland.

Family: married, first, Sophia Malloy in 1859, died 1873, four children; second, Mary E. Harding in April 1874, three children.

Died: August 8, 1895, West Meade, Tenn.

Personal Background

In 1830 Alexander Jackson left his medical practice in Virginia and moved to Paris, Tenn., with his wife Mary (Hurt) Jackson, the daughter of a Baptist minister. Two years later their eldest son, Howell Edmunds, was born. Howell grew up in Jackson, Tenn., and studied classics at Western Tennessee College, graduating at the age of 18. He continued his education at the University of Virginia from 1851-52. After completing a year in the legal department of Cumberland University in Lebanon, Tenn., Jackson passed the bar and began practicing law in his hometown.

In 1859 Jackson moved to Memphis, formed the partnership, Currin & Jackson, specializing in corporate, railroad and banking cases, and married a local woman, Sophia Malloy. After her death in 1873, Jackson wed Mary E. Harding, the daughter of General W. G. Harding, the owner of a 3,000-acre thoroughbred stock farm near Nashville. The western part of the property, West Meade, became Jackson's home, where he lived with his second wife, their three children and the four children of his previous marriage.

Although opposed to secession, Jackson served the Confederacy as the receiver of confiscated property and after the Civil War was twice appointed to the Court of Arbitration of western Tennessee. His younger brother, William Hicks — the husband of General Harding's daughter Selene, who inherited the Belle Meade plantation — was a famous brigadier general in the Confederate Army, known by his men as the "red fox."

Public Career

In 1881 Jackson, a respected lawyer and anti-repudiation Tennessean during the Reconstruction, was elected to the state house of representatives. Because of factions within the Democratic Party over the state debt, he was elected the following year to the U.S. Senate. A Whig before the war, Jackson had been able to win the needed support of Republicans and "state-credit" Democrats. In the Senate he served on the Post Office, Pensions, Claims, and Judiciary Committees and loyally defended President Grover Cleveland's tariff measures.

At the president's request, Jackson reluctantly resigned before his Senate term expired to fill a vacancy on the sixth judicial federal circuit. When the circuit court of appeals was established in 1891, Jackson became its first presiding judge. During his Senate career, Jackson was seated next to a Republican senator from Indiana, Benjamin Harrison. As president, Harrison remembered his former colleague and friend and nominated him to the Supreme Court on February 2, 1893, to fill the vacancy created by the death of Justice Lucius Q. C. Lamar. Grover Cleveland had been elected to a second term in November, and the lame-duck president realized Senate confirmation of a Republican nominee was unlikely. With the strong backing of Supreme Court Justice Henry Billings Brown, who had known him on the sixth federal circuit, Jackson was confirmed by the Senate Feb. 18, 1893.

One year after his appointment, Justice Jackson contracted a severe case of tuberculosis. Hoping to recuperate in the West, Jackson left Washington in October 1894. In May 1895 a full court was needed to rehear a case on the constitutionality of income taxes, the eight active justices having been evenly divided on the question. Unwell but unwilling to resign, Jackson returned to Washington. Three months after his dissent from the court's decision ruling income taxes unconstitutional, Jackson succumbed to tuberculosis at his home in Nashville.

Edward Douglass White
(1894-1921)

Born: Nov. 3, 1845, Parish of Lafourche, La.

Education: Mount St. Mary's College, Emmitsburg, Md., 1856; Georgetown College, Washington, D.C., 1857-61; studied law under Edward Bermudez, admitted to the bar in 1866.

Official Positions: Louisiana state senator, D, 1874; associate justice, Louisiana Supreme Court, 1878-80; United States Senator, D-La., 1891-94.

Supreme Court Appointment: nominated associate justice by President Grover Cleveland Feb. 19, 1894, to replace Samuel Blatchford, who died; confirmed by the Senate Feb. 19, 1894, by a voice vote.

Nominated Chief Justice of the United States by President Taft Dec. 12, 1910, to replace Melville Fuller, who died; confirmed by the Senate Dec. 12, 1910, by a voice vote; replaced as Chief Justice by ex-president Taft, appointed by President Harding.

Family: married Virginia Montgomery Kent, November 1894.

Died: May 19, 1921, in Washington, D.C.

Personal Background

White was born and raised in the deep South. His Irish-Catholic ancestors originally settled in Pennsylvania, but his peripatetic father moved the family farther into frontier country until they finally reached Louisiana. There the family prospered on a large farm. White's father, a Whig, spent four years as a judge on the New Orleans city court and served five terms in the U.S. House of Representatives (1829-34; 1839-43) and one term as governor of Louisiana (1834-38).

White received his early education at local Jesuit schools. In 1856 he enrolled for one year at Mount St. Mary's College, Emmitsburg, Md., and then entered Georgetown College (now University) in Washington, D.C. His academic career was interrupted by the Civil War; White joined the Confederate Army. He was captured in 1863 and spent the remainder of the war as a prisoner.

Public Career

After the war he began his legal career by reading law under the direction of Edward Bermudez, a successful New Orleans lawyer. Admitted to the Louisiana bar in 1868, White established a lucrative practice in New Orleans and became involved in Democratic politics. He was elected to the state senate in 1874, and his support of Francis T. Nicholls in the 1877 gubernatorial election gained him at age 33 an appointment to the Louisiana Supreme Court in 1878. Nicholls' successor, however, engineered White's removal from the court in 1880 through the passage of a law setting a minimum age requirement for justices which the youthful White failed to meet. Retribution came in 1888 when Nicholls was again elected governor and the state legislature gave one of Louisiana's U.S. Senate seats to Edward D. White.

White's short Senate career was marked by efforts to restrict the power of the federal government, except in matters protecting sugar farmers in the south from foreign competition. White himself farmed a large sugar-beet plantation. His unexpected appointment to the Supreme Court came in 1894. Beleaguered President Cleveland had sought to replace Justice Samuel Blatchford (who died July 7, 1893) with appointees from New York, Blatchford's home state. On two separate occasions, however, Cleveland's choices were rejected by the Senate in deference to the wishes of New York's senators, who were two of the president's chief detractors. In frustration, Cleveland nominated White, who was approved immediately.

White's appointment to the Chief Justiceship was equally surprising. Chief Justice Melville Fuller died July 4, 1910, and President Taft, on Dec. 12, 1910, elevated White to the post. He was the first associate justice successfully to be elevated to Chief Justice.

Historians tend to explain Taft's selection of White as Chief Justice in one of two ways. One side holds that Taft chose White, a southern Catholic, as a symbol of the president's desire to reduce lingering anti-South and anti-Catholic sentiments and to gain southern and Catholic support in the next election. The other, less sympathetic, view argues that Taft reckoned that he would have a better chance to receive appointment to the Chief Justiceship himself (a lifelong ambition) after he left the White House if he appointed the aging White (65) instead of the other contender for the post, the relatively young (48) Charles Evans Hughes.

White was 75 years old and had been on the Supreme Court for 26 years — and Chief Justice for the last ten years — when Warren G. Harding was elected president in 1920. White was suddenly taken ill May 13, 1921, and died May 19. His replacement on the court was the ever-eager William Howard Taft.

Rufus Wheeler Peckham

(1895-1909)

Born: Nov. 8, 1838, Albany, N.Y.

Education: Albany Boys' Academy; studied privately in Philadelphia.

Official Positions: district attorney, Albany County, 1869-72; corporation counsel, City of Albany, 1881-83; judge, New York Supreme Court, 1883-86; judge, New York court of appeals, 1886-95.

Supreme Court Appointment: nominated associate justice by President Grover Cleveland Dec. 3, 1895, to replace Howell E. Jackson, who died; confirmed by U.S. Senate Dec. 9, 1895, by a voice vote; replaced on court by Horace Harmon Lurton, nominated by President Taft.

Family: married Harriette M. Arnold, Nov. 14, 1866; two sons.

Died: Oct. 24, 1909, Altamont, N.Y.

Personal Background

Peckham was born in Albany in 1838, the son of Rufus Wheeler and Isabella (Lacey) Peckham, members of an old New York family. His father and his older brother, Wheeler Hazard Peckham, were both prominent lawyers and active in state Democratic politics. As district attorney for Albany County, Peckham Sr. was elected to the U.S. House of Representatives. He also served on the state supreme court and the New York court of appeals. During a vacation in 1873, Judge Peckham was lost at sea.

Rufus Wheeler Peckham the younger was educated at the Albany Boys' Academy and studied privately in Philadelphia. After a year in Europe with his brother, Rufus returned to Albany to read law in his father's firm, Peckham & Tremain. He joined the firm at the age of 27 and in 1866 married Harriette M. Arnold, the daughter of a wealthy New York merchant.

Peckham's elder son, a one-time president of the New York Bar Association, served as special counsel in the prosecution of the Tweed Ring in the city's political corruption trials.

Public Career

Like his father before him, Peckham began his public career as district attorney for Albany County. In this post he gained recognition for his skillful prosecution and conviction of criminals involved in railroad express-car robberies. First as county attorney and then as corporation counsel for the city of Albany from 1881-83, Peckham participated actively in upstate New York politics and became well-acquainted with Governor Grover Cleveland. Peckham's political connections, his legal reputation and his respected name helped win him election to the state supreme court in 1883 and to the New York court of appeals three years later.

After Justice Jackson's death, President Grover Cleveland nominated his friend associate justice of the Supreme Court. Peckham was confirmed without objection although his brother's nomination three months before to fill Justice Blatchford's seat had been rejected due to political infighting. (Senator David B. Hill, D-N.Y., Wheeler's chief opponent, also succeeded in blocking the confirmation of William B. Hornblower, President Cleveland's second choice for the Blatchford seat.)

During his 13 years on the bench, Peckham vigorously upheld the individual's right to contract and favored state regulation only when interstate commerce was directly and substantially affected. He dissented from the court's decision in 1898 to uphold a Utah statute limiting the working day in mines, smelters and oil refineries to eight hours and also questioned the validity of a state law requiring compulsory vaccination.

On the whole, Peckham was considered a conservative justice out of touch with the Industrial Revolution.

Justice Peckham died in Altamont, N.Y., on October 24, 1909, at the age of 70.

Joseph McKenna
(1898-1925)

Born: August 10, 1843, Philadelphia, Pa.

Education: Benicia Collegiate Institute, graduated in 1865; admitted to the bar in 1866.

Official Positions: district attorney, Solano County, Calif., 1866-70; member, California house of representatives, 1875-76; member, U.S. House of Representatives, 1885-92; judge, U.S. ninth judicial circuit, 1892-97; U.S. attorney general, 1897.

Supreme Court Appointment: nominated associate justice by President William McKinley Dec. 16, 1897, to replace Stephen J. Field, who resigned; confirmed by U.S. Senate Jan. 21, 1898, by a voice vote; replaced on court by Harlan F. Stone, nominated by President Coolidge.

Family: married Amanda F. Bornemann, June 10, 1869; three daughters.

Died: Nov. 21, 1926, Washington, D.C.

Personal Background

Joseph McKenna, the first child of Irish immigrants John and Mary Ann (Johnson) McKenna, was born in 1843 in the Irish quarter of Philadelphia. The growing popularity in Philadelphia of the staunchly anti-immigrant, anti-Catholic American Party contributed to the failure of John McKenna's bakery business. Hoping for success on the frontier, he took his family west, travelling third class on a Panamanian steamship to Benicia, Calif. In this small coastal town he succeeded in obtaining a better life for his family before his death when Joseph was 15 years old.

Young McKenna attended public schools, graduated from the law department of the Benicia Collegiate Institute in 1865, and the following year was admitted to the California bar. Republicans were becoming increasingly powerful in California. In 1861 the state elected railroad pioneer Leland Stanford as its first Republican governor. McKenna switched his membership to the Republican party, became acquainted with Stanford, and participated actively in political affairs. He was elected district attorney for Solano County in 1866 and three years later married Amanda F. Bornemann of San Francisco, his wife for 55 years.

Public Career

After his initial political success, election to the state legislature in 1875, McKenna suffered a string of defeats. He was an unsuccessful candidate for the speakership of the California house of representatives, from which he resigned after one term. Although twice nominated by his party for the U.S. Congress, he suffered two defeats prior to his election in 1885.

During four terms in the House, McKenna won passage of legislation extending railroad land grants, improving port facilities and restricting the freedoms of Chinese workers. Considering his own immigrant parentage, McKenna's support for the latter is surprising, despite its popularity with his constituents.

As a member of the House Ways and Means Committee, McKenna became friends with its chairman, William McKinley. Another political ally in Congress was Senator Leland Stanford. On Stanford's recommendation, President Harrison appointed McKenna to California's ninth judicial circuit. A circuit court judge for five years, McKenna was then promoted to attorney general. Within a year of assuming the post, he was nominated to the Supreme Court. When Justice Field resigned, President McKinley chose McKenna, another Californian and a trusted friend, to fill the vacancy. Over the objections of many to McKenna's ties with Leland Stanford and western railroad interests, the Senate confirmed the appointment.

Realizing his own need for further legal training, McKenna studied for a few months at Columbia University Law School before taking office. Nevertheless, his early years on the bench proved difficult because of his lack of knowledge of the law and his inability to construct an opinion that expressed the convictions of his colleagues.

McKenna served on the court for 26 years. He was 82 years old and in failing health when Chief Justice Taft and the other members of the court finally persuaded him to step down. The following year he died in his sleep at his home in Washington, D.C.

Oliver Wendell Holmes Jr.
(1902-1932)

Born: March 8, 1841, Boston, Mass.

Education: Harvard College, A.B., 1861; LL.B., 1866.

Official Positions: associate justice, Massachusetts Supreme Court, 1882-99, chief justice, 1899-1902.

Supreme Court Appointment: nominated associate justice by President Theodore Roosevelt Dec. 2, 1902, to replace Horace Gray, who resigned; confirmed by U.S. Senate Dec. 4, 1902, by a voice vote; replaced on court by Benjamin N. Cardozo, nominated by President Hoover.

Family: married Fanny Bowdich Dixwell, June 17, 1872; no children.

Died: March 6, 1935; Washington, D.C.

Personal Background

Born in Boston in 1841, Holmes was named after his father, a professor of anatomy at Harvard Medical School as well as a poet, essayist and novelist in the New England literary circle that included Longfellow, Emerson, Lowell and Whittier. Dr. Holmes' wife, Amelia Lee (Jackson) Holmes, was the third daughter of Massachusetts Supreme Court Justice Charles Jackson. Young Holmes attended a private Latin school in Cambridge run by Epes Sargent Dixwell and received his undergraduate education at Harvard, graduating as class poet in 1861 as had his father 32 years before him.

Commissioned after graduation a second lieutenant in the Massachusetts Twentieth Volunteers, known as the Harvard Regiment, Holmes was wounded three times in battle. At the end of his three-year enlistment, he was mustered out a captain in recognition of his bravery and gallant service. After the Civil War, Holmes returned to Harvard to study law despite his father's conviction that "a lawyer can't be a great man."

He was admitted to the Massachusetts bar in 1867, and practiced in Boston for 15 years, beginning with the firm of Chandler, Shattuck & Thayer and later forming with Shattuck his own partnership. In 1872 Holmes married Fanny Bowdich Dixwell, the daughter of his former schoolmaster and a friend since childhood. No children were born during their marriage of 57 years.

During his legal career Holmes taught constitutional law at his alma mater, edited the *American Law Review* and lectured on common law at the Lowell Institute. His 12 lectures were compiled in a volume entitled *The Common Law* and published shortly before his fortieth birthday after more than ten years of work. The London *Spectator* heralded Holmes' treatise as the most original work of legal speculation in decades. *The Common Law* was quickly translated into German, Italian and French.

Public Career

In 1882 Massachusetts' governor appointed Holmes — then a full professor at the Harvard Law School in a chair established by Boston lawyer Louis D. Brandeis — an associate justice of the Massachusetts Supreme Court. Holmes served on the state court for 20 years, the last three as chief justice, and wrote more than 1,000 opinions, many of them involving labor disputes. Holmes' progressive labor views, criticized by railroad and corporate interests, were favorably considered by President Theodore Roosevelt during his search in 1902 for someone to fill the "Massachusetts seat" on the Supreme Court, vacated by the retirement of 74-year-old Bostonian Horace Gray. Convinced of his compatibility with the administration's national policies, Roosevelt nominated Holmes associate justice December 2, 1902. The 61-year-old judge was confirmed without objection two days later.

Holmes' 29 years of service on the Supreme Court spanned the tenures of Chief Justices Fuller, White, Taft and Hughes and the administrations of Presidents Roosevelt, Taft, Wilson, Harding, Coolidge and Hoover. For 25 years he never missed a session and walked daily the 2-1/2 miles from his home to court. Like Justice Brandeis, Holmes voluntarily paid an income tax despite the majority's ruling which exempted federal judges. Unlike the idealistic and often moralistic Brandeis, with whom he is frequently compared, Holmes was pragmatic, approaching each case on its particular facts.

Although a lifelong Republican, on the court Holmes did not fulfill Roosevelt's expectations as a loyal party man. His dissent shortly after his appointment from the court's decision to break up the railroad trust of the Northern Securities Company surprised the nation and angered the president.

At the suggestion of Chief Justice Hughes and his colleagues on the bench, Holmes resigned on January 12, 1932, at the age of 90. A widower since his wife's death in 1929, he continued to spend his winters in Washington,

D.C., and his summers in Beverly Farms, Mass. He died at his Washington home two days before his 94th birthday.

William Rufus Day
(1903-1922)

Born: April 17, 1849, Ravenna, Ohio.

Education: University of Michigan, A.B., 1870; University of Michigan Law School, 1871-72.

Official Positions: judge, Court of Common Pleas, Canton, Ohio, 1886-90; first assistant U.S. secretary of state, 1897-98; U.S. secretary of state, 1898; member, United States delegation, Paris Peace Conference, 1899-99; judge, sixth circuit, United States Court of Appeals; umpire, Mixed Claims Commission, 1922-23.

Supreme Court Appointment: nominated associate justice by President Theodore Roosevelt Feb. 19, 1903, to replace George Shiras Jr., who resigned; confirmed by the U.S. Senate Feb. 23, 1903, by a voice vote; replaced on court by Pierce Butler, nominated by President Harding.

Family: married Mary Elizabeth Schaefer, 1875; four sons.

Died: July 9, 1923, Mackinac Island, Mich.

Personal Background

William Day was raised in a family with a strong judicial background. His maternal great-grandfather, Zephania Swift, was the chief justice of Connecticut; his grandfather, Rufus Spalding, was a member of the Ohio Supreme Court; his father, Luther Day, served as chief justice of Ohio. It seemed predetermined, then, that William Day, after receiving his A.B. from the University of Michigan in 1870, should enter the law school at his alma mater. Before starting law school he studied law for one year in his home town of Ravenna, Ohio, and then attended law school for a year at the University of Michigan. He returned home to Ohio in 1872 and set up a law practice in Canton, about 25 miles from Ravenna.

In Canton, Day established a solid reputation and a lucrative law practice. He also became a good friend of another young attorney in Canton, William McKinley. Day and McKinley traveled in the same Republican circles, and McKinley soon came to rely on Day for help and counsel.

While McKinley's political fortunes took him to the U.S. House of Representatives (1877-84; 1885-91) and the governor's mansion (1892-96), Day remained in Canton, married a local woman, and raised a family of four boys.

Public Career

Day's popularity was so great in the Canton area that he was elected in 1886 judge of the Court of Common Pleas after receiving both the Democratic and Republican nominations. Three years later he was appointed to the United States District Court by President Benjamin Harrison.

However, his frail health prevented him from serving in that position.

When his friend McKinley was elected president, Day was named first assistant secretary of state in the administration. His job consisted of assisting the aged and failing secretary of state, John Sherman, in performing the country's diplomatic chores. After the war between Spain and the United States over Cuba officially began April 11, 1898, Sherman was eased out of the State Department and replaced by Day, who had been closely involved in the events leading up to the outbreak of hostilities. Day served as secretary of state only from April 26 to August 26, 1898; during his brief tenure, however, he oversaw the delicate negotiations between the United States and Spain and was able to obtain assurances of neutrality and goodwill from Western European countries.

In August McKinley named Day to the U.S. commission to negotiate the terms of the peace with Spain. Day is credited with the plan to pay Spain $20 million for the Philippines.

His work on the peace commission finished, Day was named by McKinley in 1899 to the sixth circuit, United States Court of Appeals, located in Cincinnati. Day enjoyed his four years on the bench — it was close to home, and his colleagues included future president and Supreme Court Chief Justice William Howard Taft and future Associate Justice Horace H. Lurton.

Day was, of course, deeply shocked by the 1901 assassination of his longtime friend, President McKinley. As a tribute to his friend and patron, Day began to mark each of the late president's birthdays with a memorial service. It was at one of these services in January 1903 in Canton, attended by McKinley's successor, Theodore Roosevelt, that Day first learned of Roosevelt's intention to name him to the Supreme Court. After Day introduced the president to the audience, Roosevelt surprised the crowd by referring to Day as "Mr. Justice Day." His appointment was announced officially Feb. 19, 1903.

Day retired from the court Nov. 13, 1922. He accepted an appointment from President Harding to serve as an umpire on the Mixed Claims Commission, a board established to settle claims remaining from World War I. Day worked on the commission only until May 1923. He died July 9, 1923, at his summer home on Mackinac Island, Michigan.

William Henry Moody
(1906-1910)

Born: Dec. 23, 1853, Newbury, Mass.

Education: Harvard University, A.B., cum laude, 1876; Harvard University Law School, 1876-77.

Official Positions: city solicitor, Haverhill, 1888-90; district attorney, eastern district of Massachusetts, 1890-

95; U.S. House of Representatives, R-Mass., 1895-1902; secretary of the Navy, 1902-04; attorney general of the United States, 1904-06.

Supreme Court Appointment: nominated associate justice by President Theodore Roosevelt Dec. 3, 1906, to replace Henry B. Brown, who retired; confirmed by the U.S. Senate Dec. 12, 1906, by a voice vote; replaced on court by Willis Van Devanter, nominated by Taft.

Family: Unmarried.

Died: July 2, 1917, Haverhill, Mass.

Personal Background

Moody was born in a house in Newbury, Mass., that had been the Moody family home for over 200 years. He was raised in nearby Danvers, Mass., attended Phillips Academy in Andover, Mass., and graduated cum laude from Harvard University in 1876. In the fall of that year he entered the Harvard School of Law but left in January 1877. To prepare for his entry to the bar he began an 18-month course of study in the law offices of Boston lawyer and author Richard Henry Dana. Although three years of study were normally required before an applicant was allowed to take the oral examination, an exception was made in Moody's case, and he passed easily in 1878.

Moody left Boston after his admittance to the bar in 1878 and established a private practice in Haverhill, Mass. His clientele soon included most of the industries and manufacturers in the region. As his prestige grew, Moody became involved in Republican politics and in 1888 began his public career as city solicitor for Haverhill.

Public Career

Two years later he was named district attorney for the eastern district of Massachusetts. His most famous case (and the one that spread his name across the country) was the prosecution of Lizzie Borden, the alleged ax murderer of Fall River, Mass. Although Borden was acquitted by a sympathetic jury, Moody's adept handling of the state's case brought him to the attention of state Republican leaders, notably Sen. Henry Cabot Lodge (1893-1924).

In 1895 Moody won a special election to fill the U.S. House seat in Massachusetts' sixth congressional district vacated by the death of Rep. William Cogswell (1887-95). The same year, Moody made the acquaintance of New York Police Commissioner Theodore Roosevelt and the two men became close friends over the next few years.

In the House, Moody was respected for his mastery of details and facts. When Theodore Roosevelt ascended to the presidency after the assassination of President William McKinley, Moody was one of Roosevelt's first choices for his cabinet. As secretary of the Navy, Moody won increased congressional appropriations to enlarge and improve the U.S. fleet. This, of course, met with the hearty approval of President Roosevelt, who said of Moody, "we have never had as good a Secretary of the Navy...."

Moody's next assignment in the Roosevelt administration was to replace Attorney General Philander Knox in 1904 and to continue the administration's prosecution of trusts. A dedicated progressive Republican, Moody personally argued for the government in the successful suit against the beef trust, *Swift and Company v. United States, 196 U.S. 375 (1905).*

Moody's appointment to the Supreme Court was not without controversy; he was thought to be too radical. Opponents pointed to his eager prosecution of trusts and his enthusiasm for progressive reforms. Criticism notwithstanding, Moody was confirmed by the Senate Dec. 12, 1906, to replace Justice Henry B. Brown.

Moody's Supreme Court career was shortened by the onslaught of a crippling form of arthritis that forced his retirement in 1910. He returned home to Haverhill, where he died July 2, 1917.

Horace Harmon Lurton
(1909-1914)

Born: Feb. 26, 1844, Newport, Ky.

Education: University of Chicago, 1860; Cumberland Law School, L.B., 1867.

Official Positions: chancellor in equity, 1875-78; judge, Tennessee Supreme Court, 1886-93; judge, Sixth Circuit Court of Appeals, 1893-1909.

Supreme Court Appointment: nominated associate justice by President William Howard Taft Dec. 13, 1909, to replace Rufus W. Peckham, who died; confirmed by U.S. Senate Dec. 20, 1909, by a voice vote; replaced on court by James C. McReynolds, nominated by President Wilson.

Family: married Mary Francis Owens, September 1867; two sons, two daughters.

Died: July 12, 1914, Atlantic City, N.J.

Personal Background

Horace Harmon Lurton was born in Kentucky in 1844, the same year Democrat James Knox Polk defeated Whig Henry Clay for the presidency over the issue of annexation of the Republic of Texas. Lurton left Kentucky as a young boy with his mother, Sarah Ann (Harmon) Lurton, and his father, Dr. Lycurgus Leonidas Lurton, a physician who later became an Episcopal minister, and moved to Clarksville, Tenn., a town of 15,000 on the Cumberland River. At age 16, he went north and attended the University of Chicago until the outbreak of the Civil War.

Lurton served in the Confederate Army in both the Kentucky and Tennessee infantries before his capture during Gen. Grant's siege of Fort Donelson. He escaped from Camp Chase in Columbus, Ohio, and joined General John Hunt Morgan's daredevil marauders, famous throughout the South for their surprise attacks on Union railroads, bridges and telegraph stations. Lurton was captured again in July 1863. During his incarceration in one of the northernmost camps on Lake Erie he contracted tuberculosis. Fearing for her son's life, Sarah Ann Lurton went to Washington and succeeded in persuading President Lincoln to let her son return with her to Clarksville before the end of the war.

After his recuperation at home, Lurton attended Cumberland University Law School in Lebanon, Tenn. He graduated in 1867, married Mary Francis Owen, the daughter of a local physician, and returned to Clarksville to practice law. Through his partner James A. Bailey, who took Andrew Johnson's Senate seat in 1877, Lurton became involved in Democratic politics. He was appointed by the governor to the sixth chancery division of Tennessee, becoming at 31 the youngest chancellor in the state's history.

In 1878 Lurton returned to the practice of law in an eight-year partnership with ex-chancellor Charles G. Smith.

During this period Lurton became a prosperous and well-respected Clarksville citizen as president of the Farmer's and Merchants' National Bank, vestryman of Trinity Episcopal Church and trustee of the University of the South.

Public Career

Lurton was elected to the Tennessee Supreme Court in 1886 and served for seven years. Immediately following his promotion to chief justice, he was appointed to the U.S. court of appeals for the sixth circuit by President Grover Cleveland. William Howard Taft was the presiding judge. Lurton succeeded him in office when Taft left the sixth circuit court to become governor general of the Philippines. In addition to his judicial responsibilities Lurton taught constitutional law at Vanderbilt University from 1898-1905 and served as dean the following four years.

Close personal friendship as well as respect for his judicial ability prompted President Taft to make 65-year-old Lurton his first Supreme Court appointment. "There was nothing I had so much at heart in my whole administration," said Taft of his choice.

Lurton took a symbolic train ride northward to assume his new responsibilities. Explaining the personal significance of the trip he stated, "I felt that in appointing me, President Taft, aside from manifestations of his friendship, had a kindly heart for the South; that he wished to draw the South to him with cords of affection. So, being a southerner myself, I determined to go to Washington through the South — every foot of the way."

Lurton served only five years. The 70-year-old justice died of a heart attack July 12, 1914, in Atlantic City, N.J.

Charles Evans Hughes
(1910-1916; 1930-1941)

Born: April 11, 1862, Glens Falls, N.Y.

Education: Colgate University, 1876-78; Brown University, A.B., 1881, A.M., 1884; Columbia Law School, LL.B., 1884.

Official Positions: special counsel, New York state investigating commissions, 1905-06; governor of New York, 1907-10; U.S. secretary of state, 1921-25; U.S. delegate, Washington Armament Conference, 1921; U.S. member,

Permanent Court of Arbitration, 1926-30; judge, Permanent Court of International Justice, 1928-30.

Supreme Court Appointment: nominated associate justice by President William Howard Taft April 25, 1910, to replace David J. Brewer, who died; confirmed by U.S. Senate May 2, 1910, by a voice vote; resigned June 10, 1916, to become Republican presidential candidate; replaced on court by John H. Clarke, nominated by President Wilson; nominated Chief Justice Feb. 3, 1930, by President Hoover, to replace Chief Justice Taft, who resigned; confirmed by U.S. Senate Feb. 13, 1930, by a 52-26 vote; replaced on court by Harlan F. Stone, nominated by Franklin D. Roosevelt.

Family: married Antoinette Carter, Dec. 5, 1888; one son, two daughters.

Died: August 27, 1948, Osterville, Mass.

Personal Background

Charles Evans Hughes was born during the Civil War in Glens Falls, N.Y., the only child of David Charles Hughes, an abolitionist minister, and his wife Mary Catherine (Connelly) Hughes. When the Reverend Hughes became secretary of the American Bible Union, the family left the Adirondacks and moved to New York City in 1873. Charles was schooled at home by his parents until age 14 when he enrolled in Madison College (now Colgate University). Before his junior year he transferred to Brown University, chosen because of its Baptist tradition, which appealed to his parents, and its city location, which appealed to him. After graduation Hughes taught Greek, Latin and algebra at the Delaware Academy in Delhi, N.Y., and clerked for the Wall Street firm of Chamberlin, Carter & Hornblower to earn money for law school. He graduated from Columbia in 1884 and passed the bar at age 22 with a nearly perfect score.

Hughes then returned to Chamberlin, Carter & Hornblower and married Antoinette Carter, the daughter of one of the partners. Two years later the firm became Carter, Hughes & Cravath. Hughes' legal practice in New York City continued for 20 years, with an interim of three years teaching law at Cornell University.

Public Career

In 1905 Hughes began investigating illegal rate-making practices and fraudulent insurance activities in New York as special counsel for the Stevens Gas Commission and the Armstrong Insurance Committee, established by the state legislature. His successful exposure of racketeering won him national recognition. Endorsed by President Theodore Roosevelt, Hughes defeated William Randolph Hearst in a 1906 race for governor and was re-elected two years later.

When President William Howard Taft appointed Hughes to the Supreme Court to fill the vacancy left by Justice Brewer's death in 1910, his nomination met with the approval of the court and the press. According to the liberal paper *The World*, "Mr. Taft could not have made a better or more popular selection." Justifying his acceptance of the seat on the Supreme Court to New York Republicans who envisioned for him a great political future, Hughes explained, "I had no right to refuse. A refusal on the ground that some time or other I might be a candidate for the Presidency ... would have been absurd."

After six years on the court, Hughes resigned to run for president, endorsed by both the Republican and Progressive parties. "Wilson with Peace and Honor or Hughes with Roosevelt and War?" was a popular slogan of the Democrats, critical of Hughes' advocacy of military preparedness against Germany. The former Supreme Court justice lost the 1916 election by only 23 electoral votes. After his defeat he returned to the practice of law as senior partner in the New York firm, Hughes, Rounds, Schurman & Dwight.

When Warren G. Harding became president, he appointed Hughes secretary of state, a post which he also held during the Coolidge administration. At the Washington Armament Conference in 1921 Hughes was instrumental in the agreement reached by the major powers to limit the naval race, end the Anglo-Japanese Alliance and recognize China's open door diplomacy.

Unlike the general acclaim which greeted Hughes' Supreme Court appointment in 1910, his nomination as Chief Justice by President Hoover 20 years later met considerable opposition in the Senate. "No man in public life so exemplifies the influence of powerful combinations in the political and financial worlds as does Mr. Hughes," Senator Norris of Nebraska objected. Critics felt Hughes' representation of America's largest corporations after he left the State Department jeopardized his ability to defend the rights of the ordinary citizen on the court. Supporters, on the other hand, pointed to his efforts on behalf of world peace during his legal career as a member of the Permanent Court of Arbitration in the Hague and the Permanent Court of International Justice.

On Feb. 13, 1930, Hughes was confirmed as chief justice by a 52-26 vote. Hughes' son, Charles Evans Jr., resigned the same day from his position in the Hoover administration as solicitor general.

After 11 years of service as Chief Justice, Hughes informed President Roosevelt of his wish to retire due to "considerations of health and age." This announcement was followed by widespread commendation by his colleagues on the bench. Justice Frankfurter likened Hughes' ability to marshal the court to "Toscanini lead[ing] an orchestra" and Justice Douglas praised his "generosity, kindliness and forbearance."

In 1942, a year after his retirement, Hughes was awarded the American Bar Association medal for conspicuous service to jurisprudence. He died at his summer cottage on Cape Cod at the age of 86.

Willis Van Devanter
(1910-1937)

Born: April 17, 1859, Marion, Ind.

Education: Indiana Asbury University, A.B., 1878; University of Cincinnati Law School, LL.B., 1881.

Official Positions: city attorney, Cheyenne, 1887-88; member, Wyoming territorial legislature, 1888; chief justice, Wyoming Territory supreme court, 1889-90; assistant

U.S. attorney general, 1897-1903; judge, eighth circuit, U.S. Court of Appeals, 1903-10.

Supreme Court Appointment: nominated associate justice by President William Howard Taft Dec. 12, 1910, to replace William H. Moody; confirmed by U.S. Senate Dec. 15, 1910, by a voice vote; replaced on court by Hugo L. Black, nominated by President Franklin D. Roosevelt.

Family: married Dellice Burhans, Oct. 10, 1883.

Died: Feb. 8, 1941, in Washington, D.C.

Personal Background

Willis Van Devanter was born April 17, 1859, in Marion, Ind., nine years after his parents had moved west. The oldest of eight children, Van Devanter attended Indiana Asbury (now DePauw) University and the University of Cincinnati Law School.

After receiving his law degree in 1881 he joined his father's law firm in Marion. Three years later, after marrying Dellice Burhans of Michigan, he left the relative security of his native Indiana for Cheyenne in the Wyoming Territory. There he established a thriving practice and became involved in Republican politics through his close friendship with Governor (and later U.S. Senator) Francis E. Warren. Warren became head of the Republican party in Wyoming and remained an influential friend throughout Van Devanter's career.

Public Career

In 1886 Van Devanter worked on a commission that revised the territory's statutes. He served as city attorney in Cheyenne in 1887 and the following year was elected to the territorial legislature. The next year, 1889, when Van Devanter was just 30 years old, President Benjamin Harrison named him chief justice of the Wyoming Territory supreme court. He only served as chief justice for one year before resigning to resume private practice.

Van Devanter enjoyed a thriving practice and remained active in Republican politics, serving as chairman of the Wyoming state committee (1892-94) and as a member of the Republican National Committee (1896-1900). His service to the party was rewarded in 1897 when President William McKinley named him as assistant attorney general assigned to the Interior Department. There he relied on his years of experience in Wyoming to specialize in legal questions regarding public lands and Indian matters. He also found time to lecture at Columbian (now George Washington) University.

In 1903 President Theodore Roosevelt appointed Van Devanter to the eighth circuit, U.S. Court of Appeals. His years on the bench were marked by a concern for jurisdictional questions, land claims, rights of railroads and other complex technical issues.

When Justice Edward D. White was appointed Chief Justice by President Taft on Dec. 12, 1910, Van Devanter was also named to fill the associate-justice vacancy created by the retirement of William H. Moody, who resigned Nov. 20, 1910.

Van Devanter's nomination was strongly opposed by several liberals, particularly William Jennings Bryan, who said that Van Devanter was "the judge that held that two railroads running parallel to each other for two thousand miles were not competing lines, one of the roads being that of Union Pacific," one of Van Devanter's former clients.

He retired from the court June 2, 1937, and died Feb. 8, 1941, in Washington, D.C.

Joseph Rucker Lamar
(1910-1916)

Born: Oct. 14, 1857, Elbert County, Ga.

Education: University of Georgia, 1874-75; Bethany College, A.B., 1877; Washington and Lee University, 1877.

Official Positions: member, Georgia legislature, 1886-89; commissioner to codify Georgia laws, 1893; associate justice, Georgia Supreme Court, 1903-05; member, mediation conference, Niagara Falls, Canada, 1914.

Supreme Court Appointment: nominated associate justice by President William Howard Taft Dec. 12, 1910, to replace Edward D. White, who became Chief Justice; confirmed by U.S. Senate Dec. 15, 1910, by a voice vote; replaced on court by Louis D. Brandeis, nominated by President Wilson.

Family: married Clarinda Huntington Pendleton, Jan. 13, 1879; two sons, one daughter.

Died: Jan. 2, 1916, Washington, D.C.

Personal Background

Joseph Rucker Lamar was named after his maternal grandfather on whose antebellum plantation, Cedar Grove in Ruckersville, Ga., he was born and raised. Both the Ruckers and the Lamars were socially prominent Georgia families. Mary, the youngest daughter of Joseph Rucker, merchant, planter, banker and founder of Ruckersville, married James Sanford Lamar of French Huguenot ancestry.

Other notable relatives were Mirabeau Buonaparte Lamar, president of the Republic of Texas from 1838-1841, and Lucius Quintus Cincinnatus Lamar, associate justice of the Supreme Court from 1888-1893.

After his mother's death when he was eight, Joseph Lamar left Cedar Grove and moved to Augusta, where his father became a minister in the Disciples of Christ church, a new Protestant denomination founded by Alexander Campbell, the president of Bethany College during James Lamar's attendance. Greatly influenced by Campbell, Joseph's father left his legal career to join the ministry. Woodrow Wilson's father was the minister of the leading Presbyterian church in Augusta and the two boys became close friends.

Lamar attended Martin Institute and Richmond Academy in Georgia and the Penn Lucy Academy in Baltimore before enrolling in the University of Georgia. Consenting to his father's wishes, he transferred to Bethany College, from which he graduated in 1877. After reading law at Washington and Lee University and clerking for the well-known Augusta lawyer, Henry Clay Foster, Lamar passed the Georgia bar. He married Clarinda Huntington Pendleton, the daughter of the president of Bethany College, and they lived with her family for one year while he taught Latin at the college.

Public Career

Lamar's legal practice began in 1880 when Henry Clay Foster, for whom he had clerked while a law student, asked him to become a partner. During their joint practice for more than ten years, Lamar served for two terms in the Georgia legislature. As elected representative for Richmond County, he continued studying the state's history of jurisprudence, his special field of interest, and wrote a number of essays. Lamar's research on Georgia's legal history was recognized in 1893 by the governor, who asked him to help rewrite Georgia's law codes.

During his legal practice, Lamar also served on the examining board for applicants to the Georgia bar. This experience helped prepare him for a seat on the Georgia supreme court, which he occupied from 1903-05. Overworked and homesick for Augusta, Lamar resigned before his term expired and returned to private law practice, this time in a partnership specializing in railroad law with E. H. Callaway, a former superior court judge.

President Taft nominated Lamar associate justice of the Supreme Court Dec. 12, 1910, much to the Georgian's surprise. He had become acquainted with the president during two brief vacations in Augusta. Lamar did not expect to be confirmed by the Senate because he was little known outside of the South and was a member of the Democratic party. Rarely had presidents crossed party lines in making Supreme Court appointments. Lamar's fears were allayed; he was confirmed three days after his nomination.

During his last term Justice Lamar overworked himself in the performance of his judicial responsibilities. He suffered a stroke in September 1916 and died three months later at 58 after only five years on the bench. "The whole country has reason to mourn," President Wilson telegraphed Mrs. Lamar. "It has lost an able and noble servant. I have lost in him one of my most loved friends."

Mahlon Pitney
(1912-1922)

Born: Feb. 5, 1858, Morristown, N.J.

Education: College of New Jersey (Princeton), A.B., 1879; A.M., 1882.

Official Positions: U.S. House of Representatives, 1895- 99; member, New Jersey senate, 1899-1901; president, New Jersey senate, 1901; associate justice, New Jersey Supreme Court, 1901-08; chancellor of New Jersey, 1908-12.

Supreme Court Appointment: nominated associate justice Feb. 19, 1912, by President William H. Taft to replace John M. Harlan, who died; confirmed by the U.S. Senate March 13, 1912, by a 50-26 vote; replaced on court by Edward T. Sanford, nominated by President Harding.

Family: married Florence T. Shelton, Nov. 14, 1891; two sons, one daughter.

Died: Dec. 9, 1924, Washington, D.C.

Personal Background

The second son of Henry Cooper Pitney and his wife Sarah Louisa (Halsted) Pitney was born on a farm in Morristown, N.J., on Feb. 5, 1858. He was named Mahlon after his paternal great grandfather, a British descendant who fought for the Americans in the Revolution of 1776. Mahlon Pitney attended the College of New Jersey, now Princeton University, and graduated in 1879; Woodrow Wilson was a classmate.

He received his legal education from his father, "a walking encyclopedia of law," and after passing the New Jersey bar in 1882 practiced for seven years in the industrial iron town of Dover. When his father was appointed vice chancellor of New Jersey in 1889, Pitney moved back to Morristown to take over his legal practice. At the age of 33 he married a local woman, Florence T. Shelton.

Public Career

The popular choice among New Jersey Republicans, Pitney was elected to a Fourth District congressional seat in 1894. As a member of the 54th Congress, he endorsed conservative monetary policies and easily won a second term with the additional support of Democrats who favored gold-backed currency. Pitney resigned Jan. 5, 1899, after his election to the New Jersey state senate.

Party leader William J. Sewall advised Pitney to remain in the legislature for a few years before running for governor, the political office to which he most aspired. When Republicans gained control of the state senate, Pitney was elected its president. Appointment to the New Jersey Supreme Court by Governor Foster M. Voorhees in 1901 altered his gubernatorial ambitions. For the next 20 years Pitney pursued a judicial career, the culmination of which was the position of chancellor of New Jersey. His father had been vice chancellor 19 years before.

Pitney was greatly surprised when President Taft nominated him associate justice of the Supreme Court Feb. 19, 1912. They had met seven days before at a dinner party in Newark and discussed another associate justice of the New Jersey Supreme Court, Francis J. Swayze, who was being considered for the bench. After the Pitney nomination, Taft acknowledged, "I did consider with a good deal of care another lawyer from New Jersey."

The Senate confirmed the Pitney nomination within a month although there was some objection on the part of liberal senators and union leaders to Pitney's anti-labor record as a New Jersey judge. After the 50-26 vote in favor of confirmation, Pitney received a congratulatory telegram from New Jersey governor and former Princeton classmate Woodrow Wilson, who assured him "a better choice could not have been made."

"His meticulously detailed opinions," says historian Fred I. Israel, "although often repetitious and quite heavy in style, reveal a troubled man's attempt to deal with complex legal and social problems in what seemed to him a logical and consistent manner."

Mental and physical stress forced the 64-year-old justice to resign after ten years of service. He suffered a stroke in August 1922 and retired in December. Pitney's premature death two years later in Washington, D.C., has been attributed to the strain of overwork while on the court.

James Clark McReynolds
(1914-1941)

Born: Feb. 3, 1862, Elkton, Ky.

Education: Vanderbilt University, B.S., class valedictorian, 1882; University of Virginia, LL.B., 1884.

Official Positions: assistant U.S. attorney, 1903-07; U.S. attorney general, 1913-14.

Supreme Court Appointment: nominated associate justice by President Woodrow Wilson Aug. 19, 1914, to replace Horace H. Lurton, who died; confirmed by the U.S. Senate Aug. 29, 1914, by a 44-6 vote. replaced on the court by Robert H. Jackson, nominated by President Franklin D. Roosevelt.

Family: unmarried.

Died: Aug. 24, 1946, in Washington, D.C.

Personal Background

McReynolds was born in a Kentucky community that exhibited considerable sympathy for the Confederacy during the Civil War. Raised on a plantation, he was the son of highly moral parents who were members of the fundamentalist Campbellite religious sect.

After receiving his B.S. from Vanderbilt University in Nashville, Tenn., McReynolds traveled to Charlottesville to study law at the University of Virginia. He received his LL.B. there in 1884 and returned to Nashville to practice law. His legal business in Nashville went uninterrupted until 1903, except for a short stint as secretary to Sen. Howell Edmunds Jackson (D-Tenn., 1881-86, Supreme Court justice, 1893-95). McReynolds' clients included several companies and corporations in Nashville. In 1900 he took a part-time position teaching law at Vanderbilt University.

Public Career

He ran for Congress in 1896 as a "Gold Democrat" with some Republican support, but his arrogant and standoffish manners while campaigning alienated a majority of the voters. His candidacy, however, provided him with a measure of prominence in the Democratic party.

In 1903 he was appointed an assistant U.S. attorney in the Roosevelt administration. During his four years at the Justice Department, McReynolds handled several antitrust prosecutions, including the court battles with the anthracite coal trust and the tobacco trust. So involved was he in trust-busting that he once referred to the American Tobacco Co. as a group of "commercial wolves and highwaymen."

He resigned from the U.S. attorney's office in 1907 and took up law practice in New York City. He continued, however, to assist the Justice Department with antitrust cases over the next several years. A Wilson supporter in the

election of 1912, he was named U.S. attorney general in the new administration. Although he served as attorney general for little more than a year, McReynolds managed to anger several members of Congress and executive branch officials with his temper and haughtiness. To smooth the waters President Wilson named McReynolds to the Supreme Court Aug. 19, 1914, to replace Justice Horace H. Lurton, who had died in July.

McReynolds retired from the court Feb. 1, 1941. He died Aug. 24, 1946, in Washington, D.C.

Louis Dembitz Brandeis
(1916-1939)

Born: Nov. 13, 1856, Louisville, Ky.

Education: Harvard Law School, LL.B., 1877.

Official Positions: "people's attorney," Public Franchise League and Massachusetts State Board of Trade, 1897-1911; counsel, New England Policyholders' Protective Committee, 1905; special counsel, wage and hour cases in California, Illinois, Ohio and Oregon, 1907-14; counsel, Ballinger-Pinchot investigation, 1910; chairman, arbitration board, New York garment workers' labor disputes, 1910-16.

Supreme Court Appointment: nominated associate justice Jan. 28, 1916, by President Woodrow Wilson, to replace Joseph R. Lamar, who died; confirmed by the U.S. Senate June 1, 1916, by a 47-22 vote; replaced on court by William O. Douglas, nominated by President Franklin D. Roosevelt.

Family: married Alice Goldmark, March 23, 1891; two daughters.

Died: Oct. 5, 1941, Washington, D.C.

Personal Background

Louis Dembitz Brandeis was born Nov. 13, 1856, in Louisville, Ky., the son of Adolph and Fredericka Dembitz Brandeis, Jewish emigrants from Bohemia after the unsuccessful democratic revolts of 1848. His father was a prosperous grain merchant who provided his family with comfort, education and culture. Having completed two years of preparatory studies at the Annen-Realschule in Dresden, but without a college degree, Brandeis enrolled at Harvard Law School when he was 18 years of age. He graduated in 1877 with the highest average in the law school's history. After eight months practicing law in St. Louis, Brandeis returned to Cambridge — for him "the world's center" — and with Bostonian Samuel D. Warren Jr., second in their law school class, opened a one-room office downtown.

Warren & Brandeis and the successor firm Brandeis, Dunbar & Nutter handled a variety of cases and were highly successful. By the time he was 35, Brandeis was earning more than $50,000 a year. He and his wife, Alice Goldmark of New York, preferred to live simply, however, and set a ceiling on their personal expenditures of $10,000 a year. As a young lawyer Brandeis devoted many hours to his alma mater. He helped raise funds for a teaching post for Oliver Wendell Holmes Jr. and was one of the founders of the *Harvard Law Review.*

The turn of the century marked the rapid growth in America of corporate monopolies — the "curse of bigness," as Brandeis described it. He chose to protect the rights not of special interest groups but of the general public, and usually without a fee for his services. Brandeis initiated sliding scale gas rates in Boston that lowered consumer costs while raising corporate dividends and instituted savings bank insurance policies, another reform later implemented in the rest of the country. He defended municipal control of Boston's subway system and opposed the monopolistic practices of the New Haven Railroad. He arbitrated labor disputes in New York's garment industry and established the constitutionality of several state maximum hour and minimum wage statutes. For 37 years Brandeis devoted his time, energy and talents to a host of public causes. He called himself an "attorney for the situation"; the press adopted the popular title "people's attorney."

Public Career

President Wilson respected Brandeis and often sought his opinion. He nominated him associate justice of the Supreme Court Jan. 28, 1916, to fill the vacancy left by Justice Lamar's death. Vicious opposition to his appointment ensued. One particularly vituperative critic described Brandeis as a "business-baiter, stirrer up of strife, litigious lover of hate and unrest, destroyer of confidence, killer of values, commercial coyote, spoiler of pay envelopes."

Factory owners paying higher wages, New Haven Railroad stockholders, moguls in the Boston transit system, insurance and gas industries — in short, all the losers in court — united to voice their objections to the appointment. Among those seeking satisfaction for past injuries was William Howard Taft. His administration had been embarrassed by an investigation led in part by Brandeis of the conservation practices of Secretary of Interior Richard A. Ballinger.

The former president, ambitious for a justiceship himself, described the nomination as "one of the deepest wounds that I have had as an American and a lover of the Constitution" and spoke of the "indelible stain" on the Wilson administration that confirmation would bring.

Another critic, Clarence W. Barron, editor and publisher of the *Wall Street Journal,* also felt the choice was unwise, "There is only one redeeming feature in the nomination and that is that it will assist to bury Mr. Wilson in the next Presidential election."

The president viewed the political climate differently. He believed Brandeis was a smart choice who would attract the needed Progressive vote. A divided Republican party was unlikely to win him the election a second time.

During four months of acrimonious debate over his appointment, Brandeis quietly pursued his legal practice. He went to the office every day and did not resort to personal attacks against his opponents. "Your attitude while the wolves yelp is sublime," his young nephew wrote.

The hearings in the Senate Judiciary Committee turned up no valid grounds for rejection. According to Senator Thomas J. Walsh, Brandeis' only "real crime" was that "he had not stood in awe of the majesty of wealth." One of his supporters from the Harvard Law School, Arthur

Hill, attributed the opposition to the fact that "Mr. Brandeis is an outsider, successful and a Jew."

Brandeis was confirmed by the Senate on June 1, 1916, by a vote of 47-22, thus becoming the first Jew on the Supreme Court.

At 82, Brandeis resigned from the court but not from public service. After 22 years on the bench, he devoted the last two years of his life to the Zionist movement and a boycott of German products. As *The New York Times* noted upon his retirement in 1939, "the storm against him . . . seems almost incredible now."

John Hessin Clarke
(1916-1922)

Born: Sept. 18, 1857, Lisbon, Ohio.
Education: Western Reserve University, A.B., 1877, A.M., 1880; LL.D., 1916.
Official Positions: federal judge, U.S. District Court for Northern District of Ohio, 1914-16.
Supreme Court Appointment: nominated associate justice July 14, 1916, by President Woodrow Wilson, to replace Charles Evans Hughes, who resigned; confirmed by the U.S. Senate July 24, 1916, by a voice vote; replaced on court by George Sutherland, nominated by President Harding.
Family: unmarried.
Died: March 22, 1945, San Diego, Calif.

Personal Background

John Hessin Clarke, the son of Irish Protestants John and Melissa (Hessin) Clarke, was born Sept. 18, 1857, in Lisbon, Ohio. His father had left Ireland in 1830 and settled in Lisbon, the county seat, where he practiced law and participated in liberal Democratic politics. His son graduated Phi Beta Kappa from Western Reserve College in Hudson, Ohio, and returned to Lisbon to study law under his father's tutelage. He passed the bar with honors in 1878 and joined his father's practice.

Public Career

In 1880 Clarke moved to Youngstown where his career in corporate law began. Under his ownership and direction, the town newspaper the *Vindicator* became a strong voice for progressive reform. Clarke, a member of the Youngstown literary society, lectured on Shakespeare and James Russell Lowell. He was an honorary life trustee of the Youngstown Public Library and bequeathed the library $100,000 in his will.

Clarke left Youngstown and his legal practice of 17 years to join the Cleveland firm, William & Cushing, in 1897. As general counsel for the Nickel Plate Railroad he remained true to his liberal politics and advocated antitrust and anti-rebate legislation. A progressive reformer, Clarke supported suffrage for women, mandatory civil service and public disclosure of campaign expenditures.

In 1894 he ran for the U.S. Senate but was defeated by incumbent Calvin S. Brice. Chairman of the Ohio State Democratic Sound Money Convention, Clarke disagreed with William Jennings Bryan's free silver populism and split from the Democrats at the 1896 national convention over that issue. He ran for the Senate a second time in 1914 but withdrew when another Irishman, Timothy Hogan, announced his candidacy.

After more than 35 years in the legal profession and progressive politics, Clarke received his first federal post. In 1914 President Wilson appointed him federal judge for the Northern District of Ohio.

When Charles Evans Hughes resigned from the court to run against Wilson, the president considered nominating Attorney General Tom Gregory or Republican Senator Warren G. Harding to fill the vacancy. He decided instead on Judge Clarke because he wanted a decidedly progressive justice with an antitrust record on Chief Justice White's staid court.

After his nomination, Clarke was described by the *New York World* as "singularly like Brandeis in having been a successful corporation lawyer whose practice served only to quicken his sympathies and activities for the causes of political and social justice." Indeed, President Wilson had hoped that Clarke would join Brandeis "to restrain the court from the extreme reactionary course which it seem[ed] inclined to follow." He was therefore greatly disappointed when Clarke resigned from the court to promote American participation in the League of Nations, even though the League was Wilson's own dream. Clarke informed the president he would "die happier" working for world peace rather than devoting his time "to determining whether a drunken Indian had been deprived of his land before he died or whether the digging of a ditch was constitutional or not."

From 1922-30 Clarke presided over the League of Nations' Non-Partisan Association of the United States and — against the advice of his physician, who was concerned about his heart — spoke on its behalf across the country.

At the age of 80, Clarke emerged unexpectedly from his retirement in San Diego to endorse over nationwide radio President Roosevelt's court-packing plan. He died March 22, 1945, shortly before the convening of the San Francisco Conference that created the United Nations.

William Howard Taft
(1921-1930)

Born: Sept. 15, 1857, Cincinnati, Ohio.
Education: Yale University, A.B., class salutatorian, 1878; Cincinnati Law School, LL.B., 1880.

Official Positions: assistant prosecuting attorney, Hamilton County, Ohio, 1881-83; assistant county solicitor, Hamilton County, 1885-87; Ohio superior court, 1887-90; U.S. solicitor general, 1890-91; federal judge, sixth circuit, 1892-1900; chairman, Philippine Commission, 1900-01; civil governor of the Philippines, 1901-04; secretary of war, 1904-08; president of the United States, 1909-13; joint chairman, National War Labor Board, 1918-19.

Supreme Court Appointment: nominated Chief Justice by President Warren Harding June 30, 1921, to replace Chief Justice Edward D. White, who died; confirmed by the U.S. Senate June 30, 1921, by a voice vote; replaced on court by Chief Justice Charles Evans Hughes, nominated by President Hoover.

Family: married Helen Herron, June 19, 1886; two sons, one daughter.

Died: March 8, 1930, in Washington, D.C.

Personal Background

Public service was a tradition in the Taft family; William Howard Taft extended it to its limit during his lifetime. His grandfather, Peter Rawson Taft, was a judge on the probate and county courts in Windham County, Vt.; Alphonso Taft, William Howard's father, served two terms on the Ohio superior court before he was named secretary of war in the last months of the Grant administration. He also briefly served President Grant as attorney general, and later was ambassador to Austria-Hungary and Russia during the Arthur administration. William Howard's brother, Charles Phelps Taft, R-Ohio, served a term in the U.S. House of Representatives, 1895-97.

Born in Cincinnati, Taft received an A.B. in 1878 from Yale University, where he was the salutatorian of his graduating class. He returned to Ohio, entered Cincinnati Law School and took a job as a law reporter for the Cincinnati *Commercial*. He continued to report for the newspaper through 1880, the year in which he received his LL.B. and was admitted to the bar.

In 1886 he married Helen Herron. They raised one daughter and two sons, one of whom, Robert Alphonso Taft, R-Ohio, served in the U.S. Senate, 1939-53. Taft's grandson, Robert Taft Jr., R-Ohio, served in the House of Representatives, 1963-65, 1967-71, and the Senate, 1971-76.

Public Career

In 1881 Taft plunged into Republican politics and gave his support to a candidate for county prosecutor. After his candidate won, Taft was selected to be an assistant county prosecutor. He went back to private practice in 1883.

Taft was named to a two-year term as assistant county solicitor for Hamilton County in 1885 and, in 1887, when he was barely 30 years old, was appointed to the Ohio superior court.

He sat on the superior court bench until President Benjamin Harrison in 1890 named him solicitor general. In 1892, after Congress created additional judgeships for the federal circuit courts, Taft sought and received appointment to the sixth circuit.

Taft remained on the circuit court for eight years. He left reluctantly in 1900 when President McKinley asked him to head a commission established to ensure the smooth transition from military to civilian government in the Philippines in the aftermath of the Spanish-American War. In 1901 he was made civilian governor of the Philippines, a position he held until President Theodore Roosevelt named him secretary of war to replace Elihu Root in 1904.

Once in the cabinet, Taft became one of Roosevelt's closest advisers; the president increasingly relied on Taft to handle important matters for the administration. As secretary of war Taft was in command of the Panama Canal project and made a goodwill tour of the site. He also was dispatched in 1906 to Cuba to investigate for the president reports of revolutionary activity.

As Taft's prestige grew in the administration, so did his influence in the Republican party. With Roosevelt's backing he won the party's nomination for president and the subsequent election in 1908. He was sworn in as the twenty-ninth president of the United States March 4, 1909.

The presidency was a post that Taft did not particularly covet — he would have preferred a seat on the Supreme Court as Chief Justice, but he sought the presidency at the urging of his wife and Republican party regulars. His single term in office was not controversial. It saw the institution of the postal savings system and the Tariff Board, the intervention of American troops in the affairs of the Dominican Republic, the ratification of the Sixteenth Amendment to the Constitution and a continuation of the trust-busting begun under Theodore Roosevelt.

Taft also named six men to the Supreme Court, including a Chief Justice, Edward D. White. The others he named to the court were Horace A. Lurton, Charles Evans Hughes (who resigned from the court to run for president in 1916, lost, and was named Chief Justice in 1930 by President Hoover to replace Taft), Willis Van Devanter, Joseph R. Lamar and Mahlon Pitney. When Taft was named Chief Justice in 1921 only two of his appointees, Van Devanter and Pitney, were still on the bench.

Soon after he was elected president Taft began to fall out of favor with former President Roosevelt. The two men came to represent opposing sides of a division within the Republican party; when Taft was renominated in 1912, Roosevelt ran for president under the banner of his Bull Moose Party and effectively splintered the Republican vote. After the election, which was won by Democrat Woodrow Wilson, Taft described Roosevelt as "the most dangerous man that we have had in the country since its origin."

After leaving the White House, Taft taught constitutional law at Yale University, served a year as president of the American Bar Association, wrote magazine articles and was a frequent participant on the lecture circuit. He was elected president of the League to Enforce Peace in 1915. In 1916 he and four other former presidents of the American Bar Association joined with current president Elihu Root in writing to the U.S. Senate to register their disapproval of President Wilson's nomination of Louis D. Brandeis to the Supreme Court. During this period Taft also continued discreetly to publicize his desire to be named to the high court, especially as Chief Justice.

As Chief Justice, Taft was responsible for the creation of a judicial conference of senior federal judges, and passage of the Judiciary Act of 1925.

Taft served as the joint chairman of the National War Labor Board, 1918-19. An enthusiastic advocate of the League of Nations, he embarked on a 15-state tour in an attempt to rally support for the league. His greatest ambition was achieved when President Harding named him Chief Justice June 30, 1921, to replace Chief Justice Edward D. White. Taft is the only person in U.S. history to hold both the presidency and the Chief Justiceship.

George Sutherland
(1922-1938)

Born: March 25, 1862, Buckinghamshire, England.

Education: Brigham Young Academy, 1878-81; University of Michigan Law School, 1883.

Official Positions: Utah state senator, R, 1896-1900; U.S. House of Representatives, 1901-03; U.S. Senate, 1905-17; chairman, advisory committee to the Washington Conference for the Limitation of Naval Armaments, 1921; U.S. counsel, Norway-United States arbitration, The Hague, 1921-22.

Supreme Court Appointment: nominated associate justice by President Warren Harding Sept. 5, 1922, to replace Justice John H. Clarke, who resigned; confirmed by the Senate Sept. 5, 1922, by a voice vote; replaced on court by Stanley F. Reed, nominated by President Franklin D. Roosevelt.

Family: married Rosamund Lee, June 18, 1883; two daughters, one son.

Died: July 18, 1942, Stockbridge, Mass.

Personal Background

Sutherland was brought to the United States in 1863 by his parents. His father, a recent convert to the Church of Jesus Christ of Latter-day Saints, settled his family in Springville in the Utah Territory. The senior Sutherland soon deserted the Mormons, but the family remained in Utah. George Sutherland learned the value of thrift and hard work in his childhood — he left school at age 12 to help support the family. By the time he was 16, however, he had saved enough money to enroll himself at Brigham Young Academy in Provo. After three years at that school, he spent a year working for the company building the Rio Grande Western Railroad and in 1883 entered the University of Michigan Law School. He studied law for only one year before returning to Provo to start his law practice. He also returned to marry Rosamund Lee of Beaver, Utah.

Public Career

After 10 years in Provo, Sutherland in 1893 moved to Salt Lake City. When the territory achieved statehood in 1896, Sutherland, running as a Republican, was elected to the first state senate. In 1900 he was elected to the U.S. House of Representatives. He declined to run for a second term in the House but was elected in 1904 to the U.S. Senate.

During his first term in the Senate, Sutherland endorsed several reform measures, including the Pure Food and Drug Act (1906), the Postal Savings Act (1910) and a compensation bill for workers injured in interstate commerce (1911-12). He also played a major role in the revision and codification of federal criminal statutes. Among legislative programs he opposed were statehood for Arizona and New Mexico (1912), the Federal Reserve Act (1913), the

Sixteenth Amendment (1913), Clayton Antitrust Act (1914), and the Federal Trade Commission Act (1914). He also opposed the nomination of Louis D. Brandeis to the Supreme Court.

In 1916 Sutherland failed in his attempt to be renominated by the Utah Republican party. He stayed in Washington, D.C., practiced law and remained in touch with former Senate colleague Warren G. Harding. Sutherland developed into one of Harding's closest advisers and worked on his successful presidential campaign in 1920. Soon thereafter Sutherland represented the Harding administration as chairman of the advisory committee to the Washington Conference for the Limitation of Naval Armaments in 1921 and as counsel in arbitration between Norway and the United States over matters of shipping.

President Harding named Sutherland to the Supreme Court when Justice John H. Clarke unexpectedly resigned from the court to work for the cause of world peace. He retired from the court Jan. 17, 1938, and died in Stockbridge, Mass., July 18, 1942.

Pierce Butler

(1922-1939)

Born: March 17, 1866, Northfield, Minn.

Education: Carleton College, A.B., B.S., 1887; LL.D., 1923.

Official Positions: assistant county attorney, Ramsey County, Minn., 1891-93; county attorney, 1893-97.

Supreme Court Appointment: nominated associate justice Nov. 23, 1922, by President Warren Harding, to replace William R. Day, who resigned; confirmed by U.S. Senate Dec. 21, 1922, by a 61-8 vote; replaced on court by Frank Murphy, nominated by President Roosevelt.

Family: married Annie M. Cronin, Aug. 25, 1891; eight children.

Died: Nov. 16, 1939, Washington, D.C.

Personal Background

Pierce Butler was born in Northfield, Minn., on St. Patrick's Day in 1866, the sixth of Patrick and Mary Gaffrey Butler's eight children. His parents, Roman Catholics, settled on a farm in the Northwest after immigrating from Ireland during the potato famine of the 1840s. With money earned at a nearby dairy, Pierce attended Carleton College in his home town and graduated in 1887 with a bachelor of arts and a bachelor of science degree. He left Northfield to read law with the St. Paul firm of Pinch & Twohy and was admitted to the bar in 1888 at age 22.

Butler began his legal career practicing law with Stan Donnelly, the son of Ignatius Donnelly, a Minnesota congressman and future vice presidential candidate of the People's Party.

Public Career

In 1891 Butler was elected assistant attorney of Ramsey County, which includes St. Paul. While county attorney he formed the firm, How, Butler & Mitchell, and later became senior partner of Butler, Mitchell & Doherty. Attorney General George Wickersham chose Butler to represent the federal government in a number of antitrust cases around 1910. His skillful prosecution won him the attorney general's praise as the "foremost lawyer in his part of the country" and brought him to President Harding's attention.

When Justice Day's resignation in 1922 left a vacancy on the court, Butler was Chief Justice Taft's top choice for the seat. During arbitration in Canada the year before, Taft had been favorably impressed with Butler and recommended him to Harding. There were other reasons for Taft's strong preference, however. He wanted to obtain a conservative majority on the court. Butler's conservative judicial past made Taft confident that if appointed he would align himself with Justices Van Devanter, McReynolds and Sutherland. The president also was reminded by Taft of the political advantages of a Butler appointment: Taft, a Protestant, had replaced Chief Justice White, a Catholic, and another Catholic was needed on the bench.

Although Taft succeeded in convincing President Harding of Butler's merits, Senate liberals were not so easily persuaded. Their primary objection concerned Butler's defense of the Northern Pacific, Great Northern, and Chicago, Burlington and Quincy railroads during his legal practice. In the opinion of Senator-elect Henrik Shipstead of Minnesota, "the appointment of Judge Gary of the United States Steel Corporation would not ... be more unfitting or improper than the appointment of Mr. Butler."

Also criticized were Butler's actions as regent of the University of Minnesota from 1907-24. Faculty members whose economic or political views differed from his own had been dismissed or refused tenure. He was a reactionary with no tolerance for dissent, the liberal academics claimed. Despite the opposition to Butler's appointment, only eight senators voted against his confirmation Dec. 21, 1922.

Butler died in Washington, D.C., during his seventeenth year of service on the court. As anticipated, he was a staunch advocate of the court's *laissez faire* decisions during his tenure.

Edward Terry Sanford
(1923-1930)

Born: July 23, 1865, Knoxville, Tennessee.

Education: University of Tennessee, B.A. and Ph.B., 1883; Harvard, B.A., 1884, M.A., 1889; Harvard Law School, LL.B., 1889; editor of the *Harvard Law Review*.

Official Positions: special assistant to the U.S. attorney general, 1906-1907; assistant U.S. attorney general, 1907-1908; federal judge, U.S. District Court for the middle and eastern districts of Tennessee, 1908-23.

Supreme Court Appointment: nominated associate justice by President Warren Harding Jan. 24, 1923, to replace Mahlon Pitney, who retired; confirmed by the Senate Jan. 29, 1923 by a voice vote; replaced on court by Owen J. Roberts, nominated by President Hoover.

Family: married Lutie Mallory Woodruff, Jan. 6, 1891; two daughters.

Died: March 8, 1930, Washington, D.C.

Personal Background

Born in Knoxville on July 23, 1865, three months after the South had surrendered to the Union armies, Sanford grew up in one of the few Republican enclaves in the post-Civil War South. His father, Edward J. Sanford, had come to Tennessee in 1852 from Connecticut where his family had lived since 1634. In Tennessee, he rose from poverty to make a fortune in the lumber and construction business and became a prominent member of the Republican party. Sanford's mother, Emma Chavannes, of Swiss ancestry, educated her son at local private schools.

Following his education at the University of Tennessee and Harvard, Sanford studied in France and Germany for a year, returning to Knoxville, settling into the practice of law, and marrying a local woman.

Public Career

Sanford's first official position came in 1905 at the age of 41 when he accepted the post of special assistant to U.S. Attorney General William H. Moody (later appointed to the Supreme Court). Sanford's task — as one of President Theodore Roosevelt's "trustbusters" — was to prosecute the fertilizer trust under the Sherman Antitrust Act of 1890. In 1907, he became assistant attorney general. A year later, Roosevelt nominated him as federal district judge for the middle and eastern districts of Tennessee, a post Sanford held until his nomination to the Supreme Court in 1923.

After World War I, Sanford worked to mobilize support for the Treaty of Versailles and U.S. membership in the League of Nations. Although the treaty was defeated in the Senate, Sanford's efforts brought him to the attention of Chief Justice Taft — with whom he had become acquainted during his Justice Department service — and to Attorney General Harry M. Daugherty. They suggested his name to President Warren G. Harding when Justice Mahlon Pitney retired on Dec. 31, 1922, giving Harding a fourth vacancy on the court to fill during his term.

Harlan Fiske Stone
(1925-1946)

Born: Oct. 11, 1872, Chesterfield, N.H.

Education: Amherst College, A.B., 1894, M.A., 1897, LL.D., 1913; Columbia University, LL.B., 1898.

Official Positions: attorney general, 1924-25.

Supreme Court Appointment: nominated associate justice by President Calvin Coolidge Jan. 5, 1925, to replace Joseph McKenna, who resigned; confirmed by the U.S. Senate Feb. 5, 1925, by a 71-6 vote; nominated Chief Justice by President Franklin D. Roosevelt June 12, 1941, to replace Chief Justice Hughes, who resigned; confirmed by the U.S. Senate June 27, 1941, by a voice vote; replaced on court by Fred M. Vinson, nominated by President Truman.

Family: married Agnes Harvey, Sept. 7, 1899; two sons.

Died: April 22, 1946, Washington, D.C.

Personal Background

Harlan Fiske Stone was born Oct. 11, 1872, in Chesterfield, N.H., the son of Ann Sophia (Butler) and Frederick Lawson Stone, a New England farmer. Phi Beta Kappa and president of his class at Amherst College, Stone graduated with an A.B. in 1894, one year before Calvin Coolidge, and with an M.A. three years later.

A Columbia University law school graduate, Stone was admitted to the New York bar, married Agnes Harvey and began his legal practice with the firm, Sullivan & Cromwell, in 1899. For the next 25 years he divided his time between his Wall Street practice and a career as professor of law and dean at Columbia.

Public Career

In 1924 President Coolidge appointed his fellow Republican and Amherst alumnus to succeed controversial Harry M. Daugherty as attorney general. Stone began a reorganization of the Justice Department and recommended J. Edgar Hoover to head the FBI. The Supreme Court resignation of Justice McKenna in 1925 gave Coolidge the opportunity to promote his old friend to the bench after only a year in his Cabinet. Despite reservations over Stone's moderate conservatism and ties to Wall Street wealth (five years earlier he had been J. P. Morgan's counsel), Stone was confirmed by the Senate Feb. 5, 1925.

A spokesman for judicial restraint on the Taft and Hughes courts, Stone was nominated Chief Justice by President Roosevelt 16 years later.

When the Agricultural Adjustment Act was declared unconstitutional by a 6-3 majority in 1936, Stone had sided with the president, declaring that the court was not "the only agency of government that must be assumed to have the capacity to govern." Stone recognized the danger of the court's becoming a "legislative Constitution-making body," and Roosevelt needed a Chief Justice who would not thwart his programs. Moreover, a Republican appointment, the president felt, would show him to be a non-partisan leader. Favored by the press and bar, Stone's selection as Chief Justice was well received. Archibald MacLeish described the nomination as "the perfect word spoken at the perfect moment."

For Stone, the appointment was not the culmination of a lifelong ambition: "I cannot say I had any thought of being a member of the Supreme Court or any other court," said Stone recalling his ambitions as a 21-year-old college student, "for I believed then, as I do now, that the best insurance of a happy life and reasonable success in it is devotion to one's immediate job and happiness in doing it."

Stone achieved far more than "reasonable success." Progressing from the most junior to senior associate justice and finally to Chief Justice, he occupied consecutively, as none of his predecessors had done, every seat on the bench.

Stone's 21 years of service on the court ended suddenly. On April 22, 1946, while reading a dissent in a naturalization case, he was stricken, dying later in the day.

Owen Josephus Roberts
(1930-1945)

Born: May 2, 1875, Germantown, Pa.

Education: University of Pennsylvania, A.B., Phi Beta Kappa, 1895; LL.B. cum laude, 1898.

Official Positions: assistant district attorney, 1901-04; special deputy attorney general, eastern district of Pennsylvania, 1918; special United States attorney, 1924-30; chairman, Pearl Harbor Inquiry Board, 1941-42.

Supreme Court Appointment: nominated associate justice by President Herbert Hoover May 9, 1930, to replace Edward Terry Sanford, who died; confirmed by the U.S. Senate May 20, 1930, by a voice vote,; replaced by Harold H. Burton, nominated by President Truman.

Family: married Elizabeth Caldwell Rogers, 1904.

Died: May 17, 1955, West Vincent Township, Pa.

Personal Background

Roberts' ancestors left Wales in 1808 and settled in southeastern Pennsylvania. Roberts was a quiet youngster who displayed a love for books and an aptitude for debating. He attended the University of Pennsylvania, from which he graduated Phi Beta Kappa in 1895. He went on to the University of Pennsylvania Law School where he was the associate editor of the *American Law Register*, 1897-98, and graduated cum laude in 1898. Because of his distinguished academic record, Roberts was named a University Fellow in 1898, a position he held for two years. He continued to teach part-time at the university until 1919.

Public Career

Roberts entered private practice in Philadelphia in 1898. In 1901 he was named assistant district attorney in Philadelphia. Roberts returned to private practice in 1905 and built a prosperous business representing a large clientele, including several corporations.

Appointed a special deputy attorney general in 1918, Roberts prosecuted several cases in the Philadelphia area under the terms of the Espionage Act. In 1924 President Calvin Coolidge named him and former Senator Atlee Pomerene, D-Ohio (1911-23), as special United States attorneys to investigate the scandals of the Harding administration. Through thorough investigative work, Roberts uncovered a network of bribes to administration officials,

several of whom were convicted but received relatively short prison sentences. He returned to private practice once again in 1930.

In May 1930, after the Senate refused to confirm President Hoover's nomination of North Carolina judge John J. Parker to the Supreme Court because of Parker's rulings upholding "yellow dog" labor contracts and his derogatory comments on blacks, Roberts was named to replace him and was confirmed May 20, 1930.

In addition to his court duties, Roberts oversaw an investigation of the attack on Pearl Harbor and headed the Commission for the Protection and Salvage of Artistic and Historic Monuments in Europe that traced and catalogued art objects stolen or destroyed by the Germans during World War II.

After retiring from the court, he returned to his alma mater and served as dean of the University of Pennsylvania Law School from 1948 to 1951. He was involved in the world federalist movement and served in 1953 as the chairman of the Fund for the Advancement of Education. He died May 17, 1955, in West Vincent Township, Pa.

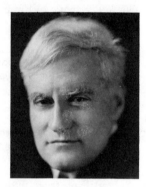

Benjamin Nathan Cardozo
(1932-1938)

Born: May 24, 1870, New York, N.Y.

Education: Columbia University, A.B., 1889; A.M., 1890; Columbia Law School, 1891 (no degree).

Official Positions: justice, supreme court of New York, 1914; judge, court of appeals for New York State., 1914-32, chief judge, 1926-32.

Supreme Court Appointment: nominated associate justice Feb. 15, 1932, by President Herbert Hoover, to replace Oliver Wendell Holmes Jr., who resigned; confirmed by the Senate Feb. 24, 1932, by a voice vote; replaced on the court by Felix Frankfurter, nominated by President Franklin D. Roosevelt.

Family: unmarried.

Died: July 9, 1938, Port Chester, N.Y.

Personal Background

The youngest son of Albert and Rebecca Washington Cardozo, Benjamin Nathan Cardozo was born in New York City on May 24, 1870. His parents were descendants of Sephardic Jews who had settled in New York in the mid-eighteenth century, and one of his ancestors authored the words at the base of the Statue of Liberty. Benjamin's childhood was spent in the aftermath of the Boss Tweed scandal, which implicated his father, a Tammany Hall judge, in the political corruption of the city government. Charged with graft, Albert Cardozo resigned rather than face impeachment.

At age 15, Benjamin Cardozo was admitted to Columbia University. He graduated with honors in 1889, completed his master's degree the following year and began to study at the law school. In 1891 he was admitted to the New York bar without a law degree — a not uncommon practice at that time — and began practicing appellate law with his older brother in the city. Cardozo remained a bachelor and had only a few close friends. He was very fond of his older unmarried sister Ellen and lived with her until her death in 1929.

Public Career

After 23 years as a private lawyer, Cardozo ran against Tammany Hall on the fusion ticket in 1914 and was elected by a narrow margin to the New York Supreme Court, the state's trial bench. Shortly thereafter, Governor Martin A. Glynn appointed him to a temporary position on the New York court of appeals, on which he was to serve for 18 years. Elected to a full term as associate judge in 1917, he became chief judge six years later and won for the court its reputation as the leading state court in the country. Cardozo's early judicial writings were used by lawyers as a handbook, and his lectures at Yale Law School on a number of topics were extended and published as *The Nature of the Judicial Process* in 1921, *The Growth of the Law* in 1924 and *The Paradoxes of Legal Science* four years later.

When 90-year-old Justice Holmes announced his retirement, Senator Robert F. Wagner, D-N.Y., presented Cardozo's name to President Hoover. University faculty, newspapermen, political leaders and members of the bar all voiced their endorsement of the New York judge. Within 10 days of Holmes' resignation, a tally of names received at the White House showed Cardozo a clear favorite. *The New York Times* described the unanimity of support for him as "quite without precedent."

Hoover was unconvinced, however. Two justices from New York, Hughes and Stone, and one Jew, Brandeis, were quite enough, he thought. Only after Stone offered his resignation (which was not accepted) on Cardozo's behalf did Hoover make his decision, appointing him Feb. 15, 1932. Harvard professor Zechariah Chafee Jr. praised the nomination: the president's choice "ignored geography and made history."

Cardozo served on the court for six years until his death in 1938 after a long illness. In *Nine Old Men*, columnists Drew Pearson and Robert S. Allen described the silver-haired justice as "the hermit philosopher." In the 1938 memorial court testimony, "the strangely compelling power of that reticent, sensitive and almost mystical personality" was remembered.

Hugo Lafayette Black
(1937-1971)

Born: Feb. 27, 1886, Harlan, Ala.
Education: Birmingham Medical College, 1903-04; University of Alabama, LL.B., 1906.
Official Positions: police court judge, Birmingham, 1910-11; solicitor, Jefferson County, Ala., 1915-17; United States Senator, D-Ala., 1927-37.
Supreme Court Appointment: nominated associate justice by President Franklin D. Roosevelt Aug. 12, 1937, to replace Willis Van Devanter, who retired; confirmed by the U.S. Senate Aug. 17, 1937, by a 63-16 vote; replaced by Lewis F. Powell Jr., nominated by President Nixon.
Family: married, first, Josephine Foster, February 1921, died 1951, two sons, one daughter; second, Elizabeth Seay DeMeritte, Sept. 11, 1957.
Died: Sept. 25, 1971, Washington, D.C.

Personal Background

The eighth child of a Baptist storekeeper and farmer, Hugo Black spent the first years of his life in the hill country near Harlan, Ala. When he was still a youngster, his family moved to Ashland, a larger community where his father's business prospered. Black attended the local schools in Ashland and after trying one year at Birmingham Medical College, decided to study law. At 18, he entered the University of Alabama Law School at Tuscaloosa.

Upon receipt of his LL.B., Black returned to Ashland and set up his first law practice. The following year a fire destroyed his office and library; Black left for Birmingham. There he quickly established a relationship with labor by defending the United Mine Workers strikers in 1908. Black also developed an expertise for arguing personal injury cases.

Public Career

He was named a part-time police court judge in Birmingham in 1911 and was elected county solicitor (public prosecutor) for Jefferson County in 1914. As solicitor, he gained a measure of local fame for his investigation of reports of the brutal means the police employed while questioning suspects at the notorious Bessemer jail. When he left the solicitor's post to enter the army in World War I, Black had succeeded in emptying a docket that had once held as many as 3,000 pending cases.

His brief military career kept him within the borders of the United States; he returned to practice in Birmingham in 1918, married a local woman the following year and continued to increase his business, still specializing in labor law and personal injury cases. In 1923 he joined the Ku Klux Klan, but resigned from the organization two years later just before announcing his intention to run for the Democratic nomination for the Senate seat held by Oscar Underwood, D-Ala. (1915-27). Campaigning as the poor man's candidate, Black won the party's endorsement and the subsequent election. He entered the Senate in 1927 and immediately began to study history and the classics at the Library of Congress to compensate for his lack of formal education.

During his two terms in the Senate Black used committee hearings to investigate several areas, including abuses of marine and airline subsidies and the activities of lobbying groups. In 1933 he introduced a bill to create a 30-hour work week. This legislation, after several alterations, was finally passed in 1938 as the Fair Labor Standards Act. One of the Senate's strongest supporters of President Roosevelt, Black spoke out in favor of Roosevelt's 1937 court-packing scheme and other New Deal programs. His support for the administration and his strong liberal instincts led the president to pick Black as his choice to fill the Supreme Court seat vacated by the retirement of Willis Van Devanter.

Black's previous affiliation with the Ku Klux Klan was widely reported in the national news media after his Senate confirmation. The furor quickly quieted, however, when the new justice admitted in a dramatic radio broadcast that he had indeed been a member of the Klan but added that he had resigned many years before and would comment no further. A man who during his court career always carried in his pocket a copy of the United States Constitution, Black retired from the court Sept. 17, 1971, after suffering a stroke. He died eight days later.

Stanley Forman Reed
(1938-1957)

Born: Dec. 31, 1884, Minerva, Ky.

Education: Kentucky Wesleyan University, A.B., 1902; Yale University, A.B., 1906; legal studies, University of Virginia and Columbia University (no degree); graduate studies, University of Paris, 1909-10.

Official Positions: general counsel, Federal Farm Board, 1929-32; general counsel, Reconstruction Finance Corporation, 1932-35; special assistant to attorney general, 1935; solicitor general, 1935-38.

Supreme Court Appointment: nominated associate justice by President Franklin D. Roosevelt Jan. 15, 1938, to replace George Sutherland, who resigned; confirmed by U.S. Senate Jan. 25, 1938, by a voice vote; replaced on court by Charles E. Whittaker, appointed by President Eisenhower.

Family: married Winifred Elgin, May 11, 1908; two sons.

Died: April 2, 1980, Huntington, N.Y.

Personal Background

Stanley Forman Reed was born Dec. 31, 1884, in tobacco-rich Mason County, Ky. His father, John A. Reed, practiced medicine and his mother, Frances Forman Reed, was active in political and social affairs and served from 1932-35 as registrar general of the National Society of Daughters of the American Revolution (DAR). Reed received undergraduate degrees from Kentucky Wesleyan and Yale Universities and studied law at the University of Virginia and Columbia University. He married Winifred Elgin from his hometown May 11, 1908, and they left the following year for Paris where he took graduate courses in civil and international law at the Sorbonne.

Reed practiced law in Maysville, Ky., population 6,500, with the firm, Browning, Reed & Zeigler, from 1910-

1917 and during this period served in the Kentucky General Assembly for four years. After a brief interim in the U.S. Army as a first lieutenant, he returned to his legal practice. The Chesapeake & Ohio Railroad and the Burley Tobacco Growers Cooperative were two of his clients.

Public Career

In 1929 Reed's experience with Burley Tobacco in market control through group sales became needed in Washington. Following the recommendation of the tobacco cooperative's president, James C. Stone, President Hoover appointed Reed general counsel for the Federal Farm Board, newly established to resell surpluses of American farm commodities abroad. After two years with the board, Reed was promoted to general counsel for the Reconstruction Finance Corporation, Hoover's loan-granting agency in the Depression to help banks, businesses and agricultural enterprises.

One of new President Roosevelt's most controversial economic policies was to raise prices by reducing the gold content of the dollar. He appointed Reed special assistant to the attorney general with the unique task of defending the government's legal right to change the requirement of certain private companies for payment in gold. Reed argued the *Gold Clause Cases* before the Supreme Court in 1935; his success with this assignment made Roosevelt confident that as solicitor general Reed would be able to argue persuasively before the Supreme Court the constitutionality of his New Deal legislation. Despite such defeats as the court's decision to invalidate the Agricultural Adjustment Act in 1936, Solicitor General Reed succeeded in defending the constitutionality of the National Labor Relations Act and other important measures of the Roosevelt era.

When Justice Sutherland retired in 1938, Roosevelt had the opportunity to add to the court the second justice of his choosing. Stanley Forman Reed, whose 10 years of government experience under both Republican and Democratic administrations and 17 years in private practice well qualified him for the bench, was his choice.

From 1939 to 1941 Justice Reed chaired President Roosevelt's Commission on Civil Service Improvement. After his resignation from the court in 1957, he also served as chairman of President Eisenhower's U.S. Civil Rights Commission. Reed soon left the commission because he felt his continued involvement with the federal judiciary disqualified him. Reed argued 35 cases before the Court of Claims and 25 cases before the Court of Appeals in the District of Columbia during his retirement. He maintained an office in the Supreme Court until his move to New York, where he resided until his death in 1980 at the age of 95.

Felix Frankfurter
(1939-1962)

Born: Nov. 15, 1882, Vienna, Austria.

Education: College of the City of New York, A.B., 1902; Harvard University School of Law, LL.B., 1906.

Official Positions: assistant United States attorney, southern New York district, 1906-09; law officer, Bureau of Insular Affairs, War Department, 1910-14; assistant to the secretary of war, secretary and counsel, President's Mediation Commission, assistant to the secretary of labor, 1917-18; chairman; War Labor Policies Board, 1918.

Supreme Court Appointment: nominated associate justice by President Franklin D. Roosevelt Jan. 5, 1939, to replace Benjamin Cardozo, who died; confirmed by the U.S. Senate Jan. 17, 1939, by a voice vote; replaced on the court by Arthur Goldberg, nominated by President Kennedy.

Family: married Marion A. Denman, Dec. 20, 1919.

Died: Feb. 22, 1965, Washington, D.C.

Personal Background

An Austrian Jew, Felix Frankfurter came to the United States with his parents in 1894 and was raised amidst the squalor of New York's Lower East Side. He attended City College and, after an impressive three years at Harvard University School of Law, took a job with a New York law firm but was soon recruited away by Henry L. Stimson, the United States attorney for the southern district of New York.

Public Career

Stimson had been appointed by President Theodore Roosevelt. At the end of the Roosevelt administration in 1909, Stimson went into private practice for a short time and brought Frankfurter with him. After an unsuccessful bid for the governorship of New York, Stimson was named secretary of war under President Taft.

Frankfurter accompanied his mentor to Washington, D.C., and was appointed legal officer in the War Department's Bureau of Insular Affairs.

In 1914 Harvard University offered Frankfurter a teaching post in the Law School and he happily returned to his alma mater. In addition to his teaching duties, Frankfurter became involved in the Zionist movement, argued a number of minimum wage and maximum hour cases for the National Consumers League and helped found the *New Republic*.

Frankfurter returned to Washington, D.C., in 1917 as an assistant to Secretary of War Newton D. Baker. That same year, President Wilson named a Mediation Commission to handle the rash of strikes obstructing the defense industry; Frankfurter was named its secretary and counsel. While serving on the commission, Frankfurter investigated the handling of the case of Tom Mooney, the alleged "Preparedness Day Parade Bomber," and the Bisbee (Ariz.) deportation case wherein approximately 1,000 miners were taken roughly from their labor camps in Arizona and dropped in a deserted town in New Mexico. In both instances Frankfurter found grounds to suspect that the rights of the individuals involved had been violated. This, as well as his highly publicized arguments in defense of Sacco and Vanzetti, his work with the National Association for the Advancement of Colored People, and the fact that he was a founding member of the American Civil Liberties Union earned him a reputation as a die-hard liberal that would follow him throughout his career.

He also served as chairman of the War Labor Policies Board. This position first introduced him to Franklin D.

Roosevelt who, as assistant secretary of the Navy, sat on the board.

At war's end, Frankfurter attended the Paris Peace Conference as a representative of the American Zionist Movement and then returned to Cambridge. In 1919, he married Marion A. Denman. The ceremony took place in Judge Learned Hand's chambers and was performed by Judge Benjamin Cardozo of the New York Court of Appeals.

At Harvard, Frankfurter enjoyed a growing reputation as an expert on the Constitution and the Supreme Court. He was offered a seat on the Massachusetts Supreme Judicial Court in 1932, which he declined. His friendship with Franklin Roosevelt grew closer; in 1933 the newly elected president asked him to be solicitor general, another post Frankfurter declined. He remained, however, a close adviser to the president and recommended to him a number of Harvard graduates eager to work in the Roosevelt administration, including Thomas G. Corcoran, one of the most influential New Dealers.

Named to the Supreme Court in 1939 to replace Justice Benjamin Cardozo, he was Roosevelt's third appointment. He continued to advise the president on a number of issues until Roosevelt's death in 1945. Frankfurter remained on the court until he suffered a debilitating stroke in 1962. He died in Washington, D.C., in 1965.

He was the author of *The Case of Sacco and Vanzetti*, 1927; *The Business of the Supreme Court* (with James M. Landis), 1928; *The Labor Injunction* (with Nathan Greene), 1930; *The Public and Its Government*, 1930; *The Commerce Clause Under Marshall, Taney and Waite*, 1937; *Mr. Justice Holmes and the Supreme Court*, 1939.

William Orville Douglas
(1939-1975)

Born: Oct. 16, 1898, Maine, Minn.

Education: Whitman College, B.A., 1920, Phi Beta Kappa; Columbia Law School, LL.B., 1925.

Official Positions: member, Securities and Exchange Commission, 1936-39, chairman, 1937-39.

Supreme Court Appointment: nominated associate justice by President Franklin D. Roosevelt March 20, 1939, to replace Louis D. Brandeis, who retired; confirmed by the Senate April 4, 1939, by a 62-4 vote; replaced on court by John Paul Stevens, nominated by President Ford.

Family: married, first, Mildred Riddle, Aug. 16, 1923, divorced 1954, one son, one daughter; second, Mercedes Hester, Dec. 14, 1954, divorced 1963; third, Joan Martin, August 1963, divorced 1966; fourth, Cathleen Heffernan, July 1966.

Died: Jan. 19, 1980, Washington, D.C.

Personal Background

Born into an impoverished farm family in Minnesota shortly before the turn of the 20th century, Douglas spent his early years in Yakima, Washington. A polio attack as a child sparked Douglas' lifelong passion for the outdoors, as he hiked the mountains near his home to build strength in his weakened legs.

After graduating from Whitman College in Walla Walla, Wash., in 1920, Douglas decided to pursue a law career. Despite his lack of funds, he determined to go east to study law at Columbia University Law School. Douglas quickly became one of the school's top students.

Following law school, a two-year stint with a prestigious Wall Street law firm convinced Douglas that representing corporate clients would not be to his liking. After a year back in Yakima, Douglas joined the law faculty of Columbia University. In 1929 he moved to New Haven, Conn., to teach law at Yale.

Public Career

By the time the Depression struck in 1929, Douglas had already developed a reputation as one of the country's foremost financial law experts. So when President Franklin D. Roosevelt needed staff for the newly formed Securities and Exchange Commission (SEC), created in 1934, he called on Douglas, who joined the commission in 1936; he became its chairman in 1937.

Douglas' 1939 Supreme Court nomination sailed through the Senate. Such easy relations with Congress, however, were not to mark Douglas' forthcoming years in Washington. Twice he faced the threat of impeachment, although neither in 1953 nor in 1970 did the move gain any real support.

Douglas' lifestyle and liberal political views — plus conservative resentment at the Senate's rejection of two of President Nixon's Supreme Court nominees — were the main spur behind the 1970 impeachment attempt. The justice's relations with the Parvin Foundation, recipient of considerable income from gambling interests, were held up for scrutiny. Anti-establishment sentiments expressed in one of his many books further fueled the attack. His controversial marital history also raised congressional eyebrows. But a special House judiciary subcommittee created to investigate the charges found no grounds for impeachment.

Douglas suffered a paralytic stroke in January 1975. At first, Douglas attempted to continue his work on the court, but in November 1975 he resigned, citing the continuing pain and physical disability. He had served 36 years and seven months, longer than any other justice. He died five years later, in January 1980, at the age of 81.

Francis William Murphy

(1940-1949)

Born: April 13, 1890, Harbor Beach, Mich.

Education: University of Michigan, A.B., 1912, LL.B., 1914; graduate study, Lincoln's Inn, London, and Trinity College, Dublin.

Official Positions: chief assistant attorney general, eastern district of Michigan, 1919-20; judge, Recorder's Court, Detroit, 1923-30; mayor of Detroit, 1930-33; governor general of Philippine Islands, 1933-35; U.S. high commissioner to Philippines, 1935-36; governor, state of Michigan, 1937-39; U.S. attorney general, 1939-40.

Supreme Court Appointment: nominated associate justice by President Franklin D. Roosevelt Jan. 4, 1940, to replace Pierce Butler, who died; confirmed by the U.S. Senate Jan. 15, 1940, by a voice vote; replaced on court by Tom C. Clark, nominated by President Truman.

Family: unmarried.

Died: July 19, 1949, Detroit, Mich.

Personal Background

Frank — christened Francis William — Murphy was born April 13, 1890, in Harbor Beach, Mich., the third child of Irish Catholic parents, John T. Murphy, a country lawyer, and his wife Mary (Brennan) Murphy. As a young boy, Frank promised his mother that he would never smoke or drink and he kept that promise until adulthood. He received his undergraduate and law degrees from the University of Michigan and after his admission to the bar in 1914 clerked for the Detroit firm, Monaghan & Monaghan, for three years, teaching law at night school. During World War I Murphy served with the American Expeditionary Force in France and with the Army of Occupation in Germany. He did not return home immediately after the war but took graduate courses at Lincoln's Inn in London and Trinity College in Dublin.

Public Career

Murphy began his career in Michigan as chief assistant attorney general for the eastern district. After practicing law in Detroit for three years, he became judge for the Recorder's Court, the principal criminal court in Detroit. In the midst of the Depression, Murphy, a pro-Labor Democrat and advocate of federal relief, was elected mayor of Detroit and served from 1930-33.

Franklin Delano Roosevelt was governor of New York during this period. The midwesterner supported Roosevelt's candidacy in 1932 and when he became president endorsed his Works Progress Administration (WPA) wholeheartedly.

In recognition of his support, Roosevelt named Murphy governor general of the Philippine Islands and in 1935, when commonwealth status was won, appointed him U.S. high commissioner. In the Far East as in the midwest, Murphy enacted such New Deal policies as maximum hour and minimum wage laws. Once the independent government was working smoothly, he returned to Michigan, but his high regard for the people of the Philippines continued. The American and Philippine flags hung side by side in his Supreme Court office.

From 1937-39 Murphy served as governor of Michigan. Immediately upon taking office, he was faced with a sit-down strike of 135,000 automotive workers. Murphy's refusal to call out the state troopers earned him many critics and cost him re-election in 1938.

Murphy aspired to be secretary of war in Roosevelt's cabinet. A bit of political juggling landed him the position of attorney general instead. Roosevelt had a lot of people to please. To Solicitor General (later Supreme Court justice) Robert H. Jackson he wrote, "I want you for my attorney general, Bob, but I want to name Murphy immediately to something and since I can't name him to what he himself wants, it is desirable to use the attorney generalship temporarily for that purpose." During his one year in that office, Murphy indicted a number of Democratic political bosses, most notably Tom Pendergast of Kansas City, brought suit against numerous trust companies and established the first civil rights unit in the Justice Department.

When Justice Butler died in 1939, President Roosevelt filled the vacancy in kind by appointing another Democrat and Catholic — Frank Murphy. Murphy did not want the job. To his parish priest he wrote, "I am not too happy about going on the court. A better choice could have been made." So anxious was he for involvement in the war effort that during court recesses Murphy served as an infantry officer in Fort Benning, Ga., much to the dismay of Chief Justice Stone.

On the court, described by Murphy as the "Great Pulpit," he preached civil liberties and his moralizing rhetoric gave birth to the saying "justice tempered with Murphy." Murphy's Catholicism did not influence his decisionmaking even where Jehovah's Witnesses, a strongly anti-Catholic sect, was concerned. He upheld their right to proselytize door to door and in the court's second flag-salute decision voted with the majority to invalidate the salute as a compulsory requirement in schools.

Frank Murphy died July 19, 1949, in Detroit, Mich., at the age of 59. With the sudden deaths that year of Murphy and Wiley B. Rutledge, the court lost two of its most consistently liberal spokesmen.

James Francis Byrnes

(1941-1942)

Born: May 2, 1879, Charleston, S.C.

Education: St. Patrick's Parochial School (never graduated); studied law privately, admitted to the bar in 1903.

Official Positions: court reporter, second circuit, S.C., 1900-08; solicitor, second circuit, S.C., 1908-10; U.S. House of Representatives, D-S.C., 1911-25; U.S. Senate, D-S.C., 1931-41; director, Office of Economic Stabilization, 1942-43; director, Office of War Mobilization and Reconversion, 1943-45; secretary of state, 1945-47; governor of South Carolina, 1951-55.

Supreme Court Appointment: nominated associate justice by President Franklin D. Roosevelt June 12, 1941, to replace James McReynolds, who retired; confirmed by the U.S. Senate June 12, 1941, by a voice vote; replaced on court by Wiley B. Rutledge, appointed by President Roosevelt.

Family: married Maude Busch, May 2, 1906; no children.

Died: April 9, 1972, Columbia, S.C.

Personal Background

The son of Irish immigrants, James Francis Byrnes was born May 2, 1879, in the Charleston of the post-Reconstruction South. He was named after his father, who died shortly before his birth. Elisabeth E. McSweeney Byrnes supported the family as a dressmaker. At age 14, James left school to work as a law clerk in a Charleston firm for $2 a week. With his mother's help he learned shorthand and won an exam for a court stenographer's job in Aiken, S.C., where he served as official court reporter for the second circuit for eight years, reading law in his spare time. Byrnes passed the bar in 1903 and the same year bought the Aiken newspaper, *Journal and Review,* and became its editor.

Public Career

As solicitor or district attorney for South Carolina's second circuit, Byrnes unexpectedly won a seat in the U.S. House of Representatives in 1910. "I campaigned on nothing but gall and gall won by 57 votes," he later reminisced. During his second term, he became well acquainted with Franklin Delano Roosevelt, Woodrow Wilson's assistant secretary of the Navy, who often appeared before the House Appropriations Committee on which Byrnes sat.

A speechwriter and political strategist for Roosevelt's campaign in 1932, he continued his loyal support of the administration during his two terms in the Senate despite his objections to certain New Deal labor and welfare policies. The president twice considered his friend as a running mate but decided in favor of Henry Wallace in 1940 and Senator Harry S Truman four years later. Byrnes' failure to obtain the vice presidential nomination was attributable in part to his unpopularity with northern liberals, and anti-Catholic sentiment despite his conversion to the Episcopalian faith.

Roosevelt rewarded Byrnes for his loyalty by nominating him to the Supreme Court June 12, 1941. So valuable was he to the president as a troubleshooter behind the scenes in the Senate that after Justice McReynolds announced his retirement in January, Roosevelt kept him in the Senate for six months before announcing him as McReynolds' successor.

Byrnes was restless on the court. "My country's at war and I want to be in it," he wrote. "I don't think I can stand the abstractions of jurisprudence at a time like this." He served only 16 months on the court, during which he wrote no concurring or dissenting opinions. Late in 1942 he resigned to take a more active part in the administration's war effort.

Both as director of the Office of Economic Stabilization from 1942-43 and as director of the Office of War Mobilization the following two years, Byrnes exercised great power in the administration. As the president himself stated when he called Byrnes from the court to the White House, "I want you to act as a judge and I will let it be known that your decision is my decision and that there is no appeal. For all practical purposes, you will be assistant President." In 1945 Byrnes accompanied Roosevelt to the meeting in Yalta with Stalin and Churchill, and as secretary of state in the Truman administration attended the Potsdam Conference.

Critical of the concentration of power in the Fair Deal government and criticized for his firm hand with the

Soviets as secretary of state, Byrnes resigned from Truman's cabinet in 1947. For four years he practiced law in South Carolina and in Washington, D.C., with the firm, Hogan & Hartson. A proponent of states' rights and separate-but-equal schooling for blacks, Byrnes was elected governor of South Carolina in 1950. This was the last public office of his distinguished career. Few justices held so many positions of responsibility after leaving the bench.

Byrnes' autobiography, *All in a Lifetime* (1958), was written during his retirement. His first book, *Speaking Frankly,* published in 1947, described his firsthand experience with postwar diplomacy. Byrnes died of a heart attack April 9, 1972, in Columbia, S.C.

Robert Houghwout Jackson
(1941-1954)

Born: Feb. 13, 1892, Spring Creek, Pa.

Education: local schools in Frewsburg, N.Y.; Albany (N.Y.) Law School, 1912.

Official Positions: general counsel, Internal Revenue Bureau, 1934-36; special counsel, Securities and Exchange Commission, 1935; assistant attorney general, 1936-38; solicitor general, 1938-39; attorney general, 1940-41; chief United States prosecutor, Nuremberg war crimes trial, 1945-46.

Supreme Court Appointment: nominated associate justice by President Franklin D. Roosevelt June 12, 1941, to replace Harlan F. Stone, who was promoted to Chief Justice; confirmed by the Senate July 7, 1941, by a voice vote; replaced on court by John Marshall Harlan, nominated by President Eisenhower.

Family: married Irene Gerhardt, April 24, 1916; one daughter, one son.

Died: Oct. 9, 1954, Washington, D.C.

Personal Background

A descendant of eighteenth-century settlers of Warren County, Pa., Jackson grew up across the border near Jamestown, N.Y., and began his law career there at 18 as an apprentice in a local firm. After a year studying law at Albany Law School, he began his career in earnest, laying the foundation for a lucrative general practice.

Public Career

Jackson entered politics at 21 when he was elected a Democratic state committeeman. His term as committeeman, marked by controversy over dispensing patronage posts, convinced Jackson that he preferred law to politics and he refused to run for re-election; he said later that politics had "filled my office with people who came there asking political favors and waging political fights."

His early contact with Roosevelt and his growing reputation as a talented advocate brought Jackson to Washington in 1934 as the counsel to the Internal Revenue Bureau, where he won a much-publicized $750,000 judgment in an income tax suit brought against the fabulously wealthy former Treasury Secretary Andrew W. Mellon. Jackson rose quickly in the Roosevelt administration: he was named assistant attorney general in 1936, solicitor general in 1938 and attorney general in 1940.

During that time, Jackson also became one of Roosevelt's closest advisers and supporters. He campaigned for the president's re-election in 1936 and was a chief assistant at the 1940 Democratic convention, supported the president's court-packing scheme and devised the legal means for Roosevelt in 1940 to give destroyers to Great Britain in exchange for American bases on British territories in the Caribbean, the West Indies and the North Atlantic.

Named to the Supreme Court in June 1941 to the seat vacated after Justice Stone was appointed Chief Justice, Jackson also served as the chief United States prosecutor at the Nuremburg war crimes trial in 1945-46. He originated the concept upon which the successful prosecution of the Nazi leaders was based, i.e., that it is a crime against international society to plan and wage an aggressive war.

While Jackson was in Germany, growing dissension among the Supreme Court justices reached a climax; it was reported that on the death of Chief Justice Harlan F. Stone, two justices had threatened to resign if Jackson was elevated to Chief Justice. Jackson exacerbated the controversy by releasing a letter he had written to President Truman castigating Justice Hugo L. Black for his participation in a case argued by Black's former law partner.

Jackson remained on the court until his death in 1954. He was the author of *The Struggle for Judicial Supremacy,* 1941; *Full Faith and Credit — The Lawyer's Clause of the Constitution,* 1945; *The Case Against the Nazi War Criminals,* 1946; *The Nuremberg Case,* 1947; and *The Supreme Court in the American System of Government,* 1955.

Wiley Blount Rutledge
(1943-1949)

Born: July 20, 1894, Cloverport, Ky.

Education: University of Wisconsin, A.B., 1914; University of Colorado, LL.B. 1922.

Official Positions: judge, Court of Appeals for District of Columbia, 1939-43.

Supreme Court Appointment: nominated associate justice by President Franklin D. Roosevelt Jan. 11, 1943, to replace James F. Byrnes, who resigned; confirmed by the Senate Feb. 8, 1943, by a voice vote; replaced on court by Sherman Minton, nominated by President Truman.

Family: married Annabel Person, August 28, 1917; two daughters, one son.

Died: Sept. 10, 1949, York, Maine.

Personal Background

In the small town of Cloverport, Ky., Mary Lou (Wigginton) Rutledge gave birth to her first son July 20, 1894, and named him for his father, Wiley Blount, a backwoods Baptist preacher. His mother's tubercular condition and his father's search for a pastorate caused the Rutledge family to move from Texas to Louisiana to North Carolina, finally settling in Asheville, N.C., where Pastor Rutledge found a position. When Wiley was nine years old, his mother died, whereupon his father took his three children and headed west again. Although raised in the conservative Christian tradition, Wiley Blount Rutledge later adopted the Unitarian faith.

An ancient-languages major and debating team captain, Rutledge transferred his junior year from Maryville College in Tennessee to the University of Wisconsin, from which he was graduated in 1914. Unable to afford legal studies there, he attended instead the University of Indiana law school part-time, supporting himself as a high school teacher in Bloomington.

Law school and teaching responsibilities proved too strenuous for Rutledge's health. He contracted a serious case of tuberculosis and went to recover in the mountains near Asheville. Two years later he married Annabel Person, a classmate at Maryville. They lived in New Mexico and Colorado, where he taught high school and continued to recuperate. He resumed his legal studies full-time at the University of Colorado and graduated in 1922, seven years after receiving his undergraduate degree. For the next two years Rutledge practiced law with the Boulder law firm, Goss, Kimbrough & Hutchinson, before returning to academia as a professor of law, and dean for more than 15 years.

Public Career

Rutledge first came to Franklin Delano Roosevelt's attention because of his outspoken support for the president's court-packing plan as dean of the University of Iowa College of Law from 1935-1939. So unpopular was the proposed judicial reorganization in the midwest that several Iowa state legislators threatened to withhold university salary increases to protest Dean Rutledge's unorthodox liberal stand. In a letter to his friend Irving Brant of the *St. Louis Star-Times* in 1936, Rutledge expressed confidence that Roosevelt would be able to gain control of the court if re-elected: "I feel sure he will have the opportunity to make a sufficient number of liberal appointments to undo the major harm."

Recommended by Justice Frankfurter and Irving Brant, Rutledge himself was appointed to the court seven years later. Although he had four years of federal judicial experience as a Roosevelt appointee to the Court of Appeals for the District of Columbia, some doubted his legal qualifications for the job. During Senate confirmation hearings Senator William Langer challenged "the wisdom of the choice of this inexperienced member of the bar. . . . Second-best generals and admirals will not bring us victory and peace. Second-best justices or legal mediocrities will not insure justice in our land."

Judicial experience, however, was not the president's deciding criterion. As he explained to his eighth and last Supreme Court appointee, "Wiley, we had a number of candidates for the court who were highly qualified, but they didn't have geography — you have that." Rutledge died suddenly September 10, 1949, after six years on the court.

Harold Hitz Burton
(1945-1958)

Born: June 22, 1888, Jamaica Plain, Mass.

Education: Bowdoin College, A.B., 1909; Harvard University LL.B., 1912.

Official Positions: Ohio House of Representatives, 1929; director of law, Cleveland, 1929-1932; acting mayor of Cleveland, Nov. 9, 1931-Feb. 20, 1932; mayor of Cleveland, 1935-40; United States Senate, 1941-45.

Supreme Court Appointment: nominated associate justice by President Harry S Truman Sept. 19, 1945, to replace Owen J. Roberts, who retired; confirmed by the U.S. Senate Sept. 19, 1945, by a voice vote; replaced by Potter Stewart, appointed by President Eisenhower.

Family: married Selma Florence Smith, June 15, 1912; two daughters, two sons.

Died: Oct. 28, 1964, Washington, D.C.

Personal Background

Burton grew up in Jamaica Plain, Mass., a suburb of Boston, in a Republican, Unitarian family. He received a B.A. from Bowdoin College, Brunswick, Maine, in 1909, and an LL.B. from Harvard University in 1912. He married a local woman, Selma Florence Smith of West Newton, Mass., and together they headed to Ohio, where Burton believed it would be easier to establish a law practice than in the East.

During the next five years, Burton engaged in private practice in Ohio (1912-14), worked for a Utah public utility (1914-16), and was an attorney for an Idaho public utility (1917). When World War I began, he was assigned to the 361st Infantry, United States Army, where he rose to the rank of captain. After the war, Burton returned to Cleveland and private practice.

Public Career

Burton served a one-year term as a Republican representative to the Ohio State legislature in 1929 and, that same year, was named Cleveland's director of law, a position he held until 1932. After a brief term as acting mayor of Cleveland in 1931-32, he won the 1935 mayoral election running as a reformer who would rid the city of gangsters. Twice re-elected by the largest majorities in the city's history, he was elected to the U.S. Senate in 1941. There he gained a reputation as an internationalist, particularly for his sponsorship of the "B²H²" resolution of 1943 which urged United States participation in a postwar international peace organization. (The resolution was named after its four sponsors, Sens. Burton, Joseph Ball, R-Minn., Carl Hatch, D-N.M., and Joseph Lister Hill, D-Ala.) Burton was also a member of the "Truman Committee" investigating fraudulent war claims against the government.

Justice Owen J. Roberts' retirement from the court July 31, 1945, gave President Truman his first opportunity to appoint a Supreme Court justice. The membership of the "New Deal" court was heavily Democratic, with the single exception of Chief Justice Harlan Fiske Stone, who had been appointed an associate justice by Republican President Calvin Coolidge. He had been named Chief Justice, however, by President Roosevelt. Truman was under considerable pressure to name a Republican to the vacant seat. By naming Burton, the president not only improved his relationship with Republican congressional leaders but also gained a justice who, though he was a member of the opposition, was at least a former colleague.

After 13 years on the bench, Burton, suffering from the debilitating Parkinson's disease, retired Oct. 13, 1958. He died six years later in Washington, D.C.

Frederick Moore Vinson

(1946-1953)

Born: January 22, 1890, Louisa, Ky.

Education: Centre College, A.B., 1909; LL.B., 1911.

Official Positions: commonwealth's attorney, 32nd judicial district, 1921-1924; U.S. House of Representatives, D-Ky., 1924-1929, 1931-1938; judge, Court of Appeals for District of Columbia, 1938-1943; director, Office of Economic Stabilization, 1943-1945; Federal Loan Administrator, 1945; director, Office of War Mobilization and Reconversion, 1945; secretary of the Treasury, 1945-1946.

Supreme Court Appointment: nominated Chief Justice by President Harry S Truman June 6, 1946, to replace Chief Justice Harlan F. Stone, who died; confirmed by the Senate June 20, 1946, by a voice vote; replaced on court by Earl Warren, nominated by President Eisenhower.

Family: married Roberta Dixson, January 24, 1923; two sons.

Died: September 8, 1953, Washington, D.C.

Personal Background

In the small town of Louisa, Ky., on Jan. 22, 1890, Fred M. — christened Frederick Moore — Vinson was born to James Vinson, the county jailer, and his wife, Virginia Ferguson Vinson. He worked his way through school, graduating with an A.B. from Centre College, Ky., in 1909 and from law school two years later. His 17 years of legal practice in the state began in 1911 when he passed the bar at the age of 21.

Public Career

Vinson's first official position came as commonwealth attorney for Kentucky's 32nd judicial district. When a vacancy occurred in Kentucky's 9th district for a U.S.

congressional seat, Vinson, a resident for 33 years and well-known for his grocery, milling and banking enterprises as well as for his legal practice, was elected. He served in the House from 1924-29 and from 1931-38, the intervening years spent practicing law in Ashland, Ky. An influential member of the House Ways and Means Committee, Vinson worked for passage of President Roosevelt's tax and coal programs.

He resigned his seat in 1938 to become judge for the Court of Appeals in the District of Columbia, a position to which he was appointed by Roosevelt in recognition of his New Deal support. After 12 years of legislative experience and five years in the federal judiciary, Vinson began his career in the executive branch as director of the Office of Economic Stabilization in the Roosevelt administration. His knowledge of tax matters and his ties with Congress well qualified him for this position.

Vinson gained further administrative experience as Federal Loan Administrator and director of the Office of War Mobilization and Reconversion, a post previously held by former congressman and Supreme Court Justice James F. Byrnes.

When Harry S Truman became president in 1945, he recognized his need for experienced advisers. Vinson's two years in the previous administration as a political organizer and congressional liaison made him valuable to Truman, who appointed him secretary of the Treasury. In this position Vinson administered the last of the war bond drives and recommended the Revenue Act of 1945 to raise taxes.

After the death of Harlan F. Stone, Vinson was appointed Chief Justice on June 6, 1946. Truman recognized in his friend and adviser someone who realized the need for strong government by the executive. As a congressman, Vinson had endorsed President Roosevelt's court-packing plan and on the court usually supported presidential authority in Truman's controversial decisions involving labor and Cold War-generated national security measures.

Such was the president's esteem for Vinson that he hoped he would succeed him in office. Vinson, however, did not aspire to the presidency.

Vinson died of a heart attack Sept. 8, 1953, ending seven years of service on the court.

Tom Campbell Clark

(1949-1967)

Born: Sept. 23, 1899, Dallas, Texas.

Education: University of Texas, A.B., 1921; L.L.B., 1922.

Official Positions: civil district attorney, Dallas County, Texas, 1927-1932; special assistant, Justice Department, 1937-1943; assistant attorney general, 1943-1945; attorney general, 1945-1949; director, Federal Judicial Center, 1968-1970; U.S. Court of Appeals, various circuits, by special arrangement, 1967-1977.

Supreme Court Appointment: nominated associate justice by President Harry S Truman Aug. 2, 1949, to replace Frank Murphy, who died; confirmed by the U.S. Senate Aug. 18, 1949, by a 73-8 vote; replaced on the court by Thurgood Marshall, nominated by President Johnson.

Family: Married Mary Jane Ramsey, Nov. 8, 1924; one daughter, two sons.

Died: June 13, 1977, New York, N.Y.

Personal Background

The son of a prominent Dallas lawyer active in Democratic politics in Texas, Tom Clark maintained a close relationship with the Democratic party throughout most of his life. After a brief stint in the infantry that failed to extend beyond training in Texas because the war ended, Clark entered the University of Texas, where he received his A.B. in 1921 and his LL.B. a year later. While a student he met Mary Jane Ramsey, the daughter of a Texas supreme court justice. They were married in 1924.

Public Career

Clark practiced law in his father's firm until his friendship with the Democratic party in general — and Tom Connally, D-Texas (House 1917-29, Senate 1929-53), in particular — resulted in his appointment as Dallas civil district attorney in 1927. He returned to private practice in 1932.

Named a special assistant in the Justice Department in 1937, Clark worked in antitrust matters, was the civilian coordinator of the program to evacuate Japanese-Americans from the West Coast, and prosecuted fraudulent war claims, an activity which brought him into contact with then-Sen. Harry S Truman, D-Mo., head of the Senate War Investigating Committee. Clark was promoted to assistant attorney general in 1943 and the following year cultivated his friendship with Truman by supporting his vice presidential bid at the Democratic convention. When Truman assumed the presidency after the death of Franklin Roosevelt in 1945, he chose Clark as his attorney general. During his four years as the president's lawyer, Clark remained active in antitrust and led the efforts of his department to prosecute the American leaders of the Communist Party and other alleged subversives. The department also drafted the first attorney general's list of dangerous political organizations. Truman relied on the anticommunist zeal of his Justice Department to defend his administration against charges of being "soft" on communism in the 1948 presidential campaign.

Truman, in his third appointment to the Supreme Court, nominated Clark Aug. 2, 1949, to replace Justice Frank Murphy, the only Roman Catholic then on the bench. The president was criticized for his choice of Clark, a Presbyterian, but Truman argued that religious considerations should not apply to the selection of Supreme Court justices.

To avoid any appearance of a conflict of interest, Clark resigned from the court in 1967 when President Johnson named his son, Ramsey Clark, attorney general.

Clark was a founder of the Federal Judicial Center, a unit within the judicial branch that studies ways to improve the administration of the courts, and served as its first director, 1968-1970. Until his death in June 1977, he accepted assignments on various circuits of the United States Court of Appeals to help ease the federal caseload.

Sherman Minton
(1949-1956)

Born: October 20, 1890, Georgetown, Ind.

Education: Indiana University, LL.B., 1915; Yale University, LL.M., 1917.

Official Positions: Indiana public counselor, 1933-1934; U.S. Senate, D-Ind., 1935-1941; administrative assistant to President Franklin Delano Roosevelt, 1941; federal judge, Seventh Circuit Court of Appeals, 1941-1949.

Supreme Court Appointment: nominated associate justice by President Harry S Truman September 15, 1949, to replace Wiley B. Rutledge, who died; confirmed by the U.S. Senate October 4, 1949, by a 48-16 vote; replaced on court by William J. Brennan Jr., nominated by President Eisenhower.

Family: married Gertrude Gurtz, August 11, 1917; two sons, one daughter.

Died: April 9, 1965, in New Albany, Ind.

Personal Background

Sherman Minton, the son of John Evan and Emma Lyvers Minton, was born on Oct. 20, 1890, in the village of Georgetown, Ind., eight miles from New Albany, his residence for many years, and was raised in a middle-class midwestern home. Tall and broad-shouldered, Shay, as he was called by his friends, attended Indiana University where he excelled in football and basketball as well as his studies. In 1925 he graduated at the top of his class at the law college; future GOP presidential candidate Wendell L. Willkie and Paul V. McNutt, who later became governor of Indiana, were classmates. After graduation Minton left the state with a $500 scholarship to attend Yale Law School for a year of graduate studies.

Public Career

McNutt appointed his former classmate and fellow liberal Democrat to his first official position, as an Indiana public counselor, in 1933. Two years later Minton successfully ran for the Senate on the New Deal ticket. "Sure I'm a New Dealer. I'd be ashamed to be an old dealer," he once explained. Minton's political career was adversely affected by his other notable classmate, Willkie. Minton lost his bid for Senate re-election in 1940 due to support for the Willkie ticket in their home state of Indiana.

Beginning his third term as president, Franklin Delano Roosevelt remembered Minton's Senate endorsement of his plan to pack the court with justices of his choosing and his support for other New Deal policies. In 1941 the president asked Minton to join his staff as an adviser in charge of coordinating military agencies and later that year appointed him to the Seventh Circuit Court of Appeals. In the White House, Minton backed Harry S Truman's efforts in the Senate to establish a new committee to investigate defense activities. The two men had become good friends in 1935 as freshman senators. "As far as you are concerned I am just as approachable as I was when we sat together in the Senate," President Truman wrote Minton ten years later.

After Wiley B. Rutledge's death it took Truman only five days to name his replacement on the Supreme Court: Sherman Minton, a fellow midwesterner, a political supporter and friend of nearly 15 years. He was appointed to the court September 15, 1949. Although a liberal legislator, Minton proved to be a conservative justice. Most of his decisions favored the restrictive powers of the government over the civil liberties of the individual.

Pernicious anemia forced Minton to resign on Oct. 15, 1956, after seven years of service. His retirement announcement suggests that perhaps his career on the court had not been as influential as he might have hoped: "There will be more interest in who will succeed me than in my passing. I'm an echo."

He spent the last nine years of his life in retirement in his hometown of New Albany, Ind., and died in 1965.

Earl Warren
(1953-1969)

Born: March 19, 1891, Los Angeles, Calif.

Education: University of California, B.L., 1912; J. D., 1914.

Official Positions: deputy city attorney of Oakland, Calif., 1919-20; deputy assistant district attorney, Alameda County, 1920-23; chief deputy district attorney, Alameda County, 1923-25; district attorney, Alameda County, 1925-39; attorney general of California, 1939-43; governor of California, 1943-53.

Supreme Court Appointment: nominated Chief Justice by President Dwight D. Eisenhower Sept. 30, 1953, to replace Chief Justice Fred M. Vinson, who died; confirmed March 1, 1954, by a voice vote; replaced on the court by Warren E. Burger, nominated by President Nixon.

Family: married Nina P. Meyers, Oct. 14, 1925; three sons, three daughters.

Died: July 9, 1974, Washington, D.C.

Personal Background

Warren was born in Los Angeles, Calif., the son of Scandinavian immigrant parents. Soon afterwards, the family moved to Bakersfield, where his father worked as a railroad car repairman. In 1938, after Warren had become active in politics, his father was bludgeoned to death in a crime that was never solved.

Warren worked his way through college and law school at the University of California. After graduation, he worked in law offices in San Francisco and Oakland, the only time in his career that he engaged in private practice.

Public Career

From 1920 until his resignation from the Supreme Court in 1969, Warren served without interruption in public office. His first post was deputy city attorney for Oakland. Then Warren was named a deputy district attorney for Alameda County, which embraces the cities of Oakland, Alameda, and Berkeley.

In 1925 Warren was appointed district attorney when the incumbent resigned. He won election to the post in his own right in 1926, 1930, and 1934. During his 14 years as district attorney, Warren developed a reputation as a crime fighter, sending a city manager and several councilmen to jail on graft charges and smashing a crooked deal involving garbage collection.

A Republican, Warren decided in 1938 to run for state attorney general. He cross-filed and won three primaries — his own party's, as well as the Democratic and Progressive Party contests.

In 1942 Warren ran for governor of California. Although he was at first rated an underdog, he wound up defeating incumbent Democratic Governor Culbert Olson by a margin of 342,000, winning 57.1 percent of the total votes cast. He was twice re-elected, winning the Democratic as well as the Republican nomination in 1946 and defeating Democrat James Roosevelt, son of President Franklin D. Roosevelt, by an almost two-to-one margin in 1950.

At first viewed as a conservative governor — he denounced "communistic radicals" and supported the wartime federal order to move all persons of Japanese ancestry away from the West Coast — Warren developed a progressive image after the war. In 1945 he proposed a state program of prepaid medical insurance and later championed liberal pension and welfare benefits.

Warren made two bids for national political office. In 1948 he ran for vice president on the Republican ticket with Gov. Thomas E. Dewey of New York. In 1952 he sought the Republican presidential nomination. But with little chance to win, he threw his support at a crucial moment behind Gen. Dwight D. Eisenhower, helping him win the battle against Sen. Robert A. Taft of Ohio for the nomination.

That support resulted in Eisenhower's political indebtedness to Warren, which the president repaid in 1953, after the death of Chief Justice Fred M. Vinson, by nominating the Californian to replace him. Reflecting on his choice years later in light of the Warren Court's liberal record, Eisenhower called the Warren appointment "the biggest damn-fool mistake I ever made."

In addition to his work on the court, Warren headed the commission which investigated the assassination of President John F. Kennedy. Warren retired in 1969, and died five years later.

John Marshall Harlan
(1955-1971)

Born: May 20, 1899, Chicago, Ill.

Education: Princeton University, B.A., 1920; Rhodes Scholar, Oxford University, Balliol College, B.A. in jurisprudence, 1923; New York Law School, LL.B., 1925.

Official Positions: assistant U.S. attorney, southern district of New York, 1925-27; special assistant attorney general of New York state, 1928-30; chief counsel, New York State Crime Commission, 1951-53; judge, U.S. Court of Appeals for the Second Circuit, 1954-55.

Supreme Court Appointment: nominated associate justice by President Dwight D. Eisenhower Nov. 8, 1954, to replace Robert Jackson, who died; Senate consideration postponed, formally renominated Jan. 10, 1955; confirmed by the U.S. Senate on March 16, 1955, by a 71-11 vote; replaced on the court by William H. Rehnquist, nominated by President Nixon.

Family: married Ethel Andrews, Nov. 10, 1928; one daughter.

Died: Dec. 29, 1971, Washington D.C.

Personal Background

The namesake and grandson of Supreme Court Justice (1877-1911) John Marshall Harlan, Harlan was born in Chicago, where his father was a prominent attorney. His father, John Maynard Harlan, was also engaged in politics, running two losing races for mayor of Chicago near the turn of the century.

The younger Harlan attended Princeton University, graduating in 1920. Awarded a Rhodes Scholarship, he spent the next three years studying jurisprudence at Balliol College, Oxford. Returning to the United States, he earned his law degree in 1924 from New York Law School.

Public Career

For the next 25 years Harlan was a member of a prominent Wall Street law firm, but took periodic leaves to serve in various public positions. In 1925 he became an assistant U.S. attorney for the southern district of New York. He returned to private practice but soon left again, this time to serve as one of the special prosecutors in a state investigation of municipal graft.

During World War II, Harlan served as head of the Operational Analysis Section of the Eighth Air Force. After the war he returned to private practice, but was soon called again to public service. From 1951 to 1953 he was chief counsel to the New York State Crime Commission, which Gov. Thomas E. Dewey had appointed to investigate the relationship between organized crime and state government.

During the same period, Harlan also became active in various professional organizations, serving as chairman of the committee on professional ethics of the Association of the Bar of the City of New York and later as chairman of its committee on the judiciary and as vice president of the association.

A lifelong Republican, Harlan was nominated in January 1954 by President Eisenhower to the U.S. court of appeals for the second circuit. Harlan had hardly begun his work there, however, when the president named him in November 1954 to the U.S. Supreme Court. The Senate, then in special session to consider the censure of Sen. Joseph R. McCarthy, postponed consideration of his nomination until the new Congress met in 1955, so Harlan remained on the appeals court until confirmed by the Senate in March 1955.

William Joseph Brennan Jr.
(1956-   )

Born: April 25, 1906, Newark, N.J.

Education: University of Pennsylvania, B.S., 1928; Harvard Law School, LL.B., 1931.

Official Positions: New Jersey superior court judge, 1949-50; appellate division, 1950-52; associate justice, New Jersey Supreme Court, 1952-56.

Supreme Court Appointment: received a recess appointment as an associate justice by President Dwight D. Eisenhower Oct. 16, 1956, to replace Sherman Minton, who resigned; nominated as an associate justice by President Eisenhower Jan. 14, 1957; confirmed by the U.S. Senate March 19, 1957 by a voice vote.

Family: married Marjorie Leonard, May 5, 1928; two sons, one daughter.

Personal Background

Brennan was born in Newark, N.J., the second of eight children of Irish parents who immigrated to the United States in 1890. Brennan displayed impressive academic abilities early in life. He was an outstanding student in high school, an honors student at the University of Pennsylvania's Wharton School of Finance, and graduated in the top 10 percent of his Harvard Law School Class in 1931.

After law school Brennan returned to Newark, where he joined a prominent law firm. After the passage of the Wagner Labor Act in 1935, he began to specialize in labor law.

With the outbreak of World War II, Brennan entered the Army, serving as a manpower troubleshooter on the staff of the undersecretary of war, Robert B. Patterson. At the conclusion of the war, Brennan returned to his old law firm. But as his practice swelled, Brennan, a devoted family man, began to resent the demands which it placed on his time.

Public Career

A desire to temper the pace of his work was one of the reasons Brennan accepted an appointment to the newly created New Jersey superior court in 1949. Brennan had been a leader in the movement to establish the court as part of a large program of judicial reform. Thus it was not surprising when Republican Gov. Alfred E. Driscoll named Brennan, a registered but inactive Democrat, to the court.

During his tenure on the superior court, Brennan's use of pre-trial procedures to speed up the disposition of cases brought him to the attention of New Jersey supreme court justice Arthur T. Vanderbilt. It was reportedly at Vanderbilt's suggestion that Brennan was moved first in 1950 to the appellate division of the superior court and then in 1952 to the state supreme court. Late in 1956, when President

Eisenhower was looking for a justice to replace Sherman Minton, Vanderbilt and others strongly recommended Brennan for the post, and Eisenhower gave him a recess appointment in October. There was some criticism that Eisenhower was playing politics by nominating a Roman Catholic Democrat to the bench so close to the election in order to curry favor with voters. But Brennan's established integrity and non-political background minimized the impact of the charges.

Charles Evans Whittaker
(1957-1962)

Born: February 22, 1901, Troy, Kansas.

Education: University of Kansas City Law School, LL.B., 1924.

Official Positions: federal judge, U.S. district court for western district of Missouri, 1954-1956; judge, Eighth Circuit Court of Appeals, 1956-1957.

Supreme Court Appointment: nominated associate justice by President Dwight D. Eisenhower March 2, 1957, to replace Stanley Reed, who resigned; confirmed by the U.S. Senate March 19, 1957, by a voice vote; replaced on court by Byron R. White, nominated by President Kennedy.

Family: married Winifred R. Pugh, July 7, 1928; three sons.

Died: November 26, 1973, Kansas City, Missouri.

Personal Background

Charles Evans Whittaker's beginnings were humble. The son of Charles and Ida Miller Whittaker, he was born in eastern Kansas on February 22, 1901, and raised on his father's farm. After his nomination to the Supreme Court, Whittaker described to the Senate Judiciary Committee his early life: "I went to school in a little white school house on the corner of my father's farm through nine grades and then I went to high school in Troy, Kansas, and rode a pony to school through six miles of mud night and morning for about a year and a half."

Whittaker quit school after his mother died on his sixteenth birthday. Four years later he applied to the University of Kansas City Law School and was accepted only after agreeing to private tutoring in the high school subjects he had missed. His education was financed from the sale of pelts of animals he trapped on the Kansas plains and from part-time work as an office boy in the law firm, Watson, Gage & Ess. In 1923 he passed the Missouri bar exams and a year later graduated from law school.

Whittaker joined the law firm that he had served as office boy and after two years became a senior partner. He represented many corporate clients including Union Pacific and Montgomery Ward.

Public Career

Whittaker served as president of the Missouri Bar Association from 1953-1954. His distinguished legal career included service as a judge on the U.S. District Court for the Western District from 1954 to 1956 and on the U.S. Court of Appeals for the Eighth Circuit in 1956 and 1957.

President Eisenhower considered previous judicial experience one of the most important criteria for a Supreme Court justice. Whittaker's outstanding qualifications as well as his ties to the Republican party made him a likely choice to fill the vacancy left by Stanley Reed's retirement. On March 19, 1957, Charles Whittaker became the first Supreme Court justice born in Kansas and appointed from Missouri.

Physically exhausted from overwork, Whittaker followed his doctor's advice and resigned from the court at the age of 61 after only five years of service.

Following his retirement Whittaker did not return to his former legal practice nor was he active in public life. In 1965 he served on the legal staff of General Motors and the following year was asked by the Senate Committee on Standards and Conduct to help devise a code of senatorial ethics. The spread of civil disobedience in the 1960s particularly disturbed him and he addressed the American Bar Association on various occasions concerning the need for "redress in the courts rather than in the streets."

Potter Stewart
(1958-1981)

Born: Jan. 23, 1915, Jackson, Mich.

Education: Yale University, B.A., cum laude, 1937; Yale Law School, LL.B., cum laude, 1941; fellow, Cambridge University, Cambridge, England, 1937-38.

Official Positions: member, Cincinnati, Ohio, city council 1950-53; vice mayor of Cincinnati, 1952-53; judge, U.S. Court of Appeals for the sixth circuit, 1954-58.

Supreme Court Appointment: received recess appointment as associate justice from President Dwight D. Eisenhower Oct. 14, 1958, to replace Harold H. Burton, who resigned; nominated associate justice by President Eisenhower Jan. 17, 1959; confirmed by the U.S. Senate May 5, 1959, by a 70-17 vote.

Family: married Mary Ann Bertles, April 24, 1943; two sons, one daughter.

Personal Background

Stewart was the son of an established middle-class Cincinnati family with a strong tradition of public service and a respect for the benefits of a good education. Stewart's father, James Garfield Stewart, was mayor of Cincinnati from 1938 to 1947 and was the Republican nominee for governor of Ohio in 1944. He served on the Ohio Supreme Court from 1947 until his death in 1959.

After early schooling in Cincinnati, Stewart was sent to two of the most prestigious eastern schools — Hotchkiss preparatory and Yale University, where he received numerous academic honors and graduated Phi Beta Kappa in 1937. After completing his undergraduate work at Yale, he spent a year abroad doing postgraduate work at Cambridge University in England. Returning to the United States in 1938, he began law school at Yale. After graduation in 1941, Stewart moved to New York, where he joined a Wall Street law firm. He had hardly begun work there, however, when World War II broke out and he joined the Navy.

After the war, Stewart at first returned to his New York law practice but soon moved to his home town of Cincinnati, where he joined one of its leading law firms.

Public Career

Once Stewart settled in Cincinnati, he took up the family's tradition of public service. He was twice elected to the city council and served one term as vice mayor. He was also actively involved in the 1948 and 1952 Republican presidential campaigns, when he supported Sen. Robert A. Taft. When Eisenhower won the party's endorsement instead in 1952, Stewart actively supported him in the fall campaign.

Stewart's appointment in 1954 to the U.S. Court of Appeals for the sixth circuit ended his direct participation in politics. He was President Eisenhower's fifth and last appointment to the Supreme Court. He received a recess appointment in 1958, and Eisenhower sent his nomination to the new Congress early in 1959.

Stewart retired July 3, 1981, saying he wished to leave the court while he was still relatively young and healthy enough to enjoy additional time with his family.

Byron Raymond White

(1962-   )

Born: June 8, 1917, Fort Collins, Colo.

Education: University of Colorado, B.A., Phi Beta Kappa, 1938; Rhodes Scholar, Oxford University, 1939; Yale Law School, LL.B., magna cum laude, 1946.

Official Positions: law clerk to Chief Justice Fred M. Vinson, 1946-47; U.S. deputy attorney general, 1961-62.

Supreme Court Appointment: nominated associate justice by President John F. Kennedy March 30, 1962, to replace Charles E. Whittaker, who resigned; confirmed by the U.S. Senate April 11, 1962, by a voice vote.

Family: married Marion Stearns, 1946; one son, one daughter.

Personal Background

White was born in Fort Collins, Colo., but grew up in Wellington, a small town in the sugar beet area of the state.

His father was in the lumber business and served as a Republican mayor of Wellington.

Ranking first in his high school class, White in 1934 won a scholarship to the University of Colorado, where he earned a reputation as an outstanding scholar-athlete. He was first in his class, a member of Phi Beta Kappa and the winner of three varsity letters in football, four in basketball and three in baseball. By the end of his college career in 1938 he had been dubbed "Whizzer" White for his prowess as a football player, a performance which earned him both a national reputation and a one-year contract with the old Pittsburgh Pirates professional football team.

But after a year as a pro football player, White sailed for England to attend Oxford University, where he had received a coveted Rhodes Scholarship. When World War II broke out in September 1939, White returned to the United States and enrolled in Yale Law School, alternating law study with playing professional football for the Detroit Lions.

When the United States entered the war, White served in the Navy in the South Pacific. He returned to Yale after the war, earning his law degree magna cum laude.

Public Career

After graduation from law school, White served as law clerk to the new Chief Justice, Fred M. Vinson. In 1947 he returned to his native Colorado, where for the next 14 years he practiced law with a prominent Denver law firm.

Several times during his adult life, White had crossed paths with the young John F. Kennedy. The two first met when White was studying at Oxford and Kennedy's father, Joseph, was ambassador to the Court of St. James. They met again during White's wartime service in the South Pacific. And when White clerked for Vinson in Washington in 1946-47, he renewed his acquaintance with Kennedy, then a freshman U.S. Representative.

In 1960, when Kennedy decided to run for president, White joined the campaign and headed the pre-convention Kennedy effort in Colorado. After Kennedy's nomination, White became chairman of the National Citizens for Kennedy organization, designed to attract independents and Republicans.

After his election, Kennedy named White to the post of deputy attorney general, a position he held until Kennedy named him to the Supreme Court in 1962.

Arthur Joseph Goldberg

(1962-1965)

Born: Aug. 8, 1908, Chicago, Ill.

Education: Northwestern University, B.S.L., 1929; J.D., summa cum laude, 1930.

Official Positions: secretary of labor, 1961-1962; United States Ambassador to the United Nations, 1965-1968.

Supreme Court Appointment: nominated associate justice by President John F. Kennedy Aug. 29, 1962, to replace Felix Frankfurter, who retired; confirmed by the U.S. Senate Sept. 25, 1962, by a voice vote. Appointed U.S. Ambassador to the United Nations July 20, 1965, by President Lyndon B. Johnson; replaced on the court by Abe Fortas, nominated by President Johnson.

Family: married Dorothy Kurgans, July 18, 1931; one daughter, one son.

Personal Background

The youngest of 11 children born to his Russian Jewish parents, Goldberg was admitted to the Illinois bar at age 20. He first gained national attention as counsel to the Chicago Newspaper Guild during its 1938 strike. After serving as a special assistant in the Office of Strategic Services during World War II, Goldberg returned to the practice of labor law, representing both the Congress of Industrial Organizations (CIO) and the United Steelworkers of America. He played a key role in the 1955 merger of the CIO with the American Federation of Labor and worked as a special counsel to the AFL-CIO until 1961.

Public Career

Appointed secretary of labor in the first year of the Kennedy administration, Goldberg's tenure saw the passage of the Area Redevelopment Act of 1961, congressional approval of an increase in the minimum wage and the reorganization of the Office of Manpower Administration (now the Employment and Training Administration).

Goldberg was President Kennedy's second Supreme Court appointment, named Aug. 29, 1962, to replace Felix Frankfurter, who had held the "Jewish seat" since 1939. It had been occupied formerly by Justice Benjamin N. Cardozo, 1932-38.

President Johnson named Goldberg U.S. Ambassador to the United Nations July 20, 1965, to replace Adlai Stevenson, who had died July 14 in London. Goldberg resigned the post in 1968. After an unsuccessful race for governor of New York against Republican incumbent Nelson Rockefeller in 1970, Goldberg returned to Washington, D.C., where he remains in private practice. A frequent guest instructor at universities and colleges, he is the author of *AFL-CIO: Labor United*, 1956; *Defenses of Freedom*, 1966; *Equal Justice: The Warren Era of the Supreme Court*, 1972.

Abe Fortas
(1965-1969)

Born: June 19, 1910, Memphis, Tenn.
Education: Southwestern College, A.B., 1930; Yale Law School, LL.B., 1933.

Official Positions: assistant director, corporate reorganization study, Securities and Exchange Commission, 1934-37; assistant director, public utilities division, Securities and Exchange Commission, 1938-39; general counsel, Public Works Administration, 1939-40, and counsel to the bituminous coal division, 1939-41; director, division of power, Department of the Interior, 1941-42; under secretary of the interior, 1942-46.

Supreme Court Appointment: nominated associate justice by President Lyndon B. Johnson July 28, 1965, to replace Arthur J. Goldberg, who resigned; confirmed by the U.S. Senate Aug. 11, 1965, by a voice vote; replaced on the court by Harry A. Blackmun, nominated by President Nixon.

Family: married Carolyn Eugenia Agger, July 9, 1935.

Personal Background

Fortas, the son of an English immigrant cabinetmaker, was born on June 19, 1910, in Memphis, Tenn. After working his way through Southwestern College in Memphis, from which he received a B.A. in 1930, Fortas went north to Yale Law School. He served as editor of the school's law journal and graduated in 1933.

Fortas developed an interest in music and began to play the violin in various string quartets, a practice he has continued throughout his life. In 1935 he married Carolyn Eugenia Agger, who became a renowned tax lawyer in her own right.

Upon graduation, Fortas became an associate professor of law at Yale. But the excitement and activity generated by President Franklin D. Roosevelt's New Deal in Washington soon enticed the young lawyer away from academic pursuits and into public affairs.

Public Career

Throughout the 1930s Fortas held a series of jobs in the Roosevelt administration, mostly involving detailed legal work in such newly created agencies as the Securities and Exchange Commission and the Public Works Administration. In 1942 he was appointed under secretary of the interior, serving under the controversial and irascible Harold L. Ickes.

Following the Second World War, Fortas helped found the law firm of Arnold, Fortas and Porter, which quickly became one of Washington's most prestigious legal institutions. The firm specialized in corporation law, but its members, including Fortas, found time to litigate some important civil and individual rights cases as well.

In 1948 Fortas successfully defended a congressman from Texas — Lyndon B. Johnson — in a challenge to Johnson's election victory in the Texas Democratic senatorial primary. That defense was the basis for an enduring friendship between the two men, and Fortas became one of Johnson's most trusted advisers.

Preferring his role as confidential adviser, Fortas in 1964 declined Johnson's offer to name him attorney general. But when Arthur J. Goldberg resigned from the Supreme Court in 1965, Johnson ignored Fortas' opposition and appointed him to the Supreme Court.

When Chief Justice Earl Warren voiced his intention to resign in 1968, Johnson decided to elevate Fortas to the Chief Justiceship. But amid charges of "cronyism," events began to unfold which ultimately led to Fortas' undoing.

In the face of strong opposition from Republicans and conservative Democrats, Johnson was finally forced to withdraw the nomination, but not before it was revealed that Fortas had received $15,000 to teach a course at a local university.

Then, in May of 1969, *Life* magazine revealed that since becoming a justice Fortas had accepted — and then returned several months later — $20,000 from a charitable foundation controlled by the family of an indicted stock manipulator.

The allegations touched off talk of impeachment proceedings against Fortas. In mid-May, despite his denial of any "wrongdoing on my part," Fortas resigned from the court. He then returned to private law practice in Washington in partnership with another attorney.

Thurgood Marshall

(1967-　　)

Born: July 2, 1908, Baltimore, Md.

Education: Lincoln University, A.B., cum laude, 1930; Howard University Law School, LL.B., 1933.

Official Positions: judge, U.S. Court of Appeals for the second circuit, 1961-65; U.S. Solicitor General, 1965-67.

Supreme Court Appointment: nominated associate justice by President Lyndon B. Johnson June 13, 1967, to replace Tom C. Clark, who resigned; confirmed by the U.S. Senate Aug. 30, 1967, by a 69-11 vote.

Family: married Vivian Burey, Sept. 4, 1929, died February 1955, two sons; married Cecelia Suryat, Dec. 17, 1955.

Personal Background

Marshall was born in Baltimore, Md., the son of a primary school teacher and a club steward. In 1926 he left Baltimore to attend the all-black Lincoln University in Chester, Pa., where he developed a reputation as an outstanding debater. After graduating cum laude in 1930, he studied law at Howard University in Washington, D.C.

During his law-school years, Marshall began to develop an interest in civil rights. After graduating first in his law school class in 1933, Marshall commenced a long and historic involvement with the National Association for the Advancement of Colored People (NAACP). In 1940 he became the head of the newly formed NAACP Legal Defense and Education Fund, a position he held for more than 20 years.

Over those two decades, Marshall coordinated the fund's attack on segregation in voting, housing, public accommodations and education. The culmination of his career as a civil rights attorney came in 1954 as chief counsel in a series of cases grouped under the title *Brown v. Board of Education*. In that historic case, which Marshall argued before the Supreme Court, civil rights advocates convinced the court to declare that segregation in public schools was unconstitutional.

Public Career

In 1961 Marshall was appointed by President Kennedy to the U.S. Court of Appeals for the second circuit, but because of heated opposition from southern Democratic senators, he was not confirmed until a year later.

Four years after he was named to the circuit court, Marshall was chosen by President Lyndon B. Johnson to be the nation's first black solicitor general. During his years as the government's chief advocate before the Supreme Court, Marshall scored impressive victories in the areas of civil and constitutional rights. He won Supreme Court approval of the 1965 Voting Rights Act, voluntarily informed the court that the government had used electronic eavesdropping devices in two cases, and joined in a suit that successfully overturned a California constitutional amendment that prohibited open housing legislation.

On June 13, 1967, President Johnson chose Marshall to become the first black appointed as a justice of the Supreme Court.

Warren Earl Burger

(1969-　　)

Born: Sept. 17, 1907, St. Paul, Minn.

Education: attended the University of Minnesota, 1925-27; St. Paul College of Law (now Mitchell College of Law), LL.B., magna cum laude, 1931.

Official Positions: U.S. assistant attorney general, civil division, Justice Department, 1953-56; judge, U.S. Court of Appeals for the District of Columbia, 1956-69.

Supreme Court Appointment: nominated Chief Justice by President Richard M. Nixon May 21, 1969, to replace Chief Justice Earl Warren, who resigned; confirmed by the U.S. Senate June 9, 1969, by a 74-3 vote.

Family: married Elvera Stromberg, Nov. 8, 1933; one son, one daughter.

Personal Background

Burger was born in St. Paul, Minn., the fourth of seven children of Swiss and German parents. Financially unable to attend college full time, Burger spent the years following his 1925 graduation from high school attending college and law school evening classes — two years at the University of Minnesota and four at St. Paul College of Law, now Mitchell College of Law. To support himself, Burger worked during the day selling life insurance.

After graduating with honors from law school in 1931, Burger joined a respected law firm in Minnesota, where he practiced until 1953. He also taught part time at his alma mater, Mitchell College of Law, from 1931 to 1948.

Burger developed a deep interest in art and is himself an accomplished sculptor; as Chief Justice, he became chairman of the board of the National Gallery of Art. He is also an antiques buff, a connoisseur of fine wines, and serves as chancellor of the Smithsonian Institution.

Public Career

Soon after beginning his law career in Minnesota, Burger became involved in state Republican politics. In 1938 he helped in the successful campaign of Harold E. Stassen for governor of Minnesota.

It was during Stassen's unsuccessful bid for the Republican presidential nomination 10 years later that Burger first met a man who was to figure largely in his future — Herbert Brownell, campaign manager for GOP presidential nominee Thomas E. Dewey, then governor of New York and later attorney general in the Eisenhower administration. It was Brownell who would bring Burger to Washington in 1953 to serve as assistant attorney general in charge of the civil division.

Burger's stint as assistant attorney general from 1953 to 1956 was not without controversy. His decision to defend the government's action in the dismissal of John F. Peters, a part-time federal employee, on grounds of disloyalty — after Solicitor General Simon E. Sobeloff had refused to do so on grounds of conscience — won Burger the enmity of many liberals.

But Burger's overall record as assistant attorney general apparently won President Eisenhower's approval, and in 1956 Burger was appointed to the U.S. Court of Appeals for the District of Columbia circuit. As an appeals-court judge, Burger developed a reputation as a conservative, especially in criminal justice cases.

Off the bench, Burger became increasingly outspoken in his support of major administrative reform of the judicial system — a cause he continued to advocate as Chief Justice. Due in large part to Burger's efforts, the American Bar Association and other legal groups established the Institute of Court Management to train court executive officers, bring new management techniques to the courts, and relieve judges of paperwork. During Burger's first years as Chief Justice, Congress also approved a number of measures to streamline and modernize the operations of the federal judiciary.

President Nixon's appointment of Burger as Chief Justice on May 21, 1969, caught most observers by surprise. For despite the white-haired nominee's years of service in the Justice Department and the court of appeals, he was little known outside the legal community. But Nixon apparently was impressed by Burger's consistent argument as an appeals judge that the Constitution should be read narrowly — a belief Nixon had stressed during his 1968 presidential campaign.

Born: Nov. 12, 1908, Nashville, Ill.

Education: Harvard University, B.A., Phi Beta Kappa, summa cum laude in mathematics, 1929; Harvard Law School, LL.B., 1932.

Official Positions: clerk, U.S. Court of Appeals for the Eighth Circuit, 1932-33; judge, U.S. Court of Appeals for the Eighth Circuit, 1959-70.

Supreme Court Appointment: nominated associate justice by President Richard M. Nixon April 14, 1970, to replace Abe Fortas, who resigned; confirmed by the U.S. Senate May 12, 1970, by a 94-0 vote.

Family: married Dorothy E. Clark, June 21, 1941; three daughters.

Personal Background

Although born in southern Illinois, Blackmun spent most of his early years in the Minneapolis-St. Paul area, where his father was an official of the Twin Cities Savings and Loan Company. It was in grade school that Blackmun began a lifelong friendship with Warren Burger, with whom he was later to serve on the Supreme Court.

After showing an early aptitude for mathematics, Blackmun went east after high school to attend Harvard University on a scholarship. At Harvard, Blackmun majored in mathematics and thought briefly of becoming a physician.

But Blackmun chose the law instead. After graduating Phi Beta Kappa from Harvard in 1929, Blackmun entered Harvard Law School, from which he graduated in 1932. During his law-school years, Blackmun supported himself with a variety of odd jobs, including tutoring in math and driving the launch for the college crew team.

After law school, Blackmun returned to St. Paul, where he served for a year and a half as a law clerk to United States Circuit Court Judge John B. Sanborn, whom Blackmun was to succeed on the court 26 years later. He left the clerkship in 1933 to teach at the Mitchell College of Law in St. Paul, Chief Justice Burger's alma mater.

After a year of teaching, Blackmun opted for private practice. In 1934 he joined the Minneapolis law firm where he was to remain for 16 years. Then, in 1950, he accepted a post as "house counsel" for the world-famous Mayo Clinic in Rochester, Minn. There, Blackmun quickly developed a reputation among his colleagues as a serious man totally engrossed in his profession.

Public Career

That reputation followed him to the bench of the U.S. Court of Appeals for the eighth circuit, to which Blackmun was appointed by President Eisenhower in 1959. As an appeals court judge, Blackmun became known for his scholarly and thorough opinions.

Blackmun's nomination for the Supreme Court was President Nixon's third try to fill the seat vacated by Justice Abe Fortas' resignation. The Senate had refused to confirm his first two nominees — Clement F. Haynsworth Jr. of South Carolina and G. Harrold Carswell of Florida. Thereupon, Nixon said that he had concluded from the rejection of his first two nominees that the Senate "as it is presently constituted" would not confirm a southern nominee who was also a judicial conservative.

Nixon then turned to Chief Justice Burger's close friend, who was confirmed without opposition. During his first years on the court, Blackmun was frequently described along with Burger as one of the "Minnesota Twins."

Harry Andrew Blackmun
(1970-   )

Lewis Franklin Powell Jr.
(1971-   )

Born: Sept. 19, 1907, Suffolk, Va.

Education: Washington and Lee University, B.S., Phi Beta Kappa, 1929; Washington and Lee University Law School, LL.B., 1931; Harvard Law School, LL.M., 1932.

Official Positions: president of the Richmond School Board, 1952-61; member, 1961-69, and president, 1968-69, Virginia state board of education; president of the American Bar Association, 1964-65; president, American College of Trial Lawyers, 1968-69.

Supreme Court Appointment: nominated associate justice by President Richard M. Nixon Oct. 21, 1971, to replace Hugo L. Black, who resigned; confirmed by the U.S. Senate Dec. 6, 1971, by an 89-1 vote.

Family: married Josephine M. Rucker, May 2, 1936; three daughters, one son.

Personal Background

Powell was born in Suffolk, in Tidewater Virginia, but spent most of his life in Richmond. He attended college and law school at Washington and Lee University in Lexington, Va., then Harvard Law School, where he earned a master's degree in 1932.

Following his year at Harvard, Powell returned to Virginia, where he joined one of the state's oldest and most prestigious law firms, located in Richmond. Powell eventually became a senior partner, continuing his association with the firm until his nomination to the Supreme Court.

Over the years, Powell's practice made him no stranger to blue-chip boardrooms. Among the companies represented during Powell's years with the law firm were the Baltimore and Ohio Railroad Co., the Prudential Insurance Company of America and the Virginia Electric and Power Co.

Public Career

Powell's reputation as a moderate stemmed from his work as president from 1952 to 1961 of the Richmond school board, and later as a member and president of the Virginia state board of education. In the face of intense pressure for "massive" resistance to desegregation, Powell consistently advocated keeping the schools open.

A one-year stint from 1964 to 1965 as president of the American Bar Association (ABA) provided Powell with a national platform from which to express his views on a variety of subjects and enhanced his reputation as a moderate. On the liberal side, Powell spoke out against inadequate legal services for the poor and worked to create the legal services program of the Office of Economic Opportunity. A more conservative tone characterized his view of social ills caused by parental permissiveness and his stern denunciations of civil disobedience and other forms of civil demonstrations. And as a member in 1966 of President Lyndon B. Johnson's Crime Commission, Powell participated in a minority statement criticizing Supreme Court rulings upholding the right of criminal suspects to remain silent.

Powell was the only Democrat among President Nixon's Supreme Court appointees.

William Hubbs Rehnquist
(1971-   )

Born: Oct. 1, 1924, Milwaukee, Wis.

Education: Stanford University, B.A., Phi Beta Kappa, "with great distinction" 1948, M.A., 1948; Harvard University, M.A. in political science, 1950; Stanford University Law School, LL.B., 1952.

Official Positions: law clerk to Supreme Court Justice Robert H. Jackson, 1952-53; U.S. assistant attorney general, office of legal counsel, 1969-1971.

Supreme Court Appointment: nominated associate justice by President Richard M. Nixon Oct. 21, 1971, to replace John Marshall Harlan, who resigned; confirmed by the U.S. Senate Dec. 10, 1971, by a 68-26 vote.

Family: married Natalie Cornell, Aug. 29, 1953; one son, two daughters.

Personal Background

Rehnquist was born in Milwaukee and grew up there. After World War II service in the Air Force, he entered Stanford University, where he received both a B.A. and an M.A. in 1948. He earned another M.A. in political science at Harvard University (conferred in 1950) before returning to Stanford to attend law school. He graduated first in his class in 1952.

Public Career

After finishing law school, Rehnquist became a law clerk to Supreme Court Justice Robert H. Jackson. In 1952 he wrote a memorandum for Jackson that would later come back to haunt him during his Senate confirmation hearings: The memorandum favored separate but equal schools for blacks and whites. Asked about those views by the Senate Judiciary Committee in 1971, Rehnquist repudiated them, declaring that they were Justice Jackson's, not his own.

Following his clerkship, Rehnquist decided to begin law practice in the economically burgeoning Southwest. In 1953 he moved to Phoenix, Ariz., and immediately became immersed in state Republican politics. From his earliest days in the state, he was associated with the party's most conservative wing. A 1957 speech denouncing the liberalism of the Warren court typified his views at the time.

During the 1964 presidential campaign, Rehnquist campaigned ardently for GOP candidate Barry Goldwater.

It was during the campaign that Rehnquist met and worked with Richard G. Kleindienst, who, as President Nixon's deputy attorney general, would later appoint Rehnquist to head the Justice Department's office of legal counsel as an assistant attorney general.

Rehnquist quickly became one of the Nixon administration's chief spokesmen on Capitol Hill, commenting on issues ranging from wiretapping to rights of the accused. It was Rehnquist's job to review the legality of all presidential executive orders and other constitutional law questions in the executive branch. He frequently testified before congressional committees in support of the administration's policies — most of which matched his own conservative philosophy. So tightly reasoned and articulate was his testimony — backing such controversial matters as government surveillance of American citizens and tighter curbs on obscene materials — that even many liberal members of Congress applauded his ability.

In 1971 the once-obscure Phoenix lawyer was nominated by President Nixon to the Supreme Court and approved by the Senate, 68-26.

John Paul Stevens
(1975-   )

Born: April 20, 1920, Chicago, Ill.

Education: University of Chicago, B.A., Phi Beta Kappa, 1941; Northwestern University School of Law, J. D. magna cum laude, 1947.

Official Positions: law clerk to Supreme Court Justice Wiley B. Rutledge, 1947-48; associate counsel, subcommittee on the study of monopoly power, U.S. House Judiciary Committee, 1951; member, U.S. Attorney General's National Committee to Study the Antitrust Laws, 1953-55; judge, U.S. Court of Appeals for the seventh circuit, 1970-75.

Supreme Court Appointment: nominated associate justice by President Gerald R. Ford Nov. 28, 1975, to replace William O. Douglas, who resigned; confirmed by the U.S. Senate Dec. 17, 1975, by a 98-0 vote.

Family: married Elizabeth Jane Sheeren, 1942, divorced; one son, three daughters; remarried, Maryan Simon.

A member of a prominent Chicago family, Stevens graduated Phi Beta Kappa from the University of Chicago in 1941. After a wartime stint in the Navy during which he earned the Bronze Star, he returned to Chicago to enter Northwestern University Law School, graduating in 1947. Stevens then served as a law clerk to Supreme Court Justice Wiley B. Rutledge. He left Washington to join a prominent Chicago law firm which specialized in antitrust law.

Stevens developed a reputation as a pre-eminent antitrust lawyer, and after three years formed his own law firm. He also taught part-time at Northwestern and the University of Chicago law schools until his appointment by President Nixon in 1970 to the U.S. Court of Appeals for the seventh circuit.

An enthusiastic pilot, Stevens flies his own small plane. He underwent open heart surgery in the early 1970s, but fully recovered.

Public Career

Stevens developed a reputation as a political moderate during his undergraduate days at the University of Chicago, then an overwhelmingly liberal campus. But although a registered Republican, he was never active in partisan politics. Nevertheless, Stevens served as Republican counsel in 1951 to a House Judiciary subcommittee's study of monopoly power. He also served from 1953 to 1955, during the Eisenhower administration, as a member of the attorney general's National Committee to Study the Antitrust Laws.

When President Ford nominated Stevens to the Supreme Court seat vacated by veteran liberal William O. Douglas, court-watchers and other observers struggled to pin an ideological label on the new nominee. But on the whole, they decided that he was neither a doctrinaire liberal nor a conservative, but a centrist whose well-crafted, scholarly opinions made him a "judge's judge." He was unanimously confirmed.

Sandra Day O'Connor

Born: March 26, 1930, El Paso, Texas.

Education: Stanford University, B.A. magna cum laude, 1950; Stanford University Law School, LL.B., with high honors, 1952.

Official Positions: deputy county attorney, San Mateo, Calif., 1952-53; assistant attorney general, Arizona, 1965-69; Arizona state senator, 1969-1975, senate majority leader, 1972-75; judge, Maricopa County Superior Court, 1974-79; judge, Arizona Court of Appeals, 1979-81.

Supreme Court Appointment: nominated associate justice by President Ronald Reagan Aug. 19, 1981, to replace Potter Stewart, who retired; confirmed by the U.S. Senate September 1981.

Family: married John J. O Connor III, Dec. 20, 1952; three sons.

Personal Background

Pioneering came naturally to Sandra Day O'Connor. Her grandfather left Kansas in 1880 to take up ranching in the desert land that would eventually become the state of

Arizona. O'Connor, born in El Paso where her mother's parents lived, was raised on the Lazy B Ranch, the 162,000-acre spread that her grandfather had founded in southeastern Arizona near Duncan. She spent her school years in El Paso, living with her grandmother and attending the schools there. She graduated from high school at age 16 and then entered Stanford University.

Six years later, in 1952, Sandra Day had won degrees, with great distinction, both from the university, in economics, and from Stanford Law School. There she met John J. O'Connor III, her future husband, and was also a classmate of William H. Rehnquist, a future colleague on the Supreme Court. During her law school years, Sandra Day was an editor of the Stanford Law Review and a member of Order of the Coif, both reflecting her academic leadership.

But despite her outstanding law school record, she found it difficult to locate a job as an attorney in 1952 when relatively few women were practicing law. She applied, among others, to the firm in which William French Smith — attorney general in the Reagan administration — was a partner, only to be offered a job as a secretary.

After a short stint as deputy county attorney for San Mateo County (Calif.) while her new husband completed law school at Stanford, the O'Connors moved with the U.S. Army to Frankfurt, Germany. There Sandra O'Connor worked as a civilian attorney for the army, while John

O'Connor served his tour of duty.

In 1957, they returned to Phoenix to live. In the next eight years, their three sons were born and O'Connor's life was a mix of mothering, home-making, volunteer work and some "miscellaneous legal tasks" on the side.

Public Career

In 1965, O'Connor resumed her legal career fulltime, taking a job as an assistant attorney general for Arizona. After four years in that post, she was appointed to fill a vacancy in the state senate, where she served on the judiciary committee. In 1970, she was elected to the senate, and two years later was chosen its majority leader; the first woman in the nation to hold such a post.

O'Connor was active in Republican Party politics and was co-chairman of the Arizona Committee to Re-Elect the President in 1972.

In 1974, she was elected to the Superior Court for Maricopa County where she served for five years. Then in 1979, Gov. Bruce Babbitt — acting, some said, to remove a potential rival for the governorship — appointed O'Connor to the Arizona Court of Appeals. It was from that seat that President Reagan chose her as his first nominee to the Supreme Court, describing her as "a person for all seasons" when he announced her selection on July 7, 1981.

Major Decisions: 1790-1981

Every Supreme Court decision begins with a dispute between persons. The interests they assert and defend may be personal ones, corporate ones, or official ones, but every case begins with a disagreement between individuals.

Early in its history the court made clear that it would not rule on theoretical situations or hypothetical cases. It would only resolve actual "cases and controversies" arising from real collisions of rights and powers. To decide a hypothetical case, said the justices, would be to exceed the function which the Constitution gave the court.

The individuals who bring their complaints before the justices are a varied group. William Marbury wished to secure his appointment as a justice of the peace. Dred Scott sought his freedom. Linda Brown wanted to attend her neighborhood school. Clarence Gideon felt he should have a lawyer to help him defend himself in court. Richard Nixon wanted to keep his White House tapes confidential.

The court resolved each of those cases, and the hundreds more which have appeared on its docket through the years, on the basis of its particular facts.

The immediate impact of each decision was simply to answer the claims of Marbury, Scott, Brown, Gideon and Nixon, settling one particular situation. Many of the court's rulings have no further impact.

But often — as in these cases — the decision has a larger significance, upholding or striking down similar laws or practices or claims, establishing the court's own power in new areas, or finding that some areas lie outside that power.

To the Supreme Court, wrote Richard Kluger in the foreword to his book *Simple Justice,*

> . . .the nation has increasingly brought its most vexing social and political problems. They come in the guise of private disputes between only the litigating parties, but everybody understands that this is a legal fiction and merely a convenient political device. American society thus reduces its most troubling controversies to the scope — and translates them into the language — of a lawsuit.

Although the progress of cases to the Supreme Court is slow, the body of issues before the court in a particular period does provide a reflection of the trends of public concern. Most of the major cases decided by the court from 1790 until 1860 dealt with questions of the balance between state and federal power. War issues were reflected in the rulings of the war years; civil rights and state powers questions marked the era of Reconstruction. As the nation's economy flourished and grew, more and more questions of business law — and the power of government over business — came to the court. And in the mid-20th century questions of individual rights and liberties began to dominate.

Decision Summaries

Following are summary descriptions of the Supreme Court's major rulings from *Chisholm v. Georgia* in 1793, through those issued in the summer of 1981. Arranged in chronological order, the summaries consist of a general subject heading, the case name, its citation, the vote by which it was decided, the date upon which the decision was announced, the name of the justice writing the major court opinion, the names of those in dissent, and a summary statement of the court's holding. (In some early cases, the vote or the exact date of its announcement are unavailable.)

Sources for Decisions

The primary source for this section on major decisions was *United States Reports,* the official record of Supreme Court decisions and opinions published by the U.S. Government Printing Office.

This source was supplemented by three unofficial records: *United States Law Week,* published by the Bureau of National Affairs; *Supreme Court Reporter,* published by West Publishing Co.; and *United States Supreme Court Reports, Lawyers' Edition,* published by Lawyers Co-operative Publishing Co.

Where specific dates and votes were not available from these sources, they were occasionally drawn from the following secondary sources:

Paul A. Freund, gen. ed. *History of the Supreme Court of the United States.* New York: Macmillan Publishing Co., 1971, 1974, 1971. Vol. I: *Antecedents and Beginnings to 1801,* by Julius Goebel Jr.; Vol. V: *The Taney Period, 1836-1864,* by Carl B. Swisher; Vol. VI: *Reconstruction and Reunion, 1864-1888, Part One,* by Charles Fairman.

Charles Warren. *The Supreme Court in United States History.* rev. ed. 2 vols. Boston: Little, Brown & Co., 1922, 1926.

1790-1799

Federal Courts

Chisholm v. Georgia (2 Dall. 419), decided by a 4-1 vote, Feb. 18, 1793. Chief Justice Jay wrote the court's major opinion; Iredell dissented.

Citizens of one state have the right — under Article III of the Constitution — to sue another state in federal court, even without the consent of the defendant state.

This ruling was reversed by adoption of the 11th Amendment, forbidding such suits without the consent of the defendant state.

Taxes

Hylton v. United States (3 Dall. 171), decided without dissent in the February 1796 term. All three participating justices — Chase, Paterson and Iredell — submitted opinions; Cushing, Wilson and Ellsworth did not participate; Wilson filed an opinion.

The court upheld a federal tax on carriages, ruling that the only taxes that were direct and therefore required by the Constitution to be apportioned among the states were head taxes and taxes on land.

This definition remained in force until 1895 when the court held that income taxes were also direct and must be apportioned; that decision was overturned by ratification of the 16th Amendment.

Treaties

Ware v. Hylton (3 Dall. 199), decided by a 4-0 vote, March 7, 1796. Chase delivered the major opinion for the court; Iredell did not participate in the decision, but did place an opinion in the record.

The court ruled that treaties made by the United States overrode any conflicting state laws.

The 1783 Treaty of Paris with Britain, ending the Revolutionary War, provided that neither Britain nor the United States would block the efforts of the other nation's citizens to secure repayment of debts in the other country. This provision rendered invalid Virginia's law allowing debts owed by Virginians to British creditors to be "paid off" through payments to the state.

Ex Post Facto Laws

Calder v. Bull (3 Dall. 386), decided by a vote of 4-0, Aug. 8, 1798. Chase wrote the court's opinion. Paterson, Iredell and Cushing also wrote opinions.

The Constitution's ban on *ex post facto* laws does not forbid a state to nullify a man's title to certain property. The court held that this ban applied only to laws making certain actions criminal after they had been committed. The ban was not intended to protect property rights, the court wrote.

1800-1809

Judicial Review

Marbury v. Madison (1 Cr. 137), decided without dissent, Feb. 24, 1803. Chief Justice Marshall wrote the opinion of the court.

Congress may not expand or contract the Supreme Court's original jurisdiction. Thus Congress exceeded its power when in Section 13 of the Judiciary Act of 1789 it authorized the Supreme Court to issue writs of *mandamus*

in original cases ordering federal officials to perform particular acts.

Therefore, the court ruled, although William Marbury had a right to receive his commission as a justice of the peace — already signed and sealed, but not delivered — the Supreme Court lacked the power, under its original jurisdiction, to order its delivery.

The immediate import of the decision was to absolve the Jefferson administration of the duty to install several of President Adams' appointments in such posts. The lasting significance was the establishment of the court's power to review acts of Congress and declare invalid those it found in conflict with the Constitution.

Federal Courts

Bank of the United States v. Deveaux (5 Cr. 61), decided without dissent, March 15, 1809. Chief Justice Marshall wrote the court's opinion; Livingston did not participate in the decision.

The court gave a strict interpretation to the "diversity" requirement in federal cases — the rule that certain cases could be heard in federal, not state, courts simply because the two parties were residents of different states. Cases involving corporations, the court held, could only come into federal courts for this reason if *all* the stockholders of the corporation lived in a state other than that of the opposing party. This strict rule resulted in very little corporate litigation in the federal courts until 1844 when the rule was revised.

1810-1819

Contracts

Fletcher v. Peck (6 Cr. 87), decided without dissent March 16, 1810. Chief Justice Marshall wrote the court's opinion; Johnson filed a separate opinion.

The Constitution forbids a state to impair the obligation of contracts. This prohibition denies a state legislature the power to annul titles to land secured under a land grant approved by a previous session of the legislature.

Judicial Review

Martin v. Hunter's Lessee (1 Wheat. 304), decided without dissent, March 20, 1816. Story wrote the court's opinion; Chief Justice Marshall did not participate in the case.

The court upheld as constitutional Section 25 of the Judiciary Act of 1789, which gave the Supreme Court the power to review, and reverse or affirm, state court rulings rejecting a federally-based challenge to a state law or state action.

Contracts

Dartmouth College v. Woodward (4 Wheat. 519), decided by a 5-1 vote, Feb. 2, 1819. Chief Justice Marshall wrote the court's opinion; Duvall dissented.

The Constitution, by its provision forbidding state action impairing the obligation of contracts, denies a state the power to alter or repeal private corporate charters, such as that between the state of New Hampshire and the trustees of Dartmouth College to establish that institution.

Sturges v. Crowninshield (4 Wheat. 122), decided without dissent, Feb. 17, 1819. Chief Justice Marshall wrote the court's opinion.

The Constitution's grant of power to Congress to enact a uniform bankruptcy law does not deny states the power to pass insolvency statutes, at least until Congress enacts a bankruptcy law.

However, the constitutional ban on state action impairing the obligation of contracts denies a state the power to enact a law freeing debtors from liability for debts contracted *before* the law's passage.

Power of Congress

McCulloch v. Maryland (4 Wheat. 316), decided without dissent, March 6, 1819. Chief Justice Marshall wrote the court's opinion.

In a broad definition of the Constitution's grant to Congress of the power to enact all laws which are "necessary and proper" to execute the responsibilities given the legislative branch by the Constitution, the court ruled that Congress had the authority to charter a national bank in the exercise of its fiscal and monetary powers. The necessary and proper clause empowered Congress to adopt any appropriate and legitimate means for achieving a legislative goal; it was not confined to using only those means that were indispensable to reaching that end.

The court also held that the national bank was immune to state taxation. Observing that the "power to tax involves the power to destroy," the court began to develop the doctrine that one government may not tax certain holdings of another government.

1820-1829

Judicial Review

Cohens v. Virginia (6 Wheat. 264), decided without dissent, March 3, 1821. Chief Justice Marshall delivered the court's opinion.

For the second time, the court reaffirmed the constitutionality of Section 25 of the Judiciary Act of 1789, under which the Supreme Court was empowered to review, and affirm or reverse, the rulings of state courts denying federal claims.

Commerce

Gibbons v. Ogden (9 Wheat. 1), decided without dissent, March 2, 1824. Chief Justice Marshall wrote the court's opinion.

In its first definition of Congress' power to regulate interstate commerce, the court ruled that Congress could regulate all commerce that extends to or affects more than one state. Furthermore, the court defined commerce as intercourse, including navigation and other modes of transportation, as well as commercial transactions. The court also declared that the congressional authority to regulate commerce is superior to state power to regulate the same commerce.

This important decision laid the foundation for the modern interpretation of the power which gives Congress virtually exclusive control over all business, even that which only indirectly affects interstate commerce.

Federal Courts

Osborn v. Bank of the United States (9 Wheat. 738), decided with one dissenting vote, March 18, 1824. Chief Justice Marshall wrote the court's opinion; Johnson dissented.

How To Read A Citation

The official version of Supreme Court decisions and opinions is contained in a series of volumes entitled *United States Reports*, published by the U.S. Government Printing Office.

While there are several unofficial compilations of court opinions, including *United States Law Week* published by the Bureau of National Affairs, *Supreme Court Reporter* published by West Publishing Co., and *United States Supreme Court Reports, Lawyers' Edition* published by Lawyers Co-operative Publishing Co., it is the official record that is generally cited. (An unofficial version or the official slip opinion might be cited if a decision has not yet been officially reported.)

A citation to a case includes, in order, the name of the parties to the case, the volume of *United States Reports* in which the decision appears, the page in the volume that the opinion begins on, the page from which any quoted material is taken and the year the decision was made.

For example, *Colegrove v. Green,* 328 U.S. 549 at 553 (1946) means that the Supreme Court decision and opinion in the case of Colegrove against Green may be found in volume 328 of *United States Reports* beginning on page 549. The specific quotation in question will be found on page 553. The case was decided in 1946.

Reporters of Decisions

Until 1875 the official reports of the court were published under the names of the court reporters and it is their names, or abbreviated versions, which appear in cites for those years. A citation such as *Marbury v. Madison,* 1 Cranch 137 (1803) means that the opinion in the case of Marbury against Madison will be found in the first volume of reporter Cranch beginning on page 137. (Between 1875 and 1883 a court reporter named William T. Otto compiled the decisions and opinions; his name appears on the volumes for those years as well as the *United States Reports* volume number, but Otto is seldom cited.)

The titles of the volumes to 1875, the names of the reporters and the corresponding *United States Reports* volumes are:

1-4	Dall.	Dallas	1-4	U.S.
1-9	Cranch or Cr.	Cranch	5-13	U.S.
1-12	Wheat.	Wheaton	14-25	U.S.
1-16	Pet.	Peters	26-41	U.S.
1-24	How.	Howard	42-65	U.S.
1-2	Black	Black	66-67	U.S.
1-23	Wall.	Wallace	68-90	U.S.

The court upheld the right of the Bank of the United States to sue state officials in federal court. It held that the 11th Amendment — allowing states to be sued in federal court by citizens of another state only with the consent of the defendant state — did not deny federal courts jurisdiction over a case brought against a state official for actions under an unconstitutional state law or in excess of his legal authority.

Power of Congress

Wayman v. Southard (10 Wheat. 1), decided without dissent, Feb. 12, 15, 1825. Chief Justice Marshall wrote the court's opinion.

In this decision the court for the first time recognized the power of Congress to delegate portions of its legislative authority. In this case the court sanctioned the right of Congress to set an objective and then authorize an administrator to promulgate rules and regulations to achieve that objective. The right to delegate such authority provides the basis for creation of the federal regulatory agencies.

Power of the President

Martin v. Mott (12 Wheat. 19), decided without dissent in the January 1827 term. Story wrote the court's opinion.

The president's decision to call out the militia was not subject to judicial review and was binding on state authorities. As a result of congressional delegation of the power to the president, the decision to call out the militia, the court said, "belongs exclusively to the President, and ... his decision is conclusive upon all other persons."

Contracts

Ogden v. Saunders (12 Wheat. 213), decided by a 4-3 vote, Feb. 18, 1827. Washington wrote the court's major opinion; Chief Justice Marshall, Story and Duvall dissented.

The constitutional ban on state action impairing the obligation of contracts does not deny states the power to enact insolvency statutes which provide for the discharge of debts contracted *after* its passage.

Mason v. Haile (12 Wheat. 370), decided by a 6-1 vote in the January 1827 term. Thompson wrote the court's opinion; Washington dissented.

The Constitution's contract clause does not prevent a state from abolishing imprisonment as a punishment for debtors who fail to pay their obligations. Modifying the remedy for defaulting on a contract does not inevitably impair the obligation incurred under the contract.

Taxes

Brown v. Maryland (12 Wheat. 419), decided by a 6-1 vote, March 12, 1827. Chief Justice Marshall wrote the court's opinion; Thompson dissented.

The court reinforced its broad interpretation of congressional power to regulate interstate commerce, ruling that a state unconstitutionally infringed on that power when it taxed imported goods that were still the property of the importer and in their original package.

Weston v. City Council of Charleston (2 Pet. 449), decided by a 4-2 vote, March 18, 1829. Chief Justice Marshall wrote the court's opinion; Johnson and Thompson dissented.

A city tax on United States stock impermissibly hinders the exercise of the federal power to borrow money.

Commerce

Willson v. Blackbird Creek Marsh Co. (2 Pet. 245), decided without dissent in the January 1829 term. Chief Justice Marshall wrote the court's opinion.

A state may exercise its police power to regulate matters affecting interstate commerce if Congress has not enacted conflicting legislation regulating the same matters.

Federal Courts

Foster v. Neilson (2 Pet. 253), decided without dissent in the January 1829 term. Chief Justice Marshall delivered the court's opinion.

The court refused to rule on a boundary dispute involving territory east of the Mississippi River claimed by both the United States and Spain. Chief Justice Marshall described the matter as a "political question" which it was not the business of the judiciary to resolve.

1830-1839

Bills of Credit

Craig v. Missouri (4 Pet. 410), decided by a 4-3 vote, March 12, 1830. Chief Justice Marshall wrote the court's opinion; Johnson, Thompson and McLean dissented.

The constitutional provision barring states from issuing bills of credit denies a state the power to authorize the issuance of state loan certificates.

State Powers

Worcester v. Georgia (6 Pet. 515), decided without dissent, March 3, 1832. Chief Justice Marshall wrote the court's opinion.

Federal jurisdiction over Indian affairs is exclusive, leaving no room for state authority. States lack any power to pass laws affecting Indians living in Indian territory within their borders. The court thus reversed the conviction, under Georgia law, of two missionaries who had failed to comply with a state law requiring the licensing of all white persons living in Indian territory.

Individual Rights

Barron v. Baltimore (7 Pet. 243), decided without dissent, in the January 1833 term. Chief Justice Marshall wrote the court's opinion.

The Bill of Rights was added to the Constitution to protect persons only against the action of the federal, not the state, government. The court rejected the effort of a wharf owner to invoke the Fifth Amendment to compel the city of Baltimore to compensate him for the value of his wharf, which he claimed had been rendered useless as a result of city action.

Commerce

New York v. Miln (11 Pet. 102), decided by a 6-1 vote, in the January 1837 term. Barbour wrote the court's opinion; Story dissented.

The court sustained a New York statute, which required all ships arriving in New York to report lists of passengers, against a challenge that the statute interfered with federal power to regulate foreign commerce. The state law was a valid exercise of state police power to protect public welfare against an influx of paupers, the majority said.

Bills of Credit

Briscoe v. Bank of the Commonwealth of Kentucky (11 Pet. 257), decided by a vote of 6-1, Feb. 11, 1837. McLean wrote the court's opinion; Story dissented.

The constitutional language forbidding states to issue bills of credit is not violated by a state law authorizing issuance of notes by a state-chartered bank, in which the state owns all the stock.

Contracts

Charles River Bridge v. Warren Bridge (11 Pet. 420), decided by a 4-3 vote, in the January 1837 term. Chief Justice Taney wrote the court's opinion; Story, Thompson and McLean dissented.

Charters granted by the state should never be assumed to limit the state's power of eminent domain. Absent an explicit grant of exclusive privilege, a corporate charter granted by the state should not be interpreted as granting such a privilege and thereby limiting the state's power to charter a competing corporation.

The court rejected the claim of the owners of the Charles River Bridge that their charter implicitly granted them a monopoly of the foot passenger traffic across the river — and was impaired by state action authorizing construction of a second bridge over that same river.

Federal Courts

Kendall v. United States ex rel. Stokes (12 Pet. 524), decided by votes of 9-0 and 6-3, in the January 1838 term. Thompson wrote the court's opinion; Chief Justice Taney, Barbour and Catron dissented in part.

The court held that federal courts — if they have jurisdiction over the controversy involved — have the power to issue a writ of *mandamus* to an executive branch official ordering him to take some ministerial action which he is required by law to perform. The court distinguished between ministerial actions of executive officials, which are prescribed by law or regulation and about which there is little discretion, and policy or political actions of those officials, which are beyond the reach of the courts.

1840-1849

Foreign Affairs

Holmes v. Jennison (14 Pet. 540), decided by a 4-4 vote in the January 1840 term. Chief Justice Taney wrote an opinion for himself, Story, McLean and Wayne; Barbour, Baldwin, Catron and Thompson filed separate opinions; McKinley did not participate.

A fugitive from Canada, detained in Vermont, sought release through a petition for a writ of *habeas corpus*. After the state supreme court denied his petition, he asked the Supreme Court to review that action. The court divided 4-4 over whether it had jurisdiction in the case. Taney, Story, McLean and Wayne held that the court did have jurisdiction; Barbour, Baldwin, Catron and Thompson disagreed.

The 4-4 vote meant that the court dismissed the case for lack of jurisdiction. But the significance of the case came in Taney's declaration that states were forbidden by the Constitution to take any independent role in foreign affairs, and thus a state governor could not surrender a fugitive within his jurisdiction to a foreign country which sought the fugitive's return.

Taxes

Dobbins v. Erie County (16 Pet. 435), decided without dissent in the January 1842 term. Wayne wrote the court's opinion.

Extending the principle adopted in *McCulloch v. Maryland* (1819) that the power to tax involves the power to destroy, the court held that states could not tax the income of federal officials.

This decision, together with that in *Collector v. Day* (11 Wall. 113, 1871), which held that the federal govern-ment, for the same reason, could not tax the incomes of state officials, led to establishment of numerous intergovernmental tax immunities that were not removed until 1939 when *Dobbins* and *Collector* were overruled.

Slavery

Prigg v. Pennsylvania (16 Pet. 539), decided by votes of 9-0 and 6-3, March 1, 1842. Story wrote the court's opinion; Chief Justice Taney, Thompson and Daniel dissented in part.

The court struck down a Pennsylvania law concerning procedures for the return of fugitive slaves to owners in other states, finding the law in conflict with the federal Fugitive Slave Act. Story declared that federal power over fugitive slaves was exclusive, denying states any power to enact any laws on that subject. On this point the three justices dissented.

Federal Courts

Louisville Railroad Company v. Letson (2 How. 497), decided without dissent, March 15, 1844. Wayne wrote the court's opinion.

Effectively overruling its 1809 decision in *Bank of the United States v. Deveaux,* the court declared that a corporation would be assumed to be a citizen of the state in which it was chartered. This assumed citizenship, for purposes of diversity jurisdiction, facilitated the movement of corporate litigation into federal courts.

Interstate Boundaries

Rhode Island v. Massachusetts (4 How. 591), decided by votes of 8-0 and 7-1 in the January 1846 term. McLean wrote the court's opinion; Chief Justice Taney dissented in part.

This was the first decision of the court resolving an interstate boundary dispute. The court affirmed its jurisdiction over these matters, a point upon which Chief Justice Taney dissented, and then resolved the dispute in favor of Massachusetts, the state which had challenged the court's jurisdiction to hear the case at all.

Commerce

Thurlow v. Massachusetts, Fletcher v. Rhode Island, Peirce v. New Hampshire (The License Cases) (5 How. 504), decided without dissent, March 6, 1847. Chief Justice Taney, McLean, Catron, Daniel, Woodbury and Grier all wrote separate opinions.

The court upheld the right of states to require that all sales of intoxicating liquors within their borders be licensed, including imported liquor. This was viewed as a valid exercise of state police power. But a majority of the justices could not agree on the line of reasoning leading to this decision. Six separate opinions were the result.

Federal Courts

Luther v. Borden (7 How. 1), decided by a 5-1 vote, Jan. 3, 1849. Chief Justice Taney delivered the court's opinion; Woodbury dissented; Catron, McKinley and Daniel did not participate.

The guaranty clause of the Constitution — stating that the United States will guarantee to each state a republican form of government — is enforceable only through the political branches, not the judiciary.

The court refused to resolve a dispute between two competing political groups, each of which asserted it was the lawful government of Rhode Island. This was a "political question," held the court, which it would leave to Congress to resolve.

Commerce

Smith v. Turner, Norris v. Boston (The Passenger Cases) (7 How. 283), decided by a 5-4 vote, Feb. 7, 1849. McLean wrote the court's opinion; Chief Justice Taney, Daniel, Nelson and Woodbury dissented.

In apparent contradiction to its decision in *New York v. Miln*, the court struck down state laws that placed a head tax on each passenger brought into a U.S. port. The revenue was intended to support immigrant paupers, but the majority held that such state laws conflicted with federal power to regulate interstate and foreign commerce even though Congress had not acted in this area.

1850-1859

Commerce

Cooley v. Board of Wardens of Port of Philadelphia (12 How. 299), decided by a 7-2 vote in the December 1851 term. Curtis wrote the court's opinion; McLean and Wayne dissented.

Adopting what is called the "selective exclusiveness doctrine," the majority ruled that Congress had exclusive power to regulate commerce that was national in nature and demanded uniform regulation. The states retained the authority to regulate commerce that was local in nature.

Pennsylvania v. Wheeling and Belmont Bridge (13 How. 518), decided by a 7-2 vote, Feb. 6, 1852. McLean wrote the court's opinion; Chief Justice Taney and Daniel dissented.

A bridge built under state direction across the Ohio River was so low that it obstructed interstate commerce, the court ruled, ordering that the bridge either be raised so that ships could pass under it or be taken down.

In its first legislative reversal of a Supreme Court decision, Congress passed a law declaring that the bridge did not interfere with interstate commerce and requiring ships to be refitted so that they could pass under the bridge. The court upheld this statute in 1856.

Due Process

Murray's Lessee v. Hoboken Land and Improvement Co. (18 How. 272), decided by a unanimous vote, Feb. 19, 1856. Curtis wrote the court's opinion.

The court held that the due process clause of the Fifth Amendment was a limitation on the legislature as well as on the executive and the judiciary.

The Fifth Amendment "cannot be construed as to leave Congress free to make any process 'due process of law' by its mere will." In this decision the court began to define due process, stating that any process in conflict with specific constitutional provisions or the "settled modes and usages" of proceedings in English and early American practice was not due process of law.

Contracts

Dodge v. Woolsey (18 How. 331), decided by a 6-3 vote, April 8, 1856. Wayne wrote the majority opinion; Campbell, Catron and Daniel dissented.

A state may not revoke a tax exemption which it has included in a charter, grant or contract. The Constitution's

ban on state action impairing the obligation of contracts forbids such revocation.

This ruling declared unconstitutional part of the Ohio constitution, the first time the court had so nullified part of a state's constitution.

Slavery

Scott v. Sandford (19 How. 393), decided by a 7-2 vote, March 6, 1857. Each justice submitted a separate opinion. Chief Justice Taney's is considered the formal opinion of the court; McLean and Curtis dissented.

In what many consider the most ill-considered decision in Supreme Court history, the majority declared unconstitutional the already-repealed Missouri Compromise of 1820. Congress, the court declared, did not have the authority to prohibit slavery in the territories. The majority also held that blacks were not and could not become citizens of the United States and therefore were not entitled to its privileges and immunities. This part of the decision was overturned by ratification of the 14th Amendment in 1868.

Federal Courts

Ableman v. Booth, United States v. Booth (21 How. 506), decided by a unanimous vote, March 7, 1859. Chief Justice Taney wrote the court's opinion.

State courts lack the power to issue writs of *habeas corpus* ordering federal courts or federal officers to justify the detention of a prisoner or release him.

The court overturned the action of state courts in using the writ to order federal officials to release a man convicted in federal court of violating the federal Fugitive Slave Act.

1860-1869

Extradition

Kentucky v. Dennison (24 How. 66), decided by a unanimous vote, March 14, 1861. Chief Justice Taney wrote the opinion.

The constitutional statement that a "person charged in any state with treason, felony or other crime, who shall flee from justice, and be found in another state, shall, on demand of the executive authority of the state from which he fled, be delivered up, to be removed to the state having jurisdiction of the crime" is not enforceable by the federal government. The Constitution imposes a moral obligation upon a governor to surrender a fugitive sought and requested by another governor, but that obligation cannot be enforced in the federal courts.

Power of the President

The Prize Cases (2 Black 635), decided by a 5-4 vote, March 10, 1863. Grier wrote the majority opinion; Chief Justice Taney, Catron, Clifford and Nelson dissented.

These cases involved the capture of four ships seized while trying to run the Union blockade of Confederate ports which Lincoln instituted in April and which Congress sanctioned in July 1861. The court sustained the president's power to proclaim the blockade without a congressional declaration of war. A state of war already existed, the majority said, and the president was obligated "to meet it in the shape it presented itself, without waiting for Congress to baptize it with a name. . . ."

Ex parte Milligan (4 Wall. 2), decided by votes of 9-0 and 5-4, April 3, 1866. Full opinions in the case were not announced until December 17, 1866. Davis wrote the majority opinion; Chief Justice Chase, Miller, Swayne and Wayne dissented in part.

The court held unanimously that the president lacks the power to authorize trial of civilians by military tribunal in wartime in areas where civil courts are still functioning.

Five justices, with Davis as their spokesman, said that even Congress and the president acting together lacked power to authorize military commissions to try civilians in areas outside the actual war zone.

Ex Post Facto Laws

Cummings v. Missouri, Ex parte Garland (4 Wall. 277, 333), decided by votes of 5-4, Jan. 14, 1867. Field wrote the majority opinion; Chief Justice Chase, Swayne, Davis and Miller dissented.

Neither the states nor the federal government may constitutionally require persons who wish to practice certain professions or exercise certain civil rights to take a "test oath" affirming past as well as present loyalty to the United States.

The court held invalid state and federal "test oaths," enacted to exclude persons who had supported the Confederacy from certain offices and certain professions. These requirements, held the court, violated the constitutional prohibitions on *ex post facto* laws and bills of attainder.

Federal Courts

Mississippi v. Johnson (4 Wall. 475), decided by a unanimous vote, April 15, 1867. Chief Justice Chase wrote the opinion.

The Supreme Court lacks jurisdiction over the political acts of the president; it has no power to issue an order directing him to stop enforcing acts of Congress, even if those acts are challenged as unconstitutional.

Ex parte McCardle (7 Wall. 506), decided by a unanimous vote, April 12, 1869. Chief Justice Chase wrote the opinion.

The Constitution authorizes Congress to make exceptions to the appellate jurisdiction of the Supreme Court. That grant includes the power to revoke the court's appellate jurisdiction over cases already argued and awaiting decision before it. Without jurisdiction over a case, the court can do nothing but dismiss it.

Congress had acted to revoke the court's jurisdiction over certain cases in which lower courts denied prisoners' petitions for release through a writ of *habeas corpus*. Congress did so because it feared that in this particular case, where a southern editor held by military authorities for "impeding" the Reconstruction effort sought his release, the court would declare the Reconstruction Acts themselves unconstitutional.

State Powers

Texas v. White (7 Wall. 700), decided by a 6-3 vote, April 12, 1869. Chief Justice Chase wrote the majority opinion. Justices Wayne, Grier and Miller dissented in part.

States lack the power to secede from the Union. From a legal point of view, Texas and the other states which had approved ordinances of secession had never left the Union.

Commerce

Paul v. Virginia (8 Wall. 168), decided by a unanimous vote, Nov. 1, 1869. Field wrote the opinion.

Insurance is a local business, not interstate commerce, the court held. Thus the states, not Congress, were responsible for regulating insurance practices even though insurance transactions crossed state lines. The court reversed this ruling in 1944 but Congress quickly returned authority to regulate insurance to the states.

Taxes

Woodruff v. Parham (8 Wall. 123), decided without dissent, Nov. 8, 1869. Miller wrote the opinion.

States are not constitutionally forbidden to tax goods "imported" from other states. The constitutional language forbidding states to tax imports or exports applies only to goods coming from or going to foreign countries.

States may tax goods from other states, once interstate transportation of those goods has ended, even if they are still in their original packages.

Veazie Bank v. Fenno (8 Wall. 533), decided by a 7-2 vote, Dec. 31, 1869. Chief Justice Chase wrote the majority opinion; Nelson and Davis dissented.

Congress may use its power to tax as a regulatory tool to support or enforce exercise of another constitutional power, even if the tax is designed to eliminate the matter taxed.

In this case, the court sustained a federal statute that placed a 10 percent tax on the circulation of state bank notes in order to give the untaxed national bank notes a competitive edge and drive the state notes out of the market. The court said the tax was a legitimate means through which Congress could exercise its constitutional authority to regulate currency.

1870-1879

Currency

Hepburn v. Griswold (First Legal Tender Case) (8 Wall. 603), decided by a 4-3 vote, Feb. 7, 1870. Chief Justice Chase wrote the majority opinion; Davis, Miller and Swayne dissented.

The court declared unconstitutional acts of Congress that substituted paper money for gold as legal tender for the payment of debts contracted prior to adoption of the first legal tender act in 1862.

The statute had been enacted to help the Union finance the Civil War, but the court held it an improper exercise of Congress' implied powers under the "necessary and proper" clause.

Knox v. Lee, Parker v. Davis (Second Legal Tender Case) (12 Wall. 457), decided by a 5-4 vote, May 1, 1871. Strong wrote the majority opinion; Chief Justice Chase, Nelson, Clifford and Field dissented.

Overturning its 1870 decision in *Hepburn v. Griswold,* the majority held that Congress had exercised its implied powers properly when it made paper money legal tender for the payment of debts. The fact that the two justices appointed to the court since the first decision supported the reversal led to charges that the court had been "packed."

Taxes

Low v. Austin (13 Wall. 29), decided by a unanimous vote, Jan. 29, 1872. Field wrote the opinion.

The constitutional language forbidding states to tax imports or exports prohibits state taxes on goods imported from foreign countries so long as those goods retain their character as imports.

Official Immunity

Bradley v. Fisher (13 Wall. 335), decided by a 7-2 vote, April 8, 1872. Field wrote the majority opinion; Davis and Clifford dissented.

Setting out the doctrine of judicial immunity, the court ruled that judges may not be sued for their official actions, no matter how erroneous or injurious those actions may be.

Privileges and Immunities

The Slaughterhouse Cases: The Butchers' Benevolent Association of New Orleans v. The Crescent City Livestock Landing and Slaughterhouse Co., Esteben v. Louisiana (16 Wall. 36), decided by a 5-4 vote, April 14, 1873. Miller wrote the majority opinion; Chief Justice Chase, Field, Swayne and Bradley dissented.

Louisiana did not violate the 14th Amendment when it granted a monopoly on the slaughterhouse business to one company for all of New Orleans. The right of other butchers to do business is neither a "privilege and immunity" of U.S. citizenship protected by the 14th Amendment nor an aspect of the "property" protected by the amendment's due process guarantee.

Bradwell v. State of Illinois (16 Wall. 130), decided by an 8-1 vote, April 15, 1873. Miller wrote the majority opinion; Chief Justice Chase dissented.

A state does not violate the 14th Amendment's guarantee of the privileges and immunities of U.S. citizenship when it refuses on the grounds of gender to license a woman to practice law in its courts. The right to practice law is not a privilege or immunity of U.S. citizenship.

Minor v. Happersett (21 Wall. 162), decided by a unanimous vote, March 29, 1875. Chief Justice Waite wrote the opinion.

The privileges and immunities clause of the 14th Amendment does not guarantee women the right to vote. A state therefore does not violate that amendment's guarantee when it denies a woman the right to vote. "[T]he Constitution of the United States does not confer the right of suffrage on anyone," the court said.

Commerce

Henderson v. Wickham, Commissioners of Immigration v. The North German Lloyd, Chy Lung v. Freeman (92 U.S. 259, 275), decided without dissent, March 20, 1876. Miller wrote the opinion.

A state may not require shipowners to give bond for each alien their ships bring into its ports. Despite the argument that this requirement would reduce the potential burden which immigrants place upon state finances, this bond requirement impermissibly interferes with the federal power to regulate foreign commerce.

This ruling resulted in the passage in 1882 of the first general federal immigration law in U.S. history.

Jury Trials

Walker v. Sauvinet (92 U.S. 90), decided by a 7-2 vote, April 24, 1876. Chief Justice Waite wrote the majority opinion; Clifford and Field dissented.

The Seventh Amendment, guaranteeing a jury trial in suits at common law involving more than $20, affects only federal, not state, trials. A trial by jury in such cases is not guaranteed in state proceedings by the 14th Amendment.

Voting Rights

United States v. Reese (92 U.S. 214), decided by an 8-1 vote, March 27, 1876. Chief Justice Waite wrote the majority opinion; Hunt dissented.

The 15th Amendment, forbidding states to deny anyone the right to vote because of race, color or previous condition of servitude, did not give anyone the right to vote. It simply guaranteed the right to be free from racial discrimination in the exercise of the right to vote — a right granted under state, not federal, laws. Therefore Congress exceeded its power to enforce the 15th Amendment when it enacted laws which penalized state officials who denied Negroes the right to vote, refused to count votes or obstructed citizens from voting.

United States v. Cruikshank (92 U.S. 542), decided by a unanimous vote, March 27, 1876. Chief Justice Waite wrote the opinion.

The court dismissed indictments brought against Louisiana citizens accused of using violence and fraud to prevent Negroes from voting. Because the indictments did not charge that these actions were motivated by racial discrimination, they were not federal offenses. "We may suspect," Waite wrote, "that race was the cause of the hostility but it is not so averred."

State Powers

Munn v. Illinois (94 U.S. 113), decided by a 7-2 vote, March 1, 1877. Chief Justice Waite wrote the majority opinion; Field and Strong dissented.

The court acknowledged the right of states to regulate private business in the exercise of their police power. The court sustained a state law setting the maximum rate that grain elevator operators could charge for grain storage. The court declared that private property dedicated to public use was subject to government regulation.

Civil Rights

Hall v. DeCuir (95 U.S. 485), decided without dissent, Jan. 14, 1878. Chief Justice Waite wrote the opinion.

A state law forbidding racial discrimination on common carriers operating in the state impermissibly infringes upon the federal power to regulate interstate commerce. Equal access to steamboat accommodations is a matter which requires national, uniform regulation and thus is outside the proper scope of state regulation.

1880-1889

Voting Rights

Ex parte Siebold (100 U.S. 371), decided by a 7-2 vote, March 8, 1880. Bradley wrote the majority opinion; Field and Clifford dissented.

Confirming federal power to protect the electoral process in congressional elections in the states, the court upheld federal laws making it a federal crime for state election officers to neglect their duty in congressional elections. The court upheld the convictions of two state officials tried and convicted for stuffing the ballot box.

Contracts

Stone v. Mississippi (101 U.S. 814), decided without dissent, May 10, 1880. Chief Justice Waite wrote the opinion.

A state may not permanently contract away any portion of its police power, its power to act to protect the general welfare. Thus, held the court, Mississippi did not act in violation of the contract clause when it amended its constitution to ban lotteries. This state action had been challenged as impairing the earlier obligation of another legislature which chartered a state lottery corporation.

Power of Congress

Kilbourn v. Thompson (103 U.S. 168), decided by a unanimous vote, Jan. 24, Feb. 28, 1881. Miller wrote the opinion.

The power of Congress to investigate is not unlimited, nor is its power to punish witnesses who refuse to cooperate with such an investigation. Investigations must be confined to subject areas over which Congress has jurisdiction, their purpose must be enactment of legislation and they may not merely inquire into the private affairs of citizens. Contempt citations issued against witnesses who refuse to cooperate in investigations that do not meet these standards are invalid.

This was the first case in which the Supreme Court asserted its authority to review the propriety of congressional investigations. The court subsequently modified the standards laid out in this case, but its basic limitations on the power of Congress to investigate remain in effect.

Civil Rights

Civil Rights Cases (109 U.S. 3), decided by an 8-1 vote, Oct. 15, 1883. Bradley wrote the court's opinion; Harlan dissented.

Neither the 13th nor the 14th Amendment empowers Congress to enact a law barring discrimination against blacks in privately owned public accommodations. The 14th Amendment prohibits only state-sponsored discrimination, not private discriminatory acts, the court held. Moreover, private discrimination does not violate the 13th Amendment because "such an act of refusal has nothing to do with slavery or involuntary servitude."

The decision effectively blocked further attempts by Congress in the post-Civil War period to end private racial discrimination; not until 1964 did Congress enact and the court sustain a federal law prohibiting discrimination in privately owned public accommodations.

Voting Rights

Ex parte Yarbrough (110 U.S. 651), decided by a unanimous court, March 3, 1884; Miller wrote the opinion.

The court upheld as a valid exercise of congressional power to enforce the 15th Amendment legislation penalizing persons who conspired to stop Negroes from exercising their right to vote. The court upheld the convictions of several members of the Ku Klux Klan for intimidating a black man in order to stop him from voting. In some cases, the court held, the 15th Amendment does confer the right to vote, as well as the right to be free of racial discrimina-

tion in voting, and Congress has the power to enforce that right.

Due Process

Hurtado v. California (110 U.S. 516), decided by a 7-1 vote, March 3, 1884. Matthews wrote the majority opinion; Harlan dissented; Field did not participate.

The due process clause of the 14th Amendment does not require states to use grand jury indictments or presentments in capital offenses.

Taxes

Head Money Cases (112 U.S. 580), decided by a unanimous vote, Dec. 8, 1884. Miller wrote the opinion.

The constitutional requirement that indirect taxes be uniform is met if the tax operates the same upon all subjects being taxed; an indirect tax is not unconstitutional simply because the subject being taxed is not distributed uniformly throughout the United States.

Search and Seizure

Boyd v. United States (116 U.S. 616), decided without dissent, Feb. 1, 1886. Bradley wrote the opinion.

The court held that a revenue statute compelling a defendant to produce in court his private papers was unconstitutional as an unreasonable search and seizure violating the Fourth Amendment and as compelled self-incrimination in violation of the Fifth Amendment.

Equal Protection

Yick Wo v. Hopkins (118 U.S. 356), decided by a unanimous vote, May 10, 1886. Matthews wrote the opinion.

The 14th Amendment protects persons, not just citizens of the United States. Holding that a city's arbitrary enforcement of a fire hazard ordinance had discriminated against Chinese laundry owners in violation of the amendment's equal protection clause, the court said that guarantee applied "to all *persons* within the territorial jurisdiction, without regard to any differences of race, of color, or of nationality...."

Santa Clara County v. Southern Pacific Railroad Co. (118 U.S. 394), decided by a unanimous vote, May 10, 1886. Harlan wrote the opinion; Chief Justice Waite made a preliminary announcement.

Before the court heard arguments in this case, involving a tax dispute between a county, a state, and a railroad, Chief Justice Waite announced that the equal protection clause of the 14th Amendment applied to protect corporations as well as individuals. Corporations were thus established to be "persons" within the meaning of that amendment, and able to invoke its protection.

Commerce

Wabash, St. Louis and Pacific Railway Co. v. Illinois (118 U.S. 557), decided by a 6-3 vote, Oct. 25, 1886. Miller wrote the majority opinion; Chief Justice Waite, Bradley and Gray dissented.

States may not regulate the rates charged by railroads which form part of an interstate network, even if the state regulates only the intrastate portion of a trip. Such state regulation infringes upon the federal power to regulate interstate commerce.

State Powers

Mugler v. Kansas (123 U.S. 623), decided by an 8-1 vote, Dec. 5, 1887. Harlan wrote the majority opinion; Field dissented.

The court upheld a state law which forbade the manufacture and sale of intoxicating liquor in the state. Rejecting a challenge to this law as abridging the privileges and immunities of U.S. citizenship, as well as the due process guarantee of the 14th Amendment, the court held the law a proper exercise of the state police power to safeguard the public health and morals.

Federal Courts

Wisconsin v. Pelican Insurance Company (127 U.S. 265), decided without dissent, May 14, 1888. Gray wrote the opinion.

States may not invoke the original jurisdiction of the Supreme Court to enforce their criminal laws against non-residents. The Supreme Court refused to enforce the order of a Wisconsin court against a Louisiana corporation for failing to comply with Wisconsin laws.

Commerce

Kidd v. Pearson (128 U.S. 1), decided without dissent, Oct. 22, 1888. Lamar wrote the opinion.

The court upheld a state law which forbade the manufacture of liquor in the state — even if it was for sale and consumption outside the state. This law did not infringe federal power to regulate interstate commerce, held the court. Manufacture of goods is not commerce and cannot be regulated as interstate commerce.

Immigration

Chinese Exclusion Cases (Chae Chan Ping v. United States) (130 U.S. 581), decided by a unanimous vote, May 13, 1889. Field wrote the opinion.

The power of Congress over the entry of aliens, derived from the need to preserve the nation's sovereign status, is exclusive and absolute. This decision sustained an act of Congress which barred the entry of Chinese aliens into the country.

1890-1899

Treaties

Geofroy v. Riggs (133 U.S. 258), decided by a unanimous vote, February 3, 1890. Field wrote the opinion.

It is within the scope of the treaty power of the United States to regulate the inheritance by aliens of land and other property in the United States. The court declared that the treaty power was unlimited except by the Constitution. Field observed: "It would not be contended that it extends so far as to authorize what the Constitution forbids. . . ."

Civil Rights

Louisville, New Orleans and Texas Railway Co. v. Mississippi (133 U.S. 587), decided by a 7-2 vote, March 3, 1890. Brewer wrote the majority opinion; Harlan and Bradley dissented.

Mississippi does not infringe on the federal power to regulate interstate commerce when it by law requires railroads doing business in the state to provide separate accommodations for black and white passengers. The state

supreme court found this to apply solely to intrastate railroad operations. The Supreme Court accepted those findings and held the requirement was no burden on interstate commerce.

Due Process

Chicago, Milwaukee & St. Paul Railway Co. v. Minnesota (134 U.S. 418), decided by a 6-3 vote, March 24, 1890. Blatchford wrote the majority opinion; Bradley, Gray and Lamar dissented.

If a state deprives a company of the power to charge reasonable rates for the use of its property and provides for no judicial review of those rate limitations, the state is depriving the company of its property without due process of law.

Courts have the power to decide on the reasonableness of rates set by states for companies to charge and due process requires that an opportunity for judicial review of these rates be provided.

Self-Incrimination

Counselman v. Hitchcock (142 U.S. 547), decided by a unanimous vote, Jan. 11, 1892. Blatchford wrote the opinion.

Only a grant of complete and absolute immunity against prosecution for an offense revealed in compelled testimony is sufficient to justify waiver of the Fifth Amendment privilege against compelled self-incrimination.

The court struck down as insufficient under this standard the existing federal immunity statute which protected a witness only against the actual use of his testimony as evidence against him, not against its indirect use to obtain other evidence against him.

Federal Courts

United States v. Texas (143 U.S. 621), decided by a 7-2 vote, Feb. 29, 1892. Harlan wrote the majority opinion; Chief Justice Fuller and Lamar dissented.

By joining the Union, states acquiesce in the constitutional provision extending federal judicial power over all cases in which the United States is a party, including those brought by the United States against a state. The court rejected Texas' argument that the court lacked jurisdiction over such a case.

Compacts

Virginia v. Tennessee (148 U.S. 503), decided without dissent, April 3, 1893. Field wrote the opinion.

A compact to resolve a boundary dispute between two states need not be approved formally by Congress in order to be permissible. The Constitution does declare that "no state shall, without the consent of Congress, . . . enter into any Agreement or Compact with another state," but this requirement of formal consent applies only to compacts tending to increase the political power of the states at the expense of national authority or the federal government.

Commerce

United States v. E. C. Knight Co. (156 U.S. 1), decided by an 8-1 vote, Jan. 21, 1895. Chief Justice Fuller wrote the majority opinion; Harlan dissented.

In its first interpretation of the Sherman Anti-trust Act, the court ruled that the act did not apply to a trust that refined more than 90 percent of the sugar sold in the country.

Congress had no constitutional power to regulate manufacture, the court stated. The fact that much of the refined sugar was intended for sale in interstate commerce made no difference. Such sales would affect interstate commerce only indirectly. Congressional authority extended only to regulation of matters that directly affected interstate commerce.

This distinction between matters affecting interstate commerce directly or indirectly was a significant modification of the court's 1824 *Gibbons v. Ogden* opinion, in which it held that the Constitution gave Congress authority to regulate intrastate matters that affected other states.

The holding in *Knight* was gradually eroded by later decisions.

Federal Courts

California v. Southern Pacific Co. (157 U.S. 229), decided by a 7-2 vote, March 18, 1895. Chief Justice Fuller wrote the majority opinion; Harlan and Brewer dissented.

The Supreme Court does not have original jurisdiction over cases brought by a state against its own citizens; such suits are generally to be brought in state courts, not federal courts.

Taxes

Pollock v. Farmers' Loan and Trust Co. (158 U.S. 601), decided by a 5-4 vote, May 20, 1895. Chief Justice Fuller wrote the majority opinion; Harlan, Jackson, Brown and White dissented.

Taxes on income derived from real estate and personal property are direct taxes and therefore must be apportioned among the states according to population. With this ruling the court struck down the first general income tax law enacted by Congress and overruled two earlier decisions which defined head taxes and taxes on land as the only two forms of direct taxation.

The decision led to adoption and ratification in 1913 of the 16th Amendment which exempted income taxes from the Constitution's apportionment requirement.

Commerce

In re Debs (158 U.S. 564) decided by a unanimous vote, May 27, 1895. Brewer wrote the court's opinion.

Eugene V. Debs and other leaders of the 1894 Pullman strike challenged their contempt convictions for violating a federal court injunction ordering them to halt the strike. A lower court upheld the validity of the injunction under the authority of the Sherman Anti-trust Act. The Supreme Court affirmed the validity of the injunction — and Debs' conviction — but on the broader grounds of national sovereignty, which the court said gave the federal government authority to remove obstructions to interstate commerce and transportation of the mails.

Civil Rights

Plessy v. Ferguson (163 U.S. 537), decided by an 8-1 vote, May 18, 1896. Brown wrote the majority opinion; Harlan dissented.

A state law requiring trains to provide separate but equal facilities for black and white passengers does not infringe upon federal authority to regulate interstate commerce nor is it in violation of the 13th or 14th Amendments. The train was local; a legal distinction between the two races did not destroy the legal equality of the two races guaranteed by the 13th Amendment, and the 14th Amend-

ment protected only political, not social, equality, the majority said.

In dissent, Justice John Marshall Harlan declared that the "Constitution is color-blind, and neither knows nor tolerates classes among citizens." The "separate but equal" doctrine remained effective until the 1954 *Brown v. Board of Education* decision.

Due Process

Allgeyer v. Louisiana (165 U.S. 578), decided without dissent, March 1, 1897. Peckham wrote the opinion.

The court declared that the liberty protected by the due process clause of the 14th Amendment against denial by the state included the freedom to make a contract. The court struck down a state law which forbade its citizens to obtain insurance from out-of-state companies.

This was the first recognition by the court of the protected "freedom of contract" which the justices would use subsequently to strike down minimum wage and maximum hour laws.

Chicago, Burlington & Quincy Railroad Company v. Chicago (166 U.S. 226), decided by a 7-1 vote, March 1, 1897. Harlan wrote the majority opinion; Brewer dissented; Chief Justice Fuller did not participate.

The 14th Amendment guarantee of due process requires a state, when it takes private property for public use, to provide just compensation to the property owner.

Holden v. Hardy (169 U.S. 366), decided by a 7-2 vote, Feb. 28, 1898. Brown wrote the majority opinion; Brewer and Peckham dissented.

The court upheld, against a due process challenge, Utah's law that limited the number of hours that miners could work in underground mines.

The "freedom of contract" is subject to certain limitations imposed by the state in the exercise of its police power to protect the health of workers in hazardous conditions, the court said.

Smyth v. Ames (169 U.S. 466), decided by a 7-0 vote, March 7, 1898. Harlan wrote the opinion; Chief Justice Fuller and McKenna did not participate in the decision.

Corporations are persons within the protection of the 14th Amendment's guarantee of due process. That guarantee requires states to set railroad rates sufficiently high to ensure the railroad companies a fair return on the value of the investment and just compensation for the use of their property.

To ensure compliance with this standard, federal courts have the power to review the rates.

Citizenship

United States v. Wong Kim Ark (169 U.S. 649) decided by a 6-2 vote, March 28, 1898. Gray wrote the majority opinion; Chief Justice Fuller and Harlan dissented; McKenna did not participate.

Children born in the United States to resident alien parents are citizens of the United States even if their parents are barred from becoming citizens because of their race.

This was the first case in which the court interpreted the clause of the 14th Amendment that defines U.S. citizens as all persons born in the United States and remaining under its jurisdiction.

Voting Rights

Williams v. Mississippi (170 U.S. 213), decided by a unanimous vote, April 25, 1898. McKenna delivered the opinion.

A state does not violate the equal protection clause of the 14th Amendment when it requires eligible voters to be able to read, write, and interpret or understand any part of the Constitution.

1900-1905

Privileges and Immunities

Maxwell v. Dow (176 U.S. 581), decided by an 8-1 vote, Feb. 25, 1900. Peckham wrote the majority opinion; Harlan dissented.

The right to be tried by a jury of 12 persons is not one of the privileges and immunities of United States citizenship protected by the 14th Amendment against violation by states.

The court upheld a state court judgment reached by a jury composed of eight persons — instead of 12 as required in federal courts.

Taxes

Knowlton v. Moore (178 U.S. 41), decided by a 5-3 vote, May 14, 1900. White wrote the majority opinion; Brewer dissented in part; Harlan and McKenna dissented; Peckham did not participate.

The constitutional requirement that indirect taxes be uniform does not require that the tax rate be uniform, only that the same rate be applied to the same class in the same manner throughout the United States.

Territories

The Insular Cases, decided May 27, 1901: **DeLima v. Bidwell** (182 U.S. 1), decided by a 5-4 vote; Brown wrote the majority opinion; Gray, McKenna, Shiras and White dissented. **Downes v. Bidwell** (182 U.S. 244), decided by a 5-4 vote; Brown wrote the majority opinion; Chief Justice Fuller, Harlan, Brewer and Peckham dissented.

In these two cases the court ruled that as a result of U.S. annexation of Puerto Rico, the island was no longer a foreign country but neither was it a part of the United States included within the full protection of the Constitution. The Constitution applied automatically only to states, the court held, and it was up to Congress, in the exercise of its power to govern territories, to determine whether the Constitution should apply in particular territories.

In a third case, *Dorr v. United States* (195 U.S. 138, 1904), the court adopted the "incorporation theory," still in effect, under which the Constitution automatically applies in territories that have been formally incorporated into the United States either through ratified treaty or act of Congress, but not to unincorporated territories.

Commerce

Champion v. Ames (188 U.S. 321), decided by a 5-4 vote, Feb. 23, 1903. Harlan wrote the majority opinion; Chief Justice Fuller, Brewer, Peckham and Shiras dissented.

In its first recognition of a federal "police" power, the court sustained a federal law banning the shipment of lottery tickets in interstate commerce. Just as states might regulate intrastate matters in order to protect the health, welfare and morals of their residents, so might Congress exercise its authority to regulate interstate commerce for the same purposes.

Northern Securities Co. v. United States (193 U.S. 197), decided by a 5-4 vote, March 14, 1904. Harlan wrote the majority opinion; Chief Justice Fuller, White, Holmes and Peckham dissented.

A holding company formed solely to eliminate competition between two railroad lines was a combination in restraint of trade and therefore in violation of the federal antitrust act.

This ruling represented a major modification of the *Knight* sugar trust decision in 1895: the majority now held that although the holding company itself was not in interstate commerce, it sufficiently affected that commerce by restraining it and thus came within the scope of the federal antitrust statute.

Taxes

McCray v. United States (195 U.S. 27), decided by a 6-3 vote, May 31, 1904. White wrote the court's opinion; Chief Justice Fuller, Brown and Peckham dissented.

Congress may use its power to tax as a regulatory "police" power. So long as the tax produces some revenue, the court will not examine the motivation for imposing the tax.

Using this reasoning, the court upheld a federal statute which placed a high tax on oleo which was colored yellow to resemble butter. That tax was obviously designed to eliminate the competition to butter, but the court held that the tax was lawful on its face and that the court had no power to "restrain the exercise of a lawful power on the assumption that a wrongful purpose or motive has caused the power to be exerted."

This ruling came little more than a year after the court held that Congress could also use its interstate commerce power as a "police" power; the two decisions substantially increased congressional power to regulate commerce in the United States.

Commerce

Swift and Co. v. United States (196 U.S 375), decided by a unanimous vote, Jan. 30, 1905. Holmes wrote the opinion.

Congress has authority to regulate local commerce that is part of an interstate current of commerce. This was the court's first enunciation of the "stream-of-commerce" doctrine.

Thus, the court held that meatpackers who combined to fix the price of livestock and meat bought and sold in Chicago stockyards were in violation of the federal antitrust act because the meatpacking operation was the middle part of an interstate transaction in which cattle were shipped from out of the state into Chicago for slaughter and packing and then shipped to other states for sale.

Due Process

Lochner v. New York (198 U.S. 45), decided by a 5-4 vote, April 17, 1905. Peckham wrote the majority opinion; Day, Harlan, Holmes and White dissented.

The court struck down a New York law limiting the hours which bakery employees could work. The majority found the law a denial of due process, infringing upon the freedom of contract. Because there was no sufficient health reason for the hours limit, the law was held to be outside the police power of the state.

1906-1910

State Powers

Georgia v. Tennessee Copper Company (206 U.S. 230), decided by a unanimous vote, May 13, 1907. Holmes wrote the opinion.

In one of the first "environmental law" cases to come to the court, the justices declared that a state could come into federal court to obtain an order directing a company in another state to cease polluting the air the two states shared.

Commerce

Adair v. United States (208 U.S. 161), decided by a 6-2 vote, Jan. 27, 1908. Harlan wrote the court's opinion; Holmes and McKenna dissented; Moody did not participate.

A federal statute prohibiting employers from making contracts that required an employee to promise not to join a labor union as a condition of employment exceeds federal authority to regulate interstate commerce. This prohibition also violates the "freedom of contract."

This decision, which was later overruled, placed these so-called "yellow dog" contracts beyond the reach of federal power. It was one of several decisions of the early 20th century in which the court ruled against the interests of the labor movement.

Loewe v. Lawler (Danbury Hatters Case) (208 U.S. 274), decided by a unanimous vote, Feb. 3, 1908. Chief Justice Fuller wrote the opinion.

A union attempting to organize workers in a factory in one state by setting up boycotts of stores in other states that sell the factory's products (secondary boycotts) becomes a combination in restraint of trade and in violation of the federal antitrust law.

This decision led to adoption of provisions in the Clayton Anti-trust Act of 1914 exempting labor unions from actions under the antitrust laws.

State Powers

Muller v. Oregon (208 U.S. 412), decided by a unanimous vote, Feb. 24, 1908. Brewer wrote the opinion.

The court upheld Oregon's law setting maximum hours for women working in laundries. The court relied on the argument that longer working hours might impair the childbearing function of women. State limitation of those hours was therefore justified as a health measure, properly within the state police power.

Federal Courts

Ex parte Young (209 U.S. 123), decided by an 8-1 vote, March 23, 1908. Peckham wrote the majority opinion; Harlan dissented.

Federal judges may properly enjoin, temporarily, the enforcement of a state law challenged as unconstitutional. The injunction may remain in effect until the validity of the law is determined.

Self-Incrimination

Twining v. New Jersey (211 U.S. 78), decided by an 8-1 vote, Nov. 9, 1908. Moody delivered the majority opinion; Harlan dissented.

The 14th Amendment does not automatically extend the Fifth Amendment privilege against compelled self-incrimination — or other provisions of the Bill of Rights — to state defendants. Thus the constitutional rights of state defendants are not impaired when a judge or prosecutor comments adversely upon their failure to testify in their own defense.

Cruel and Unusual Punishment

Weems v. United States (217 U.S. 349), decided by a 4-2 vote, May 2, 1910. McKenna wrote the majority opinion; White and Harlan dissented; Moody and Lurton did not participate.

The court held that a law of the Philippines, a U.S. territory, providing punishment of 12 years at hard labor in chains for falsifying an official document was "cruel and unusual punishment" prohibited by the Eighth Amendment.

1911-1915

Federal Courts

Muskrat v. United States (219 U.S. 346), decided by a unanimous vote, Jan. 23, 1911. Day wrote the opinion.

The court dismissed a case which Congress had authorized certain Indians to bring in order to test the constitutionality of certain laws. There was no actual dispute or conflict of rights and interests here, the court held, and thus there was no "case or controversy" properly within its power to resolve.

Commerce

Standard Oil Co. v. United States (221 U.S. 1), decided by an 8-1 vote, May 15, 1911. Chief Justice White wrote the majority opinion; Harlan dissented in part.

Only unreasonable combinations and undue restraints of trade are illegal under the federal antitrust act. In this decision, which resulted in the break-up of the Standard Oil monopoly, a majority of the court for the first time adopted the so-called "rule of reason;" it is still applied to antitrust cases today. Previously, the court had held that *any* combination which restrained trade, whether "reasonable" or "unreasonable," was a violation of the federal statute.

Contempt

Gompers v. Buck's Stove and Range Co. (221 U.S. 418), decided by a unanimous court, May 15, 1911. Lamar wrote the opinion.

Civil contempt and criminal contempt are distinguished by the character and purpose of the penalty imposed for them. The purpose of a punishment for civil contempt is remedial — to convince a witness to testify, for example — while the purpose of punishment for criminal contempt is clearly punitive, to vindicate the authority of the court. Civil contempt ends whenever the person held in contempt decides to comply with the court; criminal contempt is punished by a fixed sentence.

State Powers

Coyle v. Smith (221 U.S. 559), decided by a 7-2 vote, May 29, 1911. Lurton wrote the court's opinion; McKenna and Holmes dissented.

States are admitted into the Union on an equal footing with all other states; Congress may not place any restrictions on matters wholly under the state's control as a condition of entry. This ruling invalidated a congressional requirement that Oklahoma's state capital remain in Guthrie, Okla., for seven years after statehood was granted.

Search and Seizure

Weeks v. United States (232 U.S. 383), decided by a unanimous vote, Feb. 24, 1914. Day wrote the opinion.

A person whose Fourth Amendment rights to be secure against unreasonable search and seizure are violated by federal agents has the right to require that evidence obtained in the search be excluded from use against him in federal courts.

Commerce

Shreveport Rate Case: Houston, East and West Texas Railway Co. v. United States; Texas and Pacific Railway Co. v. United States (234 U.S. 342), decided by a 7-2 vote, June 8, 1914. Hughes wrote the majority opinion; Lurton and Pitney dissented.

Congress may regulate intrastate rail rates if they are so intertwined with interstate rail rates that it is impossible to regulate the one without regulating the other. This so-called "Shreveport Doctrine" was eventually expanded to allow regulation of other intrastate matters that affected interstate commerce.

Due Process

Frank v. Mangum (237 U.S. 309), decided by a 7-2 vote, April 12, 1915. Pitney wrote the majority opinion; Holmes and Hughes dissented.

The court upheld a state conviction for murder although the trial court atmosphere was dominated by anti-Semitism and hostility. The majority reasoned that review of the conviction by Georgia's highest state court guaranteed the defendant due process.

Interstate Relations

Virginia v. West Virginia (238 U.S. 202), decided by a unanimous vote, June 14, 1915. Hughes wrote the opinion.

In one of the longest-running disputes to come before the court, the justices held in 1915 that West Virginia owed Virginia some $12 million — its share of the pre-Civil War state debts of Virginia, which West Virginia had agreed to assume upon its becoming a separate state.

Voting Rights

Guinn v. United States (238 U.S. 347), decided by an 8-0 vote, June 21, 1915. Chief Justice White wrote the opinion; McReynolds did not participate.

The court declared an Oklahoma "grandfather clause" for voters an unconstitutional evasion of the 15th Amendment guarantee that states would not deny citizens the right to vote because of their race. Oklahoma law imposed a literacy test upon potential voters but exempted all persons whose ancestors voted in 1866. The court said that though race, color or previous servitude were not mentioned in the law, selection of a date prior to adoption of the 15th Amendment was obviously intended to disenfranchise Negroes in "direct and positive disregard" of the amendment.

United States v. Mosley (238 U.S. 383), decided by a 7-1 vote, June 21, 1915. Holmes wrote the opinion; Lamar dissented; McReynolds did not participate.

The court upheld congressional power to regulate elections tainted with fraud and corruption. For the second time the court upheld provisions of the 1870 Enforcement Act implementing the 15th Amendment. In *Ex parte Yarbrough* (1884) the court had sustained congressional power to penalize persons who used violence and intimidation to prevent Negroes from voting.

State Powers

Hadacheck v. Los Angeles (239 U.S. 394), decided by a unanimous vote, Dec. 12, 1915. McKenna wrote the opinion.

The power to pass zoning laws is part of the state police power, enabling the state to control the use to which certain lands are put. A city's use of this power to forbid brickmaking in a certain area is valid, and does not deny due process to a brickmaker, even if it puts him out of business.

1916-1920

Taxes

Brushaber v. Union Pacific Railroad Co. (240 U.S. 1), decided by a 7-2 vote, Jan. 24, 1916. Chief Justice White wrote the majority opinion; McKenna and Pitney dissented.

With two other cases decided the same day, the court in this decision sustained the 1913 general income tax law enacted after ratification of the 16th Amendment. This decision completed the action necessary to nullify the court's 1895 ruling that income taxes were direct taxes that must be apportioned among the states according to population. The 16th Amendment exempted income taxes from the apportionment requirement.

Power of Congress

Clark Distilling Co. v. Western Maryland Railway (242 U.S. 311), decided by a 7-2 vote, Jan. 8, 1917. Chief Justice White wrote the majority opinion; Holmes and Van Devanter dissented.

The court upheld the power of the states under the federal Webb-Kenyon Act of 1913 to forbid the entry of intoxicating liquor into their territory.

The act giving the states that power had been challenged as an unconstitutional delegation of power, but the court held it was permissible because the statute established the precise conditions under which the states might act.

Due Process

Bunting v. Oregon (243 U.S. 426), decided by a 5-3 vote, April 9, 1917. McKenna wrote the majority opinion; Chief Justice White, McReynolds and Van Devanter dissented; Brandeis did not participate.

Extending its 1908 decision in *Muller v. Oregon*, the court upheld an Oregon law setting 10 hours as the maximum permissible workday for all industrial workers.

Buchanan v. Warley (245 U.S. 60), decided by a unanimous vote, Nov. 5, 1917. Day wrote the opinion.

City ordinances that segregate neighborhoods by restricting some blocks to white residents only and other blocks to black residents only violate the 14th Amendment, which forbids states to deprive persons of property rights except by due process of law.

This decision led to the growth of private restrictive covenants under which neighbors would agree to sell or rent their homes only to persons of the same race. The court upheld such private covenants in the 1926 case of *Corrigan v. Buckley.*

Power of Congress

Selective Draft Law Cases (245 U.S. 366), decided by a unanimous vote, Jan. 7, 1918. Chief Justice White wrote the opinion.

Congress is authorized to institute a compulsory draft of persons into the armed forces under its power to raise armies and the "necessary and proper" clause. Moreover, service in the military is one of the duties of a citizen in a "just government." Compulsory conscription is not involuntary servitude in violation of the 13th Amendment.

Commerce

Hammer v. Dagenhart (247 U.S. 251), decided by a 5-4 vote, June 3, 1918. Day wrote the majority opinion; Holmes, McKenna, Brandeis and Clarke dissented.

Narrowing the federal "police" power substantially, the court struck down a federal statute that prohibited the shipment in interstate commerce of any goods produced by child laborers.

Labor was an aspect of manufacture, an intrastate matter not subject to federal control, the majority held. Furthermore, Congress could prohibit shipments in interstate commerce only of goods that were in themselves harmful. Because products made by children were not themselves harmful, Congress had no authority to forbid their shipment.

This decision and a 1922 ruling that Congress had used its taxing power unconstitutionally in a second law intended to bring an end to child labor were overruled in 1941.

Freedom of Expression

Schenck v. United States (249 U.S. 47), decided by a unanimous vote, March 3, 1919. Holmes wrote the opinion.

In its first decision dealing with the extent of protection afforded by the First Amendment, the court sustained the Espionage Act of 1917 against a challenge that it violated the guarantees of freedom of speech and press.

The First Amendment is not an absolute guarantee, the court said. Freedom of speech and press may be constrained if "the words used are used in such circumstances and are of such a nature as to create a clear and present danger that they will bring about the substantive evils that Congress has a right to prevent."

Treaties

Missouri v. Holland (252 U.S. 416), decided by a 7-2 vote, April 19, 1920. Holmes wrote the majority opinion; Van Devanter and Pitney dissented.

In order to implement a treaty, Congress may enact legislation that without a treaty might be an unconstitutional invasion of state sovereignty.

After lower courts ruled an act of Congress protecting migratory birds an unconstitutional invasion of powers reserved to the states, the U.S. government negotiated a treaty with Canada for the protection of the birds. After the Senate ratified it, Congress again enacted protective legislation to fulfill the terms of the treaty. Sustaining this second act, the court wrote: "It is obvious that there may

be matters of the sharpest exigency for the national well-being that an act of Congress could not deal with but that a treaty followed by such an act could. . . ."

1921-1925

Commerce

Duplex Printing Press Co. v. Deering (254 U.S. 443), decided by a 6-3 vote, Jan. 3, 1921. Pitney wrote the majority opinion. Brandeis, Holmes and Clarke dissented.

Reading the Clayton Act narrowly, the majority held that federal courts were prohibited from issuing injunctions only against legal and normal labor union operations. A secondary boycott was a combination in restraint of trade, which was illegal under the federal antitrust law. Courts therefore could use injunctions to stop illegal secondary boycotts.

Power of Congress

Newberry v. United States (256 U.S. 232), decided by a 5-4 vote, May 2, 1921. McReynolds wrote the majority opinion; Chief Justice White, Pitney, Brandeis and Clark dissented in part.

The court reversed the conviction of Truman H. Newberry for violating an act of Congress limiting campaign expenditures in a primary election. The court held that Congress lacked power to regulate primary campaigns because a primary was "in no real sense part of the manner of holding the election."

Dillon v. Gloss (256 U.S. 368), decided by a unanimous vote, May 16, 1921. Van Devanter wrote the opinion.

The power of Congress to designate the manner in which the states shall ratify proposed amendments to the Constitution includes the power to set a "reasonable" time period within which the states must act.

State Powers

Ponzi v. Fessenden (258 U.S. 254), decided by a unanimous vote, March 27, 1922. Chief Justice Taft wrote the opinion.

With the consent of the federal government, a state court may issue a writ of *habeas corpus* to federal officials, directing them to present a federal prisoner to state court for trial there on state charges.

Taxes

Bailey v. Drexel Furniture Co. (259 U.S. 20), decided by an 8-1 vote, May 15, 1922. Chief Justice Taft wrote the majority opinion; Clarke dissented.

In its second decision frustrating congressional efforts to end child labor, the court invalidated a federal law that imposed a 10 percent tax on the net profits of any company that employed children under a certain age. The court said the tax was an impermissible use of Congress' police power because Congress intended it as a penalty rather than a source of revenue. The court overruled this and its 1918 *Hammer v. Dagenhart* decision in 1941.

Double Jeopardy

United States v. Lanza (260 U.S. 377), decided by an 8-0 vote, Dec. 11, 1922. Chief Justice Taft delivered the opinion.

Where both federal and state jurisdictions make the same act a crime the double jeopardy guarantee of the Fifth

Amendment does not prohibit a federal prosecution and a state prosecution of the same defendant for the same crime.

Due Process

Moore v. Dempsey (261 U.S. 86), decided by a 6-2 vote, Feb. 19, 1923. Holmes wrote the majority opinion; McReynolds and Sutherland dissented.

Mob domination of the atmosphere of a trial can deny a defendant his right to a fair trial guaranteed by the Sixth Amendment.

Adkins v. Children's Hospital (261 U.S. 525), decided by a 5-3 vote, April 9, 1923. Sutherland wrote the majority opinion; Chief Justice Taft, Holmes and Sanford dissented; Brandeis did not participate.

The court struck down an act of Congress setting a minimum wage for women and children workers in the District of Columbia. The majority found this law a price-fixing measure, in violation of the freedom of contract protected by the Fifth Amendment against infringement by federal action.

Federal Courts

Massachusetts v. Mellon, Frothingham v. Mellon (262 U.S. 447), decided by a unanimous court, June 4, 1923. Sutherland wrote the opinion.

Rejecting a state and a taxpayer's challenges to a federal grant-in-aid program as unconstitutional, the court held that the taxpayer lacked "standing" to sue, because her share of the federal revenues expended in the challenged program was too minute to constitute the personal interest which one must have in a matter in order to bring a challenge to it in federal court.

Search and Seizure

Carroll v. United States (267 U.S. 132), decided by a 7-2 vote, March 2, 1925. Chief Justice Taft delivered the majority opinion; McReynolds and Sutherland dissented.

The ruling extended the scope of permissible searches which could be conducted without a warrant. Federal agents could make warrantless searches of automobiles when they had a reasonable suspicion of illegal actions.

Personal Liberty

Pierce v. Society of Sisters (268 U.S. 510), decided by a unanimous vote, June 1, 1925. McReynolds wrote the opinion.

A state law which requires all children in the first eight grades to attend public, rather than private or parochial, schools violates the 14th Amendment due process guarantee of "personal liberty." Implicit in this liberty is the right of parents to choose the kind of education they want for their children.

Freedom of Speech

Gitlow v. New York (268 U.S. 652), decided by a 7-2 vote, June 8, 1925. Sanford wrote the majority opinion; Holmes and Brandeis dissented.

The First Amendment prohibition against government abridgment of the freedom of speech applies to the states as well as to the federal government. The freedoms of speech and press "are among the fundamental personal rights and 'liberties' protected by the due process clause of the 14th

Amendment from impairment by the states," the court asserted. This decision was the first of a long line of rulings which held that the 14th Amendment extended the guarantees of the Bill of Rights to state, as well as federal, action.

1926-1930

Civil Rights

Corrigan v. Buckley (271 U.S. 323), decided by a unanimous vote, May 24, 1926. Sanford wrote the opinion.

Civil rights are not protected by the Fifth, 13th or 14th Amendments against the discriminatory actions of private individuals. Therefore there is no constitutional protection for individuals who have been discriminated against as a result of the use of private restrictive covenants, under which residents of one race living in a neighborhood agree among themselves not to sell or rent their homes to members of another race.

Power of the President

Myers v. United States (272 U.S. 52), decided by a 6-3 vote, Oct. 25, 1926. Chief Justice Taft wrote the majority opinion; Holmes, Brandeis and McReynolds dissented.

This decision upheld the president's power to remove certain classes of postmasters from office without congressional consent. The court held that the statute creating the positions — which also provided for removal only with congressional consent — was an unconstitutional incursion upon executive power. The court implied that the president's removal power was virtually unlimited, extending even to members of independent regulatory agencies.

State Powers

Euclid v. Ambler Realty Co. (272 U.S. 365), decided by a 6-3 vote, Nov. 22, 1926. Sutherland wrote the majority opinion; Butler, McReynolds and Van Devanter dissented.

A city's zoning ordinance excluding apartment houses from certain neighborhoods is an appropriate use of the police power and does not violate the due process guarantee in denying an individual the right to use his property as he desires. If the classification of land use in a zoning ordinance is "fairly debatable," it will be upheld.

Due Process

Tumey v. Ohio (273 U.S. 510), decided by a unanimous vote, March 7, 1927. Chief Justice Taft wrote the opinion.

The 14th Amendment guarantee of due process assures a defendant a trial before an impartial judge. A state, therefore, may not allow a city's mayor to serve as judge in cases, when half the fines collected go into the city treasury. A defendant is denied due process when he is tried before a judge with a direct, personal, pecuniary interest in ruling against him.

Voting Rights

Nixon v. Herndon (273 U.S. 536), decided by a unanimous vote, March 7, 1927. Holmes wrote the opinion.

The court invalidated a Texas law that excluded Negroes from voting in primary elections of the Democratic Party. The court declared the Texas "white primary" law unconstitutional as a violation of the equal protection clause of the 14th Amendment.

Due Process

Buck v. Bell (274 U.S. 200), decided by an 8-1 vote, May 2, 1927. Holmes wrote the majority opinion; Butler dissented.

The court held that Virginia did not violate the 14th Amendment's due process guarantee when it sterilized, without her consent, a mentally defective mother.

Freedom of Association

Whitney v. California (274 U.S. 357), decided by a unanimous vote, May 16, 1927. Sanford wrote the opinion.

The court upheld a state law that made it a crime to organize and participate in a group that advocated the overthrow by force of the established political system. The law was challenged as a violation of the First Amendment freedoms of speech and assembly.

Taxes

J. W. Hampton Jr. & Co. v. United States (276 U.S. 394), decided by a unanimous vote, April 9, 1928. Chief Justice Taft wrote the opinion.

Imposition of protective tariffs is a permissible exercise of the power to tax, a power which may be used to regulate as well as to raise revenue.

Search and Seizure

Olmstead v. United States (277 U.S. 438), decided by a 5-4 vote, June 4, 1928. Chief Justice Taft wrote the majority opinion; Brandeis, Holmes, Butler and Stone dissented.

Wiretaps do not violate the Fourth Amendment's prohibition against unreasonable searches and seizures where no entry of private premises occurred.

Jury Trials

Patton v. United States (281 U.S. 276), decided by a 7-0 vote, April 14, 1930. Sutherland wrote the opinion; Chief Justice Hughes did not participate.

The three essential elements of a jury trial required in federal courts by the Sixth Amendment are a panel of 12 jurors, supervision by a judge and a unanimous verdict.

1931-1934

Freedom of Speech

Stromberg v. California (283 U.S. 359), decided by a 7-2 vote, May 18, 1931. Chief Justice Hughes wrote the majority opinion; McReynolds and Butler dissented.

A state violates the First Amendment guarantee of free speech when it penalizes persons who raise a red flag as a symbol of opposition to organized government. The court did not directly address the First Amendment issue in this case but held instead that the language of the statute was impermissibly vague. Although aimed at curbing symbolic speech that advocated the unlawful overthrow of the government, the statute's language conceivably permitted punishment for the flying of any banner symbolizing advocacy of a change in government, even through peaceful means.

Freedom of the Press

Near v. Minnesota (283 U.S. 697), decided by a 5-4 vote, June 1, 1931. Chief Justice Hughes wrote the majority opinion; Butler, Van Devanter, McReynolds and Sutherland dissented.

A state law which bars continued publication of a newspaper that prints malicious or defamatory articles is a prior restraint of the press in violation of the First Amendment. This was the first time that the court specifically enforced the First Amendment's guarantee of freedom of the press against abridgment by a state.

Voting Rights

Nixon v. Condon (286 U.S. 73), decided by a 5-4 vote, May 2, 1932. Cardozo wrote the majority opinion; McReynolds, Butler, Sutherland and Van Devanter dissented.

Exclusion of Negroes from voting in primary elections — as a result of action by the Democratic Party — constituted denial of equal protection of the laws and was impermissible under the 14th Amendment. The political party, the court held, acted as the agent of the state in denying Negroes access to primary elections.

After the court's decision in *Nixon v. Herndon* (1927), the Texas legislature authorized the state party executive committee to set voting qualifications for its primary. The party excluded Negroes. The court held this action unconstitutional, saying that neither the state nor political parties could exclude Negroes from primaries on the basis of race alone.

Wood v. Broom (287 U.S. 1), decided by a 5-4 vote, Oct. 18, 1932. Chief Justice Hughes wrote the majority opinion; Brandeis, Stone, Cardozo and Roberts dissented.

When Congress in the Apportionment Act of 1929 omitted the requirement that electoral districts for congressional elections be contiguous, compact and equal, it effectively repealed similar requirements in previous laws. Thus, federal courts could not act to correct malapportionment in state districts.

Right to Counsel

Powell v. Alabama (287 U.S. 45), decided by a 7-2 vote, Nov. 7, 1932. Sutherland wrote the majority opinion; Butler and McReynolds dissented.

Under the particular circumstances of this — the "First Scottsboro Case" — in which a number of young black men charged with raping two white women were tried in a hostile community atmosphere — the failure of the trial court to provide the defendants the effective aid of an attorney in presenting their defense constituted a denial of due process guaranteed them by the 14th Amendment.

Contracts

Home Building and Loan Assn. v. Blaisdell (290 U.S. 398), decided by a 5-4 vote, Jan. 8, 1934. Chief Justice Hughes wrote the majority opinion; Sutherland, Van Devanter, Butler and McReynolds dissented.

The court upheld an emergency state mortgage moratorium law against the challenge that it violated the constitutional ban on state action impairing the obligation of contracts.

State Powers

Nebbia v. New York (291 U.S. 502), decided by a 5-4 vote, March 5, 1934. Roberts wrote the majority opinion; McReynolds, Butler, Van Devanter and Sutherland dissented.

The court abandoned its "public interest" rationale for determining which areas of business were properly subject to state regulation — a line of cases begun in *Munn v. Illinois* in 1877.

In this case the court upheld a New York law which set an acceptable range of prices to be charged for milk within the state. The majority declared that states could regulate almost any business in the interest of the public good, so long as the regulation was reasonable and effected through appropriate means.

1935

Power of Congress

Panama Refining Co. v. Ryan (293 U.S. 388), decided by an 8-1 vote, Jan. 7, 1935. Chief Justice Hughes wrote the majority opinion; Cardozo dissented.

The court declared invalid a provision of the National Industrial Recovery Act that authorized the president to prohibit from interstate commerce oil produced in violation of state regulations controlling the amount of production. The court said this congressional delegation of power was unconstitutionally broad because it left too much to the discretion of the president. This was the first of the court's rulings striking down New Deal legislation.

Currency

Gold Clause Cases: Norman v. Baltimore and Ohio Railroad Co. (294 U.S. 240), *Nortz v. United States* (294 U.S. 317), *Perry v. United States* (294 U.S. 330), decided by 5-4 votes, Feb. 18, 1935. Chief Justice Hughes wrote the majority opinion; McReynolds, Butler, Sutherland and Van Devanter dissented.

The power of Congress to regulate the value of currency permits it to abrogate clauses in private contracts requiring payment in gold. But the federal power to borrow money "on the credit of the United States" prohibits Congress from abrogating such clauses contained in government bonds and other federal contracts.

Voting Rights

Grovey v. Townsend (295 U.S. 45), decided by a unanimous vote, April 1, 1935. Roberts wrote the opinion.

The court held that the Texas Democratic Party did not violate the 14th Amendment by deciding to confine membership in the party to white citizens. A political party was a private organization, the court ruled, and the 14th Amendment's guarantee did not reach private action.

Jury Trials

Norris v. Alabama (294 U.S. 587), decided by an 8-0 vote, April 1, 1935. Chief Justice Hughes wrote the opinion; McReynolds did not participate.

In the "Second Scottsboro Case," the court set aside the conviction of the Negro defendant because blacks had been consistently barred from service on both the grand jury and trial jury in this case.

Commerce

Railroad Retirement Board v. Alton Railroad Co. (295 U.S. 330), decided by a 5-4 vote, May 6, 1935. Roberts wrote the majority opinion; Chief Justice Hughes, Brandeis, Cardozo and Stone dissented.

Congress exceeded its authority when it enacted the Railroad Retirement Act of 1934, which set up a comprehensive pension system for railroad workers, the court held, invalidating the act. The pension plan was unrelated to interstate commerce, the majority said, and, in addition, several parts of it violated the guarantee of due process.

Schechter Poultry Corp. v. United States (295 U.S. 495), decided by a unanimous vote, May 27, 1935. Chief Justice Hughes wrote the opinion.

Congress exceeded its authority to delegate legislative powers and to regulate interstate commerce when it enacted the National Industrial Recovery Act. The section of the statute that permitted the president to approve "fair competition" codes under certain conditions left the chief executive with too much discretionary power. Furthermore, the statute regulated matters of intrastate commerce that affected interstate commerce only indirectly and so were not within federal power to regulate.

Power of the President

Humphrey's Executor v. United States (295 U.S. 602), decided by a unanimous vote, May 27, 1935. Sutherland wrote the opinion.

The court denied the president the power to remove members of independent regulatory agencies without the consent of Congress and limited sharply the executive removal power given such broad scope in the 1926 decision in *Myers v. United States.*

1936

The Spending Power

United States v. Butler (297 U.S. 1), decided by a 6-3 vote, Jan. 6, 1936. Roberts wrote the majority opinion; Stone, Brandeis and Cardozo dissented.

In its first interpretation of the power of Congress to spend for the general welfare, the court held that Congress could not combine that power with the power to tax in order to regulate a matter that was outside the scope of federal authority — in this instance, agricultural production.

The ruling declared unconstitutional the Agricultural Adjustment Act of 1933, which sought to regulate agricultural production by taxing processors of basic food commodities and then using the revenue from that tax to pay benefits to farmers who reduced their production of those commodities.

Freedom of the Press

Grosjean v. American Press Co. (297 U.S. 233), decided by a unanimous vote, Feb. 10, 1936. Sutherland wrote the opinion.

A state law that places a 2 percent tax on the gross receipts of certain newspapers, and not others, is a prior restraint on the press in violation of the First Amendment. Although labeled a tax on the privilege of doing business, the law had actually been written so that the tax fell only on those newspapers that opposed the administration of the state governor.

Power of Congress

Ashwander v. Tennessee Valley Authority (297 U.S. 288), decided by votes of 8-1 and 5-4, Feb. 17, 1936. Chief Justice Hughes wrote the majority opinion; McReynolds, Brandeis, Stone, Roberts and Cardozo dissented in part.

The court implicitly upheld the statute authorizing the establishment of the Tennessee Valley Authority when it sustained the authority of the TVA to enter into a contract for the sale of the excess energy generated by a TVA-operated dam. The court observed that construction of the dam was within the federal government's powers to defend the nation and improve navigation and that the Constitution gave the federal government unfettered power to dispose of government property.

This statute was one of only two major early New Deal laws declared valid by the court.

Carter v. Carter Coal Co. (298 U.S. 238), decided by a 6-3 vote, May 18, 1936. Sutherland wrote the majority opinion; Chief Justice Hughes wrote a separate opinion; Cardozo, Brandeis and Stone dissented.

Striking down the Bituminous Coal Conservation Act of 1935, the court found that Congress had unconstitutionally delegated its legislative powers to private parties in that statute when it allowed a majority of coal mine operators to set mandatory wage and hours standards for the entire coal industry.

The court also held unconstitutional the statute's provisions providing collective bargaining rights for miners. Such labor relations were local in nature and not subject to regulation by Congress under its interstate commerce powers.

Due Process

Brown v. Mississippi (297 U.S. 278), decided by a unanimous court, Feb. 17, 1936. Chief Justice Hughes wrote the opinion.

States may not use coerced confessions as evidence at the trial of persons from whom the confessions were obtained by torture. Use of a person's involuntary statements to convict him is a clear denial of due process of law.

Morehead v. New York ex rel. Tipaldo (298 U.S. 587), decided by a 5-4 vote, June 1, 1936. Butler wrote the majority opinion; Chief Justice Hughes, Brandeis, Cardozo and Stone dissented.

The court struck down a New York minimum wage law for women and children workers, declaring all minimum wage laws a violation of due process. The decision was overruled in the 1937 decision of *West Coast Hotel Co. v. Parrish.*

Power of the President

United States v. Curtiss-Wright Export Corp. (299 U.S. 304), decided by a 7-1 vote, Dec. 21, 1936. Sutherland wrote the majority opinion; McReynolds dissented; Stone did not participate.

The court upheld an act of Congress authorizing the president, at his discretion, to embargo arms shipments to foreign belligerents in a South American war.

The plenary nature of the federal government's power over foreign affairs permitted Congress greater latitude in delegating power to the president in international relations than in internal matters. Sutherland described the power of the president in foreign affairs as "plenary and exclusive." The president is "the sole organ of the federal government in . . . international relations."

1937

Freedom of Assembly

DeJonge v. Oregon (299 U.S. 353), decided by an 8-0 vote, Jan. 4, 1937. Chief Justice Hughes wrote the opinion; Stone did not participate.

The First Amendment guarantee of the freedom of peaceable assembly prohibits a state from convicting a person under its criminal syndicalism act for organizing and participating in a meeting at which no illegal action was discussed, even if the meeting was held under the auspices of an association which had as its goal the overthrow by force of the federal government.

This was the first decision in which the court recognized that the right of assembly was on an equal plane with the rights of free speech and free press and that the First Amendment guarantee of freedom of assembly was applicable to the states through the due process clause of the 14th Amendment.

Due Process

West Coast Hotel Co. v. Parrish (300 U.S. 379), decided by a 5-4 vote, March 29, 1937. Chief Justice Hughes wrote the majority opinion; Butler, McReynolds, Sutherland and Van Devanter dissented.

The court upheld Washington state's law setting minimum wages for women and children workers. The court overruled its 1923 decision in *Adkins v. Children's Hospital* in which it had declared minimum wage laws to be price-fixing in violation of freedom of contract and the guarantee of due process, and its 1936 decision in *Morehead v. Tipaldo.*

Palko v. Connecticut (302 U.S. 319), decided by an 8-1 vote, Dec. 6, 1937. Cardozo wrote the majority opinion; Butler dissented.

The due process clause of the 14th Amendment does not require states to observe the double jeopardy guarantee of the Fifth Amendment. The promise that an individual will not be tried twice for the same crime is "not of the very essence of a scheme of ordered liberty" and thus due process does not mandate its application to the states.

Commerce

National Labor Relations Board v. Jones & Laughlin Steel Corp. (301 U.S. 1), decided by a 5-4 vote, April 12, 1937. Chief Justice Hughes wrote the majority opinion; McReynolds, Butler, Sutherland and Van Devanter dissented.

The federal power to regulate interstate commerce permits Congress to regulate intrastate matters that directly burden or obstruct interstate commerce. In this case, the court found that a dispute between management and labor that threatened to close down a Pennsylvania steel factory directly affected interstate commerce because the factory was in a stream of commerce.

This decision, in which the court finally abandoned its narrow view of the federal power to regulate interstate commerce, sustained the constitutionality of the National Labor Relations Act of 1935.

The Spending Power

Steward Machine Co. v. Davis (301 U.S. 548), decided by a 5-4 vote, May 24, 1937. Cardozo wrote the majority opinion; McReynolds, Butler, Sutherland and Van Devanter dissented.

A system to induce employers to participate in the federal unemployment compensation program by taxing them and then giving those who participate a tax credit is a valid exercise of the taxing and spending powers to regulate interstate commerce. While not in commerce, employment affects commerce and therefore falls within the reach of federal regulation.

Helvering v. Davis (301 U.S. 619), decided by a 7-2 vote, May 24, 1937. Cardozo wrote the majority opinion; McReynolds and Butler dissented.

Effectively overturning its 1936 *Butler* ruling, the court sustained the Social Security Act of 1935. This statute placed a tax on employees and employers, the revenue from which was used to pay benefits to retired employees. Such a program was an appropriate combination of the power to tax and the power to spend for the general welfare, the court said.

Voting Rights

Breedlove v. Suttles (302 U.S. 277), decided by a unanimous vote, Dec. 6, 1937. Butler wrote the opinion.

The court upheld a Georgia law that required all inhabitants of the state between the ages of 21 and 60 to pay an annual poll tax of $1.00. Under the state constitution payment of the tax was a prerequisite to voting in any election. The court ruled that the tax did not constitute denial of equal protection in violation of the 14th Amendment nor did it violate the 15th Amendment ban on racial discrimination in voting.

1938

Freedom of the Press

Lovell v. Griffin (303 U.S. 444), decided by an 8-0 vote, March 28, 1938. Chief Justice Hughes wrote the opinion; Cardozo did not participate.

A city ordinance which prohibits circulation on public streets of handbills or literature of any kind without written permission from the city manager is an unconstitutional prior restraint on freedom of the press. (In subsequent cases, the court said that a city could regulate the manner of distributing handbills.)

Right to Counsel

Johnson v. Zerbst (304 U.S. 458), decided by a 6-2 vote, May 23, 1938. Black wrote the majority opinion; McReynolds and Butler dissented; Cardozo did not participate.

The Sixth Amendment guarantee that in "all criminal prosecutions, the accused shall enjoy the right . . . to have the Assistance of Counsel for his defence" means that federal courts may not deprive anyone of liberty or life unless he has been provided the aid of an attorney at his trial or has explicitly waived his right to that aid.

Civil Rights

Missouri ex rel. Gaines v. Canada (305 U.S. 337), decided by a 7-2 vote, Dec. 12, 1938. Chief Justice Hughes wrote the majority opinion; McReynolds and Butler dissented.

A state denies equal protection of the laws to a black student when it refuses him admission to its all-white law school, even though it volunteers to pay his tuition at any law school in an adjacent state. By providing a law school for whites but not for blacks the state has created a privilege which one race can enjoy but the other cannot.

This was the first in a series of decisions which resulted in abandonment of the "separate but equal" doctrine of *Plessy v. Ferguson* (1896).

1939

Taxes

Graves v. New York ex rel. O'Keefe (306 U.S. 466), decided by a 7-2 vote, March 27, 1939. Stone wrote the court's opinion; Butler and McReynolds dissented.

The court specifically overruled two earlier decisions (*Collector v. Day*, 1871, and *Dobbins v. Erie County*, 1842), which had held that the income of state and federal government employees was immune to taxation by the non-employing governing body. The *Graves* decision led to the demise of most intergovernmental tax immunities.

Commerce

Mulford v. Smith (307 U.S. 38), decided by a 7-2 vote, April 17, 1939. Roberts wrote the majority opinion; Butler and McReynolds dissented.

Congress has authority to limit the amount of any commodity to be shipped in interstate commerce, the court said. The imposition of marketing quotas on certain agricultural commodities is therefore valid because such quotas are at the "throat" of interstate commerce.

By this decision the court sustained the validity of the second agricultural adjustment act against a challenge that the marketing quotas actually served to limit production, an area which Congress had no authority to regulate.

Voting Rights

Lane v. Wilson (307 U.S. 268), decided by a 6-2 vote, May 22, 1939. Frankfurter wrote the majority opinion; McReynolds and Butler dissented; Douglas did not participate.

In *Guinn v. United States* (1915), the court held unconstitutional an Oklahoma "grandfather clause" exemption to a literacy test requirement for voters. The state legislature then adopted a second voting registration law which exempted from registration all those who had voted in the 1914 election, conducted while the "grandfather clause" was still in effect. The new law required all other potential voters to register within a two-week period. The court held the second law invalid as a violation of the 15th Amendment ban on racial discrimination in voting.

Federal Courts

Coleman v. Miller (307 U.S. 433), decided by a 7-2 vote, June 5, 1939. Chief Justice Hughes wrote the majority opinion; Butler and McReynolds dissented.

The question of what constitutes a "reasonable" time period for the ratification by states of proposed constitutional amendments is a political question for Congress, not the court, to resolve.

The question of whether a state which has rejected a constitutional amendment may later reverse itself and ratify the amendment is also a political question which Congress must answer.

Freedom of Assembly

Hague v. C.I.O. (307 U.S. 496), decided by a 5-2 vote, June 5, 1939. There was no majority opinion; Roberts, Stone and Chief Justice Hughes wrote separate concurring opinions; McReynolds and Butler dissented; Frankfurter and Douglas did not participate.

The right to speak and assemble peaceably in public may not be arbitrarily prohibited by federal, state or local governments. Three members of the majority found this right to be a privilege and immunity of national citizenship; two justices found it implicit in the personal liberty protected by the 14th Amendment's due process clause. This latter, broader view, which secured the right to all persons, not just citizens, was eventually accepted by a majority of the court's members.

1940

Freedom of Religion

Cantwell v. Connecticut (310 U.S. 296), decided by a unanimous vote, May 20, 1940. Roberts wrote the opinion.

States may limit the free exercise of religion only by statutes which are narrowly drawn and applied in a nondiscriminatory manner. Therefore, a state may not convict a sidewalk preacher for breach of the peace under a general ordinance which sweeps in "a great variety of conduct under a general and indefinite characterization" and leaves too much discretion to the officials applying it. Furthermore, such a person may not be convicted under a general breach of the peace statute if there is no evidence that his speech, although insulting to some religions, caused any disturbance or threatened any "clear and present menace to public peace."

Likewise, a state statute which requires persons who wish to solicit for religious causes to obtain permits, but allows state officials discretion in determining which causes are religious is arbitrary and therefore violates the First Amendment guarantee of the free exercise of religion.

This was the first decision in which the court specifically applied the First Amendment's guarantee of free exercise of religion against state action.

Minersville School District v. Gobitis (310 U.S. 586), decided by an 8-1 vote, June 3, 1940. Frankfurter wrote the majority opinion; Stone dissented.

In this first "flag-salute" case, the court sustained a state law requiring all school children to pledge allegiance to the U.S. flag. The requirement had been challenged because participation in such a pledge conflicted with the religious beliefs of Jehovah's Witnesses. They therefore argued that the compulsory pledge violated the First Amendment's guarantee of free exercise of religion.

Religious liberty must give way to political authority so long as that authority is not used directly to promote or restrict religion, the court said. The "mere possession of religious convictions . . . does not relieve the citizen from the discharge of political responsibilities."

In 1943 the court reversed this decision with its ruling in the case of *West Virginia State Board of Education v. Barnette.*

Taxes

Sunshine Anthracite Coal Co. v. Adkins (310 U.S. 381), decided by an 8-1 vote, May 20, 1940. Douglas wrote the majority opinion; McReynolds dissented.

The use of the tax power as a penalty is an appropriate means for Congress to employ in regulating interstate commerce, the court said. The court in this ruling upheld the second coal conservation act, which placed a high tax on coal sold in interstate commerce but exempted from payment those producers who agreed to abide by industry price and competition regulations.

1941

Commerce

United States v. Darby Lumber Co. (312 U.S. 100), decided by a unanimous vote, Feb. 3, 1941. Stone wrote the opinion.

Congress has authority to prohibit the shipment in interstate commerce of any goods manufactured in violation of federally established minimum wage and maximum hours standards. In this decision the court also overruled the 1918 decision in *Hammer v. Dagenhart,* in which it had held that Congress had no power to prohibit the shipment in interstate commerce of goods made by children.

Edwards v. California (314 U.S. 160), decided by a unanimous vote, Nov. 24, 1941. Byrnes wrote the opinion.

A state impermissibly obstructs interstate commerce when it penalizes persons who bring indigent persons into the state to reside there. The court in this ruling struck down California's "anti-Okie" law.

In a concurring opinion, four justices held the right to travel to be one of the privileges and immunities of national citizenship protected by the 14th Amendment from abridgment by the states.

Freedom of Assembly

Cox v. New Hampshire (312 U.S. 569), decided by a unanimous vote, March 31, 1941. Chief Justice Hughes wrote the opinion.

The First Amendment guarantees of free speech and peaceable assembly do not bar states from setting the time, place and manner of parades on public streets in order that they do not interfere unduly with other use of the streets. Such ordinances must be precisely drawn and applied in a non-discriminatory fashion.

Voting Rights

United States v. Classic (313 U.S. 299), decided by a 5-3 vote, May 26, 1941. Stone wrote the majority opinion; Black, Murphy and Douglas dissented. Chief Justice Hughes did not participate.

Congress has the power to regulate primary elections when the primary is an integral part of the process of selecting candidates for federal office.

This decision overruled the 1921 *Newberry* decision holding that Congress could regulate only general elections, not primary elections.

1942

Freedom of Speech

Chaplinsky v. New Hampshire (315 U.S. 568), decided by a unanimous vote, March 9, 1942. Murphy wrote the opinion.

A state does not violate the First Amendment by enacting a precisely drawn and narrowly applied law making it a crime to use, in public, "fighting words" — words so insulting as to provoke violence from the person to whom they are directed. Fighting words, the lewd and obscene, profanity and libelous statements are among the classes of speech that have so little value in advancing thought or ideas that they fall outside the protection of the First Amendment guarantees of freedom of speech and press, the court said.

Right to Counsel

Betts v. Brady (316 U.S. 455), decided by a 6-3 vote, June 1, 1942. Roberts wrote the majority opinion; Black, Douglas and Murphy dissented.

The 14th Amendment's due process clause does not require states to supply defense counsel to defendants too poor to employ their own attorney.

Equal Protection

Skinner v. Oklahoma (316 U.S. 535), decided by a unanimous vote, June 1, 1942. Douglas wrote the opinion.

A state law that provides for involuntary sterilization of certain felons violates the equal protection clause of the 14th Amendment because it does not treat all persons convicted of the same crime in the same manner.

This was the first decision in which the court recognized that individuals have certain constitutionally protected "fundamental interests," in this case, procreation, with which a state may interfere only if it shows a compelling need to do so.

War Powers

Ex parte Quirin (317 U.S. 1), decided by an 8-0 vote, July 31, 1942. Chief Justice Stone wrote the opinion; Murphy did not participate.

The Supreme Court upheld the jurisdiction of a presidentially established military commission, instead of a civilian jury, to try seven Nazi saboteurs. Congress had already provided for the trial of spies by military commission and the acts charged against the saboteurs were acts of war. The guarantee of jury trial under the Sixth Amendment applies to civilian — not military — courts.

This decision firmly established the power of civil courts to review the jurisdiction of presidential military commissions.

Commerce

Wickard v. Filburn (317 U.S. 111), decided by a unanimous vote, Nov. 9, 1942. Jackson wrote the opinion.

The federal power to prevent burdens on interstate commerce permits the federal government to regulate matters that are neither interstate nor commerce. The court made this point in a decision sustaining a penalty levied against a farmer who had produced for his own consumption more wheat than he was allotted under the 1938 Agricultural Adjustment Act. The court held that Congress had the power to prevent home-grown wheat from competing with wheat sold in interstate commerce.

This decision is regarded as the high point in the court's broad interpretation of federal regulatory powers authorized under the interstate commerce clause of the Constitution.

1943

Due Process

McNabb v. United States (318 U.S. 332), decided by a 7-1 vote, March 1, 1943. Frankfurter wrote the majority opinion; Reed dissented; Rutledge did not participate.

The court established the federal rule that a person accused of a federal crime must be taken before a judicial officer for arraignment without delay after arrest.

Freedom of Religion

Murdock v. Pennsylvania (319 U.S. 105), decided by a 5-4 vote, May 3, 1943. Douglas wrote the majority opinion; Reed, Frankfurter, Roberts and Jackson dissented.

A city ordinance which requires all persons taking orders for or delivering goods door-to-door to obtain a license from the city and which places a tax of $1.50 a day on the privilege of door-to-door solicitation is unconstitutional as applied to Jehovah's Witnesses who go from house to house soliciting new members and selling religious literature. "A state may not impose a charge for the enjoyment of a right granted by the federal Constitution," the majority said.

This decision specifically overruled the previous year's decision in *Jones v. Opelika* (316 U.S. 584, 1942) in which the court upheld such license fees as applied to Jehovah's Witnesses on the grounds that these activities were primarily commercial and so fell outside the protection of the First Amendment.

West Virginia State Board of Education v. Barnette (319 U.S. 624), decided by a 6-3 vote, June 14, 1943. Jackson wrote the majority opinion; Roberts, Reed and Frankfurter dissented.

The First Amendment guarantee of the free exercise of religion protects the right of persons to remain silent and forbids the government to compel them to participate in a symbolic display of patriotic unity that conflicts with their religious beliefs.

With this ruling the court upheld the right of Jehovah's Witnesses' children to refuse to participate in compulsory flag salute ceremonies in public schools. The decision overruled the 1940 holding in *Minersville School District v. Gobitis* in which a majority held that religious liberty must give way to political authority so long as that authority was not used directly to promote or restrict religion.

War Powers

Hirabayashi v. United States (320 U.S. 810), decided by a unanimous vote, June 21, 1943. Chief Justice Stone wrote the opinion.

The court upheld the wartime curfew law placed on Japanese-Americans living on the west coast as an appropriate exercise by the president and Congress of the federal war powers.

Nor did the curfew law, by making a classification based solely on race, violate the Fifth Amendment. In this instance, consideration of race was relevant to the national security.

1944

Power of Congress

Yakus v. United States (321 U.S. 414), decided by a 6-3 vote, March 27, 1944. Chief Justice Stone wrote the majority opinion; Roberts, Murphy and Rutledge dissented.

The court sustained portions of the Emergency Price Control Act of 1942 giving the federal price administrator discretionary power to enforce the act, including the maximum prices set under it. The law was challenged as an unconstitutional delegation of legislative power. The court held that the standards for decisions under the law were "sufficiently definite and precise" and said it was "unable to find in them an unauthorized delegation of legislative power."

Voting Rights

Smith v. Allwright (321 U.S. 649), decided by an 8-1 vote, April 3, 1944. Reed wrote the majority opinion; Roberts dissented.

When party primaries are part of the machinery for choosing state and national officials, the action of any political party to exclude Negroes from voting in primaries is "state action" within the prohibitions of the 14th and 15th Amendments. This decision reversed *Grovey v. Townsend* (1935).

Commerce

United States v. South-Eastern Underwriters Assn. (322 U.S. 533), decided by a 4-3 vote, June 5, 1944. Black wrote the majority opinion; Chief Justice Stone and Frankfurter dissented; Jackson dissented in part; Roberts and Reed did not participate.

Insurance transactions are matters in interstate commerce subject to regulation under the federal antitrust act.

This ruling overturned a long line of decisions, beginning in 1869, which held that purely financial and contractual transactions, such as insurance, were not in commerce, even if they involved parties in different states, and were therefore not subject to federal regulation.

Because this decision called into question the validity of all state insurance regulations, Congress quickly passed a statute permitting states to continue to regulate insurance. The court upheld that statute in *Prudential Insurance Co. v. Benjamin* (328 U.S. 408, 1946).

War Powers

Korematsu v. United States (323 U.S. 214), decided by a 6-3 vote, December 18, 1944. Black wrote the majority opinion; Roberts, Murphy and Jackson dissented.

The court upheld the 1942 removal of Japanese-Americans to relocation centers at inland camps away from the west coast. It held that the removal program was within the combined war powers of the president and the Congress.

In this case, for the first time, a majority of the court said it would give classifications by race increased attention to ensure that racial antagonism did not lie at the base of the classification. In this instance, however, the court held that military necessity warranted the racial classification.

1946

Freedom of Religion

Girouard v. United States (328 U.S. 61), decided by a 5-3 vote, April 22, 1946. Douglas wrote the majority opinion; Chief Justice Stone, Reed and Frankfurter dissented; Jackson did not participate.

The oath that persons must swear to become naturalized citizens does not expressly require them to swear to bear arms in defense of the United States. Thus a person who meets all other qualifications for naturalization should not be barred from citizenship because he is unwilling to bear arms, an activity that conflicts with his religious beliefs.

This decision overturned three earlier rulings in which the court had interpreted the naturalization oath to require a willingness to bear arms. The decisions had barred from citizenship two women, who would not have been required to serve in the armed forces in any event, and a 54-year old divinity school professor unlikely to be called for duty because of his age.

Bills of Attainder

United States v. Lovett (328 U.S. 303), decided by a 7-0 vote, June 3, 1946. Black wrote the court's opinion; Jackson did not participate.

The court declared invalid, as an unconstitutional bill of attainder, a section of an appropriations law that prohibited payment of salaries to three specifically named federal employees unless they were re-nominated and reconfirmed to their positions.

Civil Rights

Morgan v. Virginia (328 U.S. 373), decided by a 6-1 vote, June 3, 1946. Reed wrote the court's opinion; Burton dissented; Jackson did not participate.

A state law requiring segregated seating on buses traveling interstate places an unconstitutional burden on interstate commerce. Where interstate commerce is involved, bus seating requires uniform national rules; otherwise the constant shifting of seats and rearrangement demanded by various state laws will burden interstate commerce.

Voting Rights

Colegrove v. Green (328 U.S. 549), decided by a 4-3 vote, June 10, 1946. Frankfurter wrote the majority opinion; Black, Douglas and Murphy dissented; Jackson did not participate.

The court declined to intervene to compel the rural-dominated Illinois legislature to redistrict congressional election districts. The districts had not been redrawn since 1901, creating population disparities of as much as nine to one between rural and urban regions within the state.

The problem presented a political question beyond judicial power to resolve, the court said.

1947

Cruel and Unusual Punishment

Louisiana ex rel. Francis v. Resweber (329 U.S. 459), decided by a 5-4 vote, Jan. 13, 1947. Reed wrote the majority opinion; Burton, Douglas, Murphy and Rutledge dissented.

Assuming without argument that the Eighth Amendment ban on cruel and unusual punishment applied to state as well as federal actions, the court nevertheless held that this ban was not violated by the state's execution of a man whose first execution attempt failed due to a malfunctioning electric chair.

Freedom of Religion

Everson v. Board of Education of Ewing Township (330 U.S. 1), decided by a 5-4 vote, Feb. 10, 1947. Black wrote the majority opinion; Jackson, Frankfurter, Rutledge and Burton dissented.

State reimbursement of parents for the cost of transporting their children to parochial schools does not violate the First Amendment clause barring government establishment of religion. Such reimbursements aid parents and children, not the church-affiliated schools.

This was the first case in which the court specifically applied the First Amendment's establishment clause to state as well as federal action.

Power of Congress

United Public Workers v. Mitchell (330 U.S. 75), decided by a 4-3 vote, Feb. 10, 1947. Reed wrote the majority opinion; Black, Douglas and Rutledge dissented; Murphy and Jackson did not participate.

The court sustained the 1939 Hatch Act, upholding the power of Congress to impose limitations on the political activity of government employees.

Contempt

United States v. United Mine Workers (330 U.S. 258), decided by a divided court, March 6, 1947. Chief Justice Vinson wrote the majority opinion; Murphy and Rutledge dissented; Black, Frankfurter, Douglas and Jackson dissented in part.

The same action may constitute civil and criminal contempt. The justices upheld the conviction of the United Mine Workers of America and its president, John L. Lewis, for both types of contempt for failure to obey a court order forbidding a strike.

Offshore Lands

United States v. California (332 U.S. 19), decided by a 6-2 vote, June 23, 1947. Black wrote the majority opinion; Frankfurter and Reed dissented; Jackson did not participate.

The federal government, not the states, owns the tidelands immediately adjacent to the states and the oil therein. The court reaffirmed this opinion in two subsequent cases, but then sustained — as an exercise of Congress' unrestricted power to dispose of government property — an act of Congress giving coastal states right to the tidelands oil (*Alabama v. Texas,* 347 U.S. 272, 1954).

Jury Trials

Fay v. New York (332 U.S. 261), decided by a 5-4 vote, June 23, 1947. Jackson wrote the majority opinion; Murphy, Black, Douglas and Rutledge dissented.

The court upheld New York's "blue ribbon" jury system, saying that panels of specially qualified jurors disproportionately representing upper economic and social strata were not deliberately discriminatory and did not violate the Constitution.

1948

Freedom of Religion

Illinois ex rel. McCollum v. Board of Education (333 U.S. 203), decided by an 8-1 vote, March 8, 1948. Black wrote the majority opinion; Reed dissented.

The First Amendment clause barring government establishment of religion is violated by a voluntary "released time" program in which religious instruction is given to public school students in the public school during school time.

The court in 1952 sustained a released time program in which students left the school premises to receive religious instruction (*Zorach v. Clauson,* 343 U.S. 306, 1952).

Equal Protection

Shelley v. Kraemer (334 U.S. 1), decided by a 6-0 vote, May 3, 1948. Chief Justice Vinson wrote the opinion; Reed, Jackson and Rutledge did not participate.

The 14th Amendment does not bar private parties from entering into racially restrictive covenants, which exclude blacks from buying or renting homes in "covenanted" neighborhoods, but it does prohibit state courts from enforcing such covenants. Such enforcement constitutes state action denying equal protection of the laws.

1949

Freedom of Speech

Terminiello v. Chicago (337 U.S. 1), decided by a 5-4 vote, May 16, 1949. Douglas wrote the majority opinion; Chief Justice Vinson, Frankfurter, Jackson and Burton dissented.

The court reversed the conviction, for breach of the peace, of a speaker whose remarks in a meeting hall provoked a near-riot among protesters gathered outside the hall.

Without reaching the issue of whether the First Amendment guarantee of free speech protected such inciteful speech, the majority held that the trial court's definition of breach of the peace was so broad that it included speech that was clearly protected by the First Amendment.

Search and Seizure

Wolf v. Colorado (338 U.S. 25), decided by a 6-3 vote, June 27, 1949. Frankfurter wrote the majority opinion; Douglas, Murphy and Rutledge dissented.

The Fourth Amendment protection of individuals against unreasonable searches and seizures by government agents applies against searches by state, as well as federal, agents.

State judges, however, are not required to exclude from use evidence obtained by searches in violation of this guarantee.

1950

Search and Seizure

United States v. Rabinowitz (339 U.S. 56), decided by a 5-3 vote, Feb. 20, 1950. Minton wrote the majority opinion; Frankfurter, Jackson and Black dissented; Douglas did not participate.

The Fourth Amendment guarantee of security against unreasonable searches is not violated by the warrantless search, incident to a lawful arrest, of the person arrested and the premises on which the arrest takes place if they are subject to the control of the suspect.

Freedom of Association

American Communications Assn. v. Douds (339 U.S. 382), decided by a 5-1 vote, May 8, 1950. Chief Justice Vinson wrote the majority opinion; Black dissented. Douglas, Clark and Minton did not participate.

The court upheld the provision of the Taft-Hartley Act which required each officer of a labor union to file an affidavit swearing that he was not a member of or affiliated with the Communist Party. The court held that Congress could properly impose this requirement as part of its power to prevent political strikes obstructing interstate commerce.

Civil Rights

Sweatt v. Painter (339 U.S. 629), decided by a unanimous vote, June 5, 1950. Chief Justice Vinson wrote the opinion.

A state may not deny admission to a state law school to a black even if there is a "black" law school available to the applicant. The court found the facilities of the "black" school inferior to those provided by the "white" school, and therefore in violation of the "separate but equal" doctrine established by the court in 1896.

McLaurin v. Oklahoma State Regents for Higher Education (339 U.S. 637), decided by a unanimous vote, June 5, 1950. Chief Justice Vinson wrote the opinion.

Going beyond its ruling in *Sweatt v. Painter* and eroding the "separate but equal" doctrine even more, the court ruled that once a black was admitted to a state university, the state could not deny him the right to use all its facilities, including the library, lunchroom and classrooms.

1951

Freedom of Speech

Kunz v. New York (340 U.S. 290), decided by an 8-1 vote, Jan. 15, 1951. Chief Justice Vinson wrote the majority opinion; Jackson dissented.

A New York City ordinance that barred worship services on public streets without a permit is an unconstitutional prior restraint on the exercise of the First Amendment rights of free speech and free exercise of religion.

Feiner v. New York (340 U.S. 315), decided by a 6-3 vote, Jan. 15, 1951. Chief Justice Vinson wrote the majority opinion; Black, Douglas and Minton dissented.

In this case, the court sustained the conviction, for breach of the peace, of a street speaker who refused to stop speaking after police asked him to desist. The majority held that the police had acted not to suppress speech but to preserve public order, a legitimate reason for limiting speech.

This decision, read with the decisions in *Terminiello v. Chicago* (1949) and *Kunz v. New York* (1951) demonstrate the difficulty the court had in defining precisely the circumstances in which a state might properly curtail free speech.

Dennis v. United States (341 U.S. 494), decided by a 6-2 vote, June 4, 1951. Chief Justice Vinson wrote the majority opinion; Black and Douglas dissented; Clark did not participate.

The court upheld convictions under the Smith Act of 1940 for speaking and teaching about communist theory advocating forcible overthrow of the government. Communist Party members challenged these convictions as abridgments of First Amendment rights.

Freedom of Association

Joint Anti-Fascist Refugee Committee v. McGrath (341 U.S. 123), decided by a 5-3 vote, April 30, 1951. Burton wrote the majority opinion; Chief Justice Vinson, Reed and Minton dissented; Clark did not participate.

The court upheld the power of the attorney general to prepare and distribute a list of subversive organizations to aid the work of the federal Loyalty Review Board.

Garner v. Board of Public Works (341 U.S. 716), decided by a 5-4 vote, June 4, 1951. Clark wrote the majority opinion; Burton, Frankfurter, Black and Douglas dissented.

The court upheld a loyalty oath requirement for public employees. Such a requirement was not a denial of due process or invalid as a bill of attainder or an *ex post facto* law.

Excessive Bail

Stack v. Boyle (342 U.S. 1), decided by an 8-0 vote, Nov. 5, 1951. Chief Justice Vinson wrote the opinion; Minton did not participate.

The court held that the amount of bail required of twelve Communist leaders prosecuted under the Smith Act of 1940 was excessive and violated the Eighth Amendment's prohibition of excessive bail.

1952

Search and Seizure

Rochin v. California (342 U.S. 165), decided by an 8-0 vote, Jan. 2, 1952. Frankfurter wrote the opinion; Minton did not participate.

The court held that state police officers who used a stomach pump to obtain evidence of drugs — which a suspect had swallowed in their presence — violated Fourth Amendment prohibitions against unreasonable searches and seizures.

Excessive Bail

Carlson v. Landon (342 U.S. 524), decided by a 5-4 vote, March 10, 1952. Reed wrote the majority opinion; Black, Frankfurter, Burton and Douglas dissented.

The court ruled that five alien members of the Communist Party could be detained without bail pending the outcome of deportation proceedings. Denial of bail was justified because deportation was not a criminal proceeding.

Power of the President

Youngstown Sheet and Tube Co. v. Sawyer (343 U.S. 579), decided by a 6-3 vote, June 2, 1952. Black wrote the majority opinion; Chief Justice Vinson, Reed and Minton dissented.

The court held that President Truman had exceeded his power in seizing the nation's steel mills to prevent a strike. The president had based the seizure order on his general powers as commander in chief and chief executive. But the court held he could not take such action without express authorization from Congress.

1953

Voting Rights

Terry v. Adams (345 U.S. 461), decided by an 8-1 vote, May 4, 1953. Black wrote the majority opinion; Minton dissented.

The court held unconstitutional the all-white Texas Jaybird Party primary — held before the regular Democratic Party primary — whose winners usually then won the Democratic nomination and election to county offices. The court ruled that the Jaybird primary was an integral part of the election process and that the exclusion of blacks from this process violated the 15th Amendment.

War Powers

Rosenberg v. United States (346 U.S. 273), decided by a 6-3 vote, June 19, 1953. Chief Justice Vinson wrote the majority opinion; Frankfurter, Black and Douglas dissented.

The court, after meeting in special session, lifted a stay of execution for Julius and Ethel Rosenberg, convicted of violating the Espionage Act of 1917 and sentenced to death.

Justice Douglas had granted the stay in order that lower courts might consider the argument of the Rosenbergs' attorney that the espionage act had been repealed by subsequent passage of the Atomic Energy Act of 1946. The Rosenbergs were convicted of having conveyed atomic secrets to the Soviet Union. They were executed as soon as the court lifted the stay.

1954

Civil Rights

Brown v. Board of Education of Topeka (347 U.S. 483), decided by a unanimous vote, May 17, 1954. Chief Justice Warren wrote the opinion.

In this historic school desegregation decision, the court declared that separate public schools for black and white students were inherently unequal. State-sanctioned segregation in public schools therefore violated the equal protection guarantee of the 14th Amendment.

In the companion case of *Bolling v. Sharpe* (347 U.S. 497), the court ruled that the congressionally-mandated segregated public school system in the District of Columbia violated the Fifth Amendment's due process guarantee of personal liberty.

In *Brown*, the court specifically overruled the "separate but equal" doctrine first enunciated in *Plessy v. Ferguson* (1896) so far as it applied to public schools. The ruling also led to the abolition of state-sponsored segregation in other public facilities.

1955

Civil Rights

Brown v. Board of Education of Topeka (349 U.S. 294), decided by a unanimous vote, May 31, 1955. Chief Justice Warren wrote the opinion.

In this case, the court laid out guidelines for ending segregation in public schools. The court placed primary responsibility on local school officials, recognizing that local factors would call for different treatment and timing, but admonishing the boards to proceed toward desegregation "with all deliberate speed."

Federal district courts were to retain jurisdiction of school desegregation cases. These courts could grant school districts additional time to complete desegregation once the process was begun, but the school boards were given the burden of justifying such delays.

1956

Self-Incrimination

Ullmann v. United States (350 U.S. 422), decided by a 7-2 vote, March 26, 1956. Frankfurter wrote the majority opinion; Douglas and Black dissented.

The court sustained the Immunity Act of 1950, which provided that witnesses cannot claim their privilege against self-incrimination if the government grants them immunity from prosecution for any crimes revealed in their testimony.

Slochower v. Board of Education of New York City (350 U.S. 551) decided by a 5-4 vote, April 9, 1956. Clark wrote the majority opinion; Reed, Burton, Harlan and Minton dissented.

The court held invalid a provision of the New York City charter which provided for summary dismissal of employees who invoked the Fifth Amendment privilege against self-incrimination. Such a practice violated the due process guarantee of the 14th Amendment, the court said.

State Powers

Pennsylvania v. Nelson (350 U.S. 497), decided by a 6-3 vote, April 2, 1956. Chief Justice Warren wrote the majority opinion; Reed, Minton and Burton dissented.

States may not pass laws punishing persons for seditious activity against the federal government; Congress has pre-empted that field by passing federal legislation on that subject.

1957

Power of Congress

Watkins v. United States (354 U.S. 178), decided by a 6-1 vote, June 17, 1957. Chief Justice Warren wrote the majority opinion; Clark dissented; Burton and Whittaker did not participate.

Declaring that "there is no congressional power to expose for the sake of exposure," the court held that congressional investigations may be undertaken only in aid of the legislative function. House and Senate instructions to their investigating committees must therefore fully spell out the investigating committee's purpose and jurisdiction.

Furthermore, a witness may refuse with impunity to answer questions if they are not pertinent to the investigation. "It is the duty of the investigative body, upon objection of the witness on grounds of pertinency, to state . . . the subject under inquiry at the time and the manner in which the propounded questions are pertinent thereto," the majority said.

This ruling reversed the contempt conviction of a labor union officer who answered questions about his own association with the Communist Party but refused to answer similar questions about other people.

Freedom of Speech

Yates v. United States (354 U.S. 298), decided by votes of 6-1 and 4-3, June 17, 1957. Harlan wrote the majority opinion; Clark dissented; Black and Douglas dissented in part; Brennan and Whittaker did not participate.

The court held that in prosecuting persons for violating the Smith Act by advocating the forcible overthrow of the government the United States must show active engagement on the part of the defendant in such an effort, not simply passive action — overt acts, not just abstract arguments.

The decision made it much more difficult for the government to obtain convictions under the Smith Act.

Due Process

Mallory v. United States (354 U.S. 449), decided by a unanimous vote, June 24, 1957. Frankfurter delivered the opinion.

The court reversed a criminal conviction of a man interrogated by law enforcement officials without being informed of his constitutional rights and held for an unnecessarily long period between his arrest and arraignment. Such practices, held the court, deprived him of his liberty without due process of law.

Obscenity

Roth v. United States, Alberts v. California (354 U.S. 476), decided by votes of 7-1 and 6-3, June 24, 1957. Brennan wrote the majority opinion; Harlan dissented in part; Black and Douglas dissented.

Obscene material is not protected by the First Amendment guarantees of freedom of speech and press. Material is obscene, the court said, if the average person would consider that its dominant theme appealed to prurient interest.

This was the first definition of obscenity offered by the court. It was modified in several subsequent decisions and finally replaced with another standard in the 1973 case of *Miller v. California.*

1958

Cruel and Unusual Punishment

Trop v. Dulles (356 U.S. 86), decided by a 5-4 vote, March 31, 1958. Chief Justice Warren wrote the majority opinion; Frankfurter, Burton, Clark and Harlan dissented.

The Eighth Amendment ban on cruel and unusual punishment prohibits the use of expatriation or denaturalization as punishment for persons found guilty of desertion from the armed forces in wartime.

Personal Liberty

Kent v. Dulles (357 U.S. 117), decided by a 5-4 vote, June 16, 1958. Douglas wrote the majority opinion; Clark, Harlan, Burton and Whittaker dissented.

The freedom to travel is part of the personal liberty protected by the due process guarantee of the Fifth and 14th Amendments.

Congress has not authorized the secretary of State to withhold passports from citizens because of their beliefs or associations.

Power of the President

Wiener v. United States (357 U.S. 349), decided by a unanimous vote, June 30, 1958. Frankfurter wrote the opinion.

This decision reinforced the "nature of the office" approach to the presidential removal power. The court held that where the duties of the office included quasi-judicial functions — and where there was no statutory provision for removal — the president lacked the power to remove an incumbent official from his post simply to replace him with a person of his own choice.

Freedom of Association

NAACP v. Alabama ex rel. Patterson (357 U.S. 449), decided by a unanimous vote, June 30, 1958. Harlan wrote the opinion.

The freedom to associate with others is implicit in the freedoms of speech and assembly guaranteed by the First Amendment. The right to associate carries with it the right of privacy in that association.

A state court order requiring the NAACP to produce its membership lists is therefore an unconstitutional restraint on NAACP members' right of association. The state did not show a sufficient interest in the disclosure of the lists to justify the limitation such disclosure placed on freedom of association.

Civil Rights

Cooper v. Aaron (358 U.S. 1), decided by a unanimous vote, Sept. 12, 1958. Chief Justice Warren wrote the opinion; each justice personally signed it.

Standing firm against defiance of its 1954 and 1955 decisions declaring public school segregation unconstitutional, the court refused a request by Little Rock, Ark., school officials for a delay in desegregation of their public schools. Local school officials had made the request after Gov. Orval Faubus called out the state national guard to block the entrance to a Little Rock high school to prevent entry by black students. Federal troops were eventually sent to the city to restore order and protect the black students, and the school board asked for delay of further desegregation efforts. The court convened a special session in late summer of 1958 to hear the case.

In a sharp rebuke to Faubus and state legislators, the court said that the rights of black children could "neither be nullified openly and directly by state legislators or state executive officials nor nullified indirectly by them by evasive schemes for segregation."

1959

Voting Rights

Lassiter v. Northampton County Board of Elections (360 U.S. 45), decided by a unanimous vote, June 8, 1959. Douglas delivered the opinion.

The court upheld North Carolina's requirement that all persons must be able to read and write a section of the state constitution in English before being allowed to vote. Such a provision, applied in a non-discriminatory way, did not violate the 14th, 15th or 17th Amendments, the court held.

Power of Congress

Barenblatt v. United States (360 U.S. 109), decided by a 5-4 vote, June 8, 1959. Harlan wrote the majority opinion; Chief Justice Warren, Black, Brennan and Douglas dissented.

Retreating from its ruling in the 1957 *Watkins* case, the court held that the First Amendment rights of witnesses appearing before congressional investigating committees may be limited when the public interest outweighs the private interest.

In this case, the federal government's interest in preserving itself against those who advocated the forceful overthrow of that government outweighed the right of the witness, a teacher, to conduct a classroom discussion on the theoretical nature of communism.

1960

Search and Seizure

Elkins v. United States (364 U.S. 206), decided by a 5-4 vote, June 27, 1960. Stewart wrote the majority opinion; Frankfurter, Clark, Harlan and Whittaker dissented.

In this decision the court abandoned the "silver platter" doctrine that permitted use — in federal court — of evidence illegally seized by state authorities and handed over to federal authority. The court held that such a practice violated the Fourth Amendment prohibition against unreasonable search and seizure.

Voting Rights

Gomillion v. Lightfoot (364 U.S. 339), decided by a unanimous vote, Nov. 4, 1960. Frankfurter wrote the opinion.

The court held unconstitutional, as a violation of the 15th Amendment guarantee of the right to vote, a state legislative districting plan that excluded almost all black voters from voting in city elections in Tuskegee, Ala.

1961

Freedom of Association

Communist Party v. Subversive Activities Control Board (367 U.S. 1), decided by a 5-4 vote, June 5, 1961. Harlan wrote the majority opinion; Chief Justice Warren, Black, Douglas and Brennan dissented.

The court upheld provisions of the Subversive Activities Control Act of 1950 requiring the Communist Party to register with the Justice Department, list its officials and file financial statements. The court rejected the party's arguments that the registration provisions were unconstitutional as a bill of attainder and a violation of the First Amendment guarantees of freedom of speech and association.

Scales v. United States, Noto v. United States (367 U.S. 203, 290), decided by 5-4 votes, June 5, 1961. Harlan wrote the majority opinions; Chief Justice Warren, Black, Douglas and Brennan dissented.

The First Amendment freedoms of speech and association are not violated by laws providing penalties for active membership in a group specifically intending to bring about the violent overthrow of the government.

Search and Seizure

Mapp v. Ohio (367 U.S. 643), decided by a 5-4 vote, June 19, 1961. Clark wrote the majority opinion; Stewart, Harlan, Frankfurter and Whittaker dissented.

Evidence obtained in violation of the Fourth Amendment guarantee against unreasonable search and seizure must be excluded from use at state as well as federal trials. The court overruled *Wolf v. Colorado* (1949) on this point.

Equal Protection

Hoyt v. Florida (368 U.S. 57), decided by a unanimous vote, Nov. 20, 1961. Harlan wrote the opinion.

The court sustained, against a challenge that it violated the equal protection guarantee, a state law generally excluding women from jury duty. The exclusion was rational in light of the state's interest in preventing interference with women's traditional functions as wives, homemakers and mothers, the court said.

1962

Voting Rights

Baker v. Carr (369 U.S. 186), decided by a 6-2 vote, March 26, 1962. Brennan wrote the majority opinion;

Frankfurter and Harlan dissented; Whittaker did not participate.

The court for the first time held that constitutional challenges to the maldistribution of voters among legislative districts might properly be resolved by federal courts. The court rejected the doctrine — set out in *Colegrove v. Green* in 1946 — that all such apportionment challenges were "political questions" beyond the proper reach of the federal courts.

Freedom of Religion

Engel v. Vitale (370 U.S. 421), decided by a 6-1 vote, June 25, 1962. Black wrote the majority opinion; Stewart dissented; Frankfurter and White did not participate.

Public school officials may not require pupils to recite a state-composed prayer at the beginning of each school day, even though the prayer is denominationally neutral and pupils who so desire may be excused from reciting it. Official state sanction of religious prayers or utterances constitutes an unconstitutional attempt to establish religion, the majority held.

The court reaffirmed this decision in the 1963 case of *School District of Abington Township v. Schempp* (374 U.S. 203), in which the court held that the state-ordered recitation of the Lord's Prayer and the reading of the Bible in the public school system as part of a devotional exercise also violated the establishment clause.

Cruel and Unusual Punishment

Robinson v. California (370 U.S. 660), decided by a 6-2 vote, June 25, 1962. Stewart wrote the majority opinion; Clark and White dissented; Frankfurter did not participate.

It is a violation of the Eighth Amendment ban on cruel and unusual punishment for a state to make narcotics addiction a criminal offense.

1963

Freedom of Association

NAACP v. Button (371 U.S. 415), decided by a 6-3 vote, Jan. 14, 1963. Brennan wrote the majority opinion; Harlan, Clark and Stewart dissented.

A state law, directed against the NAACP, which forbids solicitation of clients by an agent of an organization that litigates cases in which it is not a party and has no pecuniary interest, impermissibly infringes on the First Amendment right of association. "Abstract discussion is not the only species of communication which the Constitution protects; the First Amendment also protects vigorous advocacy, certainly of lawful ends, against government intrusion," the court wrote.

Freedom of Speech

Edwards v. South Carolina (372 U.S. 229), decided by an 8-1 vote, Feb. 25, 1963. Stewart wrote the majority opinion; Clark dissented.

The court reversed the breach-of-the-peace convictions of student demonstrators who had marched peacefully to protest racial discrimination. The court held that the breach-of- the-peace statute was unconstitutionally broad and had been used in this case to penalize the exercise of free speech, assembly and petition for redress of grievances "in their most pristine and classic form," a clear violation of the First Amendment.

Right to Counsel

Gideon v. Wainwright (372 U.S. 335), decided by a unanimous vote, March 18, 1963. Black delivered the opinion.

The due process clause of the 14th Amendment extends to state as well as federal defendants the Sixth Amendment guarantee that all persons charged with serious crimes will be provided the aid of an attorney. *Betts v. Brady* (1942) is overruled. States are required to appoint counsel for defendants who can not afford to pay their own attorneys' fees.

Federal Courts

Fay v. Noia (372 U.S. 391), decided by a 6-3 vote, March 18, 1963. Brennan wrote the majority opinion; Harlan, Clark and Stewart dissented.

In some circumstances, a state prisoner may challenge his imprisonment through a federal writ of *habeas corpus* even if he has not appealed his conviction through the state court system. The requirement that a state prisoner "exhaust" all state remedies before challenging his conviction in federal courts simply means that a state prisoner must have tried all state remedies still available to him at the time he comes into federal court seeking the writ of *habeas corpus.*

Voting Rights

Gray v. Sanders (372 U.S. 368), decided by an 8-1 vote, March 18, 1963. Douglas wrote the majority opinion; Harlan dissented.

Georgia's "county unit" system of electing officers to state posts violates the equal protection guarantee of the 14th Amendment by giving more weight to the votes of persons in rural, than in urban, counties. The basic idea of political equality, inherent in the American system, held the court, "can mean only one thing — one person, one vote."

Search and Seizure

Ker v. California (374 U.S. 23), decided by a 5-4 vote, June 10, 1963. Clark wrote the majority opinion; Chief Justice Warren, Brennan, Douglas and Goldberg dissented in part.

The same standards apply to determine whether federal and state searches and seizures are reasonable and thus permissible under the Fourth Amendment. (The justices disagreed over whether the warrantless search at issue in this case was reasonable.)

1964

Voting Rights

Wesberry v. Sanders (376 U.S. 1), decided by a 6-3 vote, Feb. 17, 1964. Black wrote the majority opinion; Clark dissented in part; Harlan and Stewart dissented.

Substantial disparity in the population of congressional districts in a state is unconstitutional, violating the provision for election of members of the House of Representatives "by the people of the several states." Congressional voting districts within states must be as nearly equal in population as possible.

Reynolds v. Sims (377 U.S. 533), decided by an 8-1 vote, June 15, 1964. Chief Justice Warren wrote the majority opinion; Harlan dissented.

The equal protection clause of the 14th Amendment requires application of the "one person, one vote" apportionment rule to both houses of a state legislature.

Freedom of the Press

New York Times Co. v. Sullivan (376 U.S. 254), decided by a unanimous vote, March 9, 1964. Brennan wrote the opinion.

The First Amendment guarantee of freedom of the press protects the press from libel suits for defamatory reports on public officials unless the officials prove that the reports were made with actual malice. Actual malice is defined as "with knowledge that it [the defamatory statement] was false or with reckless disregard of whether it was false or not."

Until this decision, libelous statements had not been protected by the First Amendment.

Civil Rights

Griffin v. County School Board of Prince Edward County (377 U.S. 218), decided by a 7-2 vote, May 25, 1964. Black wrote the majority opinion; Clark and Harlan dissented in part.

Finally losing patience with state defiance of its school desegregation decisions, the court declared that there had been "entirely too much deliberation and not enough speed." The court declared unconstitutional, as a violation of the 14th Amendment's equal protection clause, the closing of all the public schools in Prince Edward County, Va., to avoid the impact of desegregation.

Heart of Atlanta Motel v. United States (379 U.S. 241), decided by a unanimous vote, Dec. 14, 1964. Clark wrote the opinion.

Under its authority to regulate interstate commerce, Congress has the power to prohibit racial discrimination in privately owned public accommodations. This ruling, which effectively overturned the court's 1883 decision in the *Civil Rights Cases,* sustained Title II of the Civil Rights Act of 1964. That section prohibited discrimination, on the basis of race, religion or national origin, in accommodations that catered to interstate travelers or that served food or provided entertainment, a substantial portion of which was shipped through interstate commerce.

Self-Incrimination

Malloy v. Hogan (378 U.S. 1), decided by a 5-4 vote, June 15, 1964. Brennan wrote the majority opinion; Harlan, Clark, White and Stewart dissented.

The Fifth Amendment protection against self-incrimination is extended to state defendants through the due process clause of the 14th Amendment.

Murphy v. The Waterfront Commission of New York Harbor (378 U.S. 52), decided by a unanimous vote, June 15, 1964. Goldberg wrote the opinion.

The Fifth Amendment privilege against compelled self-incrimination protects witnesses granted immunity by either state or federal officials from prosecution in either jurisdiction based on their testimony.

Freedom of Association

Aptheker v. Secretary of State (378 U.S. 500), decided by a 7-2 vote, June 22, 1964. Goldberg wrote the majority opinion; Clark and White dissented.

The court declared unconstitutional a section of the Subversive Activities Control Act of 1950 that denied passports — and thus the right to travel — to persons who belonged to organizations listed as subversive by the attorney general. The court found the law too broad because it failed to distinguish between persons who joined such organizations with the full knowledge of their subversive purpose and those persons who were "unknowing." Nor did the law take into account the purpose of the intended travel.

Right to Counsel

Escobedo v. Illinois (378 U.S. 478), decided by a 5-4 vote, June 22, 1964. Goldberg wrote the majority opinion; Harlan, Stewart, White and Clark dissented.

The court expanded a suspect's right to counsel under the Sixth Amendment, holding that confessions obtained by police who had not advised the suspect of his right to counsel — or acceded to his requests for counsel — were inadmissible as evidence in court.

1965

Due Process

Pointer v. Texas (380 U.S. 400), decided by a unanimous vote, April 5, 1965. Black wrote the opinion.

The Sixth Amendment guarantee of the right to confront and cross-examine witnesses is applied to state defendants by the 14th Amendment's due process clause.

Federal Courts

Dombrowski v. Pfister (380 U.S. 479), decided by a 5-2 vote, April 26, 1965. Brennan wrote the majority opinion; Harlan and Clark dissented; Black and Stewart did not participate.

Federal courts need not abstain from ordering state officials to halt enforcement of a law justifiably attacked as in violation of the First Amendment, even if the person seeking the order has not yet exhausted all state procedures for challenging that law.

Voting Rights

Harman v. Forssenius (380 U.S. 528), decided by a unanimous vote, April 27, 1965. Chief Justice Warren wrote the opinion.

A Virginia law imposing special registration requirements on persons not paying the state's poll tax violates the 24th Amendment's ban on poll taxes in federal elections.

Self-Incrimination

Griffin v. California (380 U.S. 609), decided by a 7-1 vote, April 28, 1965. Douglas wrote the majority opinion; Stewart dissented; Chief Justice Warren did not participate.

The Fifth Amendment privilege against compelled self-incrimination, as applied to the states through the due process guarantee of the 14th Amendment, is infringed when a judge or prosecutor comments adversely during a trial upon a defendant's failure to testify in his own behalf.

Albertson v. Subversive Activities Control Board (382 U.S. 70), decided by an 8-0 vote, Nov. 15, 1965. Brennan delivered the opinion; White did not participate.

The court overturned convictions of Communist Party members ordered to register personally with the attorney general under provisions of the Subversive Activities Control Act of 1950. The registration orders, the court said, violated the Fifth Amendment privilege against self-incrimination.

Personal Privacy

Griswold v. Connecticut (381 U.S. 479), decided by a 7-2 vote, June 7, 1965. Douglas wrote the majority opinion; Stewart and Black dissented.

A state unconstitutionally interferes with personal privacy in the marriage relationship when it prohibits anyone, including married couples, from using contraceptives. The majority agreed that a right of personal privacy is implicit in the Constitution, but did not concur on the exact source of this right.

1966

Voting Rights

South Carolina v. Katzenbach (383 U.S. 301), decided by an 8-1 vote, March 7, 1966. Chief Justice Warren wrote the majority opinion; Black dissented.

The court upheld provisions of the Voting Rights Act of 1965 as a proper exercise of congressional power to enforce the 15th Amendment ban on racial discrimination in voting.

Harper v. Virginia State Board of Elections (383 U.S. 663), decided by a 7-2 vote, March 24, 1966. Douglas wrote the majority opinion; Black and Harlan dissented.

State laws which make the right to vote contingent upon payment of a tax violate the equal protection clause of the Fourteenth Amendment.

Freedom of Association

Elfbrandt v. Russell (384 U.S. 11), decided by a 5-4 vote, April 18, 1966. Douglas wrote the majority opinion; White, Clark, Harlan and Stewart dissented.

The court declared an Arizona loyalty oath unconstitutional because it violated the First Amendment right of freedom of association by penalizing persons for membership in certain groups whether or not they joined the group with the specific intent of engaging in unlawful acts.

Self-Incrimination

Miranda v. Arizona (384 U.S. 436), decided by a 5-4 vote, June 13, 1966. Chief Justice Warren wrote the majority opinion; Clark, Harlan, Stewart and White dissented.

The guarantee of due process requires that suspects in police custody be informed of their right to remain silent, that anything they say may be used against them, and that they have the right to counsel — before any questioning of the suspect can permissibly take place.

1967

Freedom of Association

Keyishian v. Board of Regents (385 U.S. 589), decided by a 5-4 vote, Jan. 23, 1967. Brennan wrote the majority opinion; Clark, Harlan, Stewart and White dissented.

The court invalidated New York State's teacher loyalty oath requirement holding that the law was too vague and uncertain. Membership in the Communist Party alone was not sufficient grounds to disqualify a teacher from public school employment.

United States v. Robel (389 U.S. 258), decided by a 6-2 vote, Dec. 11, 1967. Chief Justice Warren wrote the majority opinion; White and Harlan dissented; Marshall did not participate.

The court nullified a section of the Subversive Activities Control Act of 1950 which forbade a member of a group listed as subversive by the attorney general to take a job in a defense industry. The court held that the provision violated the individual's First Amendment right of association.

Due Process

Klopfer v. North Carolina (386 U.S. 213), decided by a unanimous vote, March 13, 1967. Chief Justice Warren wrote the opinion.

The Sixth Amendment right to a speedy trial applies in state, as well as federal, proceedings.

In re Gault (387 U.S. 1), decided by a 7-2 vote, May 15, 1967. Fortas wrote the majority opinion; Harlan and Stewart dissented.

The court extended some — but not all — due process privileges to juvenile court proceedings. The privilege against self-incrimination and the right to counsel were among the rights extended.

Washington v. Texas (388 U.S. 14), decided by a unanimous vote, June 12, 1967. Chief Justice Warren wrote the opinion.

Compulsory process to obtain witnesses in the defendant's favor is so fundamental to the Sixth Amendment guarantee of a fair trial that it is applicable to state trials through the due process clause of the 14th Amendment.

Search and Seizure

Warden v. Hayden (387 U.S. 294), decided by an 8-1 vote, May 29, 1967. Brennan wrote the majority opinion; Douglas dissented.

The decision upheld as reasonable and constitutional law enforcement searches for mere evidence as well as for implements and products of crime.

Katz v. United States (389 U.S. 347), decided by a 7-1 vote, Dec. 18, 1967. Stewart wrote the majority opinion for the court; Black dissented; Marshall did not participate.

The court abandoned its view, set out in the 1928 decision in *Olmstead v. United States,* that electronic surveillance and wiretapping were not "searches and seizures" within the scope of the Fourth Amendment. The amendment protects people, not places; it protects what an individual seeks to preserve as private, even in a place accessible to the public, held the court.

Civil Rights

Loving v. Virginia (388 U.S. 1), decided by a unanimous vote, June 12, 1967. Chief Justice Warren wrote the opinion.

A state law providing punishment for persons who enter into interracial marriages violates both the equal protection and due process clauses of the 14th Amendment. "Under our Constitution, the freedom to marry or not

marry a person of another race resides with the individual and cannot be infringed by the state," the court declared.

This was the first decision in which the court explicitly stated that classifications by race were "inherently suspect" and therefore justifiable only by compelling reasons.

Right to Counsel

United States v. Wade (388 U.S. 218), decided by a unanimous vote, June 12, 1967. Brennan wrote the opinion.

A police line-up identification of a suspect — made without the suspect's attorney present — is inadmissable as evidence at trial.

1968

Due Process

Duncan v. Louisiana (391 U.S. 145), decided by an 8-1 vote, May 20, 1968. White wrote the majority opinion; Harlan dissented.

The 14th Amendment's guarantee of due process requires states to provide trial by jury to persons accused of serious crimes.

Civil Rights

Green v. County School Board of New Kent County, Va. (391 U.S. 430), decided by a unanimous vote, May 27, 1968. Brennan wrote the opinion.

Local school district officials have an affirmative duty to eliminate segregation "root and branch" from public schools, the court said, striking down a "freedom-of-choice" plan that would have maintained segregated schools in New Kent County, Va. "The burden on a school board today is to come forward with a [desegregation] plan that promises realistically to work and ... to work *now,*" the court declared.

Jones v. Alfred H. Mayer Co. (392 U.S. 409), decided by a 7-2 vote, June 17, 1968. Stewart wrote the majority opinion; Harlan and White dissented.

The 1866 Civil Rights Act bars private as well as state-backed racial discrimination in the sale and rental of housing. This decision reinterpreted congressional authority to enforce the 13th Amendment adopted to remove "the badges of slavery." In the *Civil Rights Cases* of 1883, the court had held that Congress had no authority to enforce the guarantees of the 13th Amendment against private acts of discrimination.

Search and Seizure

Terry v. Ohio (392 U.S. 1), decided by an 8-1 vote, June 10, 1968. Chief Justice Warren wrote the majority opinion; Douglas dissented.

The court upheld the police practice of "stop and frisk," saying that when a police officer observes unusual conduct and suspects a crime is about to be committed, he may "frisk" a suspect's outer clothing for dangerous weapons. Such searches do not violate the Fourth Amendment's prohibition against unreasonable searches and seizures.

Federal Courts

Flast v. Cohen (392 U.S. 83), decided by an 8-1 vote, June 10, 1968. Chief Justice Warren wrote the majority opinion; Harlan dissented.

Modifying its 1923 ruling in *Frothingham v. Mellon,* the court held that a federal taxpayer may have the requisite standing to bring a federal challenge to federal spending and taxing programs which he charges are unconstitutional.

To prove the necessary personal interest in such programs, the court ruled, the taxpayer must establish a logical connection between his taxpayer status and the claim before the court. This connection or "nexus" must be shown to prevent federal courts from becoming merely forums for the airing of generalized grievances about government programs and policies.

1969

Freedom of Speech

Tinker v. Des Moines Independent Community School District (393 U.S. 503), decided by a 7-2 vote, Feb. 24, 1969. Fortas wrote the majority opinion; Harlan and Black dissented.

Students have the right to engage in peaceful nondisruptive protest, the court said, recognizing that the First Amendment guarantee of freedom of speech protects symbolic as well as oral speech. The wearing of black armbands to protest the Vietnam War was "closely akin" to the "pure speech" protected by the First Amendment, the majority said, and therefore a public school ban on this form of protest, which did not disrupt the school's work or offend the rights of others, violated these students' rights.

Voting Rights

Kirkpatrick v. Preisler (394 U.S. 526), decided by a 6-3 vote, April 7, 1969. Brennan wrote the majority opinion; Harlan, Stewart and White dissented.

Congressional districts with population variances of 3.1 percent from mathematical equality are unconstitutional unless the state can show that such variations are unavoidable.

Gaston County v. United States (395 U.S. 285), decided by a 7-1 vote, June 2, 1969. Harlan wrote the majority opinion; Black dissented.

The court denied a county's request — under provisions of the 1965 Voting Rights Act — to reinstate a literacy test for voters. The combination of such a test, the court ruled, with previous deprivation of educational opportunity for blacks in the county, would abridge the right to vote on account of race.

Personal Liberty

Shapiro v. Thompson, Washington v. Legrant, Reynolds v. Smith (394 U.S. 618), decided by a 6-3 vote, April 21, 1969. Brennan wrote the majority opinion; Chief Justice Warren, Black and Harlan dissented.

The right to travel is constitutionally protected. State or federal requirements that a person reside within a jurisdiction for one year before becoming eligible for welfare assistance violates individual rights to due process and equal protection of the laws; no compelling government interest was presented to justify this infringement on the right to travel.

Power of Congress

Powell v. McCormack (395 U.S. 486), decided by a 7-1 vote, June 16, 1969. Chief Justice Warren wrote the majority opinion; Stewart dissented.

The House of Representatives does not have the authority to exclude from membership a duly elected representative who meets the constitutional qualifications of age, residence and citizenship. The House had acted unconstitutionally when it voted to exclude Rep. Adam Clayton Powell, D-N.Y., for misconduct and misuse of public funds.

The court did not deny the unquestionable interest of Congress in maintaining its own integrity, but said such interest could be maintained by the use of each chamber's power to punish and expel its members. The court did reject the argument that the case presented a "political question," holding that a determination of Powell's right to his seat required only the interpretation of the Constitution, the traditional function of the court.

Due Process

Benton v. Maryland (395 U.S. 784), decided by a 6-2 vote, June 23, 1969. Marshall wrote the opinion; Stewart and Harlan dissented in part.

The court overruled *Palko v. Connecticut* (1937) to declare that the 14th Amendment due process guarantee extends the double jeopardy guarantee of the Fifth Amendment against state, as well as federal, action.

Search and Seizure

Chimel v. California (395 U.S. 752), decided by a 6-2 vote, June 23, 1969. Stewart wrote the opinion; White and Black dissented.

The court narrowed the limits of permissible searches conducted without a warrant incident to lawful arrest. Police may search only the immediate area around the suspect from which he could obtain a weapon or destroy evidence. A person's entire dwelling cannot be searched simply because he is arrested there.

This decision overruled *United States v. Rabinowitz* (1950).

1970

Due Process

In re Winship (397 U.S. 358), decided by a 5-3 vote, March 31, 1970. Brennan wrote the majority opinion; Chief Justice Burger, Black and Stewart dissented.

The 14th Amendment guarantee of due process requires that juveniles, like adult defendants, be found guilty "beyond a reasonable doubt." The court forbade states to use a lesser standard of proof in juvenile proceedings.

Williams v. Florida (399 U.S. 78), decided by a 7-1 vote, June 22, 1970. White wrote the majority opinion; Marshall dissented; Blackmun did not participate.

A six-member jury in non-capital state cases is constitutional. The number twelve is an "historical accident;" a jury can perform as well with six as with twelve members.

Voting Rights

Oregon v. Mitchell, Texas v. Mitchell, U.S. v. Idaho, U.S. v. Arizona (400 U.S. 112), decided by a 5-4 vote on lowered voting age, by an 8-1 vote on residency requirements and by a unanimous vote on literacy test ban, Dec. 21, 1970. Black wrote the opinion; Chief Justice Burger, Harlan, Stewart and Blackmun dissented on the question of age; Harlan dissented on the residency issue.

Congress has the power to lower the voting age for federal — but not for state and local — elections, to restrict state residency requirements to 30 days for voters in presidential elections, and to ban literacy tests as voter qualification devices in any election.

1971

Federal Courts

Younger v. Harris (401 U.S. 37), decided by an 8-1 vote, Feb. 23, 1971. Black wrote the majority opinion; Douglas dissented.

Federal judges should not normally issue orders to state officials to halt enforcement of a state law or ongoing state proceedings — at least without a showing that continued enforcement of the law threatens to do irreparable injury to the person seeking the order.

Self-Incrimination

Harris v. New York (401 U.S. 222), decided by a 5-4 vote, Feb. 24, 1971. Chief Justice Burger wrote the majority opinion; Black, Douglas, Brennan and Marshall dissented.

Voluntary statements made by a defendant not properly warned of his constitutional rights may be used in court to impeach his credibility if he takes the witness stand in his own defense and contradicts the earlier statements.

Civil Rights

Griggs v. Duke Power Co. (401 U.S. 424), decided by an 8-0 vote, March 8, 1971. Chief Justice Burger wrote the opinion; Brennan did not participate.

In its first case implicitly upholding the right of Congress to bar employment discrimination based on race, the court held that the Civil Rights Act of 1964 prohibits employers from requiring a high school diploma or score on a general intelligence test as a condition for employment or promotion if neither test is related to job skills and if both tend to disqualify more black than white applicants.

Swann v. Charlotte-Mecklenburg County Board of Education (402 U.S. 1), decided by a unanimous vote, April 20, 1971. Chief Justice Burger wrote the opinion.

Busing, racial balance ratios and gerrymandered school districts are all permissible interim methods of eliminating the vestiges of state-imposed segregation from southern schools.

There were limits to the remedies which might be used to eliminate the remnants of segregation, the court said, but no fixed guidelines setting such limits could be established. The court acknowledged that there might be valid objections to busing when so much time or distance is involved as to risk the children's health or to impinge significantly on the education process.

Equal Protection

Graham v. Richardson (403 U.S. 365), decided by a unanimous vote, June 14, 1971. Blackmun wrote the opinion.

Extending the protection of the equal protection guarantee to aliens, the court struck down state laws denying welfare benefits to aliens who lived in the United States less than 15 years and denying benefits to all resident aliens. The court held that all classification by alienage was "suspect," requiring an especially close scrutiny by the court to ensure compliance with the equal protection guarantee.

Reed v. Reed (404 U.S. 71), decided by a 7-0 vote, Nov. 22, 1971. Chief Justice Burger wrote the opinion.

The 14th Amendment guarantee of equal protection invalidates a state law which automatically prefers a father over a mother as executor of a son's estate. "To give a mandatory preference to members of either sex over members of the other . . . is to make the very kind of arbitrary legislative choice forbidden by the equal protection clause," the court said in its first opinion declaring a state law unconstitutional on the grounds that it discriminated against women.

Due Process

McKeiver v. Pennsylvania, In re Burrus (403 U.S. 528), decided by votes of 6-3 and 5-4, June 21, 1971. Blackmun wrote the majority opinion; Douglas, Black and Marshall dissented, joined in *Burrus* by Brennan.

The Sixth Amendment right to trial by jury does not extend to juvenile defendants.

Freedom of Religion

Lemon v. Kurtzman (403 U.S. 602), decided by an 8-0 vote, June 28, 1971. Chief Justice Burger wrote the opinion; Marshall did not participate.

In this case, the court established a three-part test to determine whether state aid to parochial schools violated the First Amendment's ban on government action "establishing" religion.

State aid is permissible, the court said, if it is intended to achieve a secular legislative purpose, if its primary effect neither advances nor inhibits religion, and if it does not foster excessive government entanglement with religion.

Applying this test, the court declared invalid a state law authorizing supplemental salary grants to certain parochial school teachers and another state law authorizing reimbursement to parochial schools for teachers' salaries, textbooks and instructional materials; the court found that both laws fostered an excessive entanglement between government and religion.

Freedom of the Press

New York Times Co. v. United States, United States v. The Washington Post (403 U.S. 713), decided by a 6-3 vote, June 30, 1971. The opinion was unsigned; each justice wrote a separate opinion expressing his individual views. Chief Justice Burger, Blackmun and Harlan dissented.

The court in its brief *per curiam* opinion denied the government's request for a court order barring continued publication in *The New York Times* and *The Washington Post* of articles based on classified documents detailing the history of U.S. involvement in Indochina, popularly known as the Pentagon Papers.

Any request for prior restraint of the press bears a "heavy presumption against its constitutional validity," the court said, and the government had failed to show sufficient justification for imposing such restraint.

1972

Self-Incrimination

Kastigar v. United States (406 U.S. 441), decided by a 5-2 vote, May 22, 1972. Powell wrote the opinion; Douglas and Marshall dissented; Rehnquist and Brennan did not participate.

The narrowed witness immunity provisions of the 1970 Organized Crime Control Act do not infringe upon the Fifth Amendment privilege against self-incrimination. In any subsequent prosecution of an immunized witness, the government must demonstrate that the evidence is derived from sources independent of testimony given under a grant of immunity.

Due Process

Johnson v. Louisiana, Apodaca v. Oregon (406 U.S. 356, 404), decided by 5-4 votes, May 22, 1972. White wrote the majority opinion; Douglas, Brennan, Stewart and Marshall dissented.

The constitutional guarantee of a jury trial applied to state courts does not require that the jury's verdict be unanimous. Lack of unanimity on the question of guilt does not constitute evidence of a reasonable doubt of guilt.

Furman v. Georgia, Jackson v. Georgia, Branch v. Texas (408 U.S. 238), decided by a 5-4 vote, June 29, 1972. The court's opinion was unsigned; each justice filed a separate opinion. Chief Justice Burger, Blackmun, Powell and Rehnquist dissented.

The court nullified all death penalty statutes in the United States. It held that the procedures they provided for judges and juries to follow in deciding when and whether to impose a sentence of death upon a defendant left so much discretion to the judge and jury that the result was arbitrary, irrational and deprived defendants of due process of law.

Right to Counsel

Argersinger v. Hamlin (407 U.S. 25), decided by a unanimous vote, June 12, 1972. Douglas wrote the opinion.

The right of counsel applies in trials for all offenses, state and federal, where a jail sentence is a possible penalty.

Official Immunity

United States v. Brewster (408 U.S. 501), decided by a 6-3 vote, June 29, 1972. Chief Justice Burger wrote the opinion; Brennan, Douglas and White dissented.

The constitutional immunity conferred on members of Congress by the "speech or debate clause" does not protect them from prosecution for accepting a bribe in order to vote a certain way on a legislative matter.

The holding cleared the way for prosecution of former Sen. Daniel B. Brewster (D Md. 1963-69), who had been indicted in 1969 on charges of accepting $24,000 in bribes from the mail order firm of Spiegel Inc. to influence his vote on changes in postal rates. Taking a bribe is illegal, the majority wrote, and is no part of the legislative process. It is therefore subject to prosecution and punishment in the nation's courts.

Freedom of the Press

Branzburg v. Hayes, In re Pappas, United States v. Caldwell (408 U.S. 665), decided by a 5-4 vote, June 29, 1972. White wrote the majority opinion; Douglas, Brennan, Stewart and Marshall dissented.

The constitutional guarantee of freedom of the press does not privilege news reporters to refuse — without risking contempt charges — to provide information to grand juries concerning a crime or the sources of evidence concerning a crime.

1973

Personal Privacy

Roe v. Wade (410 U.S. 113), *Doe v. Bolton* (410 U.S. 179), decided by 7-2 votes, Jan. 22, 1973. Blackmun wrote the majority opinions; Rehnquist and White dissented.

The right to privacy, grounded in the 14th Amendment's due process guarantee of personal liberty, encompasses and protects a woman's decision whether or not to bear a child. This right is impermissibly abridged by state laws which make abortion a crime.

During the first trimester of pregnancy, the decision to have an abortion should be left entirely to a woman and her physician. The state can forbid abortions by non-physicians.

During the second trimester, the state may regulate the abortion procedure in ways reasonably related to maternal health. And during the third trimester, the state may, if it wishes, forbid all abortions except those necessary to save the mother's life.

Voting Rights

Mahan v. Howell, City of Virginia Beach v. Howell, Weinberg v. Prichard (410 U.S. 315), decided by a 5-3 vote, February 21, 1973. Rehnquist wrote the opinion; Brennan, Douglas and Marshall dissented; Powell did not participate.

The court's decision in this case relaxed the requirement that state legislative districts be as nearly equal as possible — holding that states may apply more flexible standards in drawing new state legislative districts than in congressional redistricting.

The decision approved a Virginia plan permitting a 16 percent variation between the largest and smallest population districts.

Equal Protection

San Antonio Independent School District v. Rodriguez (411 U.S. 1), decided by a 5-4 vote, March 21, 1973. Powell wrote the majority opinion; Marshall, Douglas, Brennan and White dissented.

The right to an education is not a fundamental right guaranteed by the Constitution. Wealth is not a suspect way of classifying persons.

Therefore, the equal protection guarantee does not require that courts give the strictest scrutiny to a state decision to finance public schools from local property taxes, a decision resulting in wide disparities among districts in the amount spent per pupil.

States do not deny anyone the opportunity for an education by adopting this means of financing public education. Financing public schools from local property taxes rationally furthers a legitimate state purpose and so is upheld.

Due Process

Strunk v. United States (412 U.S. 434), decided by a unanimous vote, June 11, 1973. Chief Justice Burger wrote the opinion.

The court ruled that the only remedy for denial of a defendant's right to a speedy trial is dismissal of the charges against him. The court rejected the attempt of a judge to remedy a 10-month delay in trial by reducing the eventual sentence imposed on the defendant by that length of time.

Civil Rights

Keyes v. Denver School District No. 1 (413 U.S. 189), decided by a 7-1 vote, June 21, 1973. Brennan wrote the majority opinion; Rehnquist dissented; White did not participate.

This was the first time the court had defined the responsibility of school officials, in a district where racial segregation had never been required by law *(de jure)*, to act to desegregate public schools.

The court held that school officials were constitutionally obligated to desegregate a school system if the segregation there had resulted from intentional school board policies. In the case of racially segregated schools within a system, the burden of proof was on the school board to prove such segregation was not a result of intentional board actions.

Obscenity

Miller v. California (413 U.S. 15), decided by a 5-4 vote, June 21, 1973. Chief Justice Burger wrote the majority opinion; Brennan, Stewart, Marshall and Douglas dissented.

States have the power, without violating the First Amendment, to regulate material which is obscene in its depiction or description of sexual conduct. Material is obscene if the average person, applying contemporary local community standards, would find that it appeals to the prurient interest, and if it depicts in a patently offensive way, sexual conduct specifically defined by the applicable state law, and if the work, taken as a whole, lacks serious literary, artistic, political or scientific value.

This was the first definition of obscenity to command the approval of a majority of the justices since 1957; it was less stringent than the prevailing standard and consequently gave the states more control over obscene materials.

1974

Federal Courts

Edelman v. Jordan (415 U.S. 651), decided by a 5-4 vote, March 25, 1974. Rehnquist wrote the majority opinion; Brennan, Douglas, Marshall and Blackmun dissented.

The 11th Amendment immunity of states from federal lawsuits brought by citizens without the state's consent protects a state from a federal court order directing it to spend money to remedy past abuses.

Federal judges may order a state to halt enforcement of a law which violates due process and equal protection but that order may only reach future action — it may not require the state to remedy past damages inflicted under the invalid law.

In 1976 the court substantially modified the reach of this decision, holding unanimously in *Fitzpatrick v. Bitzer, Bitzer v. Matthews* (427 U.S. 445) that federal courts could order states to pay retroactive benefits to persons against whom the state had discriminated in violation of the 14th Amendment.

Equal Protection

Geduldig v. Aiello (417 U.S. 484), decided by a 6-3 vote, June 17, 1974. Stewart wrote the majority opinion; Douglas, Brennan and Marshall dissented.

California did not violate the constitutional guarantee of equal protection by excluding from its disability insurance program women unable to work because of pregnancy-related disabilities.

Women were not denied equal protection by this exclusion because, the majority said, "there is no risk from which men are protected and women are not." The decision to exclude the risk of pregnancy from the risks insured by the state plan was a rational one in light of the state interest in maintaining a low-cost, self-supporting insurance fund.

Power of the President

United States v. Nixon (418 U.S. 683), decided by an 8-0 vote, July 24, 1974. Chief Justice Burger wrote the opinion; Rehnquist did not participate.

Neither the separation of powers nor the need to preserve the confidentiality of presidential communications can alone justify an absolute executive privilege of immunity from judicial demands for evidence to be used in a criminal trial.

The court held that President Richard M. Nixon must comply with a subpoena for tapes of certain White House conversations, sought for use as evidence against White House aides charged with obstruction of justice in regard to the investigation of the break-in at the Democratic National Headquarters in the Watergate Office Building in June 1972.

Civil Rights

Milliken v. Bradley (418 U.S. 717), decided by a 5-4 vote, July 25, 1974. Chief Justice Burger wrote the majority opinion; Douglas, Brennan, Marshall and White dissented.

A multi-district remedy for school segregation, such as busing school children across district lines, can only be ordered by a federal court when there has been a finding that all the districts involved have been responsible for the segregation to be remedied.

The court reversed a lower court's order directing busing across city, county and district lines in order to desegregate the schools of Detroit, Mich. The majority ordered the lower court to devise a remedy that would affect only the city schools.

1975

Jury Trials

Taylor v. Louisiana (419 U.S. 522), decided by an 8-1 vote, Jan. 21, 1975. White wrote the majority opinion; Rehnquist dissented.

State laws generally exempting women from jury duty are unconstitutional because they violate the Sixth Amendment requirement that juries be drawn from a fair cross-section of the community.

The court overruled its 1961 decision in *Hoyt v. Florida*, which upheld this general exclusion of women from jury duty as rational in light of the state's interest in preventing interference with women's traditional functions as wives, homemakers and mothers.

Equal Protection

Weinberger v. Wiesenfeld (420 U.S. 636), decided by an 8-0 vote, March 19, 1975. Brennan wrote the opinion; Douglas did not participate.

Social Security law which pays widows with small children, but not widowers with small children, survivors' benefits violates the guarantee of due process by providing working women with fewer benefits for their Social Security contributions than it provides to working men. "It is no less important for a child to be cared for by its sole surviving parent when that parent is male rather than female," wrote Brennan, pointing out that the intended purpose of this benefit was to allow a mother not to work but to stay home and care for her young children.

Freedom of Speech

Bigelow v. Virginia (421 U.S. 809), decided by a 7-2 vote, June 16, 1975. Blackmun wrote the opinion; Rehnquist and White dissented.

Commercial advertising enjoys some First Amendment protection; *Valentine v. Chrestensen* (1942) held that the manner in which such ads were distributed could be regulated — not that advertising was itself unprotected.

The court reversed the conviction of a newspaper editor in Virginia for violating a state law against "encouraging" abortions by running an advertisement including information on legal abortions available in New York. This law was an improper effort by the state to control what its citizens could hear or read, the court held.

Commerce

Goldfarb v. Virginia State Bar (421 U.S. 773), decided by an 8-0 vote, June 16, 1975. Chief Justice Burger wrote the opinion; Powell did not participate.

Lawyers are not exempt from the provisions of federal antitrust laws. Minimum fee schedules adopted by bar associations and enforced to regulate the prices charged by attorneys for their services constitute price-fixing in violation of the antitrust laws.

Civil Rights

Albemarle Paper Co. v. Moody (422 U.S. 405), decided by a 7-1 vote, June 25, 1975. Stewart wrote the majority opinion; Chief Justice Burger dissented; Powell did not participate.

Back pay awards to victims of employment discrimination are the rule, not the exception, in cases won by employees under Title VII of the 1964 Civil Rights Act. Back pay awards are warranted to carry out the intent of Congress to make persons whole for injuries suffered on account of unlawful discrimination and should not be restricted to cases in which the employer is found to have acted in bad faith.

1976

Taxes

Michelin Tire Corp. v. Wages (423 U.S. 276), decided by an 8-0 vote, Jan. 14, 1976. Brennan wrote the opinion; Stevens did not participate.

The court overruled its 1872 decision in the case of *Low v. Austin*, which forbade states to tax imported goods so long as those goods retained their character as imports.

The court held that the export-import clause of the Constitution did not bar a county from imposing a property tax on imported goods stored prior to sale, so long as the tax does not discriminate against imported goods.

Freedom of Speech

Buckley v. Valeo (424 U.S. 1), decided by votes of 8-0, 7-1, and 6-2, Jan. 31, 1976. The opinion was unsigned; Chief Justice Burger, Blackmun, Rehnquist, White and Marshall all dissented in part; Stevens did not participate.

The First Amendment guarantee of freedom of expression is impermissibly infringed by the limits placed by the 1974 Federal Election Campaign Act Amendments on the amounts which a candidate for federal office may spend. The vote was 7-1; White dissented. The majority did find the limits permissible for candidates who accepted public financing of their campaigns for the presidency.

The court upheld, 6-2, the limits which the law placed on the amount individuals and political committees could contribute to candidates. This was only a marginal restriction on a contributor's First Amendment freedom, justified by the interest in preventing corruption, the majority said. Burger and Blackmun dissented.

The court upheld, 6-2, the system of public financing set up by the law for presidential campaigns and elections. Burger and Rehnquist dissented. Burger also dissented from the majority's decision to uphold the law's requirements for public disclosure of campaign contributions of more than $100 and campaign expenditures of more than $10.

The court unanimously agreed that the Federal Election Commission, as set up by the 1974 law, was unconstitutional as a violation of the separation of powers.

Civil Rights

Hills v. Gautreaux (425 U.S. 284), decided by an 8-0 vote, April 20, 1976. Stewart wrote the opinion; Stevens did not participate.

Federal courts have the power to order housing officials who have contributed to the racial segregation of public housing in a city to remedy that situation by developing public housing throughout the metropolitan area. The court upheld a federal court order for such an area-wide solution to the segregation of public housing in Chicago, a situation for which federal Housing and Urban Development officials had been found partially responsible.

Washington v. Davis (426 U.S. 229), decided by a 7-2 vote, June 7, 1976. White wrote the majority opinion; Brennan and Marshall dissented.

Job qualification tests are not unconstitutional simply because more black than white job applicants fail them. Some racially discriminatory purpose must be found in order for such a test to be in violation of the constitutional guarantees of due process and equal protection. "Disproportionate impact is not irrelevant, but it is not the sole touchstone of an invidious racial discrimination forbidden by the Constitution."

Runyon v. McCrary, Fairfax-Brewster School, Inc. v. Gonzales, Southern Independent School Association v. McCrary (427 U.S. 160), decided by a 7-2 vote, June 25, 1976. Stewart wrote the majority opinion; White and Rehnquist dissented.

Racially segregated private schools which refuse to admit black students violate the Civil Rights Act of 1866, which gave "all persons within the jurisdiction of the United States the same right . . . to make and enforce contracts . . . as is enjoyed by white citizens."

Pasadena City Board of Education v. Spangler (427 U.S. 424), decided by a 6-2 vote, June 28, 1976. Rehnquist wrote the opinion; Brennan and Marshall dissented; Stevens did not participate.

Once a school board has implemented a racially neutral plan for attendance of students at city schools, it is not constitutionally required to continue juggling student assignments in order to maintain a certain racial balance in the student body of each school.

Commerce

National League of Cities v. Usery, California v. Usery (426 U.S. 833), decided by a 5-4 vote, June 24, 1976. Rehnquist wrote the majority opinion; Brennan, White, Marshall and Stevens dissented.

Congress exceeded its power to regulate interstate commerce when it extended federal minimum wage and overtime standards to cover state and local government employees by its 1974 amendments to the Fair Labor Standards Act. Determination of state government employees' wages and hours is one of the "attributes of sovereignty attaching to every state government, which may not be impaired by Congress."

Freedom of Association

Elrod v. Burns (427 U.S. 347), decided by a 5-3 vote, June 28, 1976. Brennan wrote the majority opinion; Chief Justice Burger, Powell and Rehnquist dissented; Stevens did not participate.

The First Amendment freedom of political association is violated by the practice of patronage firing — the discharge by a new officeholder of those public employees not belonging to his political party.

Freedom of the Press

Nebraska Press Association v. Stuart (427 U.S. 539), decided by a unanimous vote, June 30, 1976. Chief Justice Burger wrote the opinion.

A gag order limiting severely what the press can report about pre-trial proceedings in a mass murder case violates the First Amendment guarantee of a free press.

If ever permissible, this sort of prior restraint of publication can be justified only by the most extreme circumstances. In most situations, judges concerned about preserving a defendant's right to a fair trial by an unbiased jury have many less drastic means of ensuring that potential jurors are not prejudiced by publicity.

Cruel and Unusual Punishment

Gregg v. Georgia (428 U.S. 153), *Proffitt v. Florida* (428 U.S. 242), *Jurek v. Texas* (428 U.S. 262), decided by 7-2 votes, July 2, 1976. Stewart wrote the majority decision in *Gregg;* Stevens wrote the majority decision in *Jurek;* Powell wrote the majority decision in *Proffitt;* Brennan and Marshall dissented.

Death, as a punishment for persons convicted of first degree murder, is not in and of itself cruel and unusual punishment in violation of the Eighth Amendment. That amendment, however, requires that the sentencing judge or jury consider the individual character of the offender and the circumstances of the particular crime before deciding whether or not to impose the death sentence. A two-part proceeding — one for the determination of guilt or innocence and a second for determining the sentence — provides an opportunity for such individualized consideration prior to sentencing.

Woodson v. North Carolina (428 U.S. 280), *Roberts v. Louisiana* (428 U.S. 325), decided by votes of 5-4, July 2,

1976. Stewart wrote the majority opinion in *Woodson;* Stevens wrote the majority opinion in *Roberts;* Chief Justice Burger, White, Rehnquist and Blackmun dissented.

States may not make death the mandatory penalty for first-degree murder. Such mandatory sentences fail to meet the constitutional requirement for consideration of the individual offender and offense prior to the decision to impose the death penalty.

Federal Courts

Stone v. Powell, Wolff v. Rice (428 U.S. 465), decided by a 6-3 vote, July 6, 1976. Powell wrote the majority opinion; Brennan, Marshall and White dissented.

A state prisoner's claim that illegally obtained evidence was used to convict him cannot serve as a basis for a federal court order of his release through a writ of *habeas corpus* — unless the state failed to provide the prisoner an opportunity for full and fair hearing of his challenge to the evidence.

Equal Protection

Craig v. Boren (429 U.S. 190), decided by a 7-2 vote, Dec. 20, 1976. Brennan wrote the majority opinion; Chief Justice Burger and Rehnquist dissented.

A classification based on gender is invalid unless it is substantially related to the achievement of an important governmental objective.

Using this rule, the court declared unconstitutional a state law that permitted the sale of 3.2 beer to women at age 18 but not to men until age 21. The law was not substantially related to the state's expressed goal of promoting traffic safety.

1977

Civil Rights

Village of Arlington Heights v. Metropolitan Housing Development Corporation (429 U.S. 252), decided by a 5-3 vote, Jan. 11, 1977. Powell wrote the majority opinion; Brennan and Marshall dissented in part; White dissented; Stevens did not participate.

Without any showing of discriminatory motive, the refusal of a village to rezone property to permit building of a housing development for low- and moderate-income persons of both races does not violate the 14th Amendment guarantee of equal protection.

Voting Rights

United Jewish Organizations of Williamsburgh v. Carey (430 U.S. 144), decided by a 7-1 vote, March 1, 1977. White wrote the majority opinion; Chief Justice Burger dissented; Marshall did not participate.

The court upheld the use of racial criteria by the state of New York in its 1974 state legislative redistricting plan drawn to comply with the 1965 Voting Rights Act. The court said that even if the result of the redistricting diluted the vote of a white ethnic minority — in this case the Hasidic Jewish community of Brooklyn — the Constitution "does not prevent a state subject to the Voting Rights Act from deliberately creating or preserving black majorities in particular districts in order to ensure that its reapportionment plan" complies with the act.

Taxes

Complete Auto Transit Inc. v. Brady (430 U.S. 274), decided by a unanimous vote, March 8, 1977. Blackmun wrote the opinion.

The commerce clause — granting Congress the power to regulate interstate and foreign commerce — does not forbid a state to tax an interstate enterprise doing business within the state for the "privilege" of doing business there.

Such taxes are permissible so long as the taxed activity has a sufficient nexus with the taxing state; the tax does not discriminate against interstate commerce, is fairly apportioned and is related to services provided by the state.

Cruel and Unusual Punishment

Coker v. Georgia (433 U.S. 584), decided by a 7-2 vote, June 29, 1977. White wrote the majority opinion; Burger and Rehnquist dissented.

The court held that the sentence of death for the crime of rape is an excessive and disproportionate penalty forbidden by the Eighth Amendment ban on cruel and unusual punishments.

1978

Search and Seizure

Marshall v. Barlows, Inc. (436 U.S. 307), decided by a 5-3 vote, May 23, 1978. White wrote the majority opinion; Stevens, Blackmun and Rehnquist dissented; Brennan did not participate.

The court held unconstitutional the provision of the Occupational Safety and Health Act of 1970 which allowed warrantless inspection of covered businesses. Searches of business premises without a warrant and without the owner's consent violate the Fourth Amendment's guarantee against unreasonable searches and seizures. An OSHA inspector must obtain a search warrant when the businessman objects to a warrantless search.

Zurcher v. The Stanford Daily (436 U.S. 547), decided by a 5-3 vote, May 31, 1978. White wrote the majority opinion; Stewart, Marshall and Stevens dissented; Brennan did not participate.

The Fourth Amendment does not preclude or limit the use of search warrants for searches of places owned or occupied by innocent third parties not suspected of any crime.

The First Amendment guarantee of freedom of the press does not require that information concerning a crime which is suspected to be in the possession of a newspaper be sought by a subpoena rather than a search warrant.

Jury Trials

Ballew v. Georgia (435 U.S. 223), decided by a unanimous vote, March 21, 1978. Blackmun wrote the opinion.

In order to fulfill the constitutional guarantee of trial by jury, state juries must be composed of at least six members.

Freedom of Speech

First National Bank of Boston v. Bellotti (435 U.S. 765), decided by a 5-4 vote, April 26, 1978. Powell wrote the majority opinion; White, Brennan, Marshall and Rehnquist dissented.

State law banning corporate expenditures relative to a referendum issue which does not materially affect corporations' business impermissibly abridges political speech protected by the First Amendment. "If the speakers here were not corporations, no one would suggest that the state could silence their proposed speech. It is the type of speech indispensable to decisionmaking in a democracy, and this is no less true because the speech comes from a corporation rather than an individual," the majority said.

Federal Courts

Monell v. Department of Social Services, City of New York (436 U.S. 658), decided by a 7-2 vote, June 6, 1978. Brennan wrote the majority opinion; Chief Justice Burger and Rehnquist dissented.

City officials, municipalities and municipal agencies are not immune from civil rights damage suits filed under the Civil Rights Act of 1871. Cities may be held liable for damages if action pursuant to official policy violates someone's constitutional rights. Cities are not liable simply because their employees or agents infringe upon such rights in the course of their duties.

Civil Rights

Regents of University of California v. Bakke (438 U.S. 265), decided by votes of 5-4 and 5-4, June 28, 1978. Powell announced the judgment of the court; Stevens and Brennan filed separate opinions; Stevens was joined by Chief Justice Burger, Rehnquist and Stewart; Brennan was joined by Marshall, White and Blackmun.

A special admissions program for a state medical school under which a set number of places were set aside for minority group members — and white applicants were denied the opportunity to compete for those seats — clearly violated Title VI of the 1964 Civil Rights Act which forbids the exclusion of anyone, because of race, from participation in a federally funded program.

Admissions programs which consider race as one of a complex of factors involved in the decision to admit or reject an applicant are not unconstitutional in and of themselves. "Government may take race into account when it acts not to demean or insult any racial group, but to remedy disadvantages cast on minorities by past racial prejudice, at least when appropriate findings have been made by judicial, legislative, or administrative bodies with competence to act in this area."

Official Immunity

Butz v. Economou (438 U.S. 478), decided by a 5-4 vote, June 29, 1978. White wrote the majority opinion; Chief Justice Burger, Rehnquist, Stewart and Stevens dissented.

Federal officials are not absolutely immune from damage suits based upon their performance of official duties. Even when carrying out directives from Congress, federal officials are subject to the restraints of the Constitution.

1979

Right to Counsel

Scott v. Illinois (440 U.S. 367), decided by a 5-4 vote, March 5, 1979. Rehnquist wrote the majority opinion; Brennan, Marshall, Stevens and Blackmun dissented.

A state defendant is guaranteed the right to legal counsel, paid by the state if necessary, only in cases that actually lead to imprisonment, not in all cases where imprisonment is a potential penalty.

Equal Protection

Orr v. Orr (440 U.S. 268), decided by a 6-3 vote, March 5, 1979. Brennan wrote the majority opinion; Powell, Rehnquist and Burger dissented.

States violate the 14th Amendment guarantee of equal protection when they allow women, but not men, to receive alimony as part of a divorce settlement.

Jury Trial

Burch v. Louisiana (441 U.S. 130), decided by a unanimous vote, April 17, 1979. Rehnquist wrote the opinion.

A state deprives a defendant of his constitutional right to a jury trial when it allows him to be convicted by the non-unanimous vote of a six-person jury.

Due Process

Davis v. Passman (442 U.S. 228), decided by a 5-4 vote, June 5, 1979. Brennan wrote the majority opinion; Chief Justice Burger, Powell, Rehnquist and Stewart dissented.

An individual who has been denied the rights of due process and equal protection under the Fifth Amendment guarantee against federal action can bring a federal suit for damages based on that amendment.

This decision for the first time provided a constitutional basis for job discrimination charges by congressional employees, who are not protected by the guarantees of the federal civil rights laws.

Official Immunity

United States v. Helstoski (442 U.S. 477), decided by a 5-3 vote, June 18, 1979. Chief Justice Burger wrote the majority opinion, Brennan dissented; Stevens and Stewart dissented in part; Powell did not participate.

The Constitution's provision that members of Congress may not be questioned outside Congress "for any Speech or Debate in either House" forbids the government, in prosecuting a member for accepting a bribe in return for a legislative act, to introduce evidence of the legislative act. The constitutional provision was intended to preclude prosecution of members for legislative acts.

Hutchinson v. Proxmire (443 U.S. 111), decided by a 7-2 vote, June 26, 1979. Chief Justice Burger wrote the majority opinion; Brennan dissented; Stewart dissented in part.

The Constitution's "Speech or Debate clause" does not protect a senator from being sued for libel as a result of statements made in press releases and newsletters.

An individual who does not seek to thrust himself into the public eye or otherwise draw public attention, but who is drawn into public notice by events outside his control, is not a public figure subject to the "actual malice" standard set out by the Supreme Court for libel suits brought by public officials.

Civil Rights

United Steelworkers of America v. Weber, Kaiser Aluminum v. Weber, United States v. Weber (443 U.S. 193), decided by a 5-2 vote, June 27, 1979. Brennan wrote the majority opinion; Chief Justice Burger and Rehnquist dissented; Powell and Stevens did not participate.

Title VII of the 1964 Civil Rights Act — which forbids racial discrimination in employment — does not forbid employers to adopt voluntarily race-conscious affirmative action programs to encourage minority participation in areas of work in which they have traditionally been under-represented.

Columbus Board of Education v. Penick, Dayton Board of Education v. Brinkman (443 U.S. 449), decided by votes of 7-2 and 5-4, July 2, 1979. White wrote the majority opinion in both cases; Rehnquist and Powell dissented in both; Chief Justice Burger and Stewart dissented in the *Dayton* case.

School boards operating segregated school systems at the time of the 1954 decision in *Brown v. Board of Education* are under an affirmative duty to end that segregation — even if it was not imposed as a result of state law. The court upheld system-wide busing orders for Dayton and Columbus, Ohio, where segregated schools had not been required by law since 1888.

Freedom of the Press

Gannett v. DePasquale (443 U.S. 368), decided by a 5-4 vote, July 2, 1979. Stewart wrote the majority opinion; Blackmun, Brennan, White and Marshall dissented in part.

The Constitution's guarantee of the right to a public trial is intended for the benefit of the defendant, not the public.

Members of the public do not have a constitutional right to attend a criminal trial, and thus a judge may constitutionally exclude press and public from a pretrial hearing in order to avoid publicity prejudicial to the defendant and thus protect his right to a fair trial.

1980

Power of Congress

Harris v. McRae (448 U.S. 297), decided by a 5-4 vote, June 30, 1980. Stewart wrote the opinion; Brennan, Marshall, Blackmun and Stevens dissented.

Congress did not exceed its powers nor infringe upon the constitutional guarantees of due process, equal protection or the free exercise of religion when it adopted the Hyde Amendment restricting the federal funding of medically necessary abortions. (The amendment denied reimbursement for abortions through the Medicaid program except when the abortion was necessary to save the mother's life or to terminate a pregnancy which was the result of rape or incest.)

States are not obligated by the Social Security Act, which authorizes the Medicaid program, to pay for those medically necessary abortions for which federal reimbursement is unavailable because of the Hyde Amendment.

Right of Access

Richmond Newspapers Inc. v. Commonwealth of Virginia (448 U.S. 555), decided by a 7-1 vote, July 2, 1980. Chief Justice Burger wrote an opinion announcing the decision and setting out the views of three justices; Brennan, Marshall, Stewart and Blackmun concurred. Rehnquist dissented. Powell did not participate.

The First Amendment guarantees citizens and members of the press the right to attend criminal trials. The right is not absolute and in some cases a judge may find it necessary to limit this access of press and public to a trial in order to preserve the defendant's right to a fair trial, but when he does so he must make public his reasons in writing.

Civil Rights

Fullilove v. Klutznick (448 U.S. 448), decided by a 6-3 vote, July 2, 1980. Chief Justice Burger wrote an opinion announcing the decision and setting out the views of three justices; Marshall, Brennan and Blackmun concurred; Stewart, Rehnquist and Stevens dissented.

Congress acted within constitutional limits when it enacted, in 1977, a provision setting aside for minority businesses 10 percent of the federal funds the law provided for local public works projects. Congress has the power to make some limited use of racial quotas to remedy past discrimination against black businesses.

1981

Power of Congress

United States v. Will (449 U.S. 200), decided by an 8-0 vote, Dec. 15, 1980. Chief Justice Burger wrote the opinion; Blackmun did not participate.

The court held unconstitutional two Acts of Congress rescinding cost-of-living increases for high-level federal officials, including judges and Supreme Court justices in fiscal 1977 and fiscal 1980.

The Constitution provides that the salaries of federal judges "shall not be diminished during their Continuance in Office." Once Congress in 1975 approved a law providing such cost-of-living increases, it could only rescind them — without violating this "compensation" clause — if it acted to do so before they took effect on the first day of each new fiscal year. Tested by this standard, Congress successfully rescinded the increases for fiscal 1978 and 1979, but failed to act in time to rescind those for 1977 and 1980.

Hodel v. Indiana, Hodel v. Virginia Surface Mining and Reclamation Association, decided by a 9-0 vote, June 15, 1981. Marshall wrote the opinion.

Congress did not overstep its authority to regulate interstate commerce when it enacted the Surface Mining Control and Reclamation Act of 1977, imposing severe restrictions on the use of land for strip mining. Nor did Congress in passing this law infringe on the powers of the states guaranteed by the Constitution or the rights of landowners.

Rostker v. Goldberg, decided by a 6-3 vote, June 25, 1981. Rehnquist wrote the opinion; Brennan, White and Marshall dissented.

The court upheld the decision of Congress to exclude women from the military draft. Because women are barred from combat duty by law and by military policy, they are not "similarly situated" with men and thus the Constitution does not require that they be treated in the same way.

Due Process

Chandler v. Florida, decided by an 8-0 vote, Jan. 26, 1981. Chief Justice Burger wrote the opinion; Stevens did not participate.

Nothing in the U.S. Constitution forbids states to experiment with television coverage of criminal trials. The mere presence of television cameras in the courtroom does not invariably deny a defendant his right to due process or a fair trial.

Occupational Safety

American Textile Manufacturers Institute v. Donovan, National Cotton Council v. Donovan, decided by a vote of 5-3, June 17, 1981. Brennan wrote the opinion; Rehnquist, Stewart and Burger dissented; Powell did not participate.

Congress, in enacting the 1970 Occupational Safety and Health Act required the Occupational Safety and Health Administration (OSHA) to set worker safety and health standards that would assure "to the extent feasible" that no worker "will suffer material impairment of health" from exposure to a hazardous substance throughout his working life. In light of this requirement, OSHA is not obligated to balance the costs of such safety standards against the benefits they will produce before imposing them. The court upheld the cotton dust exposure standards which OSHA had imposed, in 1978, upon the textile industry.

Self-Incrimination

Estelle v. Smith, decided by a 9-0 vote, May 18, 1981. Chief Justice Burger wrote the opinion.

A defendant must be advised of his right to counsel and his right to remain silent before he undergoes a court-ordered psychiatric examination, the results of which may be used by the state in its effort to obtain a sentence of death. The court set aside a death sentence imposed on a man, in part as a result of such an examination, before which he did not receive these warnings.

Edwards v. Arizona, decided by a 9-0 vote, May 18, 1981. White wrote the opinion.

Once a suspect in custody, who has been advised of his right to remain silent and his right to an attorney, asks for his lawyer, police must halt their questioning and may not resume it until the lawyer is present or until the accused himself initiates further conversation.

Personal Liberty

Haig v. Agee, decided by a 7-2 vote, June 29, 1981. Burger wrote the opinion; Brennan and Marshall dissented.

The secretary of state acted within the law when he revoked the passport of a former agent of the Central Intelligence Agency (CIA), who had engaged in a campaign abroad of publicizing the names of CIA agents and CIA activities. This activity presents a serious threat to national security and is not protected by the Constitution. The freedom to travel outside the United States is not synonymous with the right to travel within the country.

Power of the President

Dames & Moore v. Regan, decided by a 9-0 vote, July 2, 1981. Rehnquist wrote the opinion.

Congress in passing the International Emergency Economic Powers Act of 1977 and several earlier laws gave the president the power to conclude executive agreements nullifying court orders attaching Iranian assets in the United States and transferring all claims against Iran from U.S. court to an international tribunal for resolution.

The court's decision upheld the agreement reached by President Carter in the last days of his term with Iran under which Iran agreed to return the U.S. citizens held hostage by that country for more than a year.

Constitution of the United States

We the People of the United States, in Order to form a more perfect Union, establish Justice, insure domestic Tranquility, provide for the common defence, promote the general Welfare, and secure the Blessings of Liberty to ourselves and our Posterity, do ordain and establish this Constitution for the United States of America.

Article I

Section 1. All legislative Powers herein granted shall be vested in a Congress of the United States, which shall consist of a Senate and House of Representatives.

Section 2. The House of Representatives shall be composed of Members chosen every second Year by the People of the several States, and the Electors in each State shall have the Qualifications requisite for Electors of the most numerous Branch of the State Legislature.

No Person shall be a Representative who shall not have attained to the age of twenty five Years, and been seven Years a Citizen of the United States, and who shall not, when elected, be an Inhabitant of that State in which he shall be chosen.

[Representatives and direct Taxes shall be apportioned among the several States which may be included within this Union, according to their respective Numbers, which shall be determined by adding to the whole Number of free Persons, including those bound to Service for a Term of Years, and excluding Indians not taxed, three fifths of all other Persons.][1] The actual Enumeration shall be made within three Years after the first Meeting of the Congress of the United States, and within every subsequent Term of ten Years, in such Manner as they shall by Law direct. The Number of Representatives shall not exceed one for every thirty Thousand, but each State shall have at Least one Representative; and until such enumeration shall be made, the State of New Hampshire shall be entitled to chuse three, Massachusetts eight, Rhode-Island and Providence Plantations one, Connecticut five, New-York six, New Jersey four, Pennsylvania eight, Delaware one, Maryland six, Virginia ten, North Carolina five, South Carolina five, and Georgia three.

When vacancies happen in the Representation from any State, the Executive Authority thereof shall issue Writs of Election to fill such Vacancies.

The House of Representatives shall chuse their Speaker and other Officers; and shall have the sole Power of Impeachment.

Section 3. The Senate of the United States shall be composed of two Senators from each State, [chosen by the Legislature thereof,][2] for six Years; and each Senator shall have one Vote.

Immediately after they shall be assembled in Consequence of the first Election, they shall be divided as equally as may be into three Classes. The Seats of the Senators of the first Class shall be vacated at the Expiration of the second Year, of the second Class at the Expiration of the fourth Year, and of the third Class at the Expiration of the sixth Year, so that one third may be chosen every second Year; [and if Vacancies happen by Resignation, or otherwise, during the Recess of the Legislature of any State, the Executive thereof may make temporary Appointments until the next Meeting of the Legislature, which shall then fill such Vacancies.][3]

No Person shall be a Senator who shall not have attained to the Age of thirty Years, and been nine Years a Citizen of the United States, and who shall not, when elected, be an Inhabitant of that State for which he shall be chosen.

The Vice President of the United States shall be President of the Senate, but shall have no Vote, unless they be equally divided.

The Senate shall chuse their other Officers, and also a President pro tempore, in the Absence of the Vice President, or when he shall exercise the Office of President of the United States.

The Senate shall have the sole Power to try all Impeachments. When sitting for that Purpose, they shall be on Oath or Affirmation. When the President of the United States is tried the Chief Justice shall preside: And no Person shall be convicted without the Concurrence of two thirds of the Members present.

Judgment in Cases of Impeachment shall not extend further than to removal from Office, and disqualification to hold and enjoy any Office of honor, Trust or Profit under the United States: but the Party convicted shall nevertheless be liable and subject to Indictment, Trial, Judgment and Punishment, according to Law.

Section 4. The Times, Places and Manner of holding Elections for Senators and Representatives, shall be prescribed in each State by the Legislature thereof; but the Congress may at any time by Law make or alter such Regulations, except as to the Places of chusing Senators.

The Congress shall assemble at least once in every Year, and such Meeting shall [be on the first Monday in December],[4] unless they shall by Law appoint a different Day.

Section 5. Each House shall be the Judge of the Elections, Returns and Qualifications of its own Members, and a Majority of each shall constitute a Quorum to do Business; but a smaller Number may adjourn from day to day, and may be authorized to compel the Attendance of absent Members, in such Manner, and under such Penalties as each House may provide.

Each House may determine the Rules of its Proceedings, punish its Members for disorderly Behaviour, and, with the Concurrence of two thirds, expel a Member.

Each House shall keep a Journal of its Proceedings, and from time to time publish the same, excepting such Parts as may in their Judgment require Secrecy; and the Yeas and Nays of the Members of either House on any question shall, at the Desire of one fifth of those Present, be entered on the Journal.

Neither House, during the Session of Congress, shall, without the Consent of the other, adjourn for more than three days, nor to any other Place than that in which the two Houses shall be sitting.

Section 6. The Senators and Representatives shall receive a Compensation for their Services, to be ascertained by Law, and paid out of the Treasury of the United States. They shall in all Cases, except Treason, Felony and Breach of the Peace, be privileged from Arrest during their Attendance at the Session of their respective Houses, and in going to and returning from the same; and for any Speech or Debate in either House, they shall not be questioned in any other Place.

No Senator or Representative shall, during the Time for which he was elected, be appointed to any civil Office under the Authority of the United States, which shall have been created, or the Emoluments whereof shall have been encreased during such time; and no Person holding any Office under the United States, shall be a Member of either House during his Continuance in Office.

Section 7. All Bills for raising Revenue shall originate in the House of Representatives; but the Senate may propose or concur with amendments as on other Bills.

Every Bill which shall have passed the House of Representatives and the Senate, shall, before it become a Law, be presented to the President of the United States; If he approve he shall sign it, but if not he shall return it, with his Objections to that House in which it shall have originated, who shall enter the Objections at large on their Journal, and proceed to reconsider it. If after such Reconsideration two thirds of that House shall agree to pass the Bill, it shall be sent, together with the Objections, to the other House, by which it shall likewise be reconsidered, and if approved by two thirds of that House, it shall become a Law. But in all such Cases the Votes of both Houses shall be determined by yeas and Nays, and the Names of the Persons voting for and against the Bill shall be entered on the Journal of each House respectively. If any Bill shall not be returned by the President within ten Days (Sunday excepted) after it shall have been presented to him, the Same shall be a Law, in like Manner as if he had signed it, unless the Congress by their Adjournment prevent its Return, in which Case it shall not be a Law.

Every Order, Resolution, or Vote to which the Concurrence of the Senate and House of Representatives may be necessary (except on a question of Adjournment) shall be presented to the President of the United States; and before the Same shall take Effect, shall be approved by him, or being disapproved by him, shall be repassed by two thirds of the Senate and House of Representatives, according to the Rules and Limitations prescribed in the Case of a Bill.

Section 8. The Congress shall have Power To lay and collect Taxes, Duties, Imposts and Excises, to pay the Debts and provide for the common Defence and general Welfare of the United States; but all Duties, Imposts and Excises shall be uniform throughout the United States;

To borrow Money on the credit of the United States;

To regulate Commerce with foreign Nations, and among the several States, and with the Indian Tribes;

To establish an uniform Rule of Naturalization, and uniform Laws on the subject of Bankruptcies throughout the United States;

To coin Money, regulate the Value thereof, and of foreign Coin, and fix the Standard of Weights and Measures;

To provide for the Punishment of counterfeiting the Securities and current Coin of the United States;

To establish Post Offices and post Roads;

To promote the Progress of Science and useful Arts, by securing for limited Times to Authors and Inventors the exclusive Right to their respective Writings and Discoveries;

To constitute Tribunals inferior to the supreme Court;

To define and punish Piracies and Felonies commited on the high Seas, and Offences against the Law of Nations;

To declare War, grant Letters of Marque and Reprisal,and make Rules concerning Captures on Land and Water;

To raise and support Armies, but no Appropriation of Money to that Use shall be for a longer Term than two Years;

To provide and maintain a Navy;

To make Rules for the Government and Regulation of the land and naval Forces;

To provide for calling forth the Militia to execute the Laws of the Union, suppress Insurrections and repel Invasions;

To provide for organizing, arming, and disciplining, the Militia, and for governing such Part of them as may be employed in the Service of the United States, reserving to the States respectively, the Appointment of the Officers, and the Authority of training the Militia according to the discipline prescribed by Congress;

To exercise exclusive Legislation in all Cases whatsoever, over such District (not exceeding ten Miles square) as may, by Cession of Particular States, and the Acceptance of Congress, become the Seat of the Government of the United States, and to exercise like Authority over all Places purchased by the Consent of the Legislature of the State in which the Same shall be, for the Erection of Forts, Magazines, Arsenals, dock-Yards, and other needful Buildings; — And

To make all Laws which shall be necessary and proper for carrying into Execution the foregoing Powers, and all other Powers vested by this Constitution in the Government of the United States, or in any Department or Officer thereof.

Section 9. The Migration or Importation of such Persons as any of the States now existing shall think proper to admit, shall not be prohibited by the Congress prior to the Year one thousand eight hundred and eight, but a Tax or duty may be imposed on such Importation, not exceeding ten dollars for each Person.

The Privilege of the Writ of Habeas Corpus shall not be suspended, unless when in Cases of Rebellion or Invasion the public Safety may require it.

No Bill of Attainder or ex post facto Law shall be passed.

No capitation, or other direct, Tax shall be laid, unless in Proportion to the Census of Enumeration herein before directed to be taken.[5]

No Tax or Duty shall be laid on Articles exported from any State.

No Preference shall be given by any Regulation of Commerce or Revenue to the Ports of one State over those of another; nor shall Vessels bound to, or from, one State, be obliged to enter, clear or pay Duties in another.

No Money shall be drawn from the Treasury, but in Consequence of Appropriations made by Law; and a regular Statement and Account of the Receipts and Expenditures of all public Money shall be published from time to time.

No Title of Nobility shall be granted by the United States: And no Person holding any Office of Profit or Trust under them, shall, without the Consent of the Congress, accept of any present, Emolument, Office, or Title, of any kind whatever, from any King, Prince or foreign State.

Section 10. No State shall enter into any Treaty, Alliance, or Confederation; grant Letters of Marque and Reprisal; coin Money; emit Bills of Credit; make any Thing but gold and silver Coin a Tender in Payment of Debts;

pass any Bill of Attainder, ex post facto Law, or Law impairing the Obligation of Contracts, or grant any Title of Nobility.

No State shall, without the Consent of the Congress, lay any Imposts or Duties on Imports or Exports, except what may be absolutely necessary for executing it's inspection Laws: and the net Produce of all Duties and Imposts, laid by any State on Imports or Exports, shall be for the Use of the Treasury of the United States; and all such Laws shall be subject to the Revision and Controul of the Congress.

No State shall, without the Consent of Congress, lay any Duty of Tonnage, keep Troops, or Ships of War in time of Peace, enter into any Agreement or Compact with another State, or with a foreign Power, or engage in War, unless actually invaded, or in such imminent Danger as will not admit of delay.

Article II

Section 1. The executive Power shall be vested in a President of the United States of America. He shall hold his Office during the Term of four Years, and, together with the Vice President, chosen for the same Term, be elected, as follows.

Each State shall appoint, in such Manner as the Legislature thereof may direct, a Number of Electors, equal to the whole Number of Senators and Representatives to which the State may be entitled in the Congress: but no Senator or Representative, or Person holding an Office of Trust or Profit under the United States, shall be appointed an Elector.

[The Electors shall meet in their respective States, and vote by Ballot for two Persons, of whom one at least shall not be an Inhabitant of the same State with themselves. And they shall make a List of all the Persons voted for, and of the Number of Votes for each; which List they shall sign and certify, and transmit sealed to the Seat of the Government of the United States, directed to the President of the Senate. The President of the Senate shall, in the Presence of the Senate and House of Representatives, open all the Certificates, and the Votes shall then be counted. The Person having the greatest Number of Votes shall be the President, if such Number be a Majority of the whole Number of Electors appointed; and if there be more than one who have such Majority, and have an equal Number of Votes, then the House of Representatives shall immediately chuse by Ballot one of them for President; and if no Person have a Majority, then from the five highest on the list the said House shall in like Manner chuse the President. But in chusing the President, the Votes shall be taken by States, the Representation from each State having one Vote; a quorum for this Purpose shall consist of a Member or Members from two thirds of the States, and a Majority of all the States shall be necessary to a Choice. In every Case, after the Choice of the President, the Person having the greatest Number of Votes of the Electors shall be the Vice President. But if there should remain two or more who have equal Votes, the Senate shall chuse from them by Ballot the Vice President.][6]

The Congress may determine the Time of chusing the Electors, and the Day on which they shall give their Votes; which Day shall be the same throughout the United States.

No Person except a natural born Citizen, or a Citizen of the United States, at the time of the Adoption of this Constitution, shall be eligible to the Office of President; neither shall any Person be eligible to that Office who shall not have attained to the Age of thirty five Years, and been fourteen Years a Resident within the United States.

In Case of the Removal of the President from Office, or of his Death, Resignation, or Inability to discharge the Powers and Duties of the said Office,[7] the Same shall devolve on the Vice President, and the Congress may by Law provide for the Case of Removal, Death, Resignation or Inability, both of the President and Vice President, declaring what Officer shall then act as President, and such Officer shall act accordingly, until the Disability be removed, or a President shall be elected.

The President shall, at stated Times, receive for his Services, a Compensation, which shall neither be encreased nor diminished during the Period for which he shall have been elected, and he shall not receive within that Period any other Emolument from the United States, or any of them.

Before he enter on the Execution of his Office, he shall take the following Oath or Affirmation: — "I do solemnly swear (or affirm) that I will faithfully execute the Office of President of the United States, and will to the best of my Ability, preserve, protect and defend the Constitution of the United States."

Section 2. The President shall be Commander in Chief of the Army and Navy of the United States, and of the Militia of the several States, when called into the actual Service of the United States; he may require the Opinion, in writing, of the principal Officer in each of the executive Departments, upon any Subject relating to the Duties of their respective Offices, and he shall have Power to grant Reprieves and Pardons for Offenses against the United States, except in Cases of Impeachment.

He shall have Power, by and with the Advice and Consent of the Senate, to make Treaties, provided two thirds of the Senators present concur; and he shall nominate, and by and with the Advice and Consent of the Senate, shall appoint Ambassadors, other public Ministers and Consuls, Judges of the supreme Court, and all other Officers of the United States, whose Appointments are not herein otherwise provided for, and which shall be established by Law: but the Congress may by Law vest the Appointment of such inferior Officers, as they think proper, in the President alone, in the Courts of Law, or in the Heads of Departments.

The President shall have Power to fill up all Vacancies that may happen during the Recess of the Senate, by granting Commissions which shall expire at the End of their next Session.

Section 3. He shall from time to time give to the Congress Information of the State of the Union, and recommend to their Consideration such Measures as he shall judge necessary and expedient; he may, on extraordinary Occasions, convene both Houses, or either of them, and in Case of Disagreement between them, with Respect to the Time of Adjournment, he may adjourn them to such Time as he shall think proper; he shall receive Ambassadors and other public Ministers; he shall take Care that the Laws be faithfully executed, and shall Commission all the Officers of the United States.

Section 4. The President, Vice President and all Civil Officers of the United States, shall be removed from office on Impeachment for, and Conviction of, Treason, Bribery, or other high Crimes and Misdemeanors.

Article III

Section 1. The judicial Power of the United States, shall be vested in one supreme Court, and in such inferior Courts as the Congress may from time to time ordain and establish. The Judges, both of the supreme and inferior Courts, shall hold their Offices during good Behaviour, and shall, at stated Times, receive for their Services, a Compensation, which shall not be diminished during their Continuance in Office.

Section 2. The judicial Power shall extend to all Cases, in Law and Equity, arising under this Constitution, the Laws of the United States, and Treaties made, or which shall be made, under their Authority; — to all Cases affecting Ambassadors, other public Ministers and Consuls; — to all Cases of admiralty and maritime Jurisdiction; — to Controversies to which the United States shall be a Party; — to Controversies between two or more States; — between a State and Citizens of another State;[8] — between Citizens of different States; — between Citizens of the same State claiming Lands under Grants of different States, and between a State, or the Citizens thereof, and foreign States, Citizens or Subjects.[8]

In all Cases affecting Ambassadors, other public Ministers and Consuls, and those in which a State shall be Party, the supreme Court shall have original Jurisdiction. In all the other Cases before mentioned, the supreme Court shall have appellate Jurisdiction, both as to Law and Fact, with such Exceptions, and under such Regulations as the Congress shall make.

The Trial of all Crimes, except in cases of Impeachment, shall be by Jury; and such Trial shall be held in the State where the said Crimes shall have been committed; but when not committed within any State, the Trial shall be at such Place or Places as the Congress may by Law have directed.

Section 3. Treason against the United States, shall consist only in levying War against them, or in adhering to their Enemies, giving them Aid and Comfort. No Person shall be convicted of Treason unless on the Testimony of two Witnesses to the same overt Act, or on Confession in open Court.

The Congress shall have Power to declare the Punishment of Treason, but no Attainder of Treason shall work Corruption of Blood, or Forfeiture except during the Life of the Person attainted.

Article IV

Section 1. Full Faith and Credit shall be given in each State to the public Acts, Records, and judicial Proceedings of every other State. And the Congress may by general Laws prescribe the Manner in which such Acts, Records and Proceedings shall be proved, and the Effect thereof.

Section 2. The Citizens of each State shall be entitled to all Privileges and Immunities of Citizens in the several States.

A Person charged in any State with Treason, Felony, or other Crime, who shall flee from Justice, and be found in another State, shall on Demand of the executive Authority of the State from which he fled, be delivered up, to be removed to the State having Jurisdiction of the Crime.

[No Person held to Service or Labour in one State, under the Laws thereof, escaping into another, shall, in Consequence of any Law or Regulation therein, be discharged from such Service or Labour, but shall be delivered up on Claim of the Party to whom such Service or Labour may be due.][9]

Section 3. New States may be admitted by the Congress into this Union; but no new State shall be formed or erected within the Jurisdiction of any other State; nor any State be formed by the Junction of two or more States, or Parts of States, without the Consent of the Legislatures of the States concerned as well as of the Congress.

The Congress shall have Power to dispose of and make all needful Rules and Regulations respecting the Territory or other Property belonging to the United States; and nothing in this Constitution shall be so construed as to Prejudice any Claims of the United States, or of any particular State.

Section 4. The United States shall guarantee to every State in this Union a Republican Form of Government, and shall protect each of them against Invasion; and on Application of the Legislature, or of the Executive (when the Legislature cannot be convened) against domestic Violence.

Article V

The Congress, whenever two thirds of both Houses shall deem it necessary, shall propose Amendments to this Constitution, or, on the Application of the Legislatures of two thirds of the several States, shall call a Convention for proposing Amendments, which, in either Case, shall be valid to all Intents and Purposes, as Part of this Constitution, when ratified by the Legislatures of three fourths of the several States, or by Conventions in three fourths thereof, as the one or the other Mode of Ratification may be proposed by the Congress; Provided [that no Amendment which may be made prior to the Year One thousand eight hundred and eight shall in any Manner affect the first and fourth Clauses in the Ninth Section of the first Article; and][10] that no State, without its Consent, shall be deprived of its equal Suffrage in the Senate.

Article VI

All Debts contracted and Engagements entered into, before the Adoption of this Constitution, shall be as valid against the United States under this Constitution, as under the Confederation.

This Constitution, and the Laws of the United States which shall be made in Pursuance thereof; and all Treaties made, or which shall be made, under the Authority of the United States, shall be the supreme Law of the Land; and the Judges in every State shall be bound thereby, any Thing in the Constitution or Laws of any State to the Contrary notwithstanding.

The Senators and Representatives before mentioned, and the Members of the several State Legislatures, and all executive and judicial Officers, both of the United States and of the several States, shall be bound by Oath or Affirmation, to support this Constitution; but no religious Test shall ever be required as a Qualification to any Office or public Trust under the United States.

Article VII

The Ratification of the Conventions of nine States, shall be sufficient for the Establishment of this Constitution between the States so ratifying the Same. Done in Convention by the Unanimous Consent of the States present the Seventeenth Day of September in the Year of our Lord one thousand seven hundred and Eighty seven and of the Independence of the United States of America the Twelfth In witness whereof We have hereunto subscribed our Names, George Washington, President and deputy from Virginia.

New Hampshire: John Langdon,
                     Nicholas Gilman.

Massachusetts: Nathaniel Gorham,
                    Rufus King.

Connecticut: William Samuel Johnson,
                  Roger Sherman.

New York: Alexander Hamilton

New Jersey: William Livingston,
                 David Brearley,
                 William Paterson,
                 Jonathan Dayton.

Pennsylvania: Benjamin Franklin,
                   Thomas Mifflin,
                   Robert Morris,
                   George Clymer,
                   Thomas FitzSimons,
                   Jared Ingersoll,
                   James Wilson,
                   Gouverneur Morris.

Delaware: George Read,
               Gunning Bedford Jr.,
               John Dickinson,
               Richard Bassett,
               Jacob Broom.

Maryland: James McHenry,
               Daniel of St. Thomas Jenifer,
               Daniel Carroll.

Virginia: John Blair,
               James Madison Jr.

North Carolina: William Blount,
                     Richard Dobbs Spaight,
                     Hugh Williamson.

South Carolina: John Rutledge,
                     Charles Cotesworth Pinckney,
                     Charles Pinckney,
                     Pierce Butler.

Georgia: William Few,
              Abraham Baldwin.

[The language of the original Constitution, not including the Amendments, was adopted by a convention of the states on Sept. 17, 1787, and was subsequently ratified by the states on the following dates: Delaware, Dec. 7, 1787; Pennsylvania, Dec. 12, 1787; New Jersey, Dec. 18, 1787; Georgia, Jan. 2, 1788; Connecticut, Jan. 9, 1788; Massachusetts, Feb. 6, 1788; Maryland, April 28, 1788; South Carolina, May 23, 1788; New Hampshire, June 21, 1788.

Ratification was completed on June 21, 1788.

The Constitution subsequently was ratified by Virginia, June 25, 1788; New York, July 26, 1788; North Carolina, Nov. 21, 1789; Rhode Island, May 29, 1790; and Vermont, Jan. 10, 1791.]

Amendments

Amendment I

(First ten amendments ratified Dec. 15, 1791.)

Congress shall make no law respecting an establishment of religion, or prohibiting the free exercise thereof; or abridging the freedom of speech, or of the press; or the right of the people peaceably to assemble, and to petition the Government for a redress of grievances.

Amendment II

A well regulated Militia, being necessary to the security of a free State, the right of the people to keep and bear Arms, shall not be infringed.

Amendment III

No Soldier shall, in time of peace be quartered in any house, without the consent of the Owner, nor in time of war, but in a manner to be prescribed by law.

Amendment IV

The right of the people to be secure in their persons, houses, papers, and effects, against unreasonable searches and seizures, shall not be violated, and no Warrants shall issue, but upon probable cause, supported by Oath or affirmation, and particularly describing the place to be searched, and the persons or things to be seized.

Amendment V

No person shall be held to answer for a capital, or otherwise infamous crime, unless on a presentment or indictment of a Grand Jury, except in cases arising in the land or naval forces, or in the Militia, when in actual service in time of War or public danger; nor shall any person be subject for the same offence to be twice put in jeopardy of life or limb; nor shall be compelled in any criminal case to be a witness against himself, nor be deprived of life, liberty, or property, without due process of law; nor shall private property be taken for public use, without just compensation.

Amendment VI

In all criminal prosecutions, the accused shall enjoy the right to a speedy and public trial, by an impartial jury of the State and district wherein the crime shall have been committed, which district shall have been previously ascertained by law, and to be informed of the nature and cause of the accusation; to be confronted with the witnesses against him; to have compulsory process for obtaining witnesses in his favor, and to have the Assistance of Counsel for his defence.

Amendment VII

In Suits at common law, where the value in controversy shall exceed twenty dollars, the right of trial by jury shall be preserved, and no fact tried by a jury, shall be otherwise re-examined in any Court of the United States, than according to the rules of the common law.

Amendment VIII

Excessive bail shall not be required, nor excessive fines imposed, nor cruel and unusual punishments inflicted.

Amendment IX

The enumeration in the Constitution, of certain rights, shall not be construed to deny or disparage others retained by the people.

Amendment X

The powers not delegated to the United States by the Constitution, nor prohibited by it to the States, are reserved to the States respectively, or to the people.

Amendment XI *(Ratified Feb. 7, 1795)*

The Judicial power of the United States shall not be construed to extend to any suit in law or equity, commenced or prosecuted against one of the United States by Citizens of another State, or by Citizens or Subjects of any Foreign State.

Amendment XII *(Ratified June 15, 1804)*

The Electors shall meet in their respective states and vote by ballot for President and Vice-President, one of whom, at least, shall not be an inhabitant of the same state with themselves; they shall name in their ballots the person voted for as President, and in distinct ballots the person voted for as Vice-President, and they shall make distinct lists of all persons voted for as President, and of all persons voted for as Vice-President, and of the number of votes for each, which lists they shall sign and certify, and transmit sealed to the seat of the government of the United States, directed to the President of the Senate; — The President of the Senate shall, in the presence of the Senate and House of Representatives, open all the certificates and the votes shall then be counted; — The person having the greatest number of votes for President, shall be the President, if such number be a majority of the whole number of Electors appointed; and if no person have such majority, then from the persons having the highest numbers not exceeding three on the list of those voted for as President, the House of Representatives shall choose immediately, by ballot, the President. But in choosing the President, the votes shall be taken by states, the representation from each state having one vote; a quorum for this purpose shall consist of a member or members from two-thirds of the states, and a majority of all the states shall be necessary to a choice. [And if the House of Representatives shall not choose a President whenever the right of choice shall devolve upon them, before the fourth day of March next following, then the Vice-President shall act as President, as in the case of the death or other constitutional disability of the President —][11] The person having the greatest number of votes as Vice-President, shall be the Vice-President, if such number be a majority of the whole number of Electors appointed, and if no person have a majority, then from the two highest numbers on the list, the Senate shall choose the Vice-President; a quorum for the purpose shall consist of two-thirds of the whole number of Senators, and a majority of the whole number shall be necessary to a choice. But no person constitutionally ineligible to the office of President shall be eligible to that of Vice-President of the United States.

Amendment XIII *(Ratified Dec. 6, 1865)*

Section 1. Neither slavery nor involuntary servitude, except as a punishment for crime whereof the party shall have been duly convicted, shall exist within the United States, or any place subject to their jurisdiction.

Section 2. Congress shall have power to enforce this article by appropriate legislation.

Amendment XIV *(Ratified July 9, 1868)*

Section 1. All persons born or naturalized in the United States and subject to the jurisdiction thereof, are citizens of the United States and of the State wherein they reside. No State shall make or enforce any law which shall abridge the privileges or immunities of citizens of the United States; nor shall any State deprive any person of life, liberty, or property, without due process of law; nor deny to any person within its jurisdiction the equal protection of the laws.

Section 2. Representatives shall be apportioned among the several States according to their respective numbers, counting the whole number of persons in each State, excluding Indians not taxed. But when the right to vote at any election for the choice of electors for President and Vice President of the United States, Representatives in Congress, the Executive and Judicial officers of a State, or the members of the Legislature thereof, is denied to any of the male inhabitants of such State, being twenty-one years of age,[12] and citizens of the United States, or in any way abridged, except for participation in rebellion, or other crime, the basis of representation therein shall be reduced in the proportion which the number of such male citizens shall bear to the whole number of male citizens twenty-one years of age in such State.

Section 3. No person shall be a Senator or Representative in Congress, or elector of President and Vice President, or hold any office, civil or military, under the United States, or under any State, who, having previously taken an oath, as a member of Congress, or as an officer of the United States, or as a member of any State legislature, or as an executive or judicial officer of any State, to support the Constitution of the United States, shall have engaged in insurrection or rebellion against the same, or given aid or comfort to the enemies thereof. But Congress may by a vote of two-thirds of each House, remove such disability.

Section 4. The validity of the public debt of the United States, authorized by law, including debts incurred for payment of pensions and bounties for services in suppressing insurrection or rebellion, shall not be questioned. But neither the United States nor any State shall assume or pay any debt or obligation incurred in aid of insurrection or rebellion against the United States, or any claim for the loss or emancipation of any slave; but all such debts, obligations and claims shall be held illegal and void.

Section 5. The Congress shall have power to enforce, by appropriate legislation, the provisions of this article.

Amendment XV *(Ratified Feb. 3, 1870)*

Section 1. The right of citizens of the United States to vote shall not be denied or abridged by the United States or by any State on account of race, color, or previous condition of servitude.

Section 2. The Congress shall have power to enforce this article by appropriate legislation.

Amendment XVI *(Ratified Feb. 3, 1913)*

The Congress shall have power to lay and collect taxes on incomes, from whatever source derived, without apportionment among the several States, and without regard to any census or enumeration.

Amendment XVII *(Ratified Apr. 8, 1913)*

The Senate of the United States shall be composed of two Senators from each State, elected by the people thereof, for six years; and each Senator shall have one vote. The electors in each State shall have the qualifications requisite for electors of the most numerous branch of the State legislatures.

When vacancies happen in the representation of any State in the Senate, the executive authority of such State shall issue writs of election to fill such vacancies: *Provided,* That the legislature of any State may empower the executive thereof to make temporary appointments until the people fill the vacancies by election as the legislature may direct.

This amendment shall not be so construed as to affect the election or term of any Senator chosen before it becomes valid as part of the Constitution.

[Amendment XVIII *(Ratified Jan. 16, 1919)*

Section. 1. After one year from the ratification of this article the manufacture, sale, or transportation of intoxicating liquors within, the importation thereof into, or the exportation thereof from the United States and all territory subject to the jurisdiction thereof for beverage purposes is hereby prohibited.

Section 2. The Congress and the several States shall have concurrent power to enforce this article by appropriate legislation.

Section 3. This article shall be inoperative unless it shall have been ratified as an amendment to the Constitution by the legislatures of the several States, as provided in the Constitution, within seven years from the date of the submission hereof to the States by the Congress.][13]

Amendment XIX *(Ratified Aug. 18, 1920)*

The right of citizens of the United States to vote shall not be denied or abridged by the United States or by any State on account of sex.

Congress shall have power to enforce this article by appropriate legislation.

Amendment XX *(Ratified Jan. 23, 1933)*

Section 1. The terms of the President and Vice President shall end at noon on the 20th day of January, and the terms of Senators and Representatives at noon on the 3d day of January, of the years in which such terms would have ended if this article had not been ratified; and the terms of their successors shall then begin.

Section 2. The Congress shall assemble at least once in every year, and such meeting shall begin at noon on the 3d day of January, unless they shall by law appoint a different day.

Section 3.[14] If, at the time fixed for the beginning of the term of the President, the President elect shall have died, the Vice President elect shall become President. If a President shall not have been chosen before the time fixed for the beginning of his term, or if the President elect shall have failed to qualify, then the Vice President elect shall act as President until a President shall have qualified; and the Congress may by law provide for the case wherein neither a President elect nor a Vice President elect shall have qualified, declaring who shall then act as President, or the manner in which one who is to act shall be selected, and such person shall act accordingly until a President or Vice President shall have qualified.

Section 4. The Congress may by law provide for the case of the death of any of the persons from whom the House of Representatives may choose a President whenever the right of choice shall have devolved upon them, and for the case of the death of any of the persons from whom

the Senate may choose a Vice President whenever the right of choice shall have devolved upon them.

Section 5. Sections 1 and 2 shall take effect on the 15th day of October following the ratification of this article.

Section 6. This article shall be inoperative unless it shall have been ratified as an amendment to the Constitution by the legislatures of three-fourths of the several States within seven years from the date of its submission.

Amendment XXI *(Ratified Dec. 5, 1933)*

Section 1. The eighteenth article of amendment to the Constitution of the United States is hereby repealed.

Section 2. The transportation or importation into any State, Territory or possession of the United States for delivery or use therein of intoxicating liquors, in violation of the laws thereof, is hereby prohibited.

Section 3. This article shall be inoperative unless it shall have been ratified as an amendment to the Constitution by conventions in the several States, as provided in the Constitution, within seven years from the date of the submission hereof to the States by the Congress.

Amendment XXII *(Ratified Feb. 27, 1951)*

Section 1. No person shall be elected to the office of the President more than twice, and no person who has held the office of President, or acted as President, for more than two years of a term to which some other person was elected President shall be elected to the office of the President more than once. But this Article shall not apply to any person holding the office of President when this Article was proposed by the Congress, and shall not prevent any person who may be holding the office of President, or acting as President, during the term within which this Article become operative from holding the office of President or acting as President during the remainder of such term.

Section 2. This Article shall be inoperative unless it shall have been ratified as an amendment to the Constitution by the legislatures of three-fourths of the several States within seven years from the date of its submission to the States by the Congress.

Amendment XXIII *(Ratified March 29, 1961)*

Section 1. The District constituting the seat of Government of the United States shall appoint in such manner as the Congress may direct:

A number of electors of President and Vice President equal to the whole number of Senators and Representatives in Congress to which the District would be entitled if it were a State, but in no event more than the least populous State; they shall be in addition to those appointed by the States, but they shall be considered, for the purposes of the election of President and Vice President, to be electors appointed by a State; and they shall meet in the District and perform such duties as provided by the twelfth article of amendment.

Section 2. The Congress shall have power to enforce this article by appropriate legislation.

Amendment XXIV *(Ratified Jan. 23, 1964)*

Section 1. The right of citizens of the United States to vote in any primary or other election for President or Vice President, for electors for President or Vice President, or for Senator or Representative in Congress, shall not be denied or abridged by the United States or any State by reason of failure to pay any poll tax or other tax.

Section 2. The Congress shall have power to enforce this article by appropriate legislation.

Amendment XXV *(Ratified Feb. 10, 1967)*

Section 1. In case of the removal of the President from office or of his death or resignation, the Vice President shall become President.

Section 2. Whenever there is a vacancy in the office of the Vice President, the President shall nominate a Vice President who shall take office upon confirmation by a majority vote of both Houses of Congress.

Section 3. Whenever the President transmits to the President pro tempore of the Senate and the Speaker of the House of Representatives his written declaration that he is unable to discharge the powers and duties of his office, and until he transmits to them a written declaration to the contrary, such powers and duties shall be discharged by the Vice President as Acting President.

Section 4. Whenever the Vice President and a majority of either the principal officers of the executive departments or of such other body as Congress may by law provide, transmit to the President pro tempore of the Senate and the Speaker of the House of Representatives their written declaration that the President is unable to discharge the powers and duties of his office, the Vice President shall immediately assume the powers and duties of the office as Acting President.

Thereafter, when the President transmits to the Presi-

dent pro tempore of the Senate and the Speaker of the House of Representatives his written declaration that no inability exists, he shall resume the powers and duties of his office unless the Vice President and a majority of either the principal officers of the executive department or of such other body as Congress may by law provide, transmit within four days to the President pro tempore of the Senate and the Speaker of the House of Representatives their written declaration that the President is unable to discharge the powers and duties of his office. Thereupon Congress shall decide the issue, assembling within forty-eight hours for that purpose if not in session. If the Congress, within twenty-one days after receipt of the latter written declaration, or, if Congress is not in session, within twenty-one days after Congress is required to assemble, determines by two-thirds vote of both houses that the President is unable to discharge the powers and duties of his office, the Vice President shall continue to discharge the same as Acting President; otherwise, the President shall resume the powers and duties of his office.

Amendment XXVI *(Ratified July 1, 1971)*

Section 1. The right of citizens of the United States, who are eighteen years of age or older, to vote shall not be denied or abridged by the United States or by any State on account of age.

Section 2. The Congress shall have power to enforce this article by appropriate legislation.

Footnotes

1. The part in brackets was changed by section 2 of the Fourteenth Amendment.

2. The part in brackets was changed by section 1 of the Seventeenth Amendment.

3. The part in brackets was changed by the second paragraph of the Seventeenth Amendment.

4. The part in brackets was changed by section 2 of the Twentieth Amendment.

5. The Sixteenth Amendment gave Congress the power to tax incomes.

6. The material in brackets has been superseded by the Twelfth Amendment.

7. This provision has been affected by the Twenty-fifth Amendment.

8. These clauses were affected by the Eleventh Amendment.

9. This paragraph has been superseded by the Thirteenth Amendment.

10. Obsolete.

11. The part in brackets has been superseded by section 3 of the Twentieth Amendment.

12. See the Twenty-sixth Amendment.

13. This Amendment was repealed by section 1 of the Twenty-first Amendment.

14. See the Twenty-fifth Amendment.

Source: U.S. Congress, House, Committee on the Judiciary, *The Constitution of the United States of America, As Amended Through July 1971,* H. Doc. 93-215, 93rd Cong., 2nd sess., 1974.

Acts of Congress Held Unconstitutional in Whole or in Part by the Supreme Court

Sources: compiled from Library of Congress, *The Constitution of the United States of America; Analysis and Interpretation,* S. Doc., 92-82, 92d Cong., 2d sess., 1973; 1976 Supplement, S. Doc. 94-200, 94th Cong. 2d sess., 1976; Library of Congress, Congressional Research Service.

1. Act of September 24, 1789 (1 Stat. 81, § 13, in part).

   Provision that "...[the Supreme Court] shall have power to issue...writs of mandamus, in cases warranted by the principles and usages of law, to any...persons holding office, under authority of the United States" as applied to the issue of mandamus to the Secretary of State requiring him to deliver to plaintiff a commission (duly signed by the President) as justice of the peace in the District of Columbia, *held* an attempt to enlarge the original jurisdiction of the Supreme Court, fixed by Article III, § 2.

   Marbury v. *Madison,* 1 Cr. (5 U.S.) 137 (1803).

2. Act of February 20, 1812 (2 Stat. 677).

   Provisions establishing board of revision to annul titles conferred many years previously by governors of the Northwest Territory were *held* violative of the due process clause of the Fifth Amendment.

   Reichart v. *Felps,* 6 Wall. (73 U.S.) 160 (1868).

3. Act of March 6, 1820 (3 Stat. 548, § 8, proviso).

   The Missouri Compromise, prohibiting slavery within the Louisiana Territory north of 36° 30′, except Missouri, *held* not warranted as a regulation of Territory belonging to the United States under Article IV, § 3, clause 2 (and *see* Fifth Amendment).

   Scott v. *Sandford,* 19 How. (60 U.S.) 393 (1857).

4. Act of February 25, 1862 (12 Stat. 345, § 1); July 11, 1862 (12 Stat. 532, § 1); March 3, 1863 (12 Stat. 711, § 3), each in part only.

   "Legal tender clauses," making noninterest-bearing United States notes legal tender in payment of "all debts, public and private," so far as applied to debts contracted before passage of the act, *held* not within express or implied powers of Congress under Article I, § 8, and inconsistent with Article I, § 10, and Fifth Amendment.

   Hepburn v. *Griswold,* 8 Wall. (75 U.S.) 603 (1870); overruled in *Knox* v. *Lee (Legal Tender Cases),* 12 Wall. (79 U.S.) 457 (1871).

5. Act of March 3, 1863 (12 Stat. 756, § 5).

   "So much of the fifth section...as provides for the removal of a judgment in a State court, and in which the cause was tried by a jury to the circuit court of the United States for a retrial on the facts and law, is not in pursuance of the Constitution, and is void" under the Seventh Amendment.

   The Justices v. *Murray,* 9 Wall. (76 U.S.) 274 (1870).

6. Act of March 3, 1863 (12 Stat. 766, § 5).

   Provision for an appeal from the Court of Claims to the Supreme Court—there being, at the time, a further provision (§ 14) requiring an estimate by the Secretary of the Treasury before payment of final judgments, *held* to contravene the judicial finality intended by the Constitution, Article III.

   Gordon v. *United States,* 2 Wall. (69 U.S.) 561 (1865). (Case was dismissed without opinion; the grounds upon which this decision was made were stated in a posthumous opinion by Chief Justice Taney printed in the appendix to volume 117 U.S. 697.)

7. Act of June 30, 1864 (13 Stat. 311, § 13).

   Provision that "any prize cause now pending in any circuit court shall, on the application of all parties in interest...be transferred by that court to the Supreme Court....," as applied in a case where no action had been taken in the Circuit Court on the appeal from the district court, *held* to propose an appeal procedure not within Article III, § 2.

   The Alicia, 7 Wall. (74 U.S.) 571 (1869).

8. Act of January 24, 1865 (13 Stat. 424).

   Requirement of a test oath (disavowing actions in hostility to the United States) before admission to appear as attorney in a federal court by virtue of any previous admission, *held* invalid as applied to an attorney who had been pardoned by the President for all offenses during the Rebellion—as *ex post facto* (Article I, § 9, clause 3) and an interference with the pardoning power (Article II, § 2, clause 1).

   Ex parte Garland, 4 Wall. (71 U.S.) 333 (1867).

9. Act of March 2, 1867 (14 Stat. 484, § 29).

   General prohibition on sale of naphtha, etc., for illuminating purposes, if inflammable at less temperature than 110° F., *held* invalid "except so far as the section named operates within the United States, but without the limits of any State," as being a mere police regulation.

   United States v. *Dewitt,* 9 Wall. (76 U.S.) 41 (1870).

10. Act of May 31, 1870 (16 Stat. 140, §§ 3, 4).

    Provisions penalizing (1) refusal of local election officials to permit voting by persons offering to qualify under State laws, applicable to any citizens; and (2) hindering of any person from qualifying or voting, *held* invalid under Fifteenth Amendment.

    United States v. *Reese,* 92 U.S. 214 (1876).

11. Act of July 12, 1870 (16 Stat. 235).

    Provision making Presidential pardons inadmissible in evidence in Court of Claims, prohibiting their use by that court in deciding claims or appeals, and requiring dismissal of appeals by the Supreme Court in cases where proof of loyalty had been made otherwise than as prescribed by law, *held* an interference with judicial power under Article III, § 1, and with the pardoning power under Article II, § 2, clause 1.

    United States v. *Klein,* 13 Wall. (80 U.S.) 128 (1872).

12. Act of June 22, 1874 (18 Stat. 1878, § 4).

    Provision authorizing federal courts, in suits for forfeitures under revenue and custom laws, to require production of documents, with allegations expected to be proved therein to be taken as proved on failure to produce such documents, was *held* violative of the search and seizure provision of the Fourth Amendment and the self-incrimination clause of the Fifth Amendment.

    Boyd v. *United States,* 116 U.S. 616 (1886).

13. Revised Statutes 1977 (Act of May 31, 1870, 16 Stat. 144).

    Provision that "all persons within the jurisdiction of the United States shall have the same right in every State and Territory to make and enforce contracts...as is enjoyed by white citizens...," *held* invalid under the Thirteenth Amendment.

    Hodges v. *United States,* 203 U.S. 1 (1906).

14. Revised Statutes 4937-4947 (Act of July 8, 1870, 16 Stat. 210), and Act of August 14, 1876 (19 Stat. 141).

    Original trademark law, applying to marks "for exclusive use within the United States," and a penal act designed solely for the protection of rights defined in the earlier measure, *held* not supportable by Article I, § 8, clause 8 (copyright clause), nor Article I, § 8, clause 3, by reason of its application to intrastate as well as interstate commerce.

    Trade-Mark Cases, 100 U.S. 82 (1879).

15. Revised Statutes 5132, subdivision 9 (Act of March 2, 1867, 14 Stat. 539).

    Provision penalizing "any person respecting whom bankruptcy proceedings are commenced...who, within 3 months before the commencement of proceedings in bankruptcy, under the false color and pretense of carrying on business and dealing in the ordinary course of trade, obtains on credit from any person any goods or chattels with intent to defraud...," *held* a police regulation not within the bankruptcy power (Article I, § 4, clause 4).

    United States v. *Fox,* 95 U.S. 670 (1878).

16. Revised Statutes 5507 (Act of May 31, 1870, 16 Stat. 141, § 4).

    Provision penalizing "every person who prevents, hinders, controls, or intimidates another from exercising...the right of suffrage, to whom that right is guaranteed by the Fifteenth Amendment to the Constitution of the United States, by means of bribery...," *held* not authorized by the Fifteenth Amendment.

    James v. *Bowman,* 190 U.S. 127 (1903).

17. Revised Statutes 5519 (Act of April 20, 1871, 17 Stat. 13, § 2).

    Section providing punishment in case "two or more persons in any State...conspire...for the purpose of depriving...any person...of the equal protection of the laws...or for the purpose of preventing or hindering the constituted authorities of any State...from giving or securing to all persons within such State...the equal protection of the laws...," *held* invalid as not being directed at state action proscribed by the Fourteenth Amendment.

    United States v. *Harris,* 106 U.S. 629 (1883).

    In *Baldwin* v. *Franks,* 120 U.S. 678 (1887), an attempt was made to distinguish the *Harris* case and to apply the statute to a conspiracy directed at aliens within a State, but the provision was *held* not enforceable in such limited manner.

18. Revised Statutes of the District of Columbia, § 1064 (Act of June 17, 1870, 16 Stat. 154, § 3).

Provision that "prosecutions in the police court [of the District of Columbia] shall be by information under oath, without indictment by grand jury or trial by petit jury," as applied to punishment for conspiracy held to contravene Article III, § 2, clause 3, requiring jury trial of all crimes.

Callan v. *Wilson*, 127 U.S. 540 (1888).

19. Act of March 1, 1875 (18 Stat. 336, §§ 1, 2).

Provision "That all persons within the jurisdiction of the United States shall be entitled to the full and equal enjoyment of the accommodations...of inns, public conveyances on land or water, theaters, and other places of public amusement; subject only to the conditions and limitations established by law, and applicable alike to citizens of every race and color, regardless of any previous condition of servitude"—subject to penalty, *held* not to be supported by the Thirteenth or Fourteenth Amendments.

Civil Rights Cases, 109 U.S. 3 (1883), as to operation within States.

20. Act of March 3, 1875 (18 Stat. 479, § 2).

Provision that "if the party [i.e., a person stealing property from the United States] has been convicted, then the judgment against him shall be conclusive evidence in the prosecution against [the] receiver that the property of the United States therein described has been embezzled, stolen, or purloined," *held* to contravene the Sixth Amendment.

Kirby v. *United States*, 174 U.S. 47 (1899).

21. Act of July 12, 1876 (19 Stat. 80, sec. 6, in part).

Provision that "postmasters of the first, second, and third classes...may be removed by the President by and with the advice and consent of the Senate," *held* to infringe the executive power under Article II, § 1, clause 1.

Myers v. *United States*, 272 U.S. 52 (1926).

22. Act of August 14, 1876 (19 Stat. 141, Trademark Act). *See* Revised Statutes 4937, above, No. 14.

23. Act of August 11, 1888 (25 Stat. 411).

Clause, in a provision for the purchase or condemnation of a certain lock and dam in the Monongahela River, that "...in estimating the sums to be paid by the United States, the franchise of said corporation to collect tolls shall not be considered or estimated...," *held* to contravene the Fifth Amendment.

Monongahela Navigation Co. v. *United States*, 148 U.S. 312 (1893).

24. Act of May 5, 1892 (27 Stat. 25, § 4).

Provision of a Chinese exclusion act, that Chinese persons "convicted and adjudged to be not lawfully entitled to be or remain in the United States shall be imprisoned at hard labor for a period not exceeding 1 year and thereafter removed from the United States...(such conviction and judgment being had before a justice, judge, or commissioner upon a summary hearing), *held* to contravene the Fifth and Sixth Amendments.

Wong Wing v. *United States*, 163 U.S. 228 (1896).

25. Joint Resolution of August 4, 1894 (28 Stat. 1018, No. 41).

Provision authorizing the Secretary of the Interior to approve a second lease of certain land by an Indian chief in Minnesota (granted to lessor's ancestor by art. 9 of a treaty with the Chippewa Indians), *held* an interference with judicial interpretation of treaties under Article III, § 2, clause 1 and repugnant to the Fifth Amendment).

Jones v. *Meehan*, 175 U.S. 1 (1899).

26. Act of August 27, 1894 (28 Stat. 553-560, §§ 27-37).

Income tax provisions of the tariff act of 1894. "The tax imposed by §§ 27 and 37, inclusive...so far as it falls on the income of real estate and of personal property, being a direct tax within the meaning of the Constitution, and, therefore, unconstitutional and void because not apportioned according to representation [Article I, § 2, clause 3], all those sections, constituting one entire scheme of taxation, are necessarily invalid" (158 U.S. 601, 637).

Pollock v. *Farmers' Loan & Trust Co.*, 157 U.S. 429 (1895), and rehearing, 158 U.S. 601 (1895).

27. Act of January 30, 1897 (29 Stat. 506).

Prohibition on sale of liquor "...to any Indian to whom allotment of land has been made while the title to the same shall be held in trust by the Government...," *held* a police regulation infringing state powers, and not warranted by the commerce clause, Article I, § 8, clause 3.

Matter of Heff, 197 U.S. 488 (1905), overruled in *United States* v. *Nice*, 241 U.S. 591 (1916).

28. Act of June 1, 1898 (30 Stat. 428).

Section 10, penalizing "any employer subject to the provisions of this act" who should "threaten any employee with loss of employment...because of his membership in...a labor corporation, association, or organization" (the act being applicable "to any common carrier...engaged in the transportation of passengers or property...from one State...to another State...," etc.), *held* an infringement of the Fifth Amendment and not supported by the commerce clause.

Adair v. *United States*, 208 U.S. 161 (1908).

29. Act of June 13, 1898 (30 Stat. 451, 459).

Stamp tax on foreign bills of lading, *held* a tax on exports in violation of Article I, § 9.

Fairbank v. *United States*, 181 U.S. 283 (1901).

30. Same (30 Stat. 451, 460).

Tax on charter parties, as applied to shipments exclusively from ports in United States to foreign ports, *held* a tax on exports in violation of Article I, § 9.

United States v. *Hvoslef*, 237 U.S. 1 (1915).

31. Act of June 6, 1900 (31 Stat. 359, § 171).

Section of the Alaska Code providing for a six-person jury in trials for misdemeanors, *held* repugnant to the Sixth Amendment, requiring "jury" trial of crimes.

Rassmussen v. *United States*, 197 U.S. 516 (1905).

32. Act of March 3, 1901 (31 Stat. 1341, § 935).

Section of the District of Columbia Code granting the same right of appeal, in criminal cases, to the United States or the District of Columbia as to the defendant, but providing that a verdict was not to be set aside for error bound in rulings during trial, *held* an attempt to take an advisory opinion, contrary to Article III, § 2.

United States v. *Evans*, 213 U.S. 297 (1909).

33. Act of June 11, 1906 (34 Stat. 232).

Act providing that "every common carrier engaged in trade or commerce in the District of Columbia...or between the several States...shall be liable to any of its employees...for all damages which may result from the negligence of any of its officers...or by reason of any defect...due to its negligence in its cars, engines...roadbed," etc., *held* not supportable under Article I, § 8, clause 3 because it extended to intrastate as well as interstate commercial activities.

The Employers' Liability Cases, 207 U.S. 463 (1908). (The act was upheld as to the District of Columbia in *Hyde* v. *Southern R. Co.*, 31 App. D.C. 466 (1908); and as to the Territories, in *El Paso & N.E. Ry.* v. *Gutierrez*, 215 U.S. 87 (1909).)

34. Act of June 16, 1906 (34 Stat. 269, § 2).

Provision of Oklahoma Enabling Act restricting relocation of the State capital prior to 1913, *held* not supportable by Article IV, § 3, authorizing admission of new States.

Coyle v. *Smith*, 221 U.S. 559 (1911).

35. Act of February 20, 1907 (34 Stat. 889, § 3).

Provision in the Immigration Act of 1907 penalizing "whoever...shall keep, maintain, control, support, or harbor in any house or other place, for the purpose of prostitution...any alien woman or girl, within 3 years after she shall have entered the United States," *held* an exercise of police power not within the control of Congress over immigration (whether drawn from the commerce clause or based on inherent sovereignty).

Keller v. *United States*, 213 U.S. 138 (1909).

36. Act of March 1, 1907 (34 Stat. 1028).

Provisions authorizing certain Indians "to institute their suits in the Court of Claims to determine the validity of any acts of Congress passed since...1902, insofar as said acts...attempt to increase or extend the restrictions upon alienation...of allotments of lands of Cherokee citizens...," and giving a right of appeal to the Supreme Court, *held* an attempt to enlarge the judicial power restricted by Article III, § 2, to cases and controversies.

Muskrat v. *United States*, 219 U.S. 346 (1911).

37. Act of May 27, 1908 (35 Stat. 313, § 4).

Provision making locally taxable "all land [of Indians of the Five Civilized Tribes] from which restrictions have been or shall be removed," *held* a violation of the Fifth Amendment, in view of the Atoka Agreement, embodied in the Curtis Act of June 28, 1898, providing tax-exemption for allotted lands while title in original allottee, not exceeding 21 years.

Choate v. *Trapp*, 224 U.S. 665 (1912).

38. Act of February 9, 1909, § 2, 35 Stat. 614, as amended.

Provision of Narcotic Drugs Import and Export Act creating a presumption that possessor of cocaine knew of its illegal importation into the United States *held*, in light of the fact that more cocaine is produced domestically than is brought into the country and in absence of any showing that defendant could have known his cocaine was imported, if it was, inapplicable to support conviction from mere possession of cocaine.

Turner v. *United States*, 396 U.S. 398 (1970).

39. Act of August 19, 1911 (37 Stat. 28).

A proviso in § 8 of the Federal Corrupt Practices Act fixing a maximum authorized expenditure by a candidate for Senator "in any campaign for his nomination and election," as applied to a primary election, *held* not supported by Article I, § 4, giving Congress power to regulate the manner of holding elections for Senators and Representatives.

> *Newberry* v. *United States,* 256 U.S. 232 (1921), overruled in *United States* v. *Classic,* 313 U.S. 299 (1941).

40. Act of June 18, 1912 (37 Stat. 136, § 8).

Part of § 8 giving the Juvenile Court of the District of Columbia (proceeding upon information) concurrent jurisdiction of desertion cases (which were, by law, punishable by fine or imprisonment in the workhouse at hard labor for 1 year), *held* invalid under the Fifth Amendment, which gives right to presentment by a grand jury in case of infamous crimes.

> *United States* v. *Moreland,* 258 U.S. 433 (1922).

41. Act of March 4, 1913 (37 Stat. 988, part of par. 64).

Provision of the District of Columbia Public Utility Commission Act authorizing appeal to the United States Supreme Court from decrees of the District of Columbia Court of Appeals modifying valuation decisions of the Utilities Commission, *held* an attempt to extend the appellate jurisdiction of the Supreme Court to cases not strictly judicial within the meaning of Article III, § 2.

> *Keller* v. *Potomac Elec. Co.,* 261 U.S. 428 (1923).

42. Act of September 1, 1916 (39 Stat. 675).

The original Child Labor Law, providing "that no producer...shall ship...in interstate commerce...any article or commodity the product of any mill...in which within 30 days prior to the removal of such product therefrom children under the age of 14 years have been employed or permitted to work more than 8 hours in any day or more than 6 days in any week...," *held* not within the commerce power of Congress.

> *Hammer* v. *Dagenhart,* 247 U.S. 251 (1918).

43. Act of September 8, 1916 (39 Stat. 757, § 2(a), in part).

Provision of the income tax law of 1916, that a "stock dividend shall be considered income, to the amount of its cash value," *held* invalid (in spite of the Sixteenth Amendment) as an attempt to tax something not actually income, without regard to apportionment under Article I, § 2, clause 3.

> *Eisner* v. *Macomber,* 252 U.S. 189 (1920).

44. Act of October 6, 1917 (40 Stat. 395).

The amendment of §§ 24 and 256 of the Judicial Code (which prescribe the jurisdiction of district courts) "saving...to claimants the rights and remedies under the workmen's compensation law of any State," *held* an attempt to transfer federal legislative powers to the States—the Constitution, by Article III, § 2, and Article I, § 8, having adopted rules of general maritime law.

> *Knickerbocker Ice Co.* v. *Stewart,* 253 U.S. 149 (1920).

45. Act of September 19, 1918 (40 Stat. 960).

Specifically, that part of the Minimum Wage Law of the District of Columbia which authorized the Wage Board "to ascertain and declare...(a) Standards of minimum wages for women in any occupation within the District of Columbia, and what wages are inadequate to supply the necessary cost of living to any such women workers to maintain them in good health and to protect their morals...," *held* to interfere with freedom of contract under the Fifth Amendment.

> *Adkins* v. *Children's Hospital,* 261 U.S. 525 (1923), overruled in *West Coast Hotel Co. v. Parrish,* 300 U.S. 379 (1937).

46. Act of February 24, 1919 (40 Stat. 1065, § 213, in part).

That part of § 213 of the Revenue Act of 1918 which provided that "...for the purposes of this title...the term 'gross income'...includes gains, profits, and income derived from salaries, wages, or compensation for personal service (including in the case of...judges of the Supreme and inferior courts of the United States...the compensation received as such)..." as applied to a judge in office when the act was passed, *held* a violation of the guaranty of judges' salaries, in Article III, § 1.

> *Evans* v. *Gore,* 253 U.S. 245 (1920).
> *Miles* v. *Graham,* 268 U.S. 501 (1925), held it invalid as applied to a judge taking office subsequent to the date of the act.

47. Act of February 24, 1919 (40 Stat. 1097, § 402(c)).

That part of the estate tax law providing that "gross estate" of a decedent should include value of all property "to the extent of any interest therein of which the decedent has at any time made a transfer or with respect to which he had at any time created a trust, in contemplation of or intended to take effect in possession or enjoyment at or after his death (whether such transfer or trust is made or created before or after the passage of this act), except in case of a *bona fide* sale..." as applied to a transfer of property made prior to the act and intended to take effect "in possession or enjoyment" at death of grantor, but not in fact testamentary or designed to evade taxation, *held* confiscatory, contrary to Fifth Amendment.

> *Nicholds* v. *Coolidge,* 274 U.S. 531 (1927).

48. Act of February 24, 1919, title XII (40 Stat. 1138, entire title).

The Child Labor Tax Act, providing that "every person...operating...any...factory...in which children under the age of 14 years have been employed or permitted to work...shall pay...in addition to all other taxes imposed by law, an excise tax equivalent to 10 percent of the entire net profits received...for such year from the sale...of the product of such...factory...," *held* beyond the taxing power under Article I, § 8, clause 1, and an infringement of state authority.

> *Bailey* v. *Drexel Furniture Co. (Child Labor Tax Case),* 259 U.S. 20 (1922).

49. An Act of October 22, 1919 (41 Stat. 298, § 2), amending Act of August 10, 1917 (40 Stat. 277, § 4).

(a) § 4 of the Lever Act, providing in part "that it is hereby made unlawful for any person willfully...to make any unjust or unreasonable rate or charge in handling or dealing in or with any necessaries..." and fixing a penalty, *held* invalid to support an indictment for charging an unreasonable price on sale—as not setting up an ascertainable standard of guilt within the requirement of the Sixth Amendment.

> *United States* v. *Cohen Grocery Co.,* 255 U.S. 81 (1921).

(b) That provision of § 4 making it unlawful "to conspire, combine, agree, or arrange with any other person to...exact excessive prices for any necessaries" and fixing a penalty, *held* invalid to support an indictment, on the reasoning of the *Cohen Grocery* case.

> *Weeds, Inc.* v. *United States,* 255 U.S. 109 (1921).

50. Act of August 24, 1921 (42 Stat. 187, Future Trading Act).

(a) § 4 (and interwoven regulations) providing a "tax of 20 cents a bushel on every bushel involved therein, upon each contract of sale of grain for future delivery, except...where such contracts are made by or through a member of a board of trade which has been designated by the Secretary of Agriculture as a 'contract market'...," *held* not within the taxing power under Article I, § 8.

> *Hill* v. *Wallace,* 259 U.S. 44 (1922).

(b) § 3, providing "That in addition to the taxes now imposed by law there is hereby levied a tax amounting to 20 cents per bushel on each bushel involved therein, whether the actual commodity is intended to be delivered or only nominally referred to, upon each...option for a contract either of purchase or sale of grain...," *held* invalid on the same reasoning.

> *Trusler* v. *Crooks,* 269 U.S. 475 (1926).

51. Act of November 23, 1921 (42 Stat. 261, § 245, in part).

Provision of Revenue Act of 1921 abating the deduction (4 percent of mean reserves) allowed from taxable income of life insurance companies in general by the amount of interest on their tax-exempts, and so according no relative advantage to the owners of the tax-exempt securities, *held* to destroy a guaranteed exemption.

> *National Life Ins.* v. *United States,* 277 U.S. 508 (1928).

52. Act of June 10, 1922 (42 Stat. 634).

A second attempt to amend §§ 24 and 256 of the Judicial Code, relating to jurisdiction of district courts, by saving "to claimants for compensation for injuries to or death of persons other than the master or members of the crew of a vessel, their rights and remedies under the workmen's compensation law of any State..." *held* invalid on authority of *Knickerbocker Ice Co.* v. *Stewart.*

> *Washington* v. *Dawson & Co.,* 264 U.S. 219 (1924).

53. Act of June 2, 1924 (43 Stat. 313).

The gift tax provisions of the Revenue Act of 1924, applicable to gifts made during the calendar year, were *held* invalid under the Fifth Amendment insofar as they applied to gifts made before passage of the act.

> *Untermeyer* v. *Anderson,* 276 U.S. 440 (1928).

54. Act of February 26, 1926 (44 Stat. 70, § 302, in part).

Stipulation creating a conclusive presumption that gifts made within two years prior to the death of the donor were made in contemplation of death of donor and requiring the value thereof to be included in computing the death transfer tax on decedent's estate was *held* to effect an invalid deprivation of property without due process.

> *Heiner* v. *Donnan,* 285 U.S. 312 (1932).

55. Act of February 26, 1926 (44 Stat. 95, § 701).

Provision imposing a special excise tax of $1,000 on liquor dealers operating in States where such business is illegal, was *held* a penalty, without constitutional support following repeal of the Eighteenth Amendment.

> *United States* v. *Constantine,* 296 U.S. 287 (1935).

56. Act of March 20, 1933 (48 Stat. 11, § 17, in part).

Clause in the Economy Act of 1933 providing "...all laws granting or pertaining to yearly renewable term war risk insurance are hereby repealed," *held* invalid to abrogate an outstanding contract of insurance, which is a vested right protected by the Fifth Amendment.

> *Lynch* v. *United States,* 292 U.S. 571 (1934).

57. Act of May 12, 1933 (48 Stat. 31).

Agricultural Adjustment Act providing for processing taxes on agricultural commodities and benefit payments therefrom to farmers, *held* not within the taxing power under Article I, § 8, clause 1.

United States v. *Butler,* 297 U.S. 1 (1936).

58. Joint Resolution of June 5, 1933 (48 Stat. 113, § 1).

Abrogation of gold clause in Government obligations, *held* a repudiation of the pledge implicit in the power to borrow money (Article I, § 8, clause 2), and within the prohibition of the Fourteenth Amendment, against questioning the validity of the public debt. (The majority of the Court, however, held plaintiff not entitled to recover under the circumstances.)

Perry v. *United States,* 294 U.S. 330 (1935).

59. Act of June 16, 1933 (48 Stat. 195, the National Industrial Recovery Act).

(a) Title I, except § 9.

Provisions relating to codes of fair competition, authorized to be approved by the President in his discretion "to effectuate the policy" of the act, *held* invalid as a delegation of legislative power (Article I, § 1) and not within the commerce power (Article I, § 8, clause 3).

Schechter Corp. v. *United States,* 295 U.S. 495 (1935).

(b) § 9(c).

Clause of the oil regulation section authorizing the President "to prohibit the transportation in interstate...commerce of petroleum...produced or withdrawn from storage in excess of the amount permitted...by any State law..." and prescribing a penalty for violation of orders issued thereunder, *held* invalid as a delegation of legislative power.

Panama Refining Co. v. *Ryan,* 293 U.S. 388 (1935).

60. Act of June 16, 1933 (48 Stat. 307, § 13).

Temporary reduction of 15 percent in retired pay of judges, retired from service but subject to performance of judicial duties under the Act March 1, 1929 (45 Stat. 1422), was *held* a violation of the guaranty of judges' salaries in Article III, § 1.

Booth v. *United States,* 291 U.S. 339 (1934).

61. Act of April 27, 1934 (48 Stat. 646, § 6), amending § 5(i) of Home Owners' Loan Act of 1933.

Provision for conversion of state building and loan associations into federal associations, upon vote of 51 percent of the votes cast at a meeting of stockholders called to consider such action, *held* an encroachment on reserved powers of State.

Hopkins Savings Assn. v. *Cleary,* 296 U.S. 315 (1935).

62. Act of May 24, 1934 (48 Stat. 798).

Provision for readjustment of municipal indebtedness, though "adequately related" to the bankruptcy power, was *held* invalid as an interference with state sovereignty.

Ashton v. *Cameron County Dist.,* 298 U.S. 513 (1936).

63. Act of June 27, 1934 (48 Stat. 1283).

The Railroad Retirement Act, establishing a detailed compulsory retirement system for employees of carriers subject to the Interstate Commerce Act, *held* not a regulation of commerce within the meaning of Article I, § 8, clause 3, and violative of the due process clause (Fifth Amendment).

Railroad Retirement Board v. *Alton R. Co.,* 295 U.S. 330 (1935).

64. Act of June 28, 1934 (48 Stat. 1289, ch. 869).

The Frazier-Lemke Act, adding subsection (s) to § 75 of the Bankruptcy Act, designed to preserve to mortgagors the ownership and enjoyment of their farm property and providing specifically, in paragraph 7, that a bankrupt left in possession has the option at any time within 5 years of buying at the appraised value—subject meanwhile to no monetary obligation other than payment of reasonable rental, *held* a violation of property rights, under the Fifth Amendment.

Louisville Bank v. *Radford,* 295 U.S. 555 (1935).

65. Act of August 24, 1935 (49 Stat. 750).

Amendments of Agricultural Adjustment Act *held* not within the taxing power.

Rickert Rice Mills v. *Fontenot,* 297 U.S. 110 (1936).

66. Act of August 30, 1935 (49 Stat. 991).

Bituminous Coal Conservation Act of 1935, *held* to impose, not a tax within Article I, § 8, but a penalty not sustained by the commerce clause (Article I, § 8, clause 3).

Carter v. *Carter Coal Co.,* 298 U.S. 238 (1936).

67. Act of June 25, 1938 (52 Stat. 1040).

Federal Food, Drug, and Cosmetic Act of 1938, § 301(f), prohibiting the refusal to permit entry or inspection of premises by federal officers *held* void for vagueness and as violative of the due process clause of the Fifth Amendment.

United States v. *Cardiff,* 344 U.S. 174 (1952).

68. Act of June 30, 1938 (52 Stat. 1251).

Federal Firearms Act, § 2(f), establishing a presumption of guilt based on a prior conviction and present possession of a firearm, *held* to violate the test of due process under the Fifth Amendment.

Tot v. *United States,* 319 U.S. 463 (1943).

69. Act of October 14, 1940 (54 Stat. 1169, § 401(g)); as amended by Act of January 20, 1944 (58 Stat. 4, § 1).

Provision of Aliens and Nationality Code (8 U.S.C. § 1481(a) (8)), derived from the Nationality Act of 1940, as amended, that citizenship shall be lost upon conviction by court martial and dishonorable discharge for deserting the armed services in time of war, *held* invalid as imposing a cruel and unusual punishment barred by the Eighth Amendment and not authorized by the war powers conferred by Article I, § 8, clauses 11 to 14.

Trop v. *Dulles,* 356 U.S. 86 (1958).

70. Act of November 15, 1943 (57 Stat. 450).

Urgent Deficiency Appropriation Act of 1943, § 304, providing that no salary should be paid to certain named federal employees out of moneys appropriated, *held* to violate Article I, § 9, clause 3, forbidding enactment of bill of attainder or *ex post facto* law.

United States v. *Lovett,* 328 U.S. 303 (1946).

71. Act of September 27, 1944 (58 Stat. 746, § 401 (J)); and Act of June 27, 1952 (66 Stat. 163, 267-268, § 349(a) (10)).

§ 401 (J) of Immigration and Nationality Act of 1940, added in 1944, and § 49(a) (10) of the Immigration and Nationality Act of 1952 depriving one of citizenship, without the procedural safeguards guaranteed by the Fifth and Sixth Amendments, for the offense of leaving or remaining outside the country, in time of war or national emergency, to evade military service *held* invalid.

Kennedy v. *Mendoza-Martinez,* 372 U.S. 144 (1963).

72. Act of July 31, 1946 (ch. 707, § 7, 60 Stat. 719).

District court decision holding invalid under First and Fifth Amendments statute prohibiting parades or assemblages on United States Capitol grounds is summarily affirmed.

Chief of Capitol Police v. *Jeanette Rankin Brigade,* 409 U.S. (1972).

73. Act of June 25, 1948 (62 Stat. 760).

Provision of Lindbergh Kidnapping Act which provided for the imposition of the death penalty only if recommended by the jury *held* unconstitutional inasmuch as it penalized the assertion of a defendant's assertion of his Sixth Amendment right to a jury trial.

United States v. *Jackson,* 390 U.S. 570 (1968).

74. Act of May 5, 1950 (64 Stat. 107).

Article 3(a) of the Uniform Code of Military Justice subjecting civilian ex-servicemen to court martial for crime committed while in military service *held* to violate Article III, § 2, and the Fifth and Sixth Amendments.

Toth v. *Quarles,* 350 U.S. 11 (1955).

75. Act of May 5, 1950 (64 Stat. 107).

Insofar as Article 2(11) of the Uniform Code of Military Justice subjects civilian dependents accompanying members of the armed forces overseas in time of peace to trial, in capital cases, by court martial, it is violative of Article III, § 2, and the Fifth and Sixth Amendments.

Reid v. *Covert,* 354 U.S. 1 (1957).

Insofar as the aforementioned provision is invoked in time of peace for the trial of noncapital offenses committed on land bases overseas by employees of the armed forces who have not been inducted or who have not voluntarily enlisted therein, it is violative of the Sixth Amendment.

McElroy v. *United States,* 361 U.S. 281 (1960).

Insofar as the aforementioned provision is invoked in time of peace for the trial of noncapital offenses committed by civilian dependents accompanying members of the armed forces overseas, it is violative of Article III, § 2, and the Fifth and Sixth Amendments.

Kinsella v. *United States,* 361 U.S. 234 (1960).

Insofar as the aforementioned provision is invoked in time of peace for the trial of a capital offense committed by a civilian employee of the armed forces overseas, it is violative of Article III, § 2, and the Fifth and Sixth Amendments.

Grisham v. *Hagan,* 361 U.S. 278 (1960).

76. Act of August 16, 1950 (64 Stat. 451, as amended).

Statutory scheme authorizing the Postmaster General to close the mails to distributors of obscene materials *held* unconstitutional in the absence of procedural provisions which would assure prompt judicial determination that protected materials were not being restrained.

Blount v. *Rizzi,* 400 U.S. 410 (1971).

77. Act of August 28, 1950 (§ 202(f)(1)(E), 64 Stat. 485, 42 U.S.C. § 402(f)(1)(D)).

Social Security Act provision awarding survivors' benefits based on the earnings of a deceased wife to widower only if he was receiving at least half of his support from her at the time of her death, whereas widow receives benefits regardless of dependency violates equal protection element of Fifth Amendment's due process clause because of its impermissible gender classification.

Califano v. *Goldfarb,* 430 U.S. 199 (1977).

78. Act of September 23, 1950 (Title I, § 5, 64 Stat. 992).

Provision of Subversive Activities Control Act making it unlawful for member of Communist front organization to work in a defense plant *held* to be an overbroad infringement of the right of association protected by the First Amendment.

United States v. *Robel,* 389 U.S. 258 (1967).

79. Act of September 23, 1950 (64 Stat. 993, § 6).

Subversive Activities Control Act of 1950, § 6, providing that any member of a Communist organization, which has registered or has been ordered to register, commits a crime if he attempts to obtain or use a passport, *held* violative of due process under the Fifth Amendment.

Aptheker v. *Secretary of State,* 378 U.S. 500 (1964).

80. Act of September 23, 1950 (Title I, §§ 7, 8, 64 Stat. 993).

Provisions of Subversive Activities Control Act of 1950 requiring registration by party members in lieu of registration by the Communist Party may not be applied to compel registration of or to prosecute for refusal to register, alleged members who have asserted their privilege against self-incrimination in as much as registration would expose such persons to criminal prosecution under other laws.

Albertson v. *Subversive Activities Control Board,* 382 U.S. 70 (1965).

81. Act of October 30, 1951 (§ 5(f)(ii), 65 Stat. 683, 45 U.S.C. §231a(c)(3)(ii)).

Provision of Railroad Retirement Act similar to section voided in *Goldfarb.*

Railroad Retirement Board v. *Kalina* 431 U.S. 909 (1977).

82. Act of June 27, 1952 (Title III, § 349, 66 Stat. 267).

Provision of Immigration and Nationality Act of 1952 providing for revocation of United States citizenship of one who votes in a foreign election *held* unconstitutional under § 1 of the Fourteenth Amendment.

Afroyim v. *Rusk,* 387 U.S. 253 (1967).

83. Act of June 27, 1952 (66 Stat. 163, 269, § 352(a) (1)).

§ 352(a) (1) of the Immigration and Nationality Act of 1952 depriving a naturalized person of citizenship for "having a continuous residence for three years" in state of his birth or prior nationality *held* violative of the due process clause of the Fifth Amendment.

Schneider v. *Rusk,* 377 U.S. 163 (1964).

84. Act of August 26, 1954 (68A Stat. 525, Int. Rev. Code of 1954, §§ 4401-4423).

Provisions of tax laws requiring gamblers to pay occupational and excise taxes may not be used over an assertion of one's privilege against self-incrimination either to compel extensive reporting of activities, leaving the registrant subject to prosecution under the laws of all the States with the possible exception of Nevada, or to prosecute for failure to register and report, because the scheme abridged the Fifth Amendment privilege.

Marchetti v. *United States,* 390 U.S. 39 (1968), and *Grosso* v. *United States,* 390 U.S. 62 (1968).

85. Act of August 16, 1954 (68A Stat. 560, Marijuana Tax Act, §§ 4741, 4744, 4751, 4753).

Provisions of tax laws requiring possessors of marijuana to register and to pay a transfer tax may not be used over an assertion of the privilege against self-incrimination to compel registration or to prosecute for failure to register.

Leary v. *United States,* 395 U.S. 6 (1969).

86. Act of August 16, 1954 (68A Stat. 728, Int. Rev. Code of 1954, §§ 5841, 5851).

Provisions of tax laws requiring the possessor of certain firearms, which it is made illegal to receive or to possess, to register with the Treasury Department may not be used over an assertion of the privilege against self-incrimination to prosecute one for failure to register or for possession of an unregistered firearm since the statutory scheme abridges the Fifth Amendment privilege.

Haynes v. *United States,* 390 U.S. 85 (1968).

87. Act of August 16, 1954 (68A Stat. 867, Int. Rev. Code of 1954, § 7302).

Provisions of tax laws providing for forfeiture of property used in violating internal revenue laws may not be constitutionally used in face of invocation of privilege against self-incrimination to condemn money in possession of gambler who had failed to comply with the registration and reporting scheme held void in *Marchetti* v. *United States,* 390 U.S. 39 (1968).

United States v. *United States Coin & Currency,* 401 U.S. 715 (1971).

88. Act of July 18, 1956 (§ 106, Stat. 570).

Provision of Narcotic Drugs Import and Export Act creating a presumption that possessor of marijuana knew of its illegal importation into the United States *held,* in absence of showing that all marijuana in United States was of foreign origin and that domestic users could know that their marijuana was more likely than not of foreign

origin, unconstitutional under the due process clause of the Fifth Amendment.

Leary v. *United States,* 395 U.S. 6 (1969).

89. Act of August 10, 1956 (70A Stat. 65, Uniform Code of Military Justice, Articles 80, 130, 134).

Servicemen may not be charged under the Act and tried in military courts because of the commission of non-service connected crimes committed off-post and off-duty which are subject to civilian court jurisdiction where the guarantees of the Bill of Rights are applicable.

O'Callahan v. *Parker,* 395 U.S. 258 (1969).

90. Act of August 10, 1956 (70A Stat. 35, § 772(f)).

Provision of statute permitting the wearing of United States military apparel in theatrical productions only if the portrayal does not tend to discredit the armed force imposes an unconstitutional restraint upon First Amendment freedoms and precludes a prosecution under 18 U.S.C. § 702 for unauthorized wearing of uniform in a street skit disrespectful of the military.

Schacht v. *United States,* 398 U.S. 58 (1970).

91. Act of September 2, 1958 (§ 5601(b) (1), 72 Stat. 1399).

Provision of Internal Revenue Code creating a presumption that one's presence at the site of an unregistered still shall be sufficient for conviction under a statute punishing possession, custody, or control of an unregistered still unless defendant otherwise explained his presence at the site to the jury is unconstitutional because the presumption is not a legitimate, rational, or reasonable inference that defendant was engaged in one of the specialized functions prescribed by the statute.

United States v. *Romano,* 382 U.S. 136 (1965).

92. Act of September 2, 1958 (§ 1(25)(b), 72 Stat. 1446), and Act of September 7, 1962 (§ 401, 76 Stat. 469).

Federal statutes providing that spouses of female members of the Armed Forces must be dependent in fact in order to qualify for certain dependent's benefits, whereas spouses of male members are statutorily deemed dependent and automatically qualified for allowances, whatever their actual status, is an invalid gender classification under the equal protection principles of the Fifth Amendment's due process Clause.

Frontiero v. *Richardson,* 411 U.S. 677 (1973).

93. Act of September 14, 1959 (§ 504, 73 Stat. 536).

Provision of Labor-Management Reporting and Disclosure Act of 1959 making it a crime for a member of the Communist Party to serve as an officer or, with the exception of clerical or custodial positions, as an employee of a labor union *held* to be a bill of attainder and unconstitutional.

United States v. *Brown,* 381 U.S. 437 (1965).

94. Act of October 11, 1962 (§ 305, 76 Stat. 840).

Provision of Postal Services and Federal Employees Salary Act of 1962 authorizing Post Office Department to detain material determined to be "communist political propaganda" and to forward it to the addressee only if he requested it after notification by the Department, the material to be destroyed otherwise, *held* to impose on the addressee an affirmative obligation which amounted to an abridgment of First Amendment rights.

Lamont v. *Postmaster General,* 381 U.S. 301 (1965).

95. Act of October 15, 1962 (76 Stat. 914).

Provision of District of Columbia laws requiring that a person to be eligible to receive welfare assistance must have resided in the District for at least one year impermissibly classified persons on the basis of an assertion of the right to travel interstate and therefore *held* to violate the due process clause of the Fifth Amendment.

Shapiro v. *Thompson,* 394 U.S. 618 (1969).

96. Act of December 16, 1963 (77 Stat. 378, 20 U.S.C. § 754).

Provision of Higher Education Facilities Act of 1963 which in effect removed restriction against religious use of facilities constructed with federal funds after 20 years *held* to violate the establishment clause of the First Amendment inasmuch as the property will still be of considerable value at the end of the period and removal of the restriction would constitute a substantial governmental contribution to religion.

Tilton v. *Richardson,* 403 U.S. 672 (1971).

97. Act of July 20, 1965 (§ 339, 79 Stat. 409).

Section of Social Security Act qualifying certain illegitimate children for disability insurance benefits by presuming dependence but disqualifying other illegitimate children, regardless of dependency, if the disabled wage earner parent did not contribute to the child's support before the onset of the disability or if the child did not live with the parent before the onset of disability denies latter class of children equal protection as guaranteed by the due process clause of the Fifth Amendment.

—*Jimenez* v. *Weinberger,* 417 U.S. 628 (1974).

98. Act of September 3, 1966 (§ 102(b), 80 Stat. 831), and Act of April 8, 1974 (§§ 6(a)(1) (amending § 3(d) of Act), 6(a)(2) (amending 3(e)(2)(C), 6(a)(5) (amending § (s)(5), and 6(a)(6) (amending § 3(x)).

Those sections of the Fair Labor Standards Act extending wage and hour coverage to the employees of state and local governments are invalid because Congress lacks the authority under the commerce clause to regulate employee activities in areas of traditional governmental functions of the States.

—*National League of Cities* v. *Usery,* 426 U.S. 833 (1976).

99. Act of January 2, 1968 (§ 163(a)(2), 81 Stat. 872).

District court decisions holding unconstitutional under Fifth Amendment's due process clause section of Social Security Act that reduced, perhaps to zero, benefits coming to illegitimate children upon death of parent in order to satisfy the maximum payment due the wife and legitimate children are summarily affirmed.

—*Richardson* v. *Davis,* 409 U.S. 1069 (1972).

Richardson v. *Griffin,* 409 U.S. 1069 (1972).

100. Act of January 2, 1968 (§ 407, 81 Stat. 882, 42 U.S.C. § 607).

Provision of Social Security Act awarding benefits to families when dependent children have been deprived of parental support because of the unemployment of the father violates the equal protection principle of the Fifth Amendment due process clause because of the impermissible gender classification.

Califano v. *Westcott* (June 25, 1979).

101. Act of June 22, 1970 (ch. III, 84 Stat. 318).

Provision of Voting Rights Act Amendments of 1970 which set a minimum voting age qualification of 18 in state and local elections *held* to be unconstitutional because beyond the powers of Congress to legislate.

Oregon v. *Mitchell,* 400 U.S. 223 (1970).

102. Act of December 29, 1970 (§ 8(a), 84 Stat. 1598, 29 U.S.C. § 657 (a)).

Provision of Occupational Safety and Health Act authorizing inspections of covered work places in industry without warrant violates Fourth Amendment.

Marshall v. *Barlow's, Inc.,* 436 U.S. 307 (1978).

103. Act of January 11, 1971 (§ 2, 84 Stat. 2048).

Provision of Food Stamp Act disqualifying from participation in program any household containing an individual unrelated by birth, marriage, or adoption to any other member of the household violates the due process clause of the Fifth Amendment.

Department of Agriculture v. *Moreno,* 413 U.S. 528 (1973).

104. Act of January 11, 1971 (§ 4, 84 Stat. 2049).

Provision of Food Stamp Act disqualifying from participation in program any household containing a person 18 years or older who had been claimed as a dependent child for income tax purposes in the present or preceding tax year by a taxpayer not a member of the household violates the due process clause of the Fifth Amendment.

Dept. of Agriculture v. *Murry,* 413 U.S. 508 (1973).

105. Federal Election Campaign Act of February 7, 1972 (86 Stat. 3), as amended by the Federal Election Campaign Act Amendments of 1974 (88 Stat. 1263), adding or amending 18 U.S.C. §§ 608(a), 608(e), and 2 U.S.C. § 437c.

Provisions of election law that forbid a candidate or the members of his immediate family from expending personal funds in excess of specified amounts, that limit to $1,000 the independent expenditures of any person relative to an identified candidate, and that forbid expenditures by candidates for federal office in excess of specified amounts violate the First Amendment speech guarantees; provisions of the law creating a commission to oversee enforcement of the Act are an invalid infringement of constitutional separation of powers in that they devolve responsibilities upon a commission four of whose six members are appointed by Congress and all six of whom are confirmed by the House of Representatives as well as by the Senate, not in compliance with the appointments clause.

Buckley v. *Valeo,* 424 U.S. 1 (1976).

106. Act of Oct. 1, 1976 (Title II, part, 96 Stat. 1446), Act of Oct. 12, 1979 (§ 101(c), 93 Stat. 657).

Provisions of Legislative Appropriations Act operating to reduce judicial salaries after salaries had gone into effect violated Security of Compensation Clause of Article III.

United States v. *Will,* 449 U.S. 200 (1980).

Supreme Court Nominations, 1789-1981**

Name	State	Date of Birth	Nomi-nated by	To Replace	Date of Ap-pointment	Confirmation or Other Action*		Date Resigned	Date of Death	Years Service
John Jay	N.Y.	12/12/1745	Washington		9/24/1789	9/26/1789		6/29/1795	5/17/1829	6
John Rutledge	S.C.	1739	Washington		9/24/1789	9/26/1789		3/5/1791	6/21/1800	1
William Cushing	Mass.	3/1/1732	Washington		9/24/1789	9/26/1789			9/13/1810	21
Robert H. Harrison	Md.	1745	Washington		9/24/1789	9/26/1789	(D)		4/20/1790	
James Wilson	Pa.	9/14/1742	Washington		9/24/1789	9/26/1789			8/21/1798	9
John Blair	Va.	1732	Washington		9/24/1789	9/26/1789		1/27/1796	8/31/1800	6
James Iredell	N.C.	10/5/1751	Washington	Harrison	2/8/1790	2/10/1790			10/20/1799	9
Thomas Johnson	Md.	11/4/1732	Washington	Rutledge	11/1/1791	11/7/1791		3/4/1793	10/26/1819	1
William Paterson	N.J.	12/24/1745	Washington	Johnson	2/27/1793	2/28/1793	(W)			
William Paterson†			Washington	Johnson	3/4/1793	3/4/1793			9/9/1806	13
John Rutledge#			Washington	Jay	7/1/1795	12/15/1795	(R, 10-14)			
William Cushing#			Washington	Jay	1/26/1796	1/27/1796	(D)			
Samuel Chase	Md.	4/17/1741	Washington	Blair	1/26/1796	1/27/1796			6/19/1811	15
Oliver Ellsworth	Conn.	4/29/1745	Washington	Jay	3/3/1796	3/4/1796	(21-1)	9/30/1800	11/26/1807	4
Bushrod Washington	Va.	6/5/1762	Adams	Wilson	12/19/1798	12/20/1798			11/26/1829	31
Alfred Moore	N.C.	5/21/1755	Adams	Iredell	12/6/1799	12/10/1799		1/26/1804	10/15/1810	4
John Jay#			Adams	Ellsworth	12/18/1800	12/19/1800	(D)			
John Marshall	Va.	9/24/1755	Adams	Ellsworth	1/20/1801	1/27/1801			7/6/1835	34
William Johnson	S.C.	12/27/1771	Jefferson	Moore	3/22/1804	3/24/1804			8/4/1834	30
H. Brockholst Livingston	N.Y.	11/25/1757	Jefferson	Paterson	12/13/1806	12/17/1806			3/18/1823	16
Thomas Todd	Ky.	1/23/1765	Jefferson	New Seat	2/28/1807	3/3/1807			2/7/1826	19
Levi Lincoln	Mass.	5/15/1749	Madison	Cushing	1/2/1811	1/3/1811	(D)		4/14/1820	
Alexander Wolcott	Conn.	9/15/1758	Madison	Cushing	2/4/1811	2/13/1811	(R, 9-24)		6/26/1828	
John Quincy Adams	Mass.	7/11/1767	Madison	Cushing	2/21/1811	2/22/1811	(D)		2/23/1848	
Joseph Story	Mass.	9/18/1779	Madison	Cushing	11/15/1811	11/18/1811			9/10/1845	34
Gabriel Duvall	Md.	12/6/1752	Madison	Chase	11/15/1811	11/18/1811		1/10/1835	3/6/1844	23
Smith Thompson	N.Y.	1/17/1768	Monroe	Livingston	12/8/1823	12/19/1823			12/18/1843	20
Robert Trimble	Ky.	11/17/1776	J. Q. Adams	Todd	4/11/1826	5/9/1826	(27-5)		8/25/1828	2
John J. Crittenden	Ky.	9/10/1787	J. Q. Adams	Trimble	12/17/1828	2/12/1829	(P)		7/26/1863	
John McLean	Ohio	3/11/1785	Jackson	Trimble	3/6/1829	3/7/1829			4/4/1861	32
Henry Baldwin	Pa.	1/14/1780	Jackson	Washington	1/4/1830	1/6/1830	(41-2)		4/21/1844	14
James M. Wayne	Ga.	1790	Jackson	Johnson	1/7/1835	1/9/1835			7/5/1867	32
Roger B. Taney	Md.	3/17/1777	Jackson	Duvall	1/15/1835	3/3/1835	(P)			
Roger B. Taney†			Jackson	Marshall	12/28/1835	3/15/1836	(29-15)		10/12/1864	28
Philip P. Barbour	Va.	5/25/1783	Jackson	Duvall	12/28/1835	3/15/1836	(30-11)		2/25/1841	5
William Smith	Ala.	1762	Jackson	New Seat	3/3/1837	3/8/1837	(23-18) (D)		6/10/1840	
John Catron	Tenn.	1786	Jackson	New Seat	3/3/1837	3/8/1837	(28-15)		5/30/1865	28
John McKinley	Ala.	5/1/1780	Van Buren	New Seat	9/18/1837	9/25/1837			7/19/1852	15
Peter V. Daniel	Va.	4/24/1784	Van Buren	Barbour	2/26/1841	3/2/1841	(22-5)		5/31/1860	19
John C. Spencer	N.Y.	1/8/1788	Tyler	Thompson	1/9/1844	1/31/1844	(R, 21-26)		5/18/1855	
Reuben H. Walworth	N.Y.	10/26/1788	Tyler	Thompson	3/13/1844	6/17/1844	(W)		11/27/1867	
Edward King	Pa.	1/31/1794	Tyler	Baldwin	6/5/1844	6/15/1844	(P)			
Edward King†			Tyler	Baldwin	12/4/1844	2/7/1845	(W)		5/8/1873	
Samuel Nelson	N.Y.	11/10/1792	Tyler	Thompson	2/4/1845	2/14/1845		11/28/1872	12/13/1873	27
John M. Read	Pa.	2/21/1797	Tyler	Baldwin	2/7/1845	No action			11/29/1874	
George W. Woodward	Pa.	3/26/1809	Polk	Baldwin	12/23/1845	1/22/1846	(R, 20-29)		5/10/1875	
Levi Woodbury	N.H.	12/22/1789	Polk	Story	12/23/1845	1/3/1846			9/4/1851	5
Robert C. Grier	Pa.	3/5/1794	Polk	Baldwin	8/3/1846	8/4/1846		1/31/1870	9/26/1870	23
Benjamin R. Curtis	Mass.	11/4/1809	Fillmore	Woodbury	12/11/1851	12/29/1851		9/30/1857	9/15/1874	5
Edward A. Bradford	La.	9/27/1813	Fillmore	McKinley	8/16/1852	No action			11/22/1872	
George E. Badger	N.C.	4/13/1795	Fillmore	McKinley	1/10/1853	2/11/1853	(P)		5/11/1866	
William C. Micou	La.	1806	Fillmore	McKinley	2/24/1853	No action			4/16/1854	
John A. Campbell	Ala.	6/24/1811	Pierce	McKinley	3/22/1853	3/25/1853		4/26/1861	3/13/1889	8

Boldface - Chief Justice
Italics - Did not serve
 # Earlier court service. See above.
† Earlier nomination not confirmed. See above.
D Declined

W *Withdrawn*
P *Postponed*
R *Rejected*
* Where no vote is listed, confirmation was by voice vote or otherwise
unrecorded.
** As of September 1, 1981.

Name	State	Date of Birth	Nominated by	To Replace	Date of Appointment	Confirmation or Other Action*	Date Resigned	Date of Death	Years Service
Nathan Clifford	Maine	8/18/1803	Buchanan	Curtis	12/9/1857	1/12/1858 (26-23)		7/25/1881	23
Jeremiah S. Black	Pa.	1/10/1810	Buchanan	Daniel	2/5/1861	2/21/1861 (R, 25-26)		8/19/1883	
Noah H. Swayne	Ohio	12/7/1804	Lincoln	McLean	1/21/1862	1/24/1862 (38-1)	1/24/1881	6/8/1884	19
Samuel F. Miller	Iowa	4/5/1816	Lincoln	Daniel	7/16/1862	7/16/1862		10/13/1890	28
David Davis	Ill.	3/9/1815	Lincoln	Campbell	12/1/1862	12/8/1862	3/7/1877	6/26/1886	14
Stephen J. Field	Calif.	11/4/1816	Lincoln	New Seat	3/6/1863	3/10/1863	12/1/1897	4/9/1899	34
Salmon P. Chase	Ohio	1/13/1808	Lincoln	Taney	12/6/1864	12/6/1864		5/7/1873	8
Henry Stanbery	Ohio	2/20/1803	Johnson	Catron	4/16/1866	No action		6/26/1881	
Ebenezer R. Hoar	Mass.	2/21/1816	Grant	New Seat	12/15/1869	2/3/1870 (R, 24-33)		1/31/1895	
Edwin M. Stanton	Pa.	12/19/1814	Grant	Grier	12/20/1869	12/20/1869 (46-11)		12/24/1869	
William Strong	Pa.	5/6/1808	Grant	Grier	2/7/1870	2/18/1870	12/14/1880	8/19/1895	10
Joseph P. Bradley	N.J.	3/14/1813	Grant	New Seat	2/7/1870	3/21/1870 (46-9)		1/22/1892	21
Ward Hunt	N.Y.	6/14/1810	Grant	Nelson	12/3/1872	12/11/1872	1/7/1882	3/24/1886	9
George H. Williams	Ore.	3/23/1823	Grant	Chase	12/1/1873	1/8/1874 (W)		4/4/1910	
Caleb Cushing	Mass.	1/17/1800	Grant	Chase	1/9/1874	1/13/1874 (W)		1/2/1879	
Morrison R. Waite	Ohio	11/29/1816	Grant	Chase	1/19/1874	1/21/1874 (63-0)		3/23/1888	14
John M. Harlan	Ky.	6/1/1833	Hayes	Davis	10/17/1877	11/29/1877		10/14/1911	34
William B. Woods	Ga.	8/3/1824	Hayes	Strong	12/15/1880	12/21/1880 (39-8)		5/14/1887	6
Stanley Matthews	Ohio	7/21/1824	Hayes	Swayne	1/26/1881	No action			
Stanley Matthews†			Garfield	Swayne	3/14/1881	5/12/1881 (24-23)		3/22/1889	7
Horace Gray	Mass.	3/24/1828	Arthur	Clifford	12/19/1881	12/20/1881 (51-5)	7/9/1902	9/15/1902	20
Roscoe Conkling	N.Y.	10/30/1829	Arthur	Hunt	2/24/1882	3/2/1882 (39-12) (D)		4/18/1888	
Samuel Blatchford	N.Y.	3/9/1820	Arthur	Hunt	3/13/1882	3/27/1882		7/7/1893	11
Lucius Q. C. Lamar	Miss.	9/17/1825	Cleveland	Woods	12/6/1887	1/16/1888 (32-28)		1/23/1893	5
Melville W. Fuller	Ill.	2/11/1833	Cleveland	Waite	4/30/1888	7/20/1888 (41-20)		7/4/1910	22
David J. Brewer	Kan.	1/20/1837	Harrison	Matthews	12/4/1889	12/18/1889 (53-11)		3/28/1910	20
Henry B. Brown	Mich.	3/2/1836	Harrison	Miller	12/23/1890	12/29/1890	5/28/1906	9/4/1913	15
George Shiras Jr.	Pa.	1/26/1832	Harrison	Bradley	7/19/1892	7/26/1892	2/23/1903	8/2/1924	10
Howell E. Jackson	Tenn.	4/8/1832	Harrison	Lamar	2/2/1893	2/18/1893		8/8/1895	2
William B. Hornblower	N.Y.	5/13/1851	Cleveland	Blatchford	9/19/1893	1/15/1894 (R, 24-30)		6/16/1914	
Wheeler H. Peckham	N.Y.	1/1/1833	Cleveland	Blatchford	1/22/1894	2/16/1894 (R, 32-41)		9/27/1905	
Edward D. White	La.	11/3/1845	Cleveland	Blatchford	2/19/1894	2/19/1894		5/19/1921	17
Rufus W. Peckham	N.Y.	11/8/1838	Cleveland	Jackson	12/3/1895	12/9/1895		10/24/1909	13
Joseph McKenna	Calif.	8/10/1843	McKinley	Field	12/16/1897	1/21/1898	1/5/1925	11/21/1926	26
Oliver W. Holmes	Mass.	3/8/1841	Roosevelt	Gray	12/2/1902	12/4/1902	1/12/1932	3/6/1935	29
William R. Day	Ohio	4/17/1849	Roosevelt	Shiras	2/19/1903	2/23/1903	11/13/1922	7/9/1923	19
William H. Moody	Mass.	12/23/1853	Roosevelt	Brown	12/3/1906	12/12/1906	11/20/1910	7/2/1917	3
Horace H. Lurton	Tenn.	2/26/1844	Taft	Peckham	12/13/1909	12/20/1909		7/12/1914	4
Edward D. White#			Taft	Fuller	12/12/1910	12/12/1910			10#
Charles E. Hughes	N.Y.	4/11/1862	Taft	Brewer	4/25/1910	5/2/1910	6/10/1916	8/27/1948	6
Willis Van Devanter	Wyo.	4/17/1859	Taft	Moody	12/12/1910	12/15/1910	6/2/1937	2/8/1941	26
Joseph R. Lamar	Ga.	10/14/1857	Taft	White	12/12/1910	12/15/1910		1/2/1916	5
Mahlon Pitney	N.J.	2/5/1858	Taft	Harlan	2/19/1912	3/13/1912 (50-26)	12/31/1922	12/9/1924	10
James C. McReynolds	Tenn.	2/3/1862	Wilson	Lurton	8/19/1914	8/29/1914 (44-6)	1/31/1941	8/24/1946	26
Louis D. Brandeis	Mass.	11/13/1856	Wilson	Lamar	1/28/1916	6/1/1916 (47-22)	2/13/1939	10/5/1941	22
John H. Clarke	Ohio	9/18/1857	Wilson	Hughes	7/14/1916	7/24/1916	7/18/1922	3/22/1945	6
William H. Taft	Ohio	9/15/1857	Harding	White	6/30/1921	6/30/1921	2/3/1930	3/8/1930	8
George Sutherland	Utah	3/25/1862	Harding	Clarke	9/5/1922	9/5/1922	1/17/1938	7/18/1942	15
Pierce Butler	Minn.	3/17/1866	Harding	Day	11/23/1922	12/21/1922 (61-8)		11/16/1939	17
Edward T. Sanford	Tenn.	7/23/1865	Harding	Pitney	1/24/1923	1/29/1923		3/8/1930	7
Harlan F. Stone	N.Y.	10/11/1872	Coolidge	McKenna	1/5/1925	2/5/1925 (71-6)		4/22/1946	16
Charles E. Hughes#			Hoover	Taft	2/3/1930	2/13/1930 (52-26)	7/1/1941		11#
John J. Parker	N.C.	11/20/1885	Hoover	Sanford	3/21/1930	5/7/1930 (R, 39-41)		3/17/1958	
Owen J. Roberts	Pa.	5/2/1875	Hoover	Sanford	5/9/1930	5/20/1930	7/31/1945	5/17/1955	15
Benjamin N. Cardozo	N.Y.	5/24/1870	Hoover	Holmes	2/15/1932	2/24/1932		7/9/1938	6
Hugo L. Black	Ala.	2/27/1886	Roosevelt	Van Devanter	8/12/1937	8/17/1937 (63-16)	9/17/1971	10/25/1971	34
Stanley F. Reed	Ky.	12/31/1884	Roosevelt	Sutherland	1/15/1938	1/25/1938	2/26/1957	4/2/1980	19
Felix Frankfurter	Mass.	11/15/1882	Roosevelt	Cardozo	1/5/1939	1/17/1939	8/28/1962	2/22/1965	23

Name	State	Date of Birth	Nomi- nated by	To Replace	Date of Ap- pointment	Confirmation or Other Action*		Date Resigned	Date of Death	Years Service
William O. Douglas	Conn.	10/16/1898	Roosevelt	Brandeis	3/20/1939	4/4/1939	(62-4)	11/12/1975	1/19/1980	36
Frank Murphy	Mich.	4/13/1890	Roosevelt	Butler	1/4/1940	1/15/1940			7/19/1949	9
Harlan F. Stone#			Roosevelt	Hughes	6/12/1941	6/27/1941			4/22/1946	5#
James F. Byrnes	S.C.	5/2/1879	Roosevelt	McReynolds	6/12/1941	6/12/1941		10/3/1942	4/9/1972	1
Robert H. Jackson	N.Y.	2/13/1892	Roosevelt	Stone	6/12/1941	7/7/1941			10/9/1954	13
Wiley B. Rutledge	Iowa	7/20/1894	Roosevelt	Byrnes	1/11/1943	2/8/1943			9/10/1949	6
Harold H. Burton	Ohio	6/22/1888	Truman	Roberts	9/19/1945	9/19/1945		10/13/1958	10/28/1964	13
Fred M. Vinson	Ky.	1/22/1890	Truman	Stone	6/6/1946	6/20/1946			9/8/1953	7
Tom C. Clark	Texas	9/23/1899	Truman	Murphy	8/2/1949	8/18/1949	(73-8)	6/12/1967	6/13/1977	18
Sherman Minton	Ind.	10/20/1890	Truman	Rutledge	9/15/1949	10/4/1949	(48-16)	10/15/1956	4/9/1965	7
Earl Warren	Calif.	3/19/1891	Eisenhower	Vinson	9/30/1953	3/1/1954		6/23/1969	6/9/1974	15
John M. Harlan	N.Y.	5/20/1899	Eisenhower	Jackson	1/10/1955	3/16/1955	(71-11)	9/23/1971	12/29/1971	16
William J. Brennan Jr.	N.J.	4/25/1906	Eisenhower	Minton	1/14/1957	3/19/1957				
Charles E. Whittaker	Mo.	2/22/1901	Eisenhower	Reed	3/2/1957	3/19/1957		4/1/1962	11/26/73	5
Potter Stewart	Ohio	1/23/1915	Eisenhower	Burton	1/17/1959	5/5/1959	(70-17)	7/3/1981		22
Byron R. White	Colo.	6/8/1917	Kennedy	Whittaker	3/30/1962	4/11/1962				
Arthur J. Goldberg	Ill.	8/8/1908	Kennedy	Frankfurter	8/29/1962	9/25/1962		7/25/1965		3
Abe Fortas	Tenn.	6/19/1910	Johnson	Goldberg	7/28/1965	8/11/1965		5/14/1969		4
Thurgood Marshall	N.Y.	6/2/1908	Johnson	Clark	6/13/1967	8/30/1967	(69-11)			
Abe Fortas#			Johnson	Warren	6/26/1968	10/4/1968	(W)			
Homer Thornberry	Texas	1/9/1909	Johnson	Fortas	6/26/1968	No action				
Warren E. Burger	Minn.	9/17/1907	Nixon	Warren	5/21/1969	6/9/1969	(74-3)			
Clement Haynsworth Jr.	S.C.	10/30/1912	Nixon	Fortas	8/18/1969	11/21/1969	(R, 45-55)			
G. Harrold Carswell	Fla.	12/22/1919	Nixon	Fortas	1/19/1970	4/8/1970	(R, 45-51)			
Harry A. Blackmun	Minn.	11/12/1908	Nixon	Fortas	4/14/1970	5/12/1970	(94-0)			
Lewis F. Powell Jr.	Va.	9/19/1907	Nixon	Black	10/21/1971	12/6/1971	(89-1)			
William H. Rehnquist	Ariz.	10/1/1924	Nixon	Harlan	10/21/1971	12/10/1971	(68-26)			
John Paul Stevens	Ill.	4/20/1920	Ford	Douglas	11/28/1975	12/17/1975	(98-0)			
Sandra Day O'Connor	Ariz.	3/26/1930	Reagan	Stewart	8/19/1981	9/1981				

Sources: Leon Friedman and Fred L. Israel, eds., *The Justices of the United States Supreme Court, 1789-1969;* Executive Journal of the U.S. Senate, 1789-1975; Congressional Quarterly, 1971 and 1975 Almanacs.

Glossary of Common Legal Terms

Accessory. In criminal law, a person not present at the commission of an offense who commands, advises, instigates or conceals the offense.

Acquittal. Discharge of a person from a charge of guilt. A person is acquitted when a jury returns a verdict of not guilty. A person may also be acquitted when a judge determines that there is insufficient evidence to convict him or that a violation of due process precludes a fair trial.

Adjudicate. To determine finally by the exercise of judicial authority, to decide a case.

Affidavit. A voluntary written statement of facts or charges affirmed under oath.

A fortiori. With stronger force, with more reason.

Amicus curiae. A friend of the court, a person not a party to litigation, who volunteers or is invited by the court to give his views on a case.

Appeal. To take a case to a higher court for review. Generally, a party losing in a trial court may appeal once to an appellate court as a matter of right. If he loses in the appellate court, appeal to a higher court is within the discretion of the higher court. Most appeals to the U.S. Supreme Court are within the court's discretion.

However, when the highest court in a state rules that a U.S. statute is unconstitutional or upholds a state statute against the claim that it is unconstitutional, appeal to the Supreme Court is a matter of right.

Appellant. The party that appeals a lower court decision to a higher court.

Appellee. One who has an interest in upholding the decision of a lower court and is compelled to respond when the case is appealed to a higher court by the appellant.

Arraignment. The formal process of charging a person with a crime, reading him the charge, asking whether he pleads guilty or not guilty, and entering his plea.

Attainder, Bill of. A legislative act pronouncing a particular individual guilty of a crime without trial or conviction and imposing a sentence upon him.

Bail. The security, usually money, given as assurance of a prisoner's due appearance at a designated time and place (as in court) in order to procure in the interim his release from jail.

Bailiff. A minor officer of a court usually serving as an usher or a messenger.

Brief. A document prepared by counsel to serve as the basis for an argument in court, setting out the facts of and the legal arguments in support of his case.

Burden of proof. The need or duty of affirmatively proving a fact or facts which are disputed.

Case Law. The law as defined by previously decided cases, distinct from statutes and other sources of law.

Cause. A case, suit, litigation or action, civil or criminal.

Certiorari, Writ of. A writ issued from the Supreme Court, at its discretion, to order a lower court to prepare the record of a case and send it to the Supreme Court for review.

Civil law. Body of law dealing with the private rights of individuals, as distinguished from criminal law.

Class action. A lawsuit brought by one person or group on behalf of all persons similarly situated.

Code. A collection of laws, arranged systematically.

Comity. Courtesy, respect; usually used in the legal sense to refer to the proper relationship between state and federal courts.

Common law. Collection of principles and rules of action, particularly from unwritten English law, which derive their authority from longstanding usage and custom or from courts recognizing and enforcing these customs. Sometimes used synonymously with case law.

Consent decree. A court-sanctioned agreement settling a legal dispute and entered into by the consent of the parties.

Contempt (civil and criminal). Civil contempt consists in the failure to do something which the party is ordered by the court to do for the benefit of another party. Criminal contempt occurs when a person willfully exhibits disrespect for the court or obstructs the administration of justice.

Conviction. Final judgment or sentence that the defendant is guilty as charged.

Criminal law. That branch of law which deals with the enforcement of laws and the punishment of persons who, by breaking laws, commit crimes.

Declaratory judgment. A court pronouncement declaring a legal right or interpretation but not ordering a specific action.

De facto. In fact, in reality.

Defendant. In a civil action, the party denying or defending itself against charges brought by a plaintiff. In a criminal action, the person indicted for commission of an offense.

De jure. As a result of law, as a result of official action.

Deposition. Oral testimony from a witness taken out of court in response to written or oral questions, committed to writing, and intended to be used in the preparation of a case.

Dicta. See Obiter dictum.

Dismissal. Order disposing of a case without a trial.

Docket. See Trial docket.

Due process. Fair and regular procedure. The Fifth and 14th Amendments guarantee persons that they will not be deprived of life, liberty or property by the government until fair and usual procedures have been followed.

Error, Writ of. A writ issued from an appeals court to a lower court requiring it to send to the appeals court the record of a case in which it has entered a final judgment and which the appeals court will now review for error.

Ex parte. Only from, or on, one side. Application to a court for some ruling or action on behalf of only one party.

Ex post facto. After the fact; an *ex post facto* law makes an action a crime after it has already been committed, or otherwise changes the legal consequences of some past action.

Ex rel. Upon information from; usually used to describe legal proceedings begun by an official in the name of the state, but at the instigation of, and with information from, a private individual interested in the matter.

Grand jury. Group of 12 to 23 persons impanelled to hear in private evidence presented by the state against persons accused of crime and to issue indictments when a majority of the jurors find probable cause to believe that the accused has committed a crime. Called a "grand" jury because it consists of more persons than does a "petit jury."

Grand jury report. A public report released by a grand jury after an investigation into activities of public officials that fall short of criminal actions. Grand jury reports are often called "presentments."

Guilty. A word used by a defendant in entering a plea or by a jury in returning a verdict, indicating that the defendant is legally responsible as charged for a crime or other wrongdoing.

Habeas corpus. Literally, "you have the body"; a writ issued to inquire whether a person is lawfully imprisoned or detained. The writ demands that the persons holding the prisoner justify his detention or release him.

Immunity. A grant of exemption from prosecution in return for evidence or testimony.

In camera. "In chambers." Refers to court hearings in private without spectators.

In forma pauperis. In the manner of a pauper, without liability for court costs.

In personam. Done or directed against a particular person.

In re. In the affair of, concerning. Frequent title of judicial proceedings in which there are no adversaries, but rather where the matter itself — as a bankrupt's estate — requires judicial action.

In rem. Done or directed against the thing, not the person.

Indictment. A formal written statement based on evidence presented by the prosecutor from a grand jury decided by a majority vote, charging one or more persons with specified offenses.

Information. A written set of accusations, similar to an indictment, but filed directly by a prosecutor.

Injunction. A court order prohibiting the person to whom it is directed from performing a particular act.

Interlocutory decree. A provisional decision of the court which temporarily settles an intervening matter before completion of a legal action.

Judgment. Official decision of a court based on the rights and claims of the parties to a case which was submitted for determination.

Jurisdiction. The power of a court to hear a case in question, which exists when the proper parties are present, and when the point to be decided is within the issues authorized to be handled by the particular court.

Juries. See grand jury and petit jury.

Magistrate. A judicial officer having jurisdiction to try minor criminal cases and conduct preliminary examinations of persons charged with serious crimes.

Mandamus. "We command." An order issued from a superior court directing a lower court or other authority to perform a particular act.

Moot. Unsettled, undecided. A moot question is also one which is no longer material; a moot case is one which has become hypothetical.

Motion. Written or oral application to a court or a judge to obtain a rule or an order.

Nolo contendere. "I will not contest it." A plea entered by a defendant at the discretion of the judge with the same legal effect as a plea of guilty, except that it may not be cited in other proceedings as an admission of guilt.

Obiter dictum. Statements by a judge or justice expressing an opinion and included with, but not essential to, an opinion resolving a case before the court. Dicta are not necessarily binding in future cases.

Parole. A conditional release from imprisonment under conditions that if the prisoner abides by the law and other restrictions that may be placed upon him, he will not have to serve the remainder of his sentence. But if he does not abide by specified rules, he will be returned to prison.

Per curiam. "By the court." An unsigned opinion of the court, or an opinion written by the whole court.

Petit jury. A trial jury, originally a panel of 12 persons who tried to reach a unanimous verdict on questions of fact in criminal and civil proceedings. Since 1970, the Supreme Court has upheld the legality of state juries with fewer than 12 persons. Because it comprises fewer persons than a "grand jury," it is called a "petit" jury.

Petitioner. One who files a petition with a court seeking action or relief, including a plaintiff or an appellant. But a petitioner is also a person who files for other court action where charges are not necessarily made; for example, a party may petition the court for an order requiring another person or party to produce documents. The opposite party is called the respondent.

When a writ of certiorari is granted by the Supreme Court, the parties to the case are called petitioner and respondent in contrast to the appellant and appellee terms used in an appeal.

Plaintiff. A party who brings a civil action or sues to obtain a remedy for injury to his rights. The party against whom action is brought is termed the defendant.

Plea Bargaining. Negotiations between prosecutors and the defendant aimed at exchanging a plea of guilty from the defendant for concessions by the prosecutors, such as reduction of charges or a request for leniency.

Pleas. See Guilty and Nolo contendere.

Presentment. See Grand jury report.

Prima facie. At first sight; referring to a fact or other evidence presumably sufficient to establish a defense or a claim unless otherwise contradicted.

Probation. Process under which a person convicted of an offense, usually a first offense, receives a suspended sentence and is given his freedom, usually under the guardianship of a probation officer.

Quash. To overthrow, annul or vacate; as to quash a subpoena.

Recognizance. An obligation entered into before a court or magistrate requiring the performance of a specified act — usually to appear in court at a later date. It is an alternative to bail for pre-trial release.

Remand. To send back. In the event of a decision being remanded, it is sent back by a higher court to the court from which it came for further action.

Respondent. One who is compelled to answer the claims or questions posed in court by a petitioner. A defendant and an appellee may be called respondents, but the term also includes those parties who answer in court during actions where charges are not necessarily brought or where the Supreme Court has granted a writ of certiorari.

Seriatim. Separately, individually, one by one.

Stare Decisis. "Let the decision stand." The principle of adherence to settled cases, the doctrine that principles of law established in earlier judicial decisions should be accepted as authoritative in similar subsequent cases.

Statute. A written law enacted by a legislature. A collection of statutes for a particular governmental division is called a code.

Stay. To halt or suspend further judicial proceedings.

Subpoena. An order to present one's self before a grand jury, court or legislative hearing.

Subpoena duces tecum. An order to produce specified documents or papers.

Tort. An injury or wrong to the person or property of another.

Transactional immunity. Protects a witness from prosecution for any offense mentioned in or related to his testimony, regardless of independent evidence against him.

Trial docket. A calendar prepared by the clerks of the court listing the cases set to be tried.

Use immunity. Protects a witness against the use of his own testimony against him in prosecution.

Vacate. To make void, annul or rescind.

Writ. A written court order commanding the designated recipient to perform or not perform acts specified in the order.

Rules of the Supreme Court
of the United States

Source: The Bureau of National Affairs, Inc., Washington, D.C.
The United States Law Week

PART I. THE COURT.

Rule 1

Clerk

1. The Clerk shall have custody of all the records and papers of the Court and shall not permit any of them to be taken from his custody except as authorized by the Court. After the conclusion of the proceedings in this Court, any original records and papers transmitted as the record on appeal or certiorari will be returned to the court from which they were received. Pleadings, papers, and briefs filed with the Clerk may not be withdrawn by litigants.

2. The office of the Clerk will be open, except on a federal legal holiday, from 9 a.m. to 5 p.m. Monday through Friday, and from 9 a.m. to noon Saturday.

3. The Clerk shall not practice as any attorney or counselor while holding his office. See 28 U.S.C. § 955.

Rule 2

Library

1. The Bar library will be open to the appropriate personnel of this Court, members of the Bar of this Court, Members of Congress, members of their legal staffs, and attorneys for the United States, its departments and agencies.

2. The library will be open during such times as the reasonable needs of the Bar require and shall be governed by regulations made by the Librarian with the approval of the Chief Justice or the Court.

3. Books may not be removed from the building, except by a Justice or a member of his legal staff.

Rule 3

Term

1. The Court will hold an annual Term commencing on the first Monday in October, and may hold a special term whenever necessary. See 28 U.S.C. § 2.

2. The Court at every Term will announce the date after which no case will be called for argument at that Term unless otherwise ordered for special cause shown.

3. At the end of each Term, all cases on the docket will be continued to the next Term.

Rule 4

Sessions, Quorum, and Adjournments

1. Open sessions of the Court will be held at 10 a.m. on the first Monday in October of each year, and thereafter as announced by the Court. Unless otherwise ordered, the Court will sit to hear arguments from 10 a.m. until noon and from 1 p.m. until 3 p.m.

2. Any six Members of the Court shall constitute a quorum. See 28 U.S.C. § 1. In the absence of a quorum on any day appointed for holding a session of the Court, the Justices attending, or if no Justice is present the Clerk or a Deputy Clerk, may announce that the Court will not meet until there is a quorum.

3. The Court in appropriate circumstances may direct the Clerk or the Marshal to announce recesses and adjournments.

PART II. ATTORNEYS AND COUNSELORS

Rule 5

Admission to the Bar

1. It shall be requisite to the admission to practice in this Court that the applicant shall have been admitted to practice in the highest court of a State, Territory, District, Commonwealth, or Possession for the three years immediately preceding the date of application, and that the applicant appears to the Court to be of good moral and professional character.

2. Each applicant shall file with the Clerk (1) a certificate from the presiding judge, clerk, or other duly authorized official of the proper court evidencing the applicant's admission to practice there and present good standing, and (2) an executed copy of the form approved by the Court and furnished by the Clerk containing (i) the applicant's personal statement and (ii) the statement of two sponsors (who must be members of the Bar of this Court and must personally know, but not be related to, the applicant) endorsing the correctness of the applicant's statement, stating that the applicant possesses all the qualifications required for admission, and affirming that the applicant is of good moral and professional character.

3. If the documents submitted by the applicant demonstrate that the applicant possesses the necessary qualifications, the Clerk shall so notify the applicant. Upon the applicant's signing the oath or affirmation and paying the fee required under Rule 45 (e), the Clerk shall issue a certificate of admission. If the applicant desires, however, the applicant may be admitted in open court on oral motion by a member of the Bar, provided that the requirements for admission have been satisfied.

4. Each applicant shall take or subscribe the following oath or affirmation:

I, ... , do solemnly swear (or affirm) that as an attorney and as counselor of this Court I will conduct myself uprightly and according to law, and that I will support the Constitution of the United States.

Rule 6

Argument Pro Hac Vice

1. An attorney admitted to practice in the highest court of a State, Territory, District, Commonwealth, or Possession who has not been such for three years, but who is otherwise eligible for admission to practice in this Court under Rule 5.1, may be permitted to present oral argument *pro hac vice* in a particular case.

2. An attorney, barrister, or advocate who is qualified to practice in the courts of a foreign state may be permitted to present oral argument *pro hac vice* in a particular case.

3. Oral argument *pro hac vice* shall be allowed only on motion of the attorney of record for the party on whose behalf leave is sought. Such motion must briefly and distinctly state the appropriate qualifications of the attorney for whom permission to argue orally is sought; it must be filed with the Clerk, in the form prescribed by Rule 42, no later than the date on which the appellee's or respondent's brief on the merits is due to be filed and it must be accompanied by proof of service as prescribed by Rule 28.

Rule 7

Prohibition Against Practice

No one serving as a law clerk or secretary to a Justice of this Court and no other employee of this Court shall practice as an attorney or counselor in any court or before any agency of Government while holding that position; nor shall such person after separating from that position participate, by way of any form of professional consultation or assistance, in any case before this Court until two years have elapsed after such separation; nor shall such person ever participate, by way of any form of professional consultation or assistance, in any case that was pending in this Court during the tenure of such position.

Rule 8

Disbarment

Where it is shown to the Court that any member of its Bar has been disbarred or suspended from practice in any court of record, or has engaged in conduct unbecoming a member of the Bar of this Court, such member forthwith may be suspended from practice before this Court. Such member thereupon will be afforded the opportunity to show good cause, within 40 days, why disbarment should not be effectuated. Upon his response, or upon the expiration of the 40 days if no response is made, the Court will enter an appropriate order.

PART III. ORIGINAL JURISDICTION

Rule 9

Procedure in Original Actions

1. This Rule applies only to actions within the Court's original jurisdiction under Article III of the Constitution of the United States. Original applications for writs in aid of the Court's appellate jurisdiction are governed by Part VII of these Rules.

2. The form of pleadings and motions in original actions shall be governed, so far as may be, by the Federal Rules of Civil Procedure, and in other respects those Rules, where their application is appropriate, may be taken as a guide to procedure in original actions in this Court.

3. The initial pleading in any original action shall be prefaced by a motion for leave to file such pleading, and both shall be printed in conformity with Rule 33. A brief in support of the motion for leave to file, which shall comply with Rule 33, may be filed with the motion and pleading. Sixty copies of each document, with proof of service as prescribed by Rule 28, are required, except that, when an adverse party is a State, service shall be made on the Governor and Attorney General of such State.

4. The case will be placed upon the original docket when the motion for leave to file is filed with the Clerk. The docket fee must be paid at that time, and the appearance of counsel for the plaintiff entered.

5. Within 60 days after receipt of the motion for leave to file and allied documents, any adverse party may file, with proof of service as prescribed by Rule 28, 60 printed copies of a brief in opposition to such motion. The brief shall conform to Rule 33. When such brief in opposition has been filed, or when the time within which it may be filed has expired, the motion, pleading, and briefs will be distributed to the Court by the Clerk. The Court may thereafter grant or deny the motion, set it down for argument, or take other appropriate action.

6. Additional pleadings may be filed, and subsequent proceedings had, as the Court may direct.

7. A summons issuing out of this Court in any original action shall be served on the defendant 60 days before the return day set out therein; and if the defendant, on such service, shall not respond by the return day, the plaintiff shall be at liberty to proceed *ex parte*.

8. Any process against a State issued from the Court in an original action shall be served on the Governor and Attorney General of such State.

PART IV. JURISDICTION ON APPEAL

Rule 10

Appeal — How Taken — Parties — Cross-Appeal

1. An appeal to this Court permitted by law shall be taken by filing a notice of appeal in the form, within the time, and at the place prescribed by this Rule, and shall be perfected by docketing the case in this Court as provided in Rule 12.

2. The notice of appeal shall specify the parties taking the appeal, shall designate the judgment or part thereof appealed from, giving the date of its entry, and shall specify the statute or statutes under which the appeal to this Court is taken. A copy of the notice of appeal shall be served on all parties to the proceeding in the court where the judgment appealed from was issued, in the manner prescribed by Rule 28, and proof of service shall be filed with the notice of appeal.

3. If the appeal is taken from a federal court, the notice of appeal shall be filed with the clerk of that court. If the appeal is taken from a state court, the notice of appeal shall be filed with the clerk of the court from whose judgment the appeal is taken, and a copy of the notice of appeal shall be filed with the court possessed of the record.

4. All parties to the proceeding in the court from whose judgment the appeal is being taken shall be deemed parties in this Court, unless the appellant shall notify the Clerk of this Court in writing of appellant's belief that one or more of the parties below has no interest in the outcome of the appeal. A copy of such notice shall be served on all parties to the proceeding below and a party noted as no longer interested may remain a party here by notifying the Clerk, with service on the other parties, that he has an interest in the appeal. All parties other than appellants shall be appellees, but any appellee who supports the position of an appellant shall meet the time schedule for filing papers which is provided for that appellant, except that any response by such appellee to a jurisdictional statement shall be filed within 20 days after receipt of the statement.

5. The Court may permit an appellee, without filing a cross-appeal, to defend a judgment on any ground that the law and record permit and that would not expand the relief he has been granted.

6. Parties interested jointly, severally, or otherwise in a judgment may join in an appeal therefrom; or any one or more of them may appeal separately; or any two or more of them may join in an appeal. Where two or more cases that involve identical or closely related questions are appealed from the same court, it will suffice to file a single jurisdictional statement covering all the issues.

7. An appellee may take a cross-appeal by perfecting an appeal in the normal manner or, without filing a notice of appeal, by docketing the cross-appeal within the time permitted by Rule 12.4.

Rule 11

Appeal, Cross-Appeal — Time for Taking

1. An appeal to review the judgment of a state court in a criminal case shall be in time when the notice of appeal prescribed by Rule 10 is filed with the clerk of the court from whose judgment the appeal is taken within 90 days after the entry of such judgment and the case is docketed within the time provided in Rule 12. See 28 U.S.C. § 2101 (d).

2. An appeal in all other cases shall be in time when the notice of appeal prescribed by Rule 10 is filed with the clerk of the appropriate court within the time allowed by law for taking such appeal and the case is docketed within the time provided in Rule 12. See 28 U.S.C. §§ 2101 (a), (b), and (c).

3. The time for filing the notice of appeal runs from the date the judgment or decree sought to be reviewed is rendered, and not from the date of the issuance of the mandate (or its equivalent under local practice). However, if a petition for rehearing is timely filed by any party in the case, the time for filing the notice of appeal for all parties (whether or not they requested rehearing or joined in the petition for rehearing, or whether or not the petition

for rehearing relates to an issue the other parties would raise) runs from the date of the denial of rehearing or the entry of a subsequent judgment.

4. The time for filing a notice of appeal may not be extended.

5. A cross-appeal shall be in time if it complies with this Rule or if it is docketed as provided in Rule 12.4.

Rule 12

Docketing Cases

1. Not more than 90 days after the entry of the judgment appealed from, it shall be the duty of the appellant to docket the case in the manner set forth in paragraph 3 of this Rule, except that in the case of appeals pursuant to 28 U.S.C. §§ 1252 or 1253, the time limit for docketing shall be 60 days from the filing of the notice of appeal. See 28 U.S.C. § 2101 (a). The Clerk will refuse to receive any jurisdictional statement in a case in which the notice of appeal has obviously not been timely filed.

2. For good cause shown, a Justice of this Court may extend the time for docketing a case for a period not exceeding 60 days. An application for extension of time within which to docket a case must set out the grounds on which the jurisdiction of this Court is invoked, must identify the judgment sought to be reviewed, must have appended a copy of the opinion, must specify the date and place of filing of the notice of appeal and appended a copy thereof, and must set forth with specificity the reasons why the granting of an extension of time is thought justified. For the time and manner of presenting such an application, see Rules 29, 42.2, and 43. Such applications are not favored.

3. Counsel for the appellant shall enter an appearance, pay the docket fee, and file, with proof of service as prescribed by Rules 28, 40 copies of a printed statement as to jurisdiction, which shall comply in all respects with Rule 15. The case then will be placed on the docket. It shall be the duty of counsel for appellant to notify all appellees, on a form supplied by the Clerk, of the date of docketing and of the docket number of the case. Such notice shall be served as required by Rule 28.

4. Not more than 30 days after receipt of the statement of jurisdiction, counsel for an appellee wishing to cross-appeal shall enter an appearance, pay the docket fee, and file, with proof of service as prescribed by Rule 28, 40 copies of a printed statement as to jurisdiction on cross-appeal, which shall comply in all respects with Rule 15. The cross-appeal will then be placed on the docket. The issues tendered by a timely cross-appeal docketed under this paragraph may be considered by the Court only in connection with a separate and duly perfected appeal over which this Court has jurisdiction without regard to this paragraph. It shall be the duty of counsel for the cross-appellant to notify the cross-appellee on a form supplied by the Clerk of the date of docketing and of the docket number of the cross-appeal. Such notice shall be served as required by Rule 28. A statement of jurisdiction on cross-appeal may not be joined with any other pleading. The Clerk shall not accept any pleadings so joined. The time for filing a cross-appeal may not be extended.

Rule 13

Certification of the Record

1. An appellant at any time prior to action by this Court on the jurisdictional statement, may request the Clerk of the court possessed of the record to certify it, or any part of it, and to provide for its transmission to this Court, but the filing of the record in this Court is not required for the docketing of an appeal. If the appellant has not done so, the appellee may request such clerk to certify and transmit the record or any part of it. Thereafter, the Clerk of this Court or any party to the appeal may request that additional parts of the record be certified and transmitted to this Court. Copies of all requests for certification and transmission shall be sent to all parties. Such requests to certify the record prior to action by the Court on the jurisdictional statement, however, shall not be made as a matter of course but only

when the record is deemed essential to a proper understanding of the case by this Court.

2. When requested to certify and transmit the record, or any part of it, the Clerk of the court possessed of the record shall number the documents to be certified and shall transmit with the record a numbered list of the documents, identifying each with reasonable definiteness.

3. The record may consist of certified copies. But whenever it shall appear necessary or proper, in the opinion of the presiding judge of the court from which the appeal is taken, that original papers of any kind should be inspected in this Court in lieu of copies, the presiding judge may make any rule or order for safe-keeping, transporting, and return of the original papers as may seem proper to him. If the record or stipulated portions thereof have been printed for the use of the court below, this printed record plus the proceedings in the court below may be certified as the record unless one of the parties or the Clerk of this Court otherwise requests.

4. When more than one appeal is taken to this Court from the same judgment, it shall be sufficient to prepare a single record containing all the matter designated by the parties or the Clerk of this Court, without duplication.

Rule 14

Dismissing Appeals

1. After a notice of appeal has been filed, but before the case has been docketed in this Court, the parties may dismiss the appeal by stipulation filed in the court whose judgment is the subject of the appeal, or that court may dismiss the appeal upon motion and notice by the appellant. For dismissal after the case has been docketed, see Rule 53.

2. If a notice of appeal has been filed but the case has not been docketed in this Court within the time for docketing, plus any enlargement thereof duly granted, the court whose judgment is the subject of the appeal may dismiss the appeal upon motion of the appellee and notice to the appellant, and may make such order thereon with respect to costs as may be just.

3. If a notice of appeal has been filed but the case has not been docketed in this Court within the time for docketing, plus any enlargement thereof duly granted, and the court whose judgment is the subject of the appeal has denied for any reason an appellee's motion to dismiss the appeal, made as provided in the foregoing paragraph, the appellee may have the cause docketed and may seek to have the appeal dismissed in this Court, by producing a certificate, whether in term or vacation, from the Clerk of the Court whose judgment is the subject of the appeal, establishing the foregoing facts, and by filing a motion to dismiss, which shall conform to Rule 42, and be accompanied by proof of service as prescribed by Rule 28. The Clerk's certificate shall be attached to the motion, but it shall not be necessary for the appellee to file the record. In the event that the appeal is thereafter dismissed, the Court may give judgment for costs against the appellant and in favor of appellee. The appellant shall not be entitled to docket the cause after the appeal shall have been dismissed under this paragraph, except by special leave of Court.

Court 15

Jurisdictional Statement

1. The jurisdictional statement required by Rule 12 shall contain, in the order here indicated:

(a) The questions presented by the appeal, expressed in the terms and circumstances of the case but without unnecessary detail. The statement of the questions should be short and concise and should not be argumentative or repetitious. The statement of a question presented will be deemed to comprise every subsidiary question fairly included therein. Only the questions set forth in the jurisdictional statement or fairly included therein will be considered by the Court.

(b) A list of all parties to the proceeding in the court

whose judgment is sought to be reviewed, except where the caption of the case in this Court contains the names of all such parties. This listing may be done in a footnote.

(c) A table of contents and table of authorities, if required by Rule 33.5.

(d) A reference to the official and unofficial reports of any opinions delivered in the courts or administrative agency below.

(e) A concise statement of the grounds on which the jurisdiction of this Court is invoked, showing:

(i) The nature of the proceeding and, if the appeal is from a federal court, the statutory basis for federal jurisdiction.

(ii) The date of the entry of the judgment or decree sought to be reviewed, the date of any order respecting a rehearing, the date the notice of appeal was filed, and the court in which it was filed. In the case of a cross-appeal docketed under Rule 12.4, reliance upon that Rule shall be expressly noted, and the date of receipt of the appellant's jurisdictional statement by the appellee-cross-appellant shall be stated.

(iii) The statutory provision believed to confer jurisdiction of the appeal on this Court, and, if deemed necessary, the cases believed to sustain jurisdiction.

(f) The constitutional provisions, treaties, statutes, ordinances, and regulations that the case involves, setting them out verbatim, and giving the appropriate citation therefor. If the provisions involved are lengthy, their citation alone will suffice at this point, and their pertinent text then shall be set forth in the appendix referred to in subparagraph 1 (j) of this Rule.

(g) A *concise* statement of the case containing the facts material to consideration of the questions presented. The statement of the case shall also specify the stage in the proceedings (both in the court of first instance and in the appellate court) at which the questions sought to be reviewed were raised; the method or manner of raising them; and the way in which they were passed upon by the court.

(h) A statement of the reasons why the questions presented are so substantial as to require plenary consideration, with briefs on the merits and oral argument, for their resolution.

(i) If the appeal is from a decree of a district court granting or denying a preliminary injunction, a showing of the matters in which it is contended that the court has abused its discretion by such action. See *United States v. Corrick*, 298 U.S. 435 (1936); *Mayo v. Lakeland Highlands Canning Co.*, 309 U.S. 310 (1940).

(j) An appendix containing, in the following order:

(i) Copies of any opinions, orders, findings of fact, and conclusions of law, whether written or oral (if recorded and transcribed), delivered upon the rendering of the judgment or decree by the court whose decision is sought to be reviewed.

(ii) Copies of any other such opinions, orders, findings of fact, and conclusions of law rendered by courts or administrative agencies in the case, and, if reference thereto is necessary to ascertain the grounds of the judgment or decree, of those in companion cases. Each of these documents shall include the caption showing the name of the issuing court or agency, the title and number of the case, and the date of its entry.

(iii) A copy of the judgment or decree appealed from and any order or rehearing, including in each the caption showing the name of the issuing court or agency, the title and number of the case, and the date of entry of the judgment, decree, or order on rehearing.

(iv) A copy of the notice of appeal showing the date it was filed and the name of the court where it was filed.

(v) Any other appended materials.

If what is required by this paragraph to be appended to the statement is voluminous, it may, if more convenient, be separately presented.

2. The jurisdictional statement shall be produced in conformity with Rule 33. The Clerk shall not accept any jurisdictional statement that does not comply with this Rule and with Rule 33, except that a party proceeding *in forma pauperis* may proceed in the manner provided in Rule 46.

3. The jurisdictional statement shall be as short as possible, but may not exceed 30 pages, excluding the subject index, table of authorities, any verbatim quotations required by subparagraph 1 (f) of this Rule, and the appendices.

Rule 16

Motion to Dismiss or Affirm — Reply — Supplemental Briefs

1. Within 30 days after receipt of the jurisdictional statement, unless the time is enlarged by the Court or a Justice thereof, or by the Clerk under the provisions of Rule 29.4, the appellee may file a motion to dismiss, or a motion to affirm. Where appropriate, a motion to affirm may be united in the alternative with a motion to dismiss, provided that a motion to affirm or dismiss shall not be joined with any other pleading. The Clerk shall not accept any motion so joined.

(a) The Court will receive a motion to dismiss an appeal on the ground that the appeal is not within this Court's jurisdiction, or because not taken in conformity with statute or with these Rules.

(b) The Court will receive a motion to dismiss an appeal from a state court on the ground that it does not present a substantial federal question; or that the federal question sought to be reviewed was not timely or properly raised and was not expressly passed on; or that the judgment rests on an adequate non-federal basis.

(c) The Court will receive a motion to affirm the judgment sought to be reviewed on appeal from a federal court on the ground that it is manifest that the questions on which the decision of the cause depends are so unsubstantial as not to need further argument.

(d) The Court will receive a motion to dismiss or affirm on any other ground the appellee wishes to present as a reason why the Court should not set the case for argument.

2. A motion to dismiss or affirm shall comply in all respects with Rules 33 and 42. Forty copies, with proof of service as prescribed by Rule 28, shall be filed with the Clerk. The Clerk shall not accept a motion or brief that does not comply with this Rule and with Rules 33 and 42, except that a party proceeding *in forma pauperis* may proceed in the manner provided in Rule 46.

3. A motion to dismiss or affirm shall be as short as possible and may not, either separately or cumulatively, exceed 30 pages, excluding the subject index, table of authorities, any verbatim quotations included in accordance with Rule 34.1 (f), and any appendix.

4. Upon the filing of such motion, or the expiration of the time allowed therefor, or express waiver of the right to file, the jurisdictional statement and the motion, if any, will be distributed by the Clerk to the Court for its consideration. However, if a jurisdictional statement on cross-appeal has been docketed under Rule 12.4, distribution of both it and the jurisdictional statement on appeal will be delayed until the filing of a motion to dismiss or affirm by the cross-appellee, or the expiration of the time allowed therefor, or express waiver of the right to file.

5. A brief opposing a motion to dismiss or affirm may be filed by any appellant, but distribution of the jurisdictional statement and consideration thereof by this Court will not be delayed pending the filing of any such brief. Such brief shall be as short as possible but may not exceed 10 pages. Forty copies of any such brief, prepared in accordance with Rule 33 and served as prescribed by Rule 28, shall be filed.

6. Any party may file a supplemental brief at any time while a jurisdictional statement is pending, calling attention to new cases or legislation or other intervening matter not available at the time of the party's last filing. A supplemental brief, restricted to such new matter, may not exceed 10 pages. Forty copies of any such brief, prepared in accordance with Rule 33 and served as prescribed by Rule 28, shall be filed.

7. After consideration of the papers distributed pursuant to this Rule, the Court will enter an appropriate order. The order may be a summary disposition on the merits. If the order notes probable jurisdiction or postpones consideration of jurisdiction to the hearing on the merits, the Clerk forthwith shall notify the court below and counsel of record of the noting or postponement. The case then will stand for briefing and oral argument. If the record has not previously been filed, the Clerk of this Court shall request the Clerk of the Court possessed of the record to certify it and transmit it to this Court.

8. If consideration of jurisdiction is postponed, counsel, at the outset of their briefs and oral argument, shall address the question of jurisdiction.

PART V. JURISDICTION ON WRIT OF CERTIORARI

Rule 17

Considerations Governing Review on Certiorari

1. A review on writ of certiorari is not a matter of right, but of judicial discretion, and will be granted only when there are special and important reasons therefor. The following, while neither controlling nor fully measuring the Court's discretion, indicate the character of reasons that will be considered.

(a) When a federal court of appeals has rendered a decision in conflict with the decision of another federal court of appeals on the same matter; or has decided a federal question in a way in conflict with a state court of last resort; or has so far departed from the accepted and usual course of judicial proceedings, or so far sanctioned such a departure by a lower court, as to call for an exercise of this Court's power of supervision.

(b) When a state court of last resort has decided a federal question in a way in conflict with the decision of another state court of last resort or of a federal court of appeals.

(c) When a state court or a federal court of appeals has decided an important question of federal law which has not been, but should be, settled by this Court, or has decided a federal question in a way in conflict with applicable decisions of this Court.

2. The same general considerations outlined above will control in respect of petitions for writs of certiorari to review judgments of the Court of Claims, of the Court of Customs and Patent Appeals, and of any other court whose judgments are reviewable by law on writ of certiorari.

Rule 18

Certiorari to a Federal Court of Appeals Before Judgment

A petition for writ of certiorari to review a case pending in a federal court of appeals, before judgment is given in such court, will be granted only upon a showing that the case is of such imperative public importance as to justify the deviation from normal appellate practice and to require immediate settlement in this Court. See 28 U.S.C. § 2101 (e); see also, *United States v. Bankers Trust Co.*, 294 U.S. 240 (1935); *Railroad Retirement Board v. Alton R. Co.*, 295 U.S. 330 (1935); *Rickert Rice Mills v. Fontenot*, 297 U.S. 110 (1936); *Carter v. Carter Coal Co.*, 298 U.S. 238 (1936); *Ex parte Quirin*, 317 U.S. 1 (1942); *United States v. Mine Workers*, 330 U.S. 258 (1947); *Youngstown Sheet & Tube Co. v. Sawyer*, 343 U.S. 579 (1952); *Wilson v. Girard*, 354 U.S. 524 (1957); *United States v. Nixon*, 418 U.S. 683 (1974).

Rule 19

Review on Certiorari — How Sought — Parties

1. A party intending to file a petition for certiorari, prior to filing the case in this Court or at any time prior to action by this Court on the petition, may request the Clerk of the Court possessed of the record to certify, it, or any part of it, and to provide for its transmission to this Court, but the filing of the record in this Court is not a requisite for docketing the petition. If the petitioner has not done so, the respondent may request such Clerk to certify and transmit the record or any part of it. Thereafter, the Clerk of this Court or any party to the case may request that additional parts of the record be certified and transmitted to this Court. Copies of all requests for certification and transmission shall be sent to all parties to the proceeding. Such requests to certify the record prior to action by the Court on the petition for certiorari, however, should not be made as a matter of course but only when the record is deemed essential to a proper understanding of the case by this Court.

2. When requested to certify and transmit the record, or any part of it, the Clerk of the Court possessed of the record shall number the documents to be certified and shall transmit with the record a numbered list of the documents, identifying each with reasonable definiteness. If the record, or stipulated portions thereof, has been printed for the use of the court below, such printed record plus the proceedings in the court below may be certified as the record unless one of the parties or the Clerk of this Court otherwise requests. The provisions of Rule 13.3 with respect to original papers shall apply to all cases sought to be reviewed on writ of certiorari.

3. Counsel for the petitioner shall enter an appearance, pay the docket fee, and file, with proof of service as provided by Rule 28, 40 copies of a petition which shall comply in all respects with Rule 21. The case then will be placed on the docket. It shall be the duty of counsel for the petitioner to notify all respondents, on a form supplied by the Clerk, of the date of filing and of the docket number of the case. Such notice shall be served as required by Rule 28.

4. Parties interested jointly, severally, or otherwise in a judgment may join in a petition for a writ of certiorari therefrom; or any one or more of them may petition separately; or any two or more of them may join in a petition. When two or more cases are sought to be reviewed on certiorari to the same court and involve identical or closely related questions, it will suffice to file a single petition for writ of certiorari covering all the cases.

5. Not more than 30 days after receipt of the petition for certiorari, counsel for a respondent wishing to file a cross-petition that would otherwise be untimely shall enter an appearance, pay the docket fee, and file, with proof of service as prescribed by Rule 28, 40 copies of a cross-petition for certiorari, which shall comply in all respects with Rule 21. The cross-petition will then be placed on the docket subject, however, to the provisions of Rule 20.5. It shall be the duty of counsel for the cross-petitioner to notify the cross-respondent on a form supplied by the Clerk of the date of docketing and of the docket number of the cross-petition. Such notice shall be served as required by Rule 28. A cross-petition for certiorari may not be joined with any other pleading. The Clerk shall not accept any pleadings so joined. The time for filing a cross-petition may not be extended.

6. All parties to the proceeding in the court whose judgment is sought to be reviewed shall be deemed parties in this Court, unless the petitioner shall notify the Clerk of this Court in writing of petitioner's belief that one or more of the parties below has no interest in the outcome of the petition. A copy of such notice shall be served on all parties to the proceeding below and a party noted as no longer interested may remain a party here by notifying the Clerk, with service on the other parties, that he has an interest in the petition. All parties other than petitioners shall be respondents, but any respondent who supports the position of a petitioner shall meet the time schedule for filing papers which is provided for that petitioner, except that any response by such respondent to the petition shall be filed within 20 days after receipt of the petition. The time for filing such response may not be extended.

Rule 20

Review on Certiorari — Time for Petitioning

1. A petition for writ of certiorari to review the judgment in a criminal case of a state court of last resort or of a federal court of appeals shall be deemed in time when it is filed with the Clerk

within 60 days after the entry of such judgment. A Justice of this Court, for good cause shown, may extend the time for applying for a writ of certiorari in such cases for a period not exceeding 30 days.

2. A petition for writ of certiorari in all other cases shall be deemed in time when it is filed with the Clerk within the time prescribed by law. See 28 U.S.C. § 2101 (c).

3. The Clerk will refuse to receive any petition for a writ of certiorari which is jurisdictionally out of time.

4. The time for filing a petition for writ of certiorari runs from the date the judgment or decree sought to be reviewed is rendered, and not from the date of the issuance of the mandate (or its equivalent under local practice). However, if a petition for rehearing is timely filed by any party in the case, the time for filing the petition for writ of certiorari for all parties (whether or not they requested rehearing or joined in the petition for rehearing) runs from the date of the denial of rehearing or of the entry of a subsequent judgment entered on the rehearing.

5. A cross-petition for writ of certiorari shall be deemed in time when it is filed as provided in paragraphs 1, 2, and 4 of this Rule or in Rule 19.5. However, no cross-petition filed untimely except for the provision of Rule 19.5 shall be granted unless a timely petition for writ of certiorari of another party to the case is granted.

6. An application for extension of time within which to file a petition for writ of certiorari must set out, as in a petition for certiorari (see Rule 21.1, subparagraphs (e) and (h)), the grounds on which the jurisdiction of this Court is invoked, must identify the judgment sought to be reviewed and have appended thereto a copy of the opinion, and must set forth with specificity the reasons why the granting of an extension of time is thought justified. For the time and manner of presenting such an application, see Rules 29, 42, and 43. Such applications are not favored.

Rule 21

The Petition for Certiorari

1. The petition for writ of certiorari shall contain, in the order here indicated:

(a) The questions presented for review, expressed in the terms and circumstances of the case but without unnecessary detail. The statement of the questions should be short and concise and should not be argumentative or repetitious. The statement of a question presented will be deemed to comprise every subsidiary question fairly included therein. Only the questions set forth in the petition or fairly included therein will be considered by the Court.

(b) A list of all parties to the proceeding in the Court whose judgment is sought to be reviewed, except where the caption of the case in this Court contains the names of all parties. This listing may be done in a footnote.

(c) A table of contents and table of authorities, if required by Rule 33.5.

(d) A reference to the official and unofficial reports of any opinions delivered in the courts or administrative agency below.

(e) A concise statement of the grounds on which the jurisdiction of this Court is invoked showing:

(i) The date of the judgment or decree sought to be reviewed, and the time of its entry;

(ii) The date of any order respecting a rehearing, and the date and terms of any order granting an extension of time within which to petition for certiorari; and

(iii) Where a cross-petition for writ of certiorari is filed under Rule 19.5, reliance upon that Rule shall be expressly noted and the cross-petition shall state the date of receipt of the petition for certiorari in connection with which the cross-petition is filed.

(iv) The statutory provision believed to confer on this Court jurisdiction to review the judgment or decree in question by writ of certiorari.

(f) The constitutional provisions, treaties, statutes, ordinances, and regulations which the case involves, setting them out verbatim, and giving the appropriate citation therefor. If the provisions involved are lengthy, their citation alone will suffice at this point, and their pertinent text then shall be set forth in the appendix referred to in subparagraph 1 (k) of this Rule.

(g) A *concise* statement of the case containing the facts material to the consideration of the questions presented.

(h) If review of the judgment of a state court is sought, the statement of the case shall also specify the stage in the proceedings, both in the court of first instance and in the appellate court, at which the federal questions sought to be reviewed were raised; the method or manner of raising them and the way in which they were passed upon by the court; such pertinent quotation of specific portions of the record, or summary thereof, with specific reference to the places in the record where the matter appears (*e.g.,* ruling on exception, portion of court's charge and exception thereto, assignment of errors) as will show that the federal question was timely and properly raised so as to give this Court jurisdiction to review the judgment on writ of certiorari.

Where the portions of the record relied upon under this subparagraph are voluminous, they shall be included in the appendix referred to in subparagraph 1 (k) of this Rule.

(i) If review of the judgment of a federal court is sought, the statement of the case shall also show the basis for federal jurisdiction in the court of first instance.

(j) A direct and concise argument amplifying the reasons relied on for the allowance of the writ. See Rule 17.

(k) An appendix containing, in the following order:

(i) Copies of any opinions, orders, findings of fact, and conclusions of law, whether written or oral (if recorded and transcribed), delivered upon the rendering of the judgment or decree by the court whose decision is sought to be reviewed.

(ii) Copies of any other such opinions, orders, findings of fact, and conclusions of law rendered by courts or administrative agencies in the case, and, if reference thereto is necessary to ascertain the grounds of the judgment or decree, of those in companion cases. Each of these documents shall include the caption showing the name of the issuing court or agency and the title and number of the case, and the date of its entry.

(iii) A copy of the judgment or decree sought to be reviewed and any order on rehearing, including in each the caption showing the name of the issuing court or agency, the title and number of the case, and the date of entry of the judgment, decree, or order on rehearing.

(iv) Any other appended materials.

If what is required by this paragraph or by subparagraphs 1 (f) and (h) of this Rule, to be included in the petition is voluminous, it may, if more convenient, be separately presented.

2. The petition for writ of certiorari shall be produced in conformity with Rule 33. The Clerk shall not accept any petition for writ of certiorari that does not comply with this Rule and with Rule 33, except that a party proceeding *in forma pauperis* may proceed in the manner provided in Rule 46.

3. All contentions in support of a petition for writ of certiorari shall be set forth in the body of the petition, as provided in subparagraph 1 (j) of this Rule. No separate brief in support of a petition for a writ of certiorari will be received, and the Clerk will refuse to file any petition for a writ of certiorari to which is annexed or appended any supporting brief.

4. The petition for writ of certiorari shall be as short as possible, but may not exceed 30 pages, excluding the subject index, table of authorities, any verbatim quotations required by subparagraph 1 (f) of this Rule, and the appendix.

5. The failure of a petitioner to present with accuracy, brevity, and clearness whatever is essential to a ready and adequate understanding of the points requiring consideration will be a sufficient reason for denying his petition.

Rule 22

Brief in Opposition — Reply — Supplemental Briefs

1. Respondent shall have 30 days (unless enlarged by the Court or a Justice thereof or by the Clerk pursuant to Rule 29.4) after receipt of a petition, within which to file 40 printed copies of an opposing brief disclosing any matter or ground why the cause should not be reviewed by this Court. See Rule 17. Such brief in opposition shall comply with Rule 33 and with the requirements of Rule 34 governing a respondent's brief, and shall be served as prescribed by Rule 28. The Clerk shall not accept a brief which does not comply with this Rule and with Rule 33, except that a party proceeding *in forma pauperis* may proceed in the manner provided in Rule 46.

2. A brief in opposition shall be as short as possible and may not, in any single case, exceed 30 pages, excluding the subject index, table of authorities, any verbatim quotations included in accordance with Rule 34.1 (f), and any appendix.

3. No motion by a respondent to dismiss a petition for writ of certiorari will be received. Objections to the jurisdiction of the Court to grant the writ of certiorari may be included in the brief in opposition.

4. Upon the filing of a brief in opposition, or the expiration of the time allowed therefor, or express waiver of the right to file, the petition and brief, if any, will be distributed by the Clerk to the Court for its consideration. However, if a cross-petition for certiorari has been filed, distribution of both it and the petition for certiorari will be delayed until the filing of a brief in opposition by the cross-respondent, or the expiration of the time allowed therefor, or express waiver of the right to file.

5. A reply brief addressed to arguments first raised in the brief in opposition may be filed by any petitioner but distribution under paragraph 4 hereof will not be delayed pending the filing of any such brief. Such brief shall be as short as possible, but may not exceed 10 pages. Forty copies of any such brief, prepared in accordance with Rule 33 and served as prescribed by Rule 28, shall be filed.

6. Any party may file a supplemental brief at any time while a petition for writ of certiorari is pending calling attention to new cases or legislation or other intervening matter not available at the time of the party's last filing. A supplemental brief, restricted to such new matter, may not exceed 10 pages. Forty copies of any such brief, prepared in accordance with Rule 33 and served as prescribed by Rule 28, shall be filed.

Rule 23

Disposition of Petition for Certiorari

1. After consideration of the papers distributed pursuant to Rule 22, the Court will enter an appropriate order. The order may be a summary disposition on the merits.

2. Whenever a petition for writ of certiorari to review a decision of any court is granted, an order to that effect shall be entered, and the Clerk forthwith shall notify the court below and counsel of record. The case then will stand for briefing and oral argument. If the record has not previously been filed, the Clerk of this Court shall request the Clerk of the Court possessed of the record to certify it and transmit it to this Court. A formal writ shall not issue unless specially directed.

3. Whenever a petition for writ of certiorari to review a decision of any court is denied, an order to that effect will be entered and the Clerk forthwith will notify the Court below and counsel of record. The order of denial will not be suspended pending disposition of a petition for rehearing except by order of the Court or a Justice thereof.

PART VI. JURISDICTION OF CERTIFIED QUESTIONS

Rule 24

Questions Certified by a Court of Appeals or By the Court of Claims

1. When a federal court of appeals or the Court of Claims shall certify to this Court a question or proposition of law concerning which it desires instruction for the proper decision of a cause (see 28 U.S.C. §§ 1254 (3), 1255 (2)), the certificate shall contain a statement of the nature of the cause and the facts on which such question or proposition of law arises. Questions of fact cannot be certified. Only questions or propositions of law may be certified, and they must be distinct and definite.

2. When a question is certified by a federal court of appeals, and if it appears that there is special reason therefor, this Court, on application or on its own motion, may consider and decide the entire matter in controversy. See 28 U.S.C. § 1254 (3).

Rule 25

Procedure in Certified Cases

1. When a case is certified, the Clerk will notify the respective parties and shall docket the case. Counsel shall then enter their appearances.

2. After docketing, the certificate shall be submitted to the Court for a preliminary examination to determine whether the case shall be briefed, set for argument, or the certificate dismissed. No brief may be filed prior to the preliminary examination of the certificate.

3. If the Court orders that the case be briefed or set down for argument, the parties shall be notified and permitted to file briefs. The Clerk of this Court shall request the clerk of the court from which the case comes to certify the record and transmit it to this Court. Any portion of the record to which the parties wish to direct the Court's particular attention shall be printed in a joint appendix prepared by the appellant or plaintiff in the court below under the procedures provided in Rule 30, but the fact that any part of the record has not been printed shall not prevent the parties or the Court from relying on it.

4. Briefs on the merits in a case on certificate shall comply with Rules 33, 34, and 35, except that the brief of the party who was appellant or plaintiff below shall be filed within 45 days of the order requiring briefs or setting the case down for argument.

PART VII. JURISDICTION TO ISSUE EXTRAORDINARY WRITS

Rule 26

Considerations Governing Issuance of Extraordinary Writs

The issuance by the Court of any extraordinary writ authorized by 28 U.S.C. § 1651 (a) is not a matter of right, but of discretion sparingly exercised. To justify the granting of any writ under that provision, it must be shown that the writ will be in aid of the Court's appellate jurisdiction, that there are present exceptional circumstances warranting the exercise of the Court's discretionary powers, and that adequate relief cannot be had in any other form or from any other court.

Rule 27

Procedure in Seeking an Extraordinary Writ

1. The petition in any proceeding seeking the issuance by this Court of a writ authorized by 28 U.S.C. §§ 1651 (a), 2241, or 2254 (a), shall comply in all respects with Rule 33, except that a party proceeding *in forma pauperis* may proceed in the manner provided in Rule 46. The petition shall be captioned "In re (name of petitioner)." All contentions in support of the petition shall be included in the petition. The case will be placed upon the docket

when 40 copies, with proof of service as prescribed by Rule 28 (subject to paragraph 3 (b) of this Rule), are filed with the Clerk and the docket fee is paid. The appearance of counsel for the petitioner must be entered at this time. The petition shall be as short as possible, and in any event may not exceed 30 pages.

2. (a) If the petition seeks issuance of a writ of prohibition, a writ of mandamus, or both in the alternative, it shall identify by names and office or function all persons against whom relief is sought and shall set forth with particularity why the relief sought is not available in any other court. There shall be appended to such petition a copy of the judgment or order in respect of which the writ is sought, including a copy of any opinion rendered in that connection, and such other papers as may be essential to an understanding of the petition.

(b) The petition shall follow, insofar as applicable, the form for the petition for writ of certiorari prescribed by Rule 21. The petition shall be served on the judge or judges to whom the writ is sought to be directed, and shall also be served on every other party to the proceeding in respect of which relief is desired. The judge or judges, and the other parties, within 30 days after receipt of the petition, may file 40 copies of a brief or briefs in opposition thereto, which shall comply fully with Rules 22.1 and 22.2, including the 30-page limit. If the judge or judges concerned do not desire to respond to the petition, they shall so advise the Clerk and all parties by letter. All persons served pursuant to this paragraph shall be deemed respondents for all purposes in the proceedings in this Court.

3. (a) If the petition seeks issuance of a writ of habeas corpus, it shall comply with the requirements of 28 U.S.C. § 2242, and in particular with the requirement in the last paragraph thereof that it state the reasons for not making application to the district court of the district in which the petitioner is held. If the relief sought is from the judgment of a state court, the petition shall set forth specifically how and wherein the petitioner has exhausted his remedies in the state courts or otherwise comes within the provisions of 28 U.S.C. § 2254 (b). To justify the granting of a writ of habeas corpus, it must be shown that there are present exceptional circumstances warranting the exercise of the Court's discretionary powers and that adequate relief cannot be had in any other form or from any other court. Such writs are rarely granted.

(b) Proceedings under this paragraph 3 will be *ex parte*, unless the Court requires the respondent to show cause why the petition for a writ of habeas corpus should not be granted. If a response is ordered, it shall comply fully with Rules 22.1 and 22.2, including the 30-page limit. Neither denial of the petition, without more, nor an order of transfer under authority of 28 U.S.C. § 2241 (b), is an adjudication on the merits, and the former action is to be taken as without prejudice to a further application to any other court for the relief sought.

4. If the petition seeks issuance of a common-law writ of certiorari under 28 U.S.C. § 1651 (a), there may also be filed, at the time of docketing, a certified copy of the record, including all proceedings in the court to which the writ is sought to be directed. However, the filing of such record is not required. The petition shall follow, insofar as applicable, the form for a petition for certiorari prescribed by Rule 21, and shall set forth with particularity why the relief sought is not available in any other court, or cannot be had through other appellate process. The respondent, within 30 days after receipt of the petition, may file 40 copies of a brief in opposition, which shall comply fully with Rules 22.1 and 22.2, including the 30-page limit.

5. When a brief in opposition under paragraph 2 and 4 has been filed, or when a response under paragraph 3 has been ordered and filed, or when the time within which it may be filed has expired, or upon an express waiver of the right to file, the papers will be distributed to the Court by the Clerk.

6. If the Court orders the cause set down for argument, the Clerk will notify the parties whether additional briefs are required, when they must be filed, and, if the case involves a petition for common-law certiorari, that the parties shall proceed to print a joint appendix pursuant to Rule 30.

PART VIII. PRACTICE

Rule 28

Filing and Service — Special Rule for Service Where Constitutionality of Act of Congress or State Statute is in Issue

1. Pleadings, motions, notices, briefs, or other documents or papers required or permitted to be presented to this Court or to a Justice shall be filed with the Clerk. Any document filed by or on behalf of counsel of record whose appearance has not previously been entered must be accompanied by an entry of appearance.

2. To be timely filed, a document must be received by the Clerk within the time specified for filing, except that any document shall be deemed timely filed if it has been deposited in a United States post office or mailbox, with first-class postage prepaid, and properly addressed to the Clerk of this Court, within the time allowed for filing, and if there is filed with the Clerk a notarized statement by a member of the Bar of this Court, setting forth the details of the mailing, and stating that to his knowledge the mailing took place on a particular date within the permitted time.

3. Whenever any pleading, motion, notice, brief, or other document is required by these Rules to be served, such service may be made personally or by mail on each party to the proceeding at or before the time of filing. If the document has been produced under Rule 33, three copies shall be served on each other party separately represented in the proceeding. If the document is typewritten, service of a single copy on each other party separately represented shall suffice. If personal service is made, it may consist of delivery, at the office of counsel of record, to counsel or an employee therein. If service is by mail, it shall consist of depositing the document in a United States post office or mailbox, with first-class postage prepaid, addressed to counsel of record at his post office address. Where a party is not represented by counsel, service shall be upon the party, personally or by mail.

4. (a) If the United States or any department, office, agency, officer, or employee thereof is a party to be served, service must be made upon the Solicitor General, Department of Justice, Washington, D.C. 20530; and if a response is required or permitted within a prescribed period after service, the time does not begin to run until the document actually has been received by the Solicitor General's office. Where an agency of the United States is authorized by law to appear in its own behalf as a party, or where an officer or employee of the United States is a party, in addition to the United States, such agency, officer, or employee also must be served, in addition to the Solicitor General; and if a response is required or permitted within a prescribed period, the time does not begin to run until the document actually has been received by both the agency, officer, or employee and the Solicitor General's office.

(b) In any proceeding in this Court wherein the constitutionality of an Act of Congress is drawn in question, and the United States or any department, office, agency, officer, or employee thereof is not a party, the initial pleading, motion, or paper in this Court shall recite that 28 U.S.C. § 2403 (a) may be applicable and shall be served upon the Solicitor General, Department of Justice, Washington, D.C. 20530. In proceedings from any court of the United States, as defined by 28 U.S.C. § 451, the initial pleading, motion, or paper shall state whether or not any such court, pursuant to 28 U.S.C. § 2403 (a), has certified to the Attorney General the fact that the constitutionality of such Act of Congress was drawn in question.

(c) In any proceeding in this Court wherein the constitutionality of any statute of a State is drawn in question, and the State or any agency, officer, or employee thereof is not a party, the initial pleading, motion, or paper in this Court shall recite that 28 U.S.C. § 2403 (b) may be applicable and shall be served upon the Attorney General of the State. In proceedings from any court of the United States as defined by 28 U.S.C. § 451, the initial pleading, motion, or paper shall state whether or not any such court, pursuant to 28 U.S.C. § 2403 (b), has certified to the State Attorney

General the fact that the constitutionality of such statute of the State was drawn in question.

5. Whenever proof of service is required by these Rules, it must accompany or be endorsed upon the document in question at the time the document is presented to the Clerk for filing. Proof of service shall be shown by any one of the methods set forth below, and it must contain or be accompanied by a statement that all parties required to be served have been served, together with a list of the names and addresses of those parties; it is not necessary that service on each party required to be served be made in the same manner or evidenced by the same proof:

(a) By an acknowledgment of service of the document in question, signed by counsel of record for the party served.

(b) By a certificate of service of the document in question, reciting the facts and circumstances of service in compliance with the appropriate paragraph or paragraphs of this Rule, and signed by a member of the Bar of this Court representing the party on whose behalf such service has been made. (If counsel certifying to such service has not yet entered an appearance in this Court in respect of the cause in which such service is made, an entry of appearance shall accompany the certificate of service.)

(c) By an affidavit of service of the document in question, reciting the facts and circumstances of service in compliance with the appropriate paragraph or paragraphs of this Rule, whenever such service is made by any person not a member of the Bar of this Court.

Rule 29

Computation and Enlargement of Time

1. In computing any period of time prescribed or allowed by these Rules, by order of Court, or by an applicable statute, the day of the act, event, or default after which the designated period of time begins to run is not to be included. The last day of the period so computed is to be included, unless it is a Sunday or a federal legal holiday, in which event the period runs until the end of the next day which is neither a Sunday nor a federal legal holiday.

2. Whenever any Justice of this Court or the Clerk is empowered by law or under any provision of these Rules to extend the time for filing any document or paper, an application seeking such extension must be presented to the Clerk within the period sought to be extended. However, an application for extension of time to docket an appeal or to file a petition for certiorari shall be submitted at least 10 days before the specified final filing date and will not be granted, except in the most extraordinary circumstances, if filed less than 10 days before that date.

3. An application to extend the time within which a party may docket an appeal or file a petition for a writ of certiorari shall be presented in the form prescribed by Rules 12.2 and 20.6, respectively. An application to extend the time within which to file any other document or paper may be presented in the form of a letter to the Clerk setting forth with specificity the reasons why the granting of an extension of time is thought justified. Any application seeking an extension of time must be presented and served upon all other parties as provided in Rule 43, and any such application, if once denied, may not be renewed.

4. Any application for extension of time to file a brief, motion, joint appendix, or other paper, to designate parts of a record for printing in the appendix, or otherwise to comply with a time limit provided by these Rules (except an application for extension of time to docket an appeal, to file a petition for certiorari, to file a petition for rehearing, or to issue a mandate) shall in the first instance be acted upon by the Clerk, whether addressed to him, to the Court, or to a Justice. Any party aggrieved by the Clerk's action on such application may request that it be submitted to a Justice or to the Court. The Clerk's action under this Rule shall be reported by him to the Court in accordance with the instructions that may be issued to him by the Court.

Rule 30

The Joint Appendix

1. Unless the parties agree to use the deferred method allowed in paragraph 4 of this Rule, or the Court so directs, the appellant or petitioner, within 45 days after the order noting or postponing probable jurisdiction or granting the writ of certiorari, shall file 40 copies of a joint appendix, duplicated in the manner prescribed by Rule 33, which shall contain: (1) the relevant docket entries in the courts below; (2) any relevant pleading, jury instruction, finding, conclusion, or opinion; (3) the judgment, order, or decision in question; and (4) any other parts of the record to which the parties wish to direct the Court's attention. However, any of the foregoing items which have already been reproduced in a jurisdictional statement or the petition for certiorari complying with Rule 33.1 need not be reproduced again in the joint appendix. The appellant or petitioner shall serve at least three copies of the joint appendix on each of the other parties to the proceeding.

2. The parties are encouraged to agree to the contents of the joint appendix. In the absence of agreement, the appellant or petitioner, not later than 10 days after the order noting or postponing jurisdiction or granting the writ of certiorari, shall serve on the appellee or respondent a designation of the parts of the record which he intends to include in the joint appendix. If in the judgment of the appellee or respondent the parts of the record so designated are not sufficient, he, within 10 days after receipt of the designation, shall serve upon the appellant or petitioner a designation of additional parts to be included in the joint appendix, and the appellant or petitioner shall include the parts so designated, unless, on his motion in a case where the respondent has been permitted by this Court to proceed *in forma pauperis*, he is excused from supplementing the record.

In making these designations, counsel should include only those materials the Court should examine. Unnecessary designations should be avoided. The record is on file with the Clerk and available to the Justices, and counsel may refer in their briefs and oral argument to relevant portions of the record that have not been printed.

3. At the time that the joint appendix is filed or promptly thereafter, the appellant or petitioner shall file with the Clerk a statement of the costs of preparing the same, and shall serve a copy thereof on each of the other parties to the proceeding. Unless the parties otherwise agree, the cost of producing the joint appendix shall initially be paid by the appellant or petitioner; but if he considers that parts of the record designated by the appellee or respondent are unnecessary for the determination of the issues presented, he may so advise the appellee or respondent who then shall advance the cost of including such parts unless the Court or a Justice otherwise fixes the initial allocation of the costs. The cost of producing the joint appendix shall be taxed as costs in the case, but if a party shall cause matter to be included in the joint appendix unnecessarily, the Court may impose the cost of producing such matter on that party.

4. (a) If the parties agree or if the Court shall so order, preparation of the joint appendix may be deferred until after the briefs have been filed, and in that event the appellant or petitioner shall file the joint appendix within 14 days after receipt of the brief of the appellee or respondent. The provisions of paragraphs 1, 2, and 3 of this Rule shall be followed except that the designations referred to therein shall be made by each party at the time his brief is served.

(b) If the deferred method is used, reference in the briefs to the record may be to the pages of the parts of the record involved, in which event the original paging of each part of the record shall be indicated in the joint appendix by placing in brackets the number of each page at the place in the joint appendix where that page begins. Or if a party desires to refer in his brief directly to pages of the joint appendix, he may serve and file typewritten or page-proof copies of his brief within the time required by Rule 35, with appropriate references to the pages of the parts of the record involved. In that event, within 10 days after the joint appendix is filed he shall serve and file copies of the brief in the form prescribed by Rule 33 containing references to the pages of the joint appendix in place of or in addition to the initial references to the pages of the parts of the record involved. No other change may be made in the brief as initially served and filed, except that typographical errors may be corrected.

5. At the beginning of the joint appendix there shall be inserted a table of the parts of the record which it contains, in the order in which the parts are set out therein, with references to the pages of the joint appendix at which each part begins. The relevant docket entries shall be set out following the table of contents. Thereafter, the other parts of the record shall be set out in chronological order. When matter contained in the reporter's transcript of proceedings is set out in the joint appendix, the page of the transcript at which such matter may be found shall be indicated in brackets immediately before the matter which is set out. Omissions in the text of papers or of the transcript must be indicated by asterisks. Immaterial formal matters (captions, subscriptions, acknowledgments, etc.) shall be omitted. A question and its answer may be contained in a single paragraph.

6. Exhibits designated for inclusion in the joint appendix may be contained in a separate volume, or volumes, suitably indexed. The transcript of a proceeding before an administrative agency, board, commission, or officer used in an action in a district court or a court of appeals shall be regarded as an exhibit for the purpose of this paragraph.

7. The Court by order may dispense with the requirement of a joint appendix and may permit a case to be heard on the original record (with such copies of the record, or relevant parts thereof, as the Court may require), or on the appendix used in the court below, if it conforms to the requirements of this Rule.

8. For good cause shown, the time limits specified in this Rule may be shortened or enlarged by the Court, by a Justice thereof, or by the Clerk under the provisions of Rule 29.4.

Rule 31

Translations

Whenever any record transmitted to this Court contains any document, paper, testimony, or other proceeding in a foreign language without a translation made under the authority of the lower court or admitted to be correct, the clerk of the court transmitting the record shall report the fact immediately to the Clerk of this Court, to the end that this Court may order that a translation be supplied and, if necessary, printed as a part of the joint appendix.

Rule 32

Models, Diagrams, and Exhibits of Material

1. Models, diagrams, and exhibits of material forming part of the evidence taken in a case, and brought up to this Court for its inspection, shall be placed in the custody of the Clerk at least two weeks before the case is heard or submitted.

2. All such models, diagrams, and exhibits of material placed in the custody of the Clerk must be taken away by the parties within 40 days after the case is decided. When this is not done, it shall be the duty of the Clerk to notify counsel to remove the articles forthwith; and if they are not removed within a reasonable time after such notice, the Clerk shall destroy them, or make such other disposition of them as to him may seem best.

Rule 33

Form of Jurisdictional Statements, Petitions, Briefs, Appendices, Motions, and Other Documents Filed With the Court

1. (a) Except for typewritten filings permitted by Rules 42.2 (c), 43, and 46, all jurisdictional statements, petitions, briefs, appendices, and other documents filed with the Court shall be produced by standard typographic printing, which is preferred, or by any photostatic or similar process which produces a clear, black image on white paper; but ordinary carbon copies may not be used.

(b) The text of documents produced by standard typographic printing shall appear in print as 11-point or larger type with 2-point or more leading between lines. Footnotes shall appear in print as 9-point or larger type with 2-point or more leading between lines. Such documents shall be printed on both sides of the page.

(c) The text of documents produced by a photostatic or similar process shall be done in pica type at no more than 10 characters per inch with the lines double-spaced, except that indented quotations and footnotes may be single-spaced. In footnotes, elite type at no more than 12 characters per inch may be used. Such documents may be duplicated on both sides of the page, if practicable. They shall not be reduced in duplication.

(d) Whether duplicated under subparagraph (b) or (c) of this paragraph, documents shall be produced on opaque, unglazed paper 6⅛ by 9¼ inches in size, with type matter approximately 4⅛ by 7⅛ inches, and margins of at least ¾ inch on all sides. The paper shall be firmly bound in at least two places along the left margin so as to make an easily opened volume, and no part of the text shall be obscured by the binding. However, appendices in patent cases may be duplicated in such size as is necessary to utilize copies of patent documents.

2. (a) All documents filed with the Court must bear on the cover, in the following order, from the top of the page: (1) the number of the case or, if there is none, a space for one; (2) the name of this Court; (3) the Term; (4) the caption of the case as appropriate in this Court; (5) the nature of the proceeding and the name of the court from which the action is brought (e.g., On Appeal from the Supreme Court of California; On Writ of Certiorari to the United States Court of Appeals for the Fifth Circuit); (6) the title of the paper (e.g., Jurisdictional Statement, Brief for Respondent, Joint Appendix); (7) the name, post office address, and telephone number of the member of the Bar of this Court who is counsel of record for the party concerned, and upon whom service is to be made. The individual names of other members of the Bar of this Court or of the Bar of the highest court in their respective states and, if desired, their post office addresses, may be added, but counsel of record shall be clearly identified. The foregoing shall be displayed in an appropriate typographic manner and, except for the identification of counsel, may not be set in type smaller than 11-point or in upper case pica.

(b) The following documents shall have a suitable cover consisting of heavy paper in the color indicated: (1) jurisdictional statements and petitions for writs of certiorari, white; (2) motions, briefs, or memoranda filed in response to jurisdictional statements or petitions for certiorari, light orange; (3) briefs on the merits for appellants or petitioners, light blue; (4) briefs on the merits for appellees or respondents, light red; (5) reply briefs, yellow; (6) intervenor or amicus curiae briefs (or motions for leave to file, if bound with brief), green; (7) joint appendices, tan; (8) documents filed by the United States, by any department, office, or agency of the United States, or by any officer or employee of the United States, represented by the Solicitor General, gray. All other documents shall have a tan cover. Counsel shall be certain that there is adequate contrast between the printing and the color of the cover.

3. All documents produced by standard typographic printing or its equivalent shall comply with the page limits prescribed by these Rules. See Rules 15.3; 16.3, 16.5, and 16.6; 21.4; 22.2, 22.5, and 22.6; 27.1, 27.2 (b), 27.3 (b), and 27.4; 34.3 and 34.4; 36.1 and 36.2. Where documents are produced by photostatic or similar process, the following page limits shall apply:

Jurisdictional Statement (Rule 15.3)	65 pages;
Motion to Dismiss or Affirm (Rule 16.3)	65 pages;
Brief Opposing Motion to Dismiss or Affirm (Rule 16.5)	20 pages;
Supplemental Brief (Rule 16.6)	20 pages;
Petition for Certiorari (Rule 21.4)	65 pages;
Brief in Opposition (Rule 22.2)	65 pages;
Reply Brief (Rule 22.5)	20 pages;
Supplemental Brief (Rule 22.6)	20 pages;
Petition Seeking Extraordinary Writ (Rule 27.1)	65 pages;

Brief in Opposition (Rule 27.2 (b))   65 pages;
Response to Petition for Habeas Corpus
  (Rule 27.3 (b))   65 pages;
Brief in Opposition (Rule 27.4)   65 pages;
Brief on the Merits (Rule 34.3)   110 pages;
Reply Brief (Rule 34.4)   45 pages;
Brief of *Amicus Curiae* (Rule 36.2)   65 pages.

4. The Court or a Justice, for good cause shown, may grant leave for the filing of a document in excess of the page limits, but such an application is not favored. An application for such leave shall comply in all respects with Rule 43; and it must be submitted at least 15 days before the filing date of the document in question, except in the most extraordinary circumstances.

5. (a) All documents filed with the Court which exceed five pages, regardless of method of duplication (other than joint appendices, which in this respect are governed by Rule 30), shall be preceded by a table of contents, unless the document contains only one item.

(b) All documents which exceed three pages, regardless of method of duplication, shall contain, following the table of contents, a table of authorities (*i.e.*, cases (alphabetically arranged), constitutional provisions, statutes, textbooks, etc.) with correct references to the pages where they are cited.

6. The body of all documents at their close shall bear the name of counsel of record and such other counsel identified on the cover of the document in conformity with Rule 33.2 (a) as may be desired. One copy of every motion and application (other than one to dismiss or affirm under Rule 16) in addition must bear at its close the manuscript signature of counsel of record.

7. The Clerk shall not accept for filing any document presented in a form not in compliance with this Rule, but shall return it indicating to the defaulting party wherein he has failed to comply: the filing, however, shall not thereby be deemed untimely provided that new and proper copies are promptly substituted. If the Court shall find that the provisions of this Rule have not been adhered to, it may impose, in its discretion, appropriate sanctions including but not limited to dismissal of the action, imposition of costs, or disciplinary sanction upon counsel. See also Rule 38 respecting oral argument.

Rule 34

Briefs on the Merits — In General

1. A brief of an appellate or petitioner on the merits shall comply in all respects with Rule 33, and shall contain in the order here indicated:

(a) The questions presented for review, stated as required by Rule 15.1 (a) or Rule 21.1 (a), as the case may be. The phrasing of the questions presented need not be identical with that set forth in the jurisdictional statement or the petition for certiorari, but the brief may not raise additional questions or change the substance of the questions already presented in those documents. At its option, however, the Court may consider a plain error not among the questions presented but evident from the record and otherwise within its jurisdiction to decide.

(b) A list of all parties to the proceeding in the court whose judgment is sought to be reviewed, except where the caption of the case in this Court contains the names of all such parties. This listing may be done in a footnote.

(c) The table of contents and table of authorities, as required by Rule 33.5.

(d) Citations to the opinions and judgments delivered in the courts below.

(e) A concise statement of the grounds on which the jurisdiction of this Court is invoked, with citation to the statutory provision and to the time factors upon which such jurisdiction rests.

(f) The constitutional provisions, treaties, statutes, ordinances, and regulations which the case involves, setting them out verbatim, and giving the appropriate citation therefor. If the provisions involved are lengthy, their citation alone will suffice at this point, and their pertinent text, if not already set forth in the jurisdictional statement or petition for certiorari, shall be set forth in an appendix to the brief.

(g) A concise statement of the case containing all that is material to the consideration of the questions presented, with appropriate references to the Joint Appendix, *e.g.* (J. A. 12) or to the record, *e.g.* (R. 12).

(h) A summary of argument, suitably paragraphed, which should be a succinct, but accurate and clear, condensation of the argument actually made in the body of the brief. It should not be a mere repetition of the headings under which the argument is arranged.

(i) The argument, exhibiting clearly the points of fact and of law being presented, citing the authorities and statutes relied upon.

(j) A conclusion, specifying with particularity the relief to which the party believes himself entitled.

2. The brief filed by an appellee or respondent shall conform to the foregoing requirements, except that no statement of the case need be made beyond what may be deemed necessary in correcting any inaccuracy or omission in the statement by the other side, and except that items (a), (b), (d), (e), and (f) need not be included unless the appellee or respondent is dissatisfied with their presentation by the other side.

3. A brief on the merits shall be as short as possible, but, in any event, shall not exceed 50 pages in length.

4. A reply brief shall conform to such portions of the Rule as are applicable to the brief of an appellee or respondent, but need not contain a summary of argument, if appropriately divided by topical headings. A reply brief shall not exceed 20 pages in length.

5. Whenever, in the brief of any party, a reference is made to the Joint Appendix or the record, it must be accompanied by the appropriate page number. If the reference is to an exhibit, the page numbers at which the exhibit appears, at which it was offered in evidence, and at which it was ruled on by the judge must be indicated, *e.g.* (Pl. Ex. 14; R. 199, 2134).

6. Briefs must be compact, logically arranged with proper headings, concise, and free from burdensome, irrelevant, immaterial, and scandalous matter. Briefs not complying with this paragraph may be disregarded and stricken by the Court.

Rule 35

Briefs on the Merits — Time for Filing

1. Counsel for the appellant or petitioner shall file with the Clerk 40 copies of the printed brief on the merits within 45 days of the order noting or postponing probable jurisdiction, or of the order granting the writ of certiorari.

2. Forty printed copies of the brief of the appellee or respondent shall be filed with the Clerk within 30 days after the receipt by him of the brief filed by the appellant or petitioner.

3. A reply brief will be received no later than one week before the date of oral argument, and only by leave of Court thereafter.

4. The periods of time stated in paragraphs 1 and 2 of this Rule may be enlarged as provided in Rule 29, upon application duly made; or, if a case is advanced for hearing, the time for filing briefs may be abridged as circumstances require, pursuant to order of the Court on its own or a party's application.

5. Whenever a party desires to present late authorities, newly enacted legislation, or other intervening matters that were not available in time to have been included in his brief in chief, he may file 40 printed copies of a supplemental brief, restricted to such new matter and otherwise in conformity with these Rules, up to the time the case is called for hearing, or, by leave of Court, thereafter.

6. No brief will be received through the Clerk or otherwise after a case has been argued or submitted, except from a party and upon leave of the Court.

7. No brief will be received by the Clerk unless the same shall be accompanied by proof of service as required by Rule 28.

Rule 36

Brief of An Amicus Curiae

1. A brief of an *amicus curiae* prior to consideration of the jurisdictional statement or of the petition for writ of certiorari, accompanied by written consent of the parties, may be filed only if submitted within the time allowed for the filing of the motion to dismiss or affirm or the brief in opposition to the petition for certiorari. A motion for leave to file such a brief when consent has been refused is not favored. Any such motion must be filed within the time allowed for filing of the brief and must be accompanied by the proposed brief. In any event, no such brief shall exceed 20 pages in length.

2. A brief of an *amicus curiae* in a case before the Court for oral argument may be filed when accompanied by written consent of all parties to the case and presented within the time allowed for the filing of the brief of the party supported and if in support of neither party, within the time allowed for filing appellant's or petitioner's brief. Any such brief must identify the party supported, shall be as concise as possible, and in no event shall exceed 30 pages in length. No reply brief of an *amicus curiae* will be received.

3. When consent to the filing of a brief of an *amicus curiae* in a case before the Court for oral argument is refused by a party to the case, a motion for leave to file, accompanied by the proposed brief, complying with the 30-page limit, may be presented to the Court. No such motion shall be received unless submitted within the time allowed for the filing of an *amicus* brief on written consent. The motion shall concisely state the nature of the applicant's interest, set forth facts or questions of law that have not been, or reasons for believing that they will not adequately be, presented by the parties, and their relevancy to the disposition of the case; and it shall in no event exceed five pages in length. A party served with such motion may seasonably file an objection concisely stating the reasons for withholding consent.

4. Consent to the filing of a brief of an *amicus curiae* need not be had when the brief is presented for the United States sponsored by the Solicitor General; for any agency of the United States authorized by law to appear in its own behalf, sponsored by its appropriate legal representative; for a State, Territory, or Commonwealth sponsored by its attorney general; or for a political subdivision of a State, Territory, or Commonwealth sponsored by the authorized law officer thereof.

5. All briefs, motions, and responses filed under this Rule shall comply with the applicable provisions of Rules 33, 34, and 42 (except that it shall be sufficient to set forth the interest of the *amicus curiae*, the argument, the summary of argument, and the conclusion); and shall be accompanied by proof of service as required by Rule 28.

Rule 37

Call and Order of the Calendar

1. The Clerk, at the commencement of each Term, and periodically thereafter, shall prepare a calendar consisting of cases available for argument. Cases will be calendared so that they will not normally be called for argument less than two weeks after the brief of the appellee or respondent is due. The Clerk shall keep the calendar current throughout the Term, adding cases as they are set down for argument, and making rearrangements as required.

2. Unless otherwise ordered, the Court, on the first Monday of each Term, will commence calling cases for argument in the order in which they stand on the calendar, and proceed from day to day during the Term in the same order, except that the arrangement of cases on the calendar shall be subject to modification in the light of the availability of appendices, extensions of time to file briefs, orders advancing, postponing or specially setting arguments, and other relevant factors. The Clerk will advise counsel seasonably when they are required to be present in the Court. He shall periodically publish hearing lists in advance of each argument session, for the convenience of counsel and the information of the public.

3. On the Court's own motion, or on motion of one or more parties, the Court may order that two or more cases, involving what appear to be the same or related questions, be argued together as one case, or on such terms as may be prescribed.

Rule 38

Oral Argument

1. Oral argument should undertake to emphasize and clarify the written argument appearing in the briefs theretofore filed. Counsel should assume that all Members of the Court have read the briefs in advance of argument. *The Court looks with disfavor on any oral argument that is read from a prepared text.* The Court is also reluctant to accept the submission of briefs, without oral argument, of any case in which jurisdiction has been noted or postponed to the merits or certiorari has been granted. Notwithstanding any such submission, the Court may require oral argument by the parties.

2. The appellant or petitioner is entitled to open and conclude the argument. When there is a cross-appeal or a cross-writ of certiorari it shall be argued with the initial appeal or writ as one case and in the time of one case, and the Court will advise the parties which one is to open and close.

3. Unless otherwise directed, one-half hour on each side is allowed for argument. Counsel is not required to use all the allotted time. Any request for additional time shall be presented by motion to the Court filed under Rule 42 not later than 15 days after service of appellant's or petitioner's brief on the merits, and shall set forth with specificity and conciseness why the case cannot be presented within the half-hour limitation.

4. Only one counsel will be heard for each side, except by special permission granted upon a request presented not later than 15 days after service of the petitioner's or appellant's brief on the merits. Such request shall be by a motion to the Court under Rule 42, and shall set forth with specificity and conciseness why more than one counsel should be heard. Divided arguments are not favored.

5. In any case, and regardless of the number of counsel participating, counsel having the opening will present his case fairly and completely and not reserve points of substance for rebuttal.

6. Oral argument will not be heard on behalf of any party for whom no brief has been filed.

7. By leave of Court, and subject to paragraph 4 of this Rule, counsel for an *amicus curiae* whose brief has been duly filed pursuant to Rule 36 may, with the consent of a party, argue orally on the side of such party. In the absence of such consent, argument by counsel for an *amicus curiae* may be made only by leave of Court, on motion particularly setting forth why such argument is thought to provide assistance to the Court not otherwise available. Any such motion will be granted only in the most extraordinary circumstances.

Rule 39

Form of Typewritten Papers

1. All papers specifically permitted by these Rules to be presented to the Court without being printed shall, subject to Rule 46.3, be typewritten or otherwise duplicated upon opaque, unglazed paper, 8½ by 13 inches in size (legal cap), and shall be stapled or bound at the upper left-hand corner. The typed matter, except quotations, must be double-spaced. All copies presented to the Court must be legible.

2. The original of any such motion or application, except a motion to dismiss or affirm, must be signed in manuscript by the party or by counsel of record.

Rule 40

Death, Substitution, and Revivor—Public Officers, Substitution and Description

1. Whenever any party shall die after filing a notice of appeal to this Court or a petition for writ of certiorari, the proper repre-

sentative of the deceased may appear and, upon motion, may be substituted in an appropriate case as a party to the proceeding. If such representative shall not voluntarily become a party, the other party may suggest the death on the record, and on motion obtain an order that, unless such representative shall become a party within a designated time, the party moving for such an order, if appellee or respondent, shall be entitled to have the appeal or petition for writ of certiorari dismissed or the judgment vacated for mootness, as may be appropriate. The party so moving, if an appellant or petitioner, shall be entitled to proceed as in other cases of nonappearance by appellee or respondent. Such substitution, or, in default thereof, such suggestion, must be made within six months after the death of the party, or the case shall abate.

2. Whenever, in the case of a suggestion made as provided in paragraph 1 of this Rule, the case cannot be revived in the court whose judgment is sought to be reviewed because the deceased party has no proper representative within the jurisdiction of that court, but does have a proper representative elsewhere, proceedings then shall be had as this Court may direct.

3. When a public officer is a party to a proceeding here in his official capacity and during its pendency dies, resigns, or otherwise ceases to hold office, the action does not abate and his successor is automatically substituted as a party. Proceedings following the substitution shall be in the name of the substituted party, but any misnomer not affecting the substantial rights of the parties shall be disregarded. An order of substitution may be entered at any time, but the omission to enter such an order shall not affect the substitution.

4. When a public officer is a party in a proceeding here in his official capacity, he may be described as a party by his official title rather than by name; but the Court may require his name to be added.

Rule 41

Custody of Prisoners in Habeas Corpus Proceedings

1. Pending review in this Court of a decision in a habeas corpus proceeding commenced before a court, Justice, or judge of the United States for the release of a prisoner, a person having custody of the prisoner shall not transfer custody to another unless such transfer is directed in accordance with the provisions of this Rule. Upon application of a custodian showing a need therefor, the court, Justice, or judge rendering the decision under review may make an order authorizing transfer and providing for the substitution of the successor custodian as a party.

2. Pending such review of a decision failing or refusing to release a prisoner, the prisoner may be detained in the custody from which release is sought, or in other appropriate custody, or may be enlarged upon his recognizance, with or without surety, as may appear fitting to the court, Justice, or judge rendering the decision, or to the court of appeals or to this Court or to a judge or Justice of either court.

3. Pending such review of a decision ordering release, the prisoner shall be enlarged upon his recognizance, with or without surety, unless the court, Justice, or judge rendering the decision, or the court of appeals or this Court, or a judge or Justice of either court, shall otherwise order.

4. An initial order respecting the custody or enlargement of the prisoner, and any recognizance or surety taken, shall govern review in the court of appeals and in this Court unless for reasons shown to the court of appeals or to this Court, or to a judge or Justice of either court, the order shall be modified or an independent order respecting custody, enlargement, or surety shall be made.

Rule 42

Motions to the Court

1. Every motion to the Court shall state clearly its object, the facts on which it is based, and (except for motions under Rule 27) may present legal argument in support thereof. No separate briefs may be filed. All motions shall be as short as possible, and shall comply with any other applicable page limit. For an application or motion addressed to a single Justice, see Rule 43.

2. (a) A motion in any action within the Court's original jurisdiction shall comply with Rule 9.3.

(b) A motion to dismiss or affirm made under Rule 16, a motion to dismiss as moot (or a suggestion of mootness), a motion for permission to file a brief *amicus curiae*, any motion the granting of which would be dispositive of the entire case or would affect the final judgment to be entered (other than a motion to docket or dismiss under Rule 14, or a motion for voluntary dismissal under Rule 53), and any motion to the Court longer than five pages, shall be duplicated as provided in Rule 33, and shall comply with all other requirements of that Rule. Forty copies of the motion shall be filed.

(c) Any other motion to the Court may be typewritten in accordance with Rule 39, but the Court may subsequently require any such motion to be duplicated by the moving party in the manner provided by Rule 33.

3. A motion to the Court shall be filed with the Clerk, with proof of service as provided by Rule 28, unless *ex parte* in nature. No motion shall be presented in open court, other than a motion for admission to the Bar, except when the proceeding to which it refers is being argued. Oral argument will not be heard on any motion unless the Court so directs.

4. A response to a motion shall be made as promptly as possible considering the nature of the relief asked and any asserted need for emergency action, and, in any event, shall be made within 10 days of receipt, unless otherwise ordered by the Court or a Justice, or by the Clerk under the provisions of Rule 29.4. A response to a printed motion shall be printed if time permits. However, in appropriate cases, the Court in its discretion may act on a motion without waiting for a response.

Rule 43

Motions and Applications to Individual Justices

1. Any motion or application addressed to an individual Justice shall normally be submitted to the Clerk, who will promptly transmit it to the Justice concerned. If oral argument on the application is deemed imperative, request therefor shall be included in the application.

2. Any motion or application addressed to an individual Justice shall be filed in the form prescribed by Rule 39, and shall be accompanied by proof of service on all other parties.

3. The Clerk in due course will advise all counsel concerned, by means as speedy as may be appropriate, of the time and place of the hearing, if any, and of the disposition made of the motion or application.

4. The motion or application will be addressed to the Justice allotted to the Circuit within which the case arises. When the Circuit Justice is unavailable, for any reasons, a motion or application addressed to that Justice shall be distributed to the Justice then available who is next junior to the Circuit Justice; the turn of the Chief Justice follows that of the most junior Justice.

5. A Justice denying a motion or application made to him will note his denial thereon. Thereafter, unless action thereon is restricted by law to the Circuit Justice or is out of time under Rule 29.3, the party making the motion or application, except in the case of an application for extension of time, may renew it to any other Justice, subject to the provisions of this Rule. Except where the denial has been without prejudice, any such renewed motion or application is not favored.

6. Any Justice to whom a motion or application for a stay or for bail is submitted may refer it to the Court for determination.

Rule 44

Stays

1. A stay may be granted by a Justice of this Court as permitted by law; and a writ of injunction may be granted by any Justice in a case where it might be granted by the Court.

2. Whenever a party desires a stay pending review in this

Court, he may present for approval to a judge of the court whose decision is sought to be reviewed, or to such court when action by that court is required by law, or to a Justice of this Court, a motion to stay the enforcement of the judgment of which review is sought. If the stay is to act as a supersedeas, a supersedeas bond shall accompany the motion and shall have such surety or sureties as said judge, court, or Justice may require. The bond shall be conditioned on satisfaction of the judgment in full, together with costs, interest, and damages for delay, if for any reason the appeal is dismissed or if the judgment is affirmed, and on full satisfaction of any modified judgment and such costs, interest, and damages as this Court may adjudge and award. When the judgment is for the recovery of money not otherwise secured, the amount of bond shall be fixed at such sum as will cover the whole amount of the judgment remaining unsatisfied, costs, interest, and damages for delay, unless the judge, court or, Justice, after notice and hearing and for good cause shown, fixes a different amount or orders security other than the bond. When the judgment determines the disposition of the property in controversy, as in a real action, replevin, or an action to foreclose a mortgage, or when the property is in the custody of the court, or when the proceeds of such property or a bond for its value is in the custody or control of any court wherein the proceeding appealed from was had, the amount of the bond shall be fixed at such sum as will secure only the amount recovered for the use and detention of the property, costs, interest, and damages for delay.

3. A petitioner entitled thereto may present to a Justice of this Court an application to stay the enforcement of the judgment sought to be reviewed on certiorari. 28 U.S.C. § 2101 (f).

4. An application for a stay or injunction to a Justice of this Court shall not be entertained, except in the most extraordinary circumstances, unless application for the relief sought first has been made to the appropriate court or courts below, or to a judge or judges thereof. Any application must identify the judgment sought to be reviewed and have appended thereto a copy of the order and opinion, if any, and a copy of the order, if any, of the court or judge below denying the relief sought, and must set forth with specificity the reasons why the granting of a stay or injunction is deemed justified. Any such application is governed by Rule 43.

5. If an application for a stay addressed to the Court is received in vacation, the Clerk will refer it pursuant to Rule 43.4.

Rule 45

Fees

In pursuance of 28 U.S.C. § 1911, the fees to be charged by the Clerk are fixed as follows:

(a) For docketing a case on appeal (except a motion to docket and dismiss under Rule 14.3, wherein the fee is $50) or on petition for writ of certiorari, or docketing any other proceeding, except cases involving certified questions, $200, to be increased to $300 in a case on appeal, or writ of certiorari, or in other circumstances when oral argument is permitted.

(b) For filing a petition for rehearing, $50.

(c) For a photographic reproduction and certification of any record or paper, $1 per page; and for comparing with the original thereof any photographic reproduction of any record or paper, when furnished by the person requesting its certification, 5 cents per page.

(d) For a certificate and seal, $10.

(e) For admission to the Bar and certificate under seal, $100.

(f) For a duplicate certificate of an admission to the Bar under seal, $10.

PART IX. SPECIAL PROCEEDINGS

Rule 46

Proceedings In Forma Pauperis

1. A party desiring to proceed in this Court *in forma pauperis* shall file a motion for leave so to proceed, together with his affidavit in the form prescribed in Fed. Rules App. Proc., Form 4 (as adapted, if the party is seeking a writ of certiorari), setting forth with particularity facts showing that he comes within the statutory requirements. See 28 U.S.C. § 1915. However, the affidavit need not state the issues to be presented, and if the district court or the court of appeals has appointed counsel under the Criminal Justice Act of 1964, as amended, the party need not file an affidavit. See 18 U.S.C. § 3006A (d) (6). The motion shall also state whether or not leave to proceed *in forma pauperis* was sought in any court below and, if so, whether leave was granted.

2. With the motion, and affidavit if required, there shall be filed the appropriate substantive document — jurisdictional statement, petition for writ of certiorari, or motion for leave to file, as the case may be — which shall comply in every respect with the Rules governing the same, except that it shall be sufficient to file a single copy thereof.

3. All papers and documents presented under this Rule shall be clearly legible and should, whenever possible, comply with Rule 39. While making due allowance for any case presented under this Rule by a person appearing *pro se*, the Clerk will refuse to receive any document sought to be filed that does not comply with the substance of these Rules, or when it appears that the document is obviously and jurisdictionally out of time.

4. When the papers required by paragraphs 1 and 2 of this Rule are presented to the Clerk, accompanied by proof of service as prescribed by Rule 28, he, without payment of any docket or other fees, will file them, and place the case on the docket.

5. The appellee or respondent in a case *in forma pauperis* may respond in the same manner and within the same time as in any other case of the same nature, except that the filing of a single response, typewritten or otherwise duplicated, with proof of service as required by Rule 28, will suffice whenever petitioner or appellant has filed typewritten papers. The appellee or respondent, in such response or in a separate document filed earlier, may challenge the grounds for the motion to proceed *in forma pauperis*.

6. Whenever the Court appoints a member of the Bar to serve as counsel for an indigent party in a case set for oral argument, the briefs prepared by such counsel, unless he requests otherwise, will be printed under the supervision of the Clerk. The Clerk also will reimburse such counsel for necessary travel expenses to Washington, D.C., and return, in connection with the argument.

7. Where this Court has granted certiorari or noted or postponed probable jurisdiction in a federal case involving the validity of a federal or state criminal judgment, and where the defendant in the original criminal proceeding is financially unable to obtain adequate representation or to meet the necessary expenses in this Court, the Court will appoint counsel who may be compensated, and whose necessary expenses may be repaid, to the extent provided by the Criminal Justice Act of 1964, as amended (18 U.S.C. § 3006A).

Rule 47

Veterans' and Seamen's Cases

1. A veteran suing to establish reemployment rights under 28 U.S.C. § 2022, or under similar provisions of law exempting veterans from the payment of fees or court costs, may proceed upon typewritten papers as under Rule 46, except that the motion shall ask leave to proceed as a veteran, and the affidavit shall set forth the moving party's status as a veteran.

2. A seaman suing pursuant to 28 U.S.C. § 1916 may proceed without prepayment of fees or costs or furnishing security therefor, but he is not relieved of printing costs nor entitled to proceed on

typewritten papers except by separate motion, or unless, by motion and affidavit, he brings himself within Rule 46.

PART X. DISPOSITION OF CASES

Rule 48

Opinions of the Court

1. All opinions of the Court shall be handed to the Clerk immediately upon delivery thereof. He shall deliver copies to the Reporter of Decisions and shall cause the opinions to be issued in slip form. The opinions shall be filed by the Clerk for preservation.

2. The Reporter of Decisions shall prepare the opinions for publication in preliminary prints and bound volumes of the United States Reports.

Rule 49

Interest and Damages

1. Unless otherwise provided by law, if a judgment for money in a civil case is affirmed, whatever interest is allowed by law shall be payable from the date the judgment below was entered. If a judgment is modified or reversed with a direction that a judgment for money be entered below, the mandate shall contain instructions with respect to allowance of interest. Interest will be allowed at the same rate that similar judgments bear interest in the courts of the State where the judgment was entered or was directed to be entered.

2. When an appeal or petition for writ of certiorari is frivolous, the Court may award the appellee or the respondent appropriate damages.

Rule 50

Costs

1. In a case of affirmance of any judgment or decree by this Court, costs shall be paid by appellant or petitioner, unless otherwise ordered by the Court.

2. In a case of reversal or vacating of any judgment or decree by this Court, costs shall be allowed to appellant or petitioner, unless otherwise ordered by the Court.

3. The fees of the Clerk and the costs of serving process and printing the joint appendix in this Court are taxable items. The costs of the transcript of record from the court below is also a taxable item, but shall be taxable in that court as costs in the case. The expenses of printing briefs, motions, petitions, or jurisdictional statements are not taxable.

4. In a case where a question has been certified, including a case where the certificate is dismissed, costs shall be equally divided unless otherwise ordered by the Court; but where a decision is rendered on the whole matter in controversy (see Rule 24.2), costs shall be allowed as provided in paragraphs 1 and 2 of this Rule.

5. In a civil action commenced on or after July 18, 1966, costs under this Rule shall be allowed for or against the United States, or an officer or agent thereof, unless expressly waived or otherwise ordered by the Court. See 28 U.S.C. § 2412. In any other civil action, no such costs shall be allowed, except where specifically authorized by statute and directed by the Court.

6. When costs are allowed in this Court, it shall be the duty of the Clerk to insert the amount thereof in the body of the mandate or other proper process sent to the court below, and annex to the same the bill of items taxed in detail. The prevailing side in such a case is not to submit to the Clerk any bill of costs.

7. In an appropriate instance, the Court may adjudge double costs.

Rule 51

Rehearings

1. A petition for rehearing of any judgment or decision other than one on a petition for writ of certiorari, shall be filed within 25 days after the judgment or decision, unless the time is shortened or enlarged by the Court or a Justice. Forty copies, produced in conformity with Rule 33, must be filed (except where the party is proceeding *in forma pauperis* under Rule 46), accompanied by proof of service as prescribed by Rule 28. Such petition must briefly and distinctly state its grounds. Counsel must certify that the petition is presented in good faith and not for delay; one copy of the certificate shall bear the manuscript signature of counsel. A petition for rehearing is not subject to oral argument, and will not be granted except at the instance of a Justice who concurred in the judgment or decision and with the concurrence of a majority of the Court. See also Rule 52.2.

2. A petition for rehearing of an order denying a petition for writ of certiorari shall comply with all the form and filing requirements of paragraph 1, but its grounds must be limited to intervening circumstances of substantial or controlling effect or to other substantial grounds not previously presented. Counsel must certify that the petition is restricted to the grounds specified in this paragraph and that it is presented in good faith and not for delay; one copy of the certificate shall bear the manuscript signature of counsel or of the party when not represented by counsel. A petition for rehearing without such certificate shall be rejected by the Clerk. Such petition is not subject to oral argument.

3. No response to a petition for rehearing will be received unless requested by the Court, but no petition will be granted without an opportunity to submit a response.

4. Consecutive petitions for rehearings, and petitions for rehearing that are out of time under this Rule, will not be received.

Rule 52

Process; Mandates

1. All process of this Court shall be in the name of the President of the United States, and shall contain the given names, as well as the surnames, of the parties.

2. In a case coming from a state court, mandate shall issue as of course after the expiration of 25 days from the day the judgment is entered, unless the time is shortened or enlarged by the Court or a Justice, or unless the parties stipulate that it be issued sooner. The filing of a petition for rehearing, unless otherwise ordered, will stay the mandate until disposition of such petition, and if the petition is then denied, the mandate shall issue forthwith. When, however, a petition for rehearing is not acted upon prior to adjournment, or is filed after the Court adjourns, the judgment or mandate of the Court will not be stayed unless specifically ordered by the Court or a Justice.

3. In a case coming from a federal court, a formal mandate will not issue, unless specially directed; instead, the Clerk will send the proper court a copy of the opinion or order of the Court and a certified copy of the judgment (which shall include provisions for the recovery of costs, if any are awarded). In all other respects, the provisions of paragraph 2 apply.

Rule 53

Dismissing Clauses

1. Whenever the parties thereto, at any stage of the proceedings, file with the Clerk an agreement in writing that any cause be dismissed, specifying the terms with respect to costs, and pay to the Clerk any fees that may be due, the Clerk, without further reference to the Court, shall enter an order of dismissal.

2.(a) Whenever an appellant or petitioner in this Court files with the Clerk a motion to dismiss a cause to which he is a party, with proof of service as prescribed by Rule 28, and tenders to the Clerk any fees and costs that may be due, the adverse party, within 15 days after service thereof, may file an objection, limited to the quantum of damages and costs in this Court alleged to be payable, or, in a proper case, to a showing that the moving party does not represent all appellants or petitioners if there are more than one. The Clerk will refuse to receive any objection not so limited.

(b) Where the objection goes to the standing of the moving

party to represent the entire side, the party moving for dismissal, within 10 days thereafter, may file a reply, after which time the matter shall be laid before the Court for its determination.

(c) If no objection is filed, or if upon objection going only to the quantum of damages and costs in this Court, the party moving for dismissal, within 10 days thereafter, shall tender the whole of such additional damages and costs demanded, the Clerk, without further reference to the Court, shall enter an order of dismissal. If, after objection as to quantum of damages and costs in this Court, the moving party does not respond with such a tender within 10 days, the Clerk shall report the matter to the Court for its determination.

3. No mandate or other process shall issue on a dismissal under this Rule without an order of the Court.

PART XI. APPLICATION OF TERMS
Rule 54
Term ''State Court''

The term "state court" when used in these Rules normally includes the District of Columbia Court of Appeals and the Supreme Court of the Commonwealth of Puerto Rico (see 28 U.S.C. §§ 1257, 1258), and references in these Rules to the law and statutes of a State normally include the law and statutes of the District of Columbia and of the Commonwealth of Puerto Rico.

Rule 55
Effective Date of Amendments

The amendments to these Rules adopted April 14, 1980, shall become effective June 30, 1980.

Selected Bibliography

Abraham, Henry J. *The Judicial Process.* 2d ed. rev. New York: Oxford University Press, 1968.

Bickel, Alexander M. *The Least Dangerous Branch.* Indianapolis: Bobbs-Merrill Co., 1962.

Curtis, Charles P. Jr. *Lions Under the Throne.* Fairfield, N.J.: Kelley Press, 1947.

Frank, John P. *Marble Palace: The Supreme Court in American Life.* New York: Alfred A. Knopf, 1958.

Freund, Paul A., gen. ed *History of the Supreme Court of the United States.* New York: MacMillan Publishing Co. Inc., 1971, 1974, 1971. Vol. I: *Antecedents and Beginnings to 1801,* by Julius Goebel Jr.; Vol. V: *The Taney Period, 1836-1864,* by Carl B. Swisher; Vol. VI: *Reconstruction and Reunion, 1864-1888, Part One,* by Charles Fairman.

Freund, Paul A. *The Supreme Court of the United States.* Cleveland and New York: Meridian Books, 1961.

Friedman, Leon and Israel, Fred L., eds. *The Justices of the United States Supreme Court, 1789-1969, Their Lives and Major Opinions.* 5 Vols. New York and London: Chelsea House Publishers, 1969-1978.

Garraty, John A., ed. *Quarrels That Have Shaped the Constitution.* New York: Harper and Row, 1964.

Harrell, Mary Ann. *Equal Justice Under Law: The Supreme Court in American Life.* Washington, D.C.: The Foundation of the Federal Bar Association with the cooperation of the National Geographic Society, 1975.

Hughes, Charles Evans. *The Supreme Court of the United States: Its Foundations, Methods and Achievements, an Interpretation.* New York: Columbia University Press, 1928.

Jackson, Robert H. *The Struggle for Judicial Supremacy: A Study of a Crisis in American Power Politics.* New York: Random House, Vintage Books, 1941.

Kluger, Richard. *Simple Justice: The History of Brown v. Board of Education and Black America's Struggle for Equality.* New York: Alfred A. Knopf, 1976.

Lewis, Anthony. *Gideon's Trumpet.* New York: Random House, 1964.

Madison, James; Hamilton, Alexander; and Jay, John. *The Federalist Papers.* Introduction by Clinton Rossiter. New York: The New American Library, Mentor Books, 1961.

Mason, Alpheus T. *The Supreme Court from Taft to Warren.* rev. ed. Baton Rouge: Louisiana State University Press, 1968.

Mason, Alpheus T. and Beaney, William M. *The Supreme Court in a Free Society.* Englewood Cliffs, N.J.: Prentice-Hall Inc., 1959.

McCloskey, Robert G. *The American Supreme Court.* Chicago History of American Civilization series. Chicago: University of Chicago Press, 1960.

Pfeffer, Leo. *This Honorable Court: A History of the United States Supreme Court.* Boston: Beacon Press, 1965.

Pollak, Louis H. ed. *The Constitution and the Supreme Court: A Documentary History.* 2 vols. Cleveland: The World Publishing Co., 1966.

Pritchett, C. Herman. *The American Constitution.* 3rd ed. New York: McGraw-Hill Book Co., Inc., 1977.

Rodell, Fred. *Nine Men: A Political History of the Supreme Court of the United States from 1790-1955.* New York: Random House, 1955.

Swindler, William F. *Court and Constitution in the Twentieth Century: The Old Legality, 1889-1932.* Indianapolis: The Bobbs-Merrill Co., 1969.

———. *Court and Constitution in the Twentieth Century: The New Legality, 1932-1968.* Indianapolis: The Bobbs-Merrill Co., 1970.

Swisher, Carl Brent. *American Constitutional Development.* 2nd ed. Cambridge: Houghton Mifflin Co., The Riverside Press, 1954.

United States Congress. Library of Congress, Congressional Reference Service. *The Constitution of the United States of America: Analysis and Interpretation.* Washington, D.C.: Government Printing Office, 1973; together with the 1976 Supplement. Washington, D.C.: Government Printing Office, 1977.

Warren, Charles. *The Supreme Court in United States History.* 2 vols. rev. ed. Boston: Little, Brown & Co., 1926.

Williams, Richard L. "Justices Run 'Nine Little Law Firms' at Supreme Court," *Smithsonian* Magazine, February 1977.

———. "Supreme Court of the United States: The Staff That Keeps It Operating." *Smithsonian* Magazine, January 1977.

Case Index

XYZ

Subject Index

5/82